COLLINS REFERENCE
An Imprint of HarperCollinsPublishers
www.harpercollins.com

UNITED STATES
POSTAL SERVICE ®

D1571433

THE POSTAL SERVICE

GUIDE *to*

36th edition

U.S. STAMPS

UPDATED STAMP VALUES

THE POSTAL SERVICE GUIDE TO U.S. STAMPS 36th Edition.
© 2009 United States Postal Service. All rights reserved.
Printed in the United States of America. Certain values,
quotations, photographs, and the Scott numbering system
are owned exclusively by Amos Philatelics, Inc., dba Scott
Publishing Co. © 2008. All rights thereto are reserved by Amos
Philatelics, Inc., dba Scott Publishing Co., and such materials
and information are reproduced and used herein under license
from Scott Publishing Co. No use may be made of the material
in this publication that is represented from a copyrighted
publication of or made available by Amos Philatelics, Inc.,
without the express written permission of Amos Philatelics,
Inc., dba Scott Publishing Co., Sidney, Ohio.

The designs of stamps and postal stationery issued since
January 1, 1978, are the subject of individual copyrights by
the United States Postal Service. UNITED STATES POSTAL
SERVICE, the Eagle Logo, and POSTAL SERVICE are
trademarks of the United States Postal Service.

HarperCollins books may be purchased for educational,
business, or sales promotional use. For information, please
write: Special Markets Department, HarperCollins Publishers,
10 East 53rd Street, New York, NY 10022.

ISBN 978-0-06-185158-2

Table of Contents

2009 STAMPS

U.S. POSTAGE STAMPS AND POSTAL STATIONERY

In this year's stamp program, the U.S. Postal Service commemorates an exciting array of subjects and people, from the author said to be the originator of the detective story to 12 pioneers of the civil rights movement, and from the inhabitants of an undersea kelp forest to classic shows from television's early years. A preview of these fascinating new stamps follows; their dates and places of issue are listed on page 11, while details about each stamp appear throughout the book.

Alaska Statehood

Celebrating Lunar New Year: Year of the Ox

Oregon Statehood

Edgar Allan Poe

Redwood Forest Priority Mail®

Old Faithful Express Mail®

Abraham Lincoln

Historic Preservation:
Miami University Stamped Card

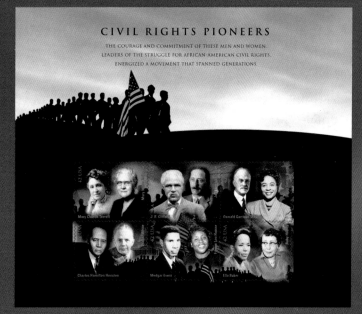

Official Mail

Civil Rights Pioneers

Patriotic Banner

Forever™

Literary Arts: Richard Wright

Polar Bear

Koi Stamped Cards

Purple Heart

Tiffany Lamp

U.S. Flag

Weddings: Rings

Weddings: Cake

The Simpsons

Love: King and Queen of Hearts

Seabiscuit Stamped Envelope

Forever™ Stamped Envelope

VISIT US ONLINE AT *THE POSTAL STORE*

AT *WWW.USPS.COM*

OR CALL *1 800 STAMP-24*

**Distinguished
Americans:
Mary Lasker**

Bob Hope

Celebrate!

Dolphin

**Scenic American
Landscapes:
Grand Teton
National Park, Wyoming**

**Scenic American
Landscapes:
Zion National Park, Utah**

**Black Heritage:
Anna Julia Cooper**

Gulf Coast Lighthouses

Flags of Our Nation (Set 3)

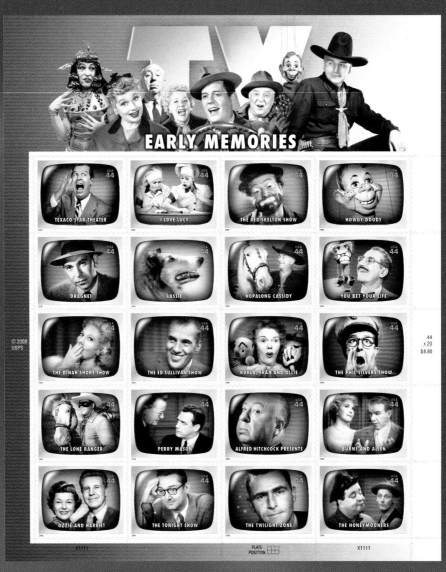

Early TV Memories

Hawai`i Statehood

Eid

**Legends of
Hollywood:
Gary Cooper**

Thanksgiving Day Parade

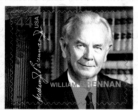

UNITED STATES SUPREME COURT JUSTICES

United States Supreme Court Justices

Nature of America: Kelp Forest

Winter Holidays

Hanukkah

Kwanzaa

Madonna and Sleeping Child by Sassoferrato

2009 STAMPS

Stamp Issue Dates & Locations. To learn more about each stamp, turn to the page listed under its information.

Alaska Statehood
January 3, 2009
Anchorage, AK
See page 194.

Celebrating Lunar New Year:
Year of the Ox
January 8, 2009
New York, NY
See page 181.

Oregon Statehood
January 14, 2009
Portland, OR
See page 57.

Edgar Allan Poe
January 16, 2009
Richmond, VA
See page 254.

Redwood Forest
Priority Mail® Envelope
January 16, 2009
San Diego, CA
See page 233.

Old Faithful Express Mail®
January 16, 2009
San Diego, CA
See page 210.

Redwood Forest
Priority Mail®
January 16, 2009
Kansas City, MO

Abraham Lincoln
February 9, 2009
Springfield, IL
See page 242.

Historic Preservation:
Miami University
Stamped Card
February 17, 2009
Oxford, OH
See page 285.

Civil Rights Pioneers
February 21, 2009
New York, NY
See page 261.

Official Mail
February 24, 2009
Washington, D C
See page 250.

Patriotic Banner
February 24, 2009
Washington, DC
See page 205.

Forever™
February 24, 2009
Washington, DC
See page 137.

Literary Arts: Richard Wright
April 9, 2009
Chicago, IL
See page 258.

Polar Bear
April 16, 2009
New York, NY
See page 225.

Koi Stamped Cards
April 17, 2009
New York, NY
See page 238.

Purple Heart
April 28, 2009
Washington, DC
See page 221.

Tiffany Lamp
April 28, 2009
Washington, DC

U.S. Flag
May 1, 2009, May 8, 2009,
June 5, 2009
Washington, DC & McLean, VA
See page 237.

Weddings: Rings
May 1, 2009
Washington, DC
See page 262.

Weddings: Cake
May 1, 2009
Washington, DC
See page 262.

The Simpsons
May 7, 2009
Los Angeles, CA
See page 189.

Love: King and Queen
of Hearts
May 8, 2009
Washington, DC
See page 142.

Seabiscuit Stamped Envelope
May 11, 2009
Kansas City, MO
See page 241.

Forever Stamped Envelope
May 11, 2009
Kansas City, MO
See page 137.

Distinguished Americans:
Mary Lasker
May 15, 2009
Washington, DC
See page 94.

Bob Hope
May 29, 2009
San Diego, CA
See page 269.

Celebrate!
June 10, 2009
Washington, DC
See page 246.

Dolphin
June 12, 2009
Washington, DC
See page 122.

Scenic American Landscapes:
Grand Teton National Park,
Wyoming
June 28, 2009
Washington, DC
See page 161.

Scenic American Landscapes:
Zion National Park, Utah
June 28, 2009
Washington, DC
See page 118.

Black Heritage:
Anna Julia Cooper
June 11, 2009
Washington, DC
See page 157.

Gulf Coast Lighthouses
July 23, 2009
Biloxi, MS
See page 257.

Flags of Our Nation (Set 3)
August 6, 2009
Pittsburgh, PA
See page 294.

Early TV Memories
August 11, 2009
North Hollywood, CA
See page 274.

Hawai`i Statehood
August 21, 2009
Honolulu, HI
See page 198.

Eid
September 3, 2009
Washington, DC
See page 141.

Thanksgiving Day Parade
September 9, 2009
New York, NY
See page 209.

Legends of Hollywood:
Gary Cooper
September 10, 2009
Los Angeles, CA
See page 169.

United States
Supreme Court Justices
September 22, 2009
Washington, DC
See page 186.

Nature of America: Kelp Forest
October 1, 2009
Monterey, CA
See page 322.

Winter Holidays
October 8, 2009
New York, NY
See page 273.

Hanukkah
October 9, 2009
New York, NY
See page 121.

Kwanzaa
October 9, 2009
New York, NY
See page 61.

Christmas: "Madonna
and Sleeping Child"
by Sassoferrato
October 20, 2009
San Simeon, CA
See page 190.

Explanation of Catalog Prices

The United States Postal Service sells only the commemoratives and special issues released during the past few years. Current postal stationery and regular issues remain on sale for longer periods of time. Prices in this book are called "catalog prices" by stamp collectors. Collectors use catalog prices as guidelines when buying or trading stamps. *It is important to remember the prices are simply guidelines to the stamp values. Stamp condition is very important in determining the actual value of a stamp.*

Prices are Estimated

Listed prices are estimates of how much you can expect to pay for a stamp from a dealer. *A 20-cent minimum valuation has been established that represents a fair-market price to have a dealer locate and provide a single stamp to a customer. Dealers may charge less per stamp to provide a group of such stamps, and may charge less for such a single stamp. Similarly, a $1.00 minimum has been established for First Day Covers (FDCs).* If you sell a stamp to a dealer, they may offer you much less than the catalog price. Dealers pay based on their interest in owning a particular stamp. If they already have a full supply, they may only buy additional stamps at a low price.

Condition Affects Value

The catalog prices are given for unused stamps and used (canceled) stamps that have been hinged and are in "very fine" condition. Stamps in "superb" condition that have never been hinged may cost more than the listed price. Stamps in less than "fine" condition may cost less. A never-hinged stamp will have full original gum with no hinge mark or disturbance. *Stamp values after No. 771 to present are priced as "unused stamps that have never been hinged."* Hinged unused stamps may be worth considerably less.

The prices for used stamps are based on a light cancellation; a heavy cancellation lessens a stamp's value. Canceled stamps may be worth more than uncanceled stamps. This happens if the cancellation is of a special type or for a significant date. Therefore, it is important to study an envelope before removing a stamp and discarding its "cover."

Understanding the Listings

■ Prices in *regular type* for single unused and used stamps are taken from the *Scott 2009 Specialized Catalogue of U.S. Stamps & Covers*, whose editors have based these prices on *actual retail values* as they found them in the marketplace. The Scott numbering system for stamps is used in this book. Prices quoted for unused and used stamps are for "very fine" condition, except where "very fine" is not available.

■ Stamp values in *italic* type generally refer to items difficult to value accurately.

■ A dash (—) in a value column means the item is known to exist but information is insufficient for establishing a value.

■ The stamp listings contain a number of additions designated "a," "b," "c," etc. These represent recognized variations of stamps as well as errors. These listings are as complete as space permits.

Occasionally, a new stamp or major variation may be inserted by the catalog editors into a series or sequence where it was not originally anticipated. These additions are identified by capital letters "A," "B" and so forth. For example, a new stamp which logically belonged between 1044 and 1045 is designated 1044A, even though it is entirely different from 1044. The insertion was preferable to a complete renumbering of the series.

■ Prices for Plate Blocks, First Day Covers, American Commemorative Panels and Souvenir Pages are taken from the *Scott 2009 Specialized Catalogue of U.S. Stamps & Covers.*

Sample Listing

	Issue	Date	Un	U	PB/LP/PNC	#	FDC	Q(M)
3069	32¢ Georgia O'Keefe	05/23/96	.85	.20	5.00	(4)	1.50	156

- Scott Catalog Number (bold type indicates stamp is pictured)
- Description
- Denomination
- Date of Issue
- Unused Catalog Price
- Used Catalog Price
- Plate Block Price, Line Pair Price or Plate Number Coil Price
- Number of stamps in Plate Block, Line Pair or Plate Number Coil
- First Day Cover Price
- Quantity Issued in Millions (where known)

3069

Sample Variation Listing

	Issue	Date	Un	U	PB/LP/PNC	#	FDC	Q(M)
2281	25¢ Honeybee	09/02/88	.45	.20	3.50	(5)	1.25	
a	Imperf. pair		45.00					
b	Black omitted		50.00	—				
d	Pair, imperf. between		700.00					

2281

The Art of Stamp Collecting

Stamp collecting can be a life-time hobby. It's fun and educational for all ages and it's easy to start without a big investment.

The study of stamps and postal materials is called *philately* and collectors are sometimes called *philatelists*.

How do I start collecting stamps?

You can start by saving stamps from letters, packages, and postcards. Many beginning collectors choose a favorite subject like art, history, sports, transportation, or animals as the theme of their collection. You can have a great time on a limited budget with just a few inexpensive accessories such as an album and stamp hinges.

What kinds of stamps are there?

There are many types of stamps—for example, commemorative, definitive, and special—and formats such as sheets, booklets, or coils. Stamps may be conventional adhesive ("lick-and-stick") or self-adhesive ("no-lick, peel-and-stick"). *Definitive stamps* are the most common. Generally less than an inch square, they are printed in large quantities, and often more than once. *Commemorative stamps,* larger and more colorful than definitives, are printed in smaller quantities and typically only once. They honor people, events, or subjects of importance to American life and culture. *Special stamps*—Christmas and Love, Holiday Celebration, international rate, Priority Mail, and Express Mail—usually are on sale for a limited time.

How do I remove stamps from an envelope?

Soaking is the best way to remove stamps from envelopes. Tear the envelope around the stamp, leaving a small margin. With the stamp facing down, place into a pan of warm, not hot, water. After a few minutes (self-adhesive gum may take longer), the stamp should sink to the bottom. When all adhesive is dislodged, remove the stamp preferably using stamp tongs. Place the stamp between two paper towels and put a heavy object, such as a book, on top to keep the stamp from curling as it dries. Leave overnight.

How can I store my stamps?

The best way to store stamps is in a *stamp album* or on loose-leaf paper in a binder. Affix your stamps by using *stamp hinges,* glassine strips with gum on one side, or *stamp mounts,* clear plastic sleeves that offer better protection for unused stamps.

Is there anything else I need?

Collectors use a variety of other materials and accessories. Transparent *glassine envelopes* protect stamps from grease and air. A *stamp catalog* is a reference book (like this one) with illustrations and stamp values. A *magnifying glass* is useful when examining stamps; *tongs* are used to pick up and move stamps. A *perforation gauge* measures perforations along the edges of stamps. *Watermark fluid* will enhance a watermark, a design or pattern that is pressed into some stamp paper during manufacturing.

How can I tell what a stamp is worth?

When figuring the value of a stamp, ask yourself two questions: "How rare is it?" and "What condition is it in?" Stamp catalog prices will give you an idea of the stamp's rarity. However, the stamp may sell at more or less than the catalog price, depending on its condition. Stamp dealers categorize stamps according to their condition. A stamp in *mint condition* is the same as when purchased from the Post Office. Hinge marks on mint stamps can reduce value, which is why stamp mounts are recommended for mint stamps.

How should I judge the condition of a stamp?

To evaluate the condition of a stamp, first look at the front. Are the colors bright or faded? Is the stamp clean, dirty, or stained? Is it torn or creased? Torn stamps are not considered "collectible," but they can be used as space fillers until you get better ones. Are the perforations intact? Has the stamp been canceled? A stamp with a light cancellation is in better condition than one with heavy marks across it. Is the stamp design centered, crooked, or off to one side? Centering can range from "superb" (perfectly centered on the stamp) to "good" (the design on at least one side is marred somewhat by the perfs). Anything less would be graded "fair" or "poor" and, like torn copies, should be saved only as space fillers. Centering varies widely on older stamps. An examination of the back of the stamp will reveal whether it has been carelessly treated and thus is less valuable.

The values listed in this book are for used and unused stamps in "very fine" condition.

What other stamp materials can I collect?

Many philatelists collect postal stationery—products with a printed or embossed stamp design—such as *Stamped Envelopes*, *Stamped Cards* (or postal cards), and *Aerogrammes*. Other philatelic collectibles include: *Plate numbers* (including *plate blocks*) appear on or adjacent to stamps. Found most often on sheet stamps, plate blocks are the stamps—usually a group of 4—that have the printing plate numbers in the adjoining selvage, or margin. *Booklet panes* are panes of stamps affixed in, or as part of, a thin folder to form a booklet. Collectors of booklet panes usually save the entire pane or booklet. *Marginal blocks* (including *copyright blocks*) feature marginal inscriptions other than plate numbers. The most common is the copyright block, which features the copyright symbol ©, copyright date, and U.S. Postal Service. All U.S. stamp designs since 1978 are copyrighted. *First Day Covers* (FDCs) are envelopes bearing new stamps postmarked on the first day of sale. For each new issuance, the U.S. Postal Service generally selects one location, usually related to the stamp subject, as the place for the first day dedication ceremony and the first day postmark. *First Day Ceremony Programs* are given to those who attend first day ceremonies. They contain a list of participants, information on the stamp subject, and the actual stamp attached and postmarked.

Are there any stamp groups I can join?

Stamp clubs are a great source for new stamps and stamp collecting advice. Ask your local postmaster or librarian about stamp clubs in your area and contact information including Internet sites.

Superb

Very Fine

Fine

Good

Light Cancel–Very Fine

Medium Cancel–Fine

Heavy Cancel

1   2   3   4

5   11   12   14   17

30   37   38   39   40   62B

Postmasters' Provisionals

1845-1847

9X1

Issue		Date	Un	U
Imperf., Typeset				
1X1	5¢ black, *buff*, type I	1846		—
1X2	5¢ black, *blue*, type I	1846		—
2XU1	5¢ carmine red, *white*	1846		300,000.00
Engraved, Imperf.				
3X1	5¢ black	1845		6,000.00
3X2	10¢ black, on cover	1845		70,000.00
3X3	5¢ black, *bluish*	1845	65,000.00	6,000.00
3X4	10¢ black, *bluish*	1845		60,000.00
Various Papers, Handstamped				
3XU1	5¢ blue	1845		6,500.00
3XU2	5¢ red	1845		10,000.00
3XU3	10¢ blue	1845		16,000.00
3XU4	10¢ blue	1845		20,000.00
Imperf., Typeset				
4X1	5¢ dull blue, *yellowish*, on cover	1846(?)		300,000.00
Imperf., Thick Soft Wove Paper, Color Coming Through				
5X1	5¢ black, *buff*	1846		11,000.00
Imperf., Handstamped				
6X1	5¢ red, *buff, on cover*	1846		300,000.00

Issue		Date	Un	U
Imperf.				
7X1	5¢ black, *bluish*	1846	130,000.00	50,000.00
8XU1	5¢ red (Bl or M)	1845		100,000.00
8XU2	5¢ red, *light bluish (Bk)*	1845		125,000.00
8XU3	5¢ dull blue, *buff (Bl)*	1845		125,000.00
8XU4	5¢ dull blue, *(Bl)*	1845		125,000.00
Engraved, Imperf., Bluish Wove Paper				
9X1	5¢ black	1846	1,500.00	525.00
9X2	5¢ black	1847	6,500.00	3,500.00
Engraved, Imperf., Gray Wove Paper				
9X3	5¢ black	1847	5,250.00	2,250.00
Engraved, Imperf., Yellowish White Paper				
10X1	5¢ gray black	1846	350.00	1,750.00
10X2	10¢ gray black	1846	1,150.00	15,000.00
Imperf., Wove Paper Colored Through				
11X1	5¢ black, *greenish*	1845-46	50,000.00	8,000.00
11X2	10¢ black, *greenish*	1845-46	50,000.00	8,000.00
11X3	20¢ black, *greenish*	1845-46		160,000.00
11X4	5¢ black, *gray lilac*	1846	—	55,000.00
11X5	10¢ black, *gray lilac*	1846	50,000.00	8,000.00
11X6	20¢ black, *gray lilac*	1846	100,000.00	50,000.00
Pelure Paper				
11X7	5¢ black, *bluish*	1846	—	11,000.00
11X8	10¢ black, *bluish*	1846		13,000.00

Issues of 1847-1875

Thin, Bluish Wove Paper, Imperf., Unwmkd.

		Un	U
1	5¢ Benjamin Franklin	6,750.00	600.00
a	5¢ dark brown	8,750.00	800.00
b	5¢ orange brown	9,000.00	900.00
c	5¢ red orange	25,000.00	9,500.00
	Pen cancel		300.00
	Double transfer of top and bottom frame lines	—	725.00
	Double transfer of top, bottom and left frame lines and numerals		3,250.00
2	10¢ George Washington	35,000.00	1,400.00
	Pen cancel		750.00
	Vertical line through second "F" of "OFFICE"	—	2,000.00
	With "stick pin" in tie, or with "harelip"	—	3,000.00
	Double transfer in lower right "X"	70,000.00	2,400.00
	Double transfer of left and bottom frame lines	—	2,400.00
	Double transfer in "POST OFFICE"	—	3,500.00

Issues of 1875, Reproductions of 1 and 2, Bluish Paper, Without Gum, Imperf.

		Un	U
3	5¢ red brown Franklin	800.00	
4	10¢ black Washington	975.00	

5¢. On the originals, the left side of the white shirt frill touches the oval on a level with the top of the "F" of "Five." On the reproductions, it touches the oval about on a level with the top of the figure "5."

10¢. On the originals, line of coat points to "T" of TEN and right line of coat points between "T" and "S" of CENTS.

On the reproductions left, line of coat points to right tip of "X" and right line of coat points to center of "S" of CENTS.

On the reproductions, the eyes have a sleepy look, the line of the mouth is straighter, and in the curl of hair near the left cheek is a strong black dot, while the originals have only a faint one.

Issues of 1851-1852, Imperf.

		Un	U
5	1¢ Franklin, type I	225,000.00	85,000.00
5A	1¢ blue, type Ib	22,500.00	9,500.00
	#6-9: Franklin (5), 1851		
6	1¢ blue, type Ia	45,000.00	13,000.00
7	1¢ blue, type II	1,150.00	170.00
	Cracked plate	1,450.00	390.00
8	1¢ blue, type III	25,000.00	3,500.00
8A	1¢ blue, type IIIa	6,000.00	1,200.00
9	1¢ blue, type IV, 1852	850.00	130.00
	Triple transfer, one inverted	1,000.00	180.00

Issues of 1851-1861

#10-11, 25-26a all had plates on which at least four outer frame lines (and usually much more) were recut, adding to their value.

		Un	U
10	3¢ orange brown Washington, type I (11)	4,000.00	160.00
10A	Copper brown	4,750.00	1,250.00
	On part-India paper		1,250.00
11	3¢ Washington, dull red	300.00	15.00
11A	3¢ Washington, double transfer, "GENTS" for "CENTS"	450.00	55.00
12	5¢ Jefferson, type I	30,000.00	900.00
13	10¢ green Washington, type I (14)	18,000.00	950.00
14	10¢ green, type II	5,000.00	200.00
15	10¢ green, type III	5,000.00	200.00
16	10¢ green, type IV (14)	35,000.00	1,700.00
17	12¢ black	6,500.00	350.00

Issues of 1857-1861, Perf. 15.5

(Issued in 1857 except #18, 27, 28A, 29, 30, 30A, 35, 36b, 37, 38, 39)

#18-24: Franklin (5)

		Un	U
18	1¢ blue, type I	2,400.00	700.00
19	1¢ blue, type Ia	40,000.00	11,000.00
20	1¢ blue, type II	1,200.00	300.00
21	1¢ blue, type III	17,500.00	2,750.00
22	1¢ blue, type IIIa	2,600.00	550.00
23	1¢ blue, type IV	10,000.00	850.00
24	1¢ blue, type V	170.00	45.00
	"Curl" on shoulder	230.00	72.50
	"Earring" below ear	600.00	100.00
	Long double "curl" in hair	290.00	85.00
b	Laid paper		1,750.00
	#25-26a: Washington (11)		
25	3¢ rose, type I	3,000.00	125.00
	Major cracked plate	5,000.00	750.00
26	3¢ dull red, type II	75.00	9.00
	Brownish carmine	150.00	20.00
	Claret	170.00	25.00
	Left or right frame line double	110.00	20.00
	Cracked plate	750.00	250.00
26A	3¢ dull red, type IIa	500.00	110.00
	Double transfer	575.00	180.00
	Left frame line double	—	210.00

Perf. 15.5

#27-29: Jefferson (12)

		Un	U
27	5¢ brick red, type I	80,000.00	1,800.00
28	5¢ red brown, type I	10,000.00	1,200.00
b	Bright red brown	12,500.00	1,750.00
28A	5¢ Indian red, type I	175,000.00	3,750.00
29	5¢ brown, type I	3,500.00	450.00
30	5¢ orange brown, type II	1,250.00	1,300.00
30A	5¢ brown, type II (30)	2,400.00	325.00
b	Printed on both sides		40,000.00
	#31-35: Washington (15)		
31	10¢ green, type I	30,000.00	1,300.00

Issues of 1857-1875

Perf. 15.5

		Un	U
32	10¢ green, type II	6,250.00	300.00
33	10¢ green, type III	6,250.00	300.00
	"Curl" on forehead or in left "X"	—	375.00
34	10¢ green, type IV	50,000.00	2,500.00
35	10¢ green, type V	260.00	65.00
	Small "curl" on forehead	310.00	77.50
	"Curl" in "e" or "t" of "Cents"	340.00	90.00
	Plate I Outer frame lines complete		
36	12¢ blk. Washington (17), plate I	1,900.00	325.00
	Triple transfer	2,300.00	—
36B	12¢ black, plate III	825.00	375.00
	Vertical line through rosette	1,000.00	450.00
37	24¢ gray lilac	1,600.00	400.00
a	24¢ gray	1,600.00	400.00
38	30¢ orange Franklin	2,400.00	500.00
	Recut at bottom	2,900.00	625.00
39	90¢ blue Washington	3,500.00	9,500.00
	Double transfer at top or bottom	3,750.00	—
	Pen cancel		2,900.00

Note: Beware of forged cancellations of #39. Genuine cancellations are rare

Issues of 1875, Government Reprints, White Paper Without Gum, Perf. 12

		Un	U
40	1¢ bright blue Franklin (5)	625.00	
41	3¢ scarlet Wash. (11)	3,250.00	
42	5¢ orange brown Jefferson (30)	1,400.00	
43	10¢ blue green Washington (14)	3,000.00	—
44	12¢ greenish black Washington (17)	3,250.00	
45	24¢ blackish violet Washington (37)	3,250.00	—
46	30¢ yellow orange Franklin (38)	3,250.00	
47	90¢ deep blue Washington (39)	4,750.00	
48-54	Not assigned		

Issue of 1861, Thin, Perf. 12 Semi-Transparent Paper

#55-62 are no longer considered postage stamps. Many experts consider them to be essays and/or trial color proofs.

		Un	U
62B	10¢ dark green Washington (58)	8,000.00	1,500.00

Details

5

Bust of Benjamin Franklin.

Detail of **#5a** Type Ib

Lower scrollwork is incomplete, the little balls are not so clear.

Detail of **#5, 18, 40** Type I

Has curved, unbroken lines outside labels. Scrollwork is substantially complete at top, forms little balls at bottom.

Detail of **#6, 19** Type Ia

Same as Type I at bottom but top ornaments and outer line partly cut away. Lower scrollwork is complete.

Detail of **#5a** Type Ib

Lower scrollwork is incomplete, the little balls are not so clear.

Detail of **#7, 20** Type II

Lower scrollwork incomplete (lacks little balls and lower plume ornaments). Side ornaments are complete.

Detail of **#8, 21** Type III

Outer lines broken in the middle. Side ornaments are substantially complete.

Detail of **#8A, 22** Type IIIa

Outer lines broken top or bottom but not both.

Detail of **#9, 23** Type IV

Similar to Type II, but outer lines recut top, bottom or both.

Detail of **#24** Type V

Similar to Type III of 1851-1857 but with side ornaments partly cut away.

2008 Digital Color Postmark First Day Covers

Enliven your postmark collectibles! These beautiful miniature works of art are uniquely created for each stamp cover they adorn. Collect them as they're issued or get them all at once—these inexpensive beauties now come in annual sets!

Item #990868 (2008 Random Set of 12 Covers) $18.00
Item #990879 (2008 Complete Set of 41 Covers) $61.50
Item #990768 (2007 Random Set of 14 Covers) $21.00
Item #990779 (2007 Complete Set of 61 Covers) $91.50
Item #990668 (2006 Random Set of 14 Covers) $27.83
Item #990679 (2006 Complete Set of 105 Covers) $164.33
Item #990568 (2005 Random Set of 17 Covers) $25.50

To order call **1 800 STAMP-24** or visit us online at **www.usps.com**

3¢ Washington Types I-IIa, Series 1851-1857, 1857-1861, 1875

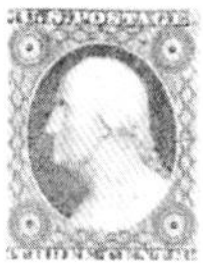

10
Bust of George Washington

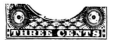

Detail of **#10, 11, 25, 41**
Type I

There is an outer frame line at top and bottom.

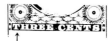

Detail of **#26**
Type II

The outer frame line has been removed at top and bottom. The side frame lines were recut so as to be continuous from the top to the bottom of the plate.

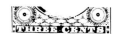

Detail of **#26a**
Type IIa

The side frame lines extended only to the bottom of the stamp design.

5¢ Jefferson Types I-II, Series 1851-1857, 1857-1861

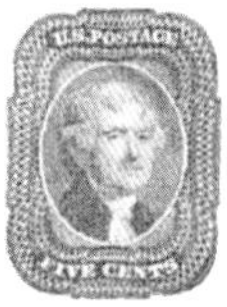

12
Portrait of Thomas Jefferson

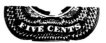

Detail of **#12, 27-29**
Type I

There are projections on all four sides.

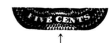

Detail of **#30-30a**
Type II

The projections at top and bottom are partly cut away.

10¢ Washington Types I-IV, Series 1851-1857, 1857-1861, 1875

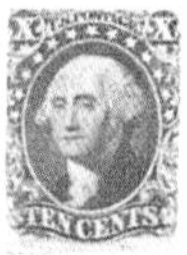

15
Portrait of George Washington

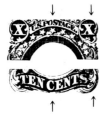

Detail of **#13, 31, 43**
Type I

The "shells" at the lower corners are practically complete. The outer line below the label is very nearly complete. The outer lines are broken above the middle of the top label and the "X" in each upper corner.

Detail of **#14, 32**
Type II

The design is complete at the top. The outer line at the bottom is broken in the middle. The shells are partly cut away.

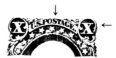

Detail of **#15, 33**
Type III

The outer lines are broken above the top label and the "X" numerals. The outer line at the bottom and the shells are partly cut away, as in Type II.

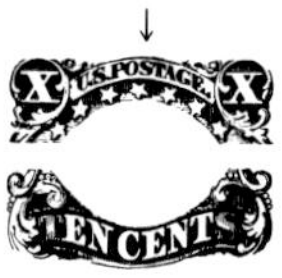

Detail of **#16, 34**
Type IV

The outer lines have been recut at top or bottom or both. Types I, II, III and IV have complete ornaments at the sides of the stamps and three pearls at each outer edge of the bottom panel.

Detail of **#35**
Type V
(Two typical examples.)

Ornaments slightly cut away. Outer lines complete at top except over right "X." Outer lines complete at bottom and shells nearly so.

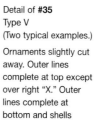

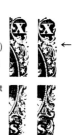

Issues of 1861-1863		Un	U
	Perf. 12		
63	1¢ blue Franklin	350.00	50.00
	Double transfer	—	62.50
	Dot in "U"	375.00	55.00
a	1¢ ultramarine	2,500.00	650.00
b	1¢ dark blue	800.00	400.00
c	Laid paper	11,000.00	9,000
d	Vert. pair, imperf. horizontally		—
e	Printed on both sides	—	4,000.00
64	3¢ pink Washington	14,000.00	1,000.00
a	3¢ pigeon blood pink	45,000.00	4,000.00
b	3¢ rose pink	600.00	160.00
65	3¢ rose Washington	140.00	3.00
	Double transfer	170.00	6.00
b	Laid paper	—	500.00
d	Vertical pair, imperf. horizontally	6,000.00	750.00
e	Printed on both sides	22,500.00	5,000.00
f	Double impression		7,500.00
66	3¢ lake Washington is considered a Trial Color Proof		2,000.00
67	5¢ buff Jefferson	27,500.00	1,100.00
68	10¢ yellow green Washington	1,200.00	62.50
	Deep yellow green on thin paper	1,400.00	70.00
	Double transfer	1,300.00	65.00
a	10¢ dark green	1,450.00	85.00
b	Vert. pair, imperf. horizontally		3,500.00
69	12¢ blk. Washington	2,000.00	120.00
	Intense black	2,100.00	135.00
	Double transfer of top or bottom frame line	2,100.00	150.00
	Double transfer of top and bottom frame lines	2,200.00	155.00
70	24¢ red lilac Washington	3,000.00	300.00
	Scratch under "A" of "POSTAGE"		—
a	24¢ brown lilac	3,250.00	225.00
b	24¢ steel blue	16,500.00	900.00
c	24¢ violet	35,000.00	2,100.00
d	24¢ grayish lilac	17,500.00	2,600.00

Issues of 1861-1867		Un	U
	Perf. 12		
71	30¢ orange Franklin	2,400.00	200.00
a	Printed on both sides		—
72	90¢ bl. Washington	3,500.00	600.00
a	90¢ pale blue	3,500.00	600.00
b	90¢ dark blue	4,250.00	750.00
73	2¢ blk. Andrew Jackson	375.00	70.00
	Double transfer	425.00	75.00
	Major double transfer of top left corner and "POSTAGE"		15,000.00
	#74 3¢ scarlet Washington was not regularly issued and is considered a Trial Color Proof.		
75	5¢ red brown Jefferson (67)	5,750.00	600.00
76	5¢ brown Jefferson (67)	1,750.00	150.00
a	5¢ black brown	2,250.00	300.00
	Double transfer of top or bottom frame line	1,850.00	160.00
	Double transfer of top and bottom frame lines	1,900.00	175.00
77	15¢ blk. Lincoln	4,500.00	225.00
	Double transfer	4,750.00	250.00
78	24¢ lilac Washington (70)	2,600.00	250.00
a	24¢ grayish lilac	2,600.00	300.00
b	24¢ gray	2,600.00	300.00
c	24¢ blackish violet	60,000.00	15,000.00
d	Printed on both sides		25,000.00
	Grills on U.S. Stamps		
	Between 1867 and 1870, postage stamps were embossed with pyramid-shaped grills that absorbed cancellation ink to prevent reuse of canceled stamps.		
	Issues of 1867, With Grills, Perf. 12		
	Grills A, B and with C: Points Up		
	A. Grill Covers Entire Stamp		
79	3¢ rose Washington (56)	8,500.00	1,750.00
b	Printed on both sides		—
80	5¢ brown Jefferson (57)	—	130,000.00
a	5¢ dark brown		130,000.00
81	30¢ orange Franklin (61)		100,000.00
	B. Grill about 18 x 15mm		
82	3¢ rose Washington (56)		240,000.00
	C. Grill about 13 x 16mm		
83	3¢ rose Washington (56)	6,500.00	1,100.00
	Double grill	7,750.00	2,400.00

Issues of 1867		Un	U
	With Grills, Perf. 12		
	Grills, D, Z, E, F with Points Down		
	D. Grill about 12 x 14mm		
84	2¢ black Jackson (73)	16,000.00	4,500.00
85	3¢ rose Washington (56)	6,750.00	1,250.00
	Split grill		1,350.00
	Z. Grill about 11 x 14mm		
85A	1¢ blue Franklin (55)	3,000,000.00	
85B	2¢ black Jackson (73)	15,000.00	1,500.00
	Double transfer	16,000.00	1,600.00
85C	3¢ rose Washington (56)	25,000.00	3,750.00
	Double grill	27,000.00	
85D	10¢ grn. Washington (58)		225,000.00
85E	12¢ blk. Washington (59)	14,000.00	2,500.00
	Double transfer of top frame line		2,600.00
85F	15¢ black Lincoln (77)		1,000,000.00
	E. Grill about 11 x 13mm		
86	1¢ blue Franklin (55)	3,750.00	550.00
a	1¢ dull blue	3,750.00	525.00
	Double grill	—	675.00
	Split grill	4,000.00	600.00
87	2¢ black Jackson (73)	1,850.00	200.00
	Intense black	1,950.00	225.00
	Double grill	—	—
	Double transfer	2,000.00	210.00
88	3¢ rose Washington (65)	1,100.00	27.50
	Double grill	—	—
	Very thin paper	1,150.00	32.50
a	3¢ lake red	1,300.00	50.00
89	10¢ grn. Washington (68)	5,500.00	325.00
	Double grill	7,000.00	525.00
90	12¢ blk. Washington (69)	5,250.00	400.00
	Double transfer of top or bottom frame line	5,500.00	425.00
91	15¢ black Lincoln (77)	13,500.00	700.00
	Double grill	—	1,000.00
	F. Grill about 9 x 13mm		
92	1¢ blue Franklin (63)	3,500.00	550.00
a	1¢ pale blue	3,000.00	475.00
	Double transfer	3,750.00	600.00
	Double grill	—	925.00

63   **64**    **65**    **67**    **68**

69    **70**    **71**    **72**    **73**    **77**

Details

Issues of 1861-1862, 1861-1866, 1867 and 1875

Detail of #63, 86, 92

There is a dash in #63, 86 and 92 added under the tip of the ornament at the right of the numeral in upper left corner.

Detail of #67, 75, 80, 95

There is a leaf in #67, 75, 80 and 95 added to the foliated ornaments at each corner.

Detail of #69, 85E, 90, 97

In #69, 85E, 90 and 97, ovals and scrolls have been added at the corners.

Detail of #64-66, 74, 79, 82-83, 85, 85C, 88, 94

In 64-66, 74, 79, 82-83, 85, 85C, 88 and 94, ornaments at corners have been enlarged and end in a small ball.

Detail of #68, 85D, 89, 96

There is an outer line in #68, 85D, 89 and 96 cut below the stars and an outer line added to the ornaments above them.

Detail of #72, 101

In #72 and 101, parallel lines form an angle above the ribbon containing "U.S. Postage"; between these lines a row of dashes has been added, along with a point of color to the apex of the lower line.

112

113

114

115

116

117

118

120

121

122

Details

15¢ Landing of Columbus, Types I-III, Series 1869-1875

Detail of #118 Type I
Picture unframed.

Detail of #119 Type II
Picture framed.

#129 Type III
Same as Type I but without fringe of brown shading lines around central vignette.

Issues of 1867

		Un	U
Issues of 1867, With Grills, Perf. 12			
F. Grill about 9 x 13mm			
93	2¢ black Jackson (73)	525.00	60.00
	Double grill	—	180.00
	Very thin paper	575.00	65.00
94	3¢ red Washington (65)	400.00	10.00
a	3¢ rose	400.00	10.00
	Double grill		—
	End roller grill		350.00
	Quadruple split grill	725.00	130.00
c	Vertical pair, imperf. horizontally	1,500.00	
d	Printed on both sides	7,500.00	
95	5¢ brown Jefferson (67)	3,750.00	900.00
a	5¢ black brown	4,500.00	1,200.00
96	10¢ yellow green Washington (68)	3,250.00	275.00
	Dark green	3,250.00	350.00
	Quadruple split grill		725.00
97	12¢ blk. Washington (69)	3,500.00	300.00
	Double transfer of top or bottom frame line	3,900.00	325.00
	Triple grill		—
98	15¢ black Lincoln (77)	4,500.00	375.00
	Double transfer of upper right corner	—	—
	Double grill	—	525.00
	Quadruple split grill	5,250.00	700.00
99	24¢ gray lilac Washington (70)	8,500.00	1,300.00
100	30¢ orange Franklin (71)	8,500.00	900.00
	Double grill	11,000.00	1,800.00
101	90¢ bl. Washington (72)	14,500.00	2,200.00
	Double grill	19,000.00	

Issues of 1869-1875

		Un	U
Issues of 1875			
Reissue of 1861-1866 Issues			
Without Grill, Perf. 12			
102	1¢ blue Franklin (63)	900.00	1,250.00
103	2¢ black Jackson (73)	4,250.00	7,000.00
104	3¢ brown red Washington (65)	4,750.00	12,500.00
105	5¢ brown Jefferson (67)	3,250.00	6,000.00
106	10¢ grn. Washington (68)	4,000.00	20,000.00
107	12¢ blk. Washington (69)	4,750.00	9,500.00
108	15¢ black Lincoln (77)	5,250.00	16,000.00
109	24¢ deep violet Washington (70)	6,500.00	17,500.00
110	30¢ brownish orange Franklin (71)	6,750.00	17,500.00
111	90¢ bl. Washington (72)	7,250.00	110,000.00
Issues of 1869			
With Grill, Perf. 12, Hard Wove Paper,			
G. Grill about 9.5 x 9mm			
112	1¢ buff Franklin	800.00	175.00
	Double grill	1,200.00	350.00
b	Without grill	10,000.00	
113	2¢ brown Post Horse and Rider	750.00	100.00
	Split grill	900.00	125.00
	Double transfer		120.00
114	3¢ ultra. Locomotive	325.00	20.00
	Triple grill	—	—
	Sextuple grill	—	7,000.00
	Gray paper	—	100.00
a	Without grill	12,500.00	
115	6¢ ultra. Washington	3,000.00	250.00
	Quadruple split grill	—	850.00

Issues of 1869-1880

		Un	U
Issues of 1869			
With Grill, Perf. 12, Hard Wove Paper,			
G. Grill about 9.5 x 9mm			
116	10¢ yel. Shield and Eagle	2,500.00	150.00
	End roller grill	—	—
117	12¢ green S.S. Adriatic	2,500.00	160.00
	Split grill	3,000.00	190.00
118	15¢ brown & blue Landing of Columbus, type I	10,000.00	750.00
a	Without grill	15,000.00	
119	15¢ brown & blue type II (118)	3,750.00	275.00
b	Center inverted	1,250,000.00	17,500.00
c	Center double, one inverted		80,000.00
120	24¢ grn. & violet Declaration of Independence	9,500.00	775.00
a	Without grill	13,500.00	
b	Center inverted	750,000.00	22,500.00
121	30¢ Shield, Eagle and Flags	7,500.00	550.00
	Double grill	—	1,250.00
a	Without grill	12,000.00	
b	Flags inverted	1,000,000.00	100,000.00
122	90¢ Lincoln	13,000.00	2,500.00
	Split grill	—	—
Issues of 1875			
Reissue of 1869 Issue			
Without Grill, Perf. 12, Hard White Paper			
123	1¢ buff (112)	650.00	400.00
124	2¢ brown (113)	750.00	875.00
125	3¢ blue (114)	5,500.00	27,500.00
126	6¢ blue (115)	2,000.00	2,750.00
127	10¢ yellow (116)	2,000.00	2,000.00
128	12¢ green (117)	2,750.00	3,250.00
129	15¢ brown and blue, type III (118)	1,750.00	1,300.00
a	Imperf. horizontally	6,250.00	7,000
130	24¢ grn. & violet (120)	2,500.00	1,750.00
131	30¢ ultra. & carmine (121)	3,000.00	3,000.00
132	90¢ car. & black (122)	4,500.00	6,500.00
Issue of 1880			
Reissue of 1869			
Without Grill, Soft Porous Paper			
133	1¢ buff (112)	350.00	350.00
a	1¢ brown orange, issued without gum	225.00	300.00

Issues of 1870-1871		Un	U

With Grill, Perf. 12, White Wove Paper, No Secret Marks

H. Grill about 10 x 12mm

		Un	U
134	1¢ ultramarine Franklin	2,500.00	200.00
	End roller grill		725.00
135	2¢ red brown Jackson	1,250.00	80.00
136	3¢ green Washington	750.00	27.50
	Cracked plate	—	100.00
137	6¢ Lincoln	6,000.00	525.00
	Double grill	—	900.00
138	7¢ Edwin M. Stanton	5,000.00	525.00
139	10¢ Jefferson	7,500.00	800.00
140	12¢ Henry Clay	27,500.00	3,500.00
141	15¢ Daniel Webster	9,000.00	1,400.00
142	24¢ Gen. Winfield Scott	—	7,500.00
143	30¢ Alexander Hamilton	20,000.00	3,750.00
144	90¢ Commodore Perry	25,000.00	2,500.00
	Split grill		2,600.00

Without Grill, Perf. 12, White Wove Paper, No Secret Marks

		Un	U
145	1¢ ultra. Franklin (134)	675.00	20.00
146	2¢ red brown Jackson (135)	375.00	17.50
147	3¢ green Washington (136)	300.00	1.75
148	6¢ carmine Lincoln (137)	1,200.00	35.00
	Brown carmine	1,250.00	65.00
	Violet carmine	1,400.00	90.00
149	7¢ vermilion Stanton (138)	1,250.00	95.00
150	10¢ brown Jefferson (139)	1,750.00	30.00
151	12¢ dull violet Clay (140)	3,000.00	200.00
152	15¢ bright orange Webster (141)	3,250.00	200.00
153	24¢ purple Scott (142)	2,200.00	200.00
154	30¢ black Hamilton (143)	7,500.00	275.00
155	90¢ carmine Perry (144)	5,500.00	350.00

Issues of 1873-1875		Un	U

Issues of 1873, Without Grill, Perf. 12, White Wove Paper, Thin to Thick, Secret Marks

		Un	U
156	1¢ ultramarine Franklin	275.00	5.00
	Paper with silk fibers	—	27.50
e	With grill	2,000.00	
f	Imperf. pair	—	1,500.00
157	2¢ brown Jackson	425.00	22.50
	Double paper	1,050.00	105.00
c	With grill	1,850.00	750.00
158	3¢ green Washington	140.00	1.00
	Olive green	375.00	15.00
	Cracked plate	—	32.50

Without Grill, White Wove Paper, Thin to Thick, Secret Marks

		Un	U
159	6¢ dull pink Lincoln	475.00	20.00
b	With grill	1,800.00	
160	7¢ orange vermilion Stanton	1,500.00	90.00
	Ribbed paper	—	105.00
161	10¢ brown Jefferson	1,300.00	25.00
162	12¢ blackish violet Clay	2,750.00	125.00
163	15¢ yellow orange Webster	3,000.00	140.00
a	With grill	5,750.00	
164	24¢ purple Scott		357,500
165	30¢ gray black Hamilton	3,500.00	130.00
166	90¢ rose carmine Perry	2,750.00	275.00

Issues of 1875, Special Printing, Perf. 12, Hard, White Wove Paper, Without Gum, Secret Marks, Perf. 12

Although perforated, these stamps were usually cut apart with scissors. As a result, the perforations are often much mutilated and the design is frequently damaged.

		Un	U
167	1¢ ultramarine Franklin (156)	20,000.00	
168	2¢ dark brown Jackson (157)	10,000.00	

Issues of 1875-1879		Un	U
169	3¢ blue green Washington (158)	25,000.00	—
170	6¢ dull rose Lincoln (159)	24,000.00	
171	7¢ reddish vermilion Stanton (160)	6,250.00	
172	10¢ pale brown Jefferson (161)	23,000.00	
173	12¢ dark violet Clay (162)	8,000.00	
174	15¢ bright orange Webster (163)	23,000.00	
175	24¢ dull purple Scott (142)	5,500.00	17,500.00
176	30¢ greenish black Hamilton (143)	19,000.00	
177	90¢ violet carmine Perry (144)	30,000.00	

Regular Issue, Yellowish Wove Paper, Perf. 12

		Un	U
178	2¢ vermilion Jackson (157)	425.00	12.50
b	Half used as 1¢ on cover		750.00
c	With grill	900.00	2,750.00
179	5¢ blue Zachary Taylor	800.00	25.00
	Cracked plate	—	170.00
	Double paper	950.00	
	Paper with silk fibers	—	37.50
c	With grill	4,500.00	

Special Printing, Hard, White Wove Paper, Without Gum

		Un	U
180	2¢ carmine vermilion Jackson (157)	80,000.00	
181	5¢ bright blue Taylor (179)	450,000.00	

Issues of 1879, Soft, Porous Paper, Thin to Thick, Perf. 12

		Un	U
182	1¢ dark ultramarine Franklin (156)	325.00	4.50
183	2¢ vermilion Jackson (157)	130.00	3.25
a	Double impression	—	5,500.00

Details

Detail of **#134, 145**

Detail of **#135, 146**

Detail of **#136, 147**

Detail of **#137, 148**

Detail of **#138**, **149**

Detail of **#156, 167, 182, 192**

1¢. In the pearl at the left of the numeral "1" there is a small crescent.

Detail of **#157, 168, 178, 180, 183, 193**

2¢. Under the scroll at the left of "U.S." there is a small diagonal line. This mark seldom shows clearly.

Detail of **#158, 169, 184, 194**

3¢. The under part of the upper tail of the left ribbon is heavily shaded.

Detail of **#159, 170, 186, 195**

6¢. The first four vertical lines of the shading in the lower part of the left ribbon have been strengthened.

Detail of **#190**

30¢. In the "S" of "CENTS," the vertical spike across the middle section of the letter has been broadened.

134

135

136

137

138

139

140

141

142

143

144

156

157

158

159

160

161

162

163

179

Details

Detail of #139,150,187, 151

Detail of #140, 151

Detail of #141, 152

Detail of #143, 154, 165, 176

Detail of #161, 172, 188, 197

10¢. There is a small semi-circle in the scroll at the right end of the upper label.

Detail of #162, 173, 198

12¢. The balls of the figure "2" are crescent-shaped.

Detail of #163, 174, 189, 199

15¢. In the lower part of the triangle in the upper left corner two lines have been made heavier, forming a "V." This mark can be found on some of the Continental and American (1879) printings, but not all stamps show it.

Detail of #190

30¢. In the "S" of "CENTS," the vertical spike across the middle section of the letter has been broadened.

205

206

207

208

209

210

211

212

219

220

221

222

223

225

226

227

228

229

Details

Issues of 1881-1882, Re-engravings of 1873 Designs

Detail of #206

1¢. Upper vertical lines have been deepened, creating a solid effect in parts of background. Upper arabesques shaded.

Detail of #207

3¢. Shading at sides of central oval is half its previous width. A short horizontal dash has been cut below the "TS" of "CENTS."

Detail of #208

6¢. Has three vertical lines instead of four between the edge of the panel and the outside of the stamp.

Detail of #209

10¢. Has four vertical lines instead of five between left side of oval and edge of the shield. Horizontal lines in lower part of background strengthened.

Issues of 1879-1880	Un	U
Issues of 1879, Soft, Porous Paper, Thin to Thick, Perf. 12		
184 3¢ grn. Washington (158)	110.00	.80
Double transfer	—	—
Short transfer	—	6.25
185 5¢ blue Taylor (179)	525.00	15.00
186 6¢ pink Lincoln (159)	1,050.00	27.50
187 10¢ brown Jefferson (139) (no secret mark)	3,500.00	32.50
188 10¢ brown Jefferson (161) (with secret mark)	2,250.00	27.50
Black brown	2,500.00	40.00
Double transfer		47.50
189 15¢ red orange Webster (163)	325.00	25.00
190 30¢ full black Hamilton (143)	1,100.00	80.00
191 90¢ carmine Perry (144)	2,500.00	325.00
Issues of 1880, Special Printing, Soft Porous Paper, Without Gum, Perf. 12		
192 1¢ dark ultramarine Franklin (156)	75,000.00	
193 2¢ black brown Jackson (157)	27,500.00	
194 3¢ blue green Washington (158)	110,000.00	
195 6¢ dull rose Lincoln (159)	100,000.00	
196 7¢ scarlet vermilion Stanton (160)	9,000.00	
197 10¢ deep brown Jefferson (161)	55,000.00	
198 12¢ black purple Clay (162)	15,000.00	
199 15¢ orange Webster (163)	50,000.00	
200 24¢ dark violet Scott (142)	14,000.00	
201 30¢ greenish black Hamilton (143)	35,000.00	
202 90¢ dull carmine Perry (144)	45,000.00	
203 2¢ scarlet vermilion Jackson (157)	150,000.00	
204 5¢ deep blue Taylor (179)	350,000.00	

Issues of 1880-1887	Un	U
Perf. 12		
205 5¢ Garfield, 04/10	300.00	10.00
Special Printing, Soft Porous Paper, Without Gum, Perf. 12		
205C 5¢ gray brown Garfield (205)	85,000.00	
Issues of 1881-1882, Designs of 1873 Re-engraved		
206 1¢ Franklin, 08/81	90.00	1.00
Double transfer	115.00	6.00
207 3¢ Washington, 07/16/81	95.00	.55
Double transfer	—	12.00
Cracked plate	—	
208 6¢ Lincoln, 06/82	850.00	100.00
a 6¢ deep brown red	650.00	160.00
209 10¢ Jefferson, 04/82	190.00	6.00
b 10¢ black brown	2,500.00	325.00
Issues of 1883, Perf. 12		
210 2¢ Washington, 01/01/83	47.50	.60
Double transfer	52.50	2.25
211 4¢ Jackson, 01/01/83	325.00	22.50
Cracked plate	—	
Special Printing, Soft Porous Paper, Perf. 12		
211B 2¢ pale red brown Washington (210)	400.00	—
c Horizontal pair, imperf. between	2,000.00	
211D 4¢ deep blue green Jackson (211) no gum	80,000.00	
Issues of 1887, Perf. 12		
212 1¢ Franklin, 06/87	110.00	2.25
Double transfer	—	
213 2¢ green Washington (210), 09/10/87	47.50	.50
Double transfer	—	3.25
b Printed on both sides	—	
214 3¢ vermilion Washington (207), 09/03/87	75.00	62.50

Issues of 1888-1890	Un	U
Issues of 1888, Perf. 12		
215 4¢ carmine Jackson (211), 11/88	240.00	22.50
216 5¢ indigo Garfield (205), 02/88	275.00	15.00
217 30¢ orange brown Hamilton (165), 01/88	425.00	120.00
218 90¢ pur. Perry (166), 02/88	1,100.00	260.00
Issues of 1890, Perf. 12		
219 1¢ Franklin, 02/22/90	28.00	.60
Double transfer	—	—
219D 2¢ lake Washington (220), 02/22/90	240.00	5.00
Double transfer	—	—
220 2¢ Washington, 1890	25.00	.55
Double transfer	—	3.25
a Cap on left "2"	140.00	10.00
c Cap on both "2s"	675.00	30.00
221 3¢ Jackson, 02/22/90	85.00	7.50
222 4¢ Lincoln, 06/02/90	110.00	4.00
Double transfer	125.00	—
223 5¢ Grant, 06/02/90	90.00	4.00
Double transfer	105.00	3.75
224 6¢ Garfield, 06/02/90	80.00	22.50
225 8¢ Sherman, 06/02/90	65.00	15.00
226 10¢ Webster, 06/22/90	210.00	3.75
Double transfer	—	—
227 15¢ Clay, 02/22/90	275.00	25.00
Double transfer	—	—
Triple transfer	—	—
228 30¢ Jefferson, 02/22/90	425.00	37.50
Double transfer	—	—
229 90¢ Perry, 02/22/90	650.00	140.00
Short transfer at bottom	—	—

25

Issues of 1893	Date	Un	U	PB #	FDC	Q(M)

Columbian Exposition, Printed by The American Bank Note Co., Perf. 12

230	1¢ Columbus in Sight of Land	01/02/93	20.00	.40	500.00 (6)	*5,000.00*	449
	Double transfer		25.00	.75			
	Cracked plate		90.00				
231	2¢ Landing of Columbus	01/02/93	20.00	.30	425.00 (6)	*5,000.00*	1,464
	Double transfer		25.00	.35			
	Triple transfer		60.00	—			
	Quadruple transfer		95.00				
	Broken hat on third figure left of Columbus		60.00	3.50			
	Broken frame line		22.50	.45			
	Recut frame lines		22.50	—			
	Cracked plate		85.00	—			
232	3¢ *Santa Maria,* Flagship	01/02/93	55.00	15.00	800.00 (6)	*7,000.00*	12
	Double transfer		75.00	—			
233	4¢ ultramarine, Fleet	01/02/93	80.00	7.50	1,100.00 (6)	*14,000.00*	19
	Double transfer		115.00	—			
a	Blue (error)		19,000.00	16,500.00	200,000.00 (4)		
234	5¢ Columbus Soliciting Aid from Queen Isabella	01/02/93	85.00	8.00	1,400.00 (6)	*17,500.00*	35
	Double transfer		145.00	—			
235	6¢ Columbus Welcomed at Barcelona	01/02/93	80.00	22.50		*22,500.00*	5
a	Red violet		80.00	22.50	1,200.00 (6)		
	Double transfer		105.00	30.00			
236	8¢ Columbus Restored to Favor	03/93	72.50	11.00	1,100.00 (6)		11
	Double transfer		80.00	—			
237	10¢ Columbus Presenting Natives	01/02/93	135.00	8.00	3,750.00 (6)	*27,500.00*	17
	Double transfer		160.00	12.50			
	Triple transfer		—				
238	15¢ Columbus Announcing His Discovery	01/02/93	240.00	75.00	*4,250.00* (6)		2
	Double transfer		—	—			
239	30¢ Columbus at La Rábida	01/02/93	275.00	90.00	*9,000.00* (6)		0.6
240	50¢ Recall of Columbus	01/02/93	600.00	180.00	*15,000.00* (6)		0.2
	Double transfer		—	—			
	Triple transfer		—	—			
241	$1 Queen Isabella Pledging Her Jewels	01/02/93	1,200.00	650.00	*52,500.00* (6)		0.05
	Double transfer		—	—			
242	$2 Columbus in Chains	01/02/93	1,250.00	650.00	*75,000.00* (6)	*65,000.00*	0.05
243	$3 Columbus Describing His Third Voyage	01/02/93	1,900.00	1,000.00			0.03
a	Olive green		1,900.00	1,000.00	*95,000.00* (6)		

Issues of 1893-1894	Date	Un	U	PB #	FDC	Q(M)

Columbian Exposition, Printed by The American Bank Note Co., Perf. 12

244	$4 Queen Isabella and Columbus	01/02/93	2,600.00	1,300.00			0.03
a	Rose carmine		2,600.00	1,300.00	*300,000.00* (6)		
245	$5 Portrait of Columbus	01/02/93	3,000.00	1,500.00	*250,000.00* (6)		0.03

Unwmkd., Perf. 12

Bureau Issues Starting in 1894 and continuing until 1979, the Bureau of Engraving and Printing in Washington produced all U.S. postage stamps except #909-21, 1335, 1355, 1410-18 and 1789. Beginning in 1979, security printers in addition to the Bureau of Engraving and Printing started producing postage stamps under contract with the U.S. Postal Service.

246	1¢ Franklin	10/94	32.50	5.00	450.00 (6)		
	Double transfer		40.00	6.00			
247	1¢ blue Franklin (246)	11/94	75.00	3.00	900.00 (6)		
	Double transfer		—	4.50			
248	2¢ pink Washington type I	10/94	30.00	7.50	300.00 (6)		
	Double transfer		—	—			
a	Vertical pair, imperf. horizontally		5,500.00				
249	2¢ carmine lake type I (248)	10/94	175.00	5.50	2,500.00 (6)		
	Double transfer		—	6.50			
250	2¢ carmine type I (248)	10/94	30.00	2.50			
a	Rose		30.00	4.50			
b	Scarlet		30.00	2.50	375.00 (6)		
	Double transfer		—	5.00			
d	Horizontal pair, imperf. between		2,000.00				
251	2¢ carmine type II (248)	02/95	350.00	12.00			
a	Scarlet		350.00	9.00	3,250.00 (6)		
252	2¢ carmine type III (248)	03/95	130.00	12.00			
a	Scarlet		130.00	12.00	1,900.00 (6)		
b	Horizontal pair, imperf. vertically		5,000.00				
c	Horizontal pair, imperf. between		5,500.00				
253	3¢ Jackson	09/94	125.00	11.00	1,500.00 (6)		
254	4¢ Lincoln	09/94	175.00	7.50	2,000.00 (6)		
255	5¢ Grant	09/94	125.00	7.00	1,350.00 (6)		
	Worn plate diagonal lines missing in oval background		125.00	5.00			
	Double transfer		150.00	6.50			
c	Vertical pair, imperf. horiz.		4,000.00				
256	6¢ Garfield	07/94	175.00	25.00	2,750.00 (6)		
a	Vertical pair, imperf. horizontally		3,000.00		*21,500.00* (6)		
257	8¢ Sherman	03/94	175.00	18.50	2,500.00 (6)		
258	10¢ Webster	09/94	325.00	16.00	3,500.00 (6)		
	Double transfer		375.00	15.00			
259	15¢ Clay	10/94	325.00	60.00	5,000.00 (6)		

230

231

232

233

234

235

236
237

238
239
240 

241

242

243

244

245

246

248

253

254

255

256

257

258

259

Details

2¢ Washington Types I-III, Series 1894-1898

Triangle of **#248-50, 265** Type I

Horizontal lines of uniform thickness run across the triangle.

Triangle of **#251, 266,** Type II

Horizontal lines cross the triangle, but are thinner within than without.

Triangle of **#252, 267, 279B-279Be** Type III

The horizontal lines do not cross the double frame lines of the triangle.

*VISIT US ONLINE AT **THE POSTAL STORE***
*AT **WWW.USPS.COM***
*OR CALL **1 800 STAMP-24***

20th Century Stamps 1900-1950

260    **261**    **262**    **263**    **277**    **282C**

285    **286**    **287**   **288**   **289**

290    **291**    **292**    **293**

Details

10¢ Webster Types I-II, Series 1898

Watermark 191
Double-line
"USPS" in
capital letters;
detail at right.

Detail of **#282C**
Type I

The tips of the foliate
ornaments do not
impinge on the white
curved line below
"TEN CENTS."

Detail of **#283**
Type II

The tips of the ornaments
break the curved line
below the "E" of "TEN"
and the "T" of "CENTS."

$1 Perry, Types I-II, Series 1894

Detail of **#261, 276**
Type I

The circles enclosing
$1 are broken.

Detail of **#261A, 276A**
Type I

The circles enclosing
$1 are complete.

Issues	Date	Un	U	PB	#	FDC	Q(M)
Unwmkd., Perf. 12							
260 50¢ Jefferson	11/94	600.00	140.00	20,000.00	(6)		
261 $1 Perry, type I	11/94	1,200.00	350.00	20,000.00	(6)		
261A $1 black Perry type II (261)	11/94	2,400.00	800.00	40,000.00	(6)		
262 $2 James Madison	12/94	3,250.00	1,250.00	45,000.00	(6)		
263 $5 John Marshall	12/94	5,000.00	2,750.00	25,000.00	(3)		
Wmkd. 191, Horizontally or Vertically, Perf. 12							
264 1¢ Franklin (246)	04/95	6.50	.50	250.00	(6)		
265 2¢ Washington, type I (248)	05/95	30.00	3.00	400.00	(6)		
Double transfer		45.00	6.75				
266 2¢ Washington, type II (248)	05/95	35.00	5.00	500.00	(6)		
267 2¢ Washington, type III (248)	05/95	5.50	.40	190.00	(6)		
268 3¢ purple Jackson (253)	10/95	37.50	2.00	725.00	(6)		
Double transfer		45.00	4.50				
269 4¢ Lincoln (254)	06/95	50.00	3.00	825.00	(6)		
Double transfer		55.00	5.00				
270 5¢ Grant (255)	06/11/95	37.50	3.00	700.00	(6)		
Double transfer		45.00	4.50				
Worn plate, diagonal lines missing in oval background		40.00	3.25				
271 6¢ Garfield (256)	08/95	130.00	7.50	3,000.00	(6)		
Very thin paper		150.00	7.50				
a Wmkd. USIR		12,500.00	10,000.00				
272 8¢ Sherman (257)	07/95	75.00	2.50	1,000.00	(6)		
Double transfer		90.00	4.00				
a Wmkd. USIR		6,000.00	1,000.00	20,000.00	(3)		
273 10¢ Webster (258)	06/95	100.00	2.00	1,750.00	(6)		
Double transfer		125.00	4.50				
274 15¢ Clay (259)	09/95	250.00	16.00	3,750.00	(6)		
275 50¢ orange Jefferson (260)	11/95	300.00	35.00	6,000.00	(6)		
a Red orange		360.00	42.50	6,500.00	(6)		
276 $1 Perry type I (261)	08/95	700.00	100.00	40,000.00	(6)		
276A $1 Perry type II (261)	08/95	1,500.00	225.00	125,000.00	(6)		
277 $2 bright blue Madison (262)	08/95	1,100.00	450.00				
a Dark blue		1,100.00	450.00	75,000.00	(6)		
278 $5 Marshall (263)	08/95	2,400.00	650.00	200,000.00	(6)		
279 1¢ Franklin (246)	01/98	9.00	.50	185.00	(6)		
Double transfer		12.00	1.10				
279B 2¢ red Washington type IV (248)	05/99	9.00	.40	200.00	(6)		
c Rose carmine type III	03/99	300.00	200.00	3,250.00	(6)		
d Orange red, type IV	06/1900	11.50	.55	220.00	(6)		

Issues	Date	Un	U	PB	#	FDC	Q(M)
Wmkd. 191, Horizontally or Vertically, Perf. 12							
280 4¢ rose brn. Lincoln (254)	10/98	30.00	3.00				
a Lilac brown		30.00	3.00				
b Orange brown		30.00	3.00	700.00	(6)		
Extra frame line at top		50.00	9.00				
281 5¢ Grant (255)	03/98	35.00	2.00	650.00	(6)		
Double transfer		45.00	4.00				
Worn plate, diagonal lines missing in oval background		40.00	2.25				
282 6¢ lake Garfield (256)	12/98	50.00	6.00	900.00	(6)		
Double transfer		60.00	8.50				
a Purple lake		75.00	14.00	1,250.00	(6)		
282C 10¢ Webster (258), type I	11/98	210.00	6.00	2,600.00	(6)		
Double transfer		240.00	10.00				
283 10¢ orange brown Webster (258), type II	11/98	160.00	5.00	1,900.00	(6)		
284 15¢ Clay (259)	11/98	175.00	12.00	2,250.00	(6)		
Trans-Mississippi Exposition, Wmkd. 191, Perf. 12							
285 1¢ Jacques Marquette on the Mississippi	06/17/98	27.50	6.50	450.00	(6)	12,000.00	71
Double transfer		37.50	7.50				
286 2¢ Farming in the West	06/17/98	27.50	2.50	450.00	(6)	14,000.00	160
Double transfer		42.50	3.75				
Worn plate		30.00	3.00				
287 4¢ Indian Hunting Buffalo	06/17/98	130.00	24.00	1,750.00	(6)	27,500.00	5
288 5¢ John Charles Frémont on the Rocky Mountains	06/17/98	130.00	22.50	1,600.00	(6)	16,000.00	8
289 8¢ Troops Guarding Wagon Train	06/17/98	190.00	45.00	3,250.00	(6)	22,500.00	3
a Vertical pair, imperf. horizontally		27,500.00		125,000.00	(4)		
290 10¢ Hardships of Emigration	06/17/98	175.00	32.50	3,500.00	(6)	27,500.00	5
291 50¢ Western Mining Prospector	06/17/98	700.00	190.00	27,500.00	(6)	50,000.00	0.5
292 $1 Western Cattle in Storm	06/17/98	1,250.00	650.00	50,000.00	(6)	55,000.00	0.06
293 $2 Mississippi River Bridge	06/17/98	2,100.00	1,050.00	150,000.00	(6)		0.06

Pan-American Exposition, Wmkd. 191, Perf. 12

	Issue	Date	Un	U	PB/LP #	FDC	Q(M)
294	1¢ Fast Lake Navigation	05/01/01	17.50	3.00	300.00 (6)	4,000.00	91
a	Center inverted		12,500.00	14,000.00	150,000.00 (4)		
295	2¢ Empire State Express	05/01/01	16.50	1.00	300.00 (6)	2,500.00	210
a	Center inverted		55,000.00	60,000.00			
296	4¢ Electric Automobile	05/01/01	80.00	17.50	2,100.00 (6)		6
a	Center inverted		70,000.00	—	550,000.00 (4)		
297	5¢ Bridge at Niagara Falls	05/01/01	90.00	16.00	2,250.00 (6)	35,000.00	7
298	8¢ Canal Locks at Sault Ste. Marie	05/01/01	110.00	50.00	4,000.00 (6)		5
299	10¢ Fast Ocean Navigation	05/01/01	145.00	27.50	6,750.00 (6)		5

Wmkd. 191, Perf. 12

	Issue	Date	Un	U	PB/LP #	FDC	Q(M)
300	1¢ Franklin	02/03	12.00	.25	225.00 (6)		
	Double transfer		17.50	1.00			
	Worn plate		13.00	.35			
	Cracked plate		14.00	.30			
b	Booklet pane of 6	03/06/07	600.00	12,500.00			
301	2¢ Washington	01/17/03	16.00	.40	275.00 (6)		
	Double transfer		27.50	1.25			
	Cracked plate		—	1.25			
c	Booklet pane of 6	01/24/03	500.00	2,250.00			
302	3¢ Jackson	02/03	55.00	3.50	800.00 (6)		
	Double transfer		77.50	4.75			
303	4¢ Grant	02/03	60.00	2.30	825.00 (6)		
	Double transfer		77.50	2.75			
304	5¢ Lincoln	01/03	60.00	2.00	825.00 (6)		
305	6¢ Garfield	02/03	67.50	5.00	925.00 (6)		
	Brownish lake		67.50	5.00			
	Double transfer		72.50	4.50			
306	8¢ Martha Washington	12/02	42.50	3.00	750.00 (6)		
	Lavender		52.50	3.75			
307	10¢ Daniel Webster	02/03	70.00	2.80	1,100.00 (6)		
308	13¢ Benjamin Harrison	11/18/02	45.00	9.00	700.00 (6)		
309	15¢ Henry Clay	05/27/03	200.00	12.00	3,400.00 (6)		
	Double transfer		230.00	14.00			
310	50¢ Jefferson	03/23/03	475.00	30.00	7,500.00 (6)		
311	$1 David G. Farragut	06/05/03	700.00	80.00	20,000.00 (6)		
312	$2 Madison	06/05/03	1,100.00	225.00	32,500.00 (6)		
313	$5 Marshall	06/05/03	2,800.00	750.00	180,000.00 (6)		

For listings of #312 and 313 with perf. 10, see #479 and 480.

Imperf.

	Issue	Date	Un	U	PB/LP #	FDC	Q(M)
314	1¢ blue green Franklin (300)	10/02/06	16.00	16.50	200.00 (6)		
314A	4¢ brown Grant (303)	04/08	90,000.00	50,000.00			

#314A was issued imperforated, but all copies were privately perforated at the sides.

	Issue	Date	Un	U	PB/LP #	FDC	Q(M)
315	5¢ blue Lincoln (304)	05/12/08	220.00	1,250.00	2,750.00 (6)		

Coil, Perf. 12 Horizontally

	Issue	Date	Un	U	PB/LP #	FDC	Q(M)
316	1¢ Franklin (300)	02/18/08	70,000.00		325,000.00 (2)		

Coil, Perf. 12 Horizontally

	Issue	Date	Un	U	PB/LP #	FDC	Q(M)
317	5¢ Lincoln (304)	02/24/08	6,000.00	—	70,000.00 (2)		

Coil, Perf. 12 Vertically

	Issue	Date	Un	U	PB/LP #	FDC	Q(M)
318	1¢ Franklin (300)	07/31/08	6,000.00		35,000.00 (2)		

Wmkd. 191, Perf. 12

	Issue	Date	Un	U	PB/LP #	FDC	Q(M)
319	2¢ Washington	11/12/03	6.00	.25	180.00 (6)		
a	Lake, type I		—	—			
b	Carmine rose, type I		10.00	.40	250.00 (6)		
c	Scarlet, type I		10.00	.30	250.00 (6)		
d	Vertical pair, imperf. horiz.		7,500.00				
e	Vertical pair, imperf. between		2,500.00				

Washington 319, Imperf.

	Issue	Date	Un	U	PB/LP #	FDC	Q(M)
320	2¢ carmine	10/02/06	16.00	17.50	200.00 (6)		
	Double transfer		24.00	21.50			
a	Lake, type II		45.00	50.00	725.00 (6)		
b	Scarlet		18.50	15.00	225.00 (6)		
c	Carmine rose, type I		60.00	42.50			
d	Carmine, type II		120.00	250.00			

Coil, Perf. 12 Horizontally

	Issue	Date	Un	U	PB/LP #	FDC	Q(M)
321	2¢ carmine pair, type I	02/18/08	450,000.00		—		

Coil, Perf. 12 Vertically

	Issue	Date	Un	U	PB/LP #	FDC	Q(M)
322	2¢ carmine pair, type II	07/31/08	7,000.00	—	35,000.00 (2)		

Louisiana Purchase Exposition, Wmkd. 191, Perf. 12

	Issue	Date	Un	U	PB/LP #	FDC	Q(M)
323	1¢ Robert R. Livingston	04/30/04	27.50	5.00	350.00 (6)	7,500.00	80
	Diagonal line through left "1"			50.00	12.50		
324	2¢ Thomas Jefferson	04/30/04	27.50	2.00	350.00 (6)	5,000.00	193
325	3¢ James Monroe	04/30/04	85.00	30.00	950.00 (6)	20,000.00	5
326	5¢ William McKinley	04/30/04	87.50	25.00	1,000.00 (6)	22,500.00	7
327	10¢ Map of Louisiana Purchase	04/30/04	160.00	30.00	2,250.00 (6)	24,000.00	4

Jamestown Exposition, Wmkd. 191, Perf. 12

	Issue	Date	Un	U	PB/LP #	FDC	Q(M)
328	1¢ Captain John Smith	04/26/07	27.50	5.00	500.00 (6)	10,000.00	78
	Double transfer		35.00	6.00			
329	2¢ Founding of Jamestown, 1607	04/26/07	32.50	4.50	550.00 (6)	15,000.00	149
330	5¢ Pocahontas	04/26/07	140.00	32.50	2,750.00 (6)		

294    295    296    297    298    299

300   301    302    303    304    305    306    307

308    309    310    311    312    313    319

323   324    325   326   327

328    329    330

Details

2¢ Washington Die I-II, Series 1903

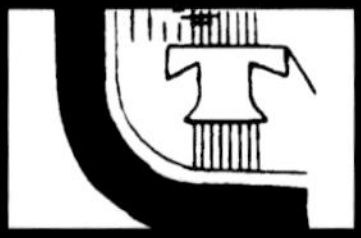

Detail of #319a, 319b, 319g Die I.    Detail of #319c, 319f, 319h, 319i Die II.

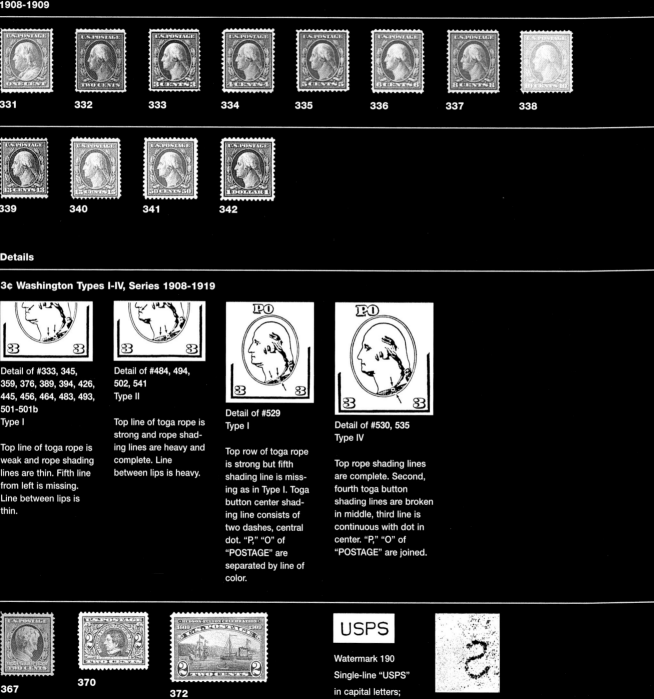

331 **332** **333** **334** **335** **336** **337** **338**

339 **340** **341** **342**

Details

3¢ Washington Types I-IV, Series 1908-1919

Detail of #333, 345, 359, 376, 389, 394, 426, 445, 456, 464, 483, 493, 501-501b
Type I

Top line of toga rope is weak and rope shading lines are thin. Fifth line from left is missing. Line between lips is thin.

Detail of #484, 494, 502, 541
Type II

Top line of toga rope is strong and rope shading lines are heavy and complete. Line between lips is heavy.

Detail of #529
Type I

Top row of toga rope is strong but fifth shading line is missing as in Type I. Toga button center shading line consists of two dashes, central dot. "P," "O" of "POSTAGE" are separated by line of color.

Detail of #530, 535
Type IV

Top rope shading lines are complete. Second, fourth toga button shading lines are broken in middle, third line is continuous with dot in center. "P," "O" of "POSTAGE" are joined.

367 **370** **372**

USPS

Watermark 190
Single-line "USPS"
in capital letters;

Issue	Date	Un	U	PB/LP	#	FDC	Q(M)

The Postal Service Guide to U.S. Stamps is no longer listing the so-called "china clay" paper varieties. Information about this paper can be found in the 2009 Scott Specialized Catalog.

Wmkd. 191, Perf. 12

	Issue	Date	Un	U	PB/LP	#	FDC	Q(M)
331	1¢ Franklin	12/08	7.25	.40	100.00	(6)		
	Double transfer		9.50	.75				
a	Booklet pane of 6	12/02/08	160.00	450.00				
332	2¢ Washington	11/08	6.75	.35	90.00	(6)		
	Double transfer		12.50	—				
a	Booklet pane of 6	11/16/08	135.00	400.00				
333	3¢ Washington, type I	12/08	35.00	3.00	400.00	(6)		
334	4¢ Washington	12/08	42.50	1.50	450.00	(6)		
	Double transfer		55.00	—				
335	5¢ Washington	12/08	55.00	2.50	550.00	(6)		
336	6¢ Washington	01/09	70.00	6.50	750.00	(6)		
337	8¢ Washington	12/08	50.00	3.00	525.00	(6)		
	Double transfer		57.50	—				
338	10¢ Washington	01/09	75.00	2.00	800.00	(6)		
339	13¢ Washington	01/09	42.50	19.00	500.00	(6)		
	Line through "TAG" of "POSTAGE"		70.00	—				
340	15¢ Washington	01/09	70.00	6.50	650.00	(6)		
341	50¢ Washington	01/13/09	350.00	20.00	7,000.00	(6)		
342	$1 Washington	01/29/09	550.00	100.00	20,000.00	(6)		

Imperf.

	Issue	Date	Un	U	PB/LP	#	FDC	Q(M)
343	1¢ green Franklin (331)	12/08	4.25	5.00	47.50	(6)		
	Double transfer		11.00	7.75				
344	2¢ carmine Washington (332)	12/10/08	5.25	3.25	77.50	(6)		
	Double transfer		12.50	4.00				
	Foreign entry, design of 1¢		1,250.00	—				

#345-347: Washington (Designs of 333-335)

	Issue	Date	Un	U	PB/LP	#	FDC	Q(M)
345	3¢ deep violet, type I	1909	10.00	22.50	155.00	(6)		
	Double transfer		22.50	—				
346	4¢ orange brown	02/25/09	15.00	25.00	175.00	(6)		
	Double transfer		35.00	—				
347	5¢ blue	02/25/09	30.00	37.50	275.00	(6)		

Coil, Perf. 12 Horizontally

#350-351, 354-356: Washington (Designs of 334-335, 338)

	Issue	Date	Un	U	PB/LP	#	FDC	Q(M)
348	1¢ green Franklin (331)	12/29/08	37.50	50.00	275.00	(2)		
349	2¢ carmine Washington (332)	01/09	80.00	100.00	550.00	(2)		
	Foreign entry, design of 1¢		—	3,000.00				
350	4¢ orange brown	08/15/10	150.00	210.00	1,250.00	(2)		
351	5¢ blue	01/09	160.00	275.00	1,150.00	(2)		

Coil, Perf. 12 Vertically

	Issue	Date	Un	U	PB/LP	#	FDC	Q(M)
352	1¢ green Franklin (331)	01/09	95.00	190.00	825.00	(2)		
353	2¢ carmine Washington (332)	01/12/09	95.00	220.00	750.00	(2)		
354	4¢ orange brown	02/23/09	220.00	275.00	1,500.00	(2)		

Coil, Perf. 12 Vertically

	Issue	Date	Un	U	PB/LP	#	FDC	Q(M)
355	5¢ blue	02/23/09	225.00	300.00	1,500.00	(2)		
356	10¢ yellow	01/07/09	3,250.00	4,500.00	17,500.00	(2)		

Bluish Paper, Perf. 12, #359-366: Washington (Designs of 333-340)

	Issue	Date	Un	U	PB/LP	#	FDC	Q(M)
357	1¢ green Franklin (331)	02/16/09	100.00	100.00	3,100.00	(6)		
358	2¢ carmine Washington (332)	02/16/09	90.00	100.00	1,000.00	(6)		
359	3¢ deep violet, type I	1909	2,000.00	5,000.00	22,500.00	(6)		
360	4¢ orange brown	1909	27,500.00		140,000.00	(3)		
361	5¢ blue	1909	6,000.00	15,000.00	90,000.00	(6)		
362	6¢ red orange	1909	1,500.00	15,000.00	16,000.00	(6)		
363	8¢ olive green	1909	30,000.00		150,000.00	(3)		
364	10¢ yellow	1909	1,900.00	7,000.00	33,500.00	(6)		
365	13¢ blue green	1909	3,000.00	2,250.00	30,000.00	(6)		
366	15¢ pale ultramarine	1909	1,500.00	11,000.00	11,500.00	(6)		

Lincoln Memorial, Wmkd. 191, Perf. 12

	Issue	Date	Un	U	PB/LP	#	FDC	Q(M)
367	2¢ Bust of Abraham Lincoln	02/12/09	5.25	2.00	200.00	(6)	500.00	148
	Double transfer		7.25	2.75				

Imperf.

	Issue	Date	Un	U	PB/LP	#	FDC	Q(M)
368	2¢ carmine (367)	02/12/09	17.00	22.50	200.00	(6)	13,000.00	1
	Double transfer		42.50	30.00				

Bluish Paper, Perf. 12

	Issue	Date	Un	U	PB/LP	#	FDC	Q(M)
369	2¢ carmine (367)	02/09	200.00	275.00	3,000.00	(6)		0.6

Alaska-Yukon-Pacific Exposition, Wmkd. 191, Perf. 12

	Issue	Date	Un	U	PB/LP	#	FDC	Q(M)
370	2¢ Willam H. Seward	06/01/09	8.00	2.25	200.00	(6)	3,000.00	153
	Double transfer		10.50	5.00				

Imperf.

	Issue	Date	Un	U	PB/LP	#	FDC	Q(M)
371	2¢ carmine (370)	06/09	19.00	24.00	225.00	(6)		0.5
	Double transfer		32.50	30.00				

Hudson-Fulton Celebration, Wmkd. 191, Perf. 12

	Issue	Date	Un	U	PB/LP	#	FDC	Q(M)
372	2¢ Half Moon & Clermont	09/25/09	11.50	4.75	280.00	(6)	900.00	73
	Double transfer		16.00	5.00				

Imperf.

	Issue	Date	Un	U	PB/LP	#	FDC	Q(M)
373	2¢ carmine (372)	09/25/09	22.50	27.50	240.00	(6)	8,000.00	0.2
	Double transfer		45.00	32.50				

Wmkd. 190, #376-382: Washington (Designs of 333-338, 340) Perf. 12

	Issue	Date	Un	U	PB/LP	#	FDC	Q(M)
374	1¢ green Franklin (331)	11/23/10	7.00	.25	100.00	(6)		
	Double transfer		14.00	—				
a	Booklet pane of 6	10/07/10	225.00	300.00				
375	2¢ carmine Washington (332)	11/23/10	7.00	.25	125.00	(6)		
	Double transfer		12.00	—				
	Foreign entry, design of 1¢		—	1,450.00				
a	Booklet pane of 6	11/30/10	125.00	200.00				
b	2¢ lake		900.00					
376	3¢ deep violet, type I	01/16/11	21.50	2.00	300.00	(6)		

Issue	Date	Un	U	PB/LP	#	FDC	Q(M)
Wmkd. 190, Perf. 12							
377 4¢ Washington	01/20/11	32.50	1.00	350.00	(6)		
378 5¢ Washington	01/25/11	32.50	.75	350.00	(6)		
379 6¢ Washington	01/25/11	37.50	1.00	500.00	(6)		
380 8¢ Washington	02/08/11	115.00	15.00	1,100.00	(6)		
381 10¢ Washington	01/24/11	110.00	6.00	1,250.00	(6)		
382 15¢ Washington	03/01/11	275.00	19.00	2,500.00	(6)		
Imperf.							
383 1¢ Franklin (331)	12/10	2.10	2.00	45.00	(6)		
Double transfer		6.50	—				
384 2¢ Washington (332)	12/10	3.50	2.50	130.00	(6)		
Double transfer		7.50	—				
Rosette plate, crack on head		150.00	—				
Coil, Perf. 12 Horizontally							
385 1¢ Franklin (331)	11/01/10	45.00	45.00	450.00	(2)		
386 2¢ Washington (332)	11/01/10	110.00	100.00	1,400.00	(2)		
Coil, Perf. 12 Vertically							
387 1¢ Franklin (331)	11/01/10	200.00	140.00	1,200.00	(2)		
388 2¢ Washington (332)	11/01/10	1,500.00	2,250.00	8,750.00	(2)		
389 3¢ Washington, type I (333)	01/24/11	110,000.00	11,000.00				
Coil, Perf. 8.5 Horizontally							
390 1¢ Franklin (331)	12/12/10	5.00	14.00	37.50	(2)		
391 2¢ Washington (332)	12/23/10	42.50	50.00	260.00	(2)		
Coil, Perf. 8.5 Vertically #394-396: Washington (Designs of 333-335)							
392 1¢ Franklin (331)	12/12/10	30.00	55.00	200.00	(2)		
393 2¢ Washington (332)	12/16/10	47.50	45.00	300.00	(2)		
394 3¢ Washington, type I	09/18/11	60.00	67.50	425.00	(2)		
395 4¢ Washington	04/15/12	62.50	70.00	475.00	(2)		
396 5¢ Washington	03/13	60.00	67.50	425.00	(2)		
Panama Pacific Exposition, Wmkd. 190, Perf. 12							
397 1¢ Vasco Nunez de Balboa	01/01/13	17.50	2.00	300.00	(6)	5,000.00	335*
Double transfer		22.50	3.25				
398 2¢ Pedro Miguel Locks, Panama Canal	01/13	20.00	1.00	400.00	(6)		504*
Double transfer		40.00	3.50				
a Carmine lake		1,500.00					
b Lake		5,000.00					
399 5¢ Golden Gate	01/01/13	80.00	10.00	1,900.00	(6)	31,000.00	29*
400 10¢ Discovery of San Francisco Bay	01/01/13	135.00	22.50	2,350.00	(6)	10,000.00	17*
400A 10¢ orange (400)	08/13	225.00	20.00	12,000.00	(6)		
*Includes perf. 10 printing quantities.							
Wmkd. 190, Perf. 10							
401 1¢ green (397)	12/14	27.50	7.00	400.00	(6)		335
402 2¢ carmine (398)	01/15	75.00	2.75	1,950.00	(6)		504
Wmkd. 190, Perf. 10							
403 5¢ blue (399)	02/15	175.00	20.00	4,000.00	(6)		29
404 10¢ orange (400)	07/15	850.00	70.00	14,000.00	(6)		17

Issue	Date	Un	U	PB/LP	#	FDC	Q(M)
Wmkd. 190, Perf. 12							
405 1¢ Washington	02/12	7.00	.25	110.00	(6)		
Cracked plate		14.50	—				
Double transfer		8.50	—				
a Vertical pair, imperf. horizontally		2,000.00	—				
b Booklet pane of 6	02/08/12	65.00	75.00				
406 2¢ Washington, type I	02/12	7.00	.25	125.00	(6)		
Double transfer		9.00	—				
a Booklet pane of 6	02/08/12	65.00	90.00				
b Double impression		—					
c Lake		2,000.00	2,750.00				
407 7¢ Washington	04/14	80.00	14.00	1,200.00	(6)		
Imperf. #408-413: Washington (Designs of 405-406)							
408 1¢ Washington	03/12	1.00	1.00	18.00	(6)		
Double transfer		2.40	2.40				
409 2¢ Washington, type I	02/12	1.20	1.20	35.00	(6)		
Cracked plate		14.00	—				
Coil, Perf. 8.5 Horizontally							
410 1¢ Washington	03/12	6.00	12.50	30.00	(2)		
411 2¢ Washington, type I	03/12	10.00	15.00	55.00	(2)		
Double transfer		12.50	—				
Coil, Perf. 8.5 Vertically							
412 1¢ Washington	03/18/12	25.00	25.00	120.00	(2)		
413 2¢ Washington, type I	03/12	55.00	25.00	300.00	(2)		
Double transfer		52.50	—				
Wmkd. 190, Perf. 12							
414 8¢ Franklin	02/12	45.00	2.00	475.00	(6)		
415 9¢ Franklin	04/14	55.00	14.00	650.00	(6)		
416 10¢ Franklin	01/12	45.00	.80	500.00	(6)		
417 12¢ Franklin	04/14	50.00	5.00	625.00	(6)		
Double transfer		55.00	—				
Triple transfer		72.50	—				
418 15¢ Franklin	02/12	85.00	4.50	1,000.00	(6)		
Double transfer		—	—				
419 20¢ Franklin	04/14	200.00	19.00	2,000.00	(6)		
420 30¢ Franklin	04/14	125.00	19.00	1,450.00	(6)		
421 50¢ Franklin	08/14	450.00	30.00	10,000.00	(6)		
Wmkd. 191							
422 50¢ Franklin (421)	02/12/12	260.00	22.50	4,750.00	(6)		
423 $1 Franklin	02/12/12	550.00	75.00	13,500.00	(6)		
Double transfer		550.00	—				
Wmkd. 190, Perf. 12 x 10							
423A 1¢ Washington	1914	20,000.00	10,000.00				
Wmkd. 190, Perf. 10 #424-430: Wash. (Designs of 405-406, 333-336, 407)							
424 1¢ Washington	09/05/14	2.50	.20	60.00	(6)		
Double transfer		4.75	—				
c Vertical pair, imperf. horiz.		2,800.00	2,500.00				
d Booklet pane of 6		5.25	7.50				
e As "d", imperf.		2,000.00					
425 2¢ Washington, type I	09/05/14	2.30	.20	40.00	(6)		
Cracked plate		9.50	—				
e Booklet pane of 6	01/06/14	17.50	25.00				

397   398   399   400

405   406   407   414   415   416

417   418   419   420

421   423

Pacific Lighthouses Commemorative Booklet and Print Set

434

After 1915 (from 1916 to date), all postage stamps, except #519 and 832b, are on unwatermarked paper.

Details

2¢ Washington, Types I-VII, Series 1912-1921

Detail of #406-406a, 411, 413, 425-425e, 442, 444, 449, 453, 461, 463-463a, 482, 499-499f Type I

One shading line in first curve of ribbon above left "2" and one in second curve of ribbon above right "2." Toga button has only a faint outline. Top line of toga rope, from button to front of the throat, is very faint. Shading lines of face end in the front of the ear, with little or no joining, to form lock of hair.

Detail of #482a, 500 Type Ia

Similar to Type I but all lines are shorter.

Detail of #454, 487, 491, 539 Type II

Shading lines in ribbons as in Type I. Toga button, rope and rope shading lines are heavy. Shading lines of face at lock of hair end in strong vertical curved line.

Detail of #450, 455, 488, 492, 540, 546 Type III

Two lines of shading in curves of ribbons.

Detail of #526, 532 Type IV

Top line of toga rope is broken. Toga button shading lines form "DID." Line of color in left "2" is very thin and usually broken.

Detail of #527, 533 Type V

Top line of toga rope is complete. Toga button has five verticle shading lines. Line of color in left "2" is very thin and usually broken. Nose shading dots are as shown.

Detail of #528, 534 Type Va

Same as Type V except third row from bottom of nose shading dots has four dots instead of six. Overall height of design is 1⁄3mm shorter than Type V.

Detail of #528A, 534A Type VI

Generally same as Type V except line of color in left "2" is very heavy.

Detail of #528B, 534B Type VII

Line of color in left "2" is continuous, clearly defined and heavier than in Type V or Va but not as heavy as Type VI. An additional vertical row of dots has been added to upper lip. Numerous additional dots appear in hair at top of head.

	Issue	Date	Un	U	PB/LP # FDC	Q(M)
	Wmkd. 190, Perf. 10					
426	3¢ deep violet, type I	09/18/14	15.00	1.50	250.00	(6)
427	4¢ brown	09/07/14	35.00	1.00	475.00	(6)
	Double transfer		45.00	—		
428	5¢ blue	09/14/14	35.00	1.00	425.00	(6)
429	6¢ red orange	09/28/14	50.00	2.00	525.00	(6)
430	7¢ black	09/10/14	100.00	5.00	1,000.00	(6)
	#431-433, 435, 437-440: Franklin (Designs of 414-421, 423)					
431	8¢ pale olive green	09/26/14	37.50	3.00	550.00	(6)
432	9¢ salmon red	10/06/14	50.00	9.00	725.00	(6)
433	10¢ orange yellow	09/09/14	50.00	1.00	825.00	(6)
434	11¢ Franklin	08/11/15	25.00	8.50	300.00	(6)
435	12¢ claret brown	09/10/14	27.50	6.00	350.00	(6)
	Double transfer		35.00	—		
	Triple transfer		40.00	—		
a	Copper red		32.50	7.00	350.00	(6)
436	Not assigned					
437	15¢ gray	09/16/14	135.00	7.25	1,125.00	(6)
438	20¢ ultramarine	09/19/14	220.00	6.00	3,250.00	(6)
439	30¢ orange red	09/19/14	260.00	17.50	4,100.00	(6)
440	50¢ violet	12/10/15	575.00	17.50	15,000.00	(6)
	Coil, Perf. 10 Horizontally					
	#441-459: Washington (Designs of 405-406, 333-435; Flat Press, 18.5-19 x 22mm)					
441	1¢ green	11/14/14	1.00	1.50	8.00	(2)
442	2¢ carmine, type I	07/22/14	10.00	45.00	60.00	(2)
	Coil, Perf. 10 Vertically					
443	1¢ green	05/29/14	30.00	45.00	155.00	(2)
444	2¢ carmine, type I	04/25/14	50.00	40.00	325.00	(2)
445	3¢ violet, type I	12/18/14	250.00	250.00	1,300.00	(2)
446	4¢ brown	10/02/14	140.00	150.00	750.00	(2)
447	5¢ blue	07/30/14	50.00	115.00	260.00	(2)
	Coil, Perf. 10 Horizontally (Rotary Press, Designs 18.5-19 x 22.5mm)					
448	1¢ green	12/12/15	7.50	17.50	60.00	(2)
449	2¢ red, type I	12/05/15	3,000.00	650.00	16,000.00	(2)
450	2¢ carmine, type III	02/16	12.50	22.50	230.00	(2)
451	Not assigned					
	Coil, Perf. 10 Vertically (Rotary Press, Designs 19.5 20 x 22mm)					
452	1¢ green	11/11/14	10.00	17.50	75.00	(2)
453	2¢ carmine rose, type I	07/03/14	150.00	17.50	725.00	(2)
454	2¢ red, type II	06/15	75.00	22.50	425.00	(2)
455	2¢ carmine, type III	12/15	8.50	3.50	50.00	(2)
456	3¢ violet, type I	02/02/16	250.00	170.00	1,250.00	(2)
457	4¢ brown	02/18/16	25.00	30.00	150.00	(2)
	Cracked plate		35.00	—		
458	5¢ blue	03/09/16	30.00	30.00	175.00	(2)
	Horizontal Coil, Imperf.					
459	2¢ carmine, type I	06/30/14	200.00	1,300.00	1,000.00	(2)
	Wmkd. 191, Perf. 10					
460	$1 Franklin (423)	02/08/15	850.00	150.00	13,500.00	(6)
	Double transfer		900.00	175.00		
	Wmkd. 190, Perf. 11					
461	2¢ Washington (406), type I	06/17/15	150.00	360.00	1,500.00	(6)

Privately perforated copies of #409 have been made to resemble 461.

	Issue	Date	Un	U	PB/LP # FDC	Q(M)
	Unwmkd., Perf. 10 #462-469: Washington (Designs of 405-406, 333-336, 407)					
462	1¢ green	09/27/16	7.00	.35	160.00	(6)
	Experimental precancel, Springfield, MA, or New Orleans, LA			10.00		
a	Booklet pane of 6	10/15/16	9.50	12.50		
463	2¢ carmine, type I	09/25/16	4.50	.40	150.00	(6)
	Experimental precancel, Springfield, MA			22.50		
	Double transfer			6.50	—	
a	Booklet pane of 6	10/08/16	110.00	110.00		
464	3¢ violet, type I	11/11/16	75.00	19.00	1,350.00	(6)
	Double transfer in "CENTS"			90.00	—	
465	4¢ orange brown	10/07/16	45.00	2.50	650.00	(6)
466	5¢ blue	10/17/16	75.00	2.50	950.00	(6)
	Experimental precancel, Springfield, MA			175.00		
467	5¢ carmine (error in plate of 2¢)		525.00	850.00		
468	6¢ red orange	10/10/16	95.00	9.00	1,350.00	(6)
	Experimental precancel, Springfield, MA			175.00		
469	7¢ black	10/10/16	130.00	15.00	1,350.00	(6)
	Experimental precancel, Springfield, MA			175.00		
	#470-478: Franklin (Designs of 414-416, 434, 417-421, 423)					
470	8¢ olive green	11/13/16	60.00	8.00	600.00	(6)
	Experimental precancel, Springfield, MA			165.00		
471	9¢ salmon red	11/16/16	60.00	18.50	750.00	(6)
472	10¢ orange yellow	10/17/16	110.00	2.50	1,350.00	(6)
473	11¢ dark green	11/16/16	45.00	18.50	360.00	(6)
	Experimental precancel, Springfield, MA			575.00		
474	12¢ claret brown	10/10/16	60.00	7.50	625.00	(6)
	Double transfer		65.00	8.50		
	Triple transfer		77.50	11.00		
475	15¢ gray	11/16/16	200.00	16.00	3,000.00	(6)
476	20¢ light ultramarine	12/05/16	250.00	17.50	3,600.00	(6)
476A	30¢ orange red		3,750.00		67,500.00	(6)
477	50¢ light violet	03/02/17	1,100.00	80.00	57,500.00	(6)
478	$1 violet black	12/22/16	800.00	25.00	13,500.00	(6)
	Double transfer		825.00	32.50		
	Unwmkd., Perf. 10					
479	$2 Madison (312)	03/22/17	250.00	42.50	4,250.00	(6)
480	$5 Marshall (313)	03/22/17	200.00	40.00	3,300.00	(6)
	Imperf. #481-496: Washington (Designs of 405-406, 333-335)					
481	1¢ green	11/16	.95	.95	30.00	(6)
	Double transfer		2.50	2.50		
482	2¢ carmine, type I	12/08/16	1.30	1.30	30.00	(6)
482A	2¢ deep rose, type Ia		65,000.00			
483	3¢ violet, type I	10/13/17	10.00	10.00	115.00	(6)
	Double transfer		17.50	—		
484	3¢ violet, type II		8.00	8.00	87.50	(6)
	Double transfer		12.50	—		
485	5¢ carmine (error in plate of 2¢)	03/17	12,000.00		130.00	(6)

	Issue	Date	Un	U	PB/LP #	FDC Q(M)
	Coil, Perf. 10 Horizontally					
	#481-496: Washington (Designs of 405-406, 333-335)					
486	1¢ green	01/18	.85	.85	4.50 (2)	
	Double transfer		2.25	—		
487	2¢ carmine, type II	11/15/16	12.50	14.00	110.00 (2)	
488	2¢ carmine, type III	1919	3.00	5.00	40.00 (2)	
	Cracked plate		12.50	10.00		
489	3¢ violet, type I	10/10/17	4.50	2.25	32.50 (2)	
	Coil, Perf. 10 Vertically (Designs 19.5 x 20 x 22mm)					
	#481-496: Washington (Designs of 405-406, 333-335)					
490	1¢ green	11/17/16	.50	.60	3.25 (2)	
	Cracked plate (horizontal)		7.50	—		
	Cracked plate (vertical) retouched		9.00	—		
	Rosette crack		60.00	—		
491	2¢ carmine, type II	11/17/16	2,600.00	750.00	14,000.00 (2)	
492	2¢ carmine, type III		9.00	1.00	55.00 (2)	
493	3¢ violet, type I	07/23/17	14.00	4.50	110.00 (2)	
494	3¢ violet, type II	02/04/18	10.00	2.50	75.00 (2)	
495	4¢ orange brown	04/15/17	10.00	7.00	75.00 (2)	
	Cracked plate		25.00	—		
496	5¢ blue	01/15/19	3.25	2.50	30.00 (2)	
497	10¢ Franklin (416)	01/31/22	19.00	17.50	130.00 (2) 6,000.00	
	Unwmk., Perf. 11, #498-507: Washington (Designs of 405-406, 333-336, 407)					
498	1¢ green	03/17	.35	.25	22.50 (6)	
	Cracked plate		7.50	—		
a	Vertical pair, imperf. horizontally		900.00			
b	Horizontal pair, imperf. between		575.00			
c	Vertical pair, imperf. between		700.00	—		
d	Double impression		250.00	4,000.00		
e	Booklet pane of 6	04/06/17	2.50	2.00		
f	Booklet pane of 30	09/17	1,150.00			
g	Perf. 10 top or bottom		15,000.00	45,000		
499	2¢ rose, type I	03/17	.35	.25	22.50 (6)	
	Double transfer		6.00	—		
a	Vertical pair, imperf. horizontally		600.00			
b	Horizontal pair, imperf. vertically		375.00	225.00		
c	Vertical pair, imperf. between		1,000.00	300.00		
e	Booklet pane of 6	03/31/17	4.00	2.50		
f	Booklet pane of 30	09/17	28,000.00	—		
g	Double impression		200.00	—		

	Issue	Date	Un	U	PB/LP #	FDC Q(M)
	Unwmk., Perf. 11					
	#498-507: Washington (Designs of 405-406, 333-336, 407)					
500	2¢ deep rose, type Ia		275.00	240.00	2,150.00 (6)	
	Pair, types I and Ia		1,275.00			
501	3¢ light violet, type I	03/17	11.00	.40	140.00 (6)	
b	Booklet pane of 6	10/17/17	75.00	60.00		
c	Vertical pair, imperf. horizontally, type I		2,500.00			
d	Double impression		3,500.00	2,750.00		
502	3¢ dark violet, type II		14.00	.75	160.00 (6)	
b	Booklet pane of 6	02/28/18	60.00	55.00		
c	Vertical pair, imperf. horizontally		1,400.00	750.00		
d	Double impression		750.00	750.00		
e	Perf. 10, top or bottom		15,000.00	12,500.00		
503	4¢ brown	03/17	10.00	.40	150.00 (6)	
504	5¢ blue	03/17	9.00	.35	140.00 (6)	
	Double transfer		11.00	—		
505	5¢ rose (error in plate of 2¢)		325.00	550.00		
506	6¢ red orange	03/17	12.00	.40	180.00 (6)	
a	Perf. 10, top or bottom		5,000.00	9,000.00		
507	7¢ black	03/17	27.50	1.25	250.00 (6)	
	#508-518: Franklin (Designs of 414-416, 434, 417-421, 423)					
508	8¢ olive bister	03/17	12.00	.65	140.00 (6)	
b	Vertical pair, imperf. between		—	—		
c	Perf. 10 top or bottom			16,000.00		
509	9¢ salmon red	03/17	13.00	1.75	150.00 (6)	
510	10¢ orange yellow	03/17	17.50	.25	200.00 (6)	
511	11¢ light green	05/17	9.00	2.50	150.00 (6)	
	Double transfer		12.50	3.25		
512	12¢ claret brown	05/17	9.00	.40	150.00 (6)	
a	Brown carmine		10.00	.50		
b	Perf. 10, top or bottom		17,500.00	6,000.00		
513	13¢ apple green	01/10/19	11.00	6.00	140.00 (6)	
	Deep apple green		12.50	6.50		
514	15¢ gray	05/17	37.50	1.50	550.00 (6)	
515	20¢ light ultramarine	05/17	45.00	.45	600.00 (6)	
	Deep ultramarine		50.00	.55		
b	Vertical pair, imperf. between		2,000.00	1,750.00		
c	Double impression		1,250.00			
d	Perf. 10 at top or bottom		—	15,000.00		
516	30¢ orange red	05/17	37.50	1.50	600.00 (6)	
a	Perf. 10 top or bottom		20,000.00	7,500.00		

Celebrating Lunar New Year: Year of the Ox — Digital Color Postmark Covers

498   499   500   501   502   503

504   505   506   507

508   509   510   511   512

512a   513   514   515   516

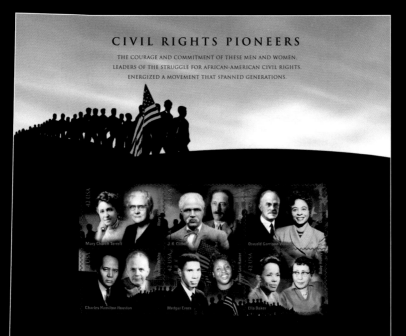

Civil Rights Pioneers

With this souvenir sheet, the U.S. Postal Service honors the courage, commitment and achievements of 12 leaders of the struggle for African-American civil rights.

Item #573940 $2.52

To know more about these and other philatelic products call **1 800 STAMP-24** *or visit us online at* **www.usps.com**

517

523

524

537

547

548

549

550

551

552

553

554

555

556

Flags of Our Nation — An Exciting New Multi-Stamp Series!

Flags of Our Nation (Set 2)

In 2008, the U.S. Postal Service introduced a new multi-stamp series featuring the Stars and Stripes, the fifty state flags, five territorial flags, and the District of Columbia flag. A total of sixty stamps will be issued in sets of ten, with the last issuance in 2012. Start your collection today with these exciting sets!

Flags of Our Nation Set 2: Coil of 50 (only)   Item #786640 $21.00

To order this item and other philatelic products call **1 800 STAMP-24** or visit us on-line at **www.usps.com.**

	Issue	Date	Un	U	PB/LP #	FDC	Q(M)
	Olympic Games, Perf. 11						
716	2¢ Ski Jumper	01/25/32	.40	.20	10.00 (6)	6.00	51
	Recut		3.50	1.50			
	Colored "snowball"		25.00	5.00			
	Perf. 11 x 10.5						
717	2¢ Arbor Day	04/22/32	.20	.20	5.50 (4)	4.00	100
	Olympic Games, Perf. 11 x 10.5						
718	3¢ Runner at Starting Mark	06/15/32	1.40	.20	12.00 (4)	6.00	169
	Gripper cracks		4.25	.75			
719	5¢ Myron's Discobolus	06/15/32	2.20	.20	20.00 (4)	8.00	52
	Gripper cracks		4.25	1.00			
	Perf. 11 x 10.5						
720	3¢ Washington	06/16/32	.20	.20	1.60 (4)	7.50	
	Pair with full vertical or horizontal gutter between		200.00				
	Recut lines on face		2.00	.75			
b	Booklet pane of 6	07/25/32	35.00	12.50		100.00	
c	Vertical pair, imperf. between		700.00	1,350.00			
	Coil, Perf. 10 Vertically						
721	3¢ Washington (720)	06/24/32	2.75	.20	10.00 (2)	15.00	
	Coil, Perf. 10 Horizontally						
722	3¢ Washington (720)	10/12/32	1.50	.35	6.25 (2)	15.00	
	Coil, Perf. 10 Vertically						
723	6¢ Garfield (558)	08/18/32	11.00	.30	60.00 (2)	15.00	
	Perf. 11						
724	3¢ William Penn	10/24/32	.45	.20	8.50 (6)	3.25	50
725	3¢ Daniel Webster	10/24/32	.45	.25	16.00 (6)	3.25	50
726	3¢ Georgia Settlement	02/12/33	.45	.20	10.00 (6)	3.25	62
	American Revolution Sesquitennial, Perf. 10.5 x 11						
727	3¢ Peace of 1783	04/19/33	.20	.20	3.00 (4)	3.50	73
	Century of Progress, Perf. 10.5 x 11						
728	1¢ Restoration of Fort Dearborn	05/25/33	.20	.20	1.75 (4)	3.00 (3)	348
	Gripper cracks		2.00	—			
729	3¢ Federal Building at Chicago	05/25/33	.25	.20	2.40 (4)	3.00	480
	American Philatelic Society Souvenir Sheets, Without Gum, Imperf.						
730	1¢ sheet of 25 (728)	08/25/33	27.50	27.50	100.00		0.4
a	Single stamp		.75	.50			11
731	3¢ sheet of 25 (729)	08/25/33	25.00	25.00	100.00		0.4
a	Single stamp from sheet		.65	.50		3.25	11
	Perf. 10.5 x 11						
732	3¢ National Recovery Act	08/15/33	.20	.20	1.50 (4)	3.25	1,978
	Gripper cracks		1.50	—			
	Recut at right		4.00				
	Perf. 11						
733	3¢ Byrd Antarctic Expedition II	10/09/33	.50	.50	12.00 (6)	10.00	6
	Double transfer		2.75	1.00			
	American Revolution Sesquitennial, Perf. 11						
734	5¢ General Tadeusz Kosciuszko	10/13/33	.55	.25	27.50 (6)	4.50	45
a	Horizontal pair, imperf. vertically		2,250.00		35,000.00 (8)		

	Issue	Date	Un	U	PB #	FDC	Q(M)
	National Stamp Exhibition Souvenir Sheet, Without Gum, Imperf.						
735	3¢ Byrd sheet of 6 (733)	02/10/34	11.00	10.00		40.00	0.8
a	Single stamp from sheet		1.85	1.65		5.00	5
	Perf. 11						
736	3¢ Maryland Tercentenary	03/23/34	.25	.20	6.25 (6)	1.60	46
	Perf. 11 x 10.5						
737	3¢ Portrait of his Mother, by James A. McNeill Whistler	05/02/34	.20	.20	1.00 (4)	1.60	193
	Perf. 11						
738	3¢ Portrait of his Mother, by James A. McNeill Whistler (737)	05/02/34	.20	.20	4.25 (6)	1.60	15
739	3¢ Wisconsin Tercentenary	07/07/34	.25	.20	2.90 (6)	1.10	64
a	Vert. pair, imperf. horizontally		350.00				
b	Horiz. pair, imperf. vertically		500.00		2,250.00 (6)		
	National Parks, Unwmkd., Perf. 11						
740	1¢ El Capitan, Yosemite (California)	07/16/34	.20	.20	1.00 (6)	2.25	85
	Recut		1.50	.50			
a	Vertical pair, imperf. horizontally, with gum		1,500.00				
741	2¢ Grand Canyon (Arizona)	07/24/34	.20	.20	1.50 (6)	2.25	74
	Double transfer		1.25		—		
a	Vertical pair, imperf. horizontally, with gum		575.00				
b	Horizontal pair, imperf. vertically, with gum		600.00				
742	3¢ Mt. Rainier, and Mirror Lake, (Washington)	08/03/34	.20	.20	1.80 (6)	2.50	95
a	Vertical pair, imperf. horizontally, with gum		700.00				
743	4¢ Cliff Palace, Mesa Verde (Colorado)	09/25/34	.40	.40	7.00 (6)	2.25	19
a	Vertical pair, imperf. horizontally, with gum		1,000.00				
744	5¢ Old Faithful, Yellowstone (Wyoming)	07/30/34	.70	.65	9.00 (6)	2.25	31
a	Horizontal pair, imperf. vertically, with gum		600.00				
745	6¢ Crater Lake (Oregon)	09/05/34	1.10	.85	17.50 (6)	3.00	17
746	7¢ Great Head, Acadia Park (Maine)	10/02/34	.60	.75	9.00 (6)	3.00	16
a	Horizontal pair, imperf. vertically, with gum		600.00				
747	8¢ Great White Throne, Zion Park (Utah)	09/18/34	1.60	1.50	17.50 (6)	3.25	15
748	9¢ Glacier National Park (Montana)	08/27/34	1.50	.65	15.00 (6)	3.50	17
749	10¢ Great Smoky Mountains (North Carolina)	10/08/34	3.00	1.25	22.50 (6)	6.00	19
	American Philatelic Society Souvenir Sheet, Imperf.						
750	3¢ sheet of 6 (742)	08/28/34	30.00	27.50		40.00	0.5
a	Single stamp		3.50	3.25		3.25	3
	Trans-Mississippi Philatelic Exposition Souvenir Sheet						
751	1¢ sheet of 6 (740)	10/10/34	12.50	12.50		35.00	0.8
a	Single stamp		1.40	1.60			5

Issue		Date	Un	U	PB	#	FDC	Q(M)
American Revolution Sesquitennial, Special Printing (#752-771), **Without Gum, Unwmk., Perf. 10.5 x 11**								
752	3¢ Peace of 1783 (727)	03/15/35	.25	.20	30.00	(4)	5.00	3
	Perf. 11							
753	3¢ Byrd Expedition II (733)	03/15/35	.50	.45	20.00	(6)	6.00	2
	Imperf.							
754	3¢ Whistler's Mother (737)	03/15/35	.60	.60	12.00	(6)	6.00	2
755	3¢ Wisconsin (739)	03/15/35	.60	.60	12.00	(6)	6.00	2
	National Parks, Imperf.							
756	1¢ Yosemite (740)	03/15/35	.20	.20	4.50	(6)	6.00	3
757	2¢ Grand Canyon (741)	03/15/35	.25	.25	5.75	(6)	6.00	3
758	3¢ Mt. Rainier (742)	03/15/35	.50	.45	14.00	(6)	6.00	2
759	4¢ Mesa Verde (743)	03/15/35	.95	.95	22.50	(6)	6.50	2
760	5¢ Yellowstone (744)	03/15/35	1.50	1.40	27.50	(6)	6.50	2
761	6¢ Crater Lake (745)	03/15/35	2.25	2.25	37.50	(6)	6.50	2
762	7¢ Acadia (746)	03/15/35	1.50	1.40	30.00	(6)	6.50	2
763	8¢ Zion (747)	03/15/35	1.80	1.50	37.50	(6)	7.50	2
764	9¢ Glacier (748)	03/15/35	1.90	1.75	42.50	(6)	7.50	2
765	10¢ Smoky Mts. (749)	03/15/35	3.75	3.50	50.00	(6)	7.50	2
	Imperf.							
766	1¢ Restoration of Fort Dearborn (728), pane of 25	03/15/35	25.00	25.00			250.00	0.1
a	Single stamp		.70	.50			5.50 (3)	2
767	3¢ Federal Building, Chicago (729), pane of 25	03/15/35	23.50	23.50			250.00	0.1
a	Single stamp		.60	.50			5.50	2
768	3¢ Byrd Antarctic Expedition II (733), pane of 6	03/15/35	20.00	15.00			250.00	0.3
a	Single stamp		2.80	2.40			6.50	2
769	1¢ El Capitan, Yosemite (California) (740), pane of 6	03/15/35	12.50	11.00			250.00	0.3
a	Single stamp		1.85	1.80			4.00	2
770	3¢ Cliff Palace, Mesa Verde (Colorado) (742), pane of 6	03/15/35	30.00	24.00			250.00	0.2
a	Single stamp from pane		3.25	3.10			5.00	1
771	6¢ Great Seal of U.S.	03/15/35	2.60	2.60	55.00	(6)	12.50	1

Issue		Date	Un	U	PB	#	FDC	Q(M)
Beginning with #772 to the end of the catalog, "unused" values are for "never-hinged" stamps.								
	Unwmk., Perf. 11 x 10.5							
772	3¢ Connecticut Tercentenary	04/26/35	.30	.20	2.00	(4)	14.00	71
	Defect in cent design		5.00	4.00				
773	3¢ California Pacific International Expo	05/29/35	.30	.20	1.30	(4)	14.00	101
	Unwmk., Perf. 11							
774	3¢ Boulder Dam	09/30/35	.30	.20	1.65	(6)	15.00	74
	Unwmk., Perf. 11 x 10.5							
775	3¢ Michigan Centenary	11/01/35	.30	.20	1.75	(4)	15.00	76
776	3¢ Texas Centennial	03/02/36	.30	.20	1.50	(4)	20.00	124
	Unwmk., Perf. 10.5 x 11							
777	3¢ Rhode Island Tercentenary	05/04/36	.35	.20	1.25	(4)	12.50	67
	Pair with full gutter between		200.00					
	Third International Philatelic Exhibition Souvenir Sheet, Unwmk., Imperf.							
778	Sheet of 4 different stamps (#772, 773, 775 and 776)	05/09/36	1.75	1.25			14.00	3
a-d	Single stamp from sheet		.40	.30				3
779-781	Not assigned							
	Unwmk., Perf. 11 x 10.5							
782	3¢ Arkansas Statehood	06/15/36	.30	.20	1.40	(4)	13.00	73
783	3¢ Oregon Territory	07/14/36	.25	.20	1.10	(4)	10.00	74
	Double transfer		4.00	2.50				
784	3¢ Susan B. Anthony	08/26/36	.25	.20	1.10	(4)	15.00	270
	Period missing after "B"		4.00	2.00				

A number of position pieces can be collected from the panes or sheets of the 1935 Special Printing issues, including horizontal and vertical gutter (#752, 766-770) or line (#753-765, 771) blocks of four (HG/L and VG/L), arrow-and-guideline blocks of four (AGL) and crossed-gutter or centerline blocks of four (CG/L). Pairs sell for half the price of blocks of four. Arrow-and-guideline blocks are *top or bottom only.*

	HG/L	VG/L	AGL	CG/L
752	5.75	9.50		60.00
753	2.25	30.00	62.50	75.00
754	1.75	1.50	3.25	7.25
755	1.75	1.50	3.25	7.25
756	.45	.55	1.25	3.00
757	.70	.55	1.25	4.00
758	1.40	1.25	2.75	5.25
759	2.75	2.25	4.75	8.50
760	3.50	4.25	9.00	15.00
761	6.00	5.00	11.00	17.50
762	4.25	3.75	8.25	14.00
763	4.25	5.25	15.00	20.00
764	5.00	4.50	10.50	22.50
765	9.00	10.50	24.00	30.00
766	5.00	7.00		16.00
767	5.00	6.50		17.50
768	7.00	8.00		20.00
769	5.50	7.50		15.00
770	12.50	10.50		27.50
771	7.75	6.50	15.00	65.00

1335

1336

1337

1338

1339

1340

1341

1342

1343

1344

1345

1346

1355

1356

1357

1358

1359

1347

1348

1360

1361

1362

1363

1364

1349

1350

1351

1352

1365 1366

1367 1368

1368a

1369

1370

1371

1353

1354

1354a

1372

1373

1374

1375

1376 1377
1378 1379 1379a

1380

1381

1382

1383

1384

1384 Precancel

1385

1386

1387 1388
1389 1390 1390a

1391

1392

1393

1393D

1394

1396

1397

1398

1399

1400

1405

1406

1407

1408

1409

1410 1411
1412 1413
1413a

Examples of Special Printing Position Blocks

Gutter Block 752

Centerline Block 754

Line Block 756

Arrow Block 763

Cross-Gutter Block 768

772

773

774

775

776

777

782

783

784

785   786   787   788   789

790   791   792   793   794

795   796   798   799   800   801

802   803   804   805   806   807   808   809

810   811   812   813   814   815   816   817   818

819   820   821   822   823   824   825   826   827

828   829   830   831   832   833   834

	Issue	Date	Un	U	PB #	FDC	Q(M)
	Army, Unwmk., Perf. 11 x 10.5						
785	1¢ George Washington, Nathanael Greene and Mount Vernon	12/15/36	.25	.20	1.10 (4)	8.00	105
786	2¢ Andrew Jackson, Winfield Scott and The Hermitage	01/15/37	.25	.20	1.10 (4)	8.00	94
787	3¢ Generals Sherman, Grant and Sheridan	02/18/37	.35	.20	1.75 (4)	8.00	88
788	4¢ Generals Robert E. Lee and "Stonewall" Jackson and Stratford Hall	03/23/37	.55	.20	8.50 (4)	8.00	36
789	5¢ U.S. Military Academy at West Point	05/26/37	.65	.25	8.00 (4)	8.00	37
	Navy, Unwmk., Perf. 11 x 10.5						
790	1¢ John Paul Jones, John Barry, *Bon Homme Richard* and *Lexington*	12/15/36	.25	.20	1.10 (4)	8.00	105
791	2¢ Stephen Decatur, Thomas MacDonough and *Saratoga*	01/15/37	.25	.20	1.10 (4)	8.00	92
792	3¢ David G. Farragut and David D. Porter, *Hartford* and *Powhatan*	02/18/37	.35	.20	1.10 (4)	8.00	93
793	4¢ Admirals William T. Sampson, George Dewey and Winfield S. Schley	03/23/37	.55	.20	9.00 (4)	8.00	35
794	5¢ Seal of U.S. Naval Academy and Naval Cadets	05/26/37	.65	.25	8.75 (4)	8.00	37
	Perf. 11 x 10.5						
795	3¢ Northwest Territory Ordinance	07/13/37	.30	.20	1.40 (4)	9.00	85
	Unwmk., Perf. 11						
796	5¢ Virginia Dare and Parents	08/18/37	.35	.20	6.50 (6)	11.00	25
	Society of Philatelic Americans Souvenir Sheet, Unwmk., Imperf.						
797	10¢ blue green (749)	08/26/37	.60	.40		11.00	5
	Perf. 11 x 10.5						
798	3¢ Constitution Sesquicentennial	09/17/37	.35	.20	1.60 (4)	9.00	100
	Territorial, Unwmk., Perf. 10.5 x 11						
799	3¢ Hawaii	10/18/37	.30	.20	1.40 (4)	11.00	78
	Territorial, Perf. 11 x 10.5						
800	3¢ Alaska	11/12/37	.30	.20	1.40 (4)	10.00	77
801	3¢ Puerto Rico	11/25/37	.30	.20	1.40 (4)	10.00	81
802	3¢ Virgin Islands	12/15/37	.30	.20	1.40 (4)	10.00	76
	Pair with full vertical gutter between		275.00				
	Presidential, Unwmk., Perf. 11 x 10.5						
	(#804b, 806b, 807a issued in 1939, 832b in 1951, 832c in 1954, rest in 1938)						
803	½¢ Benjamin Franklin	05/19/38	.20	.20	.50 (4)	3.50	
804	1¢ George Washington	04/25/38	.20	.20	.50 (4)	3.50	
	Pair with full vertical gutter between		160.00	—			
b	Booklet pane of 6	01/27/39	2.00	*.50*			
805	1½¢ Martha Washington	05/05/38	.20	.20	.30 (4)	3.50	
	Pair with full horizontal gutter between		175.00				
b	Horizontal pair, imperf. between		150.00	20.00			

	Issue	Date	Un	U	PB #	FDC	Q(M)
	Presidential Unwmk., Perf. 11 x 10.5 continued						
806	2¢ John Adams	06/03/38	.20	.20	.40 (4)	3.50	
	Recut at top of head		3.00	1.50			
b	Booklet pane of 6	01/27/39	5.50	*1.00*		15.00	
807	3¢ Thomas Jefferson	06/16/38	.20	.20	.35 (4)	3.50	
a	Booklet pane of 6	01/27/39	8.50	*2.00*		17.50	
b	Horizontal pair, imperf. between		2,000.00	—			
c	Imperf., pair		2,750.00				
808	4¢ James Madison	07/01/38	.75	.20	3.25 (4)	3.50	
809	4½¢ The White House	07/11/38	.25	.20	1.50 (4)	3.50	
810	5¢ James Monroe	07/21/38	.30	.20	1.25 (4)	3.50	
811	6¢ John Quincy Adams	07/28/38	.35	.20	1.50 (4)	3.50	
812	7¢ Andrew Jackson	08/04/38	.40	.20	1.75 (4)	3.50	
813	8¢ Martin Van Buren	08/11/38	.40	.20	1.75 (4)	3.50	
814	9¢ William H. Harrison	08/18/38	.35	.20	1.60 (4)	3.50	
	Pair with full vertical gutter between		—				
815	10¢ John Tyler	09/02/38	.40	.20	1.80 (4)	3.50	
816	11¢ James K. Polk	09/08/38	.75	.20	3.25 (4)	5.00	
817	12¢ Zachary Taylor	09/14/38	1.00	.20	5.00 (4)	5.00	
818	13¢ Millard Fillmore	09/22/38	1.30	.20	7.00 (4)	5.00	
819	14¢ Franklin Pierce	10/06/38	1.00	.20	4.50 (4)	5.00	
820	15¢ James Buchanan	10/13/38	.55	.20	2.40 (4)	5.00	
821	16¢ Abraham Lincoln	10/20/38	1.25	.25	7.00 (4)	7.00	
822	17¢ Andrew Johnson	10/27/38	1.00	.20	4.75 (4)	6.00	
823	18¢ Ulysses S. Grant	11/03/38	2.25	.20	12.50 (4)	6.00	
824	19¢ Rutherford B. Hayes	11/10/38	1.30	.35	6.50 (4)	6.00	
825	20¢ James A. Garfield	11/10/38	1.00	.20	4.50 (4)	7.00	
826	21¢ Chester A. Arthur	11/22/38	1.30	.20	7.50 (4)	7.00	
827	22¢ Grover Cleveland	11/22/38	1.20	.40	9.00 (4)	8.00	
828	24¢ Benjamin Harrison	12/02/38	3.50	.20	15.00 (4)	8.00	
829	25¢ William McKinley	12/02/38	1.00	.20	4.50 (4)	8.00	
830	30¢ Theodore Roosevelt	12/08/38	4.00	.20	17.00 (4)	9.00	
a	30¢ Blue		17.00	—			
b	30¢ Deep blue		260.00	—			
831	50¢ William Howard Taft	12/08/38	5.00	.20	22.50 (4)	12.50	
	Perf. 11						
832	$1 Woodrow Wilson	08/29/38	7.00	.20	35.00 (4)	50.00	
a	Vertical pair, imperf. horizontally		1,500.00				
b	Watermarked "USIR"	1951	150.00	65.00	*1,800* (4)		
c	$1 red violet and black	08/31/54	6.00	.20	30.00 (4)	25.00	
d	As "c," vert. pair, imperf. horiz.		1,500.00				
e	Vertical pair, imperf. between		2,750.00				
f	As "c," vert. pair, imperf. between		8,500.00				
833	$2 Warren G. Harding	09/29/38	18.00	3.75	95.00 (4)	100.00	
834	$5 Calvin Coolidge	11/17/38	90.00	3.00	375.00 (4)	175.00	
a	$5 red, brown and black		3,000.00	7,000.00			

	Issue	Date	Un	U	PB/LP #	FDC	Q(M)
	Perf. 11 x 10.5						
835	3¢ Constitution Ratification	06/21/38	.45	.20	3.50 (4)	15.00	73
	Perf. 11						
836	3¢ Swedish-Finnish Tercentenary	06/27/38	.35	.20	2.25 (6)	15.00	59
	Perf. 11 x 10.5						
837	3¢ Northwest Territory Sesquicentennial	07/15/38	.30	.20	6.00 (4)	15.00	66
838	3¢ Iowa Territorial Centennial	08/24/38	.35	.20	6.00 (4)	15.00	47
	Coil, Perf. 10 Vertically						
839	1¢ Washington (804)	01/20/39	.30	.20	1.40 (2)	5.00	
840	1½¢ Martha Washington (805)	01/20/39	.30	.20	1.50 (2)	5.00	
841	2¢ John Adams (806)	01/20/39	.40	.20	1.75 (2)	5.00	
842	3¢ Jefferson (807)	01/20/39	.50	.20	2.00 (2)	5.00	
	Thin, translucent paper		2.50	—			
843	4¢ Madison (808)	01/20/39	7.50	.40	27.50 (2)	5.00	
844	4½¢ White House (809)	01/20/39	.70	.40	5.00 (2)	5.00	
845	5¢ James Monroe 810)	01/20/39	5.00	.35	27.50 (2)	5.00	
846	6¢ John Quincy Adams (811)	01/20/39	1.10	.20	7.50 (2)	6.50	
847	10¢ John Tyler (815)	01/20/39	11.00	1.00	42.50 (2)	9.00	
	Coil, Perf. 10 Horizontally						
848	1¢ Washington (804)	01/27/39	.85	.20	2.75 (2)	5.00	
849	1½¢ Martha Washington (805)	01/27/39	1.25	.30	4.50 (2)	5.00	
850	2¢ John Adams (806)	01/27/39	2.50	.40	7.50 (2)	5.00	
851	3¢ Thomas Jefferson (807)	01/27/39	2.50	.40	8.50 (2)	5.50	
	Perf. 10.5 x 11						
852	3¢ Golden Gate Exposition	02/18/39	.30	.20	1.40 (4)	16.00	114
853	3¢ New York World's Fair	04/01/39	.30	.20	1.75 (4)	20.00	102
	Perf. 11						
854	3¢ Washington's Inauguration	04/30/39	.55	.20	3.50 (6)	17.50	73
	Perf. 11 x 10.5						
855	3¢ Baseball Centennial	06/12/39	1.75	.20	7.50 (4)	40.00	81
	Perf. 11						
856	3¢ Panama Canal	08/15/39	.35	.20	3.50 (6)	18.00	68
	Perf. 10.5 x 11						
857	3¢ Printing	09/25/39	.25	.20	1.10 (4)	15.00	71
	Perf. 11 x 10.5						
858	3¢ 50th Anniversary of Statehood (Montana, North Dakota, South Dakota, Washington)	11/02/39	.35	.20	2.00 (4)	12.50	67

	Issue	Date	Un	U	PB/LP #	FDC	Q(M)
	Famous Americans, Perf. 10.5 x 11						
	Authors						
859	1¢ Washington Irving	01/29/40	.20	.20	.95 (4)	4.50	56
860	2¢ James Fenimore Cooper	01/29/40	.20	.20	.95 (4)	3.00	53
861	3¢ Ralph Waldo Emerson	02/05/40	.25	.20	1.25 (4)	3.00	53
862	5¢ Louisa May Alcott	02/05/40	.35	.20	8.25 (4)	4.00	22
863	10¢ Samuel L. Clemens (Mark Twain)	02/13/40	1.75	1.20	32.50 (4)	8.00	13
	Poets						
864	1¢ Henry W. Longfellow	02/16/40	.20	.20	1.75 (4)	3.00	52
865	2¢ John Greenleaf Whittier	02/16/40	.20	.20	1.75 (4)	3.00	52
866	3¢ James Russell Lowell	02/20/40	.25	.20	2.25 (4)	3.00	52
867	5¢ Walt Whitman	02/20/40	.50	.20	9.50 (4)	4.00	22
868	10¢ James Whitcomb Riley	02/24/40	1.75	1.25	32.50 (4)	6.00	12
	Educators						
869	1¢ Horace Mann	03/14/40	.20	.20	2.25 (4)	3.00	52
870	2¢ Mark Hopkins	03/14/40	.20	.20	1.50 (4)	3.00	52
871	3¢ Charles W. Eliot	03/28/40	.25	.20	2.00 (4)	3.00	52
872	5¢ Frances E. Willard	03/28/40	.50	.20	9.00 (4)	4.00	21
873	10¢ Booker T. Washington	04/07/40	2.00	1.10	27.50 (4)	10.00	14
	Scientists						
874	1¢ John James Audubon	04/08/40	.20	.20	.90 (4)	3.00	59
875	2¢ Dr. Crawford W. Long	04/08/40	.20	.20	.95 (4)	3.00	58
876	3¢ Luther Burbank	04/17/40	.25	.20	1.10 (4)	3.00	58
877	5¢ Dr. Walter Reed	04/17/40	.50	.20	5.50 (4)	4.00	24
878	10¢ Jane Addams	04/26/40	1.50	.85	16.00 (4)	6.00	15
	Composers						
879	1¢ Stephen Collins Foster	05/03/40	.20	.20	.95 (4)	3.00	57
880	2¢ John Philip Sousa	05/03/40	.20	.20	1.00 (4)	4.00	58
881	3¢ Victor Herbert	05/13/40	.25	.20	1.10 (4)	3.00	56
882	5¢ Edward A. MacDowell	05/13/40	.50	.20	9.25 (4)	4.00	21
883	10¢ Ethelbert Nevin	06/10/40	3.75	1.35	32.50 (4)	6.00	13
	Artists						
884	1¢ Gilbert Charles Stuart	09/05/40	.20	.20	1.00 (4)	3.00	54
885	2¢ James A. McNeill Whistler	09/05/40	.20	.20	.95 (4)	3.00	54
886	3¢ Augustus Saint-Gaudens	09/16/40	.30	.20	1.50 (4)	3.00	55
887	5¢ Daniel Chester French	09/16/40	.50	.20	8.00 (4)	4.00	22
888	10¢ Frederic Remington	09/30/40	1.75	1.25	20.00 (4)	7.00	14
	Inventors						
889	1¢ Eli Whitney	10/07/40	.25	.20	2.25 (4)	3.00	48
890	2¢ Samuel F.B. Morse	10/07/40	.30	.20	2.00 (4)	3.00	53
891	3¢ Cyrus Hall McCormick	10/14/40	.30	.20	1.50 (4)	3.00	54
892	5¢ Elias Howe	10/14/40	1.10	.30	12.50 (4)	4.00	20
893	10¢ Alexander Graham Bell	10/28/40	11.00	2.00	50.00 (4)	10.00	14

835

836

837

838

852

853

854

855

856

857

858

859

860

861

862

863

864

865

866

867

868

869

870

871

872

873

874

875

876

877

878

879

880

881

882

883

884

885

886

887

888

889

890

891

892

893

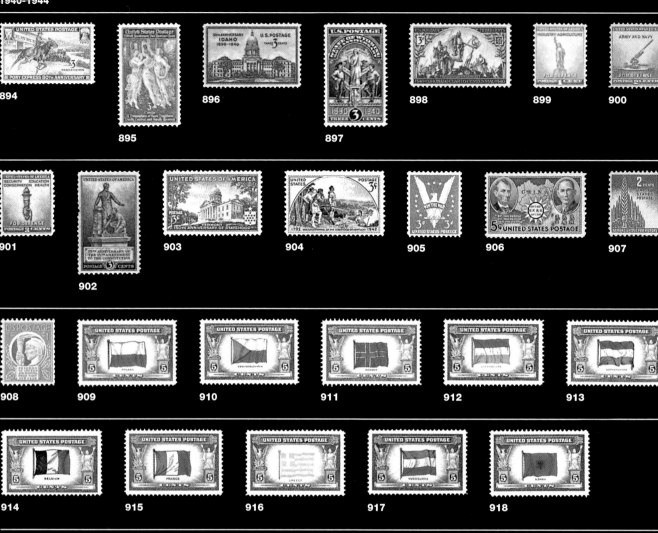

894
895
896
897
898
899
900

901
902
903
904
905
906
907

908
909
910
911
912
913

914
915
916
917
918

919
920
921
922
923

924
925
926

VISIT US ONLINE AT **THE POSTAL STORE**
AT **WWW.USPS.COM**
OR CALL **1 800 STAMP-24**

	Issue	Date	Un	U	PB	#	FDC	Q(M)
	Perf. 11 x 10.5							
894	3¢ Pony Express	04/03/40	.40	.20	3.25	(4)	12.00	46
	Perf. 10.5 x 11							
895	3¢ Pan American Union	04/14/40	.30	.20	2.75	(4)	9.50	48
	Perf. 11 x 10.5							
896	3¢ Idaho Statehood	07/03/40	.35	.20	2.00	(4)	9.50	51
	Perf. 10.5 x 11							
897	3¢ Wyoming Statehood	07/10/40	.30	.20	1.75	(4)	9.50	50
	Perf. 11 x 10.5							
898	3¢ Coronado Expedition	09/07/40	.25	.20	1.60	(4)	9.50	61
	Win the War, Perf. 11 x 10.5							
899	1¢ Statue of Liberty	10/16/40	.20	.20	.45	(4)	7.00	
	Cracked plate		3.00					
	Gripper cracks		3.00					
a	Vertical pair, imperf. between		625.00	—				
b	Horizontal pair, imperf. between		32.50	—				
900	2¢ 90mm Anti-aircraft Gun	10/16/40	.20	.20	.45	(4)	7.00	
a	Horizontal pair, imperf. between		37.50	—				
	Pair with full vertical gutter between		275.00					
901	3¢ Torch of Enlightenment	10/16/40	.20	.20	.60	(4)	7.00	
a	Horizontal pair, imperf. between		25.00	—				
	Win the War, Perf. 10.5 x 11							
902	3¢ Thirteenth Amendment	10/20/40	.30	.20	3.00	(4)	10.00	44
	Win the War, Perf. 11 x 10.5							
903	3¢ Vermont Statehood	03/04/41	.45	.20	3.00	(4)	10.00	55
904	3¢ Kentucky Statehood	06/01/42	.30	.20	1.50	(4)	10.00	64
905	3¢ Win the War	07/04/42	.20	.20	.55	(4)	10.00	
	Pair with full vertical or horizontal gutter between		175.00					
b	3¢ purple		750.00	500.00				

	Issue	Date	Un	U	PB	#	FDC	Q(M)
	Win the War, Perf. 11 x 10.5							
906	5¢ Chinese Resistance	07/07/42	1.25	.20	8.25	(4)	12.00	21
907	2¢ Allied Nations	01/14/43	.20	.20	.30	(4)	6.00	1,700
	Pair with full vertical or horizontal gutter between		225.00					
908	1¢ Four Freedoms	02/12/43	.20	.20	.70	(4)	6.00	1,200
	Overrun Countries, Perf. 12							
909	5¢ Poland	06/22/43	.25	.20	3.50	(4)	5.00	20
910	5¢ Czechoslovakia	07/12/43	.25	.20	2.75	(4)	4.00	20
911	5¢ Norway	07/27/43	.25	.20	1.30	(4)	4.00	20
912	5¢ Luxembourg	08/10/43	.25	.20	1.30	(4)	4.00	20
913	5¢ Netherlands	08/24/43	.25	.20	1.25	(4)	4.00	20
914	5¢ Belgium	09/14/43	.25	.20	1.25	(4)	4.00	20
915	5¢ France	09/28/43	.25	.20	1.25	(4)	4.00	20
916	5¢ Greece	10/12/43	.50	.25	11.00	(4)	4.00	15
917	5¢ Yugoslavia	10/26/43	.40	.20	4.25	(4)	4.00	15
918	5¢ Albania	11/09/43	.25	.20	4.25	(4)	4.00	15
919	5¢ Austria	11/23/43	.30	.20	3.50	(4)	4.00	15
920	5¢ Denmark	12/07/43	.30	.20	5.25	(4)	4.00	15
921	5¢ Korea	11/02/44	.25	.20	4.50	(4)	5.00	15
	"KORPA" plate flaw		19.00	12.50				
	Perf. 11 x 10.5							
922	3¢ Transcontinental Railroad	05/10/44	.25	.20	1.75	(4)	10.00	61
923	3¢ Steamship	05/22/44	.20	.20	1.25	(4)	9.00	61
924	3¢ Telegraph	05/24/44	.20	.20	1.00	(4)	9.00	61
	Win the War, Perf. 11 x 10.5							
925	3¢ Philippine	09/27/44	.20	.20	1.25	(4)	9.00	50
	Perf. 11 x 10.5							
926	3¢ Motion Pictures	10/31/44	.20	.20	1.10	(4)	10.00	53

OREGON STATEHOOD

In 2009, the U.S. Postal Service commemorates the sesquicentennial of Oregon's statehood with a stamp featuring a painting evocative of the state's coastline by Gregory Manchess of Beaverton. Officially welcomed as the 33rd state in the Union in 1859, today Oregon boasts a diverse population, an active and innovative urban scene, and some of the most beautiful and fertile landscapes in the country. ■ A few decades after the Lewis and Clark expedition into Columbia River country, overland immigrants from the east began to pour into the "New Eden." By the mid-1800s, thousands had followed the Oregon Trail with dreams of owning land and starting a new life. ■ For almost 30 years, the U.S. and Britain agreed on joint occupation of the territory, but tension was brewing over borders and natural resources. In 1846, the countries agreed on a boundary at the 49th parallel (now part of the U.S.-Canadian border). The new Oregon Territory included present-day Oregon, Washington, Idaho, and western Montana and Wyoming. The land was split into the Oregon and Washington Territories in 1853. Oregonians formed a provisional government and agreed on a state constitution. On February 14, 1859, President James Buchanan signed legislation granting statehood to Oregon. ■ From the rocky Pacific coast to the snowcapped Cascade Mountains and high eastern desert, Oregon's landscapes are picturesque and attract visitors year long. Crater Lake, with a depth of nearly 2,000 feet, is the deepest lake in the nation, while Mt. Hood towers over the state with an elevation of 11,239 feet. Many of Oregon's 3.7 million residents live in Portland and the Willamette Valley.

Issue		Date	Un	U	PB	#	FDC	Q(M)
	Perf. 11 x 10.5							
927	3¢ Florida Statehood Centenary	03/03/45	.20	.20	1.10	(4)	9.00	62
	Win the War, Perf. 11 x 10.5							
928	5¢ United Nations Conference	04/25/45	.20	.20	.45	(4)	9.00	76
	Win the War, Perf. 10.5 x 11							
929	3¢ Iwo Jima (Marines)	07/11/45	.30	.20	2.00	(4)	15.00	137
	Win the War, Perf. 11 x 10.5							
930	1¢ Franklin D. Roosevelt and Hyde Park Residence	07/26/45	.20	.20	.35	(4)	4.00	128
931	2¢ Franklin D. Roosevelt and "The Little White House" at Warm Springs, Ga.	08/24/45	.20	.20	.45	(4)	4.50	67
932	3¢ Roosevelt and White House	06/27/45	.20	.20	.60	(4)	4.50	134
933	5¢ Roosevelt, Map of Wester Hemisphere and Four Freedoms	01/30/46	.20	.20	.45	(4)	4.50	76
934	3¢ Army	09/28/45	.20	.20	.60	(4)	11.00	128
935	3¢ Navy	10/27/45	.20	.20	.60	(4)	11.00	139
936	3¢ Coast Guard	11/10/45	.20	.20	.70	(4)	11.00	112
937	3¢ Alfred E. Smith	11/26/45	.20	.20	.45	(4)	3.00	309
938	3¢ Texas Statehood	12/29/45	.20	.20	.50	(4)	9.00	171
939	3¢ Merchant Marine	02/26/46	.20	.20	.50	(4)	9.00	136
940	3¢ Veterans of World War II	05/09/46	.20	.20	.50	(4)	11.00	260
	Perf. 11 x 10.5							
941	3¢ Tennessee Statehood	06/01/46	.20	.20	.50	(4)	4.00	132
942	3¢ Iowa Statehood	08/03/46	.20	.20	.45	(4)	4.00	132
943	3¢ Smithsonian Institution	08/10/46	.20	.20	.40	(4)	4.00	139
944	3¢ Kearny Expedition	10/16/46	.20	.20	.40	(4)	4.00	115

Issue		Date	Un	U	PB	#	FDC	Q(M)
	Perf. 10.5 x 11							
945	3¢ Thomas A. Edison	02/11/47	.20	.20	.40	(4)	5.00	157
	Perf. 11 x 10.5							
946	3¢ Joseph Pulitzer	04/10/47	.20	.20	.40	(4)	4.00	120
947	3¢ Postage Stamps Centenary	05/17/47	.20	.20	.40	(4)	4.00	127
	Centenary International Philatelic Exhibition Souvenir Sheet, Imperf.							
948	Souvenir sheet of 2 stamps (#1-2)	05/19/47	.55	.45			4.50	10
a	5¢ single stamp from sheet		.20	.20				
b	10¢ single stamp from sheet		.25	.25				
	Perf. 11 x 10.5							
949	3¢ Doctors	06/09/47	.20	.20	.40	(4)	9.00	133
950	3¢ Utah Settlement	07/24/47	.20	.20	.60	(4)	3.00	132
951	3¢ U.S. Frigate *Constitution*	10/21/47	.20	.20	.40	(4)	8.00	131
	Perf. 10.5 x 11							
952	3¢ Everglades National Park	12/05/47	.20	.20	.40	(4)	3.00	122
953	3¢ Dr. G.W. Carver	01/05/48	.20	.20	.45	(4)	3.00	122
	Perf. 11 x 10.5							
954	3¢ California Gold	01/24/48	.20	.20	.40	(4)	3.50	131
955	3¢ Mississippi Territory	04/07/48	.20	.20	.50	(4)	2.00	123
956	3¢ Four Chaplains	05/28/48	.20	.20	.50	(4)	8.00	122
957	3¢ Wisconsin Statehood	05/29/48	.20	.20	.50	(4)	3.00	115
958	5¢ Swedish Pioneer	06/04/48	.20	.20	.45	(4)	4.00	64
959	3¢ Progress of Women	07/19/48	.20	.20	.55	(4)	3.00	118
	Perf. 10.5 x 11							
960	3¢ William Allen White	07/31/48	.20	.20	.40	(4)	2.50	78

The Art of Disney: Romance Stamped Cards and Prints*

Third in the series of three, these cards and prints honor Romance as depicted by Walt Disney and his studio animators. Featured are some of the most lovable animated characters—Mickey and Minnie Mouse, Cinderella and Prince Charming, Beauty and the Beast, and Lady and Tramp.

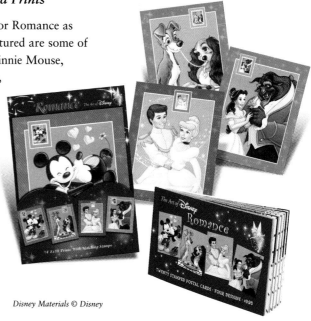

Booklet of 20 stamped cards* (four different designs)
Item #568066 $9.95

Print Set (four different designs) 8"x10"
Item #568088 $14.95

Save with complete set
Romance Stamped Cards* and Print Set
Item #568098 $19.95

For more information call **1 800 STAMP-24**

*Additional postage required for mailing.

Disney Materials © Disney

927

928

929

930

931

932

933

934

935

936

937

938

939

940

941

942

943

944

945

946

947

948

949

950

951

952

953

954

955

956

957

958

959

960

961

962

963

964

965

966

967

968

969

970

971

972

973

974

975

976

977

978

979

980

981

982

983

984

985

986

987

988

989

990

991

992

993

994

995

996

997

998

999

1000

1001

	Issue	Date	Un	U	PB	#	FDC	Q(M)
	Perf. 11 x 10.5							
961	3¢ U.S.-Canada Friendship	08/02/48	.20	.20	.40	(4)	3.00	113
962	3¢ Francis Scott Key	08/09/48	.20	.20	.40	(4)	2.50	121
963	3¢ Salute to Youth	08/11/48	.20	.20	.40	(4)	2.50	78
964	3¢ Oregon Territory	08/14/48	.20	.20	.50	(4)	3.00	52
	Perf. 10.5 x 11							
965	3¢ Harlan F. Stone	08/25/48	.20	.20	.60	(4)	2.50	54
966	3¢ Palomar Observatory	08/30/48	.20	.20	.95	(4)	5.00	61
a	Vertical pair, imperf. between		350.00					
	Perf. 11 x 10.5							
967	3¢ Clara Barton	09/07/48	.20	.20	.50	(4)	3.00	58
968	3¢ Poultry Industry	09/09/48	.20	.20	.50	(4)	3.00	53
	Perf. 10.5 x 11							
969	3¢ Gold Star Mothers	09/21/48	.20	.20	.40	(4)	2.00	77
	Perf. 11 x 10.5							
970	3¢ Fort Kearny	09/22/48	.20	.20	.60	(4)	2.00	58
971	3¢ Volunteer Firemen	10/04/48	.20	.20	.60	(4)	10.00	56
972	3¢ Indian Centennial	10/15/48	.20	.20	.60	(4)	3.50	58
973	3¢ Rough Riders	10/27/48	.20	.20	.50	(4)	2.50	54
974	3¢ Juliette Gordon Low	10/29/48	.20	.20	.50	(4)	8.00	64
	Perf. 10.5 x 11							
975	3¢ Will Rogers	11/04/48	.20	.20	.45	(4)	2.00	67
976	3¢ Fort Bliss	11/05/48	.20	.20	1.00	(4)	5.00	65
	Perf. 11 x 10.5							
977	3¢ Moina Michael	11/09/48	.20	.20	.50	(4)	2.50	64
978	3¢ Gettysburg Address	11/19/48	.20	.20	.60	(4)	2.75	63
	Perf. 10.5 x 11							
979	3¢ American Turners	11/20/48	.20	.20	.40	(4)	2.00	62
980	3¢ Joel Chandler Harris	12/09/48	.20	.20	.55	(4)	2.25	57
	Perf. 11 x 10.5							
981	3¢ Minnesota Territory	03/03/49	.20	.20	.45	(4)	2.25	99
982	3¢ Washington and Lee University	04/12/49	.20	.20	.40	(4)	2.25	105

	Issue	Date	Un	U	PB	#	FDC	Q(M)
	Perf. 11 x 10.5							
983	3¢ Puerto Rico Election	04/27/49	.20	.20	.40	(4)	2.25	109
984	3¢ Annapolis Tercentenary	05/23/49	.20	.20	.40	(4)	3.00	107
985	3¢ Grand Army of the Republic (GAR)	08/29/49	.20	.20	.40	(4)	3.25	117
	Perf. 10.5 x 11							
986	3¢ Edgar Allan Poe	10/07/49	.20	.20	.45	(4)	4.00	123
	Thin outer frame line at top, inner frame line missing		6.00					
	Perf. 11 x 10.5							
987	3¢ American Bankers	01/03/50	.20	.20	.40	(4)	2.75	131
	Perf. 10.5 x 11							
988	3¢ Samuel Gompers	01/27/50	.20	.20	.40	(4)	1.75	128
	National Capital Sesquicentennial, Perf. 10.5 x 11, 11 x 10.5							
989	3¢ Statue of Freedom on Capitol Dome	04/20/50	.20	.20	.40	(4)	1.50	132
990	3¢ Executive Mansion	06/12/50	.20	.20	.50	(4)	1.50	130
991	3¢ Supreme Court Bluilding	08/02/50	.20	.20	.30	(4)	1.50	131
992	3¢ U.S. Capital	11/22/50	.20	.20	.55	(4)	1.50	130
	Gripper cracks		4.50	3.00				
	Perf. 11 x 10.5							
993	3¢ Railroad Engineers	04/29/50	.20	.20	.50	(4)	4.00	122
994	3¢ Kansas City, MO	06/03/50	.20	.20	.40	(4)	1.50	122
995	3¢ Boy Scouts	06/30/50	.20	.20	.50	(4)	12.00	132
996	3¢ Indiana Territory	07/04/50	.20	.20	.50	(4)	1.75	122
997	3¢ California Statehood	09/09/50	.20	.20	.50	(4)	2.50	121
	United Confederate Veterans Final Reunion, Perf. 11 x 10.5							
998	3¢ United Confederate Veterans (UCV)	05/30/51	.20	.20	.45	(4)	3.00	119
	Perf. 11 x 10.5							
999	3¢ Nevada Settlement	07/14/51	.20	.20	.50	(4)	1.50	112
1000	3¢ Landing of Cadillac	07/24/51	.20	.20	.30	(4)	1.50	114
1001	3¢ Colorado Statehood	08/01/51	.20	.20	.40	(4)	1.50	114

KWANZAA

With this colorful stamp, the U.S. Postal Service celebrates Kwanzaa, a non-religious holiday that takes place over seven days from December 26 to January 1. Kwanzaa draws on African traditions and takes its name from the Swahili phrase for "first fruits." Its origins are in harvest celebrations that occurred in ancient and modern times in various places across the African continent. These traditions were synthesized and reinvented in 1966 by Maulana Karenga as the contemporary cultural festival known as Kwanzaa. ■ The holiday is intended to be a celebration of seven principles—unity, self-determination, collective work and responsibility, cooperative economics, purpose, creativity, and faith—based on values prevalent in African culture. "I believe that the principles celebrated by Kwanzaa are basic and righteous principles for all of humanity," says stamp artist Lloyd McNeill, of New York, who created a highly symbolic design to celebrate the holiday and its associated ideas. ■ The bold colors in the stamp art are complemented in the top right corner by the colors of the Kwanzaa flag—green for growth, red for blood, and black for the African people. The field of green around the borders symbolizes growth and a bountiful harvest. In the hoop that the girl holds in her hands, as well as in the family grouping of mother, father, and child, McNeill symbolized unity. "The figures are all touching in some way," he says. "Compositionally, it's not a perfect circle, but it represents the essence of a circle—an enclosed space occupied by the people." ■ This is the third Kwanzaa commemorative stamp issued by the Postal Service; the first was issued in 1997.

	Issue	Date	Un	U	PB	#	FDC	Q(M)
	Perf. 11 x 10.5							
1002	3¢ American Chemical Society	09/04/51	.20	.20	.50	(4)	1.75	117
1003	3¢ Battle of Brooklyn	12/10/51	.20	.20	.40	(4)	1.50	116
1004	3¢ Betsy Ross	01/02/52	.20	.20	.40	(4)	1.50	116
1005	3¢ 4-H Club	01/15/52	.20	.20	.50	(4)	3.25	116
1006	3¢ B&O Railroad	02/28/52	.20	.20	.45	(4)	4.50	113
1007	3¢ American Automobile Association	03/04/52	.20	.20	.40	(4)	1.75	117
1008	3¢ NATO	04/04/52	.20	.20	.40	(4)	1.50	2,900
1009	3¢ Grand Coulee Dam	05/15/52	.20	.20	.40	(4)	1.50	115
1010	3¢ Arrival of Lafayette	06/13/52	.20	.20	.45	(4)	1.50	113
	Perf. 10.5 x 11							
1011	3¢ Mt. Rushmore Memorial	08/11/52	.20	.20	.75	(4)	1.50	116
	Perf. 11 x 10.5							
1012	3¢ Engineering	09/06/52	.20	.20	.45	(4)	1.50	114
1013	3¢ Service Women	09/11/52	.20	.20	.40	(4)	1.75	124
1014	3¢ Gutenberg Bible	09/30/52	.20	.20	.40	(4)	1.50	116
1015	3¢ Newspaper Boys	10/04/52	.20	.20	.40	(4)	1.50	115
1016	3¢ International Red Cross	11/21/52	.20	.20	.40	(4)	2.00	136
1017	3¢ National Guard	02/23/53	.20	.20	.40	(4)	2.00	115
1018	3¢ Ohio Statehood	03/02/53	.20	.20	.45	(4)	1.50	119
1019	3¢ Washington Territory	03/02/53	.20	.20	.45	(4)	1.50	114
1020	3¢ Louisiana Purchase	04/30/53	.20	.20	.90	(4)	1.50	114
1021	5¢ Opening of Japan	07/14/53	.20	.20	.65	(4)	1.75	89
1022	3¢ American Bar Association	08/24/53	.20	.20	.40	(4)	6.50	115
1023	3¢ Sagamore Hill	09/14/53	.20	.20	.40	(4)	1.50	116
1024	3¢ Future Farmers	10/13/53	.20	.20	.40	(4)	1.50	115
1025	3¢ Trucking Industry	10/27/53	.20	.20	.40	(4)	1.50	124
1026	3¢ General George S. Patton, Jr.	11/11/53	.20	.20	.45	(4)	4.50	115
1027	3¢ New York City	11/20/53	.20	.20	.40	(4)	1.50	116
1028	3¢ Gadsden Purchase	12/30/53	.20	.20	.40	(4)	1.50	116
1029	3¢ Columbia University	01/04/54	.20	.20	.40	(4)	1.50	119
	Liberty, Perf. 11 x 10.5 (Designs of 1030-1059)							
1030	½¢ Benjamin Franklin	10/20/55	.20	.20	.25	(4)	1.00	
a	Wet printing		.20	.20	.35	(4)		
1031	1¢ George Washington	03/56	.20	.20	.25	(4)		
	Pair with full vertical or horizontal gutter between		150.00					
b	Wet printing		.20	.20	.25	(4)	1.00	
	Liberty, Perf. 10.5 x 11							
1031A	1¼¢ Palace of the Governors	06/17/60	.20	.20	.45	(4)	1.50	
1032	1½¢ Mt. Vernon	02/22/56	.20	.20	1.75	(4)	1.00	

	Issue	Date	Un	U	PB	#	FDC	Q(M)
	Liberty, Perf. 11 x 10.5 (Designs of 1030-1059)							
1033	2¢ Thomas Jefferson	09/15/54	.20	.20	.25	(4)	1.00	
1034	2½¢ Bunker Hill Monument and Massachusetts Flag	06/17/59	.20	.20	.50	(4)	1.00	
1035	3¢ Statue of Liberty	06/24/54	.20	.20	.30	(4)		
a	Booklet pane of 6	06/30/54	4.00	1.25			3.50	
b	Tagged	07/06/66	.35	.25	5.75	(4)	40.00	
c	Imperf., pair		2,000.00					
d	Horizontal pair, imperf. between		—					
e	Wet printing	06/24/54	.20	.20	.40	(4)	1.00	
f	As "a," dry printing		5.00	1.50				
g	As "a," vertical imperf. between		5,000.00					
1036	4¢ Abraham Lincoln	11/19/54	.20	.20	.35	(4)		
a	Booklet pane of 6	07/31/58	2.75	1.25			4.00	
b	Tagged	11/02/63	.65	.40	9.00	(4)	50.00	
	Liberty, Perf. 10.5 x 11							
1037	4½¢ The Hermitage	03/16/59	.20	.20	.65	(4)	1.00	
	Liberty, Perf. 11 x 10.5							
1038	5¢ James Monroe	12/02/54	.20	.20	.60	(4)	1.00	
	Pair with full vertical gutter between		200.00					
1039	6¢ Theodore Roosevelt	11/18/55	.25	.20	1.25	(4)		
a	Wet printing		.40	.20	2.00	(4)	1.00	
b	Imperf. block of 4 (unique)		23,000.00					
1040	7¢ Woodrow Wilson	01/10/56	.20	.20	1.00	(4)	1.00	
	Liberty, Perf. 11							
1041	8¢ Statue of Liberty	04/09/54	.25	.20	2.00	(4)	1.00	
a	Carmine double impression		575.00					
1042	8¢ Statue of Liberty, redrawn	03/22/58	.20	.20	.90	(4)	1.00	
	Liberty, Perf. 11 x 10.5							
1042A	8¢ Gen. John J. Pershing	11/17/61	.20	.20	.90	(4)	1.25	
	Liberty, Perf. 10.5 x 11							
1043	9¢ The Alamo	06/14/56	.30	.20	1.30	(4)	1.50	
1044	10¢ Independence Hall	07/04/56	.30	.20	1.40	(4)	1.00	
b	Tagged	07/06/66	.25	.20	1.10	(4)	40.00	
d	Tagged	07/06/66	2.00	1.00	35.00	(4)		
	Liberty, Perf. 11							
1044A	11¢ Statue of Liberty	06/15/61	.30	.20	1.50	(4)	1.25	
c	Tagged	01/11/67	2.50	1.60	45.00	(4)	40.00	
	Liberty, Perf. 11 x 10.5							
1045	12¢ Benjamin Harrison	06/06/59	.35	.20	1.50	(4)	1.25	
a	Tagged	1968	.35	.20	4.00	(4)	40.00	
1046	15¢ John Jay	12/12/58	.60	.20	3.00	(4)	1.25	
a	Tagged	07/06/66	1.10	.80	13.00	(4)	40.00	
	Liberty, Perf. 10.5 x 11							
1047	20¢ Monticello	04/13/56	.50	.20	2.25	(4)	1.25	

VISIT US ONLINE AT **THE POSTAL STORE**

AT **WWW.USPS.COM**

OR CALL **1 800 STAMP-24**

1002 1003 1004 1005 1006 1007

1008 1009 1010 1011 1012 1013

1014 1015 1016 1017 1018 1019

1020 1021 1022 1023 1024 1025

1026 1027 1028 1029 1030 1031 1031A

1032 1033 1034 1035 1036 1037 1038 1039 1040

1041 1042 1042A 1043 1044 1044A 1045 1046 1047

1048 1049 1050 1051 1052 1053 1060 1061

1062 1063 1064 1065 1066 1067

1068 1069 1070 1071 1072 1073

1074 1075 1076 1077

1078 1079 1080 1081 1082 1083

1084 1085 1086 1087 1088 1089

	Issue	Date	Un	U	PB	#	FDC	Q(M)
	Liberty, Perf. 11 x 10.5 (Designs of 1030-1059)							
1048	25¢ Paul Revere	04/18/58	1.10	.75	4.75	(4)	1.25	
1049	30¢ Robert E. Lee	06/57	1.00	.20	4.50	(4)		
a	Wet printing	09/21/55	1.20	.75	5.25	(4)	2.00	
1050	40¢ John Marshall	04/58	1.50	.20	7.50	(4)		
a	Wet printing	09/24/55	1.75	.25	9.00	(4)	2.00	
1051	50¢ Susan B. Anthony	04/58	1.50	.20	8.00	(4)		
a	Wet printing	08/25/55	1.75	.20	11.00	(4)	6.00	
1052	$1 Patrick Henry	10/58	4.50	.20	19.00	(4)		
a	Wet printing	10/07/55	5.25	1.00	22.50	(4)	15.00	
	Liberty, Perf. 11							
1053	$5 Alexander Hamilton	03/19/56	60.00	6.75	275.00	(4)	50.00	
	Liberty, Coil, Perf. 10 Vertically							
1054	1¢ dark Washington (1031)	08/57	.20	.20	1.00	(2)		
b	Imperf., pair		2,500.00	—				
c	Wet printing	10/08/54	.35	.20	1.75	(2)	1.00	
	Liberty, Coil, Perf. 10 Horizontally							
1054A	1¼¢ Palace of the Governors (1031A)	06/17/60	.20	.20	2.25	(2)	1.00	
	Liberty, Coil, Perf. 10 Vertically							
1055	2¢ Jefferson (1033)	05/57	.35	.20	1.50	(2)		
a	Tagged	05/06/68	.20	.20	.75	(2)	32.50	
b	Imperf., pair (Bureau precanceled)		450.00					
c	As "a," imperf., pair		550.00		1,200.00	(2)		
1056	2½¢ Bunker Hill (1034)	09/09/59	.30	.25	3.50	(2)	2.00	
1057	3¢ Statue of Liberty (1035)	10/56	.35	.20	2.75	(2)		
a	Imperf., pair		1,500.00	800.00	2,750.00	(2)		
b	Tagged	06/26/67	1.00	.50	25.00	(2)		
c	Wet printing	07/20/54	.35	.20	2.75	(2)	1.00	
1058	4¢ Lincoln (1036)	07/31/58	.50	.20	2.50	(2)	1.50	
a	Imperf., pair		85.00	70.00	200.00	(2)		
	Liberty, Coil, Perf. 10 Horizontally							
1059	4½¢ The Hermitage (1037)	05/01/59	1.50	1.00	14.00	(2)	1.75	
	Liberty, Coil, Perf. 10 Vertically							
1059A	25¢ Revere (1048)	02/25/65	.50	.30	2.00	(2)	1.25	
b	Tagged, shiney gum	04/03/73	.80	.20	3.25	(2)	40.00	
	Tagged, dull gum	1980	4.00		12.00	(2)		
c	Imperf., pair		40.00		90.00	(2)		
	Perf. 11 x 10.5							
1060	3¢ Nebraska Territory	05/07/54	.20	.20	.45	(4)	1.00	116
1061	3¢ Kansas Territory	05/31/54	.20	.20	.55	(4)	1.00	114
	Perf. 10.5 x 11							
1062	3¢ George Eastman	07/12/54	.20	.20	.40	(4)	1.00	128
	Perf. 11 x 10.5							
1063	3¢ Lewis and Clark Expedition	07/28/54	.20	.20	.75	(4)	1.50	116
	Perf. 10.5 x 11							
1064	3¢ Pennsylvania Academy of the Fine Arts	01/15/55	.20	.20	.45	(4)	1.00	116

	Issue	Date	Un	U	PB	#	FDC	Q(M)
	Perf. 11 x 10.5							
1065	3¢ Land-Grant Colleges	02/12/55	.20	.20	.45	(4)	1.25	120
1066	8¢ Rotary International	02/23/55	.25	.20	1.25	(4)	3.00	54
1067	3¢ Armed Forces Reserve	05/21/55	.20	.20	.40	(4)	1.25	176
	Perf. 10.5 x 11							
1068	3¢ New Hampshire	06/21/55	.20	.20	.70	(4)	2.00	126
	Perf. 11 x 10.5							
1069	3¢ Soo Locks	06/28/55	.20	.20	.40	(4)	1.00	122
1070	3¢ Atoms for Peace	07/28/55	.20	.20	.40	(4)	1.00	134
1071	3¢ Fort Ticonderoga	09/18/55	.20	.20	.40	(4)	1.00	119
	Perf. 10.5 x 11							
1072	3¢ Andrew W. Mellon	12/20/55	.20	.20	.40	(4)	1.00	112
1073	3¢ Benjamin Franklin	01/17/56	.20	.20	.40	(4)	1.25	129
	Perf. 11 x 10.5							
1074	3¢ Booker T. Washington	04/05/56	.20	.20	.40	(4)	2.00	121
	Fifth International Philatelic Exhibition Souvenir Sheet, Imperf.							
1075	Statue of Liberty Sheet of 2 stamps (1035, 1041)	04/28/56	2.00	1.50			5.00	3
a	3¢ (1035), single stamp from sheet		.80	.60				
b	8¢ (1041), single stamp from sheet		1.00	.75				
	Perf. 11 x 10.5							
1076	3¢ New York Coliseum and Columbus Monument	04/30/56	.20	.20	.30	(4)	1.00	120
	Wildlife Conservation, Perf. 11 x 10.5							
1077	3¢ Wild Turkey	05/05/56	.20	.20	.35	(4)	1.75	123
1078	3¢ Pronghorn Antelope	06/22/56	.20	.20	.35	(4)	1.75	123
1079	3¢ King Salmon	11/09/56	.20	.20	.35	(4)	1.75	109
	Perf. 10.5 x 11							
1080	3¢ Pure Food and Drug Laws	06/27/56	.20	.20	.50	(4)	1.00	113
	Perf. 11 x 10.5							
1081	3¢ Wheatland	08/05/56	.20	.20	.40	(4)	1.00	125
	Perf. 10.5 x 11							
1082	3¢ Labor Day	09/03/56	.20	.20	.40	(4)	1.00	118
	Perf. 11 x 10.5							
1083	3¢ Nassau Hall	09/22/56	.20	.20	.50	(4)	1.00	122
	Perf. 10.5 x 11							
1084	3¢ Devils Tower	09/24/56	.20	.20	.45	(4)	1.25	118
	Perf. 11 x 10.5							
1085	3¢ Children's Stamp	12/15/56	.20	.20	.40	(4)	1.00	101
1086	3¢ Alexander Hamilton	01/11/57	.20	.20	.40	(4)	1.00	115
	Perf. 10.5 x 11							
1087	3¢ Polio	01/15/57	.20	.20	.40	(4)	1.50	187
	Perf. 11 x 10.5							
1088	3¢ Coast and Geodetic Survey	02/11/57	.20	.20	.40	(4)	1.00	115
1089	3¢ American Institute of Architects	02/23/57	.20	.20	.40	(4)	1.25	107

	Issue	Date	Un	U	PB	#	FDC	Q(M)
	Perf. 10.5 x 11							
1090	3¢ Steel Industry	05/22/57	.20	.20	.40	(4)	1.00	112
	Perf. 11 x 10.5							
1091	3¢ International Naval Review-Jamestown Festival	06/10/57	.20	.20	.40	(4)	1.25	118
1092	3¢ Oklahoma Statehood	06/14/57	.20	.20	.50	(4)	1.00	102
1093	3¢ School Teachers	07/01/57	.20	.20	.40	(4)	2.00	102
	Perf. 11							
1094	4¢ Flag	07/04/57	.20	.20	.45	(4)	1.00	84
	Perf. 10.5 x 11							
1095	3¢ Shipbuilding	08/15/57	.20	.20	.45	(4)	1.25	126
	Champion of Liberty, Perf. 11							
1096	8¢ Bust of Ramon Magsaysay on Medal	08/31/57	.20	.20	.85	(4)	1.50	39
	Perf. 10.5 x 11							
1097	3¢ Marquis de Lafayette	09/06/57	.20	.20	.40	(4)	1.00	123
	Wildlife Conservation, Perf. 11							
1098	3¢ Whooping Cranes	11/22/57	.20	.20	.40	(4)	1.25	174
	Perf. 10.5 x 11							
1099	3¢ Religious Freedom	12/27/57	.20	.20	.40	(4)	1.00	114
1100	3¢ Gardening-Horticulture	03/15/58	.20	.20	.40	(4)	1.00	123
1101-1103	Not assigned							
	Perf. 11 x 10.5							
1104	3¢ Brussels Universal and International Exhibition	04/17/58	.20	.20	.40	(4)	1.00	114
1105	3¢ James Monroe	04/28/58	.20	.20	.45	(4)	1.00	120
1106	3¢ Minnesota Statehood	05/11/58	.20	.20	.45	(4)	1.00	121
	Perf. 11							
1107	3¢ International Geophysical Year	05/31/58	.20	.20	.40	(4)	1.00	126
	Perf. 11 x 10.5							
1108	3¢ Gunston Hall	06/12/58	.20	.20	.40	(4)	1.00	108
	Perf. 10.5 x 11							
1109	3¢ Mackinac Bridge	06/25/58	.20	.20	.50	(4)	1.00	107
	Champion of Liberty, Perf. 10.5 x 11							
1110	4¢ Bust of Simon Bolivar on Medal	07/24/58	.20	.20	.40	(4)	1.50	116
	Champion of Liberty, Perf. 11							
1111	8¢ Bust of Bolivar on Medal	07/24/58	.20	.20	1.25	(4)	2.25	40
	Plate block of four, ocher # only		—					
	Perf. 11 x 10.5							
1112	4¢ Atlantic Cable	08/15/58	.20	.20	.40	(4)	1.00	115

	Issue	Date	Un	U	PB	#	FDC	Q(M)
	Abraham Lincoln Sesquicentennial, Perf. 10.5 x 11 (Designs of 1113-1116)							
1113	1¢ Portrait by George Healy	02/12/59	.20	.20	.25	(4)	1.75	120
1114	3¢ Sculptured Head by Gutzon Borglum	02/27/59	.20	.20	.40	(4)	1.75	91
	Perf. 11 x 10.5							
1115	4¢ Lincoln and Stephen Douglas Debating, by Joseph Boggs Beale	08/27/58	.20	.20	.60	(4)	1.75	115
1116	4¢ Statue in Lincoln Memorial by Daniel Chester French	05/30/59	.20	.20	.40	(4)	1.75	126
	Champion of Liberty, Perf. 10.5 x 11							
1117	4¢ Bust of Lajos Kossuth on Medal	09/19/58	.20	.20	.40	(4)	1.25	121
	Champion of Liberty, Perf. 11							
1118	8¢ Bust of Kossuth on Medal	09/19/58	.20	.20	1.10	(4)	1.50	44
	Perf. 10.5 x 11							
1119	4¢ Freedom of the Press	09/22/58	.20	.20	.40	(4)	1.00	118
	Perf. 11 x 10.5							
1120	4¢ Overland Mail	10/10/58	.20	.20	.40	(4)	1.00	126
	Perf. 10.5 x 11							
1121	4¢ Noah Webster	10/16/58	.20	.20	.40	(4)	1.00	114
	Perf. 11							
1122	4¢ Forest Conservation	10/27/58	.20	.20	.40	(4)	1.00	157
	Perf. 11 x 10.5							
1123	4¢ Fort Duquesne	11/25/58	.20	.20	.40	(4)	1.00	124
1124	4¢ Oregon Statehood	02/14/59	.25	.20	1.10	(4)	1.00	121
	Champion of Liberty, Perf. 10.5 x 11							
1125	4¢ Bust of José de San Martin on Medal	02/25/59	.20	.20	.40	(4)	1.50	134
a	Horizontal pair, imperf. between	1,250.00						
	Champion of Liberty, Perf. 11							
1126	8¢ Bust of San Martin on Medal	02/25/59	.20	.20	.90	(4)	2.00	46
	Perf. 10.5 x 11							
1127	4¢ NATO	04/01/59	.20	.20	.40	(4)	1.25	122
	Perf. 11 x 10.5							
1128	4¢ Arctic Explorations	04/06/59	.20	.20	.40	(4)	1.00	131
1129	8¢ World Peace Through World Trade	04/20/59	.20	.20	.85	(4)	1.00	47
1130	4¢ Silver Centennial	06/08/59	.20	.20	.40	(4)	1.00	123
	Perf. 11							
1131	4¢ St. Lawrence Seaway	06/26/59	.20	.20	.40	(4)	1.25	126

1090

1091

1092

1093

1094

1095

1096

1097

1098

1099

1100

1104

1105

1106

1107

1108

1109

1110

1111

1112

1113

1114

1115

1116

1117

1118

1119

1120

1121

1122

1123

1124

1125

1126

1127

1128

1129

1130

1131

1132

1133

1134

1135

1136

1137

1138

1139

1140

1141

1142

1143

1144

1145

1146

1147

1148

1149

1150

1151

1152

1153

1154

1155

1156

1157

1158

1159

1160

1161

1162

1163

1164

1165

1166

1167

1168

1169

1170

1171

1172

1173

	Issue	Date	Un	U	PB	#	FDC	Q(M)
	Perf. 11							
1132	4¢ 49-Star Flag	07/04/59	.20	.20	.40	(4)	1.00	209
1133	4¢ Soil Conservation	08/26/59	.20	.20	.40	(4)	1.00	121
	Perf. 10.5 x 11							
1134	4¢ Petroleum Industry	08/27/59	.20	.20	.40	(4)	1.50	116
	Perf. 11 x 10.5							
1135	4¢ Dental Health	09/14/59	.20	.20	.40	(4)	3.50	118
	Champion of Liberty, Perf. 10.5 x 11							
1136	4¢ Bust of Ernst Reuter on Medal	09/29/59	.20	.20	.40	(4)	1.25	112
	Champion of Liberty, Perf. 11							
1137	8¢ Bust of Reuter on Medal	09/29/59	.20	.20	.90	(4)	1.50	43
a	Ocher missing		4,250.00					
b	Ultramarine missing		4,250.00					
c	Ocher & ultramarine missing		4,500.00					
d	All colors missing		2,500.00					
	Perf. 10.5 x 11							
1138	4¢ Dr. Ephraim McDowell	12/03/59	.20	.20	.40	(4)	1.25	115
a	Vertical pair, imperf. between		400.00					
b	Vertical pair, imperf. horizontally		275.00					
	American Credo, Perf. 11							
1139	4¢ Quotation from Washington's Farewell Address	01/20/60	.20	.20	.40	(4)	1.25	126
1140	4¢ Benjamin Franklin Quotation	03/31/60	.20	.20	.40	(4)	1.25	125
1141	4¢ Thomas Jefferson Quotation	05/18/60	.20	.20	.60	(4)	1.25	115
1142	4¢ Francis Scott Key Quotation	09/14/60	.20	.20	.50	(4)	1.25	122
1143	4¢ Abraham Lincoln Quotation	11/19/60	.20	.20	.50	(4)	1.50	121
1144	4¢ Patrick Henry Quotation	01/11/61	.20	.20	.65	(4)	1.25	113
	Perf. 11							
1145	4¢ Boy Scouts	02/08/60	.20	.20	.55	(4)	4.00	139
	Olympic Games, Perf. 10.5 x 11							
1146	4¢ Olympic Rings and Snowflake	02/18/60	.20	.20	.40	(4)	1.00	124
	Champion of Liberty, Perf. 10.5 x 11							
1147	4¢ Bust of Thomas Masaryk on Medal	03/07/60	.20	.20	.40	(4)	1.25	114
a	Vertical pair, imperf. between		2,750.00					
	Champion of Liberty, Perf. 11							
1148	8¢ Bust of Masaryk on Medal	03/07/60	.20	.20	.95	(4)	1.50	44
	Perf. 11 x 10.5							
1149	4¢ World Refugee Year	04/07/60	.20	.20	.40	(4)	1.00	113
	Perf. 11							
1150	4¢ Water Conservation	04/18/60	.20	.20	.40	(4)	1.00	122
a	Brown orange missing		2,400.00					
	Perf. 10.5 x 11							
1151	4¢ SEATO	05/31/60	.20	.20	.40	(4)	1.00	115
a	Vertical pair, imperf. between		140.00					

	Issue	Date	Un	U	PB	#	FDC	Q(M)
	Perf. 11 x 10.5							
1152	4¢ American Woman	06/02/60	.20	.20	.40	(4)	1.25	111
	Perf. 11							
1153	4¢ 50-Star Flag	07/04/60	.20	.20	.40	(4)	1.00	153
	Perf. 11 x 10.5							
1154	4¢ Pony Express	07/19/60	.20	.20	.65	(4)	1.75	120
	Perf. 10.5 x 11							
1155	4¢ Employ the Handicapped	08/28/60	.20	.20	.40	(4)	1.50	118
1156	4¢ 5th World Forestry Congress	08/29/60	.20	.20	.40	(4)	1.00	118
	Perf. 11							
1157	4¢ Mexican Independence	09/16/60	.20	.20	.40	(4)	1.00	112
1158	4¢ U.S.-Japan Treaty	09/28/60	.20	.20	.40	(4)	1.00	125
	Champion of Liberty, Perf. 10.5 x 11							
1159	4¢ Bust of Ignacy Jan Paderewski on Medal	10/08/60	.20	.20	.40	(4)	1.25	120
	Champion of Liberty, Perf. 11							
1160	8¢ Bust of Paderewski on Medal	10/08/60	.20	.20	.90	(4)	1.50	43
	Perf. 10.5 x 11							
1161	4¢ Sen. Robert A. Taft Memorial	10/10/60	.20	.20	.45	(4)	1.00	107
	Perf. 11 x 10.5							
1162	4¢ Wheels of Freedom	10/15/60	.20	.20	.40	(4)	1.00	110
	Perf. 11							
1163	4¢ Boys' Clubs of America	10/18/60	.20	.20	.40	(4)	1.00	124
1164	4¢ First Automated Post Office	10/20/60	.20	.20	.40	(4)	1.00	124
	Champion of Liberty, Perf. 10.5 x 11							
1165	4¢ Bust of Gustaf Mannerheim on Medal	10/26/60	.20	.20	.40	(4)	1.25	125
	Champion of Liberty, Perf. 11							
1166	8¢ Bust of Mannerheim on Medal	10/26/60	.20	.20	.80	(4)	1.50	42
	Perf. 11							
1167	4¢ Camp Fire Girls	11/01/60	.20	.20	.65	(4)	3.00	116
	Champion of Liberty, Perf. 10.5 x 11							
1168	4¢ Bust of Giusseppe Garibaldi on Medal	11/02/60	.20	.20	.40	(4)	1.25	126
	Champion of Liberty, Perf. 11							
1169	8¢ Bust of Garibaldi on Medal	11/02/60	.20	.20	.85	(4)	1.50	43
	Perf. 10.5 x 11							
1170	4¢ Sen. Walter F. George Memorial	11/05/60	.20	.20	.45	(4)	1.00	124
1171	4¢ Andrew Carnegie	11/25/60	.20	.20	.40	(4)	1.00	120
1172	4¢ John Foster Dulles Memorial	12/06/60	.20	.20	.40	(4)	1.00	117
	Perf. 11 x 10.5							
1173	4¢ Echo I-Communications for Peace	12/15/60	.20	.20	.65	(4)	2.50	124

Issue		Date	Un	U	PB/LP	#	FDC	Q(M)
	Champion of Liberty, Perf. 10.5 x 11							
1174	4¢ Bust of Gandhi on Medal	01/26/61	.20	.20	.40	(4)	1.25	113
	Champion of Liberty, Perf. 11							
1175	8¢ Bust of Gandhi on Medal	01/26/61	.20	.20	1.00	(4)	1.75	42
	Perf. 11							
1176	4¢ Range Conservation	02/02/61	.20	.20	.60	(4)	1.00	111
	Perf. 10.5 x 11							
1177	4¢ Horace Greeley	02/03/61	.20	.20	.45	(4)	1.00	99
	Civil War Centennial, Perf. 11 x 10.5							
1178	4¢ Fort Sumter	04/12/61	.30	.20	1.25	(4)	4.00	101
1179	4¢ Shiloh	04/07/62	.20	.20	.75	(4)	4.00	125
	Civil War Centennial, Perf. 11							
1180	5¢ Gettysburg	07/01/63	.20	.20	.85	(4)	4.00	80
1181	5¢ The Wilderness	05/05/64	.20	.20	.60	(4)	4.00	125
1182	5¢ Appomattox	04/09/65	.35	.20	1.50	(4)	4.00	113
a	Horizontal pair, imperf. vertically	4,500.00						
	Perf. 11							
1183	4¢ Kansas Statehood	05/10/61	.20	.20	.55	(4)	1.00	106
	Perf. 11 x 10.5							
1184	4¢ Sen. George W. Norris	07/11/61	.20	.20	.40	(4)	1.00	111
1185	4¢ Naval Aviation	08/20/61	.20	.20	.40	(4)	1.50	117
	Pair with full vertical gutter between	150.00						
	Perf. 10.5 x 11							
1186	4¢ Workmen's Compensation	09/04/61	.20	.20	.40	(4)	1.00	121
	With plate # inverted				.60	(4)		
	Perf. 11							
1187	4¢ Frederic Remington	10/04/61	.20	.20	.40	(4)	1.25	112
	Perf. 10.5 x 11							
1188	4¢ Republic of China	10/10/61	.20	.20	.45	(4)	5.50	111
1189	4¢ Naismith-Basketball	11/06/61	.20	.20	.50	(4)	7.50	109
	Perf. 11							
1190	4¢ Nursing	12/28/61	.20	.20	.50	(4)	10.00	145
1191	4¢ New Mexico Statehood	01/06/62	.20	.20	.50	(4)	2.00	113
1192	4¢ Arizona Statehood	02/14/62	.20	.20	.50	(4)	1.75	122
	Space, Perf. 11							
1193	4¢ Project Mercury	02/20/62	.20	.20	.40	(4)	3.00	289
	Perf. 11							
1194	4¢ Malaria Eradication	03/30/62	.20	.20	.40	(4)	1.00	120
	Perf. 10.5 x 11							
1195	4¢ Charles Evans Hughes	04/11/62	.20	.20	.40	(4)	1.00	125
	Perf. 11							
1196	4¢ Seattle World's Fair	04/25/62	.20	.20	.40	(4)	1.25	147
1197	4¢ Louisiana Statehood	04/30/62	.20	.20	.50	(4)	1.00	119

Issue		Date	Un	U	PB/LP	#	FDC	Q(M)
	Perf. 11 x 10.5							
1198	4¢ Homestead Act	05/20/62	.20	.20	.40	(4)	1.00	123
1199	4¢ Girl Scout Jubilee	07/24/62	.20	.20	.40	(4)	5.00	127
	Pair with full vertical gutter between	250.00						
1200	4¢ Sen. Brien McMahon	07/28/62	.20	.20	.40	(4)	1.00	131
1201	4¢ Apprenticeship	08/31/62	.20	.20	.40	(4)	1.00	120
	Perf. 11							
1202	4¢ Sam Rayburn	09/16/62	.20	.20	.45	(4)	1.50	121
1203	4¢ Dag Hammarskjold	10/23/62	.20	.20	.40	(4)	1.00	121
1204	4¢ Dag Hammarskjold, black, brown and yellow (yellow inverted), special printing	11/16/62	.20	.20	1.25	(4)	5.00	40
	Holiday Celebrations: Holiday, Perf. 11							
1205	4¢ Wreath and Candles	11/01/62	.20	.20	.40	(4)	1.10	862
	Perf. 11							
1206	4¢ Higher Education	11/14/62	.20	.20	.40	(4)	1.25	120
1207	4¢ Winslow Homer	12/15/62	.20	.20	.45	(4)	1.25	118
a	Horizontal pair, imperf. between	6,750.00						
1208	5¢ Flag over White House	01/09/63	.20	.20	.40	(4)	1.00	
a	Tagged	08/25/66	.20	.20	2.00	(4)	30.00	
b	Horizontal pair, imperf. between	1,500.00						
	Perf. 11 x 10.5							
1209	1¢ Andrew Jackson	03/22/63	.20	.20	.20	(4)	1.00	
a	Tagged	07/06/66	.20	.20	.40	(4)	30.00	
1210-1212	Not assigned							
1213	5¢ George Washington	11/23/62	.20	.20	.40	(4)	1.00	
a	Booklet pane of 5 + label		3.00	2.00			4.00	
b	Tagged	10/28/63	.50	.20	4.50	(4)	30.00	
c	As "a," tagged	10/28/63	2.00	1.50			100.00	
1214-1224	Not assigned							
	Coil, Perf. 10 Vertically							
1225	1¢ green Jackson (1209)	05/31/63	.20	.20	2.25	(2)	1.00	
a	Tagged	07/06/66	.20	.20	.75	(2)	30.00	
1226-1228	Not assigned							
1229	5¢ dark blue gray Washington (1213)	11/23/62	1.50	.20	4.00	(2)	1.00	
a	Tagged	10/28/63	1.80	.20	12.00	(2)	30.00	
b	Imperf., pair		350.00		900.00	(2)		
	Perf. 11							
1230	5¢ Carolina Charter	04/06/63	.20	.20	.45	(4)	1.00	130
1231	5¢ Food for Peace– Freedom from Hunger	06/04/63	.20	.20	.40	(4)	1.00	136
1232	5¢ West Virginia Statehood	06/20/63	.20	.20	.50	(4)	1.00	138

1174   **1175**   **1176**   **1177**   **1178**   **1179**   **1180**

1181   **1183**   **1184**   **1185**   **1186**   **1187**

1182

1188   **1189**   **1190**   **1191**   **1192**   **1193**   **1194**

1195   **1196**   **1197**   **1198**   **1199**   **1200**

1201   **1203**   **1204**   **1205**   **1206**

1202

1207   **1208**   **1209**   **1213**   **1230**   **1232**

1231

1233

1234

1235

1236

1238

1239

1240

1241

1242

1243

1244

1245

1246

1247

1248

1249

1250

1251

1252

1253

1254   1255

1256   1257 1257b

1258

1259

1260

1261

1262

1263

1264

1265

1266

1267

1268

1269

	Issue	Date	Un	U	PB	#	FDC	Q(M)
	Perf. 11							
1233	5¢ Emancipation Proclamation	08/16/63	.20	.20	.50	(4)	1.75	132
1234	5¢ Alliance for Progress	08/17/63	.20	.20	.40	(4)	1.00	136
	Perf. 10.5 x 11							
1235	5¢ Cordell Hull	10/05/63	.20	.20	.50	(4)	1.00	131
	Perf. 11 x 10.5							
1236	5¢ Eleanor Roosevelt	10/11/63	.20	.20	.45	(4)	1.25	133
	Perf. 11							
1237	5¢ The Sciences	10/14/63	.20	.20	.40	(4)	1.25	130
	Tagged, Perf. 11							
1238	5¢ City Mail Delivery	10/26/63	.20	.20	.50	(4)	1.25	128
a	Tagged omitted			9.50				
1239	5¢ International Red Cross	10/29/63	.20	.20	.50	(4)	2.00	119
	Holiday Celebrations: Holiday, Perf. 11							
1240	5¢ National Christmas Tree and White House	11/01/63	.20	.20	.50	(4)	1.25	1,300
a	Tagged	11/02/63	.65	.50	5.00	(4)	60.00	
	Perf. 11							
1241	5¢ John James Audubon (See also #C71)	12/07/63	.20	.20	.45	(4)	1.25	175
	Perf. 10.5 x 11							
1242	5¢ Sam Houston	01/10/64	.25	.20	1.05	(4)	1.75	126
	Perf. 11							
1243	5¢ Charles M. Russell	03/19/64	.20	.20	.40	(4)	1.25	128
	Perf. 11 x 10.5							
1244	5¢ New York World's Fair	04/22/64	.20	.20	.45	(4)	2.00	146
	Perf. 11							
1245	5¢ John Muir	04/29/64	.20	.20	.45	(4)	1.50	120
	Perf. 11 x 10.5							
1246	5¢ President John Fitzgerald Kennedy Memorial	05/29/64	.20	.20	.60	(4)	2.50	512
	Perf. 10.5 x 11							
1247	5¢ New Jersey Tercentenary	06/15/64	.20	.20	.50	(4)	1.00	124
	Perf. 11							
1248	5¢ Nevada Statehood	07/22/64	.25	.20	1.05	(4)	1.00	123
1249	5¢ Register and Vote	08/01/64	.20	.20	.45	(4)	1.25	453
	Perf. 10.5 x 11							
1250	5¢ Shakespeare	08/14/64	.20	.20	.40	(4)	2.00	123
1251	5¢ Doctors William and Charles Mayo	09/11/64	.20	.20	.70	(4)	3.00	123
	Perf. 11							
1252	5¢ American Music	10/15/64	.20	.20	.40	(4)	1.50	127
a	Blue omitted		850.00					
1253	5¢ Homemakers	10/26/64	.20	.20	.40	(4)	1.00	121
	Holiday Celebrations: Holiday, Perf. 11							
1254	5¢ Holly	11/09/64	.25	.20				352
a	Tagged, Nov. 10		.75	.50				
1255	5¢ Mistletoe	11/09/64	.25	.20				352
a	Tagged, Nov. 10		.75	.50				
1256	5¢ Poinsettia	11/09/64	.25	.20				352
a	Tagged, Nov. 10		.75	.50				
1257	5¢ Sprig of Conifer	11/09/64	.25	.20				352
a	Tagged, Nov. 10		.75	.50				
b	Block of four, #1254-1257		1.00	1.00	1.10	(4)	3.00	
c	As "b," tagged		3.00	2.25	6.00	(4)	57.50	
	Perf. 10.5 x 11							
1258	5¢ Verrazano-Narrows Bridge	11/21/64	.20	.20	.45	(4)	1.00	120
	Perf. 11							
1259	5¢ Fine Arts	12/02/64	.20	.20	.45	(4)	1.00	126
	Perf. 10.5 x 11							
1260	5¢ Amateur Radio	12/15/64	.20	.20	.70	(4)	5.00	122
	Perf. 11							
1261	5¢ Battle of New Orleans	01/08/65	.20	.20	.60	(4)	1.00	116
1262	5¢ Physical Fitness-Sokol	02/15/65	.20	.20	.50	(4)	1.25	115
1263	5¢ Crusade Against Cancer	04/01/65	.20	.20	.40	(4)	2.50	120
	Perf. 10.5 x 11							
1264	5¢ Winston Churchill Memorial	05/13/65	.20	.20	.40	(4)	2.00	125
	Perf. 11							
1265	5¢ Magna Carta	06/15/65	.20	.20	.40	(4)	1.00	120
1266	5¢ International Cooperation Year–United Nations	06/26/65	.20	.20	.40	(4)	1.00	115
1267	5¢ Salvation Army	07/02/65	.20	.20	.40	(4)	3.00	116
	Perf. 10.5 x 11							
1268	5¢ Dante Alighieri	07/17/65	.20	.20	.40	(4)	1.00	115
1269	5¢ President Herbert Hoover Memorial	08/10/65	.20	.20	.55	(4)	1.00	115

	Issue	Date	Un	U	PB	#	FDC	Q(M)
	Perf. 11							
1270	5¢ Robert Fulton	08/19/65	.20	.20	.40	(4)	1.00	116
1271	5¢ Florida Settlement	08/28/65	.20	.20	.50	(4)	1.00	117
a	Yellow omitted		250.00					
1272	5¢ Traffic Safety	09/03/65	.20	.20	.45	(4)	1.00	114
1273	5¢ John Singleton Copley	09/17/65	.20	.20	.50	(4)	1.00	115
1274	11¢ International Telecommunication Union	10/06/65	.35	.20	2.00	(4)	1.10	27
1275	5¢ Adlai E. Stevenson Memorial	10/23/65	.20	.20	.40	(4)	1.00	128
	Holiday Celebrations: Holiday, Perf. 11							
1276	5¢ Angel with Trumpet (1840 Weather Vane)	11/02/65	.20	.20	.40	(4)	1.00	1,140
a	Tagged	11/15/65	.75	.25	5.50	(4)		50.00
1277	Not assigned							
	Prominent Americans, Perf. 11 x 10.5, 10.5 x 11							
1278	1¢ Thomas Jefferson	01/12/68	.20	.20	.20	(4)	1.00	
a	Booklet pane of 8	01/12/68	1.00	.75			2.50	
b	Bklt. pane of 4 + 2 labels	05/10/71	.80	.60			11.50	
c	Untagged (Bureau precanceled)		6.25	1.25	175.00	(4)		
d	Tagging omitted		3.50	—				
1279	1¼¢ Albert Gallatin	01/30/67	.20	.20	4.50	(4)	1.00	
1280	2¢ Frank Lloyd Wright	06/08/66	.20	.20	.25	(4)	1.00	
a	Booklet pane of 5 + label	01/08/68	1.25	.80			3.50	
b	Untagged (Bureau precanceled)		1.35	.40				
c	Booklet pane of 6	05/07/71	1.00	.75			15.00	
d	Tagging omitted		4.00	—				
1281	3¢ Francis Parkman	09/16/67	.20	.20	.25	(4)	1.00	
a	Untagged (Bureau precanceled)		3.00	.75				
b	Tagging omitted		5.00	—				
1282	4¢ Abraham Lincoln	11/19/65	.20	.20	.40	(4)	1.50	
a	Tagged	12/01/65	.20	.20	.55	(4)	30.00	
	Pair with full horizontal gutter between		700.00					
1283	5¢ George Washington	02/22/66	.20	.20	.50	(4)	1.00	
a	Tagged	02/23/66	.20	.20	.60	(4)	30.00	
1283B	5¢ George Washington Tagged, shiney gum	11/17/67	.20	.20	.50	(4)	1.00	
	Dull gum		.20		1.40	(4)		
d	Untagged (Bureau precanceled)		12.50	1.00				
1284	6¢ Franklin D. Roosevelt	01/29/66	.20	.20	.60	(4)	1.00	
a	Tagged	12/29/66	.20	.20	.80	(4)	40.00	
b	Booklet pane of 8	12/28/67	1.50	1.00			2.75	
c	Booklet pane of 5 + label	01/09/68	1.50	1.00			100.00	
1285	8¢ Albert Einstein	03/14/66	.20	.20	.85	(4)	3.00	
a	Tagged	07/06/66	.20	.20	.95	(4)	40.00	
1286	10¢ Andrew Jackson	03/15/67	.20	.20	1.00	(4)	1.00	
b	Untagged (Bureau precanceled)		57.50	1.75				
1286A	12¢ Henry Ford	07/30/68	.25	.20	1.20	(4)	1.50	
c	Untagged (Bureau precanceled)		4.75	1.00	145.00	(4)		
1287	13¢ John F. Kennedy	05/29/67	.30	.20	1.50	(4)	1.75	
a	Untagged (Bureau precanceled)		6.00	1.00	100.00	(4)		
b	Tagging omitted		15.00	—				

	Issue	Date	Un	U	PB/LP	#	FDC	Q(M)
1288	15¢ Oliver Wendell Holmes	03/08/68	.30	.20	1.25	(4)	1.00	
a	Untagged (Bureau precanceled)		.75	.75	29.50	(4)		
d	Type II		.55	.20	8.00	(4)		
f	As "d", tagging omitted		7.50	—				
	Booklet, Perf. 10							
1288B	15¢ magenta, tagged (1288), Single from booklet		.35	.20			1.00	
c	Booklet pane of 8	06/14/78	2.80	1.75			3.00	
e	As "c," vert. imperf. between		1,750.00					
	Prominent Americans, Perf. 11 x 10.5, 10.5 x 11							
1289	20¢ George C. Marshall	10/24/67	.40	.20	1.75	(4)	1.10	
a	Tagged	04/03/73	.40	.20	1.75	(4)	40.00	
1290	25¢ Frederick Douglass	02/14/67	.55	.20	2.25	(4)	2.50	
a	Tagged	04/03/73	.45	.20	2.00	(4)	45.00	
b	Magenta		25.00	—	150.00			
1291	30¢ John Dewey	10/21/68	.65	.20	2.90	(4)	1.75	
a	Tagged	04/03/73	.50	.20	2.25	(4)	45.00	
1292	40¢ Thomas Paine	01/29/68	.80	.20	3.25	(4)	1.75	
a	Tagged	04/03/73	.65	.20	2.75	(4)	45.00	
1293	50¢ Lucy Stone	08/13/68	1.00	.20	4.25	(4)	2.50	
a	Tagged	04/03/73	.80	.20	3.50	(4)	45.00	
1294	$1 Eugene O'Neill	10/16/67	2.25	.20	10.00	(4)	6.00	
a	Tagged	04/03/73	1.65	.20	6.75	(4)	60.00	
1295	$5 John Bassett Moore	12/03/66	10.00	2.25	42.50	(4)	40.00	
a	Tagged	04/03/73	8.50	2.00	35.00	(4)	120.00	
1296	Not assigned							
	Prominent Americans, Coil, Tagged, Perf. 10 Horizontally							
1297	3¢ Parkman (1281)	11/04/75	.20	.20	.45	(2)	1.00	
a	Imperf., pair		22.50		45.00	(2)		
b	Untagged (Bureau precanceled)		.40	.25	62.50	(2)		
c	As "b," imperf., pair		6.00	—	22.50	(2)		
1298	6¢ Franklin D. Roosevelt (1284)	12/28/67	.20	.20	1.10	(2)	1.00	
a	Imperf., pair		1,900.00		4,750.00	(2)		
b	Tagging omitted		3.50					
	Prominent Americans, Coil, Tagged, Perf. 10 Vertically							
1299	1¢ Jefferson (1278)	01/12/68	.20	.20	.25	(2)	1.00	
a	Untagged (Bureau precanceled)		8.00	1.75	295.00	(2)		
b	Imperf., pair		25.00	—	52.50	(2)		
1300-1302	Not assigned							
1303	4¢ Lincoln (1282)	05/28/66	.20	.20	.75	(2)	1.50	
a	Untagged (Bureau precanceled)		8.75	.75	250.00	(2)		
b	Imperf., pair		700.00		1,650.00	(2)		
1304	5¢ Washington (1283)	09/08/66	.20	.20	.40	(2)	1.00	
a	Untagged (Bureau precanceled)		6.50	.65	175.00	(2)		
b	Imperf., pair		140.00		250.00	(2)		
e	As "a," imperf. pair		275.00		850.00	(2)		
1304C	5¢ redrawn (1283B)	1981	.20	.20	1.25	(2)		
d			575.00					
1305	6¢ Franklin D. Roosevelt	02/28/68	.20	.20	.55	(2)	1.00	
a	Imperf., pair		60.00		115.00	(2)		
b	Untagged (Bureau precanceled)		20.00	1.00	675.00	(2)		
1305C	$1 Eugene O'Neill (1294)	01/12/73	2.75	.40	9.00	(2)	4.00	
d			1,850.00		4,000.00	(2)		
1305E	15¢ Oliver Wendell Holmes, type I, (1288)	06/14/78	.25	.20	1.10	(2)	1.00	
	Dull finish gum		.75		4.25	(2)		

1270

1271

1272

1273

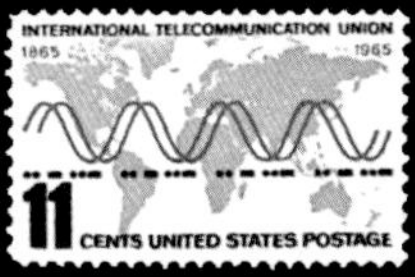

1274

1275

1276

1278

1279

1280

1281

1282

1283

1283B

1284

1285

1286

1286A

1287

1288

1289

1290

1291

1292

1293

1294

1295

1305

Vintage Black Cinema Commemorative Folio & Pane of 20 Stamps

* *Additional postage required after 5/11/09*

1306

1307

1308

1309

1310

1311

1312

1313

1314

1315

1316

1317

1318

1319

1320

1321

1322

1323

1324

1325

1326

1327

1328

1329

1330

1331

1332

1332b

1333

1334

	Issue	Date	Un	U	PB	#	FDC	Q(M)
	Perf. 11							
1306	5¢ Migratory Bird Treaty	03/16/66	.20	.20	.40	(4)	1.75	117
1307	5¢ Humane Treatment of							
	Animals	04/09/66	.20	.20	.40	(4)	1.25	117
1308	5¢ Indiana Statehood	04/16/66	.20	.20	.50	(4)	1.00	124
1309	5¢ American Circus	05/02/66	.20	.20	.50	(4)	2.00	131
	Sixth International Philatelic Exhibition, Perf. 11							
1310	5¢ Stamped Cover	05/21/66	.20	.20	.40	(4)	1.00	122
	Souvenir Sheet, Imperf.							
1311	5¢ Stamped Cover (1310) and							
	Washington, D.C., Scene	05/23/66	.20	.20			1.10	15
	Perf. 11							
1312	5¢ The Bill of Rights	07/01/66	.20	.20	.45	(4)	1.75	114
	Perf. 10.5 x 11							
1313	5¢ Poland's Millennium	07/30/66	.20	.20	.45	(4)	1.50	128
	Perf. 11							
1314	5¢ National Park Service	08/25/66	.20	.20	.50	(4)	1.00	120
a	Tagged	08/26/66	.35	.35	2.25	(4)	35.00	
1315	5¢ Marine Corps Reserve	08/29/66	.20	.20	.45	(4)	1.50	125
a	Tagged		.40	.20	2.25	(4)	35.00	
b	Black and bister omitted	16,000.00						
1316	5¢ General Federation of							
	Women's Clubs	09/12/66	.20	.20	.45	(4)	1.25	115
a	Tagged	09/13/66	.40	.20	2.25	(4)	35.00	
	American Folklore, Perf. 11							
1317	5¢ Johnny Appleseed							
	and Apple	09/24/66	.20	.20	.45	(4)	1.50	124
a	Tagged	09/26/66	.40	.20	2.25	(4)	35.00	
	Perf. 11							
1318	5¢ Beautification of							
	America	10/05/66	.20	.20	.45	(4)	1.00	128
a	Tagged		.40	.20	2.25	(4)	35.00	
1319	5¢ Great River Road	10/21/66	.20	.20	.60	(4)	1.00	128
a	Tagged	10/22/66	.40	.20	2.50	(4)	35.00	
1320	5¢ Savings Bond–Servicemen	10/26/66	.20	.20	.45	(4)	1.00	116
a	Tagged	10/27/66	.40	.20	2.00	(4)	35.00	
b	Red, dark bl. and blk. omitted	4,250.00						
c	Dark blue omitted	5,500.00						

	Issue	Date	Un	U	PB	#	FDC	Q(M)
	Holiday Celebration: Christmas, Perf. 11							
1321	5¢ Madonna and Child, by Hans Memling	11/01/66	.20	.20	.40	(4)	1.00	1,174
a	Tagged	11/02/66	.40	.20	2.00	(4)	35.00	
	Perf. 11							
1322	5¢ Mary Cassatt	11/17/66	.20	.20	.60	(4)	1.00	114
a	Tagged		.40	.25	2.00	(4)	35.00	
	Tagged, Perf. 11							
1323	5¢ National Grange	04/17/67	.20	.20	.40	(4)	1.00	121
a	Tagging omitted		6.00	—				
1324	5¢ Canada Centenary	05/25/67	.20	.20	.40	(4)	1.00	132
a	Tagging omitted		7.50	—				
1325	5¢ Erie Canal	07/04/67	.20	.20	.40	(4)	1.00	119
a	Tagging omitted		22.50	—				
1326	5¢ Search for Peace	07/05/67	.20	.20	.40	(4)	1.00	122
a	Tagging omitted		7.50	—				
1327	5¢ Henry David Thoreau	07/12/67	.20	.20	.50	(4)	1.00	112
a	Tagging omitted		200.00	—				
1328	5¢ Nebraska Statehood	07/29/67	.20	.20	.70	(4)	1.00	117
a	Tagging omitted		7.50	—				
1329	5¢ Voice of America	08/01/67	.20	.20	.40	(4)	2.00	112
a	Tagging omitted		20.00	—				
	American Folklore, Tagged, Perf. 11							
1330	5¢ Davy Crockett	08/17/67	.20	.20	.60	(4)	1.25	114
a	Vertical pair, imperf. between		7,000.00					
e	Tagging omitted		9.00	—				
	Space, Tagged, Perf. 11							
1331	5¢ Space-Walking Astronaut	09/29/67	.50	.20			3.00	60
a	Tagging omitted		25.00	—			8.00	
1332	5¢ Gemini 4 Capsule and Earth	09/29/67	.50	.20	2.25	(4)	3.00	60
a	Tagging omitted		25.00	—				
b	Pair, #1331-1332		1.10	1.25				
c	As "b", Tagging omitted		60.00	—				
	Tagged, Perf. 11							
1333	5¢ Urban Planning	10/02/67	.20	.20	.50	(4)	1.00	111
a	Tagging omitted		50.00					
1334	5¢ Finland Independence	10/06/67	.20	.20	.50	(4)	1.00	111
a	Tagging omitted		100.00					

Celebrating Lunar New Year: Year of the Ox Limited Edition Notecard Set*

Featuring three designs, this set of 12 notecards comes packaged in a special box that also includes matching envelopes and a sheet of 12 stamps.

Limited Edition Notecard Set
w/Envelopes & Stamps (12 of each)
Item #573894 $13.95

To order this item call **1 800 STAMP-24**
or visit us online at **www.usps.com**

*Additional postage required for mailing.

	Issue	Date	Un	U	PB	#	FDC	Q(M)
	Tagged, Perf. 12							
1335	5¢ Thomas Eakins	11/02/67	.20	.20	.50	(4)	1.40	114
a	Tagging omitted		40.00	—				
	Holiday Celebration: Christmas, Tagged, Perf. 11							
1336	5¢ Madonna and Child, by Hans Memling	11/06/67	.20	.20	.40	(4)	1.25	1,209
a	Tagging omitted		5.50	—				
	Tagged, Perf. 11							
1337	5¢ Mississippi Statehood	12/11/67	.20	.20	.60	(4)	1.00	113
a	Tagging omitted		10.00	—				
	Tagged, Perf. 11							
1338	6¢ Flag over White House design 19 x 22mm	01/24/68	.20	.20	.45	(4)	1.00	
k	Vertical pair, imperf. between		400.00	175.00				
m	Tagging omitted		4.50	—				
	Coil, Perf. 10 Vertically							
1338A	6¢ dk bl, rd and grn (1338), design 18.25 x 21mm	05/30/69	.20	.20	.30	(2)	1.00	
b	Imperf., pair		475.00					
q	Tagging omitted		10.00					
	Tagged, Perf. 11 x 10.5							
1338D	6¢ dark blue, red and green (1338), design 18.25 x 21mm	08/07/70	.20	.20	2.60	(20)	1.00	
e	Horizontal pair, imperf. between		125.00					
n	Tagging omitted		4.00	—				
1338F	8¢ dk bl, rd and slt grn (1338)	05/10/71	.20	.20	3.00	(20)	1.00	
i	Imperf., vertical pair		37.50					
j	Horizontal pair, imperf. between		45.00					
o	Tagging omitted		4.00	—				
	Coil, Tagged, Perf. 10 Vertically							
1338G	8¢ dk bl, rd and slt grn (1338), design 18.25 x 21mm	05/10/71	.30	.20	.60	(2)	1.00	
h	Imperf., pair		50.00					
r	Tagging omitted		5.00	—				
	Tagged, Perf. 11							
1339	6¢ Illinois Statehood	02/12/68	.20	.20	.60	(4)	1.00	141
1340	6¢ HemisFair '68	03/30/68	.20	.20	.50	(4)	1.00	144
a	White omitted		1,100.00					
	Untagged, Perf. 11							
1341	$1 Airlift	04/04/68	2.00	1.25	8.50	(4)	7.00	
	Pair with full horizontal gutter between			—				
	Tagged, Perf. 11							
1342	6¢ Support Our Youth–Elks	05/01/68	.20	.20	.55	(4)	1.00	147
a	Tagging omitted		9.50	—				
1343	6¢ Law and Order	05/17/68	.20	.20	.55	(4)	2.50	130
1344	6¢ Register and Vote	06/27/68	.20	.20	.50	(4)	1.00	159
	Historic Flags, Tagged, Perf. 11							
1345	6¢ Ft. Moultrie Flag, 1776	07/04/68	.40	.25				23
1346	6¢ Ft. McHenry (U.S.) Flag, 1795-1818	07/04/68	.40	.25				23
1347	6¢ Washington's Cruisers Flag, 1775	07/04/68	.30	.25				23
1348	6¢ Bennington Flag, 1777	07/04/68	.30	.25				23
1349	6¢ Rhode Island Flag, 1775	07/04/68	.30	.25				23
1350	6¢ First Stars and Stripes, 1777	07/04/68	.30	.25				23
1351	6¢ Bunker Hill Flag, 1775	07/04/68	.30	.25				23
1352	6¢ Grand Union Flag, 1776	07/04/68	.30	.25				23

	Issue	Date	Un	U	PB	#	FDC	Q(M)
	Historic Flags, Tagged, Perf. 11 continued							
1353	6¢ Philadelphia Light Horse Flag, 1775	07/04/68	.30	.25			3.00	23
1354	6¢ First Navy Jack, 1775	07/04/68	.30	.25			3.00	23
a	Strip of 10, #1345-1354		3.25	3.25	6.75	(20)	15.00	
	Tagged, Perf. 12							
1355	6¢ Walt Disney	09/11/68	.40	.20	1.75	(4)	25.00	153
a	Ocher omitted		500.00	—				
b	Vertical pair, imperf. horizontally		600.00					
c	Imperf., pair		500.00					
d	Black omitted		1,850.00					
e	Horizontal pair, imperf. between		4,500.00					
f	Blue omitted		1,850.00					
g	Tagging omitted		18.00	—				
	Tagged, Perf. 11							
1356	6¢ Father Marquette	09/20/68	.20	.20	.60	(4)	1.00	133
a	Tagging omitted		6.00	—				
	American Folklore, Tagged, Perf. 11							
1357	6¢ Pennsylvania Rifle, Powder Horn, Tomahawk, Pipe and Knife	09/26/68	.20	.20	.50	(4)	1.25	130
	Tagged, Perf. 11							
1358	6¢ Arkansas River Navigation	10/01/68	.20	.20	.50	(4)	1.00	132
1359	6¢ Leif Erikson	10/09/68	.20	.20	.50	(4)	1.00	129
	Tagged, Perf. 11 x 10.5							
1360	6¢ Cherokee Strip	10/15/68	.20	.20	.80	(4)	1.00	125
a	Tagging omitted		7.50	—				
	Tagged, Perf. 11							
1361	6¢ John Trumbull	10/18/68	.20	.20	.60	(4)	2.00	128
a	Tagging omitted		125.00	—				
b	Black (engr.) missing (FO)		11,000.00	—				
1362	6¢ Waterfowl Conservation	10/24/68	.20	.20	.75	(4)	1.25	142
a	Vertical pair, imperf. between		275.00	—				
b	Red and dark blue omitted		750.00					
	Holiday Celebration: Christmas, Tagged, Perf. 11							
1363	6¢ Angel Gabriel, from *The Annunciation*, by Jan Van Eyck	11/01/68	.20	.20	2.00	(10)	1.25	1,411
a	Untagged	11/02/68	.20	.20	2.00	(10)	10.00	
b	Imperf., pair (tagged)		175.00					
	Tagged, Perf. 11							
1364	6¢ American Indian	11/04/68	.20	.20	.75	(4)	1.25	125
	Beautification of America, Tagged, Perf. 11							
1365	6¢ Capitol, Azaleas and Tulips	01/16/69	.25	.20			1.00	48
1366	6¢ Washington Monument, Potomac River and Daffodils	01/16/69	.25	.20			1.00	48
1367	6¢ Poppies and Lupines along Highway	01/16/69	.25	.20			1.00	48
1368	6¢ Blooming Crabapple Trees Lining Avenue	01/16/69	.25	.20			1.00	48
a	Block of 4, #1365-1368		1.00	1.25	1.25	(4)	4.00	
1369	6¢ American Legion	03/15/69	.20	.20	.45	(4)	1.00	149
	American Folklore, Tagged, Perf. 11							
1370	6¢ "July Fourth" by Grandma Moses	05/01/69	.20	.20	.50	(4)	1.50	139
a	Horizontal pair, imperf. between		175.00	—				
b	Black and Prussian blue omitted		700.00					
c	Tagging omitted		7.50	—				
	Space, Tagged, Perf. 11							
1371	6¢ Apollo 8	05/05/69	.20	.20	1.00	(4)	2.25	187

498 499 500 501 502 503

504 505 506 507

508 509 510 511 512

512a 513 514 515 516

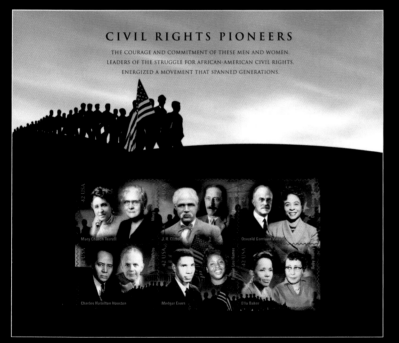

Civil Rights Pioneers

With this souvenir sheet, the U.S. Postal Service honors the courage, commitment and achievements of 12 leaders of the struggle for African-American civil rights.

Item #573940 $2.52

To know more about these and other philatelic products call **1 800 STAMP-24** *or visit us online at* **www.usps.com**

517

523

524

537

547

548

549

550

551

552

553

554

555

556

Flags of Our Nation — An Exciting New Multi-Stamp Series!

Flags of Our Nation (Set 2)

In 2008, the U.S. Postal Service introduced a new multi-stamp series featuring the Stars and Stripes, the fifty state flags, five territorial flags, and the District of Columbia flag. A total of sixty stamps will be issued in sets of ten, with the last issuance in 2012. Start your collection today with these exciting sets!

Flags of Our Nation Set 2: Coil of 50 (only)   Item #786640 $21.00

To order this item and other philatelic products call **1 800 STAMP-24**
or visit us on-line at **www.usps.com.**

Issue		Date	Un	U	PB #	FDC	Q(M)
	Unwmkd., Perf. 11						
517	50¢ Franklin	05/17	65.00	.75	1,600.00 (6)		
b	Vertical pair, imperf. between and at bottom		—	10,000.00			
c	Perf. 10, top or bottom			10,000.00			
518	$1 Franklin	05/17	50.00	1.50	1,300.00 (6)		
b	Deep brown		1,800.00	1,250.00			
	Wmkd. 191, Perf. 11						
519	2¢ carm. Washington (332)	10/10/17	425.00	1,400.00	3,500.00 (6)		
	Privately perforated copies of #344 have been made to resemble #519.						
520-522	Not assigned						
	Unwmkd., Perf. 11						
523	$2 Franklin	08/19/18	600.00	250.00	12,000.00 (8)		
524	$5 Franklin	08/19/18	190.00	35.00	4,500.00 (8)		
	#525-535: Washington (Designs of 405-406, 333)						
525	1¢ gray green	12/18	2.50	.90	30.00 (6)		
	Emerald		3.50	1.25			
a	Dark green		7.00	1.75			
c	Horizontal pair, imperf. between		100.00	700.00			
d	Double impression		40.00	—			
526	2¢ carmine, type IV	03/06/20	27.50	4.00	240.00 (6)	850.00	
	Gash on forehead		60.00	—			
	Malformed "2" at left		40.00	6.00			
527	2¢ carmine, type V	03/20/20	20.00	1.25	185.00 (6)		
	Line through "2" and "EN"		35.00	—			
a	Double impression		75.00	—			
b	Vertical pair, imperf. horizontally		850.00				
c	Horizontal pair, imperf. vertically		1,000.00	—			
528	2¢ carmine, type Va	05/04/20	9.50	.40	200.00 (6)		
c	Double impression		55.00				
g	Vertical pair, imperf. between		3,500.00				
528A	2¢ carmine, type VI	06/24/20	52.50	2.00	425.00 (6)		
d	Double impression		180.00	—			
f	Vertical pair, imperf. horizontally		—				
h	Vertical pair, imperf. between		1,000.00				
528B	2¢ carmine, type VII	11/03/20	22.50	.75	200.00 (6)		
	Retouched on cheek		750.00	—			
e	Double impression		80.00	400.00			
529	3¢ violet, type III	03/18	3.60	.50	75.00 (6)		
a	Double impression		45.00	—			
b	Printed on both sides		2,500.00				
530	3¢ purple, type IV		2.00	.30	32.50 (6)		
	"Blister" under "U.S."		5.00	—			
	Recut under "U.S."		5.00	—			
a	Double impression		35.00	—			
b	Printed on both sides		350.00				
	Imperf.						
531	1¢ green	01/19	11.00	12.00	110.00 (6)		
532	2¢ carmine rose, type IV	03/20	37.50	35.00	370.00 (6)		
533	2¢ carmine, type V	05/04/20	100.00	95.00	1,100.00 (6)		
534	2¢ carmine, type Va	05/25/20	12.50	9.00	130.00 (6)		
534A	2¢ carmine, type VI	07/26/20	42.50	32.50	400.00 (6)		
534B	2¢ carmine, type VII	12/02/20	1,900.00	1,250.00	17,000.00 (6)		
535	3¢ violet, type IV	1918	9.00	5.00	80.00 (6)		
a	Double impression		95.00	—			
	Perf. 12.5						
536	1¢ Washington (405)	08/15/19	22.50	27.50	225.00 (6)		
a	Horizontal pair, imperf. vertically			1,250.00			

Issue		Date	Un	U	PB #	FDC	Q(M)
	Unwmk., Perf. 11						
537	3¢ Allied Victory	03/03/19	10.00	3.25	275.00 (6)	800.00	100
a	Deep red violet		1,250.00	2,250.00	10,000.00 (6)		
b	Light reddish violet		125.00	45.00	1,150.00 (6)		
c	Red violet		150.00	55.00			
	Unwmkd., Perf. 11 x 10						
	#538-546: Washington						
538	1¢ green	06/19	11.00	9.00	110.00 (4)		
	Double transfer		17.50	—			
a	Vertical pair, imperf. horizontally		50.00	100.00	900.00 (4)		
539	2¢ carmine rose, type II		2,850.00	5,500.00	17,500.00 (4)		
540	2¢ carmine rose, type III	06/14/19	13.00	9.50	105.00 (4)		
	Double transfer		22.50	—			
a	Vertical pair, imperf. horizontally		50.00	100.00	1,000.00 (4)		
b	Horizontal pair, imperf. vertically		1,750.00				
541	3¢ violet, type II	06/19	45.00	32.50	360.00 (4)	9,000.00	
	Perf. 10 x 11 (Design 19 x 22.5-22.75mm)						
542	1¢ green	05/26/20	14.00	1.50	165.00 (6)	1,750.00	
	Perf. 10						
543	1¢ green	05/21	.70	.40	17.50 (4)		
a	Horizontal pair, imperf. between		2,750.00				
	Perf. 11						
544	1¢ green		22,500.00	3,750.00			
545	1¢ green	05/21	200.00	210.00	1,150.00 (4)		
546	2¢ carmine rose, type III	05/21	125.00	190.00	775.00 (4)		
	Recut in hair		140.00	210.00			
a	Perf. 10 at left		7,500.00	10,000.00			
547	$2 Franklin	11/01/20	150.00	40.00	4,500.00 (8)		
a	Lake and black		210.00	40.00			
	Pilgrim Tercentenary, Unwmk., Perf. 11						
548	1¢ The *Mayflower*	12/21/20	4.75	2.25	70.00 (6)	1,000.00	138
549	2¢ Landing of the Pilgrims	12/21/20	6.25	1.60	85.00 (6)	700.00	196
550	5¢ Signing of the Compact	12/21/20	45.50	14.00	475.00 (6)	—	11
	America, Unwmk., Perf. 11						
551	½¢ Nathan Hale	04/04/25	.25	.20	15.00 (6)	19.00(4)	
	"Cap" on fraction bar		.75	.20			
552	1¢ Franklin	01/17/23	1.30	.20	37.50 (6)	27.50(2)	
	Double transfer		3.50	—			
a	Booklet pane of 6	08/11/23	7.50	4.00			
553	1½¢ Warren G. Harding	03/19/25	2.30	.20	67.50 (6)	52.50(2)	
554	2¢ Washington	01/15/23	1.20	.20	42.50 (6)	42.50	
	Double transfer		2.50	.80			
a	Horizontal pair, imperf. vert.		275.00				
b	Vertical pair, imperf. horiz.		4,000.00				
c	Booklet pane of 6	02/10/23	7.00	3.00			
d	Perf. 10 at top or bottom		7,000.00	5,500.00			
555	3¢ Lincoln	02/12/23	17.50	1.25	225.00 (6)	40.00	
556	4¢ Martha Washington	01/15/23	20.00	.50	250.00 (6)	65.00	
a	Vertical pair, imperf. horiz.		10,500.00				
b	Perf. 10, top or bottom		3,500.00	25,000.00			

	Issue	Date	Un	U	PB	#	FDC Q(M)
	America, Unwmk., Perf. 11						
557	5¢ Theodore Roosevelt	10/27/22	20.00	.30	250.00	(6)	*135.00*
a	Imperf., pair		2,000.00				
b	Horizontal pair, imperf. vertically		—				
c	Perf. 10, top or bottom		—	11,000.00			
558	6¢ Garfield	11/20/22	37.50	1.00	400.00	(6)	235.00
	Double transfer		57.50	2.00			
	Same, recut		57.50	2.00			
559	7¢ McKinley	05/01/23	8.50	.75	125.00	(6)	185.00
560	8¢ Grant	05/01/23	50.00	1.00	575.00	(6)	190.00
561	9¢ Jefferson	01/15/23	14.00	1.25	250.00	(6)	190.00
562	10¢ Monroe	01/15/23	17.50	.35	275.00	(6)	190.00
a	Vertical pair, imperf. horizontally		2,250.00				
b	Imperf., pair		2,500.00				
c	Perf. 10 at top or bottom		—	20,000.00			
563	11¢ Rutherford B. Hayes	10/04/22	1.40	.60	55.00	(6)	650.00
a	Light bluish green		1.40	.60			
d	Imperf., pair		20,000.00				
564	12¢ Grover Cleveland	03/20/23	6.00	.35	115.00	(6)	*185.00*
a	Horizontal pair, imperf. vertically		1,750.00				
565	14¢ American Indian	05/01/23	4.00	.90	80.00	(6)	400.00
566	15¢ Statue of Liberty	11/11/22	20.00	.30	275.00	(6)	575.00
567	20¢ Golden Gate	05/01/23	20.00	.30	300.00	(6)	*600.00*
a	Horizontal pair, imperf. vertically		2,000.00				
568	25¢ Niagara Falls	11/11/22	18.00	.75	300.00	(6)	*650.00*
b	Vertical pair, imperf. horizontally		2,500.00				
c	Perf. 10 at one side		5,000.00	11,000.00			
569	30¢ Buffalo	03/20/23	30.00	.60	325.00	(6)	*800.00*
	Double transfer		55.00	—			
570	50¢ Arlington Amphitheater	11/11/22	45.00	.40	575.00	(6)	*1,250.00*
571	$1 Lincoln Memorial	02/12/23	42.50	.65	350.00	(6)	*7,000.00*
	Double transfer		95.00	1.60			
572	$2 U.S. Capitol	03/20/23	75.00	9.00	750.00	(6)	*17,500.00*
573	$5 Head of Freedom, Capitol Dome	03/20/23	100.00	15.00	2,250.00	(8)	*32,500.00*
a	Carmine lake and dark blue		190.00	20.00	3,000.00	(8)	
574	Not assigned						
	Imperf. (Design 19.25 x 22.25mm)						
575	1¢ Franklin (552)	03/20/23	5.00	5.00	80.00	(6)	
576	1½¢ Harding (553)	04/04/25	1.25	*1.50*	30.00	(6)	42.50
577	2¢ Washington (554)		1.30	1.25	30.00	(6)	
	Perf. 11 x 10						
578	1¢ Franklin (552)	1923	85.00	*160.00*	925.00	(4)	
579	2¢ Washington (554)	1923	80.00	*140.00*	600.00	(4)	
	Recut in eye		*110.00*	*150.00*			

	Issue	Date	Un	U	PB/LP	#	FDC Q(M)
	Perf. 10						
580	Not assigned						
581	1¢ Franklin (552)	04/21/23	10.00	.75	175.00	(4)	6,000.00
582	1½¢ Harding (553)	03/19/25	5.50	.65	85.00	(4)	40.00
	Pair with full horiz. gutter between		160.00				
	Pair with full vert. gutter between		210.00				
583	2¢ Washington (554)	04/14/24	2.75	.30	70.00	(4)	
a	Booklet pane of 6	08/27/26	95.00	*150.00*			1,500.00
584	3¢ Lincoln (555)	08/01/25	27.50	3.00	275.00	(4)	55.00
585	4¢ Martha Washington (556)	03/25	18.00	.65	275.00	(4)	50.00
586	5¢ T. Roosevelt (557)	12/24	18.00	.40	275.00	(4)	60.00
587	6¢ Garfield (558)	03/25	9.25	.60	225.00	(4)	60.00
588	7¢ McKinley (559)	05/29/26	12.50	6.25	200.00	(4)	60.00
589	8¢ Grant (560)	05/29/26	27.50	4.50	300.00	(4)	65.00
590	9¢ Jefferson (561)	05/29/26	6.00	2.50	150.00	(4)	77.50
591	10¢ Monroe (562)	06/08/25	55.00	.50	475.00	(4)	95.00
592-593	Not assigned						
	Perf. 11						
594	1¢ Franklin (552), design 19.75 x 22.25mm	1923	*27,500.00*	12,500.00			
595	2¢ Washington (554), design 19.75 x 22.25mm	1923	275.00	*375.00*	2,150.00	(4)	
596	1¢ Franklin (552), design 19.25 x 22.5mm	1923		130,000.00			
	Coil, Perf. 10 Vertically						
597	1¢ Franklin (552)	07/18/23	.25	.20	2.00	(2)	*600.00*
	Gripper cracks or double transfer		2.60	1.00			
598	1½¢ Harding (553)	03/19/25	.90	.20	4.50	(2)	65.00
599	2¢ Washington (554) type I	01/23	.35	.20	2.25	(2)	1,750.00
	Double transfer		1.90	1.00			
	Gripper cracks		2.30	2.00			
599A	2¢ Washington (554) type II	03/29	120.00	17.50	650.00	(2)	
600	3¢ Lincoln (555)	05/10/24	6.25	.20	22.50	(2)	90.00
601	4¢ M. Washington (556)	08/05/23	3.75	.35	27.50	(2)	
602	5¢ T. Roosevelt (557)	03/05/24	1.50	.20	10.00	(2)	95.00
603	10¢ Monroe (562)	12/01/24	3.50	.20	25.00	(2)	110.00
	Coil, Perf. 10 Horizontally						
604	1¢ yellow green Franklin (552)	07/19/24	.30	.20	3.50	(2)	90.00
605	1½¢ yellow brown Harding (553)	05/09/25	.30	.20	3.00	(2)	70.00
606	2¢ carmine Washington (554)	12/31/23	.30	.20	2.25	(2)	125.00
607-609	Not assigned						

557  558  559  560  561

562  563 564  565  566

567  568  569  570

571  572  573

599

Details

2¢ Washington, Types I-II, Series 1923-1929

Detail of #599, 634
Type I

No heavy hair lines at top center of head.

Detail of #599A, 634A
Type II

Three heavy hair lines at top center of head.

610

614

615

616

617

618

619

620

621

622

623

627

628

629

630

643

644

645

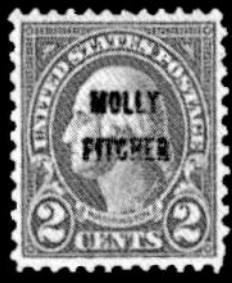

646

647

648

649

650

651

654

657

Issue	Date	Un	U	PB	#	FDC	Q(M)
Harding Memorial, Perf. 11							
610 2¢ Warren Gamaliel Harding	09/01/23	.55	.25	25.00	(6)	37.50	1,459
Double transfer		1.75	.50				
a Horizontal pair, imperf. vertically		1,750.00					
Imperf.							
611 2¢ Harding (610)	11/15/23	4.75	4.00	75.00	(6)	90.00	0.8
Perf. 10							
612 2¢ Harding (610)	09/12/23	15.00	1.75	300.00	(4)	100.00	100
Perf. 11							
613 2¢ Harding (610)	1923	45,000.00					
Huguenot-Walloon Tercentary, May 1, Perf. 11							
614 1¢ Ship Nieu Nederland	05/01/24	2.00	3.25	40.00	(6)	35.00	51
615 2¢ Walloons' Landing at Fort Orange (Albany)	01/05/24	4.25	2.25	60.00	(6)	50.00	78
Double transfer		12.00	3.50				
616 5¢ Huguenot Monument to Jan Ribault at Duval County, Florida	01/05/24	18.00	13.00	250.00	(6)	75.00	6
American Revolution Sesquitennial, Lexington-Concord, Perf. 11							
617 1¢ Washington at Cambridge	04/04/25	1.90	2.50	40.00	(6)	30.00	16
618 2¢ "The Birth of Liberty," by Henry Sandham	04/04/25	3.90	4.00	60.00	(6)	35.00	27
619 5¢ "The Minute Man," by Daniel Chester French	04/04/25	17.00	13.00	200.00	(6)	75.00	5
Line over head		42.50	19.00				
Norse-American, Perf. 11							
620 2¢ Sloop Restaurationen	05/18/25	3.50	3.00	200.00	(8)	20.00	9
621 5¢ Viking Ship	05/18/25	11.00	11.00	500.00	(8)	32.50	2
Perf. 11							
622 13¢ Benjamin Harrison	01/11/26	11.00	.75	215.00	(6)	25.00	
623 17¢ Woodrow Wilson	12/28/25	12.00	.30	250.00	(6)	15.00	
624-626 Not assigned							
American Revolution Sesquitennial, Perf. 11							
627 2¢ Independence Sesquicentennial Exposition	05/10/26	2.50	.50	37.50	(6)	15.00	308
Perf. 11							
628 5¢ John Ericsson Memorial	05/29/26	5.50	3.25	60.00	(6)	40.00	20
American Revolution Sesquitennial, Perf. 11							
629 2¢ Alexander Hamilton's Battery	10/18/26	1.90	1.70	37.50	(6)	6.25	41
International Philatelic Exhibition Souvenir Sheet, Perf. 11							
630 2¢ Battle of White Plains, sheet of 25 with selvage inscription (629)	10/18/26	375.00	450.00			1,500.00	0.1
Dot over first "S" of "States"		400.00	475.00				
631 1½¢ Harding (553)	08/27/26	1.80	1.70	57.50	(4)	35.00	
Perf. 11 x 10.5							
632 1¢ Franklin (552)	06/10/27	.20	.20	2.00	(4)	45.00	
Pair with full vertical gutter between		150.00	—				
a Booklet pane of 6	11/02/27	5.00	4.00			3,250.00	
b Vertical pair, imperf. between		4,500.00	—				
c Horizontal pair, imperf. between		5,000.00					
633 1½¢ Harding (553)	05/17/27	1.70	.20	70.00	(4)	45.00	

Issue	Date	Un	U	PB/LP	#	FDC	Q(M)
Perf. 11 x 10.5							
634 2¢ Washington (554), type I	12/10/26	.20	.20	3.75	(4)	47.50	
Pair with full vertical gutter between		200.00					
b Carmine lake, type I		225.00	—	1,500.00	(4)		
c Horizontal pair, imperf. between		7,000.00					
d Booklet pane of 6	02/25/27	1.50	1.50				
634A 2¢ Washington (554), type II	12/28/27	325.00	13.50	2,200.00	(4)		
Pair with full vertical or horizontal gutter between		850.00	—				
635 3¢ Lincoln (555)	02/03/27	.40	.20	17.50	(4)	47.50	
a Bright violet Lincoln	02/07/34	.20	.20	11.00	(4)	25.00	
Gripper cracks		3.25	2.00				
636 4¢ Martha Washington (556)	05/17/27	1.90	.20	75.00	(4)	50.00	
Pair with full vertical gutter between		200.00					
637 5¢ T. Roosevelt (557)	03/24/27	1.90	.20	15.00	(4)	50.00	
Pair with full vertical gutter between		275.00					
638 6¢ Garfield (558)	07/27/27	1.90	.20	15.00	(4)	57.50	
Pair with full vert. gutter between		200.00					
639 7¢ black McKinley (559)	03/24/27	1.90	.20	15.00	(4)	57.50	
a Vertical pair, imperf. between		325.00	250.00				
640 8¢ olive green Grant (560)	06/10/27	1.90	.20	15.00	(4)	67.50	
641 9¢ orange red Jefferson (561)	1931	1.90	.20	15.00	(4)	72.50	
642 10¢ orange Monroe (562)	02/03/27	3.10	.20	20.00	(4)	90.00	
Perf. 11							
643 2¢ Vermont Sesquicentennial	08/03/27	1.20	.80	35.00	(6)	6.00	40
American Revolution Sesquicentennial, Perf. 11							
644 2¢ Burgoyne at Saratoga	08/03/27	3.10	2.10	32.50	(6)	12.50	26
645 2¢ Valley Forge	05/26/28	.95	.50	25.00	(6)	4.00	101
Perf. 11 x 10.5							
646 2¢ Battle of Monmouth/ Molly Pitcher	10/20/28	1.00	1.00	37.50	(4)	15.00	10
Wide spacing, vertical pair		50.00	—				
Hawaii Sesquicentennial, Perf. 11 x 10.5							
647 2¢ Washington (554)	08/13/28	4.00	4.00	125.00	(4)	15.00	6
Wide spacing, vertical pair		125.00					
Perf. 11 x 10.5							
648 5¢ T. Roosevelt (557)	08/13/28	11.00	12.50	275.00	(4)	22.50	1
Aeronautics Conference, Perf. 11							
649 2¢ Wright Airplane	12/12/28	1.10	.80	12.00	(6)	7.00	51
650 5¢ Globe and Airplane	12/12/28	4.50	3.25	45.00	(6)	10.00	10
Plate flaw "prairie dog"		27.50	12.50				
American Revolution Sesquicentennial, Perf. 11							
651 2¢ George Rogers Clark	02/25/29	.70	.50	12.00	(6)	6.00	17
Double transfer		4.25	2.25				
652 Not assigned							
Perf. 11 x 10.5							
653 ½¢ Nathan Hale (551)	5/25/29	.20	.20	2.00	(4)	27.50	
Electric Light's Golden Jubilee, Perf. 11							
654 2¢ Thomas Edison's First Lamp	06/05/29	.60	.65	25.00	(6)	10.00	32
Perf. 11 x 10.5							
655 2¢ carmine rose (654)	06/11/29	.55	.20	35.00	(4)	80.00	210
Coil, Perf. 10 Vertically							
656 2¢ carmine rose (654)	06/11/29	11.00	1.75	60.00	(2)	90.00	133
American Revolution Sesquicentennial, Perf. 11							
657 2¢ Sullivan Expedition	06/17/29	.60	.60	22.50	(6)	4.00	51
a Lake		325.00	300.00	2,750.00	(6)		

	Issue	Date	Un	U	PB/LP	#	FDC	Q(M)
	Perf. 11 x 10.5 (#658-668 overprinted "Kans.,")							
658	1¢ Franklin	05/01/29	2.00	2.00	50.00	(4)	50.00	13
a	Vertical pair, one without overprint		375.00					
659	1½¢ Harding (553)	05/01/29	3.10	2.90	60.00	(4)	57.50	8
	Wide spacing, pair			70.00				
660	2¢ Washington (554)	05/01/29	3.75	1.00	60.00	(4)	57.50	87
661	3¢ Lincoln (555)	05/01/29	18.50	15.00	225.00	(4)	65.00	3
662	4¢ Martha Washington (556)	05/01/29	18.50	9.00	225.00	(4)	100.00	2
a	Vertical pair, one with overprint		500.00					
663	5¢ T. Roosevelt (557)	05/01/29	12.00	9.75	200.00	(4)	100.00	3
664	6¢ Garfield (558)	05/01/29	27.50	18.00	450.00	(4)	125.00	1
665	7¢ McKinley (559)	05/01/29	27.50	27.50	500.00	(4)	125.00	1
666	8¢ Grant (560)	05/01/29	90.00	70.00	700.00	(4)	125.00	2
667	9¢ Jefferson (561)	05/01/29	13.00	11.50	275.00	(4)	150.00	1
668	10¢ Monroe (562)	05/01/29	22.50	12.50	375.00	(4)	200.00	3
	#669-679 overprinted "Nebr."							
669	1¢ Franklin	05/01/29	3.10	2.25	60.00	(4)	50.00	8
a	Vertical pair, one without overprint		—					
670	1½¢ Harding (553)	05/01/29	2.90	2.50	65.00	(4)	52.50	9
671	2¢ Washington (554)	05/01/29	2.90	1.30	50.00	(4)	57.50	73
672	3¢ Lincoln (555)	05/01/29	12.00	12.00	200.00	(4)	70.00	2
673	4¢ Martha Washington (556)	05/01/29	17.50	15.00	275.00	(4)	100.00	2
	Wide spacing, pair		120.00					
674	5¢ T. Roosevelt (557)	05/01/29	16.00	15.00	300.00	(4)	100.00	2
675	6¢ Garfield (558)	05/01/29	37.50	24.00	525.00	(4)	125.00	1
676	7¢ McKinley (559)	05/01/29	21.00	18.00	325.00	(4)	150.00	0.8
677	8¢ Grant (560)	05/01/29	32.50	25.00	400.00	(4)	125.00	1
678	9¢ Jefferson (561)	05/01/29	35.00	27.50	525.00	(4)	150.00	0.5
a	Vertical pair, one with overprint		750.00					
679	10¢ Monroe (562)	05/01/29	115.00	22.50	925.00	(4)	200.00	2
	Warning: Excellent forgeries of the Kansas and Nebraska overprints exist.							
	American Revolution Sesquitennial, Perf. 11							
680	2¢ Battle of Fallen Timbers	09/14/29	.70	.70	20.00	(6)	3.50	29
681	2¢ Ohio River Canalization	10/19/29	.60	.60	14.00	(6)	3.50	33
682	2¢ Mass. Bay Colony	04/08/30	.50	.50	22.50	(6)	3.50	74
683	2¢ Gov. Joseph West and Chief Shadoo, a Kiowa	04/10/30	1.05	1.05	40.00	(6)	3.50	25
	Perf. 11 x 10.5							
684	1½¢ Warren G. Harding	12/01/30	.35	.20	2.00	(4)	4.50	
	Pair with full horizontal gutter between			175.00				
	Pair with full vertical gutter between			—				
685	4¢ William H. Taft	06/04/30	.80	.25	15.00	(4)	6.00	
	Gouge on right "4"		2.10	.60				
	Recut right "4"		2.10	.65				
	Pair with full horizontal gutter between			—				
	Coil, Perf. 10 Vertically							
686	1½¢ brn. Harding (684)	12/01/30	1.65	.20	7.00	(2)	5.00	
687	4¢ brown Taft (685)	09/18/30	3.00	.45	11.00	(2)	20.00	
	American Revolution Sesquitennial, Perf. 11							
688	2¢ Battle of Braddock's Field	07/09/30	.90	.85	32.50	(6)	4.00	26
689	2¢ Gen. von Steuben	09/17/30	.50	.50	17.50	(6)	4.00	66
a	Imperf., pair		2,750.00		12,500.00	(6)		

	Issue	Date	Un	U	PB	#	FDC	Q(M)
	American Revolution Sesquitennial, Perf. 11							
690	2¢ General Pulaski	01/16/31	.30	.25	10.00	(6)	4.00	97
691	Not assigned							
	Perf. 11 x 10.5							
692	11¢ Hayes (563)	09/04/31	2.50	.25	15.00	(4)	100.00	
	Retouched forehead		20.00	1.00				
693	12¢ Cleveland (564)	08/25/31	5.00	.20	22.50	(4)	100.00	
694	13¢ Harrison (622)	09/04/31	1.90	.25	15.00	(4)	100.00	
695	14¢ American Indian (565)	09/08/31	3.50	.60	26.00	(4)	100.00	
696	15¢ Statue of Liberty (566)	08/27/31	7.75	.25	37.50	(4)	120.00	
	Perf. 10.5 x 11							
697	17¢ Wilson (623)	07/25/31	4.25	.25	37.50	(4)	2,750.00	
698	20¢ Golden Gate (567)	09/08/31	7.75	.25	37.50	(4)	300.00	
	Double transfer		20.00	—				
699	25¢ Niagara Falls (568)	07/25/31	8.00	.25	42.50	(4)	2,000.00	
700	30¢ Buffalo (569)	09/08/31	13.00	.25	72.50	(4)	300.00	
	Cracked plate		26.00	.85				
701	50¢ Arlington Amphitheater (570)	09/04/31	30.00	.25	175.00	(4)	400.00	
	Perf. 11							
702	2¢ "The Greatest Mother"	05/21/31	.20	.20	2.25	(4)	3.00	99
a	Red cross omitted		40,000.00					
	American Revolution Sesquitennial, Perf. 11							
703	2¢ Yorktown	10/19/31	.35	.25	3.00	(4)	3.50	25
a	Lake and black		4.50	.75				
b	Dark lake and black		400.00		2,250.00	(4)		
c	Pair, imperf. vertically		5,000.00					
	Washington Bicentennial, Perf. 11 x 10.5							
704	½¢ Portrait by Charles W. Peale	01/01/32	.20	.20	6.50	(4)	5.00 (4)	88
	Broken circle		.75	.20				
705	1¢ Bust by Jean Antoine Houdon	01/01/32	.20	.20	4.00	(4)	4.00 (2)	1,266
706	1½¢ Portrait by Charles W. Peale	01/01/32	.45	.20	15.00	(4)	4.00 (2)	305
707	2¢ Portrait by Gilbert Stuart	01/01/32	.20	.20	1.25	(4)	4.00	4,222
	Gripper cracks		1.75	.65				
708	3¢ Portrait by Charles W. Peale	01/01/32	.55	.20	17.50	(4)	4.00	456
709	4¢ Portrait by Charles P. Polk	01/01/32	.30	.20	5.00	(4)	4.00	151
	Broken bottom frame line		1.50	.50				
710	5¢ Portrait by Charles W. Peale	01/01/32	1.50	.20	15.00	(4)	4.00	171
	Cracked plate		5.25	1.10				
711	6¢ Portrait by John Trumbull	01/01/32	3.00	.20	52.50	(4)	4.00	112
712	7¢ Portrait by John Trumbull	01/01/32	.40	.20	9.00	(4)	4.00	83
713	8¢ Portrait by Charles B.J.F. Saint Memin	01/01/32	2.75	.50	50.00	(4)	4.50	97
714	9¢ Portrait by W. Williams	01/01/32	2.25	.20	35.00	(4)	4.50	76
715	10¢ Portrait by Gilbert Stuart	01/01/32	10.00	.20	90.00	(4)	4.50	147

658

669

680

681

682

683

684

685

688

689

690

702

703

704

705

706

707

708

709

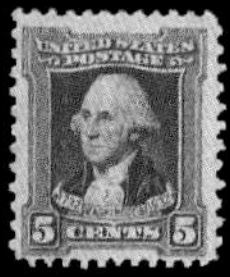

710

711

712

713

714

715

1932-1934

716

717

718

719

720

724

725

726

727

728

730

731

732

733

729

734

735

736

737

739

740

741

742

743

744

745

746

750

751

747

748

749

	Issue	Date	Un	U	PB	#	FDC	Q(M)
	Tagged, Perf. 11							
1372	6¢ W.C. Handy	05/17/69	.20	.20	.65	(4)	2.25	126
a	Tagging omitted			9.00	—			
1373	6¢ California Settlement	07/16/69	.20	.20	.60	(4)	1.00	144
a	Tagging omitted			10.00	—			
b	Red (engr.) missing			—				
1374	6¢ John Wesley Powell	08/01/69	.20	.20	.60	(4)	1.00	136
a	Tagging omitted			10.00	—			
1375	6¢ Alabama Statehood	08/02/69	.20	.20	.75	(4)	1.00	151
b	Tagging omitted		140.00	—				
	Botanical Congress, Tagged, Perf. 11							
1376	6¢ Douglas Fir (Northwest)	08/23/69	.35	.20			1.50	40
1377	6¢ Lady's Slipper (Northeast)	08/23/69	.35	.20			1.50	40
1378	6¢ Ocotillo (Southwest)	08/23/69	.35	.20			1.50	40
1379	6¢ Franklinia (Southeast)	08/23/69	.35	.20			1.50	40
a	Block of 4, #1376-1379		1.50	1.75	1.75	(4)	5.00	
	Tagged, Perf. 10.5 x 11							
1380	6¢ Dartmouth College Case	09/22/69	.20	.20	.50	(4)	1.00	130
	Tagged, Perf. 11							
1381	6¢ Professional Baseball	09/24/69	.55	.20	2.50	(4)	12.00	131
a	Black omitted		800.00					
1382	6¢ Intercollegiate Football	09/26/69	.20	.20	1.00	(4)	6.50	139
1383	6¢ Dwight D. Eisenhower	10/14/69	.20	.20	.55	(4)	1.00	151
	Holiday Celebration: Holiday, Tagged, Perf. 11 x 10.5							
1384	6¢ Winter Sunday in Norway, Maine	11/03/69	.20	.20	1.40	(10)	1.25	1,710
	Precanceled		.50	.20				
b	Imperf., pair		800.00					
c	Light green omitted		30.00					
d	Light green and yellow omitted		700.00	—				
e	Yellow omitted		2,000.00					
f	Tagging omitted		5.00	—				

Precanceled versions issued on an experimental basis in four cities whose names appear on the stamps: Atlanta, GA; Baltimore, MD; Memphis, TN; and New Haven, CT.

	Issue	Date	Un	U	PB	#	FDC	Q(M)
	Tagged, Perf. 11							
1385	6¢ Hope for the Crippled	11/20/69	.20	.20	.50	(4)	1.25	128
1386	6¢ William M. Harnett	12/03/69	.20	.20	.55	(4)	1.00	146
	Natural History, Tagged, Perf. 11							
1387	6¢ American Bald Eagle	05/06/70	.20	.20				50
1388	6¢ African Elephant Herd	05/06/70	.20	.20				50
1389	6¢ Tlingit Chief in Haida Ceremonial Canoe	05/06/70	.20	.20				50
1390	6¢ Brontosaurus, Stegosaurus and Allosaurus from Jurassic Period	05/06/70	.20	.20				50
a	Block of 4, #1387-1390		.55	.60	.70	(4)	4.00	
	Tagged, Perf. 11							
1391	6¢ Maine Statehood	07/09/70	.20	.20	.60	(4)	2.75	172
	Tagged, Perf. 11 x 10.5							
1392	6¢ Wildlife Conservation	07/20/70	.20	.20	.75	(4)	1.00	142
	Prominent Americans, Tagged, Perf. 11 x 10.5							
1393	6¢ Dwight D. Eisenhower	08/06/70	.20	.20	.50	(4)	1.00	
a	Booklet pane of 8		1.50	.75			3.00	
b	Booklet pane of 5 + label		1.50	.75			1.50	
c	Untagged (Bureau precanceled)		12.75	3.00	175.00	(4)		

	Issue	Date	Un	U	PB/LP	#	FDC	Q(M)
	Prominent Americans, Perf. 10.5 x 11							
1393D	7¢ Benjamin Franklin	10/20/72	.20	.20	.60	(4)	1.00	
e	Untagged (Bureau precanceled)		4.25	1.00	52.50	(4)		
f	Tagging omitted		4.00	—				
	Prominent Americans, Perf. 11							
1394	8¢ Eisenhower	05/10/71	.20	.20	.60	(4)	1.00	
a	Tagging omitted		4.50	—				
b	Red missing		175.00	—				
	Perf. 11 x 10.5 on 2 or 3 sides							
1395	8¢ deep claret Eisenhower (1394), Single from booklet		.20	.20			1.00	
a	Booklet pane of 8	05/10/71	1.80	1.25			2.50	
b	Booklet pane of 6	05/10/71	1.25	1.10			2.50	
c	Booklet pane of 4 + 2 labels	01/28/72	1.65	1.00			2.25	
d	Booklet pane of 7 + label	01/28/72	1.90	1.10			2.25	
	Prominent Americans, Perf. 11 x 10.5							
1396	8¢ U.S. Postal Service	07/01/71	.20	.20	2.00	(12)	1.00	
1397	14¢ Fiorello H. LaGuardia	04/24/72	.25	.20	1.15	(4)	1.00	
a	Untagged (Bureau precanceled)		140.00	17.50				
1398	16¢ Ernie Pyle	05/07/71	.35	.20	2.50	(4)	1.50	
a	Untagged (Bureau precanceled)		22.50	5.00	—			
1399	18¢ Dr. Elizabeth Blackwell	01/23/74	.35	.20	1.50	(4)	1.25	
1400	21¢ Amadeo P. Giannini	06/27/73	.40	.20	1.65	(4)	1.50	
	Coil, Tagged, Perf. 10 Vertically							
1401	6¢ dark blue gray Eisenhower (1393)	08/06/70	.20	.20	.50	(2)	1.00	
a	Untagged (Bureau precanceled)		19.50	3.00	525.00	(2)		
b	Imperf., pair		1,900.00		—			
1402	8¢ deep claret Eisenhower (1394)	05/10/71	.20	.20	.60	(2)	1.00	
a	Imperf., pair		37.50		65.00	(2)		
b	Untagged (Bureau precanceled)		6.75	.75	185.00	(2)		
c	Pair, imperf. between		6,250.00					
1403-1404	Not assigned							
	Tagged, Perf. 11							
1405	6¢ Edgar Lee Masters	08/22/70	.20	.20	.50	(4)	1.00	138
a	Tagging omitted		125.00	—				
1406	6¢ Woman Suffrage	08/26/70	.20	.20	.50	(4)	1.00	135
1407	6¢ South Carolina Settlement	09/12/70	.20	.20	.55	(4)	1.00	136
1408	6¢ Stone Mountain Memorial	09/19/70	.20	.20	.50	(4)	1.00	133
1409	6¢ Ft. Snelling	10/17/70	.20	.20	.55	(4)	1.00	135
	Anti-Pollution, Tagged, Perf. 11 x 10.5							
1410	6¢ Save Our Soil Globe and Wheat Field	10/28/70	.25	.20			1.25	40
1411	6¢ Save Our Cities Globe and City Playground	10/28/70	.25	.20			1.25	40
1412	6¢ Save Our Water Globe and Bluegill Fish	10/28/70	.25	.20			1.25	40
1413	6¢ Save Our Air Globe and Seagull	10/28/70	.25	.20			1.25	40
a	Block of 4, #1410-1413		1.10	1.25	2.25	(10)	4.00	

Issue		Date	Un	U	PB	#	FDC	Q(M)
	Holiday Celebration: Christmas, Tagged, Perf. 10.5 x 11							
1414	6¢ Nativity, by Lorenzo Lotto	11/05/70	.20	.20	1.10(8)		1.25	684*
a	Precanceled		.20	.20	1.90(8)		7.50	
b	Black omitted		450.00					
c	As "a," blue omitted		1,450.00					
d	Type II		.20	.20	2.75(8)			
e	Type II, precanceled		.25	.20	4.00(8)			

#1414a-1418a were furnished to 68 cities. Unused prices are for copies with gum and used prices are for copies with or without gum but with an additional cancellation. *Includes #1414a.

Issue		Date	Un	U	PB	#	FDC	Q(M)
	Holiday Celebration: Holiday, Tagged, Perf. 11 x 10.5							
1415	6¢ Tin and Cast-iron Locomotive	11/05/70	.30	.20			1.50	122
a	Precanceled		.75	.20				110
b	Black omitted		2,500.00					
1416	6¢ Toy Horse on Wheels	11/05/70	.30	.20			1.50	122
a	Precanceled		.75	.20				110
b	Black omitted		2,500.00					
c	Imperf., pair			2,500.00				
1417	6¢ Mechanical Tricycle	11/05/70	.30	.20			1.50	122
a	Precanceled		.75	.20				110
b	Black omitted		2,500.00					
1418	6¢ Doll Carriage	11/05/70	.30	.20			1.50	122
a	Precanceled		.75	.20			5.00	110
b	Block of 4, #1415-1418		1.25	1.40	3.00(8)		8.50 (4)	
c	Block of 4, #1415a-1418a		3.25	3.50	6.25(8)		30.00 (4)	
d	Black omitted		2,500.00					
	Tagged, Perf. 11							
1419	6¢ United Nations	11/20/70	.20	.20	.50(4)		1.50	128
a	Tagging omitted		85.00					
1420	6¢ Landing of the Pilgrims	11/21/70	.20	.20	.50(4)		1.00	130
a	Orange and yellow omitted		700.00					
1421	6¢ Disabled American Veterans Emblem	11/24/70	.20	.20			2.00	67
1422	6¢ U.S. Servicemen	11/24/70	.20	.20			2.00	67
a	Attached pair, #1421-1422		.30	.30	1.00(4)		3.00	
	Tagged, Perf. 11							
1423	6¢ American Wool Industry	01/19/71	.20	.20	.55(4)		1.00	136
a	Tagging omitted		11.00	—				
1424	6¢ Gen. Douglas MacArthur	01/26/71	.20	.20	.60(4)		1.75	135
a	Tagging omitted		125.00					
1425	6¢ Blood Donor	03/12/71	.20	.20	.50(4)		1.00	131
a	Tagging omitted		10.00	—				
	Tagged, Perf. 11 x 10.5							
1426	8¢ Missouri Statehood	05/08/71	.20	.20	3.00(12)		1.00	161
	Wildlife Conservation, Tagged, Perf. 11							
1427	8¢ Trout	06/12/71	.20	.20			1.25	44
b	Red omitted		1,250.00					
1428	8¢ Alligator	06/12/71	.20	.20			1.25	44
1429	8¢ Polar Bear and Cubs	06/12/71	.20	.20			1.25	44
1430	8¢ California Condor	06/12/71	.20	.20			1.25	44
a	Block of 4, #1427-1430		.80	.90	.90(4)		3.00	
b	As "a," light green and dark green omitted from #1427-1428		4,500.00					
c	As "a," red omitted from #1427, 1429-1430		7,000.00					

Issue		Date	Un	U	PB	#	FDC	Q(M)
	Tagged, Perf. 11							
1431	8¢ Antarctic Treaty	06/23/71	.20	.20	.65	(4)	1.00	139
a	Tagging omitted		10.00					
b	Both colors omitted		500.00					
	Prominent Americans, Tagged, Perf. 11							
1432	8¢ Bicentennial Commission Emblem	07/04/71	.20	.20	.85	(4)	1.00	138
a	Gray and black omitted		550.00					
b	Gray omitted		950.00					
c	Tagging omitted		125.00					
	Tagged, Perf. 11							
1433	8¢ John Sloan	08/02/71	.20	.20	.70	(4)	1.00	152
a	Tagging omitted		—					
c	Red missing		950.00					
	Space, Tagged, Perf. 11							
1434	8¢ Earth, Sun and Landing Craft on Moon	08/02/71	.20	.20				88
a	Tagging omitted		45.00				2.00	
1435	8¢ Lunar Rover and Astronauts	08/02/71	.20	.20				88
a	Tagging omitted		45.00					
b	Pair #1434-1435		.40	.45	.65	(4)		
c	As "b", tagging omitted		125.00					
d	As "b", blue & red omitted		1,250.00					
	Tagged, Perf. 11							
1436	8¢ Emily Dickinson	08/28/71	.20	.20	.65	(4)	1.00	143
a	Black and olive omitted		600.00					
b	Pale rose omitted		6,250.00					
1437	8¢ San Juan, Puerto Rico	09/12/71	.20	.20	.65	(4)	1.00	149
a	Tagging omitted		9.00					
	Tagged, Perf. 10.5 x 11							
1438	8¢ Prevent Drug Abuse	10/04/71	.20	.20	1.00	(6)	1.00	139
1439	8¢ CARE	10/27/71	.20	.20	1.25	(8)	1.00	131
a	Black omitted		2,500.00					
b	Tagging omitted		5.00					
	Historic Preservation, Tagged, Perf. 11							
1440	8¢ Decatur House, Washington, D.C.	10/29/71	.20	.20			1.25	43
1441	8¢ Whaling Ship Charles W. Morgan, Mystic, Connecticut	10/29/71	.20	.20			1.25	43
1442	8¢ Cable Car, San Francisco	10/29/71	.20	.20			1.25	43
1443	8¢ San Xavier del Bac Mission, Tucson, Arizona	10/29/71	.20	.20			1.25	43
a	Block of 4, #1440-1443		.75	.85	.90	(4)	3.00	
b	As "a," black brown omitted		1,650.00					
c	As "a," ocher omitted		—					
d	As "a," tagging omitted		75.00					
	Holiday Celebration: Christmas, Tagged, Perf. 10.5 x 11							
1444	8¢ Adoration of the Shepherds, by Giorgione	11/10/71	.20	.20	1.80(12)		1.25	1,074
a	Gold omitted		400.00					
	Holiday Celebration: Holiday, Tagged, Perf. 10.5 x 11							
1445	8¢ Partridge in a Pear Tree	11/10/71	.20	.20	1.80(12)		1.25	980

1414

1414a

1415 1416

Christmas 6 U.S.

Christmas 6 U.S.

Christmas 6 U.S.

Christmas 6 U.S.

1417 1418 1418b

UNITED STATES POSTAGE 6 CENTS

United Nations 25ᵗʰ Anniversary

1419

U.S. POSTAGE 6 CENTS

1420

1421 1422 1422a

UNITED STATES

AMERICA'S WOOL

1423

DOUGLAS MacARTHUR

1424

giving BLOOD saves lives

United States Postage 6

1425

1427 1428

WILDLIFE CONSERVATION

WILDLIFE CONSERVATION

WILDLIFE CONSERVATION

WILDLIFE CONSERVATION

Missouri United States

1426 1429 1430 1430a

Emily Dickinson American Poet

1436

8 U.S. ANTARCTIC TREATY 1961-1971

1431

U.S POSTAGE 8c AMERICAN REVOLUTION BICENTENNIAL 1776-1976

1432

John Sloan American Artist 1871-1951 United States 8 cents

1433

UNITED STATES IN SPACE... A DECADE OF ACHIEVEMENT

1434 1435 1435b

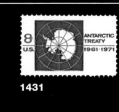

SAN JUAN, PUERTO RICO US 8

1437

Prevent drug abuse 8c United States Postage

1438

CARE 1946-1971 US 8c

1439

1440 1441

HISTORIC PRESERVATION

HISTORIC PRESERVATION

HISTORIC PRESERVATION

HISTORIC PRESERVATION

1442 1443 1443a

Christmas

1444

ON THE FIRST DAY OF CHRISTMAS MY TRUE LOVE SENT TO ME A

1445

1446

1447

1448   1449

1450   1451   1451a

1452

1453

1454

1455

1456   1457

1458   1459   1459a

1460

1461

1462

1463

1464   1465

1466   1467   1467a

1468

1469

1470

1471

1472

1473

1474

1475

1476

1477

1478

1479

1480   1481

1482   1483

1483a

Issue		Date	Un	U	PB	#	FDC	Q(M)
	Tagged, Perf. 11							
1446	8¢ Sidney Lanier	02/03/72	.20	.20	.65	(4)	1.00	137
a	Tagging omitted		55.00					
	Tagged, Perf. 10.5 x 11							
1447	8¢ Peace Corps	02/11/72	.20	.20	1.00	(6)	1.00	150
a	Tagging omitted		5.00					
	National Parks Centennial, Tagged, Perf. 11							
1448	2¢ Ship at Sea	04/05/72	.20	.20				43
1449	2¢ Cape Hatteras Lighthouse	04/05/72	.20	.20				43
1450	2¢ Laughing Gulls on Driftwood	04/05/72	.20	.20				43
1451	2¢ Laughing Gulls and Dune	04/05/72	.20	.20				43
a	Block of 4, #1448-1451		.25	.30	.50	(4)	3.00	
b	As "a," black omitted		1,400.00					
1452	6¢ Performance at Wolf Trap Farm, Shouse Pavilion	06/26/72	.20	.20	.55	(4)	1.00	104
a	Tagging omitted		10.00					
1453	8¢ Old Faithful, Yellowstone	03/01/72	.20	.20	.70	(4)	1.00	164
a	Tagging omitted		140.00					
1454	15¢ View of Mount McKinley in Alaska	07/28/72	.30	.20	1.30	(4)	1.00	54
a	Tagging omitted		125.00					

Note: Beginning with this National Parks Centennial issue, the USPS began to offer stamp collectors first day cancellations affixed to 8" x 10½" souvenir pages. The pages are similar to the stamp announcements that have appeared on Post Office bulletin boards beginning with Scott #1132. See "American Commemorative Panels" listed in the Table of Contents.

Issue		Date	Un	U	PB	#	FDC	Q(M)
	Tagged, Perf. 11							
1455	8¢ Family Planning	03/18/72	.20	.20	.65	(4)	1.00	153
a	Yellow omitted		400.00					
c	Dark brown missing		9,000.00					
d	Tagging omitted		—					
	American Bicentennial, Tagged, Perf. 11 x 10.5							
1456	8¢ Glass Blower	07/04/72	.20	.20			1.00	50
1457	8¢ Silversmith	07/04/72	.20	.20			1.00	50
1458	8¢ Wigmaker	07/04/72	.20	.20			1.00	50
1459	8¢ Hatter	07/04/72	.20	.20			1.00	50
a	Block of 4, #1456-1459		.65	.75	.80	(4)	2.50	
b	As "a," tagging omitted		150.00					
	Olympic Games, Tagged, Perf. 11 x 10.5							
1460	6¢ Bicycling and Olympic Rings	08/17/72	.20	.20	1.25	(10)	1.00	67
	Cylinder flaw (broken red ring)		10.00					
1461	8¢ Bobsledding and Olympic Rings	08/17/72	.20	.20	1.60	(10)	1.00	180
a	Tagging omitted		7.50					
1462	15¢ Running and Olympic Rings	08/17/72	.30	.20	3.00	(10)	1.00	46
	Tagged, Perf. 11 x 10.5							
1463	8¢ Parent Teachers Association	09/15/72	.20	.20	.65	(4)	1.00	180
	Wildlife Conservation, Tagged, Perf. 11							
1464	8¢ Fur Seals	09/20/72	.20	.20			1.50	50
1465	8¢ Cardinal	09/20/72	.20	.20			1.50	50
1466	8¢ Brown Pelican	09/20/72	.20	.20			1.50	50

Issue		Date	Un	U	PB	#	FDC	Q(M)
	Wildlife Conservation, Tagged, Perf. 11 continued							
1467	8¢ Bighorn Sheep	09/20/72	.20	.20			1.50	50
a	Block of 4, #1464-1467		.65	.75	.75	(4)	3.00	
b	As "a," brown omitted		3,750.00					
c	As "a," green and blue omitted		3,750.00					
d	As "a," red & brown omitted		3,750.00					

Note: With this Wildlife Conservation issue the USPS introduced the "American Commemorative Panels". Each panel contains a block of four or more mint stamps with text and background illustrations. See these pages in the Table of Contents.

Issue		Date	Un	U	PB	#	FDC	Q(M)
	Tagged, Perf. 11 x 10.5							
1468	8¢ Mail Order Business	09/27/72	.20	.20	1.75	(12)	1.00	185
	Tagged, Perf. 10.5 x 11							
1469	8¢ Osteopathic Medicine	10/09/72	.20	.20	1.10	(6)	1.50	162
	American Folklore, Tagged, Perf. 11							
1470	8¢ Tom Sawyer Whitewashing a Fence, by Norman Rockwell	10/13/72	.20	.20	.65	(4)	1.50	163
a	Horizontal pair, imperf. between		4,250.00					
b	Red and black omitted		1,350.00					
c	Yellow and tan omitted		2,000.00					
	Holiday Celebration: Christmas, Tagged, Perf. 10.5 x 11							
1471	8¢ Angels from "Mary, Queen of Heaven" by the Master of the St. Lucy Legend	11/09/72	.20	.20	1.75	(12)	1.00	1,003
a	Pink omitted		120.00					
b	Black omitted		3,250.00					
1472	8¢ Santa Claus	11/09/72	.20	.20	1.75	(12)	1.00	1,017
	Tagged, Perf. 11							
1473	8¢ Pharmacy	11/10/72	.20	.20	.65	(4)	8.00	166
a	Blue and orange omitted		700.00					
b	Blue omitted		1,750.00					
c	Orange omitted		1,750.00					
1474	8¢ Stamp Collecting	11/17/72	.20	.20	.65	(4)	1.25	167
a	Black omitted		500.00					
b	Tagging omitted		4.50					
	Love, Tagged, Perf. 11 x 10.5							
1475	8¢ Love	01/26/73	.20	.20	1.00	(6)	2.00	320
	American Bicentennial, Tagged, Perf. 11							
1476	8¢ Printer and Patriots Examining Pamphlet	02/16/73	.20	.20	.65	(4)	1.00	166
1477	8¢ Posting a Broadside	04/13/73	.20	.20	.65	(4)	1.00	163
	Pair with full horizontal gutter between		—					
1478	8¢ Postrider	06/22/73	.20	.20	.65	(4)	1.00	159
1479	8¢ Drummer	09/28/73	.20	.20	.65	(4)	1.00	147
	American Bicentennial, Boston Tea Party, Tagged, Perf. 11							
1480	8¢ British Merchantman	07/04/73	.20	.20			1.00	49
1481	8¢ British Three-Master	07/04/73	.20	.20			1.00	49
1482	8¢ Boats and Ship's Hull	07/04/73	.20	.20			1.00	49
1483	8¢ Boat and Dock	07/04/73	.20	.20			1.00	49
a	Block of 4, #1480-1483		.65	.75	.75	(4)	3.00	
b	As "a," blk. (engraved) omitted		1,100.00					
c	As "a," blk. (lithograph) omitted		1,100.00					

Issue	Date	Un	U	PB	#	FDC	Q(M)
American Arts, Tagged, Perf. 11							
1484 8¢ George Gershwin and Scene from "Porgy and Bess"	02/28/73	.20	.20	1.75	(12)	1.00	139
a Vertical pair, imperf. horizontally		175.00					
1485 8¢ Robinson Jeffers, "Man and Children of Carmel with Burro"	08/13/73	.20	.20	1.75	(12)	1.00	128
a Vertical pair, imperf. horizontally		225.00					
1486 8¢ Henry Ossawa Tanner, Palette and Rainbow	09/10/73	.20	.20	1.75	(12)	2.50	146
1487 8¢ Willa Cather, Pioneer Family and Covered Wagon	09/20/73	.20	.20	1.75	(12)	1.00	140
a Vertical pair, imperf. horizontally		225.00					
Tagged, Perf. 11							
1488 8¢ Nicolaus Copernicus	04/23/73	.20	.20	.65	(4)	1.50	159
a Orange omitted		850.00					
b Black omitted		875.00					
Postal Service Employees, Tagged, Perf. 10.5 x 11							
1489 8¢ Stamp Counter	04/30/73	.20	.20			1.00	49
1490 8¢ Mail Collection	04/30/73	.20	.20			1.00	49
1491 8¢ Letter Facing on Conveyor	04/30/73	.20	.20			1.00	49
1492 8¢ Parcel Post Sorting	04/30/73	.20	.20			1.00	49
1493 8¢ Mail Canceling	04/30/73	.20	.20			1.00	49
1494 8¢ Manual Letter Routing	04/30/73	.20	.20			1.00	49
1495 8¢ Electronic Letter Routing	04/30/73	.20	.20			1.00	49
1496 8¢ Loading Mail on Truck	04/30/73	.20	.20			1.00	49
1497 8¢ Mail Carrier	04/30/73	.20	.20			1.00	49
1498 8¢ Rural Mail Delivery	04/30/73	.20	.20			1.00	49
a Strip of 10, #1489-1498		1.75	1.90	3.75	(20)	5.00	
b As "a," tagging omitted		300.00	—				
#1489-1498 were the first United States postage stamps to have printing on the back. (See also 1559-1562.)							
Tagged, Perf. 11							
1499 8¢ Harry S. Truman	05/08/73	.20	.20	.75	(4)	1.50	157
a Tagging omitted		7.50					
Progress in Electronics, Tagged, Perf. 11							
1500 6¢ Marconi's Spark Coil and Gap	07/10/73	.20	.20	.55	(4)	1.00	53
1501 8¢ Transistors and Printed Circuit Board	07/10/73	.20	.20	.70	(4)	1.00	160
a Black inscriptions omitted		375.00					
b Tan and lilac omitted		1,000.00					
1502 15¢ Microphone, Speaker, Vacuum Tube, TV Camera Tube	07/10/73	.30	.20	1.30	(4)	1.00	39
a Black inscriptions omitted		1,250.00					
Tagged, Perf. 11							
1503 8¢ Lyndon B. Johnson	08/27/73	.20	.20	2.20	(12)	1.00	153
a Horizontal pair, imperf. vertically		275.00					

Issue	Date	Un	U	PB/LP	#	FDC	Q(M)
Rural America, Tagged, Perf. 11							
1504 8¢ Angus and Longhorn Cattle, by F.C. Murphy	10/05/73	.20	.20	.65	(4)	1.00	146
a Green and red brown omitted		800.00					
b Vertical pair, imperf. between		5,000.00					
1505 10¢ Chautauqua Tent and Buggies	08/06/74	.20	.20	.85	(4)	1.00	151
b Black (litho) omitted		1,750.00					
1506 10¢ Wheat Fields and Train	08/16/74	.20	.20	.85	(4)	1.00	141
a Black and blue omitted		650.00					
b Tagging omitted		100.00					
Holiday Celebration: Christmas, Tagged, Perf. 10.5 x 11							
1507 8¢ Small Cowper Madonna, by Raphael	11/07/73	.20	.20	1.75	(12)	1.00	885
Holiday Celebration: Holiday, Tagged, Perf. 10.5 x 11							
1508 8¢ Christmas Tree in Needlepoint	11/07/73	.20	.20	1.75	(12)	1.00	940
a Vertical pair, imperf. between		250.00					
Tagged, Perf. 11 x 10.5							
1509 10¢ 50-Star and 13-Star Flags	12/08/73	.20	.20	4.25	(20)	1.00	
a Horizontal pair, imperf. between		45.00	—				
b Blue omitted		165.00	—				
c Imperf., pair		850.00					
d Horizontal pair, imperf. vertically		900.00					
e Tagging omitted		9.00					
1510 10¢ Jefferson Memorial	12/14/73	.20	.20	.85	(4)	1.00	
a Untagged (Bureau precanceled)		4.00	1.00	50.00	(4)		
b Booklet pane of 5 + label		1.65	.90			2.25	
c Booklet pane of 8		1.65	1.00			2.50	
d Booklet pane of 6	08/05/74	5.25	1.75			3.00	
e Vertical pair, imperf. horizontally		425.00					
f Vertical pair, imperf. between		475.00					
g Tagging omitted		5.00					
1511 10¢ ZIP Code	01/04/74	.20	.20	1.75	(8)	1.00	
a Yellow omitted		45.00					
1512-1517 Not assigned							
Coil, Tagged, Perf. 10 Vertically							
1518 6.3¢ Liberty Bell	10/01/74	.20	.20	.80	(2)	1.00	
a Untagged (Bureau precanceled)		.35	.20	1.65	(2)		
b Imperf., pair		165.00		425.00	(2)		
c As "a," imperf., pair		85.00		175.00	(2)		
1519 10¢ 15-star and 13-star Flags (1509)	12/08/73	.20	.20			1.00	
a Imperf., pair		37.50					
b Tagging omitted		9.00					
1520 10¢ blue Jefferson Memorial (1510)	12/14/73	.25	.20	.75	(2)	1.00	
a Untagged (Bureau precanceled)		5.50	1.25	185.00	(2)		
b Imperf., pair		32.50		62.50	(2)		
1521-1524 Not assigned							
Tagged, Perf. 11							
1525 10¢ Veterans of Foreign Wars	03/11/74	.20	.20	.85	(4)	1.50	144
a Tagging omitted		90.00					

1484

1485

1486

1487

1488

1489   1490   1491   1492   1493

1494   1495   1496   1497   1498

1499

1500

1501

1502

1503

1504

1505

1506

1507

1508

1509

1510

1511

1518

1525

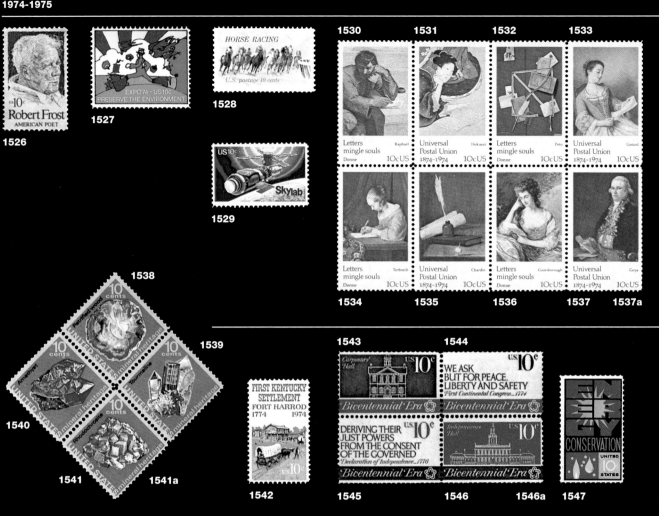

1526 — Robert Frost AMERICAN POET

1527 — EXPO'74 · US10c PRESERVE THE ENVIRONMENT

1528 — HORSE RACING U.S. postage 10 cents

1529 — US 10c Skylab

1530 / 1531 / 1532 / 1533

Letters mingle souls — Donne — Raphael — 10c US
Universal Postal Union 1874-1974 — Hokusai — 10c US
Letters mingle souls — Donne — Peto — 10c US
Universal Postal Union 1874-1974 — Liotard — 10c US

1534 / 1535 / 1536 / 1537 / 1537a

Letters mingle souls — Donne — Terborch — 10c US
Universal Postal Union 1874-1974 — Chardin — 10c US
Letters mingle souls — Donne — Gainsborough — 10c US
Universal Postal Union 1874-1974 — Goya — 10c US

1538 / 1539 / 1540 / 1541 / 1541a — UNITED STATES mineral heritage — 10 cents — Petrified wood, Amethyst, Tourmaline, Rhodochrosite

1542 — FIRST KENTUCKY SETTLEMENT FORT HARROD 1774 1974 — US 10c

1543 / 1544 / 1545 / 1546 / 1546a
Carpenters' Hall — Bicentennial Era — US 10c
WE ASK BUT FOR PEACE, LIBERTY AND SAFETY — First Continental Congress...1774 — Bicentennial Era — US 10c
DERIVING THEIR JUST POWERS FROM THE CONSENT OF THE GOVERNED — Declaration of Independence...1776 — Bicentennial Era — US 10c
Independence Hall — Bicentennial Era — US 10c

1547 — ENERGY CONSERVATION UNITED STATES 10

1548 — THE LEGEND OF SLEEPY HOLLOW — 10c US

1549 — Retarded Children Can Be Helped — 10c

1550 — us 10c — Altarpiece. Metropolitan Museum — Christmas

1551 — Christmas 10c U.S. — Currier and Ives

1552 — Peace on Earth Christmas — PRECANCELLED US 10c

1553 — Benjamin West — American artist 10 cents U.S. postage

1554 — Paul Laurence Dunbar — American poet 10 cents U.S. postage

1555 — MOVIEMAKER US 10c — D W GRIFFITH

1556 — PIONEER ★ JUPITER — US 10c

1557 — MARINER 10 ★ VENUS/MERCURY — us 10c

1558 — collective bargaining out of conflict...accord — UNITED STATES 10c

	Issue	Date	Un	U	PB	#	FDC	Q(M)
	Tagged, Perf. 10.5 x 11							
1526	10¢ Robert Frost	03/26/74	.20	.20	.85	(4)	1.00	145
	Tagged, Perf. 11							
1527	10¢ Expo '74 World's Fair	04/18/74	.20	.20	2.50	(12)	1.00	135
	Tagged, Perf. 11 x 10.5							
1528	10¢ Horse Racing	05/04/74	.25	.20	3.50	(12)	3.00	157
a	Blue omitted		800.00					
b	Red omitted		2,250.00					
	Space, Tagged, Perf. 11							
1529	10¢ Skylab	05/14/74	.20	.20	.85	(4)	1.50	165
b	Tagging omitted		10.00					
	Universal Postal Union, Tagged, Perf. 11							
1530	10¢ Michelangelo, from "School of Athens," by Raphael	06/06/74	.20	.20			1.00	25
1531	10¢ "Five Feminine Virtues," by Hokusai	06/06/74	.20	.20			1.00	25
1532	10¢ "Old Scraps," by John Fredrick Peto	06/06/74	.20	.20			1.00	25
1533	10¢ "The Lovely Reader," by Jean Etienne Liotard	06/06/74	.20	.20			1.00	25
1534	10¢ "Lady Writing Letter," by Gerard Terborch	06/06/74	.20	.20			1.00	25
1535	10¢ Inkwell and Quill, from "Boy with a Top," by Jean-Baptiste Simeon Chardin	06/06/74	.20	.20			1.00	25
1536	10¢ Mrs. John Douglas, by Thomas Gainsborough	06/06/74	.20	.20			1.00	25
1537	10¢ Don Antonio Noriega, by Francisco de Goya	06/06/74	.20	.20			1.00	25
a	Block of 8, #1530-1537		1.75	1.75	2.25	(10)	4.00	
b	As "a," imperf. vertically		7,500.00					
	Mineral Heritage, Tagged, Perf. 11							
1538	10¢ Petrified Wood	06/13/74	.20	.20			1.00	42
a	Light blue and yellow omitted		—					
1539	10¢ Tourmaline	06/13/74	.20	.20			1.00	42
a	Light blue omitted		—					
b	Black and purple omitted		—					
1540	10¢ Amethyst	06/13/74	.20	.20			1.00	42
a	Light blue and yellow omitted		—					
1541	10¢ Rhodochrosite	06/13/74	.20	.20			1.00	42
a	Block of 4, #1538-1541		.80	.90	.90	(4)	2.75	
b	As "a," light blue and yellow omitted		1,700.00					
c	Light blue omitted		—					
d	Black and red omitted		—					
	Tagged, Perf. 11							
1542	10¢ First Kentucky Settlement - Ft. Harrod	06/15/74	.20	.20	.85	(4)	1.00	156
a	Dull black omitted		650.00					
b	Green, black and blue omitted		3,000.00					
c	Green omitted		3,000.00					
d	Green and black omitted		3,000.00					
e	Tagging omitted		150.00					

	Issue	Date	Un	U	PB	#	FDC	Q(M)
	American Bicentennial: First Continental Congress, Tagged, Perf. 11							
1543	10¢ Carpenters' Hall	07/04/74	.20	.20			1.00	49
1544	10¢ "We Ask but for Peace, Liberty and Safety"	07/04/74	.20	.20			1.00	49
1545	10¢ "Deriving Their Just Powers from the Consent of the Governed"	07/04/74	.20	.20			1.00	49
1546	10¢ Independence Hall	07/04/74	.20	.20			1.00	49
a	Block of 4, #1543-1546		.80	.90	.90	(4)	2.75	
b	Tagging omitted		65.00					
	Tagged, Perf. 11							
1547	10¢ Energy Conservation	09/23/74	.20	.20	.85	(4)	1.00	149
a	Blue and orange omitted		800.00					
b	Orange and green omitted		500.00					
c	Green omitted		800.00					
d	Tagging omitted		7.00					
	American Folklore, Tagged, Perf. 11							
1548	10¢ The Legend of Sleepy Hollow	10/10/74	.20	.20	.85	(4)	3.00	157
a	Tagging omitted		200.00	—				
	Tagged, Perf. 11							
1549	10¢ Retarded Children	10/12/74	.20	.20	.85	(4)	1.00	150
a	Tagging omitted		9.00					
	Holiday Celebration: Christmas, Tagged, Perf. 10.5 x 11							
1550	10¢ Angel from Perussis Altarpiece	10/23/74	.20	.20	2.10	(10)	1.00	835
	Holiday Celebration: Holiday, Perf. 11 x 10.5							
1551	10¢ "The Road-Winter," by Currier and Ives	10/23/74	.20	.20	2.50	(12)	1.00	883
a	Buff omitted		12.50					
	Untagged, Self-Adhesive, Die-Cut (Inscribed "precanceled")							
1552	10¢ Dove Weather Vane atop Mount Vernon	11/15/74	.20	.20	4.25	(20)	1.50	213
	American Arts, Tagged, Perf. 10.5 x 11							
1553	10¢ Benjamin West, Self-Portrait	02/10/75	.20	.20	2.10	(10)	1.00	157
	American Arts, Perf. 11							
1554	10¢ Paul Laurence Dunbar and Lamp	05/01/75	.20	.20	2.10	(10)	1.50	146
a	Imperf., pair		1,000.00					
1555	10¢ D.W. Griffith and Motion-Picture Camera	05/27/75	.20	.20	.85	(4)	1.00	149
a	Brown omitted		625.00					
	Space, Tagged, Perf. 11							
1556	10¢ Pioneer 10 Passing Jupiter	02/28/75	.20	.20	.85	(4)	1.25	174
a	Red and yellow omitted		1,100.00					
b	Blue omitted		750.00					
c	Tagging omitted		11.00					
1557	10¢ Mariner 10, Venus and Mercury	04/04/75	.20	.20	.85	(4)	1.25	159
a	Red omitted		375.00					
b	Ultramarine and bister omitted		1,650.00					
c	Tagging omitted		11.00					
	Tagged, Perf. 11							
1558	10¢ Collective Bargaining	03/13/75	.20	.20	1.75	(8)	1.00	153
	Imperfs. of #1558 exist from printer's waste							

Issue	Date	Un	U	PB #	FDC	Q(M)
American Bicentennial: Contributors to the Cause, Tagged, Perf. 11 x 10.5						
1559 8¢ Sybil Ludington Riding Horse	03/25/75	.20	.20	1.50 (10)	1.00	63
a Back inscription omitted		200.00				
1560 10¢ Salem Poor Carrying Musket	03/25/75	.20	.20	2.10 (10)	1.50	158
a Back inscription omitted		175.00				
1561 10¢ Haym Salomon Figuring Accounts	03/25/75	.20	.20	2.10 (10)	1.00	167
a Back inscription omitted		175.00				
b Red omitted		225.00				
1562 18¢ Peter Francisco Shouldering Cannon	03/25/75	.35	.20	3.60 (10)	1.00	45
American Bicentennial, Battle of Lexington & Concord, Tagged, Perf. 11						
1563 10¢ "Birth of Liberty," by Henry Sandham	04/19/75	.20	.20	2.50 (12)	1.00	144
a Vertical pair, imperf. horizontally		400.00				
American Bicentennial, Tagged, Perf. 11						
1564 10¢ "Battle of Bunker Hill," by John Trumbull	06/17/75	.20	.20	2.50 (12)	1.00	140
American Bicentennial, Military Uniforms, Tagged, Perf. 11						
1565 10¢ Soldier with Flintlock Musket, Uniform Button	07/04/75	.20	.20		1.00	45
1566 10¢ Sailor with Grappling Hook, First Navy Jack, 1775	07/04/75	.20	.20		1.00	45
1567 10¢ Marine with Musket, Full-Rigged Ship	07/04/75	.20	.20		1.00	45
1568 10¢ Militiaman with Musket, Powder Horn	07/04/75	.20	.20		1.00	45
a Block of 4, #1565-1568		.85	.90	2.50 (12)	2.50	
Space, Tagged, Perf. 11						
1569 10¢ Apollo and Soyuz after Link-up and Earth	07/15/75	.20	.20		3.00	81
1570 10¢ Spacecraft before Link-up, Earth and Project Emblem	07/15/75	.20	.20		3.00	81
a Attached pair, #1569-1570		.45	.40	2.50 (12)		
b As "a", tagging omitted		30.00	—			
c As "a," vertical pair, imperf. horizontally		2,100.00				
Tagged, Perf. 11 x 10.5						
1571 10¢ International Women's Year	08/26/75	.20	.20	1.30 (6)	1.00	146
Postal Service Bicentennial, Tagged, Perf. 11 x 10.5						
1572 10¢ Stagecoach and Trailer Truck	09/03/75	.20	.20		1.00	42
1573 10¢ Old and New Locomotives	09/03/75	.20	.20		1.00	42
1574 10¢ Early Mail Plane and Jet	09/03/75	.20	.20		1.00	42
1575 10¢ Satellite for Mailgrams	09/03/75	.20	.20		1.00	42
a Block of 4, #1572-1575		.85	.90	2.50 (12)	2.50	
b As "a," red "10¢" omitted		7,500.00				
Tagged, Perf. 11						
1576 10¢ World Peace Through Law	09/29/75	.20	.20	.85 (4)	1.25	147
a Tagging omitted		7.50				
b Horizontal pair, imperf. vert.		7,500.00				
Banking and Commerce, Tagged, Perf. 11						
1577 10¢ Engine Turning, Indian Head Penny and Morgan Silver Dollar	10/06/75	.25	.20		1.00	73

Issue	Date	Un	U	PB #	FDC	Q(M)
Banking and Commerce, Tagged, Perf. 11 continued						
1578 10¢ Seated Liberty Quarter, $20 Gold Piece and Engine Turning	10/06/75	.25	.20		1.00	73
a Attached pair, #1577-1578		.50	.40	1.20 (4)	1.75	
b Brown and blue omitted		2,000.00				
c As "a", brown, blue and yel. omitted		2,500.00				
Holiday Celebration: Christmas, Tagged, Perf. 11						
1579 (10¢) Madonna and Child, by Domenico Ghirlandaio	10/14/75	.20	.20	2.50 (12)	1.00	739
a Imperf., pair		90.00				
Plate flaw ("d" damaged)		5.00	—			
Holiday Celebration: Holiday, Perf. 11.2						
1580 (10¢) Christmas Card, by Louis Prang, 1878	10/14/75	.20	.20	2.50 (12)	1.00	879
a Imperf., pair		90.00				
c Perf. 10.9		.25	.20	3.50 (12)		
Perf. 10.5 x 11.3						
1580B (10¢) Christmas Card, by Louis Prang, 1878	10/14/75	.65	.20	15.00 (12)		
Americana, Tagged, Perf. 11 x 10.5						
(Designs 18.5 x 22.5mm; #1590-1590a, 17.5 x 20mm						
1581 1¢ Inkwell & Quill	12/08/77	.20	.20	.25 (4)	1.00	
a Untagged (Bureau precanceled)		4.50	1.50	22.50 (4)		
d Tagging omitted		4.50				
1582 2¢ Speaker's Stand	12/08/77	.20	.20	.25 (4)	1.00	
a Untagged (Bureau precanceled)		4.50	1.50	22.50 (4)		
b Cream paper, dull gum, 1981		.20	.20	.25 (4)		
c Tagging omitted		4.50				
1583 Not assigned						
1584 3¢ Early Ballot Box	12/08/77	.20	.20	.30 (4)	1.00	
a Untagged (Bureau precanceled)		.75	.50	9.50 (4)		
b Tagging omitted		7.50				
1585 4¢ Books, Bookmark, Eyeglasses	12/08/77	.20	.20	.40 (4)	1.00	
a Untagged (Bureau precanceled)		1.00	.75	13.50 (4)		
1586-1589 Not assigned						
1590 9¢ Capitol Dome, single (1591) from booklet (1623a)	03/11/77	.45	.20		1.00	
Americana, Perf. 10 x 9.75						
1590A Single (1591) from booklet (1623c)		17.50	15.00			
#1590 is on white paper; #1591 is on gray paper.						
Americana, Perf. 11 x 10.5						
1591 9¢ Capitol Dome	11/24/75	.20	.20	.85 (4)	1.00	
a Untagged (Bureau precanceled)		1.75	1.00	50.00 (4)		
b Tagging omitted		5.00				
1592 10¢ Contemplation of Justice	11/17/77	.20	.20	.90 (4)	1.00	
a Untagged (Bureau precanceled)		9.50	5.00	95.00 (4)		
b Tagging omitted		7.50				
1593 11¢ Printing Press	11/13/75	.20	.20	.90 (4)	1.00	
a Tagging omitted		4.00				
1594 12¢ Torch, Statue of Liberty	04/08/81	.25	.20	1.60 (4)	1.00	
a Tagging omitted		5.00				
1595 13¢ Liberty Bell, single from booklet		.30	.20		1.00	
a Booklet pane of 6	10/31/75	2.25	1.00		2.00	
b Booklet pane of 7 + label		2.25	1.00		2.75	
c Booklet pane of 8		2.25	1.00		2.50	
d Booklet pane of 5 + label	04/02/76	1.75	.75		2.25	
e Vertical pair, imperf. between		1,250.00				

Sybil Ludington ★ *Youthful Heroine*

1559

Salem Poor ★ *Gallant Soldier*

1560

Haym Salomon ★ *Financial Hero*

1561

Peter Francisco ★ *Fighter Extraordinary*

1562

Lexington & Concord 1775 by Sandham
US Bicentennial 10cents

1563

Bunker Hill 1775 by Trumbull
US Bicentennial 10c

1564

YOUTHFUL HEROINE
On the dark night of April 26, 1777, 16-year-old Sybil Ludington rode her horse "Star" alone through the Connecticut countryside rallying her father's militia to repel a raid by the British on Danbury.

GALLANT SOLDIER
The conspicuously courageous actions of black foot soldier Salem Poor at the Battle of Bunker Hill on June 17, 1775, earned him citations for his bravery and leadership ability.

FINANCIAL HERO
Businessman and broker Haym Salomon was responsible for raising most of the money needed to finance the American Revolution and later to save the new nation from collapse.

FIGHTER EXTRAORDINARY
Peter Francisco's strength and bravery made him a legend around campfires. He fought with distinction at Brandywine, Yorktown and Guilford Court House.

1565 **1566**   **1569**   **1572** **1573**

1567   **1568** **1568a**

APOLLO SOYUZ 1975

1570   **1570a**

USA 10c INTERNATIONAL WOMEN'S YEAR

1571

1574   **1575**   **1575a**

World Peace through LAW

1576

BANKING COMMERCE

1577   **1578**   **1578a**

Ghirlandaio: National Gallery
Christmas US postage

1579

Merry Christmas!
Early Card by Louis Prang

1580

1581

1582

1584

1585

1591

1592

1593

1594

1595

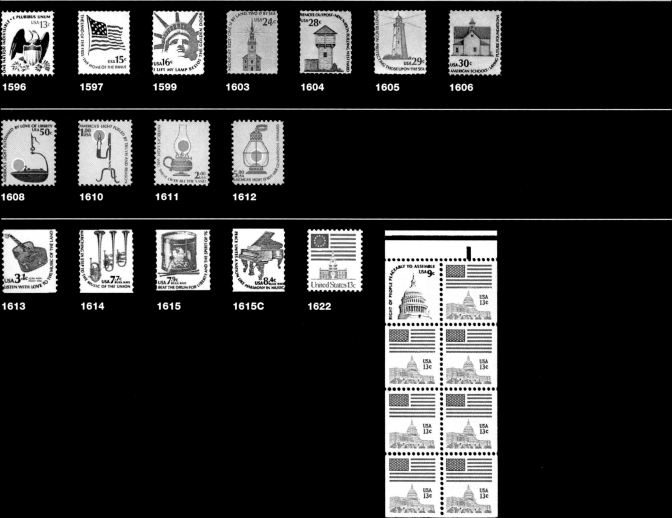

1596   1597   1599   1603   1604   1605   1606

1608   1610   1611   1612

1613   1614   1615   1615C   1622

1623a

1629   1630   1631   1631a

1632

Issue		Date	Un	U	PB/LP	#	FDC	Q(M)
	Americana, Perf. 11.2 (Designs 17.5 x 20mm; #1606, 1608, 1610-1619, 1622-1623, 1625, 1811, 1813, 1816) continued							
1596	13¢ Eagle and Shield	12/01/75	.25	.20	3.25	(12)	1.00	
a	Imperf., pair		40.00	—				
b	Yellow omitted		115.00					
d	Line perforated		27.50	—	375.00	(12)		
1597	15¢ Ft. McHenry Flag	06/30/78	.30	.20	1.90	(6)	1.00	
a	Small block tagging		.30	.20	1.90	(6)	1.00	
b	Gray omitted		425.00					
d	Tagging omitted		3.00					
	Americana, Booklet, Perf. 11 x 10.5							
1598	15¢ Ft. McHenry Flag (1597), single from booklet		.40	.20			1.00	
a	Booklet pane of 8	06/30/78	4.25	.80			2.50	
1599	16¢ Head, Statue of Liberty	03/31/78	.35	.20	1.90	(4)	1.00	
1600-1602	Not assigned							
1603	24¢ Old North Church	11/14/75	.50	.20	2.25	(4)	1.00	
a	Tagging omitted		7.50					
1604	28¢ Ft. Nisqually	08/11/78	.55	.20	2.40	(4)	1.00	
	Dull gum		1.10		10.00	(4)		
1605	29¢ Sandy Hook Lighthouse	04/14/78	.60	.20	3.00	(4)	1.50	
	Dull gum		2.00		15.00	(4)		
1606	30¢ Morris Township School No.2	08/27/79	.55	.20	2.40	(4)	1.25	
a	Tagging omitted		65.00					
1607	Not assigned							
	Americana, Perf. 11							
1608	50¢ Iron "Betty" Lamp	09/11/79	.85	.20	3.75	(4)	1.50	
a	Black omitted		250.00					
b	Vertical pair, imperf. horizontally		1,500.00					
c	Tagging omitted		16.00					
1609	Not assigned							
1610	$1 Rush Lamp and Candle	07/02/79	2.00	.20	8.50	(4)	3.00	
a	Brown omitted		225.00					
b	Tan, orange and yellow omitted		250.00					
c	Brown inverted		21,000.00					
d	Tagging omitted		12.50					
1611	$2 Kerosene Table Lamp	11/16/78	3.75	.75	16.00	(4)	5.00	
1612	$5 Railroad Conductor's Lantern	08/23/79	8.50	1.75	36.00	(4)	12.50	
	Americana, Coil, Perf. 10 Vertically							
1613	3.1¢ Six String Guitar	10/25/79	.20	.20	1.25	(2)	1.00	
a	Untagged (Bureau precanceled)		.35	.35	7.00	(2)		
b	Imperf., pair		1,250.00		2,750.00	(2)		
1614	7.7¢ Saxhorns	11/20/76	.20	.20	.90	(2)	1.00	
a	Untagged (Bureau precanceled)		.40	.30	3.25	(2)		
b	As "a," imperf., pair		1,500.00		2,750.00	(2)		
1615	7.9¢ Drum	04/23/76	.20	.20	.75	(2)	1.00	
a	Untagged (Bureau precanceled)		.40	.40	2.75	(2)		
b	Imperf., pair		550.00					
1615C	8.4¢ Steinway Grand Piano	07/13/78	.20	.20	3.25	(2)	1.00	
d	Untagged (Bureau precanceled)		.50	.40	4.25	(2)		
e	As "d," pair, imperf. between			45.00	110.00	(2)		
f	As "d," imperf., pair			15.00	25.00	(2)		
1616	9¢ slate green Capitol Dome (1591)	03/05/76	.20	.20	.90	(2)	1.00	
a	Imperf., pair		135.00		300.00	(2)		
b	Untagged (Bureau precanceled)		1.15	.75	42.50	(2)		
c	As "b," imperf., pair		650.00		—			

Issue		Date	Un	U	PB/LP	#	FDC	Q(M)
	Americana, Coil, Perf. 10 Vertically continued							
1617	10¢ purple Contemplation of Justice (1592)	11/04/77	.20	.20	1.00	(2)	1.00	
	Dull gum		.30		2.50	(2)		
a	Untagged (Bureau precanceled)		42.50	1.35	1,150.00	(2)		
b	Imperf., pair		55.00		115.00	(2)		
1618	13¢ brown Liberty Bell (1595)	11/25/75	.25	.20	.75	(2)	1.00	
a	Untagged (Bureau precanceled)		5.75	.75	90.00	(2)		
b	Imperf., pair		22.50		45.00	(2)		
1618C	15¢ Ft. McHenry Flag (1597)	06/30/78	.75	.20			1.00	
d	Imperf., pair		20.00					
e	Pair, imperf. between		135.00					
f	Gray omitted		30.00					
i	Tagging omitted		50.00					
1619	16¢ blue Head of Liberty (1599)	03/31/78	.35	.20	1.50	(2)	1.00	
a	Huck Press printing (white background with a bluish tinge, fraction of a millimeter smaller)		.50	.20				
1620-1621	Not assigned							
	Americana, Perf. 11 x 10.75							
1622	13¢ Flag over Independence Hall	11/15/75	.25	.20	5.75	(20)	1.00	
a	Horizontal pair, imperf. between		45.00					
b	Imperf., pair		425.00					
e	Horizontal pair, imperf. vertically		—					
f	Tagging omitted		4.00					
	Americana, Perf. 11.25							
1622C	13¢ Star Flag over Independence Hall		1.00	.25	20.00	(6)		
d	Vertical pair, imperf.		125.00					
	Americana, Booklet, Engr., Perf. 11 x 10.5							
1623	13¢ Flag over Capitol, single from booklet (1623a)	03/11/77	.25	.20			1.50	
a	Booklet pane of 8, (1 #1590 and 7 #1623)		2.25	1.25			25.00	
d	Attached pair, #1590 and 1623		.70	1.00				
	Americana, Booklet, Perf. 10 x 9.75							
1623B	13¢ Single from booklet		.80	.80				
c	Booklet pane of 8, (1 #1590A and 7 #1623B)		22.50	—			15.00	
e	Attached pair, #1590A and 1623B		18.50	18.50				
	#1623, 1623B issued only in booklets. All stamps are imperf. at one side or imperf. at one side and bottom.							
1624	Not assigned							
	Coil, Perf. 10 Vertically							
1625	13¢ Flag over Independence Hall (1622)	11/15/75	.35	.20			1.00	
a	Imperf. pair		20.00					
	American Bicentennial: The Spirit of '76, Tagged, Perf. 11							
1629	13¢ Drummer Boy	01/01/76	.25	.20			1.25	73
1630	13¢ Old Drummer	01/01/76	.25	.20			1.25	73
1631	13¢ Fifer	01/01/76	.25	.20			1.25	73
a	Strip of 3, #1629-1631		.75	.75	3.50	(12)	2.00	
b	As "a," imperf.		850.00					
c	Imperf., pair, #1631		700.00					
	Tagged, Perf. 11							
1632	13¢ Interphil 76	01/17/76	.20	.20	1.00	(4)	1.00	158

	Issue	Date	Un	U	FDC	Q(M)
	American Bicentennial: State Flags, Tagged, Perf. 11					
1633	13¢ Delaware	02/23/76	.30	.25	1.50	9
1634	13¢ Pennsylvania	02/23/76	.30	.25	1.50	9
1635	13¢ New Jersey	02/23/76	.30	.25	1.50	9
1636	13¢ Georgia	02/23/76	.30	.25	1.50	9
1637	13¢ Connecticut	02/23/76	.30	.25	1.50	9
1638	13¢ Massachusetts	02/23/76	.30	.25	1.50	9
1639	13¢ Maryland	02/23/76	.30	.25	1.50	9
1640	13¢ South Carolina	02/23/76	.30	.25	1.50	9
1641	13¢ New Hampshire	02/23/76	.30	.25	1.50	9
1642	13¢ Virginia	02/23/76	.30	.25	1.50	9
1643	13¢ New York	02/23/76	.30	.25	1.50	9
1644	13¢ North Carolina	02/23/76	.30	.25	1.50	9
1645	13¢ Rhode Island	02/23/76	.30	.25	1.50	9
1646	13¢ Vermont	02/23/76	.30	.25	1.50	9
1647	13¢ Kentucky	02/23/76	.30	.25	1.50	9
1648	13¢ Tennessee	02/23/76	.30	.25	1.50	9
1649	13¢ Ohio	02/23/76	.30	.25	1.50	9

	Issue	Date	Un	U	FDC	Q(M)
	American Bicentennial: State Flags, Tagged, Perf. 11 continued					
1650	13¢ Louisiana	02/23/76	.30	.25	1.50	9
1651	13¢ Indiana	02/23/76	.30	.25	1.50	9
1652	13¢ Mississippi	02/23/76	.30	.25	1.50	9
1653	13¢ Illinois	02/23/76	.30	.25	1.50	9
1654	13¢ Alabama	02/23/76	.30	.25	1.50	9
1655	13¢ Maine	02/23/76	.30	.25	1.50	9
1656	13¢ Missouri	02/23/76	.30	.25	1.50	9
1657	13¢ Arkansas	02/23/76	.30	.25	1.50	9
1658	13¢ Michigan	02/23/76	.30	.25	1.50	9
1659	13¢ Florida	02/23/76	.30	.25	1.50	9
1660	13¢ Texas	02/23/76	.30	.25	1.50	9
1661	13¢ Iowa	02/23/76	.30	.25	1.50	9
1662	13¢ Wisconsin	02/23/76	.30	.25	1.50	9
1663	13¢ California	02/23/76	.30	.25	1.50	9
1664	13¢ Minnesota	02/23/76	.30	.25	1.50	9
1665	13¢ Oregon	02/23/76	.30	.25	1.50	9
1666	13¢ Kansas	02/23/76	.30	.25	1.50	9
1667	13¢ West Virginia	02/23/76	.30	.25	1.50	9

DISTINGUISHED AMERICANS: MARY LASKER

This stamp in the Distinguished Americans series honors Mary Woodard Lasker (1900-1994), philanthropist, political strategist, and ardent advocate of medical research for major diseases. Lasker persuaded the nation's leaders to adopt dramatic increases in public funding for biomedical research, and her efforts helped make cancer research a national priority. ■ A graduate of Radcliffe College, Mary Woodard settled in New York City, where she worked as an art dealer. Soon after her marriage in 1940 to advertising mogul Albert Davis Lasker (1880-1952), she and her husband created the Albert and Mary Lasker Foundation to advance medical research into the major causes of disability and fatal disease. The Foundation's legacy includes the prestigious Lasker Awards, which recognize the contributions of scientists, physicians, and public servants who have made advances in the prevention and cure of human disease and which highlight how medical research benefits the public. Seventy-six Lasker laureates have received the Nobel Prize.

■ Skillfully coordinating the support of the media, medical experts, U.S. Presidents, Congress, and others, Mary Lasker built a powerful lobby for medical research, especially directed at the expansion of the National Institutes of Health to include research centers concentrating on specific diseases. ■ Throughout her life, Lasker fought to encourage funding for medical research for cancer, heart disease, stroke, mental illness, blindness, cerebral palsy, arthritis, osteoporosis, growth disorders, and AIDS. Especially passionate about the fight against cancer, she led the reorganization and growth of the American Cancer Society and established its research program; advocated more aggressive applied cancer research, including chemotherapy; and became the driving force behind the National Cancer Act. ■ In 1969, she was awarded the Presidential Medal of Freedom, the nation's highest civilian honor, and in 1989, she received a Congressional Gold Medal.

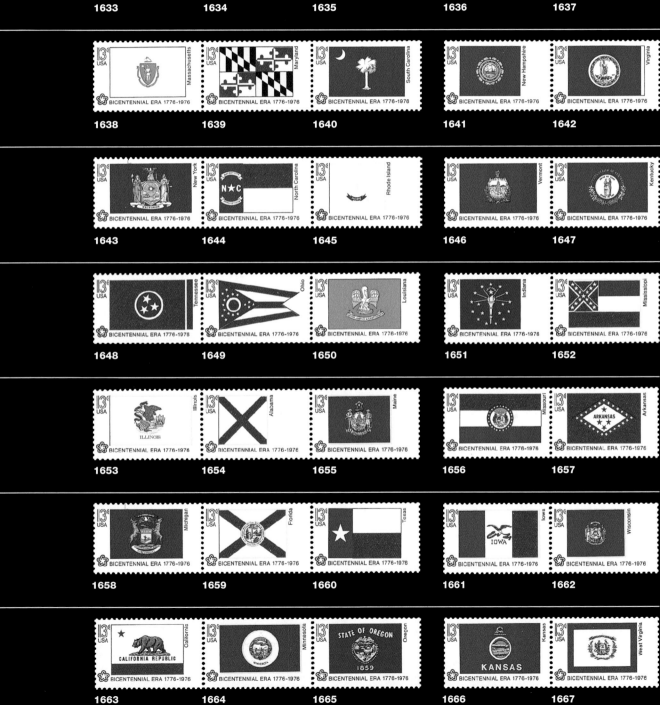

1668　　**1669**　　**1670**　　　　**1671**　　**1672**

1673　　**1674**　　**1675**　　　　**1676**　　**1677**

1678　　**1679**　　**1680**　　　　**1681**　　**1682**

1683　　　　**1684**　　　　**1685**

The Surrender of Lord Cornwallis at Yorktown
From a Painting by John Trumbull

The Declaration of Independence, 4 July 1776 at Philadelphia
From a Painting by John Trumbull

1686　　**a**　　**b**　　**c**　　**d**　　**e**　　　　**1687**　　**a**　　**b**　　**c**　　**d**　　**e**

Issue		Date	Un	U	PB	#	FDC	Q(M
American Bicentennial: State Flags Tagged, Perf. 11 continued								
1668	13¢ Nevada	02/23/76	.30	.25			1.50	9
1669	13¢ Nebraska	02/23/76	.30	.25			1.50	9
1670	13¢ Colorado	02/23/76	.30	.25			1.50	9
1671	13¢ North Dakota	02/23/76	.30	.25			1.50	9
1672	13¢ South Dakota	02/23/76	.30	.25			1.50	9
1673	13¢ Montana	02/23/76	.30	.25			1.50	9
1674	13¢ Washington	02/23/76	.30	.25			1.50	9
1675	13¢ Idaho	02/23/76	.30	.25			1.50	9
1676	13¢ Wyoming	02/23/76	.30	.25			1.50	9
1677	13¢ Utah	02/23/76	.30	.25			1.50	9
1678	13¢ Oklahoma	02/23/76	.30	.25			1.50	9
1679	13¢ New Mexico	02/23/76	.30	.25			1.50	9
1680	13¢ Arizona	02/23/76	.30	.25			1.50	9
1681	13¢ Alaska	02/23/76	.30	.25			1.50	9
1682	13¢ Hawaii	02/23/76	.30	.25			1.50	9
a	Pane of 50, #1633-1682		17.50	15.00			27.50	
Tagged, Perf. 11								
1683	13¢ Telephone Centennial	03/10/76	.25	.20	1.10	(4)	1.00	158
a	Black and purple omitted		450.00					
1684	13¢ Commercial Aviation	03/19/76	.25	.20	2.75	(10)	1.50	156
1685	13¢ Chemistry	04/06/76	.25	.20	3.25	(12)	1.50	158

Issue		Date	Un	U	PB	#	FDC	Q(M
American Bicentennial, Souvenir Sheets, Tagged, Perf. 11								
1686	13¢ The Surrender of Lord Cornwallis at Yorktown, by John Trumbull, sheet of 5	05/29/76	3.25	2.25			7.50	2
a	13¢ Two British Officers		.45	.40				2
b	13¢ Gen. Benjamin Lincoln		.45	.40				2
c	13¢ George Washington		.45	.40				2
d	13¢ John Trumbull, Col. David Cobb, General Friedrich von Steuben, Marquis de Lafayette and Thomas Nelson		.45	.40				2
e	13¢ Alexander Hamilton, John Laurens and Walter Stewart		.45	.40				2
f	"USA/13¢" omitted on "b," "c" and "d," imperf.		—	2,000.00				
g	"USA/13¢" omitted on "a" and "e"		450.00	—				
h	Imperf. (untagged)			2,250.00				
i	"USA/13¢" omitted on "b," "c" and "d"		450.00					
j	"USA/13¢" double on "b"		—					
k	"USA/13¢" omitted on "c" and "d"		750.00					
l	"USA/13¢" omitted on "e"		550.00					
m	"USA/13¢" omitted, imperf. (untagged)		—					
1687	18¢ The Declaration of Independence, 4 July 1776 at Philadelphia, by John Trumbull, sheet of 5	05/29/76	4.25	3.25			7.50	2
a	18¢ John Adams, Roger Sherman and Robert R. Livingston		.55	.55				2
b	18¢ Thomas Jefferson and Benjamin Franklin		.55	.55				2
c	18¢ Thomas Nelson, Jr., Francis Lewis, John Witherspoon and Samuel Huntington		.55	.55				2
d	18¢ John Hancock and Charles Thomson		.55	.55				2
e	18¢ George Read, John Dickinson and Edward Rutledge		.55	.55				2
f	Design and marginal inscriptions omitted		3,250.00					
g	"USA/18¢" omitted on "a" and "c"		600.00					
h	"USA/18¢" omitted on "b," "d" and "e"		450.00					
i	"USA/18¢" omitted on "d"		475.00	475.00				
j	Black omitted in design		2,000.00					
k	"USA/18¢" omitted, imperf. (untagged)		2,000.00					
m	"USA/18¢" omitted on "b" and "e"		500.00					

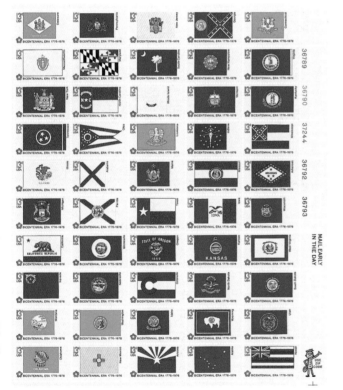

36789
36790
37244
36792
36793

MAIL EARLY IN THE DAY

USE ZIP CODE

Example of 1682a

	Issue	Date	Un	U	PB	#	FDC	Q(M)
	American Bicentennial, Souvenir Sheets, Tagged, Perf. 11 continued							
1688	24¢ Washington Crossing the Delaware, by Emanuel Leutze/ Eastman Johnson, sheet of 5	05/29/76	5.25	4.25			7.50	2
a	24¢ Boatmen		.70	.70				2
b	24¢ George Washington		.70	.70				2
c	24¢ Flagbearer		.70	.70				2
d	24¢ Men in Boat		.70	.70				2
e	24¢ Steersman and Men on Shore		.70	.70				2
f	"USA/24¢" omitted, imperf.		1,500.00					
g	"USA/24¢" omitted on "d" and "e"		450.00	450.00				
h	Design and marginal inscriptions omitted		2,750.00					
i	"USA/24¢" omitted on "a," "b" and "c"		500.00	500.00				
j	Imperf. (untagged)		1,750.00					
k	"USA/24¢" inverted on "d" and "e"		—					
l	As "i," imperf., tagging omitted		3,250.00	—				
m	Tagging omitted on "e" and "f"		—					
n	As (1688), perfs. inverted		450.00					
1689	31¢ Washington Reviewing His Ragged Army at Valley Forge, by William T. Trego, sheet of 5	05/29/76	6.25	5.25			7.50	2
a	31¢ Two Officers		.85	.85				2
b	31¢ George Washington		.85	.85				2
c	31¢ Officer and Brown Horse		.85	.85				2
d	31¢ White Horse and Officer		.85	.85				2
e	31¢ Three Soldiers		.85	.85				2
f	"USA/31¢" omitted, imperf.		1,500.00					
g	"USA/31¢" omitted on "a" and "c"		400.00					
h	"USA/31¢" omitted on "b," "d" and "e"		500.00	—				
i	"USA/31¢" omitted on "e"		450.00					
j	Black omitted in design		1,500.00					
k	Imperf. (untagged)			2,000.00				
l	"USA/31¢" omitted on "b" and "d"		600.00					
m	"USA/31¢" omitted on "a," "c" and "e"		—					
n	As "m," imperf. (untagged)		—					
p	As "h," imperf. (untagged)			2,000.00				
q	As "g," imperf. (untagged)		2,750.00					
r	"USA/31¢" omitted on "d" & "e"		600.00					
s	As "f," untagged		2,250.00					
t	"USA/13¢" omitted on "d"		750.00					
	American Bicentennial, Tagged, Perf. 11							
1690	13¢ Bust of Benjamin Franklin, Map of North America, 1776	06/01/76	.25	.20	1.10	(4)	1.00	165
a	Light blue omitted		200.00					
b	Tagging omitted		7.50					

	Issue	Date	Un	U	PB	#	FDC	Q(M)
	American Bicentennial: Declaration of Independence, Tagged, Perf. 11 continued							
1691	13¢ Delegates	07/04/76	.30	.20			1.00	41
1692	13¢ Delegates and John Adams	07/04/76	.30	.20			1.00	41
1693	13¢ Roger Sherman, Robert R. Livingston, Thomas Jefferson and Benjamin Franklin	07/04/76	.30	.20			1.00	41
1694	13¢ John Hancock, Charles Thomson, George Read, John Dickinson and Edward Rutledge	07/04/76	.30	.20			1.00	41
a	Strip of 4, #1691-1694		1.20	1.10	7.25	(20)	2.00	
	Olympic Games, Tagged, Perf. 11							
1695	13¢ Diver and Olympic Rings	07/16/76	.30	.20			1.00	46
1696	13¢ Skier and Olympic Rings	07/16/76	.30	.20			1.00	46
1697	13¢ Runner and Olympic Rings	07/16/76	.30	.20			1.00	46
1698	13¢ Skater and Olympic Rings	07/16/76	.30	.20			1.00	46
a	Block of 4, #1695-1698		1.20	1.20	4.00	(12)	2.00	
b	As "a," imperf.		575.00					
	Tagged, Perf. 11							
1699	13¢ Clara Maass	08/18/76	.25	.20	4.00	(12)	2.50	131
a	Horizontal pair, imperf. vertically		400.00					
1700	13¢ Adolph S. Ochs	09/18/76	.25	.20	1.10	(4)	1.00	158
a	Tagging omitted		50.00	—				
	Holiday Celebration: Christmas, Tagged, Perf. 11							
1701	13¢ Nativity, by John Singleton Copley	10/27/76	.25	.20	3.25	(12)	1.00	810
a	Imperf., pair		85.00					
	Holiday Celebration: Holiday, Tagged, Perf. 11							
1702	13¢ "Winter Pastime," by Nathaniel Currier	10/27/76	.25	.20	2.75	(10)	1.00	482*
a	Imperf., pair		90.00					
	*Includes #1703 printing							
1703	13¢ as #1702	10/27/76	.25	.20	6.00	(20)	1.00	
a	Imperf., pair		90.00					
b	Vertical pair, imperf. between		325.00					
c	Tagging omitted		12.50					

#1702 has overall tagging. Lettering at base is black and usually ½mm below design. As a rule, no "snowflaking" in sky or pond. Pane of 50 has margins on 4 sides with slogans. #1703 has block the size of the printed area. Lettering at base is gray-black and usually ¾mm below design. "Snowflaking" generally in sky and pond. Pane of 50 has margin only at right or left and no slogans.

	Issue	Date	Un	U	PB	#	FDC	Q(M)
	American Bicentennial, Tagged, Perf. 11							
1704	13¢ Washington, Nassau Hall, Hessian Prisoners and 13-star Flag	01/03/77	.25	.20	2.75	(10)	1.00	150
a	Horizontal pair, imperf. vertically		500.00					
	Tagged, Perf. 11							
1705	13¢ Sound Recording	03/23/77	.25	.20	1.10	(4)	1.25	177

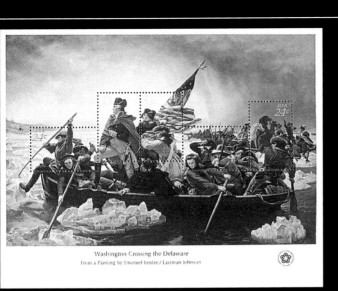

Washington Crossing the Delaware
From a Painting by Emanuel Leutze / Eastman Johnson

Washington Reviewing His Ragged Army at Valley Forge
From a Painting by William T. Trego

1688　a　b　c　d　e　　**1689**　a　b　c　d　e

1690

1691　**1692**　**1693**　**1694**

1695　**1696**

1697　**1698**　**1698a**

1699

1700

1701

1702

1703

1704

1705

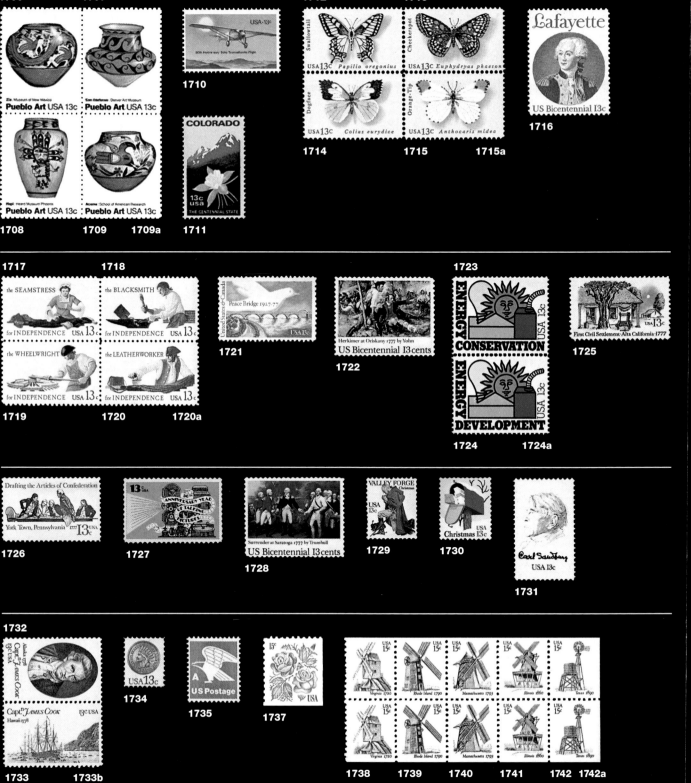

1708 **1709** **1709a** **1711**

Pueblo Art USA 13c — Zia. Museum of New Mexico
Pueblo Art USA 13c — San Ildefonso. Denver Art Museum
Pueblo Art USA 13c — Hopi. Heard Museum Phoenix
Pueblo Art USA 13c — Acoma. School of American Research

1710
USA 13c — 50th Anniversary Solo Transatlantic Flight

1711
COLORADO 13c usa — THE CENTENNIAL STATE

1714 **1715** **1715a**
Swallowtail — USA 13c *Papilio oregonius*
Checkerspot — USA 13c *Euphydryas phaeton*
Dogface — USA 13c *Colias eurydice*
Orange-Tip — USA 13c *Anthocaris midea*

1716
Lafayette — US Bicentennial 13c

1717 **1718**
1719 **1720** **1720a**
the SEAMSTRESS for INDEPENDENCE USA 13c
the BLACKSMITH for INDEPENDENCE USA 13c
the WHEELWRIGHT for INDEPENDENCE USA 13c
the LEATHERWORKER for INDEPENDENCE USA 13c

1721
United States & Canada — Peace Bridge 1927–77 — USA 13c

1722
Herkimer at Oriskany 1777 by Yohn — US Bicentennial 13 cents

1723
ENERGY CONSERVATION USA 13c

1724 **1724a**
ENERGY DEVELOPMENT USA 13c

1725
First Civil Settlement-Alta California·1777 — USA 13c

1726
Drafting the Articles of Confederation — York Town, Pennsylvania 1777 — 13c USA

1727
13c USA

1728
Surrender at Saratoga 1777 by Trumbull — US Bicentennial 13 cents

1729
VALLEY FORGE Christmas — USA 13c

1730
Christmas USA 13c

1731
Carl Sandburg — USA 13c

1732
Alaska 1778 Captⁿ JAMES COOK 13c USA

1733 **1733b**
Captⁿ JAMES COOK 13c USA — Hawaii 1778

1734
USA 13c

1735
A US Postage

1737
15c — USA

1738 **1739** **1740** **1741** **1742** **1742a**
USA 15c Virginia 1720
USA 15c Rhode Island 1790
USA 15c Massachusetts 1793
USA 15c Illinois 1860
USA 15c Texas 1890

Issue	Date	Un	U	PB	#	FDC	Q(M)
American Folk Art: Pueblo Pottery, Tagged, Perf. 11							
1706 13¢ Zia Pot	04/13/77	.25	.20			1.00	49
1707 13¢ San Ildefonso Pot	04/13/77	.25	.20			1.00	49
1708 13¢ Hopi Pot	04/13/77	.25	.20			1.00	49
1709 13¢ Acoma Pot	04/13/77	.25	.20			1.00	49
a Block of 4, #1706-1709		1.00	1.00	2.75	(10)	2.00	
b As "a," imperf. vertically		2,000.00					
Tagged, Perf. 11							
1710 13¢ Solo Transatlantic Flight	05/20/77	.25	.20	3.25	(12)	3.50	209
a Imperf. pair		850.00					
1711 13¢ Colorado Statehood	05/21/77	.25	.20	3.25	(12)	1.00	192
a Horizontal pair, imperf. between		—					
b Horizontal pair, imperf. vertically		750.00					
c Perf. 11.2		.35	.25	20.00	(12)		
Butterfly, Tagged, Perf. 11							
1712 13¢ Swallowtail	06/06/77	.25	.20			2.00	55
1713 13¢ Checkerspot	06/06/77	.25	.20			2.00	55
1714 13¢ Dogface	06/06/77	.25	.20			2.00	55
1715 13¢ Orange-Tip	06/06/77	.25	.20			2.00	55
a Block of 4, #1712-1715		1.00	1.00	3.25	(12)	2.00	
b As "a," imperf. horizontally		15,000.00					
American Bicentennial, Tagged, Perf. 11							
1716 13¢ Marquis de Lafayette	06/13/77	.25	.20	1.10	(4)	1.00	160
1717 13¢ Seamstress	07/04/77	.25	.20			1.00	47
1718 13¢ Blacksmith	07/04/77	.25	.20			1.00	47
1719 13¢ Wheelwright	07/04/77	.25	.20			1.00	47
1720 13¢ Leatherworker	07/04/77	.25	.20			1.00	47
a Block of 4, #1717-1720		1.00	1.00	3.25	(12)	2.00	
Tagged, Perf. 11 x 10.5							
1721 13¢ Peace Bridge	08/04/77	.25	.20	1.10	(4)	1.00	164
American Bicentennial, Tagged, Perf. 11							
1722 13¢ Herkimer at Oriskany, by Frederick Yohn	08/06/77	.25	.20	2.75	(10)	1.00	156
Energy, Tagged, Perf. 11							
1723 13¢ Energy Conservation	10/20/77	.25	.20			1.25	79
1724 13¢ Energy Development	10/20/77	.25	.20			1.25	79
a Attached pair, #1723-1724		.50	.50	3.25	(12)		
Tagged, Perf. 11							
1725 13¢ First Civil Settlement Alta, California	09/09/77	.25	.20	1.10	(4)	1.00	154
American Bicentennial, Tagged, Perf. 11							
1726 13¢ Articles of Confederation	09/30/77	.25	.20	1.10	(4)	1.00	168
a Tagging omitted		125.00					
b Red omitted		600.00					
c Red & brown omitted		400.00					
Tagged, Perf. 11							
1727 13¢ Talking Pictures	10/06/77	.25	.20	1.10	(4)	1.50	157
American Bicentennial, Tagged, Perf. 11							
1728 13¢ Surrender of Burgoyne, at Saratoga	10/07/77	.25	.20	2.75	(10)	1.00	154
Holiday Celebration: Christmas, Tagged, Perf. 11							
1729 13¢ Washington at Valley Forge, by J.C. Leyendecker	10/21/77	.25	.20	5.75	(20)	1.00	882
a Imperf., pair		65.00					
1730 13¢ Rural Mailbox	10/21/77	.25	.20	2.75	(10)	1.00	922
a Imperf., pair		225.00					
Tagged, Perf. 11							
1731 13¢ Carl Sandburg	01/06/78	.25	.20	1.25	(4)	1.00	157
a Brown omitted		2,250.00					
1732 13¢ Capt. James Cook Alaska, by Nathaniel Dance	01/20/78	.25	.20			1.25	101
1733 13¢ Resolution and Discovery Hawaii, by John Webber	01/20/78	.25	.20			1.25	101
a Vertical pair, imperf. horizontally		—					
b Attached pair, #1732-1733		.50	.50	1.10	(4)		
c As " b," imperf. between		4,250.00					
1734 13¢ Indian Head Penny	01/11/78	.25	.20	1.25	(4)	1.00	
a Horizontal pair, imperf. vertically		250.00					
1735 (15¢) "A" Stamp	05/22/78	.30	.20	1.40	(4)	1.00	
a Imperf., pair		85.00					
b Vertical pair, imperf. horizontally		600.00					
c Perf. 11.2		.35	.20	1.80	(4)		
Booklet, Perf. 11 x 10.5 on 2 or 3 sides							
1736 (15¢) "A" orange Eagle (1735), single from booklet	05/22/78	.30	.20			1.00	
a Booklet pane of 8	05/22/78	2.50	1.50			2.50	
b Vert. pair, imperf. between		850.00					
Booklet, Perf. 10							
1737 15¢ Roses, single from booklet	07/11/78	.30	.20			1.00	
a Booklet pane of 8	07/11/78	2.50	1.50			2.50	
b As "a," imperf.		450.00					
c As "a," imperf.		2,200.00					
d As "a," tagging omitted		50.00	—				

#1736-1737 issued only in booklets. All stamps are imperf. on one side or on one side and bottom.

Issue	Date	Un	U	PB	#	FDC	Q(M)
Windmills, Booklet, Tagged, Perf. 11 on 2 or 3 sides							
1738 15¢ Virginia, 1720	02/07/80	.30	.20			1.00	
1739 15¢ Rhode Island, 1790	02/07/80	.30	.20			1.00	
1740 15¢ Massachusetts, 1793	02/07/80	.30	.20			1.00	
1741 15¢ Illinois, 1860	02/07/80	.30	.20			1.00	
1742 15¢ Texas, 1890	02/07/80	.30	.20			1.00	
a Booklet pane of 10, #1738-1742		3.50	3.00			3.50	
b Strip of 5, #1730-1742		1.50	1.40				

#1737-1742 issued only in booklets. All stamps are imperf. top or bottom, or top or bottom and right side.

Issue	Date	Un	U	PB	#	FDC	Q(M)
Coil, Perf. 10 Vertically							
1743 (15¢) "A" orange Eagle (1735)	05/22/78	.30	.20	.75	(2)	1.00	
a Imperf., pair		80.00	—				

Issue		Date	Un	U	PB	#	FDC	Q(M)
	Black Heritage, Tagged, Perf. 10.5 x 11							
1744	13¢ Harriet Tubman and Cart Carrying Slaves	02/01/78	.25	.20	3.25	(12)	1.75	157
	American Folk Art: Quilts, Perf. 11							
1745	13¢ Basket design, red and orange	03/08/78	.25	.20			1.00	41
1746	13¢ Basket design, red	03/08/78	.25	.20			1.00	41
1747	13¢ Basket design, orange	03/08/78	.25	.20			1.00	41
1748	13¢ Basket design, brown	03/08/78	.25	.20			1.00	41
a	Block of 4, #1745-1748		1.00	1.00	3.25	(12)	2.00	
	American Dance, Tagged, Perf. 11							
1749	13¢ Ballet	04/26/78	.25	.20			1.00	39
1750	13¢ Theater	04/26/78	.25	.20			1.00	39
1751	13¢ Folk	04/26/78	.25	.20			1.00	39
1752	13¢ Modern	04/26/78	.25	.20			1.00	39
a	Block of 4, #1749-1752		1.00	1.00	3.25	(12)	2.00	
	American Bicentennial: French Alliance, Tagged, Perf. 11							
1753	13¢ King Louis XVI and Benjamin Franklin, by Charles Gabriel Sauvage	05/04/78	.25	.20	1.10	(4)	1.00	103
	Tagged, Perf. 10.5 x 11							
1754	13¢ Early Cancer Detection	05/18/78	.25	.20	1.10	(4)	1.00	152
	Performing Arts, Tagged, Perf. 11							
1755	13¢ Jimmie Rodgers with Guitar and Brakeman's Cap, Locomotive	05/24/78	.25	.20	4.00	(12)	1.00	95
1756	15¢ George M. Cohan, "Yankee Doodle Dandy" and Stars	07/03/78	.30	.20	4.00	(12)	1.25	152
	CAPEX '78 Souvenir Sheet, Tagged, Perf. 11							
1757	13¢ Souvenir sheet of 8	06/10/78	2.00	1.75	2.25	(8)	2.75	15
a	13¢ Cardinal		.25	.20				
b	13¢ Mallard		.25	.20				
c	13¢ Canada Goose		.25	.20				
d	13¢ Blue Jay		.25	.20				
e	13¢ Moose		.25	.20				
f	13¢ Chipmunk		.25	.20				
g	13¢ Red Fox		.25	.20				
h	13¢ Raccoon		.25	.20				
i	Yellow, green, red, brown and black (litho.) omitted		7,000.00					

Issue		Date	Un	U	PB	#	FDC	Q(M)
	Tagged, Perf. 11							
1758	15¢ Photography	06/26/78	.30	.20	4.00	(12)	1.00	161
	Space, Tagged, Perf. 11							
1759	15¢ Viking Missions to Mars	07/20/78	.30	.20	1.35	(4)	1.00	159
a	Tagging omitted		60.00					
	Wildlife Conservation: American Owls, Tagged, Perf. 11							
1760	15¢ Great Gray Owl	08/26/78	.30	.20			1.25	47
1761	15¢ Saw-Whet Owl	08/26/78	.30	.20			1.25	47
1762	15¢ Barred Owl	08/26/78	.30	.20			1.25	47
1763	15¢ Great Horned Owl	08/26/78	.30	.20			1.25	47
a	Block of 4, #1760-1763		1.25	1.25	1.40	(4)	2.00	
	Wildlife Conservation: American Trees, Tagged, Perf. 11							
1764	15¢ Giant Sequoia	10/09/78	.30	.20			1.25	42
1765	15¢ White Pine	10/09/78	.30	.20			1.25	42
1766	15¢ White Oak	10/09/78	.30	.20			1.25	42
1767	15¢ Gray Birch	10/09/78	.30	.20			1.25	42
a	Block of 4, #1764-1767		1.25	1.25	4.00	(12)	2.00	
b	As "a," imperf. horizontally		17,500.00					
	Holiday Celebration: Christmas, Perf. 11							
1768	15¢ Madonna and Child with Cherubim, by Andrea della Robbia	10/18/78	.30	.20	4.00	(12)	1.00	963
a	Imperf., pair		85.00					
	Holiday Celebration: Holiday, Perf. 11							
1769	15¢ Child on Hobby Horse and Christmas Trees	10/18/78	.30	.20	4.00	(12)	1.00	917
a	Imperf., pair		85.00					
b	Vertical pair, imperf. horizontally		1,600.00					
	Tagged, Perf. 11							
1770	15¢ Robert F. Kennedy	01/12/79	.35	.20	1.75	(4)	1.50	159
a	Tagging omitted		60.00					
	Black Heritage, Tagged, Perf. 11							
1771	15¢ Martin Luther King, Jr., and Civil Rights Marchers	01/13/79	.40	.20	5.75	(12)	2.00	166
a	Imperf., pair		1,400.00					
	Tagged, Perf. 11							
1772	15¢ International Year of the Child	02/15/79	.30	.20	1.40	(4)	1.00	163
	Literary Arts, Tagged, Perf. 10.5 x 11							
1773	15¢ John Steinbeck, by Philippe Halsman	02/27/79	.30	.20	1.40	(4)	1.00	155
	Tagged, Perf. 10.5 x 11							
1774	15¢ Albert Einstein	03/04/79	.35	.20	1.75	(4)	3.50	157

1744

1745 **1746**

1747 **1748** **1748a**

1750

1749 **1752**

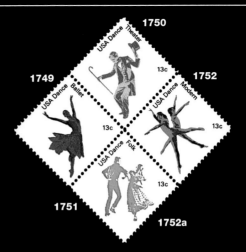

1751

1752a

1753

a **b** **c** **d**

1754

1755

1756

Canadian International Philatelic Exhibition
Toronto

1757 **e** **f** **g** **h**

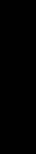

Photography USA 15c

1758

1759

1760 **1761**

1762 **1763** **1763a**

1764 **1765**

1766 **1767** **1767a**

1769

1768

1770

1771

1772

1773

1774

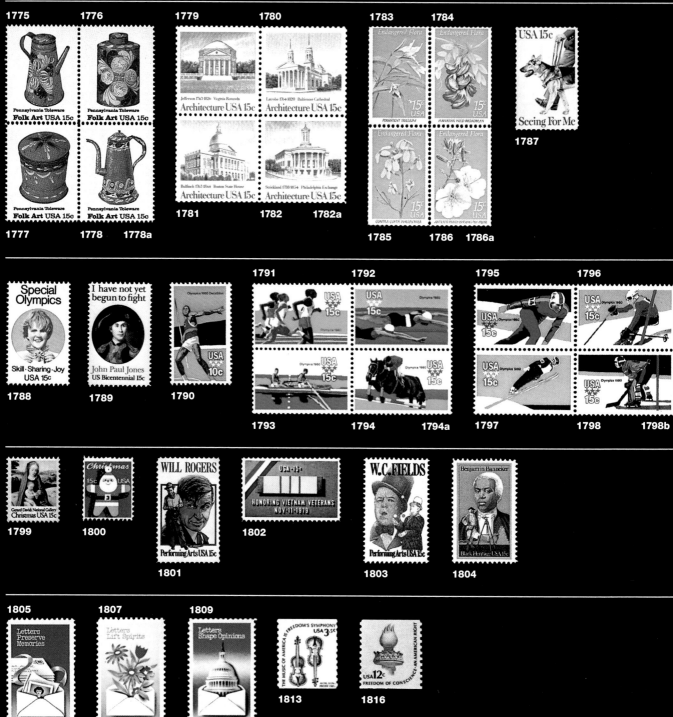

1775 **1776**

1777 **1778** **1778a**

Pennsylvania Toleware
Folk Art USA 15c

1779 **1780**

Jefferson 1743-1826 Virginia Rotunda
Architecture USA 15c

Latrobe 1764-1820 Baltimore Cathedral
Architecture USA 15c

1781 **1782** **1782a**

Bulfinch 1763-1844 Boston State House
Architecture USA 15c

Strickland 1788-1854 Philadelphia Exchange
Architecture USA 15c

1783 **1784**

Endangered Flora

1785 **1786** **1786a**

1787

USA 15c
Seeing For Me

1788

Special Olympics
Skill · Sharing · Joy
USA 15c

1789

I have not yet begun to fight
John Paul Jones
US Bicentennial 15c

1790

Olympics 1980 Decathlon
USA 10c

1791 **1792**

USA 15c

1793 **1794** **1794a**

USA 15c

1795 **1796**

USA 15c · Olympics 1980

1797 **1798** **1798b**

USA 15c

1799

Gerard David National Gallery
Christmas USA 15c

1800

Christmas 15c USA

1801

WILL ROGERS
Performing Arts USA 15c

1802

USA 15c
HONORING VIETNAM VETERANS
NOV · 11 · 1979

1803

W.C. FIELDS
Performing Arts USA 15c

1804

Benjamin Banneker
Black Heritage USA 15c

1805 **1807** **1809**

Letters Preserve Memories
USA 15c

Letters Lift Spirits
USA 15c

Letters Shape Opinions
USA 15c

1806 **1808** **1810**

P.S. Write Soon
USA 15c

1813

THE MUSIC OF AMERICA IS FREEDOM'S SYMPHONY USA 3.5c

1816

USA 12c FREEDOM OF CONSCIENCE-AN AMERICAN RIGHT

Issue		Date	Un	U	PB	#	FDC	Q(M)
American Folk Art: Pennsylvania Toleware, c.1800, Tagged, Perf. 11								
1775	15¢ Straight-Spout Coffeepot	04/19/79	.30	.20			1.00	44
1776	15¢ Tea Caddy	04/19/79	.30	.20			1.00	44
1777	15¢ Sugar Bowl	04/19/79	.30	.20			1.00	44
1778	15¢ Curved-Spout Coffeepot	04/19/79	.30	.20			1.00	44
a	Block of 4, #1775-1778		1.25	1.25	3.25	(10)	2.00	
b	As "a," imperf. horizontally		3,750.00					
American Architecture, Tagged, Perf. 11								
1779	15¢ Virginia Rotunda, by Thomas Jefferson	06/04/79	.30	.20			1.00	41
1780	15¢ Baltimore Cathedral, by Benjamin Latrobe	06/04/79	.30	.20			1.00	41
1781	15¢ Boston State House, by Charles Bulfinch	06/04/79	.30	.20			1.00	41
1782	15¢ Philadelphia Exchange, by William Strickland	06/04/79	.30	.20			1.00	41
a	Block of 4, #1779-1782		1.25	1.25	1.45	(4)	2.00	
Endangered Flora, Tagged, Perf. 11								
1783	15¢ Persistent Trillium	06/07/79	.30	.20			1.00	41
1784	15¢ Hawaiian Wild Broadbean	06/07/79	.30	.20			1.00	41
1785	15¢ Contra Costa Wallflower	06/07/79	.30	.20			1.00	41
1786	15¢ Antioch Dunes Evening Primrose	06/07/79	.30	.20			1.00	41
a	Block of 4, #1783-1786		1.25	1.25	4.00	(12)	2.00	
b	As "a," imperf.		275.00					
Tagged, Perf. 11								
1787	15¢ Seeing Eye Dogs	06/15/79	.30	.20	6.50	(20)	1.25	162
a	Imperf., pair		400.00					
b	Tagging omitted		12.00					
1788	15¢ Special Olympics	08/09/79	.30	.20	3.25	(10)	1.25	166
American Bicentennial, Tagged, Perf. 11 x 12								
1789	15¢ John Paul Jones	09/23/79	.30	.20	3.25	(10)	1.50	160
c	Vertical pair, imperf. horizontally		150.00					
American Bicentennial, Perf. 11								
1789A	15¢ John Paul Jones	09/23/79	.55	.20	4.00	(10)	1.50	
d	Vertical pair, imperf. horizontally		125.00					
American Bicentennial, Perf. 12								
1789B	15¢ John Paul Jones	09/23/79	3,500.00	3,500.00	40,000.00	(10)		
	Numerous varieties of printer's waste of #1789 exist							
Olympic Games, Summer, Tagged, Perf. 11								
1790	10¢ Javelin Thrower	09/05/79	.20	.20	3.00	(12)	1.00	67
1791	15¢ Runner	09/28/79	.30	.20			1.25	47
1792	15¢ Swimmer	09/28/79	.30	.20			1.25	47
1793	15¢ Rowers	09/28/79	.30	.20			1.25	47
1794	15¢ Equestrian Contestant	09/28/79	.30	.20			1.25	47
a	Block of 4, #1791-1794		1.25	1.25	4.00	(12)	2.00	
b	As "a," imperf.		1,400.00					
Olympic Games, Winter, Tagged, Perf. 11.25 x 10.5								
1795	15¢ Speed Skater	02/01/80	.35	.20			1.25	52
1796	15¢ Downhill Skier	02/01/80	.35	.20			1.25	52
1797	15¢ Ski Jumper	02/01/80	.35	.20			1.25	52
1798	15¢ Ice Hockey	02/01/80	.35	.20			1.25	52
b	Block of 4, #1795-1798		1.50	1.40	4.50	(12)	2.00	

Issue		Date	Un	U	PB	#	FDC	Q(M)
Olympic Games, Tagged, Perf. 11								
1795A	15¢ Speed Skater	02/01/80	1.10	.60				
1796A	15¢ Downhill Skier	02/01/80	1.10	.60				
1797A	15¢ Ski Jumper	02/01/80	1.10	.60				
1798A	15¢ Ice Hockey	02/01/80	1.10	.60				
c	Block of 4, #1795A-1798A		4.50	3.50	15.00	(12)		
Holiday Celebration: Christmas, Tagged, Perf. 11								
1799	15¢ Virgin and Child with Cherubim, by Gerard David	10/18/79	.30	.20	4.00	(12)	1.25	874
a	Imperf., pair		85.00					
b	Vertical pair, imperf. horizontally		600.00					
c	pair, imperf. between		1,100.00					
Holiday Celebration: Holiday, Tagged, Perf. 11								
1800	15¢ Santa Claus, Tree Ornament Christmas	10/18/79	.30	.20	4.00	(12)	1.25	932
a	Green and yellow omitted		500.00					
b	Green, yellow and tan omitted		500.00					
Performing Arts, Tagged, Perf. 11								
1801	15¢ Will Rogers and Rogers as a Cowboy Humorist	11/04/79	.30	.20	4.00	(12)	1.50	161
a	Imperf., pair		175.00					
Tagged, Perf. 11								
1802	15¢ Vietnam Veterans	11/11/79	.30	.20	3.25	(10)	3.25	173
Performing Arts, Tagged, Perf. 11								
1803	15¢ W.C. Fields and Fields as a Juggler	01/29/80	.30	.20	4.00	(12)	2.00	169
Black Heritage, Tagged, Perf. 11								
1804	15¢ Benjamin Banneker and Banneker as Surveyor	02/15/80	.35	.20	4.50	(12)	2.00	160
a	Horizontal pair, imperf. vertically		450.00					
Letter Writing, Tagged, Perf. 11								
1805	15¢ Letters Preserve Memories	02/25/80	.30	.20			1.00	39
1806	15¢ purple P.S. Write Soon	02/25/80	.30	.20			1.00	39
1807	15¢ Letters Lift Spirits	02/25/80	.30	.20			1.00	39
1808	15¢ green P.S. Write Soon	02/25/80	.30	.20			1.00	39
1809	15¢ Letters Shape Opinions	02/25/80	.30	.20			1.00	39
1810	15¢ red and blue P.S. Write Soon	02/25/80	.30	.20			1.00	39
a	Vertical Strip of 6, #1805-1810		1.85	2.00	13.00	(36)	2.50	
Americana, Coil, Perf. 10 Vertically								
1811	1¢ dark blue, greenish Inkwelll and Quill (1581)	03/06/80	.20	.20	.40	(2)	1.00	
a	Imperf., pair		165.00		260.00	(2)		
1812	Not assigned							
1813	3.5¢ Weaver Violins	06/23/80	.20	.20	1.00	(2)	1.00	
a	Untagged (Bureau precanceled)		.20	.20	1.95	(2)		
b	Imperf., pair		165.00		425.00	(2)		
1814-1815	Not assigned							
1816	12¢ red brown, *beige* Torch from Statue of Liberty (1594)	04/08/81	.25	.20	2.00	(2)	1.00	
a	Untagged (Bureau precanceled)		1.15	1.15	47.50	(2)		
b	Imperf., pair		165.00		300.00	(2)		
1817	Not assigned							

	Issue	Date	Un	U	PB/LP	#	FDC	Q(M)
	Tagged, Perf. 11 x 10.5							
1818	(18¢) "B" Stamp Eagle	03/15/81	.35	.20	1.60	(4)	1.25	
	Booklet, Perf. 10							
1819	(18¢) "B" Stamp (1818), single from booklet	03/15/81	.40	.20			1.00	
a	Booklet pane of 8	03/15/81	3.75	2.25			3.00	
	Coil, Perf. 10 Vertically							
1820	(18¢) "B" Stamp (1818)	03/15/81	.40	.20	1.60	(2)	1.00	
a	Imperf., pair		85.00		150.00	(2)		
	Tagged, Perf. 10.5 x 11							
1821	15¢ Frances Perkins	04/10/80	.30	.20	1.30	(4)	1.00	164
	Tagged, Perf. 11							
1822	15¢ Dolley Madison	05/20/80	.30	.20	1.40	(4)	1.00	257
1823	15¢ Emily Bissell	05/31/80	.35	.20	1.75	(4)	1.00	96
a	Vertical pair, imperf. horizontally		350.00					
1824	15¢ Helen Keller/Anne Sullivan	06/27/80	.30	.20	1.30	(4)	1.25	154
1825	15¢ Veterans Administration	07/21/80	.30	.20	1.30	(4)	1.50	160
a	Horizontal pair, imperf. vertically		425.00					
	American Bicentennial, Tagged, Perf. 11							
1826	15¢ General Bernardo de Galvez, Battle of Mobile	07/23/80	.30	.20	1.30	(4)	1.00	104
a	Red, brown and blue omitted		650.00					
b	Bl., brn., red and yel. omitted		1,150.00					
	Coral Reefs, Tagged, Perf. 11							
1827	15¢ Brain Coral, Beaugregory Fish	08/26/80	.30	.20			1.00	51
1828	15¢ Elkhorn Coral, Porkfish	08/26/80	.30	.20			1.00	51
1829	15¢ Chalice Coral, Moorish Idol	08/26/80	.30	.20			1.00	51
1830	15¢ Finger Coral, Sabertooth Blenny	08/26/80	.30	.20			1.00	51
a	Block of 4, #1827-1830		1.25	1.10	4.00	(12)	2.00	
b	As "a," imperf.		450.00					
c	As "a," imperf. between, vertically		—					
d	As "a," imperf. vertically		3,250.00					

	Issue	Date	Un	U	PB	#	FDC	Q(M)
	Tagged, Perf. 11							
1831	15¢ Organized Labor	09/01/80	.30	.20	3.50	(12)	1.00	167
a	Imperf., pair		300.00					
	Literary Arts, Tagged, Perf. 10.5 x 11							
1832	15¢ Edith Wharton Reading Letter	09/05/80	.30	.20	1.30	(4)	1.00	163
	Tagged, Perf. 11							
1833	15¢ Education	09/12/80	.30	.20	1.90	(6)	1.50	160
a	Horizontal pair, imperf. vertically		200.00					
	American Folk Art: Pacific Northwest Indian Masks, Tagged, Perf. 11							
1834	15¢ Heiltsuk, Bella Bella Tribe	09/25/80	.35	.20			1.00	38
1835	15¢ Chilkat Tlingit Tribe	09/25/80	.35	.20			1.00	38
1836	15¢ Tlingit Tribe	09/25/80	.35	.20			1.00	38
1837	15¢ Bella Coola Tribe	09/25/80	.35	.20			1.00	38
a	Block of 4, #1834-1837		1.50	1.25	5.00	(10)	2.00	
	American Architecture, Tagged, Perf. 11							
1838	15¢ Smithsonian Institution, by James Renwick	10/09/80	.30	.20			1.00	38
1839	15¢ Trinity Church, by Henry Hobson Richardson	10/09/80	.30	.20			1.00	38
1840	15¢ Pennsylvania Academy of Fine Arts, by Frank Furness	10/09/80	.30	.20			1.00	38
1841	15¢ Lyndhurst, by Alexander Jefferson Davis	10/09/80	.30	.20			1.00	38
a	Block of 4, #1838-1841		1.25	1.25	1.50	(4)	1.75	
b	As "a," red omitted on #1838,1839		375.00					
	Holiday Celebration: Christmas, Tagged, Perf. 11							
1842	15¢ Madonna and Child from Epiphany Window, Washington Cathedral	10/31/80	.30	.20	4.00	(12)	1.25	693
a	Imperf., pair		50.00					
	Pair with full vertical gutter between		—					
	Holiday Celebration: Holiday, Tagged, Perf. 11							
1843	15¢ Wreath and Toys	10/31/80	.30	.20	6.50	(20)	1.25	719
a	Imperf., pair		65.00					
b	Buff omitted		22.50					
c	Vertical pair, imperf. horizontally		—					
d	Horizontal pair, imperf. between		3,750.00					

1818

Frances Perkins
USA 15c

1821

1822

Emily Bissell
Crusader Against Tuberculosis
USA 15c

1823

HELEN KELLER
ANNE SULLIVAN

1824

Veterans Administration
Fifty Years of Service
USA 15c

1825

Gen. Bernardo de Gálvez
Battle of Mobile 1780

1826

1827   1828

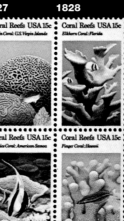

1829   1830   1830a

Organized Labor
Proud and Free
USA 15c

1831

Edith Wharton
USA 15c

1832

Edited by Josef Albers USA 15c
Learning never ends

1833

1834   1835

Heiltsuk, Bella Bella
Indian Art USA 15c

Chilkat Tlingit
Indian Art USA 15c

Tlingit
Indian Art USA 15c

Bella Coola
Indian Art USA 15c

1836   1837   1837a

1838   1839

Renwick 1818-1895 Smithsonian Washington
Architecture USA 15c

Richardson 1838-1886 Trinity Church Boston
Architecture USA 15c

Furness 1839-1912 Penn Academy Philadelphia
Architecture USA 15c

A.J. Davis 1803-1892 Lyndhurst Tarrytown NY
Architecture USA 15c

1840   1841   1841a

Christmas USA 15c

1842

USA 15c
Season's Greetings

1843

VISIT US ONLINE AT **THE POSTAL STORE**
AT **WWW.USPS.COM**
OR CALL **1 800 STAMP-24**

Dorothea Dix USA 1c
1844

Igor Stravinsky USA 2c
1845

Henry Clay USA 3c
1846

Carl Schurz 4c USA
1847

Pearl Buck USA 5c
1848

Walter Lippmann 6 USA
1849

Abraham Baldwin 7 USA
1850

Henry Knox USA 8
1851

Sylvanus Thayer USA 9
1852

Richard Russell USA 10c
1853

Alden Partridge USA 11
1854

USA 13c Crazy Horse
1855

Sinclair Lewis USA 14
1856

Rachel Carson USA 17c
1857

George Mason USA 18c
1858

USA 19c Sequoyah
1859

Ralph Bunche USA 20c
1860

Thomas H. Gallaudet USA 20c
1861

Harry S. Truman USA 20c
1862

John J. Audubon USA 22
1863

Frank C. Laubach USA 30c
1864

Charles R Drew MD USA 35c
1865

Robert Millikan 37c USA
1866

Grenville Clark USA 39
1867

Lillian M. Gilbreth USA 40c
1868

USA 50 Chester W. Nimitz
1869

USA 15c Everett Dirksen
1874

Whitney Moore Young Black Heritage USA 15c
1875

1876 **1877**

Rose USA 18c
1878

Camellia USA 18c
1879

Dahlia USA 18c

Lily USA 18c
1879a

1880 **1881**

USA 18c
1882 **1883**

USA 18c
1884 **1885**

USA 18c
1886 **1887**

USA 18c
1888 **1889**

USA 18c USA 18c
1889a

USA 18c ...for amber waves of grain

USA 18c ...from sea to shining sea

	Issue	Date	Un	U	PB	#	FDC	Q(M)
	Great Americans, Tagged, Perf. 11 x 10.5							
1844	1¢ Dorothea Dix	09/23/83	.20	.20	.35	(6)	1.00	
a	Imperf., pair		350.00					
b	Vertical pair, imperf. between		1,900.00					
c	Perf. 10.9, small or large block tagging		.20	.20	.35	(6)		
1845	2¢ Igor Stravinsky	11/18/82	.20	.20	.35	(4)	1.00	
a	Tagging omitted		150.00					
1846	3¢ Henry Clay	07/13/83	.20	.20	.55	(4)	1.00	
a	Tagging omitted		5.00					
1847	4¢ Carl Schurz	06/03/83	.20	.20	.65	(4)	1.00	
a	Tagging omitted		5.00					
1848	5¢ Pearl Buck	06/25/83	.30	.20	1.50	(4)	1.00	
	Great Americans, Tagged, Perf. 11							
1849	6¢ Walter Lippman	09/19/85	.20	.20	.85	(6)	1.00	
a	Vertical pair, imperf. between		1,900.00					
1850	7¢ Abraham Baldwin	01/25/85	.20	.20	.95	(6)	1.00	
1851	8¢ Henry Knox	07/25/85	.20	.20	.85	(4)	1.00	
1852	9¢ Sylvanus Thayer	06/07/85	.20	.20	1.30	(6)	1.25	
1853	10¢ Richard Russell	05/31/84	.25	.20	2.00	(6)	1.00	
a	Large block tagging		.30	.20	2.25	(6)		
b	Vertical pair, imperf. between and at bottom		750.00					
c	Horizontal pair, imperf. between		1,850.00					
1854	11¢ Alden Partridge	02/12/85	.40	.20	2.00	(4)	1.25	
a	Tagging omitted		35.00					
	Great Americans, Tagged, Perf. 11 x 10.5							
1855	13¢ Crazy Horse	01/15/82	.40	.20	2.25	(4)	1.50	
a	Tagging omitted		7.50					
	Great Americans, Tagged, Perf. 11							
1856	14¢ Sinclair Lewis	03/21/85	.30	.20	2.25	(6)	1.00	
a	Large block tagging		.30	.20	2.25	(6)		
b	Vertical pair, imperf. horizontally		110.00					
c	Horizontal pair, imperf. between		9.00					
d	Vertical pair, imperf. between		1,650.00					
	Great Americans, Tagged, Perf. 11 x 10.5							
1857	17¢ Rachel Carson	05/28/81	.35	.20	2.00	(4)	1.00	
a	Tagging omitted		17.50					
1858	18¢ George Mason	05/07/81	.35	.20	3.00	(4)	1.00	
a	Tagging omitted		6.50					
1859	19¢ Sequoyah	12/27/80	.45	.20	2.75	(4)	1.25	
1860	20¢ Ralph Bunche	01/12/82	.40	.20	3.75	(4)	1.75	
a	Tagging omitted		7.50					
1861	20¢ Thomas H. Gallaudet	06/10/83	.50	.20	4.00	(4)	1.25	
	Great Americans, Tagged, Perf. 11							
1862	20¢ Harry S. Truman	01/26/84	.40	.20	4.50	(6)	1.25	
a	Perf. 11.2, large block tagging, dull gum		.40	.20	3.00	(4)		
b	Perf. 11.2, overall tagging, dull gum		.40	—	3.75	(4)		
c	Perf. 11.2, tagging omitted		11.50					
1863	22¢ John J. Audubon	04/23/85	.75	.20	9.00	(6)	1.25	
a	Large block tagging		1.00	.20	12.50	(6)		
b	Perf. 11.2, large block tagging		.65	.20	7.00	(4)		
c	Tagging omitted		7.50					
d	Vertical pair, imperf. horizontally		1,900.00					
1864	30¢ Frank C. Laubach	09/02/84	.60	.20	3.50	(6)	1.25	
a	Perf. 11.2, large block tagging		.55	.20	3.25	(4)		
b	Perf. 11.2, overall tagging		2.00	.20	25.00	(4)		
	Great Americans, Tagged, Perf. 11 x 10.5							
1865	35¢ Charles R. Drew, MD	06/03/81	.75	.20	4.25	(4)	1.75	
1866	37¢ Robert Millikan	01/26/82	.80	.20	3.75	(4)	1.25	
a	Tagging omitted		12.50					

	Issue	Date	Un	U	PB	#	FDC	Q(M)
	Great Americans, Tagged, Perf. 11							
1867	39¢ Grenville Clark	03/20/85	.90	.20	5.75	(6)	1.25	
a	Vertical pair, imperf. horizontally		500.00					
b	Vertical pair, imperf. between		1,850.00					
c	Perf. 10.9, large block tagging		.90	.20	5.75	(6)		
d	Perf. 11.2, large block tagging		.90	.20	7.00	(4)		
1868	40¢ Lillian M. Gilbreth	02/24/84	.90	.20	6.50	(6)	1.50	
a	Perf. 11.2, large block tagging		.90	.20	6.50	(4)		
1869	50¢ Chester W. Nimitz	02/22/85	.95	.20	7.50	(4)	2.00	
a	Perf. 11.2, large block tagging, dull gum		.95	.20	6.25	(4)		
b	Tagging omitted		11.00					
c	Perf. 11.2, tagging omitted, dull gum		9.00					
d	Perf. 11.2, overall tagging, dull gum		2.50	.20	11.00	(4)		
e	Perf. 11.2, prephosphored uncoated paper, shiny gum		.90	.20	5.00	(4)		
1870-1873	Not assigned							
	Tagged, Perf. 11							
1874	15¢ Everett Dirksen	01/04/81	.30	.20	1.40	(4)	1.00	160
a	All color omitted		500.00					
	Black Heritage, Tagged, Perf. 11							
1875	15¢ Whitney Moore Young at Desk	01/30/81	.35	.20	1.75	(4)	1.75	160
	Flower, Tagged, Perf. 11							
1876	18¢ Rose	04/23/81	.35	.20			1.00	53
1877	18¢ Camellia	04/23/81	.35	.20			1.00	53
1878	18¢ Dahlia	04/23/81	.35	.20			1.00	53
1879	18¢ Lily	04/23/81	.35	.20			1.00	53
a	Block of 4, #1876-1879		1.40	1.25	1.75	(4)	2.50	
	American Wildlife, Tagged, Perf. 11							
1880	18¢ Bighorn Sheep	05/14/81	.80	.20			1.00	
1881	18¢ Puma	05/14/81	.80	.20			1.00	
1882	18¢ Harbor Seal	05/14/81	.80	.20			1.00	
1883	18¢ Buffalo	05/14/81	.80	.20			1.00	
1884	18¢ Brown Bear	05/14/81	.80	.20			1.00	
1885	18¢ Polar Bear	05/14/81	.80	.20			1.00	
1886	18¢ Elk (Wapiti)	05/14/81	.80	.20			1.00	
1887	18¢ Moose	05/14/81	.80	.20			1.00	
1888	18¢ White-Tailed Deer	05/14/81	.80	.20			1.00	
1889	18¢ Pronghorn Antelope	05/14/81	.80	.20			1.00	
a	Booklet pane of 10, #1880-1889		8.50	6.00			5.00	

#1880-1889 issued only in booklets. All stamps are imperf. at one side or imperf. at one side and bottom.

	Issue	Date	Un	U	PB	#	FDC	Q(M)
	Flag and Anthem, Tagged, Perf. 11							
1890	18¢ "…for amber waves of grain"	04/24/81	.35	.20	2.25	(6)	1.00	
a	Imperf., pair		90.00					
b	Vertical pair, imperf. horizontally		700.00					
	Flag and Anthem, Coil, Perf. 10 Vertically							
1891	18¢ "…from sea to shining sea"	04/24/81	.35	.20	4.00	(3)	1.50	
a	Imperf., pair		20.00	—				
b	Pair imperf., between		1,150.00					

Beginning with #1891, all coil stamps except 1947 feature a small plate number at the bottom of the design at varying intervals in a roll, depending on the press used. The basic "plate number coil" (PNC) collecting unit is a strip of three stamps, with the plate number appearing on the middle stamp. PNC values are for the most common plate number.

	Issue	Date	Un	U	PB/LP	#	FDC	Q(M)
	Flag and Anthem, Booklet, Perf. 11							
1892	6¢ USA Circle of Stars, single from booklet (1893a)	04/24/81	.50	.20			1.00	
1893	18¢ "...for purple mountain majesties," single from booklet (1893a)	04/24/81	.30	.20			1.00	
a	Booklet pane of 8 (2 #1892 & 6 #1893)		3.00	2.50			2.50	
b	As "a," imperf. vertically between		*70.00*					
c	Se-tenant pair, #1892 and #1893		.90	1.00				
	#1892-93 issued only in booklets. All stamps are imperf. at one side or imperf. at one side and bottom.							
	Tagged, Perf. 11							
1894	20¢ Flag Over Supreme Court	12/17/81	.40	.20	2.75	(6)	1.00	
a	Imperf., pair		*32.50*					
b	Vertical pair, imperf. horizontally		*450.00*					
c	Dark blue omitted		*70.00*					
d	Black omitted		*275.00*					
e	Perf. 11.2, shiny gum		.35	.20	2.50	(6)		
	Coil, Perf. 10 Vertically							
1895	20¢ Flag Over Supreme Court (1894)	12/17/81	.40	.20	2.00	(3)	1.00	
a	Narrow block tagging		.40	.20	6.00	(3)		
b	Untagged (Bureau precanceled)		.50	.50	32.50	(3)		
c	Tagging omitted		*15.00*					
d	Imperf., pair		*8.50*	—				
e	Pair, imperf. between		*800.00*	—				
f	Black omitted		*45.00*	—				
g	Blue omitted		*1,350.00*	—				
	Booklet, Perf. 11 x 10.5							
1896	20¢ Flag over Supreme Court (1894), single from booklet	12/17/81	.40	.20			1.00	
a	Booklet pane of 6	12/17/81	3.00	2.25			6.00	
b	Booklet pane of 10	06/01/82	5.25	3.25			*10.00*	
	Transportation, Coil, Tagged, Perf. 10 Vertically							
1897	1¢ Omnibus 1880s	08/19/83	.20	.20	.30	(3)	1.00	
b	Imperf., pair		*550.00*				—	
1897A	2¢ Locomotive 1870s	05/20/82	.20	.20	.45	(3)	1.50	
c	Imperf., pair		*45.00*				—	
1898	3¢ Handcar 1880s	03/25/83	.20	.20	.50	(3)	1.00	
1898A	4¢ Stagecoach 1890s	08/19/82	.20	.20	.50	(3)	1.00	
b	Untagged (Bureau precanceled)		.20	.20	3.25	(3)		
c	As "b," imperf., pair		*700.00*					
d	Imperf., pair		*750.00*				—	
1899	5¢ Motorcycle 1913	10/10/83	.20	.20	.50	(3)	2.00	
a	Imperf., pair		*2,500.00*					
1900	5.2¢ Sleigh 1880s	03/21/83	.20	.20	2.00	(3)	1.00	
a	Untagged (Bureau precanceled)		.20	.20	6.50	(3)		
1901	5.9¢ Bicycle 1870s	02/17/82	.25	.20	2.50	(3)	1.50	
a	Untagged (Bureau precanceled)		.20	.20	15.00	(3)		
b	As "a," imperf., pair		*150.00*				—	(2)
1902	7.4¢ Baby Buggy 1880s	04/07/84	.20	.20	3.50	(3)	1.00	
a	Untagged (Bureau precanceled)		.20	.20	3.50	(3)		
1903	9.3¢ Mail Wagon 1880s	12/15/81	.30	.20	2.50	(3)	1.00	
a	Untagged (Bureau precanceled)		.25	.25	8.50	(3)		
b	As "a," imperf., pair		*100.00*		175.00	(2)		

	Issue	Date	Un	U	PB	#	FDC	Q(M)
	Transportation, Coil, Tagged, Perf. 10 Vertically continued							
1904	10.9¢ Hansom Cab 1890s	03/26/82	.30	.20	6.00	(3)	1.00	
a	Untagged (Bureau precanceled)		.30	.25	11.00	(3)		
b	As "a," imperf., pair		*140.00*			(2)		
1905	11¢ RR Caboose 1890s	02/03/84	.30	.20	1.60	(3)	1.50	
a	Untagged (Bureau precanceled)		.25	.20	1.60	(3)		
1906	17¢ Electric Auto 1917	06/25/81	.35	.20	1.40	(3)	1.00	
a	Untagged (Bureau precanceled)		.35	.35	6.00	(3)		
b	Imperf., pair		*140.00*				—	
c	As "a," imperf., pair		*550.00*				—	(2)
1907	18¢ Surrey 1890s	05/18/81	.35	.20	17.00	(3)	1.00	
a	Imperf., pair		*110.00*				—	
1908	20¢ Fire Pumper 1860s	12/10/81	.35	.20	20.00	(3)	2.00	
a	Imperf., pair		*90.00*		275.00	(2)		
	Values for plate # coil strips of 3 stamps for #1897-1908 are for the most common plate numbers. Other plate #s and strips of 5 stamps may have higher values.							
	Booklet, Tagged, Perf. 10 Vertically							
1909	$9.35 Eagle and Moon, single from booklet	08/12/83	20.00	15.00			50.00	
a	Booklet pane of 3		60.00	—			*125.00*	
	#1909 issued only in booklets. All stamps are imperf. at top and bottom or imperf. at top, bottom and right side.							
	Tagged, Perf. 10.5 x 11							
1910	18¢ American Red Cross	05/01/81	.35	.20	1.50	(4)	1.75	165
	Tagged, Perf. 11							
1911	18¢ Savings and Loans	05/08/81	.35	.20	1.50	(4)	1.00	107
	Space, Tagged, Perf. 11							
1912	18¢ Exploring the Moon — Moon Walk	05/21/81	.40	.20			1.00	42
1913	18¢ Benefiting Mankind (upper left) Columbia Space Shuttle	05/21/81	.40	.20			1.00	42
1914	18¢ Benefiting Mankind— Space Shuttle Deploying Satellite	05/21/81	.40	.20			1.00	42
1915	18¢ Understanding the Sun— Skylab	05/21/81	.40	.20			1.00	42
1916	18¢ Probing the Planets— Pioneer 11	05/21/81	.40	.20			1.00	42
1917	18¢ Benefiting Mankind— Columbia Space Shuttle Lifting Off	05/21/81	.40	.20			1.00	42
1918	18¢ Benefiting Mankind— Space Shuttle Preparing to Land	05/21/81	.40	.20			1.00	42
1919	18¢ Comprehending the Universe — Telescope	05/21/81	.40	.20			1.00	42
a	Block of 8, #1912-1919		3.25	3.00	3.75	(8)	3.00	
b	As "a," imperf.		*7,500.00*					
	Tagged, Perf. 11							
1920	18¢ Professional Management	06/18/81	.35	.20	1.50	(4)	1.00	99
	Preservation of Wildlife Habitats, Tagged, Perf. 11							
1921	18¢ Save Wetland Habitats— Great Blue Heron	06/26/81	.35	.20			1.00	45
1922	18¢ Save Grassland Habitats— Badger	06/26/81	.35	.20			1.00	45
1923	18¢ Save Mountain Habitats— Grizzly Bear	06/26/81	.35	.20			1.00	45
1924	18¢ Save Woodland Habitats— Ruffled Grouse	06/26/81	.35	.20			1.00	45
a	Block of 4, #1921-1924		1.50	1.25	2.00	(4)	2.50	

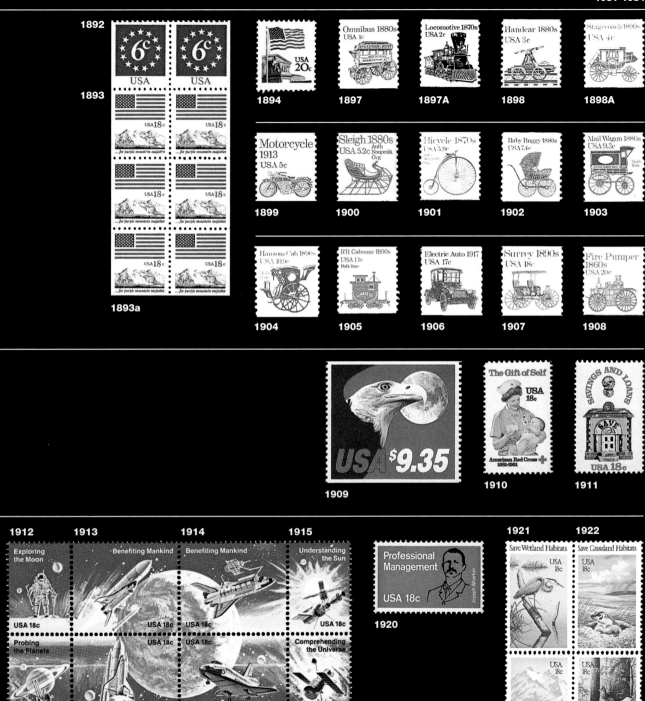

1892

1893

1893a

1894

1897

1897A

1898

1898A

1899

1900

1901

1902

1903

1904

1905

1906

1907

1908

1909

1910

1911

1912   1913   1914   1915

1916   1917   1918   1919   1919a

1920

1921   1922

1923   1924   1924a

1925

1926

1927

1928  **1929**

1930 **1931**

1931a

1932

1933

1934

1935

1936

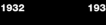

1937   **1938**   **1938a**

1939

1940

1941

1942   **1943**   **1945**

1944   **1945a**

1946

1949

1950

1951

1952

	Issue	Date	Un	U	PB	#	FDC	Q(M)
	Tagged, Perf. 11							
1925	18¢ International Year of the Disabled	06/29/81	.35	.20	1.50	(4)	1.00	100
a	Vertical pair, imperf. horizontally		2,500.00					
1926	18¢ Edna St. Vincent Millay	07/10/81	.35	.20	1.50	(4)	1.00	100
a	Black omitted		275.00	—				
1927	18¢ Alcoholism	08/19/81	.45	.20	10.00	(6)	3.00	98
a	Imperf., pair		375.00					
b	Vertical pair, imperf. horizontally		2,400.00					
	American Architecture, Tagged, Perf. 11							
1928	18¢ NYU Library, by Sanford White	08/28/81	.40	.20			1.00	42
1929	18¢ Biltmore House, by Richard Morris Hunt	08/28/81	.40	.20			1.00	42
1930	18¢ Palace of the Arts, by Bernard Maybeck	08/28/81	.40	.20			1.00	42
1931	18¢ National Farmer's Bank, by Louis Sullivan	08/28/81	.40	.20			1.00	42
a	Block of 4, #1928-1931		1.65	1.65	2.10	(4)	2.50	
	American Sports Personalities, Tagged, Perf. 10.5 x 11							
1932	18¢ Babe Zaharias	09/22/81	.40	.20	3.00	(4)	6.50	102
1933	18¢ Bobby Jones	09/22/81	.60	.20	3.25	(4)	12.50	99
	Tagged, Perf. 11							
1934	18¢ Frederic Remington	10/09/81	.35	.20	1.60	(4)	1.25	101
a	Vertical pair, imperf. between		225.00					
b	Brown omitted		375.00					
1935	18¢ James Hoban	10/13/81	.35	.20	1.60	(4)	1.00	101
1936	20¢ James Hoban	10/13/81	.35	.20	1.65	(4)	1.00	167
	American Bicentennial, Tagged, Perf. 11							
1937	18¢ Battle of Yorktown 1781	10/16/81	.35	.20			1.00	81
1938	18¢ Battle of the Virginia Capes 1781	10/16/81	.35	.20			1.00	81
a	Attached pair, #1937-1938		.90	.75	2.00	(4)	1.50	
b	As "a," black omitted		350.00					
	Holiday Celebration: Christmas, Tagged, Perf. 11							
1939	20¢ Madonna and Child, by Botticelli	10/28/81	.40	.20	1.75	(4)	1.00	598
a	Imperf., pair		100.00					
b	Vertical pair, imperf. horizontally		1,150.00					
	Holiday Celebration: Holiday, Tagged, Perf. 11							
1940	20¢ Felt Bear on Sleigh	10/28/81	.40	.20	1.75	(4)	1.00	793
a	Imperf., pair		200.00					
b	Vertical pair, imperf. horizontally		2,750.00					

	Issue	Date	Un	U	PB/LP	#	FDC	Q(M)
	American Bicentennial, Tagged, Perf. 11							
1941	20¢ John Hanson	11/05/81	.40	.20	1.75	(4)	1.00	167
	Desert Plants, Tagged, Perf. 11							
1942	20¢ Barrel Cactus	12/11/81	.35	.20			1.00	48
1943	20¢ Agave	12/11/81	.35	.20			1.00	48
1944	20¢ Beavertail Cactus	12/11/81	.35	.20			1.00	48
1945	20¢ Saguaro	12/11/81	.35	.20			1.00	48
a	Block of 4, #1942-1945		1.50	1.25	1.90	(4)	2.50	
b	As "a," deep brown omitted		4,250.00					
c	#1945 vertical pair, imperf.		3,500.00					
	Tagged, Perf. 11 x 10.5							
1946	(20¢) "C" brown Eagle	10/11/81	.40	.20	2.00	(4)	1.00	
a	Tagging omitted		7.00					
	Coil, Perf. 10 Vertically							
1947	(20¢) "C" brown Eagle (1946)	10/11/81	.60	.20	1.50	(2)	1.00	
a	Imperf., pair		950.00			—		
	Booklet, Perf. 11							
1948	(20¢) "C" brown Eagle (1946), single from booklet	10/11/81	.40	.20			1.00	
a	Booklet pane of 10	10/11/81	4.50	3.25			3.50	
	Booklet, Tagged, Perf. 11							
1949	20¢ Bighorn Sheep, single from booklet	01/08/82	.55	.20			1.25	
a	Booklet pane of 10		5.50	2.50			6.00	
b	As "a," imperf. between		95.00					
c	Type II		1.40	.20				
d	Type II, booklet pane of 10		14.00	—				
e	As #1949, tagging omitted		5.00	—				
f	As "e," booklet pane of 10		50.00	—				
	#1949 issued only in booklets. All stamps are imperf. at one side or imperf. at one side and bottom.							
	Tagged, Perf. 11							
1950	20¢ Franklin D. Roosevelt	01/30/82	.40	.20	1.75	(4)	1.00	164
	Love, Tagged, Perf. 11.25							
1951	20¢ Love	02/01/82	.40	.20	1.75	(4)	1.00	447
b	Imperf., pair		250.00					
c	Blue omitted		200.00					
d	Yellow omitted		950.00					
e	Purple omitted		—					
1951A	Perf. 11.25 x 10.5		.75	.25	3.50	(4)		
	American Bicentennial, Tagged, Perf. 11							
1952	20¢ George Washington	02/22/82	.40	.20	1.75	(4)	1.25	181

Issue		Date	Un	U	PB #	FDC	Q(M)
State Birds & Flowers, Tagged, Perf. 10.5 x 11.25							
1953	20¢ Alabama: Yellowhammer and Camellia	04/14/82	.55	.30		1.25	13
1953A	Perf. 11.25 x 11		.65	.30			
1954	20¢ Alaska: Willow Ptarmigan and Forget-Me-Not	04/14/82	.55	.30		1.25	13
1954A	Perf. 11.25 x 11		.65	.30			
1955	20¢ Arizona: Cactus Wren and Saguaro Cactus Blossom	04/14/82	.55	.30		1.25	13
1955A	Perf. 11.25 x 11		.65	.30			
1956	20¢ Arkansas: Mockingbird and Apple Blossom	04/14/82	.55	.30		1.25	13
1956A	Perf. 11.25 x 11		.65	.30			
1957	20¢ California: California Quail and California Poppy	04/14/82	.55	.30		1.25	13
1957A	Perf. 11.25 x 11		.65	.30			
1958	20¢ Colorado: Lark Bunting and Rocky Mountain Columbine	04/14/82	.55	.30		1.25	13
1958A	Perf. 11.25 x 11		.65	.30			
1959	20¢ Connecticut: Robin and Mountain Laurel	04/14/82	.55	.30		1.25	13
1959A	Perf. 11.25 x 11		.65	.30			
1960	20¢ Delaware: Blue Hen Chicken and Peach Blossom	04/14/82	.55	.30		1.25	13
1960A	Perf. 11.25 x 11		.65	.30			
1961	20¢ Florida: Mockingbird and Orange Blossom	04/14/82	.55	.30		1.25	13
1961A	Perf. 11.25 x 11		.65	.30			
1962	20¢ Georgia: Brown Thrasher and Cherokee Rose	04/14/82	.55	.30		1.25	13
1962A	Perf. 11.25 x 11		.65	.30			
1963	20¢ Hawaii: Hawaiian Goose and Hibiscus	04/14/82	.55	.30		1.25	13
1963A	Perf. 11.25 x 11		.65	.30			
1964	20¢ Idaho: Mountain Bluebird and Syringa	04/14/82	.55	.30		1.25	13
1964A	Perf. 11.25 x 11		.65	.30			

Issue		Date	Un	U	PB #	FDC	Q(M)
State Birds & Flowers Tagged, Perf. 10.5 x 11.25 continued							
1965	20¢ Illinois: Cardinal and Violet	04/14/82	.55	.30		1.25	13
1965A	Perf. 11.25 x 11		.65	.30			
1966	20¢ Indiana: Cardinal and Peony	04/14/82	.55	.30		1.25	13
1966A	Perf. 11.25 x 11		.65	.30			
1967	20¢ Iowa: Eastern Goldfinch and Wild Rose	04/14/82	.55	.30		1.25	13
1967A	Perf. 11.25 x 11		.65	.30			
1968	20¢ Kansas: Western Meadowlark and Sunflower	04/14/82	.55	.30		1.25	13
1968A	Perf. 11.25 x 11		.65	.30			
1969	20¢ Kentucky: Cardinal and Goldenrod	04/14/82	.55	.30		1.25	13
1969A	Perf. 11.25 x 11		.65	.30			
1970	20¢ Louisiana: Brown Pelican and Magnolia	04/14/82	.55	.30		1.25	13
1970A	Perf. 11.25 x 11		.65	.30			
1971	20¢ Maine: Chickadee and White Pine Cone and Tassel	04/14/82	.55	.30		1.25	13
1971A	Perf. 11.25 x 11		.65	.30			
1972	20¢ Maryland: Baltimore Oriole and Black-Eyed Susan	04/14/82	.55	.30		1.25	13
1972A	Perf. 11.25 x 11		.65	.30			
1973	20¢ Massachusetts: Black-Capped Chickadee and Mayflower	04/14/82	.55	.30		1.25	13
1973A	Perf. 11.25 x 11		.65	.30			
1974	20¢ Michigan: Robin and Apple Blossom	04/14/82	.55	.30		1.25	13
1974A	Perf. 11.25 x 11		.65	.30			
1975	20¢ Minnesota: Common Loon and Showy Lady Slipper	04/14/82	.55	.30		1.25	13
1975A	Perf. 11.25 x 11		.65	.30			
1976	20¢ Mississippi: Mockingbird and Magnolia	04/14/82	.55	.30		1.25	13
1976A	Perf. 11.25 x 11		.65	.30			
1977	20¢ Missouri: Eastern Bluebird and Red Hawthorn	04/14/82	.55	.30		1.25	13
1977A	Perf. 11.25 x 11		.65	.30			

1982

1982

| Montana USA 20c | Nebraska USA 20c | Nevada USA 20c | New Hampshire USA 20c | New Jersey USA 20c |

Western Meadowlark & Bitterroot — *Western Meadowlark & Goldenrod* — *Mountain Bluebird & Sagebrush* — *Purple Finch & Lilac* — *American Goldfinch & Violet*

1978 **1979** **1980** **1981** **1982**

| New Mexico USA 20c | New York USA 20c | North Carolina USA 20c | North Dakota USA 20c | Ohio USA 20c |

Roadrunner & Yucca Flower — *Eastern Bluebird & Rose* — *Cardinal & Flowering Dogwood* — *Western Meadowlark & Wild Prairie Rose* — *Cardinal & Red Carnation*

1983 **1984** **1985** **1986** **1987**

| Oklahoma USA 20c | Oregon USA 20c | Pennsylvania USA 20c | Rhode Island USA 20c | South Carolina USA 20c |

Scissor-tailed Flycatcher & Mistletoe — *Western Meadowlark & Oregon Grape* — *Ruffed Grouse & Mountain Laurel* — *Rhode Island Red & Violet* — *Carolina Wren & Carolina Jessamine*

1988 **1989** **1990** **1991** **1992**

| South Dakota USA 20c | Tennessee USA 20c | Texas USA 20c | Utah USA 20c | Vermont USA 20c |

Ring-Necked Pheasant & Pasqueflower — *Mockingbird & Iris* — *Mockingbird & Bluebonnet* — *California Gull & Sego Lily* — *Hermit Thrush & Red Clover*

1993 **1994** **1995** **1996** **1997**

| Virginia USA 20c | Washington USA 20c | West Virginia USA 20c | Wisconsin USA 20c | Wyoming USA 20c |

Cardinal & Flowering Dogwood — *American Goldfinch & Rhododendron* — *Cardinal & Rhododendron Maximum* — *Robin & Wood Violet* — *Western Meadowlark & Indian Paintbrush*

1998 **1999** **2000** **2001** **2002**

Issue	Date	Un	U	PB #	FDC	Q(M)
State Birds & Flowers Tagged, Perf. 10.5 x 11.25 continued						
1978 20¢ Montana: Western Meadowlark & Bitterroot	04/14/82	.55	.30		1.25	13
1978A Perf. 11.25 x 11		.65	.30			
1979 20¢ Nebraska: Western Meadowlark & Goldenrod	04/14/82	.55	.30		1.25	13
1979A Perf. 11.25 x 11		.65	.30			
1980 20¢ Nevada: Mountain Bluebird & Sagebrush	04/14/82	.55	.30		1.25	13
1980A Perf. 11.25 x 11		.65	.30			
1981 20¢ New Hampshire: Purple Finch & Lilac	04/14/82	.55	.30		1.25	13
b Black omitted		6,000.00				
1981A Perf. 11.25 x 11		.65	.30			
1982 20¢ New Jersey: American Goldfinch & Violet	04/14/82	.55	.30		1.25	13
1982A Perf. 11.25 x 11		.65	.30			
1983 20¢ New Mexico: Roadrunner & Yucca Flower	04/14/82	.55	.30		1.25	13
1983A Perf. 11.25 x 11		.65	.30			
1984 20¢ New York: Eastern Bluebird & Rose	04/14/82	.55	.30		1.25	13
1984A Perf. 11.25 x 11		.65	.30			
1985 20¢ North Carolina: Cardinal & Flowering Dogwood	04/14/82	.55	.30		1.25	13
1985A Perf. 11.25 x 11		.65	.30			
1986 20¢ North Dakota: Western Meadowlark & Wild Prairie Rose	04/14/82	.55	.30		1.25	13
1986A Perf. 11.25 x 11		.65	.30			
1987 20¢ Ohio: Cardinal & Red Carnation	04/14/82	.55	.30		1.25	13
1987A Perf. 11.25 x 11		.65	.30			
1988 20¢ Oklahoma: Scissor-tailed Flycatcher & Mistletoe	04/14/82	.55	.30		1.25	13
1980A Perf. 11.25 x 11		.65	.30			
1989 20¢ Oregon: Western Meadowlark & Oregon Grape	04/14/82	.55	.30		1.25	13
1989A Perf. 11.25 x 11		.65	.30			
1990 20¢ Pennsylvania: Ruffed Grouse & Mountain Laurel	04/14/82	.55	.30		1.25	13
1990A Perf. 11.25 x 11		.65	.30			

Issue	Date	Un	U	PB #	FDC	Q(M)
State Birds & Flowers Tagged, Perf. 10.5 x 11.25 continued						
1991 20¢ Rhode Island: Rhode Island Red & Violet	04/14/82	.55	.30		1.25	13
b Black omitted		6,000.00				
1991A Perf. 11.25 x 11		.65	.30			
1992 20¢ South Carolina: Carolina Wren & Carolina Jessamine	04/14/82	.55	.30		1.25	13
1992A Perf. 11.25 x 11		.65	.30			
1993 20¢ South Dakota: Ring-Necked Pheasant & Pasqueflower	04/14/82	.55	.30		1.25	13
1993A Perf. 11.25 x 11		.65	.30			
1994 20¢ Tennessee: Mockingbird & Iris	04/14/82	.55	.30		1.25	13
1994A Perf. 11.25 x 11		.65	.30			
1995 20¢ Texas: Mockingbird & Bluebonnet	04/14/82	.55	.30		1.25	13
1995A Perf. 11.25 x 11		.65	.30			
1996 20¢ Utah: California Gull & Sego Lily	04/14/82	.55	.30		1.25	13
1996A Perf. 11.25 x 11		.65	.30			
1997 20¢ Vermont: Hermit Thrush & Red Clover	04/14/82	.55	.30		1.25	13
1997A Perf. 11.25 x 11		.65	.30			
1998 20¢ Virginia: Cardinal & Flowering Dogwood	04/14/82	.55	.30		1.25	13
1998A Perf. 11.25 x 11		.65	.30			
1999 20¢ Washington: American Goldfinch & Rhododendron	04/14/82	.55	.30		1.25	13
1999A Perf. 11.25 x 11		.65	.30			
2000 20¢ West Virginia: Cardinal & Rhododendron Maximum	04/14/82	.55	.30		1.25	13
2000A Perf. 11.25 x 11		.65	.30			
2001 20¢ Wisconsin: Robin & Wood Violet	04/14/82	.55	.30		1.25	13
b Black omitted		6,000.00				
2001A Perf. 11.25 x 11		.65	.30			
2002 20¢ Wyoming: Western Meadowlark & Indian Paintbrush	04/14/82	.55	.30		1.25	13
b Pane of 50		27.50	20.00		30.00	
d Pane of 50, imperf.		27,500.00				
2002A Perf. 11.25 x 11		.65	.30			

Charles W. Chesnutt Cultural Diary Page, Maxi Card and Pane of 20 Stamps

The 31st stamp in the *Black Heritage* series pays tribute to Charles W. Chesnutt, a pioneering writer whose work addressed a broad range of African-American experience during the post-Civil War period.

Cultural Diary Page, Maxi Card and Pane of 20.
Item #462876 $13.95

To order call **1 800 STAMP-24** or visit us online at **www.usps.com**

	Issue	Date	Un	U	PB/LP	#	FDC	Q(M)
	Tagged, Perf. 11							
2003	20¢ USA/ The Netherlands	04/20/82	.40	.20	3.50	(6)	1.00	109
a	Imperf., pair		275.00					
2004	20¢ Library of Congress	04/21/82	.40	.20	1.75	(4)	1.00	113
	Coil, Tagged, Perf. 10 Vertically							
2005	20¢ Consumer Education	04/27/82	.55	.20	10.00	(3)	1.00	
a	Imperf., pair		95.00		375.00	(2)		
b	Tagging omitted		7.50					

Value for plate no. coil strip of 3 stamps is for most common plate nos. Other plate nos. and strips of 5 stamps may have higher values.

	Issue	Date	Un	U	PB/LP	#	FDC	Q(M)
	Knoxville World's Fair, Tagged, Perf. 11							
2006	20¢ Solar Energy	04/29/82	.45	.20			1.00	31
2007	20¢ Synthetic Fuels	04/29/82	.45	.20			1.00	31
2008	20¢ Breeder Reactor	04/29/82	.45	.20			1.00	31
2009	20¢ Fossil Fuels	04/29/82	.45	.20			1.00	31
a	Block of 4, #2006-2009		1.80	1.50	2.40	(4)	2.50	
	Tagged, Perf. 11							
2010	20¢ Horatio Alger	04/30/82	.40	.20	1.75	(4)	1.00	108
2011	20¢ Aging Together	05/21/82	.40	.20	1.75	(4)	1.00	173
	Performing Arts, Tagged, Perf. 11							
2012	20¢ John, Ethel and Lionel Barrymore	06/08/82	.40	.20	1.75	(4)	1.00	107
	Tagged, Perf. 11							
2013	20¢ Dr. Mary Walker	06/10/82	.40	.20	1.75	(4)	1.00	109
2014	20¢ International Peace Garden	06/30/82	.50	.20	2.25	(4)	1.00	183
a	Black and green omitted		225.00					
2015	20¢ America's Libraries	07/13/82	.40	.20	1.75	(4)	1.00	169
a	Vertical pair, imperf. horizontally		250.00					
b	Tagging omitted		9.00					
	Black Heritage, Tagged, Perf. 10.5 x 11							
2016	20¢ Jackie Robinson	08/02/82	1.10	.20	6.00	(4)	6.00	164
	Tagged, Perf. 11							
2017	20¢ Touro Synagogue	08/22/82	.45	.20	12.50	(20)	1.50	110
a	Imperf., pair		2,350.00					
2018	20¢ Wolf Trap Farm Park	09/01/82	.40	.20	1.75	(4)	1.00	111

	Issue	Date	Un	U	PB	#	FDC	Q(M)
	American Architecture, Tagged, Perf. 11							
2019	20¢ Fallingwater, by Frank Lloyd Wright	09/30/82	.45	.20			1.00	41
2020	20¢ Illinois Institute of Technology, by Ludwig Mies van der Rohe	09/30/82	.45	.20			1.00	41
2021	20¢ Gropius House, by Walter Gropius	09/30/82	.45	.20			1.00	41
2022	20¢ Dulles Airport by Eero Saarinen	09/30/82	.45	.20			1.00	41
a	Block of 4, #2019-2022		2.00	1.75	2.50	(4)	2.50	
	Tagged, Perf. 11							
2023	20¢ St. Francis of Assisi	10/07/82	.40	.20	1.75	(4)	1.00	174
2024	20¢ Ponce de Leon	10/12/82	.50	.20	3.50	(6)	1.00	110
a	Imperf., pair		425.00					
	Holiday Celebration: Holiday, Tagged, Perf. 11							
2025	13¢ Puppy and Kitten	11/03/82	.25	.20	1.40	(4)	1.25	234
a	Imperf., pair		475.00					
	Holiday Celebration: Christmas, Tagged, Perf. 11							
2026	20¢ *Madonna and Child,* by Tiepolo	10/28/82	.40	.20	11.00	(20)	1.00	703
a	Imperf., pair		135.00					
	Holiday Celebration: Holiday, Tagged, Perf. 11							
2027	20¢ Children Sledding	10/28/82	.60	.20			1.00	197
2028	20¢ Children Building a Snowman	10/28/82	.60	.20			1.00	197
2029	20¢ Children Skating	10/28/82	.60	.20			1.00	197
2030	20¢ Children Trimming a Tree	10/28/82	.60	.20			1.00	197
a	Block of 4, #2027-2030		2.40	1.50	2.75	(4)	2.50	
b	As "a," imperf.		1,800.00					
c	As "a," imperf. horizontally		800.00					
	Tagged, Perf. 11							
2031	20¢ Science & Industry	01/19/83	.40	.20	1.75	(4)	1.00	119
a	Black omitted		1,250.00					

ZION NATIONAL PARK, UTAH

This international rate stamp in the Scenic American Landscapes series features a photograph taken by Richard Cummins of a sandstone formation on the east side of Zion National Park in Utah. Originally established in 1909 as Mukuntuwean National Monument, the park was expanded and designated a national park in 1919. ▪ Today Zion National Park encompasses more than 229 square miles and is characterized by high plateaus and mesas with deep sandstone canyons carved into towering cliffs. Bare expanses of sandstone reveal artifacts and layers of rock that showcase the park's geological history. Diverse environments within the park include deserts, canyons, slickrock, hanging gardens, and plateaus. Zion Canyon, one of the park's largest and most visited sites, rises more than 2,000 feet above the canyon floor. One hundred sixty miles of rivers, streams, and waterfalls support a remarkable diversity of plant and animal life, including more than 270 species of birds. One hundred twenty miles of hiking trails are available to the approximately 2.5 million people who visit the park annually.

2003

2004

2005

2006   2007

2008   2009   2009a

2010

2011

2012

2013

2014

2015

2016

2017

2018

2019   2020

2021   2022   2022a

2023

2024

2025

2026

2027   2028

2029   2030   2030a

2031

2032 2033

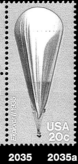

2036

2037

Joseph Priestley
USA 20c

2038

2034 2035 2035a

2039

2040

2041

2042

2043

2044

2045

2046

2047

2048 2049

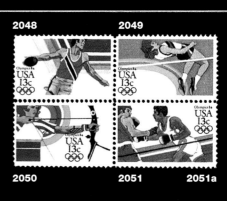

2050 2051 2051a

2052

2053

2054

2055 2056

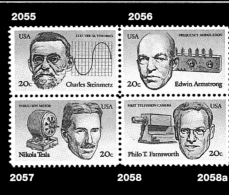

2057 2058 2058a

	Issue	Date	Un	U	PB	#	FDC	Q(M)
	Balloons, Tagged, Perf. 11							
2032	20¢ *Intrepid*, 1861	03/31/83	.50	.20			1.00	57
2033	20¢ Hot Air Ballooning (wording lower right)	03/31/83	.50	.20			1.00	57
2034	20¢ Hot Air Ballooning (wording upper left)	03/31/83	.50	.20			1.00	57
2035	20¢ Explorer II, 1935	03/31/83	.50	.20			1.00	57
a	Block of 4, #2032-2035		2.00	1.50	2.25	(4)	2.50	
b	As "a," imperf.		3,750.00					
c	As "a," right stamp perf., otherwise imperf.		4,250.00					
	Tagged, Perf. 11							
2036	20¢ U.S./Sweden Treaty	03/24/83	.40	.20	1.75	(4)	1.00	118
2037	20¢ Civilian Conservation Corps	04/05/83	.40	.20	1.75	(4)	1.00	114
a	Imperf., pair		3,000.00					
2038	20¢ Joseph Priestley	04/13/83	.40	.20	1.75	(4)	1.00	165
2039	20¢ Voluntarism	04/20/83	.40	.20	3.00	(6)	1.00	120
a	Imperf., pair		325.00					
2040	20¢ Concord-German Immigration, Apr. 29	04/29/83	.40	.20	1.75	(4)	1.00	117
	Tagged, Perf. 11							
2041	20¢ Brooklyn Bridge	05/17/83	.40	.20	1.75	(4)	1.75	182
a	Tagging omitted		150.00					
b	All color omitted		75.00					
2042	20¢ Tennessee Valley Authority	05/18/83	.40	.20	10.00	(20)	1.00	114
2043	20¢ Physical Fitness	05/14/83	.40	.20	3.00	(6)	1.25	112
	Black Heritage, Tagged, Perf. 11							
2044	20¢ Scott Joplin	06/09/83	.50	.20	2.40	(4)	1.75	115
a	Imperf., pair		425.00					
	Tagged, Perf. 11							
2045	20¢ Medal of Honor	06/07/83	.55	.20	2.50	(4)	5.50	109
a	Red omitted		225.00					

	Issue	Date	Un	U	PB	#	FDC	Q(M)
	American Sports Personalities, Tagged, Perf. 10.5 x 11							
2046	20¢ Babe Ruth	07/06/83	1.40	.20	6.25	(4)	5.00	185
	Literary Arts, Tagged, Perf. 11							
2047	20¢ Nathaniel Hawthorne	07/08/83	.45	.20	2.10	(4)	1.00	111
	Olympic Games, Summer, Tagged, Perf. 11							
2048	13¢ Discus Thrower	07/28/83	.35	.20			1.25	99
2049	13¢ High Jumper	07/28/83	.35	.20			1.25	99
2050	13¢ Archer	07/28/83	.35	.20			1.25	99
2051	13¢ Boxers	07/28/83	.35	.20			1.25	99
a	Block of 4, #2048-2051		1.50	1.25	1.75	(4)	2.50	
	American Bicentennial, Tagged, Perf. 11							
2052	20¢ Signing of Treaty of Paris (John Adams, Benjamin Franklin and John Jay observing David Hartley)	09/02/83	.40	.20	1.75	(4)	1.00	104
	Tagged, Perf. 11							
2053	20¢ Civil Service	09/09/83	.40	.20	3.00	(6)	1.00	115
2054	20¢ Metropolitan Opera	09/14/83	.40	.20	1.75	(4)	1.50	113
	American Inventors, Tagged, Perf. 11							
2055	20¢ Charles Steinmetz and Curve on Graph	09/21/83	.50	.20			1.00	48
2056	20¢ Edwin Armstrong and Frequency Modulator	09/21/83	.50	.20			1.00	48
2057	20¢ Nikola Tesla and Induction Motor	09/21/83	.50	.20			1.00	48
2058	20¢ Philo T. Farnsworth and First Television Camera	09/21/83	.50	.20			1.00	48
a	Block of 4, #2055-2058		2.00	1.50	2.75	(4)	2.50	
b	As "a," black omitted		325.00					

HANUKKAH

Spanning eight days and nights, Hanukkah is a joyous yearly festival celebrated by Jews around the world. The holiday commemorates the successful revolt of the Jews led by Judah Maccabee against the oppressive government of Antiochus IV and the Seleucid Empire in 165 B.C.E. ■ Hanukkah is the Hebrew word for "dedication." Tradition relates how a miracle took place during the rededication of the Temple in Jerusalem, which had been desecrated. The remaining supply of sacramental oil, thought to be enough for only one day, burned for eight days. ■ The eight days and nights of Hanukkah begin on the 25th of Kislev in the Hebrew calendar, a date that falls in late November or December. Hanukkah begins on December 11 in 2009 and on December 1 in 2010. ■ During Hanukkah, family members gather each night during the festival to light candles on a special candleholder called a menorah. Other Hanukkah traditions include singing, the exchange of gifts, and the spinning of the dreidel, a four-sided top. Children typically use chocolate gelt (coins) to make bets on the outcome of each spin of the dreidel. ■ The 2009 Hanukkah stamp is the third U.S. issuance to commemorate the holiday. The Postal Service issued its first Hanukkah stamp, which featured a stylized illustration of a menorah, in 1996. A design featuring an ornate dreidel followed in 2004. ■ The 2009 Hanukkah design features a photograph of a menorah with nine lit candles. The menorah was designed by Lisa Regan of the Garden Deva Sculpture Company in Tulsa, Oklahoma, and photographed by Ira Wexler of Braddock Heights, Maryland.

2164

2165

2166

2167

2168

2169

2170

2171

2172

2173

2175

2176

2177

2178

2179

2180

2181

2182

2183

2184

2185

2186

2187

2188

2189

2190

2191

2192

2193

2194

2195

2196

2198

2199

2200

2201   2201a

2202

2203

	Issue	Date	Un	U	PB	#	FDC	Q(M)
	Balloons, Tagged, Perf. 11							
2032	20¢ *Intrepid*, 1861	03/31/83	.50	.20			1.00	57
2033	20¢ Hot Air Ballooning (wording lower right)	03/31/83	.50	.20			1.00	57
2034	20¢ Hot Air Ballooning (wording upper left)	03/31/83	.50	.20			1.00	57
2035	20¢ Explorer II, 1935	03/31/83	.50	.20			1.00	57
a	Block of 4, #2032-2035		2.00	1.50	2.25	(4)	2.50	
b	As "a," imperf.		3,750.00					
c	As "a," right stamp perf., otherwise imperf.		4,250.00					
	Tagged, Perf. 11							
2036	20¢ U.S./Sweden Treaty	03/24/83	.40	.20	1.75	(4)	1.00	118
2037	20¢ Civilian Conservation Corps	04/05/83	.40	.20	1.75	(4)	1.00	114
a	Imperf., pair		3,000.00					
2038	20¢ Joseph Priestley	04/13/83	.40	.20	1.75	(4)	1.00	165
2039	20¢ Voluntarism	04/20/83	.40	.20	3.00	(6)	1.00	120
a	Imperf., pair		325.00					
2040	20¢ Concord-German Immigration, Apr. 29	04/29/83	.40	.20	1.75	(4)	1.00	117
	Tagged, Perf. 11							
2041	20¢ Brooklyn Bridge	05/17/83	.40	.20	1.75	(4)	1.75	182
a	Tagging omitted		150.00					
b	All color omitted		75.00					
2042	20¢ Tennessee Valley Authority	05/18/83	.40	.20	10.00	(20)	1.00	114
2043	20¢ Physical Fitness	05/14/83	.40	.20	3.00	(6)	1.25	112
	Black Heritage, Tagged, Perf. 11							
2044	20¢ Scott Joplin	06/09/83	.50	.20	2.40	(4)	1.75	115
a	Imperf., pair		425.00					
	Tagged, Perf. 11							
2045	20¢ Medal of Honor	06/07/83	.55	.20	2.50	(4)	5.50	109
a	Red omitted		225.00					

	Issue	Date	Un	U	PB	#	FDC	Q(M)
	American Sports Personalities, Tagged, Perf. 10.5 x 11							
2046	20¢ Babe Ruth	07/06/83	1.40	.20	6.25	(4)	5.00	185
	Literary Arts, Tagged, Perf. 11							
2047	20¢ Nathaniel Hawthorne	07/08/83	.45	.20	2.10	(4)	1.00	111
	Olympic Games, Summer, Tagged, Perf. 11							
2048	13¢ Discus Thrower	07/28/83	.35	.20			1.25	99
2049	13¢ High Jumper	07/28/83	.35	.20			1.25	99
2050	13¢ Archer	07/28/83	.35	.20			1.25	99
2051	13¢ Boxers	07/28/83	.35	.20			1.25	99
a	Block of 4, #2048-2051		1.50	1.25	1.75	(4)	2.50	
	American Bicentennial, Tagged, Perf. 11							
2052	20¢ Signing of Treaty of Paris (John Adams, Benjamin Franklin and John Jay observing David Hartley)	09/02/83	.40	.20	1.75	(4)	1.00	104
	Tagged, Perf. 11							
2053	20¢ Civil Service	09/09/83	.40	.20	3.00	(6)	1.00	115
2054	20¢ Metropolitan Opera	09/14/83	.40	.20	1.75	(4)	1.50	113
	American Inventors, Tagged, Perf. 11							
2055	20¢ Charles Steinmetz and Curve on Graph	09/21/83	.50	.20			1.00	48
2056	20¢ Edwin Armstrong and Frequency Modulator	09/21/83	.50	.20			1.00	48
2057	20¢ Nikola Tesla and Induction Motor	09/21/83	.50	.20			1.00	48
2058	20¢ Philo T. Farnsworth and First Television Camera	09/21/83	.50	.20			1.00	48
a	Block of 4, #2055-2058		2.00	1.50	2.75	(4)	2.50	
b	As "a," black omitted		325.00					

HANUKKAH

Spanning eight days and nights, Hanukkah is a joyous yearly festival celebrated by Jews around the world. The holiday commemorates the successful revolt of the Jews led by Judah Maccabee against the oppressive government of Antiochus IV and the Seleucid Empire in 165 B.C.E. ■ Hanukkah is the Hebrew word for "dedication." Tradition relates how a miracle took place during the rededication of the Temple in Jerusalem, which had been desecrated. The remaining supply of sacramental oil, thought to be enough for only one day, burned for eight days. ■ The eight days and nights of Hanukkah begin on the 25th of Kislev in the Hebrew calendar, a date that falls in late November or December. Hanukkah begins on December 11 in 2009 and on December 1 in 2010. ■ During Hanukkah, family members gather each night during the festival to light candles on a special candleholder called a menorah. Other Hanukkah traditions include singing, the exchange of gifts, and the spinning of the dreidel, a four-sided top. Children typically use chocolate gelt (coins) to make bets on the outcome of each spin of the dreidel. ■ The 2009 Hanukkah stamp is the third U.S. issuance to commemorate the holiday. The Postal Service issued its first Hanukkah stamp, which featured a stylized illustration of a menorah, in 1996. A design featuring an ornate dreidel followed in 2004. ■ The 2009 Hanukkah design features a photograph of a menorah with nine lit candles. The menorah was designed by Lisa Regan of the Garden Deva Sculpture Company in Tulsa, Oklahoma, and photographed by Ira Wexler of Braddock Heights, Maryland.

	Issue	Date	Un	U	PB	#	FDC	Q(M)
	Streetcars, Tagged, Perf. 11							
2059	20¢ First American Streetcar	10/08/83	.50	.20			1.00	52
2060	20¢ Early Electric Streetcar	10/08/83	.50	.20			1.00	52
2061	20¢ "Bobtail" Horsecar	10/08/83	.50	.20			1.00	52
2062	20¢ St. Charles Streetcar	10/08/83	.50	.20			1.00	52
a	Block of 4, #2059-2062		2.00	1.50	2.60	(4)	2.50	
b	As "a," black omitted	325.00						
c	As "a," black omitted on #2059, 2061	—						
	Holiday Celebration: Christmas, Tagged, Perf. 11							
2063	20¢ Niccolini-Cowper Madonna, by Raphael	10/28/83	.40	.20	1.75	(4)	1.00	716
	Holiday Celebration: Holiday, Tagged, Perf. 11							
2064	20¢ Santa Claus	10/28/83	.40	.20	3.00	(6)	1.00	849
a	Imperf., pair	125.00						
	Tagged, Perf. 11							
2065	20¢ Martin Luther	11/11/83	.40	.20	1.75	(4)	1.50	165
2066	20¢ Alaska Statehood	01/03/84	.40	.20	1.75	(4)	1.00	120
	Olympic Games, Winter, Tagged, Perf. 10.5 x 11							
2067	20¢ Ice Dancing	01/06/84	.55	.20			1.00	80
2068	20¢ Downhill Skiing	01/06/84	.55	.20			1.00	80
2069	20¢ Cross-country Skiing	01/06/84	.55	.20			1.00	80
2070	20¢ Hockey	01/06/84	.55	.20			1.00	80
a	Block of 4, #2067-2070		2.20	1.75	3.00	(4)	2.50	
	Tagged, Perf. 11							
2071	20¢ Federal Deposit Insurance Corporation	01/12/84	.40	.20	1.75	(4)	1.00	104
	Love, Tagged, Perf. 11 x 10.5							
2072	20¢ Love	01/31/84	.40	.20	11.50	(20)	1.00	555
a	Horizontal pair, imperf. vertically	150.00						
b	Tagging omitted	5.00						

	Issue	Date	Un	U	PB	#	FDC	Q(M)
	Black Heritage, Tagged, Perf. 11							
2073	20¢ Carter G. Woodson	02/01/84	.40	.20	2.00	(4)	1.75	120
a	Horizontal pair, imperf. vertically	1,150.00						
	Tagged, Perf. 11							
2074	20¢ Soil and Water Conservation	02/06/84	.40	.20	1.75	(4)	1.00	107
2075	20¢ 50th Anniversary of Credit Union Act	02/10/84	.40	.20	1.75	(4)	1.00	107
	Orchids, Tagged, Perf. 11							
2076	20¢ Wild Pink	03/05/84	.50	.20			1.00	77
2077	20¢ Yellow Lady's-Slipper	03/05/84	.50	.20			1.00	77
2078	20¢ Spreading Pogonia	03/05/84	.50	.20			1.00	77
2079	20¢ Pacific Calypso	03/05/84	.50	.20			1.00	77
a	Block of 4, #2076-2079		2.00	1.50	2.50	(4)	2.50	
	Tagged, Perf. 11							
2080	20¢ Hawaii Statehood	03/12/84	.40	.20	1.70	(4)	1.00	120
2081	20¢ National Archives	04/16/84	.40	.20	1.70	(4)	1.00	108
	Olympic Games, Summer, Tagged, Perf. 11							
2082	20¢ Diving	05/04/84	.55	.20			1.25	78
2083	20¢ Long Jump	05/04/84	.55	.20			1.25	78
2084	20¢ Wrestling	05/04/84	.55	.20			1.25	78
2085	20¢ Kayak	05/04/84	.55	.20			1.25	78
a	Block of 4, #2082-2085		2.40	1.90	3.50	(4)	2.50	
	Tagged, Perf. 11							
2086	20¢ Louisiana World Exposition	05/11/84	.50	.20	2.60	(4)	1.00	130
2087	20¢ Health Research	05/17/84	.40	.20	1.75	(4)	1.00	120
	Performing Arts, Tagged, Perf. 11							
2088	20¢ Douglas Fairbanks	05/23/84	.50	.20	13.00	(20)	1.00	117
a	Tagging omitted	25.00						
	American Sports Personalities, Tagged, Perf. 11							
2089	20¢ Jim Thorpe on Football Field	05/24/84	.60	.20	3.00	(4)	3.00	116
	Performing Arts, Tagged, Perf. 11							
2090	20¢ John McCormack	06/06/84	.40	.20	1.75	(4)	1.00	117

DOLPHIN

*A*n illustration by Nancy Stahl of the bottlenose dolphin *(Tursiops truncatus),* a marine mammal noted for its high intelligence and playful behavior, is featured on this 2009 stamp. The bottlenose dolphin belongs to the family *Delphinidae,* which includes some 30 species of dolphins that swim in oceans and bays around the world. ▦ Found mainly in temperate and tropical waters, bottlenose dolphins are social animals that live in groups ranging in size from two to several hundred. They are often seen from shore and by boaters, and appear to engage in play with other dolphins. Named for their short, broad snouts, their mostly gray bodies are large and stout. The corners of their mouths curve up, giving the appearance of a permanent smile. ▦ Bottlenose dolphins eat a variety of fish, as well as squid and crustaceans. They use echolocation to find potential prey. The dolphins emit sounds from the nasal region, and the echoes that bounce back provide clues about the size, density, and location of nearby objects. Dolphins also communicate with each other by making certain sounds. ▦ Mating generally occurs throughout the year. A female gives birth to a calf after a gestation period of about 12 months, and the two immediately form a close bond, staying together for up to six years.

2091
2092
a
2093

2094
2095
2096
a
b
c
d
2097
a
2098
2099
2100
2101

a
2102
2103
a
2104
a
b
2105
2106

2107

2108
a
2109

2110
a

2059   2060

2061   2062   2062a

2063

2064

2065

2066

2067   2068

2069   2070   2070a

2071

2072

2073

2074

2075

2076   2077

2078   2079   2079a

2080

2081

2082   2083

2084   2085   2085a

2086

2087

2088

2089

2090

	Issue	Date	Un	U	PB/PNC	#	FDC	Q(M)
	Transportation, Coil, Tagged, Perf. 10 Vertically							
2123	3.4¢ School Bus 1920s	06/08/85	.35	.20	.80	(5)	1.00	
a	Untagged (Bureau precanceled)		.20	.20	3.75	(5)		
2124	4.9¢ Buckboard 1880s	06/21/85	.20	.20	.75	(5)	1.00	
a	Untagged (Bureau precanceled)		.20	.20	1.50	(5)		
2125	5.5¢ Star Route Truck 1910s	11/01/86	.20	.20	1.60	(5)	1.00	
a	Untagged (Bureau precanceled)		.20	.20	1.50	(5)		
2126	6¢ Tricycle 1880s	05/06/85	.35	.20	2.00	(5)	1.25	
a	Untagged (Bureau precanceled)		.20	.20	1.75	(5)		
b	As "a," imperf., pair		210.00					
2127	7.1¢ Tractor 1920s	02/06/87	.20	.20	2.00	(5)	1.00	
a	Untagged (Bureau precanceled "Nonprofit org.")		.20	.20	2.50	(5)	5.00	
b	Untagged (Bureau precanceled "Nonprofit 5-Digit ZIP + 4")	05/26/89	.20	.20	1.75	(5)		
2128	8.3¢ Ambulance 1860s	06/21/85	.20	.20	1.50	(5)	1.00	
a	Untagged (Bureau precanceled)		.20	.20	1.50	(5)		
2129	8.5¢ Tow Truck 1920s	01/24/87	.20	.20	2.50	(5)	1.25	
a	Untagged (Bureau precanceled)		.20	.20	2.25	(5)		
2130	10.1¢ Oil Wagon 1890s	04/18/85	.55	.20	3.75	(5)	1.25	
a	Untagged (Bureau precanceled, red)		.25	.25	2.25	(5)	1.25	
	Untagged (Bureau precanceled, black)		.25	.25	2.25	(5)		
b	As "a," red precancel, imperf., pair		15.00					
	As "a," black precancel, imperf., pair		80.00					
2131	11¢ Stutz Bearcat 1933	06/11/85	.25	.20	1.40	(5)	1.25	
2132	12¢ Stanley Steamer 1909	04/02/85	.25	.20	2.00	(5)	1.25	
a	Untagged (Bureau precanceled)		.25	.25	2.00	(5)		
b	As "a," type II		.40	.30	16.00	(5)		
	Type II has "Stanley Steamer 1909" .5 mm shorter (17.5 mm) than #2132 (18mm).							
2133	12.5¢ Pushcart 1880s	04/18/85	.25	.20	2.75	(5)	1.25	
a	Untagged (Bureau precanceled)		.25	.25	2.75	(5)		
b	As "a," imperf., pair		50.00					
2134	14¢ Iceboat 1880s	03/23/85	.30	.20	2.00	(5)	1.25	
a	Imperf., pair		95.00					
b	Type II		.30	.20	2.50	(5)		
2135	17¢ Dog Sled 1920s	08/20/86	.55	.20	4.00	(5)	1.50	
a	Imperf., pair		375.00					
2136	25¢ Bread Wagon 1880s	11/22/86	.45	.20	3.00	(5)	1.25	
a	Imperf., pair		10.00					
b	Pair, imperf. between		600.00					
c	Tagging omitted		27.50					
	Black Heritage, Tagged, Perf. 11							
2137	22¢ Mary McLeod Bethune	03/05/85	.60	.20	3.25	(4)	1.50	120
	American Folk Art: Duck Decoys, Tagged, Perf. 11							
2138	22¢ Broadbill Decoy	03/22/85	1.00	.20			1.00	75
2139	22¢ Mallard Decoy	03/22/85	1.00	.20			1.00	75
2140	22¢ Canvasback Decoy	03/22/85	1.00	.20			1.00	75
2141	22¢ Redhead Decoy	03/22/85	1.00	.20			1.00	75
a	Block of 4, #2138-2141		4.00	2.75	4.50	(4)	2.50	

	Issue	Date	Un	U	PB/PNC	#	FDC	Q(M)
	Tagged, Perf. 11							
2142	22¢ Winter Special Olympics	03/25/85	.50	.20	2.25	(4)	1.00	121
a	Vertical pair, imperf. horizontally		425.00					
	Love, Tagged, Perf. 11							
2143	22¢ Love	04/17/85	.40	.20	1.70	(4)	1.00	730
a	Imperf., pair		1,250.00					
	Tagged, Perf. 11							
2144	22¢ Rural Electrification Administration	05/11/85	.50	.20	17.50	(20)	1.00	125
2145	22¢ AMERIPEX '86	05/25/85	.40	.20	1.75	(4)	1.00	203
a	Red, black and blue omitted		175.00					
b	Red and black omitted		1,150.00					
2146	22¢ Abigail Adams	06/14/85	.40	.20	2.00	(4)	1.00	126
a	Imperf., pair		225.00					
2147	22¢ Frederic A. Bartholdi	07/18/85	.40	.20	1.90	(4)	1.00	130
2148	Not assigned							
	Coil Stamps, Perf. 10 Vertically							
2149	18¢ George Washington, Washington Monument	11/06/85	.40	.20	2.75	(5)	1.00	
a	Untagged (Bureau precanceled)		.35	.35	6.00	(5)		
b	Imperf., pair		875.00					
c	As "a," imperf. pair		675.00					
d	Tagging omitted		75.00	—				
e	As "a," tagged (error), dull gum		2.00	1.75	150.00			
2150	21.1¢ Sealed Envelopes	10/22/85	.40	.20	3.00	(5)	1.00	
a	Untagged (Bureau precanceled)		.40	.40	3.50	(5)		
b	As "a," tagged (error)		.50	.50	2.50	(5)		
2151	Not assigned							
	Tagged, Perf. 11							
2152	22¢ Korean War Veterans	07/26/85	.40	.20	2.50	(4)	3.00	120
2153	22¢ Social Security Act, 50th Anniversary	08/14/85	.40	.20	1.90	(4)	1.00	120
2154	22¢ World War I Veterans	08/26/85	.40	.20	2.25	(4)	1.50	120
	American Horses, Tagged, Perf. 11							
2155	22¢ Quarter Horse	09/25/85	1.25	.20			1.50	37
2156	22¢ Morgan	09/25/85	1.25	.20			1.50	37
2157	22¢ Saddlebred	09/25/85	1.25	.20			1.50	37
2158	22¢ Appaloosa	09/25/85	1.25	.20			1.50	37
a	Block of 4, #2155-2158		6.00	4.00	7.50	(4)	2.50	
	Tagged, Perf. 11							
2159	22¢ Public Education	10/01/85	.45	.20	2.75	(4)	1.00	120
	International Youth Year, Tagged, Perf. 11							
2160	22¢ YMCA Youth Camping	10/07/85	.70	.20			1.00	33
2161	22¢ Boy Scouts	10/07/85	.70	.20			2.00	33
2162	22¢ Big Brothers/Big Sisters	10/07/85	.70	.20			1.00	33
2163	22¢ Camp Fire	10/07/85	.70	.20			1.00	33
a	Block of 4, #2160-2163		3.00	2.25	4.00	(4)	2.50	

School Bus 1920s
3.4 USA
2123

Buckboard 1880s
USA 4.9
2124

Star Route Truck
5.5 USA 1910s
2125

Tricycle 1880s
6 USA
2126

Tractor 1920s
7.1 USA
2127

Ambulance 1860s
8.3 USA
2128

Tow Truck 1920s
8.5 USA
2129

Oil Wagon 1890s
10.1 USA
2130

Stutz Bearcat 1933
11 USA
2131

Stanley Steamer 1909
USA 12
2132

Pushcart 1880s
12.5 USA
2133

Iceboat 1880s
USA 14
2134

Dog Sled 1920s
17 USA
2135

Bread Wagon 1880s
25 USA
2136

Mary McLeod Bethune
Black Heritage USA 22
2137

2138 **2139**

Broadbill Decoy — Folk Art USA 22
Mallard Decoy — Folk Art USA 22
Canvasback Decoy — Folk Art USA 22
Redhead Decoy — Folk Art USA 22
2140 **2141** **2141a**

22 USA
Winter Special Olympics
2142

Love
USA 22
2143

22 USA
Rural Electrification Administration 1935 1985
2144

AMERIPEX 86
International Stamp Show, Chicago
May 22 to June 1, 1986
US POSTAGE
USA 22
2145

Abigail Adams
USA 22
2146

USA 22
F.A. Bartholdi, Statue of Liberty Sculptor
2147

18 USA
2149

USA 21.1
2150

Veterans Korea
USA 22
2152

Social Security Act 1935-1985 USA 22
2153

Veterans World War I
USA 22
2154

2155 **2156**

USA 22 Quarter horse
USA 22 Morgan
USA 22 Saddlebred
USA 22 Appaloosa
2157 **2158** **2158a**

22 USA
Public Education
2159

2160 **2161**

YMCA Youth Camping USA 22
Boy Scouts USA 22
Big Brothers/Big Sisters USA 22
Camp Fire USA 22
2162 **2163** **2163a**

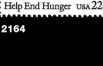
Help End Hunger USA22

2164

CHRISTMAS USA 22
Luca della Robbia, Detroit Institute of Arts

2165

Season's Greetings USA22

2166

Arkansas Statehood 1836-1986
Old State House Little Rock
USA22

2167

Margaret Mitchell USA1

2168

Mary Lyon USA 2

2169

Paul Dudley White MD USA3

2170

Father Flanagan USA 4

2171

Hugo L. Black 5USA

2172

Luis Muñoz Marín, Governor, Puerto Rico USA 05

2173

Red Cloud 10USA

2175

14USA Julia Ward Howe

2176

Buffalo Bill Cody USA 15

2177

Belva Ann Lockwood USA 17

2178

Virginia Apgar Physician 1909-1974 USA 20

2179

Chester Carlson USA 21

2180

Mary Cassatt USA 23

2181

USA 25 Jack London

2182

Sitting Bull USA 28

2183

Earl Warren Chief Justice of the US USA 29

2184

Thomas Jefferson USA 29

2185

Dennis Chavez United States Senator USA 35

2186

Claire Chennault Flying Tigers, 1940s USA40

2187

Harvey Cushing MD USA 45

2188

Hubert H. Humphrey VICE PRESIDENT USA 52

2189

John Harvard USA 56

2190

H.H."Hap"Arnold USA 65

2191

Wendell Willkie 1892-1944 Statesman 75USA

2192

Bernard Revel USA$1

2193

Johns Hopkins USA $1

2194

Bryan $2 William Jennings USA

2195

Bret Harte USA $5

2196

STAMP COLLECTING USA22

2198

STAMP COLLECTING USA22

2199

STAMP COLLECTING USA22

2200

STAMP COLLECTING Ameripex 86 USA22

2201   **2201a**

LOVE USA22

2202

Sojourner Truth 22
Black Heritage USA

2203

Issue	Date	Un	U	PB #	FDC	Q(M)
Tagged, Perf. 11						
2164 22¢ Help End Hunger	10/15/85	.45	.20	2.25 (4)	1.00	120
Holiday Celebration: Christmas, Tagged, Perf. 11						
2165 22¢ Genoa Madonna, by Luca Della Robbia	10/30/85	.40	.20	1.75 (4)	1.00	759
a Imperf., pair		70.00				
Holiday Celebration: Holiday, Tagged, Perf. 11						
2166 22¢ Poinsettia Plants	10/30/85	.40	.20	1.70 (4)	1.00	758
a Imperf., pair		110.00				
Tagged, Perf. 11						
2167 22¢ Arkansas Statehood	01/03/86	.75	.20	3.75 (4)	1.00	130
Great Americans, Tagged, Perf. 11, 11.2 x 11.1						
2168 1¢ Margaret Mitchell	06/30/86	.20	.20	.25 (4)	2.00	
a Tagging omitted		5.00				
2169 2¢ Mary Lyon	02/28/87	.20	.20	.30 (4)	1.00	
a Untagged		.20	.20	.35 (4)		
2170 3¢ Paul Dudley White, MD	09/15/86	.20	.20	.50 (4)	1.00	
a Untagged, dull gum		.20	.20	.50 (4)		
2171 4¢ Father Flanagan	07/14/86	.20	.20	.60 (4)	1.25	
a Grayish violet, untagged		.20	.20	.40 (4)		
b Deep grayish blue, untagged		.20	.20	.50 (4)		
2172 5¢ Hugo L. Black	02/27/86	.20	.20	1.00 (4)	1.00	
a Tagging omitted		150.00				
2173 5¢ Luis Munoz Marin	02/18/90	.20	.20	.75 (4)	1.00	
a Untagged		.20	.20	.60 (4)		
2174 Not assigned						
2175 10¢ Red Cloud	08/15/87	.25	.20	1.10 (4)	1.50	
a Overall tagging	1990	.60	.25	10.00 (4)		
b Tagging omitted		12.50				
c Prephosphored coated paper (solid tagging)		.90	.20	4.00 (4)		
d Prephosphored uncoated paper (mottled tagging)		.90	.20	4.00 (4)		
e Carmine, prephosphored uncoated paper (mottled tagging)		.40	.20	2.00 (4)		
2176 14¢ Julia Ward Howe	02/12/87	.30	.20	1.50 (4)	1.00	
2177 15¢ Buffalo Bill Cody	06/06/88	.35	.20	10.00 (4)	2.00	
a Overall tagging	1990	.30	—	3.25 (4)		
b Prephosphored coated paper (solid tagging)		.40	—	3.25 (4)		
c Tagging omitted		15.00	—			
2178 17¢ Belva Ann Lockwood	06/18/86	.35	.20	2.00 (4)	1.00	
a Tagging omitted		10.00				
2179 20¢ Virginia Apgar	10/24/94	.40	.20	2.00 (4)	1.00	
a Orange brown		.45	.20	2.25 (4)		
2180 21¢ Chester Carlson	10/21/88	.45	.20	2.50 (4)	1.00	
2181 23¢ Mary Cassatt	11/04/88	.45	.20	2.50 (4)	1.00	
a Overall tagging, dull gum		.75	—	5.75 (4)		
b Prephosphored coated paper (solid tagging)		.65	—	5.00 (4)		
c Prephosphored uncoated paper (mottled tagging)		.75	.20	5.75 (4)		
d Tagging omitted		7.50				
2182 25¢ Jack London	01/11/86	.50	.20	2.75 (4)	1.25	
a Booklet pane of 10	05/03/88	5.00	3.75		6.00	
2183 28¢ Sitting Bull	09/14/89	.65	.35	3.50 (4)	1.50	
2184 29¢ Earl Warren	03/09/92	.70	.20	5.00 (4)	1.25	
Great Americans, Tagged, Perf. 11.5 x 11						
2185 29¢ Thomas Jefferson	04/13/93	.65	.20	3.50 (4)	1.25	
Great Americans, Tagged, Perf. 11, 11.2 x 11.1						
2186 35¢ Dennis Chavez	04/03/91	.75	.20	4.25 (4)	1.25	

Issue	Date	Un	U	PB #	FDC	Q(M)
Great Americans, Tagged, Perf. 11, 11.2 x 11.1, continued						
2187 40¢ Claire Lee Chennault	09/06/90	.85	.20	4.50 (4)	2.00	
a Prephosphored coated paper (solid tagging)		1.00	.35	5.50 (4)		
b Prephosphored coated paper (grainy solid tagging)		.85	.35	4.50 (4)		
c Prephosphored uncoated paper (mottled tagging)		1.00	.20	10.00 (4)		
2188 45¢ Harvey Cushing, MD	06/17/88	1.00	.20	5.00 (4)	1.25	
a Overall tagging	1990	2.25	.20	22.50 (4)		
b Tagging omitted		17.50				
2189 52¢ Hubert H. Humphrey	06/03/91	1.10	.20	7.50 (4)	1.40	
a Prephosphored uncoated paper (mottled tagging)		1.25	—	8.00 (4)		
2190 56¢ John Harvard	09/03/86	1.20	.20	7.00 (4)	2.50	
2191 65¢ H.H. 'Hap' Arnold	11/05/88	1.30	.20	6.50 (4)	2.50	
a Tagging omitted		22.50				
Perf. 11						
2192 75¢ Wendell Willkie	02/16/92	1.60	.20	7.50 (4)	2.50	
a Prephosphored uncoated paper (mottled tagging)		1.75	—	9.00 (4)		
2193 $1 Bernard Revel	09/23/86	3.00	.50	15.00 (4)	5.00	
2194 $1 Johns Hopkins	06/07/89	2.25	.50	12.00 (4)	3.00	
b Overall tagging	1990	2.50	.50	13.00 (4)		
c Tagging omitted		10.00				
d Dark blue, prephosphored coated paper (solid tagging)		2.50	.50	13.00 (4)		
e Blue, prephosphored uncoated paper (mottled tagging)		2.75	.60	14.00 (4)		
f Blue, prephosphored coated paper (grainy solid tagging)		2.75	.50	14.00 (4)		
2195 $2 William Jennings Bryan	03/19/86	4.50	.50	20.00 (4)	6.00	
a Tagging omitted		250.00				
2196 $5 Bret Harte	08/25/87	9.00	1.00	42.50 (4)	15.00	
b Prephosphored paper (solid tagging)		11.00	—	45.00 (4)		
Great Americans, Booklet, Perf. 10 on 2 or 3 sides						
2197 25¢ Jack London (2182), single from booklet		.55	.20		1.00	
a Booklet pane of 6	05/03/88	3.30	2.50		4.00	
b Tagging omitted		8.00				
c As "b," booklet pane of 6		50.00				
United States — Sweden Stamp Collecting Booklet, Tagged, Perf. 10 Vertically on 1 or 2 sides						
2198 22¢ Handstamped Cover	01/23/86	.45	.20		1.00	17
2199 22¢ Boy Examining Stamp Collection	01/23/86	.45	.20		1.00	17
2200 22¢ #836 Under Magnifying Glass	01/23/86	.45	.20		1.00	17
2201 22¢ 1986 Presidents Miniature Sheet	01/23/86	.45	.20		1.00	17
a Booklet pane of 4, #2198-2201		2.00	1.75		4.00	17
b As "a," black omitted on #2198, 2201		40.00	—			
c As "a," blue omitted on #2198-2200		2,250.00				

#2198-2201 issued only in booklets. All stamps are imperf. at top and bottom or imperf. at top, bottom and right side.

Issue	Date	Un	U	PB #	FDC	Q(M)
Love, Tagged, Perf. 11						
2202 22¢ Love	01/30/86	.55	.20	2.75 (4)	1.00	947
Black Heritage, Tagged, Perf. 11						
2203 22¢ Sojourner Truth and Truth Lecturing	02/04/86	.55	.20	2.75 (4)	1.75	130

	Issue	Date	Un	U	PB	#	FDC	Q(M)
	Tagged, Perf. 11							
2204	22¢ Republic of Texas, 150th Anniversary	03/02/86	.55	.20	2.75	(4)	1.75	137
a	Horizontal pair, imperf. vertically		900.00					
b	Dark red omitted		2,350.00					
c	Dark blue omitted		8,000.00					
	Fish, Booklet, Tagged, Perf. 10 Horizontally							
2205	22¢ Muskellunge	03/21/86	1.00	.20			1.25	44
2206	22¢ Atlantic Cod	03/21/86	1.00	.20			1.25	44
2207	22¢ Largemouth Bass	03/21/86	1.00	.20			1.25	44
2208	22¢ Bluefin Tuna	03/21/86	1.00	.20			1.25	44
2209	22¢ Catfish	03/21/86	1.00	.20			1.25	44
a	Booklet pane of 5, #2205-2209		5.50	2.75			5.00	44

#2205-2209 issued only in booklets. All stamps are imperf. at sides or imperf. at sides and bottom.

	Issue	Date	Un	U	PB	#	FDC	Q(M)
	Tagged, Perf. 11							
2210	22¢ Public Hospitals	04/11/86	.40	.20	1.75	(4)	1.00	130
a	Vertical pair, imperf. horizontally		275.00					
b	Horizontal pair, imperf. vertically		1,150.00					
	Performing Arts, Tagged, Perf. 11							
2211	22¢ Duke Ellington and Piano Keys	04/29/86	.40	.20	1.90	(4)	2.25	130
a	Vertical pair, imperf. horizontally		800.00					

2212-2215 Not assigned

	Issue	Date	Un	U	PB	#	FDC	Q(M)
	AMERIPEX '86, Presidents Miniature Sheets, Tagged, Perf. 11							
2216	Sheet of 9	05/22/86	7.50	4.00			4.00	6
a	22¢ George Washington		.75	.40			1.50	
b	22¢ John Adams		.75	.40			1.50	
c	22¢ Thomas Jefferson		.75	.40			1.50	
d	22¢ James Madison		.75	.40			1.50	
e	22¢ James Monroe		.75	.40			1.50	
f	22¢ John Quincy Adams		.75	.40			1.50	
g	22¢ Andrew Jackson		.75	.40			1.50	
h	22¢ Martin Van Buren		.75	.40			1.50	
i	22¢ William H. Harrison		.75	.40			1.50	
j	Blue omitted		2,500.00					
k	Black inscription omitted		2,000.00					
l	Imperf.		10,500.00					
2217	Sheet of 9	05/22/86	7.50	4.00			4.00	6
a	22¢ John Tyler		.75	.40			1.50	
b	22¢ James Polk		.75	.40			1.50	
c	22¢ Zachary Taylor		.75	.40			1.50	
d	22¢ Millard Fillmore		.75	.40			1.50	
e	22¢ Franklin Pierce		.75	.40			1.50	
f	22¢ James Buchanan		.75	.40			1.50	
g	22¢ Abraham Lincoln		.75	.40			1.50	
h	22¢ Andrew Johnson		.75	.40			1.50	
i	22¢ Ulysses S. Grant		.75	.40			1.50	
j	Black inscription omitted		2,500.00					
k	Tagging omitted		—					

#2216

#2217

2204

2205

2206

2207

2208

2209

2209a

Muskellunge

Atlantic Cod

Largemouth Bass

Bluefin Tuna

Catfish

2210

2211

2216a

2216b

2216c

2216d

2216e

2216f

2216g

2216h

2216i

2217a

2217b

2217c

2217d

2217e

2217f

2217g

2217h

2217i

2218a 2218b 2218c 2218d 2218e 2218f 2218g 2218h

2218i 2219a 2219b 2219c 2219d 2219e 2219f 2219g

2219h 2219i

2220 2221

Elisha Kent Kane · Adolphus W. Greely
Vilhjalmur Stefansson · Robert E. Peary, Matthew Henson

2222 2223 2223a

Liberty 1886-1986 · USA 22

2224

Omnibus 1880s — 2225
Locomotive 1870s — 2226

2235 2236

Navajo Art USA 22

2237 2238 2238a

T.S. Eliot — 22 USA
2239

2240 2241

Folk Art USA 22

2242 2243 2243a

CHRISTMAS 22 USA · Perugino, National Gallery
2244

GREETINGS
2245

USA 22 · 1837-1987 Michigan Statehood
2246

22 USA · Pan American Games Indianapolis 1987
2247

Issue		Date	Un	U	PB/PNC #	FDC	Q(M)
AMERIPEX '86, Presidents Miniature Sheets, Tagged, Perf. 11 continued							
2218	Sheet of 9	05/22/86	7.50	4.00		4.00	6
a	22¢ Rutherford B. Hayes		.75	.40		1.50	
b	22¢ James A. Garfield		.75	.40		1.50	
c	22¢ Chester A. Arthur		.75	.40		1.50	
d	22¢ Grover Cleveland		.75	.40		1.50	
e	22¢ Benjamin Harrison		.75	.40		1.50	
f	22¢ William McKinley		.75	.40		1.50	
g	22¢ Theodore Roosevelt		.75	.40		1.50	
h	22¢ William H. Taft		.75	.40		1.50	
i	22¢ Woodrow Wilson		.75	.40		1.50	
j	Brown omitted		—				
k	Black inscription omitted		2,500.00				
l	Tagging omitted		—				
2219	Sheet of 9	05/22/86	7.50	4.00		4.00	6
a	22¢ Warren G. Harding		.75	.40		1.50	
b	22¢ Calvin Coolidge		.75	.40		1.50	
c	22¢ Herbert Hoover		.75	.40		1.50	
d	22¢ Franklin D. Roosevelt		.75	.40		1.50	
e	22¢ White House		.75	.40		1.50	
f	22¢ Harry S. Truman		.75	.40		1.50	
g	22¢ Dwight D. Eisenhower		.75	.40		1.50	
h	22¢ John F. Kennedy		.75	.40		2.50	
i	22¢ Lyndon B. Johnson		.75	.40		1.50	
j	Blackish blue inscription omitted		2,500.00				
k	Tagging omitted		4,000.00				
Arctic Explorers, Tagged, Perf. 11							
2220	22¢ Elisha Kent Kane	05/28/86	.65	.20		1.25	33
2221	22¢ Adolphus W. Greely	05/28/86	.65	.20		1.25	33
2222	22¢ Vilhjalmur Stefansson	05/28/86	.65	.20		1.25	33
2223	22¢ Robt. Peary, Matt. Henson	05/28/86	.65	.20		1.25	33
a	Block of 4, #2220-2223		2.75	2.25	4.50 (4)	3.75	
b	As "a," black omitted		5,000.00				
2224	22¢ Statue of Liberty	07/04/86	.40	.20	2.25 (4)	1.25	221

Issue		Date	Un	U	PB/PNC #	FDC	Q(M)
Transportation Coil, Tagged, Perf. 10 Vertically							
2225	1¢ Omnibus	11/26/86	.20	.20	.50 (5)	1.00	
a	Prephosphored uncoated paper (mottled tagging)		.20	.20	32.50 (5)		
b	Untagged, dull gum		.20	.20	.55 (5)		
c	Imperf., pair		2,000.00				
2226	2¢ Locomotive	03/06/87	.20	.20	.50 (5)	1.50	
a	Untagged, dull gum		.20	.20	1.00 (5)		
2227	Not assigned						
2228	4¢ Stagecoach (1898A)	08/86	.20	.20	1.50 (5)		
a	Overall tagging		.70	.20	11.00 (5)		
b	Imperf., pair		250.00				

On #2228, "Stagecoach 1890s" is 17mm long; on #1898A, it is 19.5mm long. On #2231, "Ambulance 1860s" is 18mm long; on #2128, it is 18.5mm long.

Issue		Date	Un	U	PB/PNC #	FDC	Q(M)
2229-2230	Not assigned						
Transportation Coil, Untagged, Perf. 10 Vertically							
2231	8.3¢ Ambulance (2128) (Bureau precanceled)	08/29/86	.50	.20	5.75 (5)		
2232-2234	Not assigned						
American Folk Art: Navajo Art, Tagged, Perf. 11							
2235	22¢ Navajo Art, four "+" marks horizontally through middle	09/04/86	.80	.20		1.00	60
2236	22¢ Navajo Art, vertical diamond pattern	09/04/86	.80	.20		1.00	60
2237	22¢ Navajo Art, horizontal diamond pattern	09/04/86	.80	.20		1.00	60
2238	22¢ Navajo Art, jagged line horizontally through middle	09/04/86	.80	.20		1.00	60
a	Block of 4, #2235-2238		3.25	2.25	4.25 (4)	2.00	
b	As "a," black omitted		325.00				
Literary Arts, Tagged, Perf. 11							
2239	22¢ T.S. Eliot	09/26/86	.55	.20	2.75 (4)	1.00	132
American Folk Art: Wood Carved Figurines, Tagged, Perf. 11							
2240	22¢ Highlander Figure	10/01/86	.50	.20		1.00	60
2241	22¢ Ship Figurehead	10/01/86	.50	.20		1.00	60
2242	22¢ Nautical Figure	10/01/86	.50	.20		1.00	60
2243	22¢ Cigar Store Figure	10/01/86	.50	.20		1.00	60
a	Block of 4, #2240-2243		2.00	1.50	3.75 (4)	2.00	
b	As "a," imperf. vertically		1,250.00				
Holiday Celebration: Christmas, Tagged, Perf. 11							
2244	22¢ Madonna and Child	10/24/86	.40	.20	2.00 (4)	1.00	690
a	Imperf. pair		600.00				
Holiday Celebration: Holiday, Tagged, Perf. 11							
2245	22¢ Village Scene	10/24/86	.40	.20	1.90 (4)	1.00	882
Tagged, Perf. 11							
2246	22¢ Michigan Statehood	01/26/87	.55	.20	2.75 (4)	1.00	167
	Pair with full vertical gutter between		—				
2247	22¢ Pan American Games	01/29/87	.40	.20	1.90 (4)	1.00	167
a	Silver omitted		1,500.00				

Presidents of the United States: III

AMERIPEX 86 International Stamp Show Chicago, Illinois May 22-June 1, 1986

#2218

Presidents of the United States: IV

AMERIPEX 86 International Stamp Show Chicago, Illinois May 22-June 1, 1986

#2219

Issue		Date	Un	U	PB/PNC #	FDC	Q(M)
	Love, Tagged, Perf. 11.5 x 11						
2248	22¢ Love	01/30/87	.40	.20	1.90 (4)	1.00	812
	Black Heritage, Tagged, Perf. 11						
2249	22¢ Jean Baptiste Point Du Sable and Chicago Settlement	02/20/87	.50	.20	2.60 (4)	1.50	143
a	Tagging omitted		10.00				
	Performing Arts, Tagged, Perf. 11						
2250	22¢ Enrico Caruso	02/27/87	.40	.20	1.90 (4)	1.00	130
a	Black (engr.) omitted		5,000.00				
	Tagged, Perf. 11						
2251	22¢ Girl Scouts	03/12/87	.40	.20	1.90 (4)	2.50	150
a	All litho colors omitted		2,450.00				
	Transportation, Coil, Tagged, Perf. 10 Vertically						
	Untagged (5.3¢, 7.6¢, 8.4¢, 13¢, 13.2¢, 16.7¢, 20.5¢, 21¢, 24.1¢)						
2252	3¢ Conestoga Wagon 1800s	02/29/88	.20	.20	.70 (5)	1.00	
a	Untagged, dull gum		.20	.20	1.50 (5)		
2253	5¢ Milk Wagon 1900s	09/25/87	.20	.20	.80 (5)	1.00	
2254	5.3¢ Elevator 1900s, Bureau precanceled	09/16/88	.20	.20	1.40 (5)	1.00	
2255	7.6¢ Carreta 1770s, Bureau precanceled	08/30/88	.20	.20	1.75 (5)	1.00	
2256	8.4¢ Wheel Chair 1920s, Bureau precanceled	08/12/88	.20	.20	1.90 (5)	1.00	
a	Imperf., pair		575.00				
2257	10¢ Canal Boat 1880s	04/11/87	.40	.20	2.00 (5)	1.00	
a	Overall tagging, dull gum		1.50	.20	12.00 (5)		
b	Prephosphored uncoated paper		.20	.20	2.75 (5)		
c	Prephosphored coated paper		.25	.20	4.75 (5)		
d	Tagging omitted		30.00				
2258	13¢ Patrol Wagon 1880s, Bureau precanceled	10/29/88	.65	.25	5.00 (5)	1.50	
2259	13.2¢ Coal Car 1870s, Bureau precanceled	07/19/88	.25	.25	2.75 (5)	1.00	
a	Imperf., pair		95.00				
2260	15¢ Tugboat 1900s	07/12/88	.25	.20	2.25 (5)	1.00	
a	Overall tagging		.25	.20	3.25 (5)		
b	Tagging omitted		3.75				
c	Imperf., pair		650.00				
2261	16.7¢ Popcorn Wagon 1902, Bureau precanceled	07/07/88	.30	.30	2.25 (5)	1.00	
a	Imperf., pair		165.00				
2262	17.5¢ Racing Car 1911	09/25/87	.65	.20	4.00 (5)	1.25	
a	Untagged (Bureau precanceled)		.65	.30	4.00 (5)		
b	Imperf., pair		2,250.00				
2263	20¢ Cable Car 1880s	10/28/88	.35	.20	3.00 (5)	1.00	
a	Imperf., pair		50.00				
b	Overall tagging		1.00	.20	8.00 (5)		
2264	20.5¢ Fire Engine 1920s, Bureau precanceled	09/28/88	.75	.40	5.75 (5)	1.50	

Issue		Date	Un	U	PB/PNC #	FDC	Q(M)
	Transportation, Coil, Untagged, Perf. 10 Vertically continued						
2265	21¢ Railroad Mail Car 1920s, Bureau precanceled	08/16/88	.40	.40	3.00 (5)	1.00	
a	Imperf., pair		42.50				
2266	24.1¢ Tandem Bicycle 1890s, Bureau precanceled	10/26/88	.80	.45	3.75 (5)	1.50	
	Special Occasions Booklet, Tagged, Perf. 10 on 1, 2 or 3 sides						
2267	22¢ Congratulations!	04/20/87	.65	.20		1.00	1,222
2268	22¢ Get Well!	04/20/87	.80	.20		1.00	611
2269	22¢ Thank you!	04/20/87	.80	.20		1.00	611
2270	22¢ Love You, Dad!	04/20/87	.80	.20		1.00	611
2271	22¢ Best Wishes!	04/20/87	.80	.20		1.00	611
2272	22¢ Happy Birthday!	04/20/87	.65	.20		1.00	1,222
2273	22¢ Love You, Mother!	04/20/87	1.40	.20		1.00	611
2274	22¢ Keep In Touch!	04/20/87	.80	.20		1.00	611
a	Booklet pane of 10, #2268-2271, #2273-2274 and 2 each of #2267, #2272		10.00	5.00		5.00	611
	#2267-2274 issued only in booklets. All stamps are imperf. at one or two sides or imperf. at sides and bottom.						
	Tagged, Perf. 11						
2275	22¢ United Way	04/28/87	.40	.20	1.90 (4)	1.00	157
2276	22¢ Flag with Fireworks	05/09/87	.40	.20	1.90 (4)	1.00	
a	Booklet pane of 20	11/30/87	8.50	—		8.00	
b	As "a," vert. pair, imperf. between		1,500.00				
2277	(25¢) "E" Stamp	03/22/88	.45	.20	2.00 (4)	1.25	
2278	25¢ Flag with Clouds	05/06/88	.45	.20	1.90 (4)	1.25	
	Pair with full vertical gutter between		125.00				
	Coil, Perf. 10 Vertically						
2279	(25¢) "E" Earth	03/22/88	.45	.20	2.75 (5)	1.25	
a	Imperf., pair		65.00	—			
2280	25¢ Flag over Yosemite	05/20/88	.45	.20	5.75 (5)	1.25	
a	Prephosphored paper	02/14/89	.45	.20	30.00 (5)	1.25	
b	Imperf., pair, large block tagging		25.00				
c	Imperf., pair, prephosphored paper		10.00				
d	Tagging omitted		5.00				
e	Black trees		100.00	—	700.00 (5)		
f	Pair, imperf. between		500.00				
2281	25¢ Honeybee	09/02/88	.45	.20	3.50 (5)	1.25	
a	Imperf., pair		45.00				
b	Black (engr.) omitted		50.00				
c	Black (litho) omitted		450.00				
d	Pair, imperf. between		700.00				
e	Yellow (litho) omitted		1,000.00				
	Booklet, Perf. 10						
2282	(25¢) "E" Earth (#2277), single from booklet		.50	.20		1.25	
a	Booklet pane of 10	03/22/88	6.50	3.50		6.00	

2248

Jean Baptiste Pointe Du Sable 22
Black Heritage USA

2249

Enrico Caruso 22 USA

2250

GIRL SCOUTS USA 22

2251

Conestoga Wagon 1800s
3 USA

2252

Milk Wagon 1900s
5 USA

2253

Elevator 1900s
5.3 USA
Nonprofit Carrier Route Sort

2254

Carreta 1770s
7.6 USA
Nonprofit

2255

Wheel Chair 1920s
8.4 USA
Nonprofit

2256

Canal Boat 1880s
10 USA

2257

Patrol Wagon 1880s
13 USA
Presorted First-Class

2258

Coal Car 1870s
13.2 USA
Bulk Rate

2259

Tugboat 1900s
15 USA

2260

Popcorn Wagon 1902
16.7 USA
Bulk Rate

2261

Racing Car 1911
USA 17.5

2262

USA 20
Cable Car 1880s

2263

Fire Engine 1900s
20.5 USA
ZIP+4 Presort

2264

Railroad Mail Car 1920s
Presorted First-Class
21 USA

2265

Tandem Bicycle 1890s
24.1 USA
ZIP+4

2266

2267

Congratulations! 22 USA

2268

Get Well! USA 22

2269

Thank You! USA 22

2270

Love You, Dad! USA 22

2271

Best Wishes! USA 22

Happy Birthday! USA 22

2272

Love You, Mother! USA 22

2273

2274

Keep In Touch! USA 22

Happy Birthday! USA 22

2272

2267

Congratulations! USA 22

2274a

United Way 1887-1987
Uniting Communities USA 22

2275

22 USA

2276

E
Earth
Domestic USA

2277

USA 25

2278

E
Earth
Domestic USA

2279

25 USA
Yosemite

2280

25 USA

2281

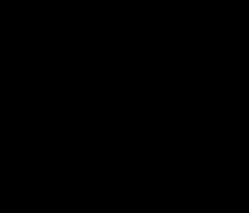

E Earth Domestic USA (block)

2282a

2283

2283c

2284   **2285**

2285b

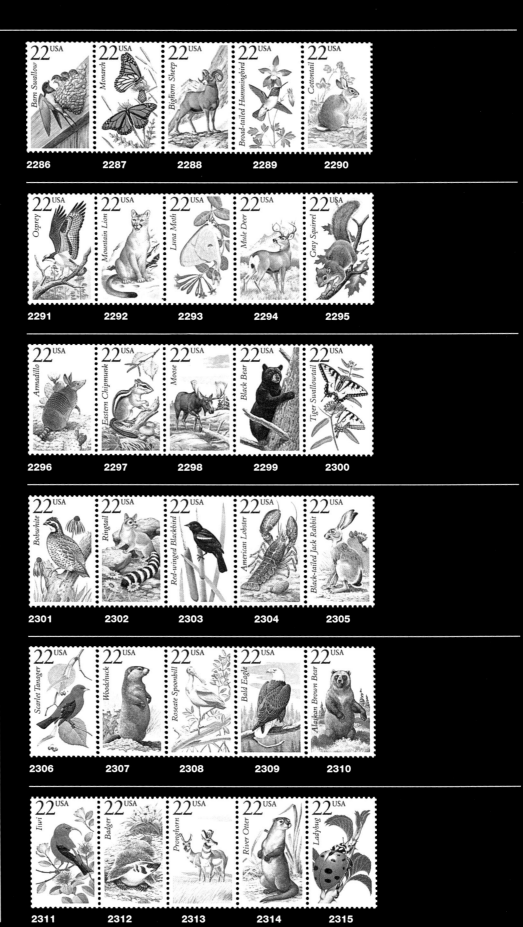

Barn Swallow	Monarch	Bighorn Sheep	Broad-tailed Hummingbird	Cottontail
2286	**2287**	**2288**	**2289**	**2290**
Osprey	Mountain Lion	Luna Moth	Mule Deer	Gray Squirrel
2291	**2292**	**2293**	**2294**	**2295**
Armadillo	Eastern Chipmunk	Moose	Black Bear	Tiger Swallowtail
2296	**2297**	**2298**	**2299**	**2300**
Bobwhite	Ringtail	Red-winged Blackbird	American Lobster	Black-tailed Jack Rabbit
2301	**2302**	**2303**	**2304**	**2305**
Scarlet Tanager	Woodchuck	Roseate Spoonbill	Bald Eagle	Alaskan Brown Bear
2306	**2307**	**2308**	**2309**	**2310**
Iiwi	Badger	Pronghorn	River Otter	Ladybug
2311	**2312**	**2313**	**2314**	**2315**

	Issue	Date	Un	U	PB #	FDC	Q(M)
	Booklet, Perf. 11						
2283	25¢ Pheasant, single from booklet		.50	.20		1.25	
a	Booklet pane of 10	04/29/88	6.00	3.50		6.00	
b	Single, red removed from sky		6.50	.20			
c	As "b," booklet pane of 10		70.00	—			
	#2283 issued only in booklets.						
	All stamps have one or two imperf. edges. Imperf. and part perf. pairs and						
	panes exist from printer's waste.						
	Booklet, Perf. 10						
2284	25¢ Grosbeak	05/28/88	.50	.20		1.25	
2285	25¢ Owl	05/28/88	.50	.20		1.25	
b	Booklet pane of 10, 5 each of #2284, 2285	05/28/88	5.00	3.50		6.00	
d	Pair, #2284, 2285		1.10	.25			
e	As "d," tagging omitted		12.50				
	#2284 and 2285 issued only in booklets. All stamps are imperf. at one side						
	or imperf. at one side and bottom.						
2285A	25¢ Flag with Clouds	07/05/88	.50	.20		1.00	
c	Booklet pane of 6		3.00	2.00		4.00	
	North American Wildlife, Tagged, Perf. 11						
2286	22¢ Barn Swallow	06/13/87	1.00	.50		1.50	13
2287	22¢ Monarch Butterfly	06/13/87	1.00	.50		1.50	13
2288	22¢ Bighorn Sheep	06/13/87	1.00	.50		1.50	13
2289	22¢ Broad-tailed Hummingbird	06/13/87	1.00	.50		1.50	13

	Issue	Date	Un	U	PB #	FDC	Q(M)
	North American Wildlife, Tagged, Perf. 11 continued						
2290	22¢ Cottontail	06/13/87	1.00	.50		1.50	13
2291	22¢ Osprey	06/13/87	1.00	.50		1.50	13
2292	22¢ Mountain Lion	06/13/87	1.00	.50		1.50	13
2293	22¢ Luna Moth	06/13/87	1.00	.50		1.50	12
2294	22¢ Mule Deer	06/13/87	1.00	.50		1.50	13
2295	22¢ Gray Squirrel	06/13/87	1.00	.50		1.50	13
2296	22¢ Armadillo	06/13/87	1.00	.50		1.50	13
2297	22¢ Eastern Chipmunk	06/13/87	1.00	.50		1.50	13
2298	22¢ Moose	06/13/87	1.00	.50		1.50	13
2299	22¢ Black Bear	06/13/87	1.00	.50		1.50	13
2300	22¢ Tiger Swallowtail	06/13/87	1.00	.50		1.50	13
2301	22¢ Bobwhite	06/13/87	1.00	.50		1.50	13
2302	22¢ Ringtail	06/13/87	1.00	.50		1.50	13
2303	22¢ Red-winged Blackbird	06/13/87	1.00	.50		1.50	13
2304	22¢ American Lobster	06/13/87	1.00	.50		1.50	13
2305	22¢ Black-tailed Jack Rabbit	06/13/87	1.00	.50		1.50	13
2306	22¢ Scarlet Tanager	06/13/87	1.00	.50		1.50	13
2307	22¢ Woodchuck	06/13/87	1.00	.50		1.50	13
2308	22¢ Roseate Spoonbill	06/13/87	1.00	.50		1.50	13
2309	22¢ Bald Eagle	06/13/87	1.00	.50		1.50	13
2310	22¢ Alaskan Brown Bear	06/13/87	1.00	.50		1.50	13
2311	22¢ Iiwi	06/13/87	1.00	.50		1.50	13
2312	22¢ Badger	06/13/87	1.00	.50		1.50	13
2313	22¢ Pronghorn	06/13/87	1.00	.50		1.50	13
2314	22¢ River Otter	06/13/87	1.00	.50		1.50	13
2315	22¢ Ladybug	06/13/87	1.00	.50		1.50	13

FOREVER™ STAMPED ENVELOPE

*I*n 2009, the U.S. Postal Service issued the first stamped envelope to feature the Forever stamp. As it is with the stamp, the value of the postage on the Forever stamped envelope is always equal to the then-current First-Class Mail one-ounce single-piece denomination. ■ The stamp art depicts the Liberty Bell, perhaps the most prominent and recognizable symbol associated with American independence. Over the years, the historic significance of the bell has transcended our national borders, and today it is an international icon of freedom. ■ In 1751 the Pennsylvania Assembly ordered a bell to be hung in the State House (now Independence Hall) in Philadelphia. Commissioned from Whitechapel Bell Foundry in England, the bell arrived the following year. While being tested, it cracked; two local foundry workers melted and recast the bell twice. Made mostly of copper and tin and weighing more than 2,000 pounds, the bell was finally hung in the tower of the State House in June 1753. ■ No one knows exactly when the Liberty Bell's familiar crack first appeared, but when the bell was rung in 1846 in celebration of George Washington's birthday the crack that had appeared some time after 1800 expanded so much that the bell could no longer be rung. Six years later the bell was removed from the State House tower and put on display. Since then its popularity as a symbol of freedom has only increased. Between 1885 and 1915 enthusiastic crowds greeted the Liberty Bell as it traveled by train to exhibitions across the nation. Today people from all over the world join American visitors at Liberty Bell Center (part of Independence National Historical Park in Philadelphia), where the taped history of the bell is available in several different languages.

Issue		Date	Un	U	PB #	FDC	Q(M)
North American Wildlife, Tagged, Perf. 11 continued							
2316	22¢ Beaver	06/13/87	1.00	.50		1.50	13
2317	22¢ White-tailed Deer	06/13/87	1.00	.50		1.50	13
2318	22¢ Blue Jay	06/13/87	1.00	.50		1.50	13
2319	22¢ Pika	06/13/87	1.00	.50		1.50	13
2320	22¢ Bison	06/13/87	1.00	.50			
2321	22¢ Snowy Egret	06/13/87	1.00	.50		1.50	13
2322	22¢ Gray Wolf	06/13/87	1.00	.50		1.50	13
2323	22¢ Mountain Goat	06/13/87	1.00	.50		1.50	13
2324	22¢ Deer Mouse	06/13/87	1.00	.50		1.50	13
2325	22¢ Black-tailed Prairie Dog	06/13/87	1.00	.50		1.50	13
2326	22¢ Box Turtle	06/13/87	1.00	.50		1.50	13
2327	22¢ Wolverine	06/13/87	1.00	.50		1.50	13
2328	22¢ American Elk	06/13/87	1.00	.50		1.50	13
2329	22¢ California Sea Lion	06/13/87	1.00	.50		1.50	13
2330	22¢ Mockingbird	06/13/87	1.00	.50		1.50	13
2331	22¢ Raccoon	06/13/87	1.00	.50		1.50	13
2332	22¢ Bobcat	06/13/87	1.00	.50		1.50	13
2333	22¢ Black-footed Ferret	06/13/87	1.00	.50		1.50	13
2334	22¢ Canada Goose	06/13/87	1.00	.50		1.50	13
2335	22¢ Red Fox	06/13/87	1.00	.50		1.50	13
a	Pane of 50, #2286-2335		50.00	35.00		50.00	
2286b-2335b Any single, red omitted			2,500.00				

Issue		Date	Un	U	PB #	FDC	Q(M)
Ratification of the Constitution, Tagged, Perf. 11							
2336	22¢ Delaware	07/04/87	.60	.20	2.75 (4)	1.50	167
2337	22¢ Pennsylvania	08/26/87	.60	.20	2.75 (4)	1.50	187
2338	22¢ New Jersey	09/11/87	.60	.20	2.75 (4)	1.50	184
a	Black omitted		5,500.00				
2339	22¢ Georgia	01/06/88	.60	.20	2.75 (4)	1.50	169
2340	22¢ Connecticut	01/09/88	.60	.20	2.75 (4)	1.50	155
2341	22¢ Massachusetts	02/06/88	.60	.20	2.75 (4)	1.50	102
2342	22¢ Maryland	02/15/88	.60	.20	2.75 (4)	1.50	103
2343	25¢ South Carolina	05/23/88	.60	.20	2.75 (4)	1.50	162
2344	25¢ New Hampshire	06/21/88	.60	.20	2.75 (4)	1.50	153
2345	25¢ Virginia	06/25/88	.60	.20	2.75 (4)	1.50	160
2346	25¢ New York	07/26/88	.60	.20	2.75 (4)	1.50	183
2347	25¢ North Carolina	08/22/89	.60	.20	2.75 (4)	1.50	180
2348	25¢ Rhode Island	05/29/90	.60	.20	3.00 (4)	1.50	164
	Tagged, Perf. 11						
2349	22¢ Friendship with Morocco	07/18/87	.55	.20	1.75 (4)	1.00	157
a	Black omitted		250.00				
	Literary Arts, Tagged, Perf. 11						
2350	22¢ William Faulkner	08/03/87	.55	.20	2.75 (4)	1.00	156
	American Folk Art: Lace Making, Tagged, Perf. 11						
2351	22¢ Squash Blossoms	08/14/87	.45	.20		1.00	41
2352	22¢ Floral Piece	08/14/87	.45	.20		1.00	41
2353	22¢ Floral Piece	08/14/87	.45	.20		1.00	41
2354	22¢ Dogwood Blossoms	08/14/87	.45	.20		1.00	41
a	Block of 4, #2351-2354		1.90	1.90	3.25 (4)	2.50	
b	As "a," white omitted		550.00				

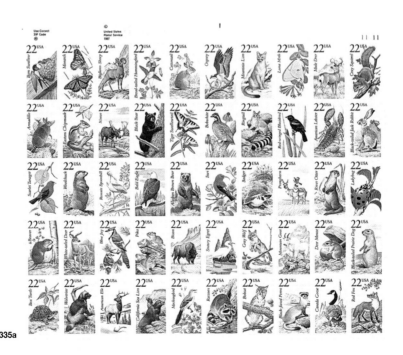

2335a

22 USA Beaver **2316**	22 USA White-tailed Deer **2317**	22 USA Blue Jay **2318**	22 USA Pika **2319**	22 USA Bison **2320**
22 USA Snowy Egret **2321**	22 USA Gray Wolf **2322**	22 USA Mountain Goat **2323**	22 USA Deer Mouse **2324**	22 USA Black-tailed Prairie Dog **2325**
22 USA Box Turtle **2326**	22 USA Wolverine **2327**	22 USA American Elk **2328**	22 USA California Sea Lion **2329**	22 USA Mockingbird **2330**
22 USA Raccoon **2331**	22 USA Bobcat **2332**	22 USA Black-footed Ferret **2333**	22 USA Canada Goose **2334**	22 USA Red Fox **2335**

Dec 7, 1787 USA Delaware 22 **2336**	Dec 12, 1787 USA Pennsylvania 22 **2337**	Dec 18, 1787 USA New Jersey 22 **2338**
22 USA January 2, 1788 Georgia **2339**	22 USA January 9, 1788 Connecticut **2340**	22 USA Feb 6, 1788 Massachusetts **2341**
April 28, 1788 USA Maryland 22 **2342**	25 USA May 23, 1788 South Carolina **2343**	25 USA June 21, 1788 New Hampshire **2344**
June 25, 1788 USA Virginia 25 **2345**	July 26, 1788 USA New York 25 **2346**	25 USA November 21, 1789 North Carolina **2347**

25 USA May 29, 1790 Rhode Island **2348**	Friendship with Morocco 1787-1987 USA 22 **2349**	William Faulkner USA 22 **2350**	Lacemaking USA 22 **2351**	Lacemaking USA 22 **2352**
			Lacemaking USA 22 **2353**	Lacemaking USA 22 **2354** / **2354a**

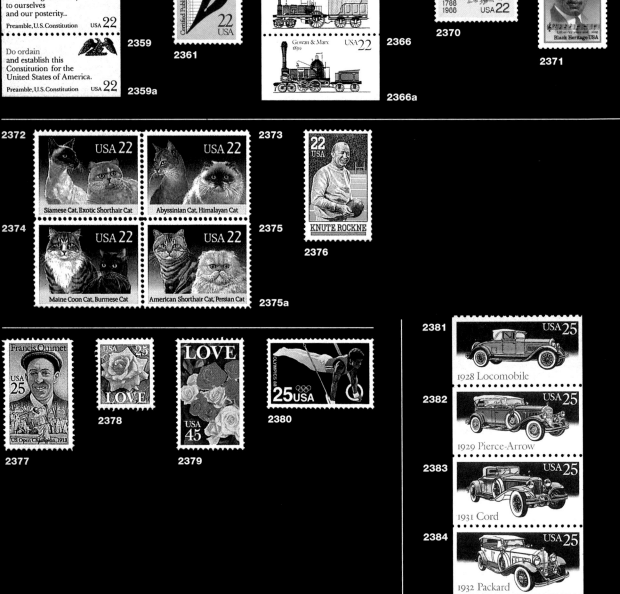

2355 The Bicentennial of the Constitution of the United States of America 1787-1987 USA 22

2356 We the people of the United States, in order to form a more perfect Union... Preamble, U.S. Constitution USA 22

2357 Establish justice, insure domestic tranquility, provide for the common defense, promote the general welfare... Preamble, U.S. Constitution USA 22

2358 And secure the blessings of liberty to ourselves and our posterity... Preamble, U.S. Constitution USA 22

2359 Do ordain and establish this Constitution for the United States of America. Preamble, U.S. Constitution USA 22

2359a

2360 U.S. Constitution We the People 1787-1987 22 USA

2361 CPA Certified Public Accountants 22 USA

2362 Stourbridge Lion 1829 USA 22

2363 Best Friend of Charleston 1830 USA 22

2364 John Bull 1831 USA 22

2365 Brother Jonathan 1832 USA 22

2366 Gowan & Marx 1839 USA 22

2366a

2367 CHRISTMAS 22 Moroni, National Gallery

2368 USA 22 GREETINGS

2369 22 OLYMPICS 88 USA

2370 Happy Bicentennial Australia! 1788 1988 USA 22

2371 James Weldon Johnson 22 Lift every voice and sing Black Heritage USA

2372 USA 22 Siamese Cat, Exotic Shorthair Cat

2373 USA 22 Abyssinian Cat, Himalayan Cat

2374 USA 22 Maine Coon Cat, Burmese Cat

2375 USA 22 American Shorthair Cat, Persian Cat

2375a

2376 22 USA KNUTE ROCKNE

2377 Francis Ouimet USA 25 US Open Champion, 1913

2378 USA 25 LOVE

2379 LOVE USA 45

2380 OLYMPICS 88 25 USA

2381 USA 25 1928 Locomobile

2382 USA 25 1929 Pierce-Arrow

2383 USA 25 1931 Cord

2384 USA 25 1932 Packard

2385 USA 25 1935 Duesenberg

2385a

	Issue	Date	Un	U	PB	#	FDC	Q(M)
	Drafting of the Constitution, Booklet, Tagged, Perf. 10 Horizontally							
2355	22¢ "The Bicentennial..."	08/28/87	.90	.20			1.25	117
2356	22¢ "We the people..."	08/28/87	.90	.20			1.25	117
2357	22¢ "Establish justice..."	08/28/87	.90	.20			1.25	117
2358	22¢ "And secure..."	08/28/87	.90	.20			1.25	117
2359	22¢ "Do ordain..."	08/28/87	.90	.20			1.25	117
a	Booklet pane of 5, #2355-2359		4.50	2.25			4.00	

#2355-2359 issued only in booklets. All stamps are imperf. at sides or imperf. at sides and bottom.

	Issue	Date	Un	U	PB	#	FDC	Q(M)
	Signing of the Constitution, Tagged, Perf. 11							
2360	22¢ Constitution and Signer's Hand-Holding Quill Pen	09/17/87	.55	.20	2.75	(4)	1.25	169
2361	22¢ Certified Public Accountants	09/21/87	1.00	.20	5.50	(4)	7.50	163
a	Black omitted		675.00					
	Locomotives Booklet, Tagged, Perf. 10 Horizontally							
2362	22¢ Stourbridge Lion, 1829	10/01/87	.55	.20			1.25	79
2363	22¢ Best Friend of Charleston, 1830	10/01/87	.55	.20			1.25	79
2364	22¢ John Bull, 1831	10/01/87	.55	.20			1.25	79
2365	22¢ Brother Jonathan, 1832	10/01/87	.55	.20			1.25	79
a	Red omitted		1,100.00	225.00				
2366	22¢ Gowan & Marx, 1839	10/01/87	.55	.20			1.25	79
a	Booklet pane of 5, #2362-2366		2.75	2.50			3.00	

#2362-2366 issued only in booklets. All stamps are imperf. at sides or imperf. at sides and bottom.

	Issue	Date	Un	U	PB	#	FDC	Q(M)
	Holiday Celebration: Christmas, Tagged, Perf. 11							
2367	22¢ Madonna and Child, by Moroni	10/23/87	.45	.20	2.25	(4)	1.25	529
	Holiday Celebration: Holiday, Tagged, Perf. 11							
2368	22¢ Christmas Ornaments	10/23/87	.45	.20	2.10	(4)	1.25	978
	Pair with full vertical gutter between		—					
	Olympic Games, Winter, Tagged, Perf. 11							
2369	22¢ Skier and Olympic Rings	01/10/88	.50	.20	2.25	(4)	1.00	159

	Issue	Date	Un	U	PB	#	FDC	Q(M)
	Tagged, Perf. 11							
2370	22¢ Australia Bicentennial	01/10/88	.45	.20	2.10	(4)	1.75	146
	Black Heritage, Tagged, Perf. 11							
2371	22¢ James Weldon Johnson	02/02/88	.50	.20	2.60	(4)	1.75	97
	American Cats, Tagged, Perf. 11							
2372	22¢ Siamese and Exotic Shorthair	02/05/88	.70	.20			2.00	40
2373	22¢ Abyssinian and Himalayan	02/05/88	.70	.20			2.00	40
2374	22¢ Maine Coon and Burmese	02/05/88	.70	.20			2.00	40
2375	22¢ American Shorthair and Persian	02/05/88	.70	.20			2.00	40
a	Block of 4, #2372-2375		2.80	1.90	4.00	(4)	4.50	
	American Sports Personalities, Tagged, Perf. 11							
2376	22¢ Knute Rockne	03/09/88	.50	.20	2.60	(4)	4.00	97
2377	25¢ Francis Ouimet	06/13/88	.60	.20	3.00	(4)	4.50	153
	Love, Tagged							
2378	25¢ Love	07/04/88	.50	.20	2.25	(4)	1.00	841
a	Imperf., pair		1,750.00					
2379	45¢ Love	08/08/88	.85	.20	3.75	(4)	1.25	170
	Olympic Games, Summer, Tagged							
2380	25¢ Gymnast on Rings	08/19/88	.50	.20	2.25	(4)	1.25	157
	Classic Cars, Booklet, Tagged, Perf. 10 Horizontally							
2381	25¢ 1928 Locomobile	08/25/88	.80	.20			1.25	127
2382	25¢ 1929 Pierce-Arrow	08/25/88	.80	.20			1.25	127
2383	25¢ 1931 Cord	08/25/88	.80	.20			1.25	127
2384	25¢ 1932 Packard	08/25/88	.80	.20			1.25	127
2385	25¢ 1935 Duesenberg	08/25/88	.80	.20			1.25	127
a	Booklet pane of 5, #2381-2385		6.00	3.50			4.00	

#2381-2385 issued only in booklets. All stamps are imperf. at sides or imperf. at sides and bottom.

EID

With the reissue of the 2001 Eid stamp, the U.S. Postal Service again commemorates the two most important holidays in the Islamic calendar: Eid al-Fitr and Eid al-Adha. ■ The first day of the Muslim lunar month of Shawwal, Eid al-Fitr signifies "The Feast of Breaking the Fast." This festival marks the end of Ramadan, the month of fasting, during which Muslims must abstain from food and drink—and also from evil thoughts, sexual activity, and smoking—from just before first light until sunset. Eid al-Fitr is observed by offering special alms with prayers, feasting, exchanging gifts, and visiting family and friends. ■ Eid al-Adha, signifying "The Feast of the Sacrifice," occurs approximately two months and ten days after Eid al-Fitr. Coming at the end of the *hajj*, the annual period of pilgrimage to the holy city of Mecca, Eid al-Adha commemorates Ibrahim's willingness to sacrifice his son Ismail. It is celebrated with prayers and social gatherings and traditionally includes the sacrifice of a lamb, or any other animal permitted for food in Islam, as an act of thanksgiving for Allah's mercy. The sacrificial animal is distributed among family, friends, and the poor. ■ Elegantly designed by renowned Islamic calligrapher Mohamed Zakariya, this stamp features the Arabic phrase *Eid mubarak* in gold calligraphy on a blue background. *Eid mubarak* translates literally as "blessed festival" but can be paraphrased in a way that people of all backgrounds and cultures can appreciate: "May your holiday be blessed."

	Issue	Date	Un	U	PB	#	FDC	Q(M)
	Antarctic Explorers, Tagged, Perf. 11							
2386	25¢ Nathaniel Palmer	09/14/88	.65	.20			1.25	41
2387	25¢ Lt. Charles Wilkes	09/14/88	.65	.20			1.25	41
2388	25¢ Richard E. Byrd	09/14/88	.65	.20			1.25	41
2389	25¢ Lincoln Ellsworth	09/14/88	.65	.20			1.25	41
a	Block of 4, #2386-2389		2.75	2.00	4.50	(4)	3.00	
b	As "a," black omitted		1,250.00					
c	As "a," imperf. horizontally		1,950.00					
	American Folk Art: Carousel Animals, Tagged, Perf. 11							
2390	25¢ Deer	10/01/88	.65	.20			1.50	76
2391	25¢ Horse	10/01/88	.65	.20			1.50	76
2392	25¢ Camel	10/01/88	.65	.20			1.50	76
2393	25¢ Goat	10/01/88	.65	.20			1.50	76
a	Block of 4, #2390-2393		3.00	2.00	4.00	(4)	3.50	
	Tagged, Perf. 11							
2394	$8.75 Express Mail	10/04/88	13.50	8.00	54.00	(4)	27.50	
	Special Occasions, Booklet, Tagged, Perf. 11							
2395	25¢ Happy Birthday	10/22/88	.50	.20			1.25	120
2396	25¢ Best Wishes	10/22/88	.50	.20			1.25	120
a	Booklet pane of 6, 3 #2395 and 3 #2396 with gutter between		3.50	3.25			4.00	
2397	25¢ Thinking of You	10/22/88	.50	.20			1.25	120
2398	25¢ Love You	10/22/88	.50	.20			1.25	120
a	Booklet pane of 6, 3 #2397 and 3 #2398 with gutter between		3.50	3.25			4.00	
b	As "a," imperf. horizontally		—					

#2395-2398a issued only in booklets. All stamps are imperf. on one side or on one side and top or bottom.

	Issue	Date	Un	U	PB	#	FDC	Q(M)
	Holiday Celebration: Christmas, Tagged, Perf. 11.5							
2399	25¢ Madonna and Child, by Botticelli	10/20/88	.50	.20	2.25	(4)	1.25	822
a	Gold omitted		25.00					
	Holiday Celebration: Holiday, Tagged, Perf. 11							
2400	25¢ One-Horse Open Sleigh and Village Scene	10/20/88	.50	.20	2.25	(4)	1.25	1,038
	Pair with full vertical gutter between		—					
	Tagged, Perf. 11							
2401	25¢ Montana Statehood	01/15/89	.55	.20	2.75	(4)	1.25	165
	Black Heritage, Tagged, Perf. 11							
2402	25¢ A. Philip Randolph	02/03/89	.50	.20	2.25	(4)	1.75	152
	Tagged, Perf. 11							
2403	25¢ North Dakota Statehood	02/21/89	.50	.20	2.25	(4)	1.00	163
2404	25¢ Washington Statehood	02/22/89	.50	.20	2.25	(4)	1.00	265
	Steamboats, Booklet, Tagged, Perf. 10 Horizontally on 1 or 2 sides							
2405	25¢ Experiment 1788-1790	03/03/89	.50	.20			1.25	41
2406	25¢ Phoenix 1809	03/03/89	.50	.20			1.25	41
2407	25¢ New Orleans 1812	03/03/89	.50	.20			1.25	41
2408	25¢ Washington 1816	03/03/89	.50	.20			1.25	41
2409	25¢ Walk in the Water 1818	03/03/89	.50	.20			1.25	41
a	Booklet pane of 5, #2405-2409		2.50	1.75			3.00	

#2405-2409 issued only in booklets. All stamps are imperf. at sides or imperf. at sides and bottom.

	Issue	Date	Un	U	PB	#	FDC	Q(M)
	Tagged, Perf. 11							
2410	25¢ World Stamp Expo '89	03/16/89	.50	.20	2.25	(4)	1.00	104
	Performing Arts, Tagged, Perf. 11							
2411	25¢ Arturo Toscanini	03/25/89	.50	.20	2.25	(4)	1.00	152

LOVE: KING AND QUEEN OF HEARTS

In 2009, the U.S. Postal Service pays clever tribute to the world's favorite "game" with the King and Queen of Hearts stamps, the latest in the Love series. The game of love draws on elements of luck, strategy—such as the bluff—and skill. As the English poet John Donne wrote, love is "got by chance" but "kept by art." With all its risks and pleasures, love is sure to keep writers busy for a long time to come. And with these stamps, love letters and other correspondence will have a delightful, playful touch. ▪ Artist Jeanne Greco used images from 18th-century French playing cards as reference for the stamp art. "I wanted to find something intriguing on two levels—visually compelling, but also conceptually smart," she says. "I thought of two stamps which addressed each other and the idea of the male and female stamps facing each other." ▪ Love stories take various forms, but they all seem to follow one of several basic patterns. Perhaps that is partly why Greco and art director Derry Noyes settled on a repeating pattern for these stamps. "I love the idea," says Noyes, "of having the design flow through the stamp perforations so it's a continuous pattern, and it doesn't stop with a white border around it. It's intriguing in the way they're kind of glancing at each other and the way her hand reaches out to hold the flower." ▪ The Postal Service began issuing its popular Love stamps in 1973. Over the years these stamps have featured a wide variety of designs, including heart motifs, colorful flowers, and the word "LOVE" itself.

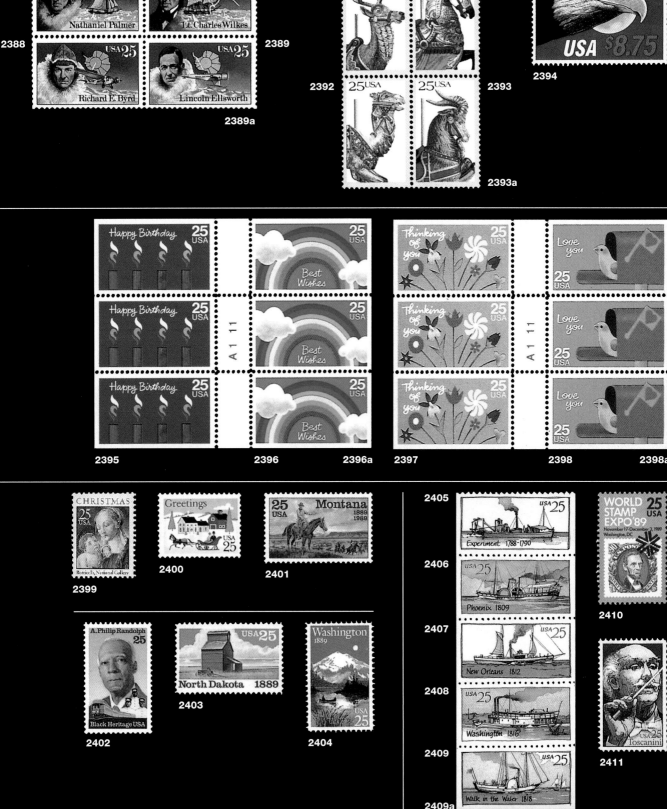

2386 2387 2390 2391 2394
2388 2389 2389a 2392 2393 2393a
2395 2396 2396a 2397 2398 2398a
2399 2400 2401 2405 2406 2407 2408 2409 2410
2402 2403 2404 2411 2409a

BICENTENNIAL
HOUSE OF REPRESENTATIVES

2412

BICENTENNIAL
UNITED STATES SENATE

2413

BICENTENNIAL
EXECUTIVE BRANCH

2414

BICENTENNIAL
U.S. SUPREME COURT

Chief Justice John Marshall

2415

South Dakota 1889 USA 25

2416

Lou Gehrig

USA 25

2417

Hemingway

USA 25

2418

USA $2.40

2419

Letter Carriers: We Deliver! USA 25

2420

Bill of Rights

USA 25

2421

2422

USA 25 Tyrannosaurus

2423

USA 25 Pteranodon

2424

USA 25 Stegosaurus

2425

USA 25 Brontosaurus

2425a

AMERICA USA 25

2426

CHRISTMAS USA 25

Carracci, National Gallery

2427

Greetings USA 25

2428

WORLD STAMP EXPO '89

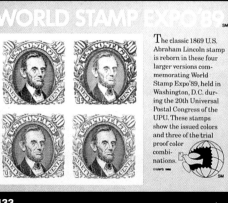

The classic 1869 U.S. Abraham Lincoln stamp is reborn in these four larger versions commemorating World Stamp Expo '89, held in Washington, D.C. during the 20th Universal Postal Congress of the UPU. These stamps show the issued colors and three of the trial proof color combinations.

2433

USA 25

2431

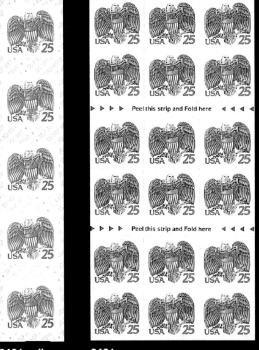

Peel this strip and Fold here

Peel this strip and Fold here

2431 coil

2431a

2434

USA 25 20th Universal Postal Congress

2435

2436

USA 25 20th Universal Postal Congress

2437

2437a

144

	Issue	Date	Un	U	PB	#	FDC	Q(M)
	Constitution Bicentennial, Tagged, Perf. 11							
2412	25¢ U.S. House of Representatives	04/04/89	.50	.20	2.25	(4)	1.25	139
2413	25¢ U.S. Senate	04/06/89	.50	.20	2.75	(4)	1.25	138
2414	25¢ Executive Branch, George Washington	04/16/89	.50	.20	2.25	(4)	1.25	139
2415	25¢ Supreme Court, Chief Justice John Marshall	02/02/90	.50	.20	2.25	(4)	1.25	151
	Tagged, Perf. 11							
2416	25¢ South Dakota Statehood	05/03/89	.60	.20	2.75	(4)	1.00	165
	American Sports Personalities, Tagged, Perf. 11							
2417	25¢ Lou Gehrig	06/10/89	.60	.20	3.00	(4)	4.00	263
	Literary Arts, Tagged, Perf. 11							
2418	25¢ Ernest Hemingway	07/17/89	.50	.20	2.25	(4)	1.25	192
a	Vertical pair, imperf. horiz.		1,750.00					
	Space, Priority Mail, Tagged, Perf. 11 x 11.5							
2419	$2.40 Moon Landing	07/20/89	4.75	2.00	20.00	(4)	7.50	
a	Black (engr.) omitted		2,000.00					
b	Imperf., pair		650.00					
c	Black (litho.) omitted		2,250.00					
	Tagged, Perf. 11							
2420	25¢ Letter Carriers	08/30/89	.50	.20	2.25	(4)	1.25	188
	Constitution Bicentennial, Tagged, Perf. 11							
2421	25¢ Bill of Rights	09/25/89	.50	.20	3.25	(4)	1.00	192
a	Black omitted		250.00					
	Prehistoric Animals, Tagged, Perf. 11							
2422	25¢ Tyrannosaurus	10/01/89	.70	.20			1.50	102
2423	25¢ Pteranodon	10/01/89	.70	.20			1.50	102
2424	25¢ Stegosaurus	10/01/89	.70	.20			1.50	102
2425	25¢ Brontosaurus	10/01/89	.70	.20			1.50	102
a	Block of 4, #2422-2425		2.80	2.00	4.00	(4)	3.00	
b	As "a," black omitted		425.00					
	America/PUAS, Tagged, Perf. 11							
2426	25¢ Southwest Carved Figure (A.D. 1150-1350), Emblem of the Postal Union of the Americas	10/12/89	.60	.20	3.00	(4)	1.00	137
	Holiday Celebration: Christmas, Tagged, Perf. 11.5							
2427	25¢ Madonna and Child, by Caracci	10/19/89	.50	.20	2.25	(4)	1.00	913
a	Booklet pane of 10		5.00	3.50			6.00	
b	Red (litho.) omitted		650.00					

	Issue	Date	Un	U	PB	#	FDC	Q(M)
	Holiday Celebration: Holiday, Tagged, Perf. 11							
2428	25¢ Sleigh Full of Presents	10/19/89	.50	.20	2.25	(4)	1.00	900
a	Vertical pair, imperf. horizontally		750.00					
	Booklet, Perf. 11.5 on 2 or 3 sides							
2429	25¢ Single from booklet pane (#2428)	10/19/89	.50	.20			1.00	399
a	Booklet pane of 10		5.00	3.50			6.00	
b	As "a," imperf. horiz. between		—					
c	Vertical pair, imperf. horizontally		—					
d	As "a," red omitted		3,250.00					
e	Imperf., pair		—					

In #2429, runners on sleigh are twice as thick as in #2428; bow on package at rear of sleigh is same color as package; board running underneath sleigh is pink.

	Issue	Date	Un	U	PB	#	FDC	Q(M)
2430	Not assigned							
	Tagged, Self-Adhesive, Die-Cut							
2431	25¢ Eagle and Shield	11/10/89	.50	.20			1.25	75
a	Booklet pane of 18		11.00					
b	Vertical pair, no die-cutting between		450.00					
c	Die-cutting omitted, pair		250.00					
2432	Not assigned							
	World Stamp Expo '89 Souvenir Sheet, Tagged, Imperf.							
2433	Reproduction of #122, 90¢ Lincoln, and three essays of #122	11/17/89	10.00	10.00			7.00	2
a-d	Single stamp from sheet		2.50	2.50				
	20th UPU Congress, Classic Mail Transportation, Tagged, Perf. 11							
2434	25¢ Stagecoach	11/19/89	.50	.20			1.25	41
2435	25¢ Paddlewheel Steamer	11/19/89	.50	.20			1.25	41
2436	25¢ Biplane	11/19/89	.50	.20			1.25	41
2437	25¢ Depot-Hack Type Automobile	11/19/89	.50	.20			1.25	41
a	Block of 4, #2434-2437		2.00	1.75	3.75	(4)	2.50	
b	As "a," dark blue omitted		475.00					

Issue	Date	Un	U	PB/PNC	#	FDC	Q(M)
Souvenir Sheet, Tagged, Imperf.							
2438 Designs of #2434-2437	11/28/89	5.00	3.75			3.00	2
a-d Single stamp from sheet		1.10	.80				
Tagged, Perf. 11							
2439 25¢ Idaho Statehood	01/06/90	.55	.20	3.00	(4)	1.25	173
Love, Tagged, Perf. 12.5 x 13							
2440 25¢ Love	01/18/90	.50	.20	2.25	(4)	1.25	886
a Imperf., pair		675.00					
Booklet, Perf. 11.5							
2441 25¢ Love, single from booklet	01/18/90	.50	.20			1.00	995
a Booklet pane of 10	01/18/90	5.00	3.50			6.00	
b bright pink omitted, single		150.00					
c As "a," bright pink omitted		1,650.00					
Black Heritage, Tagged, Perf. 11							
2442 25¢ Ida B. Wells	02/01/90	.75	.20	3.75	(4)	2.00	153
Booklet, Tagged, Perf. 11							
2443 15¢ Beach Umbrella, single from booklet	02/03/90	.30	.20			1.25	
a Booklet pane of 10	02/03/90	3.00	2.00			4.25	
b Blue omitted		125.00					
c As "a," blue omitted		1,250.00					

#2443 issued only in booklets. All stamps are imperf. at one side or imperf. at one side and bottom.

Issue	Date	Un	U	PB/PNC	#	FDC	Q(M)
Tagged, Perf. 11							
2444 25¢ Wyoming Statehood	02/23/90	.50	.20	3.25	(4)	1.00	169
a Black (engr.) omitted		1,350.00	—				
Classic Films, Tagged, Perf. 11							
2445 25¢ The Wizard of Oz	03/23/90	1.50	.20			2.50	44
2446 25¢ Gone With the Wind	03/23/90	1.50	.20			2.50	44
2447 25¢ Beau Geste	03/23/90	1.50	.20			2.50	44
2448 25¢ Stagecoach	03/23/90	1.50	.20			2.50	44
a Block of 4, #2445-2448		6.00	3.50	6.50	(4)	5.00	
Literary Arts, Tagged, Perf. 11							
2449 25¢ Marianne Moore	04/18/90	.60	.20	2.75	(4)	1.25	150
2450 Not assigned							
Transportation, Coil, Tagged, Perf. 9.8 Vertically							
Untagged (#2452B, 2452D, 2453, 2454, 2457, 2458)							
2451 4¢ Steam Carriage 1866	01/25/91	.20	.20	.80	(5)	1.25	
a Imperf., pair		550.00					
b Untagged		.20	.20	.90	(5)		
2452 5¢ Circus Wagon 1900s, intaglio printing	08/31/91	.20	.20	.85	(5)	1.50	
a Untagged, dull gum		.20	.20	3.00	(5)		
c Imperf., pair		600.00					
2452B 5¢ Circus Wagon (2452), gravure printing	12/08/92	.20	.20	1.25	(5)	1.50	
f Printed with luminescent ink		.20	.20	2.75	(5)		
2452D 5¢ Circus Wagon (2452), gravure printing	03/20/95	.20	.20	1.25	(5)	2.00	
e Imperf., pair		135.00					
g Printed with luminescent ink		.20	.20	2.25	(5)		
2453 5¢ Canoe 1800s, precanceled, intaglio printing	05/25/91	.20	.20	1.50	(5)	1.25	
a Imperf., pair		225.00					
2454 5¢ Canoe 1800s, precanceled, gravure printing	10/22/91	.45	.20	1.25	(5)	1.25	
2455-245 Not assigned							
2457 10¢ Tractor Trailer, Bureau precanceled, intaglio printing	05/25/91	.35	.20	2.50	(5)	1.25	
a Imperf., pair		130.00					

Issue	Date	Un	U	PB/PNC	#	FDC	Q(M)
Transportation Coil, Untagged, Perf. 9.8 Vertically continued							
2458 10¢ Tractor Trailer, Bureau precanceled, gravure printing	05/25/94	.45	.20	3.50	(5)	1.25	
2459-2462 Not assigned							
Tagged, Perf. 9.8 Vertically							
2463 20¢ Cog Railway Car 1870s	06/09/95	.40	.20	3.00	(5)	1.25	
a Imperf., pair		90.00					
2464 23¢ Lunch Wagon 1890s	04/12/91	.45	.20	3.25	(5)	1.25	
a Prephosphored uncoated paper		1.20	.20	9.00	(5)		
b Imperf., pair		110.00					
2465 Not assigned							
2466 32¢ Ferryboat 1900s	06/02/95	.80	.20	4.50	(5)	1.25	
a Imperf., pair		500.00					
b Bright blue, prephosphored uncoated paper		6.00	4.50	95.00	(5)		
2467 Not assigned							
2468 $1 Seaplane 1914	04/20/90	2.25	.50	13.00	(5)	2.50	
a Imperf., pair		2,500.00	—				
b Prephosphored uncoated paper		2.40	.50	13.00	(5)		
c Prephosphored coated paper		3.50	.50	18.00	(5)		
2469 Not assigned							
Lighthouses, Booklet, Tagged, Perf. 10 Vertically on 1 or 2 sides							
2470 25¢ Admiralty Head, WA	04/26/90	1.90	.20			1.50	147
2471 25¢ Cape Hatteras, NC	04/26/90	1.90	.20			1.50	147
2472 25¢ West Quoddy Head, ME	04/26/90	1.90	.20			1.50	147
2473 25¢ American Shoals, FL	04/26/90	1.90	.20			1.50	147
2474 25¢ Sandy Hook, NJ	04/26/90	1.90	.20			1.50	147
a Booklet pane of 5, #2470-2474		9.50	2.00			4.00	
b As "a," white (USA 25) omitted		80.00	—				
Untagged, Self-Adhesive, Die-Cut							
2475 25¢ Flag, single from pane	05/18/90	.55	.25			1.00	36
a Pane of 12	05/18/90	6.60					
Flora and Fauna, Untagged, Perf. 11, Perf. 11.2 (#2477)							
2476 1¢ American Kestrel	06/22/91	.20	.20	.20	(4)	1.00	
2477 1¢ American Kestrel	05/10/95	.20	.20	.20	(4)	1.00	
2478 3¢ Eastern Bluebird	06/22/91	.20	.20	.30	(4)	1.00	
Tagged, Perf. 11.5 x 11							
2479 19¢ Fawn	03/11/91	.35	.20	1.75	(4)	1.00	
a Tagging omitted		10.00					
b Red omitted		725.00					
2480 30¢ Cardinal	06/22/91	.60	.20	2.75	(4)	1.25	
Perf. 11							
2481 45¢ Pumpkinseed Sunfish	12/02/92	.90	.20	4.25	(4)	1.75	
a Black omitted		425.00	—				
2482 $2 Bobcat	06/01/90	3.50	1.25	14.00	(4)	5.00	
a Black omitted		225.00					
b Tagging omitted		12.50					
Booklet, Tagged, Perf. 10.9 x 9.8, Perf. 10 on 2 or 3 sides (#2477)							
2483 20¢ Blue Jay	06/15/95	.50	.20			1.25	
a Booklet pane of 10		5.25	2.25				
Booklet, Tagged, Perf. 10 on 2 or 3 sides							
2484 29¢ Wood Duck	04/12/91	.60	.20			1.00	
a Booklet pane of 10		6.00	3.75			4.00	
b Vertical pair, imperf. between		190.00					
c As "b," booklet pane of 10		950.00					
d Prephosphored coated paper		.60	.20				
Booklet, Tagged, Perf. 11 on 2 or 3 sides							
2485 29¢ Red and multicolored	04/12/91	.60	.20			1.00	
a Booklet pane of 10		6.00	4.00			4.00	
b Vertical pair, imperf. between		3,000.00					
c Imperf, pair		2,500.00					

#2484-2485a issued only in booklets. All stamps are imperf. top or bottom, or top or bottom and right edge.

20th Universal Postal Congress

A review of historical methods of delivering the mail in the United States is the theme of these four stamps issued in commemoration of the convening of the 20th Universal Postal Congress in Washington, D.C. from November 13 through December 15, 1989. The United States, as host nation to the Congress for the first time in ninety-two years, welcomed more than 1,000 delegates from most of the member nations of the Universal Postal Union to the major international event.

2438

2439

2440

2442

2443

2444

2445  **2446**

2447 **2448**

2448a

2449

2451

2452

2452D

2453

2454 **2457** **2463** **2464**

2466

2468

2470 **2471** **2472** **2473** **2474** **2474a**

2475

2476

2477

2478

2479

2480

2481

2482
2483

2484

2485

2486

2487

2488

2489

2490

2491

2492

2496   **2497**   **2498**   **2499**   **2500**   **2500a**

2501   **2502**   **2503**   **2504**   **2505**   **2505a**

2506   **2507**   **2507a**

2508   **2509**

2510   **2511**   **2511a**

2512

2513

2514

2515

2517

2519

2520

This U.S. stamp, along with 25¢ of additional U.S. postage, is equivalent to the 'F' stamp rate

2521

2522

2523

2523A

2524

2525

2526

2528

	Issue	Date	Un	U	PB/PNC	#	FDC	Q(M)
	Booklet, Tagged, Perf. 10 x 11 on 2 or 3 sides							
2486	29¢ African Violet	10/08/93	.60	.20			1.00	
a	Booklet pane of 10		6.00	4.00			4.00	
2487	32¢ Peach	07/08/95	.65	.20			1.50	
2488	32¢ Pear	07/08/95	.65	.20			1.50	
a	Booklet pane, 5 each #2487-2488		6.50	4.25			7.50	
b	Pair, #2487-2488		1.30	.30				
	Booklet, Tagged, Self-Adhesive, Die-Cut							
2489	29¢ Red Squirrel	06/25/93	.65	.20			1.25	
a	Booklet pane of 18		12.00					
2490	29¢ Red Rose	08/19/93	.65	.20			1.25	
a	Booklet pane of 18		12.00					
2491	29¢ Pine Cone	11/05/93	.60	.20			1.25	
a	Booklet pane of 18		11.00					
b	Horizontal pair, no die cutting between		200.00					
c	Coil with plate #B1		—	6.00	8.50	(5)		
	Serpentine Die-Cut 11.3 x 11.7 on 2, 3 or 4 sides							
2492	32¢ Pink Rose	06/02/95	.65	.20			1.25	
a	Booklet pane of 20 plus label		13.00					
b	Booklet pane of 15 plus label		9.75					
c	Horizontal pair, no die cutting between		—					
d	As "a," 2 stamps and parts of 7 others printed on backing liner		—					
e	Booklet pane of 14		21.00					
g	Coil with plate #S111		—	5.50	8.00	(5)		
	Serpentine Die-Cut 8.8 on 2, 3 or 4 sides							
2493	32¢ Peach	07/08/95	.65	.20			1.25	
2494	32¢ Pear	07/08/95	.65	.20			1.25	
a	Booklet pane, 10 each #2493-2494		13.00					
b	Pair, #2493-2494		1.30					
	Coil, Serpentine Die-Cut 8.8 Vertically							
2495	32¢ Peach	07/08/95	2.00	.20			1.25	
2495A	32¢ Pear	07/08/95	2.00	.20			1.25	
b	Pair #2495-2495A		4.00		13.00	(5)		
	Olympians, Tagged, Perf. 11							
2496	25¢ Jesse Owens	07/06/90	.60	.20			1.25	36
2497	25¢ Ray Ewry	07/06/90	.60	.20			1.25	36
2498	25¢ Hazel Wightman	07/06/90	.60	.20			1.25	36
2499	25¢ Eddie Eagan	07/06/90	.60	.20			1.25	36
2500	25¢ Helene Madison	07/06/90	.60	.20			1.25	36
a	Strip of 5, #2496-2500		3.25	2.50	8.00	(10)	4.00	
	Indian Headdresses, Booklet, Tagged, Perf. 11 on 2 or 3 sides							
2501	25¢ Assiniboine Headdress	08/17/90	1.50	.20			1.25	124
2502	25¢ Cheyenne Headdress	08/17/90	1.50	.20			1.25	124
2503	25¢ Comanche Headdress	08/17/90	1.50	.20			1.25	124
2504	25¢ Flathead Headdress	08/17/90	1.50	.20			1.25	124
2505	25¢ Shoshone Headdress	08/17/90	1.50	.20			1.25	124
a	Booklet pane of 10, 2 each of #2501-2505		15.00	7.50			6.00	
b	As "a," black omitted		3,500.00					
c	Strip of 5		7.50	2.50				
	Micronesia/Marshall Islands, Tagged, Perf. 11							
2506	25¢ Canoe and Flag of the Federated States of Micronesia	09/28/90	.50	.20			1.25	76
2507	25¢ Stick Chart, Canoe and Flag of the Marshall Islands	09/28/90	.50	.20			1.25	76
a	Pair, #2506-2507		1.00	.75	2.50	(4)	2.00	
b	As "a," black omitted		2,750.00					
	Creatures of the Sea, Tagged, Perf. 11							
2508	25¢ Killer Whales	10/03/90	.55	.20			1.25	70
2509	25¢ Northern Sea Lions	10/03/90	.55	.20			1.25	70
2510	25¢ Sea Otter	10/03/90	.55	.20			1.25	70
2511	25¢ Common Dolphin	10/03/90	.55	.20			1.25	70
a	Block of 4, #2508-2511		2.25	1.90	2.50	(4)	3.00	
b	As "a," black omitted		400.00					

	Issue	Date	Un	U	PB/PNC	#	FDC	Q(M)
	America/PUAS, Tagged, Perf. 11							
2512	25¢ Grand Canyon	10/12/90	.55	.20	2.75	(4)	1.25	144
	Tagged, Perf. 11							
2513	25¢ Dwight D. Eisenhower	10/13/90	.90	.20	4.00	(4)	1.25	143
	Holiday Celebration: Christmas, Tagged, Perf. 11.5							
2514	25¢ Madonna and Child, by Antonello	10/18/90	.50	.20	2.25	(4)	1.25	729
a	Prephosphored coated paper (solid tagging)		.50	.20				
b	Booklet pane of 10		5.00	3.25			6.00	23
	Holiday Celebration: Holiday, Tagged, Perf. 11							
2515	25¢ Christmas Tree	10/18/90	.50	.20	2.25	(4)	1.25	599
a	Vertical pair, imperf. horizontally	1,000.00						
	Booklet, Perf. 11.5 x 11 on 2 or 3 sides							
2516	Single (2515) from booklet pane	10/18/90	.50	.20			1.00	320
a	Booklet pane of 10	10/18/90	5.00	3.25			6.00	
	Tagged, Perf. 13							
2517	(29¢) "F" Stamp	01/22/91	.60	.20	2.75	(4)	1.25	
b	Horizontal pair, imperf. vertically	1,150.00						
	Coil, Perf. 10 Vertically							
2518	(29¢) "F" Tulip (2517)	01/22/91	.60	.20	3.50	(5)	1.25	
a	Imperf., pair		27.50					
	Booklet, Perf. 11 on 2 or 3 sides							
2519	(29¢) "F", single from booklet		.60	.20			1.00	
a	Booklet pane of 10	01/22/91	6.50	4.50			7.25	
2520	(29¢) "F", single from booklet		1.75	.20			1.25	
a	Booklet pane of 10	01/22/91	18.00	4.50			8.00	

#2519 has bull's-eye perforations that measure approximately 11.2.
#2520 has less-pronounced black lines in the leaf, which is a much brighter green than on #2519.

	Issue	Date	Un	U	PB/PNC	#	FDC	Q(M)
	Untagged, Perf. 11							
2521	(4¢) Makeup Rate	01/22/91	.20	.20	.40	(4)	1.25	
a	Vertical pair, imperf. horizontally		95.00					
b	Imperf., pair		60.00					
	Untagged, Self-Adhesive, Die-Cut							
2522	(29¢) F Flag, single from pane	01/22/91	.60	.25			1.25	
a	Pane of 12		7.25					
	Coil, Tagged, Perf. 10 Vertically							
2523	29¢ Flag Over Mt. Rushmore, intaglio printing	03/29/91	.65	.20	4.00	(5)	1.25	
b	Imperf., pair		20.00					
c	Blue, red and brown		3.00	—	4,000.00	(5)		
d	Prephosphored coated paper		5.00	—	1,400.00	(5)		
2523A	29¢ Flag Over Mt. Rushmore, gravure printing	07/04/91	.75	.20	4.00	(5)	1.25	
	Tagged, Perf. 11							
2524	29¢ Tulip	04/05/91	.60	.20	2.75	(4)	1.00	
	Tagged, Perf. 13 x 12.75							
2524A	29¢ Tulip		1.00	.20	50.00	(4)		
	Coil, Rouletted 10 Vertically							
2525	29¢ Tulip	08/16/91	.60	.20	4.00	(5)	1.00	
	Perf. 10 Vertically							
2526	29¢ Tulip	03/03/92	.80	.20	4.25	(5)	1.00	
	Booklet, Tagged, Perf. 11 on 2 or 3 sides							
2527	29¢ Tulip (2524), single from bklt.		.60	.20			1.00	
a	Booklet pane of 10	04/05/91	6.00	3.50			4.00	
	Olympic Games, Booklet, Tagged, Perf. 11 on 2 or 3 sides							
2528	29¢ U.S. Flag, Olympic Rings, single from booklet	04/21/91	.60	.20			1.25	
a	Booklet pane of 10	04/21/91	6.00	3.50			5.00	

Issue		Date	Un	U	PB	#	FDC	Q(M)
	Tagged, Perf. 9.8 Vertically							
2529	19¢ Fishing Boat	08/08/91	.40	.20	3.00	(5)	1.50	
a	New printing, Type II	1993	.40	.20	3.50	(5)		
b	As "a," untagged		1.00	.40	8.50	(5)		
	Tagged, Perf. 9.8							
2529C	19¢ Fishing Boat	06/25/94	.50	.20	4.00	(5)	1.50	
	Type II stamps have finer dot pattern, smoother edges along type. #2529C has only one loop of rope tying up the boat.							
	Ballooning, Booklet, Tagged, Perf. 10 on 2 or 3 sides							
2530	19¢ Overhead View of Balloon, single from booklet	05/17/91	.40	.20			1.25	
a	Booklet pane of 10	05/17/91	4.00	2.75			5.00	
	#2530 was issued only in booklets. All stamps are imperf. on one side or on one side and bottom.							
	Tagged, Perf. 11							
2531	29¢ Flags on Parade	05/30/91	.60	.20	2.75	(4)	1.00	
b	Prephosphored coated paper		.75	.25	6.50	(4)		
	Tagged, Self-Adhesive, Die-Cut, Imperf.							
2531A	29¢ Liberty Torch, single stamp from pane	06/25/91	.60	.25			1.25	
b	Pane of 18	06/25/91	11.00					
	Tagged, Perf. 11							
2532	50¢ Founding of Switzerland	02/22/91	1.00	.25	5.00	(4)	1.40	104
a	Vertical pair, imperf. horizontally	2,250.00						
2533	29¢ Vermont Statehood	03/01/91	.90	.20	4.50	(4)	1.50	180
	Tagged, Perf. 11							
2534	29¢ Savings Bonds	04/30/91	.60	.20	2.75	(4)	1.25	151
	Love, Tagged, Perf. 12.5 x 13							
2535	29¢ Love	05/09/91	.60	.20	2.75	(4)	1.25	631
a	Imperf. pair	1,850.00						
2535A	Perf. 11		.85	.20	4.00	(4)		
	Booklet, Perf. 11 on 2 or 3 sides							
2536	29¢ (2535), single from booklet		.60	.20			1.25	
a	Booklet pane of 10	05/09/91	6.00	3.50			5.00	
	Love, Perf. 11							
2537	52¢ Love	05/09/91	.90	.20	4.50	(4)	1.25	200
	Literary Arts, Tagged, Perf. 11							
2538	29¢ William Saroyan	05/22/91	.60	.20	2.75	(4)	1.50	161
	Olympic Games, Tagged, Perf. 11							
2539	$1 USPS Logo/Olympic Rings	09/29/91	1.90	.50	8.00	(4)	2.25	
	Tagged, Perf. 11							
2540	$2.90 Priority Mail	07/07/91	6.00	1.50	24.00	(4)	5.50	

Issue		Date	Un	U	PB	#	FDC	Q(M)
	Untagged, Perf. 11							
2541	$9.95 Domestic Express Mail	06/16/91	20.00	6.00	80.00	(4)	15.00	
2542	$14 International Express Mail	08/31/91	25.00	15.00	100.00	(4)	27.50	
	Space, Tagged, Perf. 11 x 10.5							
2543	$2.90 Space Vehicle	06/03/93	6.00	1.75	27.50	(4)	6.00	
	Space, Tagged, Perf. 11.2							
2544	$3 Space Shuttle *Challenger*	06/22/95	5.75	1.75	23.50	(4)	6.00	
	Space, Tagged, Perf. 11							
2544A	$10.75 Space Shuttle *Endeavour*	08/04/95	20.00	9.00	82.50	(4)	15.00	
	Fishing Flies, Booklet, Tagged, Perf. 11 Horizontally							
2545	29¢ Royal Wulff	05/31/91	2.50	.20			1.25	149
2546	29¢ Jock Scott	05/31/91	2.50	.20			1.25	149
2547	29¢ Apte Tarpon Fly	05/31/91	2.50	.20			1.25	149
2548	29¢ Lefty's Deceiver	05/31/91	2.50	.20			1.25	149
2549	29¢ Muddler Minnow	05/31/91	2.50	.20			1.25	149
a	Booklet pane of 5, #2545-2549		12.50	3.50			3.00	
	#2545-2549 were issued only in booklets. All stamps are imperf. at sides or imperf. at sides and bottom.							
	Performing Arts, Tagged, Perf. 11							
2550	29¢ Cole Porter	06/08/91	.60	.20	2.75	(4)	1.25	150
a	Vertical pair, imperf. horizontally	525.00						
	Tagged, Perf. 11							
2551	29¢ Operations Desert Shield/ Desert Storm	07/02/91	.60	.20	2.75	(4)	2.50	200
a	Vertical pair, imperf. horizontally	1,350.00						
	Booklet, Perf. 11 Vertically on 1 or 2 sides							
2552	29¢ Operations Desert Shield/ Desert Storm (2551), single from booklet	07/02/91	.60	.20			2.50	200
a	Booklet pane of 5	07/02/91	3.00	2.25			5.00	40
	Olympic Games, Summer, Tagged, Perf. 11							
2553	29¢ Pole Vaulter	07/12/91	.60	.20			1.25	34
2554	29¢ Discus Thrower	07/12/91	.60	.20			1.25	34
2555	29¢ Women Sprinters	07/12/91	.60	.20			1.25	34
2556	29¢ Javelin Thrower	07/12/91	.60	.20			1.25	34
2557	29¢ Women Hurdlers	07/12/91	.60	.20			1.25	34
a	Strip of 5, #2553-2557		3.00	2.25	8.00	(10)	3.00	
	Tagged, Perf. 11							
2558	29¢ Numismatics	08/13/91	.60	.20	2.75	(4)	1.25	150

2529

2529C

2530

2531

2531A

2532

2533

2534

2535

2537

2538

2539

2540

2541

2542

2543

2544

2544A

2545
2546
2547
2548
2549

2550

2551

2549a

2553

2554

2555

2556

2557   **2557a**

2558

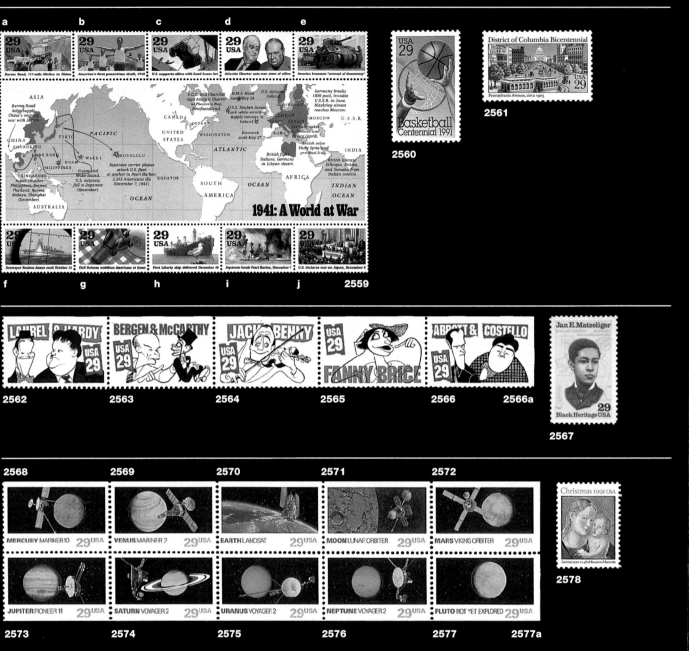

a
29 USA — Burma Road, 717-mile lifeline to China
b
29 USA — America's first peacetime draft, 1940
c
29 USA — U.S. supports allies with Lend-Lease Act
d
29 USA — Atlantic Charter sets war aims of allies
e
29 USA — America becomes "arsenal of democracy"

1941: A World at War

f
29 USA — Destroyer Reuben James sunk October 31
g
29 USA — Civil Defense mobilizes Americans at home
h
29 USA — First Liberty ship delivered December 30
i
29 USA — Japanese bomb Pearl Harbor, December 7
j
29 USA — U.S. declares war on Japan, December 8

2559

2560 — USA 29 Basketball Centennial 1991

2561 — District of Columbia Bicentennial — Pennsylvania Avenue, circa 1903 — USA 29

2562 — LAUREL & HARDY USA 29
2563 — BERGEN & McCARTHY USA 29
2564 — JACK BENNY USA 29
2565 — USA 29 FANNY BRICE
2566 — ABBOTT & COSTELLO USA 29
2566a
2567 — Jan E. Matzeliger — Black Heritage USA 29

2568 — MERCURY MARINER 10 29 USA
2569 — VENUS MARINER 2 29 USA
2570 — EARTH LANDSAT 29 USA
2571 — MOON LUNAR ORBITER 29 USA
2572 — MARS VIKING ORBITER 29 USA
2573 — JUPITER PIONEER 11 29 USA
2574 — SATURN VOYAGER 2 29 USA
2575 — URANUS VOYAGER 2 29 USA
2576 — NEPTUNE VOYAGER 2 29 USA
2577 — PLUTO NOT YET EXPLORED 29 USA
2577a
2578 — Christmas 1991 USA — Antoniazzo c.1460 Houston Museum

2579 — 1991 USA CHRISTMAS
2582 — 1991 USA CHRISTMAS
2583 — 1991 USA CHRISTMAS
2584 — 1991 USA CHRISTMAS
2585 — 1991 USA CHRISTMAS
2587 — UNITED STATES 32 CENTS
2590 — U.S. POSTAGE $1

2592 — U.S. POSTAGE $5 FIVE DOLLARS

 2593 — USA 29 I pledge allegiance...
 2594 — USA 29 I pledge allegiance...
 2595 — USA 29
 2596 — USA 29
 2597 — USA 29
 2598 — 29 USA
 2599 — USA 29

Issue	Date	Un	U	PB #	FDC	Q(M)
World War II, 1941: A World at War, Miniature Sheet, Tagged, Perf. 11						
2559 Sheet of 10 and central label 09/03/91		7.50	5.00		7.00	15
a 29¢ Burma Road			.75	.45	2.00	15
b 29¢ America's First Peacetime Draft			.75	.45	2.00	15
c 29¢ Lend-Lease Act			.75	.45	2.00	15
d 29¢ Atlantic Charter			.75	.45	2.00	15
e 29¢ Arsenal of Democracy			.75	.45	2.00	15
f 29¢ Destroyer *Reuben James*			.75	.45	2.00	15
g 29¢ Civil Defense			.75	.45	2.00	15
h 29¢ Liberty Ship			.75	.45	2.00	15
i 29¢ Pearl Harbor			.75	.45	2.00	15
j 29¢ U.S. Declaration of War			.75	.45	2.00	15
k 29¢ Black omitted		12,500.00				
2560 29¢ Basketball	08/28/91	.60	.20	2.75 (4)	2.25	150
2561 29¢ District of Columbia	09/07/91	.60	.20	2.75 (4)	1.25	149
a Black omitted		100.00				
Comedians, Booklet, Tagged, Perf. 11 on 2 or 3 sides						
2562 29¢ Stan Laurel and Oliver Hardy	08/29/91	1.00	.20		1.25	140
2563 29¢ Edgar Bergen and Dummy Charlie McCarthy	08/29/91	1.00	.20		1.25	140
2564 29¢ Jack Benny	08/29/91	1.00	.20		1.25	140
2565 29¢ Fanny Brice	08/29/91	1.00	.20		1.25	140
2566 29¢ Bud Abbott and Lou Costello	08/29/91	1.00	.20		1.25	140
a Booklet pane of 10, 2 each of #2562-2566		10.00	5.00		3.00	
b As "a," scarlet and bright violet omitted		650.00				
c Strip of 5		5.00	2.50			

#2562-2566 issued only in booklets. All stamps are imperf. at top or bottom, or at top or bottom and right side.

Issue	Date	Un	U	PB #	FDC	Q(M)
Black Heritage, Tagged, Perf. 11						
2567 29¢ Jan Matzeliger	09/15/91	.60	.20	2.75 (4)	1.75	149
a Horizontal pair, imperf. vertically		1,250.00				
b Vertical pair, imperf. horizontally		1,250.00				
c Imperf., pair		425.00				
Space, Booklet, Tagged, Perf. 11 on 2 or 3 sides						
2568 29¢ Mercury, Mariner 10	10/01/91	1.00	.20		1.25	33
2569 29¢ Venus, Mariner 2	10/01/91	1.00	.20		1.25	33
2570 29¢ Earth, Landsat	10/01/91	1.00	.20		1.25	33
2571 29¢ Moon, Lunar Orbiter	10/01/91	1.00	.20		1.25	33
2572 29¢ Mars, Viking Orbiter	10/01/91	1.00	.20		1.25	33
2573 29¢ Jupiter, Pioneer 11	10/01/91	1.00	.20		1.25	33
2574 29¢ Saturn, *Voy r 2*	10/01/91	1.00	.20		1.25	33
2575 29¢ Uranus, *Voyager 2*	10/01/91	1.00	.20		1.25	33
2576 29¢ Neptune, *Voyager 2*	10/01/91	1.00	.20		1.25	33
2577 29¢ Pluto	10/01/91	1.00	.20		1.25	33
a Booklet pane of 10, #2568-2577		10.00	4.50		5.00	

#2568-2577 issued only in booklets. All stamps are imperf. at top or bottom, or at top or bottom and right side.

Issue	Date	Un	U	PB #	FDC	Q(M)
Holiday Celebration: Christmas, Tagged, Perf. 11						
2578 29¢ *Madonna and Child*, by Antoniazzo Romano	10/17/91	.60	.20	2.75 (4)	1.25	401
a Booklet pane of 10		6.00	3.25			30
b As "a," single, red and black omitted	3,250.00					
Holiday Celebration: Holiday, Tagged, Perf. 11						
2579 29¢ Santa Claus in Chimney	10/17/91	.60	.20	2.50 (4)	1.25	900
a Horizontal pair, imperf. vertically		250.00				
b Vertical pair, imperf. horizontally		375.00				

Issue	Date	Un	U	PB #	FDC	Q(M)
Holiday Celebration: Holiday, Booklet, Perf. 11 on 2 or 3 sides						
2580 29¢ Santa Claus (2579), Type I, single from booklet	10/17/91	2.00	.20		1.25	
2581 29¢ Santa Claus (2579), Type II, single from booklet	10/17/91	2.40	.20		1.25	
a Pair, #2580, 2581	10/17/91	4.80	.50			28
b Booklet pane, 2 each		10.00	1.25		2.50	

The extreme left brick in top row of chimney is missing from Type II, #2581.

2582 29¢ Santa Claus Checking List, single from booklet	10/17/91	.60	.20		1.25	
a Booklet pane of 4	10/17/91	2.40	1.25		2.50	28
2583 29¢ Santa Claus with Present Under Tree, single from booklet	10/17/91	.60	.20		1.25	
a Booklet pane of 4	10/17/91	2.40	1.25		2.50	28
2584 29¢ Santa Claus at Fireplace, single from booklet	10/17/91	.60	.20		1.25	
a Booklet pane of 4	10/17/91	2.40	1.25		2.50	28
2585 29¢ Santa Claus and Sleigh, single from booklet	10/17/91	.60	.20		1.25	
a Booklet pane of 4	10/17/91	2.40	1.25		2.50	28

#2582-2585 issued only in booklets. All stamps are imperf. at top or bottom, or at top or bottom and right side.

Issue	Date	Un	U	PB #	FDC	Q(M)
Tagged, Perf. 11.2						
2587 32¢ James K. Polk	11/02/95	.65	.20	3.25 (4)	1.25	
Perf. 11.5						
2590 $1 Victory at Saratoga	05/05/94	1.90	.50	7.60 (4)	2.50	
2592 $5 Washington and Jackson	08/19/94	8.00	2.50	40.00 (4)	12.50	
Tagged, Perf. 10 on 2 or 3 sides						
2593 29¢ Pledge of Allegiance	09/08/92	.60	.20		1.25	
a Booklet of 10		6.00	4.25		5.00	
Perf. 11 x 10 on 2 or 3 sides						
2593B 29¢ Pledge of Allegiance, shiny gum		1.70	.50			
c Booklet pane of 10, shiny gum		17.00	7.50			
2594 29¢ Pledge of Allegiance	04/08/93	.65	.20			
a Booklet of 10		6.50	4.25			
Booklet, Tagged, Self-Adhesive, Die-Cut						
2595 29¢ Eagle and Shield (brown lettering)	09/25/92	.60	.25		1.50	
a Pane of 17 + label		13.00				
b Pair, no die-cutting		135.00				
c Brown omitted		350.00				
d As "a," no die-cutting		1,150.00				
2596 29¢ Eagle and Shield (green lettering)	09/25/92	.60	.25		1.50	
a Pane of 17 + label		12.00				
2597 29¢ Eagle and Shield (red lettering)	09/25/92	.60	.25		1.50	
a Pane of 17 + label		10.50				
2598 29¢ Eagle	02/04/94	.60	.20		1.25	
a Booklet pane of 18		11.00				
b Coil		—	5.00	9.00 (5)		
2599 29¢ Statue of Liberty	06/24/94	.60	.20		1.25	
a Booklet pane of 18		11.00				
b Coil		—	5.00	9.00 (5)		

Issue		Date	Un	U	PB	#	FDC	Q(M)
	Coil, Untagged, Perf. 10 Vertically							
2602	10¢ Eagle and Shield (inscribed "Bulk Rate USA")	12/13/91	.30	.20	2.00	(5)	1.25	
2603	10¢ Eagle and Shield (inscribed "USA Bulk Rate")	05/29/93	.30	.20	2.25	(5)	1.25	
a	Imperf., pair		20.00					
b	Tagged (error), shiny gum		2.00	1.50	10.00	(5)		
2604	10¢ Eagle and Shield (metallic, inscribed "USA Bulk Rate")	05/29/93	.30	.20	3.25	(5)	1.25	
2605	23¢ Flag, Presorted First-Class	09/27/91	.45	.40	3.25	(5)	1.25	
	Perf. 11							
2606	23¢ USA	07/21/92	.45	.40	3.75	(5)	1.25	
2607	23¢ USA (Bureau) (In #2607, "23" is 7mm long)	10/09/92	.45	.40	4.00	(5)	1.25	
a	Tagged (error), shiny gum		5.00	4.50	100.00	(5)		
c	Imperf., pair		70.00					
2608	23¢ USA (violet)	05/14/93	.75	.40	4.00	(5)	1.25	
	Tagged							
2609	29¢ Flag Over White House	04/23/92	.60	.20	4.00	(5)	1.25	
a	Imperf., pair		15.00					
b	Pair, imperf. between		90.00					
	Olympic Games, Winter, Tagged, Perf. 11							
2611	29¢ Hockey	01/11/92	.60	.20			1.25	
2612	29¢ Figure Skating	01/11/92	.60	.20			1.25	
2613	29¢ Speed Skating	01/11/92	.60	.20			1.25	
2614	29¢ Skiing	01/11/92	.60	.20			1.25	
2615	29¢ Bobsledding	01/11/92	.60	.20			1.25	
a	Strip of 5, #2611-2615		3.00	2.50	7.00	(10)	3.50	32
	Tagged, Perf. 11							
2616	29¢ World Columbian Stamp Expo	01/24/92	.60	.20	2.75	(4)	1.25	149
a	Tagging omitted		7.50					
	Black Heritage, Tagged, Perf. 11							
2617	29¢ W.E.B. DuBois	01/31/92	.60	.20	2.75	(4)	1.75	150
	Love, Tagged, Perf. 11							
2618	29¢ Love	02/06/92	.60	.20	2.75	(4)	1.25	835
a	Horizontal pair, imperf. vertically		625.00					
2619	29¢ Olympic Baseball	04/03/92	.60	.20	2.75	(4)	2.00	160

Issue		Date	Un	U	PB	#	FDC	Q(M)
	First Voyage of Christopher Columbus, Tagged, Perf. 11							
2620	29¢ Seeking Queen Isabella's Support	04/24/92	.60	.20			1.25	40
2621	29¢ Crossing The Atlantic	04/24/92	.60	.20			1.25	40
2622	29¢ Approaching Land	04/24/92	.60	.20			1.25	40
2623	29¢ Coming Ashore	04/24/92	.60	.20			1.25	40
a	Block of 4, #2620-2623		2.40	2.00	2.75	(4)	2.75	
	The Voyages of Columbus Souvenir Sheets, Perf. 10.5							
2624	First Sighting of Land, sheet of 3	05/22/92	2.00	1.25			3.50	1
a	1¢ deep blue		.20	.20			1.50	
b	4¢ ultramarine		.20	.20			1.50	
c	$1 salmon		1.75	1.00			2.50	
2625	Claiming a New World, sheet of 3	05/22/92	7.25	5.00			9.00	1
a	2¢ brown violet		.20	.20			1.50	
b	3¢ green		.20	.20			1.50	
c	$4 crimson lake		7.00	4.00			8.00	
2626	Seeking Royal Support, sheet of 3	05/22/92	1.60	1.25			3.00	1
a	5¢ chocolate		.20	.20			1.50	
b	30¢ orange brown		.60	.30			1.50	
c	50¢ slate blue		.90	.50			2.00	
2627	Royal Favor Restored, sheet of 3	05/22/92	5.75	3.50			7.50	1
a	6¢ purple		.20	.20			1.50	
b	8¢ magenta		.20	.20			1.50	
c	$3 yellow green		5.50	3.00			7.50	
2628	Reporting Discoveries, sheet of 3	05/22/92	4.00	3.00			8.50	1
a	10¢ black brown		.20	.20			1.50	
b	15¢ dark green		.30	.20			1.50	
c	$2 brown red		3.50	2.00			5.00	
2629	$5 Christopher Columbus, sheet of 1	05/22/92	8.75	6.00			12.50	1
a	$5 black		8.50	5.00				

Abraham Lincoln Commemorative Folio

The U.S. Postal Service celebrates the 200th anniversary of Abraham Lincoln's birth with four stamps depicting different aspects of his life: rail-splitter, lawyer, politician and president. Celebrate the man and his legacy with this exclusive folio that folds out with the Gettysburg Address, four (5"x7") biographical cards — perfect for framing and a pane of 20 stamps is included.

To order call **1 800 STAMP-24** or visit us online at **www.usps.com**

Item #464774
$16.95

2602

2603

2604

2605

2606

2607

2608

2609

2611

2612

2613

2614

2615

2615a

2616

2617

2618

2624

2625

2619

2620   2621

2622   2623   2623a

2626

2627

2628

2629

2630

2631   **2632**

2633   **2634**

2634a

2635   **2636**

2637   **2638**   **2639**   **2640**   **2641**   **2641a**

2642   **2643**   **2644**   **2645**   **2646**   **2646a**

2647   **2648**   **2649**   **2650**   **2651**   **2652**   **2653**   **2654**   **2655**   **2656**

2657   **2658**   **2659**   **2660**   **2661**   **2662**   **2663**   **2664**   **2665**   **2666**

Issue		Date	Un	U	PB	#	FDC	Q(M)
	Tagged, Perf. 11							
2630	29¢ New York Stock Exchange Bicentennial	05/17/92	.60	.20	2.75	(4)	2.50	148
a	Black omitted (ED)		—					
b	Brown omitted (CM)		8,000.00					
c	Center inverted		26,000.00					
	Space, Tagged, Perf. 11							
2631	29¢ Cosmonaut, US Space Shuttle	05/29/92	.60	.20			1.50	37
2632	29¢ Astronaut, Russian Space Station	05/29/92	.60	.20			1.50	37
2633	29¢ Sputnik, Vostok, Apollo Command and Lunar Modules	05/29/92	.60	.20			1.50	37
2634	29¢ Soyuz, Mercury and Gemini Spacecraft	05/29/92	.60	.20			1.50	37
a	Block of 4, #2631-2634		2.40	1.90	3.25	(4)	2.75	
	Tagged, Perf. 11							
2635	29¢ Alaska Highway, 50th Anniversary	05/30/92	.60	.20	2.75	(4)	1.25	147
a	Black (engr.) omitted		750.00					
	Tagged, Perf. 11							
2636	29¢ Kentucky Statehood Bicentennial	06/01/92	.60	.20	2.75	(4)	1.25	160
	Olympic Games, Summer, Tagged, Perf. 11							
2637	29¢ Soccer	06/11/92	.60	.20			1.25	32
2638	29¢ Gymnastics	06/11/92	.60	.20			1.25	32
2639	29¢ Volleyball	06/11/92	.60	.20			1.25	32
2640	29¢ Boxing	06/11/92	.60	.20			1.25	32
2641	29¢ Swimming	06/11/92	.60	.20			1.25	32
a	Strip of 5, #2637-2641		3.00	2.50	6.50	(10)	3.00	

Issue		Date	Un	U	PB	#	FDC	Q(M)
	Hummingbirds, Tagged, Perf. 11 Vertically on 1 or 2 sides							
2642	29¢ Ruby-Throated	06/15/92	.60	.20			1.25	88
2643	29¢ Broad-Billed	06/15/92	.60	.20			1.25	88
2644	29¢ Costa's	06/15/92	.60	.20			1.25	88
2645	29¢ Rufous	06/15/92	.60	.20			1.25	88
2646	29¢ Calliope	06/15/92	.60	.20			1.25	88
a	Booklet pane of 5, #2642-2646		3.00	2.50			3.00	
	Wildflowers, Tagged, Perf. 11							
2647	29¢ Indian Paintbrush	07/24/92	.80	.60			1.25	11
2648	29¢ Fragrant Water Lily	07/24/92	.80	.60			1.25	11
2649	29¢ Meadow Beauty	07/24/92	.80	.60			1.25	11
2650	29¢ Jack-in-the-Pulpit	07/24/92	.80	.60			1.25	11
2651	29¢ California Poppy	07/24/92	.80	.60			1.25	11
2652	29¢ Large-Flowered Trillium	07/24/92	.80	.60			1.25	11
2653	29¢ Tickseed	07/24/92	.80	.60			1.25	11
2654	29¢ Shooting Star	07/24/92	.80	.60			1.25	11
2655	29¢ Stream Violet	07/24/92	.80	.60			1.25	11
2656	29¢ Bluets	07/24/92	.80	.60			1.25	11
2657	29¢ Herb Robert	07/24/92	.80	.60			1.25	11
2658	29¢ Marsh Marigold	07/24/92	.80	.60			1.25	11
2659	29¢ Sweet White Violet	07/24/92	.80	.60			1.25	11
2660	29¢ Claret Cup Cactus	07/24/92	.80	.60			1.25	11
2661	29¢ White Mountain Avens	07/24/92	.80	.60			1.25	11
2662	29¢ Sessile Bellwort	07/24/92	.80	.60			1.25	11
2663	29¢ Blue Flag	07/24/92	.80	.60			1.25	11
2664	29¢ Harlequin Lupine	07/24/92	.80	.60			1.25	11
2665	29¢ Twinflower	07/24/92	.80	.60			1.25	11
2666	29¢ Common Sunflower	07/24/92	.80	.60			1.25	11

BLACK HERITAGE: ANNA JULIA COOPER

The 32nd stamp in the Black Heritage series honors Anna Julia Cooper (c. 1858-1964), an educator, scholar, feminist, and activist who gave voice to the African-American community during the 19th and 20th centuries—from the end of slavery to the beginning of the civil rights movement. Cooper—who once described her vocation as "the education of neglected people"—viewed learning as a means of true liberation. She is best known for her educational leadership, her challenges to the racist notion that African Americans were naturally inferior, and her groundbreaking collection of essays and speeches, *A Voice from the South by a Black Woman of the South* (1892), the first book-length volume of black feminist analysis in the United States. ▨ Born into slavery in Raleigh, North Carolina, Cooper developed a love of learning at a young age and earned a degree in mathematics from Oberlin College in Ohio, one of the first African-American women to graduate from the school. In 1887, she was invited to teach at the Preparatory High School for Colored Youth (today Dunbar High School) in Washington, D.C., the largest and most prestigious public high school for African Americans in the nation. Named principal in 1902, Cooper immediately began to strengthen the curriculum. "We are not just educating heads and hands," she stated, "we are educating the men and women of a race." ▨ In 1925, Cooper earned a doctoral degree at the Sorbonne in Paris, becoming the fourth African-American woman in the U.S. to earn a Ph.D. and the first black woman from any country to do so at the Sorbonne. ▨ Throughout her life, Cooper fought for social justice and civil rights for African-American women, young people, and the poor through her scholarship, community outreach, and innovative educational leadership.

	Issue	Date	Un	U	PB	#	FDC	Q(M)
	Wildflowers, Tagged, Perf. 11 continued							
2667	29¢ Sego Lily	07/24/92	.80	.60			1.25	11
2668	29¢ Virginia Bluebells	07/24/92	.80	.60			1.25	11
2669	29¢ Ohi'a Lehua	07/24/92	.80	.60			1.25	11
2670	29¢ Rosebud Orchid	07/24/92	.80	.60			1.25	11
2671	29¢ Showy Evening Primrose	07/24/92	.80	.60			1.25	11
2672	29¢ Fringed Gentian	07/24/92	.80	.60			1.25	11
2673	29¢ Yellow Lady's Slipper	07/24/92	.80	.60			1.25	11
2674	29¢ Passionflower	07/24/92	.80	.60			1.25	11
2675	29¢ Bunchberry	07/24/92	.80	.60			1.25	11
2676	29¢ Pasqueflower	07/24/92	.80	.60			1.25	11
2677	29¢ Round-Lobed Hepatica	07/24/92	.80	.60			1.25	11
2678	29¢ Wild Columbine	07/24/92	.80	.60			1.25	11
2679	29¢ Fireweed	07/24/92	.80	.60			1.25	11
2680	29¢ Indian Pond Lily	07/24/92	.80	.60			1.25	11
2681	29¢ Turk's Cap Lily	07/24/92	.80	.60			1.25	11
2682	29¢ Dutchman's Breeches	07/24/92	.80	.60			1.25	11
2683	29¢ Trumpet Honeysuckle	07/24/92	.80	.60			1.25	11
2684	29¢ Jacob's Ladder	07/24/92	.80	.60			1.25	11
2685	29¢ Plains Prickly Pear	07/24/92	.80	.60			1.25	11
2686	29¢ Moss Campion	07/24/92	.80	.60			1.25	11
2687	29¢ Bearberry	07/24/92	.80	.60			1.25	11
2688	29¢ Mexican Hat	07/24/92	.80	.60			1.25	11
2689	29¢ Harebell	07/24/92	.80	.60			1.25	11
2690	29¢ Desert Five Spot	07/24/92	.80	.60			1.25	11

	Issue	Date	Un	U	PB	#	FDC	Q(M)
	Wildflowers, Tagged, Perf. 11 continued							
2691	29¢ Smooth Solomon's Seal	07/24/92	.80	.60			1.25	11
2692	29¢ Red Maids	07/24/92	.80	.60			1.25	11
2693	29¢ Yellow Skunk Cabbage	07/24/92	.80	.60			1.25	11
2694	29¢ Rue Anemone	07/24/92	.80	.60			1.25	11
2695	29¢ Standing Cypress	07/24/92	.80	.60			1.25	11
2696	29¢ Wild Flax	07/24/92	.80	.60			1.25	11
a	Pane of 50, #2647-2696		40.00	—			30.00	
	World War II, 1942: Into the Battle, Miniature Sheet, Tagged, Perf. 11							
2697	Sheet of 10 and central label	08/17/92	7.50	5.00			7.00	
a	29¢ B-25s Take Off to Raid Tokyo		.75	.30			2.00	12
b	29¢ Food and Other Commodities Rationed		.75	.30			2.00	12
c	29¢ U.S. Wins Battle of the Coral Sea		.75	.30			2.00	12
d	29¢ Corregidor Falls to Japanese		.75	.30			2.00	12
e	29¢ Japan Invades Aleutian Islands		.75	.30			2.00	12
f	29¢ Allies Decipher Secret Enemy Codes		.75	.30			2.00	12
g	29¢ *Yorktown* Lost		.75	.30			2.00	12
h	29¢ Millions of Women Join War Effort		.75	.30			2.00	12
i	29¢ Marines Land on Guadalcanal		.75	.30			2.00	12
j	29¢ Allies Land in North Africa		.75	.30			2.00	12
k	Red (litho.) omitted		5,000.00					
	Literary Arts, Tagged, Perf. 11							
2698	29¢ Dorothy Parker	08/22/92	.60	.20	2.75	(4)	1.50	105
	Tagged, Perf. 11							
2699	29¢ Dr. Theodore von Karman	08/31/92	.60	.20	2.75	(4)	1.50	143

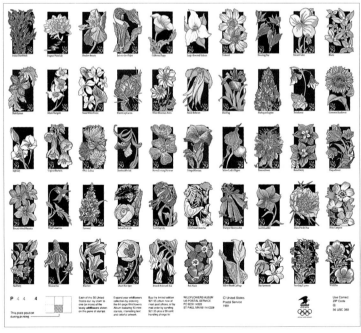

#2696a

2667	2668	2669	2670	2671
Sego Lily	Virginia Bluebells	Ohi'a Lehua	Rosebud Orchid	Showy Evening Primrose

2672	2673	2674	2675	2676
Fringed Gentian	Yellow Lady's Slipper	Passionflower	Bunchberry	Pasqueflower

2677	2678	2679	2680	2681
Round-lobed Hepatica	Wild Columbine	Fireweed	Indian Pond Lily	Turk's Cap Lily

2682	2683	2684	2685	2686
Dutchman's Breeches	Trumpet Honeysuckle	Jacob's Ladder	Plains Prickly Pear	Moss Campion

2687	2688	2689	2690	2691
Bearberry	Mexican Hat	Harebell	Desert Five Spot	Smooth Solomon's Seal

2692	2693	2694	2695	2696
Red Maids	Yellow Skunk Cabbage	Rue Anemone	Standing Cypress	Wild Flax

a b c d e

29 USA — B-25s take off to raid Tokyo April 18, 1942
29 USA — Food and other commodities rationed, 1942
29 USA — U.S. wins Battle of the Coral Sea May 1942
29 USA — Corregidor falls to Japanese May 6, 1942
29 USA — Japan invades Aleutian Islands June 1942

1942: Into the Battle

ASIA
Supplies flown to China over the "Hump"
Doolittle carries out daring raid on Tokyo with B-25s launched from U.S.S. Hornet April 18.
Farthest extent of Japanese expansion.
CANADA OTTAWA
U.S.S.R.
LENINGRAD MOSCOW BERLIN LONDON ROME
Extent of German expansion, Summer 1942.
Massive RAF raids strike German cities.
CHINA
PACIFIC
UNITED STATES
WASHINGTON
ATLANTIC
Desperate struggle waged against German U-boats at Allies convoy supplies across North Atlantic.
Russian defenders battle German forces at Stalingrad, Summer 1942.
TOKYO
Battle of Midway decisive defeat for Japan June 3–6.
HONG KONG GUAM WAKE I.
HONOLULU
OCEAN
INDIA
U.S. and Allies land more than 100,000 troops in North Africa November 8.
British defeat German forces at Battle of El Alamein October 23–November 4.
SINGAPORE PHILIPPINES
Philippines fall to Japanese; Bataan, April 9; Corregidor, May 6.
EQUATOR
SOUTH AMERICA
AFRICA
INDIAN OCEAN
Singapore falls February 15.
Battle of the Coral Sea halts Japanese advance southward May 4–8.
U.S. Marines land on Guadalcanal August 7.
AUSTRALIA
OCEAN
Note: Red areas controlled by enemy.

29 USA — Allies decipher secret enemy codes, 1942
29 USA — Yorktown lost, U.S. wins at Midway, 1942
29 USA — Millions of women join war effort, 1942
29 USA — Marines land on Guadalcanal Aug. 7, 1942
29 USA — Allies land in North Africa November 1942

29 USA
Dorothy Parker
American Writer 1893–1967

2698

Theodore von Kármán
Aerospace Scientist
USA 29

2699

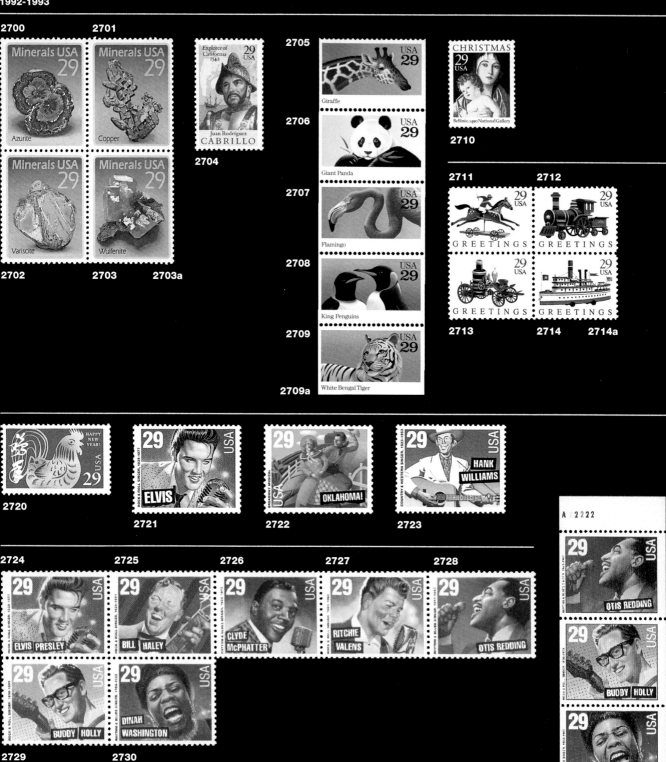

2700 2701

2704

Minerals USA 29 Azurite
Minerals USA 29 Copper
Minerals USA 29 Variscite
Minerals USA 29 Wulfenite

2702 2703 2703a

Explorer of California 1542 29 USA
Juan Rodríguez CABRILLO

2705 2706 2707 2708 2709 2709a

Giraffe
Giant Panda
Flamingo
King Penguins
White Bengal Tiger

2710

CHRISTMAS 29 USA
Bellini c.1490 National Gallery

2711 2712

2713 2714 2714a

GREETINGS
GREETINGS
GREETINGS
GREETINGS

2720

HAPPY NEW YEAR! 29 USA

2721

29 ELVIS USA

2722

29 USA OKLAHOMA!

2723

29 HANK WILLIAMS USA

2724 2725 2726 2727 2728

29 ELVIS PRESLEY
29 BILL HALEY
29 CLYDE McPHATTER
29 RITCHIE VALENS
29 OTIS REDDING

2729 2730

29 BUDDY HOLLY
29 DINAH WASHINGTON

A 22222

29 OTIS REDDING USA
29 BUDDY HOLLY USA
29 DINAH WASHINGTON USA
29 ELVIS PRESLEY USA

2737b

Issue		Date	Un	U	PB	#	FDC	Q(M)
	Minerals, Tagged, Perf. 11							
2700	29¢ Azurite	09/17/92	.60	.20			1.25	37
2701	29¢ Copper	09/17/92	.60	.20			1.25	37
2702	29¢ Variscite	09/17/92	.60	.20			1.25	37
2703	29¢ Wulfenite	09/17/92	.60	.20			1.25	37
a	Block of 4, #2700-2703		2.40	2.00	3.50	(4)	2.75	
b	As "a," silver (litho.) omitted		8,250.00					
	Tagged, Perf. 11							
2704	29¢ Juan Rodriguez Cabrillo	09/28/92	.60	.20	3.50	(4)	1.25	85
a	Black (engr.) omitted		3,250.00					
	Wild Animals, Tagged, Perf. 11 Horizontally							
2705	29¢ Giraffe	10/01/92	.65	.20			1.25	80
2706	29¢ Giant Panda	10/01/92	.65	.20			1.25	80
2707	29¢ Flamingo	10/01/92	.65	.20			1.25	80
2708	29¢ King Penguins	10/01/92	.65	.20			1.25	80
2709	29¢ White Bengal Tiger	10/01/92	.65	.20			1.25	80
a	Booklet pane of 5, #2705-2709		3.25	2.25			3.25	
b	As "a," imperf.		2,250.00					
	Holiday Celebration: Christmas, Tagged, Perf. 11.5 x 11							
2710	29¢ Madonna and Child by Giovanni Bellini	10/22/92	.60	.20	2.75	(4)	1.25	300
a	Booklet pane of 10		6.00	3.50			7.25	349
	Holiday Celebration: Holiday, Tagged, Perf. 11.5 x 11							
2711	29¢ Horse and Rider	10/22/92	.75	.20			1.25	125
2712	29¢ Toy Train	10/22/92	.75	.20			1.25	125
2713	29¢ Toy Steamer	10/22/92	.75	.20			1.25	125
2714	29¢ Toy Ship	10/22/92	.75	.20			1.25	125
a	Block of 4, #2711-2714		3.00	1.10	3.75	(4)	2.75	
	Holiday Celebration: Holiday, Booklet, Perf. 11 on 2 or 3 sides							
2715	29¢ Horse and Rider	10/22/92	.85	.20			1.25	102
2716	29¢ Toy Train	10/22/92	.85	.20			1.25	102
2717	29¢ Toy Steamer	10/22/92	.85	.20			1.25	102
2718	29¢ Toy Ship	10/22/92	.85	.20			1.25	102
a	Booklet pane of 4, #2715-2718		3.50	1.25			2.75	
2719	29¢ Toy Train (self-adhesive)	10/22/92	.60	.20			1.25	22
a	Booklet pane of 18		11.00					

Issue		Date	Un	U	PB	#	FDC	Q(M)
	Lunar New Year, Tagged, Perf. 11							
2720	29¢ Year of the Rooster	12/30/92	.60	.20	2.50	(4)	2.25	
a	Prephosphored paper (mottled tagging) + block tagging		3.00	—				
b	Prephosphored paper		100.00	—				
	Legends of American Music: Rock & Roll/Rhythm & Blues (#2721-2730), **Tagged, Perf. 11**							
2721	29¢ Elvis Presley	01/08/93	.60	.20	2.75	(4)	2.00	517
	Perf. 10							
2722	29¢ *Oklahoma*!	03/30/93	.60	.20	4.00	(4)	1.25	150
2723	29¢ Hank Williams	06/09/93	.75	.20	4.25	(4)	1.25	152
	Perf. 11.2 x 11.5							
2723A	29¢ Hank Williams		20.00	10.00	140.00	(4)	—	
	Perf. 10							
2724	29¢ Elvis Presley	06/16/93	.70	.20			1.25	14
2725	29¢ Bill Haley	06/16/93	.70	.20			1.25	14
2726	29¢ Clyde McPhatter	06/16/93	.70	.20			1.25	14
2727	29¢ Ritchie Valens	06/16/93	.70	.20			1.25	14
2728	29¢ Otis Redding	06/16/93	.70	.20			1.25	14
2729	29¢ Buddy Holly	06/16/93	.70	.20			1.25	14
2730	29¢ Dinah Washington	06/16/93	.70	.20			1.25	14
a	Vertical strip of 7, #2724-2730		5.50		10.00	(10)	5.00	
	Booklet, Perf. 11 Horizontally							
2731	29¢ Elvis Presley	06/16/93	.60	.20			1.25	99
2732	29¢ Bill Haley (2725)	06/16/93	.60	.20			1.25	33
2733	29¢ Clyde McPhatter (2726)	06/16/93	.60	.20			1.25	33
2734	29¢ Ritchie Valens (2727)	06/16/93	.60	.20			1.25	33
2735	29¢ Otis Redding	06/16/93	.60	.20			1.25	66
2736	29¢ Buddy Holly	06/16/93	.60	.20			1.25	66
2737	29¢ Dinah Washington	06/16/93	.60	.20			1.25	66
a	Booklet pane, 2 #2731, 1 each #2732-2737		5.00	2.25			5.25	
b	Booklet pane of 4, #2731, 2735-2737		2.40	1.50			2.75	
2738-40	Not assigned							

GRAND TETON NATIONAL PARK, WYOMING

This new international rate stamp in the Scenic American Landscapes series features a photograph of Grand Teton National Park in northwestern Wyoming. Originally established in 1929 to protect part of the Teton Range and lakes near its base, the park was expanded in 1950 to include much of the adjacent Jackson Hole valley. ▪ Now encompassing nearly 310,000 acres, Grand Teton National Park is characterized by the majesty of its rugged mountains that tower some 7,000 feet over glacial lakes and a valley where the Snake River runs. ▪ Renowned for its climbing and hiking trails, the park welcomes most of its nearly 2.5 million annual visitors in the warm summer months when the weather is perfect for boating, biking, horseback riding, and fishing. During the serene winter season, popular activities include ice fishing, snowshoeing, and cross-country skiing. ▪ Diverse habitats within the park provide countless opportunities to observe moose, elk, bison, pronghorn, black and grizzly bears, and hundreds of species of birds, including bald eagles, ospreys, and trumpeter swans, the largest waterfowl in North America. ▪ The stamp photograph is the work of Dennis Flaherty of Bishop, California, who snapped this image of Grand Teton National Park from the Snake River Overlook at dawn.

Issue	Date	Un	U	PB	#	FDC	Q(M)
Space, Tagged, Perf. 11 Vertically on 1 or 2 sides							
2741 29¢ Space Fantasy	01/25/93	.60	.20			1.25	140
2742 29¢ Space Fantasy	01/25/93	.60	.20			1.25	140
2743 29¢ Space Fantasy	01/25/93	.60	.20			1.25	140
2744 29¢ Space Fantasy	01/25/93	.60	.20			1.25	140
2745 29¢ Space Fantasy	01/25/93	.60	.20			1.25	140
a Booklet pane of 5, #2741-2745		3.00	2.25			3.25	
Black Heritage, Tagged, Perf. 11							
2746 29¢ Percy Lavon Julian	01/29/93	.60	.20	2.75	(4)	1.75	105
Tagged, Perf. 11							
2747 29¢ Oregon Trail	02/12/93	.60	.20	2.75	(4)	1.25	110
a Tagging omitted		22.50					
2748 29¢ World University Games	02/25/93	.60	.20	2.75	(4)	1.50	110
2749 29¢ Grace Kelly	03/24/93	.60	.20	2.75	(4)	3.00	173
Circus, Tagged, Perf. 11							
2750 29¢ Clown	04/06/93	.60	.20			1.50	66
2751 29¢ Ringmaster	04/06/93	.60	.20			1.50	66
2752 29¢ Trapeze Artist	04/06/93	.60	.20			1.50	66
2753 29¢ Elephant	04/06/93	.60	.20			1.50	66
a Block of 4, #2750-2753		2.40	1.75	5.75	(6)	3.00	
Tagged, Perf. 11							
2754 29¢ Cherokee Strip	04/17/93	.60	.20	2.50	(4)	1.25	110
Perf. 11							
2755 29¢ Dean Acheson	04/21/93	.60	.20	2.75	(4)	1.25	116
Sporting Horses, Tagged, Perf. 11 x 11.5							
2756 29¢ Steeplechase	05/01/93	.60	.20			2.00	40
2757 29¢ Thoroughbred Racing	05/01/93	.60	.20			2.00	40
2758 29¢ Harness Racing	05/01/93	.60	.20			2.00	40
2759 29¢ Polo	05/01/93	.60	.20			2.00	40
a Block of 4, #2756-2759		2.40	2.00	2.75	(4)	4.00	
b As "a," black omitted		750.00					

Issue	Date	Un	U	PB	#	FDC	Q(M)
Garden Flowers, Tagged, Perf. 11 Vertically							
2760 29¢ Hyacinth	05/15/93	.60	.20			1.50	200
2761 29¢ Daffodil	05/15/93	.60	.20			1.50	200
2762 29¢ Tulip	05/15/93	.60	.20			1.50	200
2763 29¢ Iris	05/15/93	.60	.20			1.50	200
2764 29¢ Lilac	05/15/93	.60	.20			1.50	200
a Booklet pane of 5, #2760-2764		3.00	2.25			3.00	
b As "a," black omitted		175.00					
c As "a," imperf.		1,000.00					
World War II, 1943: Turning The Tide, Miniature Sheet, Tagged, Perf. 11							
2765 Sheet of 10 and central label	05/31/93	7.50	5.00			7.00	
a 29¢ Allied Forces Battle German U-boats		.75	.40			2.00	120
b 29¢ Military Medics Treat the Wounded		.75	.40			2.00	120
c 29¢ Sicily Attacked by Allied Forces		.75	.40			2.00	120
d 29¢ B-24s Hit Ploesti Refineries		.75	.40			2.00	120
e 29¢ V-Mail Delivers Letters from Home		.75	.40			2.00	120
f 29¢ Italy Invaded by Allies		.75	.40			2.00	120
g 29¢ Bonds and Stamps Help War Effort		.75	.40			2.00	120
h 29¢ "Willie and Joe" Keep Spirits High.		.75	.40			2.00	120
i 29¢ Gold Stars Mark World War II Losses		.75	.40			2.00	120
j 29¢ Marines Assault Tarawa		.75	.40			2.00	120
American Sports Personalities, Tagged, Perf. 11							
2766 29¢ Joe Louis	06/22/93	.60	.20	2.75	(4)	3.00	160
Legends of American Music: Broadway Musicals, Tagged, Perf. 11 Horizontally on 1 or 2 sides							
2767 29¢ *Show Boat*	07/14/93	.60	.20			1.25	129
2768 29¢ *Porgy & Bess*	07/14/93	.60	.20			1.25	129
2769 29¢ *Oklahoma!*	07/14/93	.60	.20			1.25	129
2770 29¢ *My Fair Lady*	07/14/93	.60	.20			1.25	129
a Booklet pane of 4, #2767-2770		2.75	2.25			3.50	

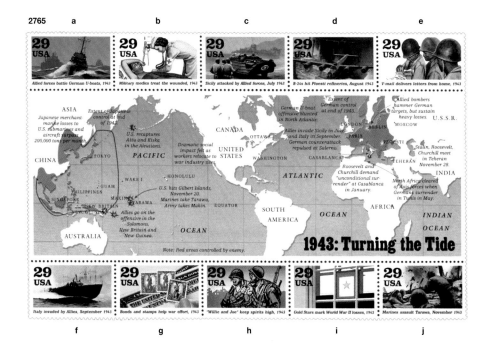

2741   2742   2743   2744   2745 2745a

2746

2747

2748

2749

2750   2751

2752   2753

2753a

2754

2755

2756   2757

2758   2759

2759a

2766

2767

2768

2769

2770

2760   2761   2762   2763   2764 2764a

1993

2771 2772

2773 2774 2774a

2775
2776
2777
2778
2778a

2779 2780

2781 2782 2782a

2783 2784 2784a

2785 2786

2787 2788 2788a

2789 2790

2791 2792

2793 2794 2794a

2795 2796

2797 2798 2798c

2803

2804

2805

Issue		Date	Un	U	PB	#	FDC	Q(M)
Legends of American Music: Country & Western, Tagged, Perf. 10								
2771	29¢ Hank Williams (2775)	09/25/93	.75	.20			1.25	25
2772	29¢ Patsy Cline (2777)	09/25/93	.75	.20			1.25	25
2773	29¢ The Carter Family (2776)	09/25/93	.75	.20			1.25	25
2774	29¢ Bob Wills (2778)	09/25/93	.75	.20			1.25	25
a	Block or horiz. strip of 4, #2771-2774		3.00	1.75	3.25	(4)	3.00	
Booklet, Perf. 11 Horizontally on 1 or 2 sides								
2775	29¢ Hank Williams	09/25/93	.60	.20			1.25	170
2776	29¢ The Carter Family	09/25/93	.60	.20			1.25	170
2777	29¢ Patsy Cline	09/25/93	.60	.20			1.25	170
2778	29¢ Bob Wills	09/25/93	.60	.20			1.25	170
a	Booklet pane of 4, #2775-2778		2.50	2.00			3.00	
National Postal Museum, Tagged, Perf. 11								
2779	Independence Hall, Benjamin Franklin, Printing Press, Colonial Post Rider	07/30/93	.60	.20			1.25	38
2780	Pony Express Rider, Civil War Soldier, Concord Stagecoach	07/30/93	.60	.20			1.25	38
2781	Biplane, Charles Lindbergh, Railway Mail Car, 1931 Model A Ford Mail Truck	07/30/93	.60	.20			1.25	38
2782	California Gold Rush Miner's Letter, Barcode and Circular Date Stamp	07/30/93	.60	.20			1.25	38
a	Block or strip of 4, #2779-2782		2.40	2.00	2.50	(4)	2.75	
c	As "a," imperf.	3,250.00						
American Sign Language, Tagged, Perf. 11.5								
2783	29¢ Recognizing Deafness	09/20/93	.60	.20			1.50	42
2784	29¢ American Sign Language	09/20/93	.60	.20			1.50	42
a	Pair, #2783-2784		1.20	.75	2.50	(4)	2.50	
Classic Books, Tagged, Perf. 11								
2785	29¢ Rebecca of Sunnybrook Farm	10/23/93	.60	.20			1.25	38
2786	29¢ Little House on the Prairie	10/23/93	.60	.20			1.25	38
2787	29¢ The Adventures of Huckleberry Finn	10/23/93	.60	.20			1.25	38
2788	29¢ Little Women	10/23/93	.60	.20			1.25	38
a	Block or horiz. strip of 4, #2785-2788		2.40	2.00	5.00	(4)	2.75	

Issue		Date	Un	U	PB	#	FDC	Q(M)
Holiday Celebration: Christmas, Tagged, Perf. 11								
2789	29¢ Madonna and Child by Giovanni Battista Cima	10/21/93	.60	.20	2.75	(4)	1.25	500
Booklet, Perf. 11.5 x 11 on 2 or 3 sides								
2790	29¢ Madonna and Child (2789)	10/21/93	.60	.20			1.25	500
a	Booklet pane of 4		2.40	1.75			2.50	
Perf. 11.5								
2791	29¢ Jack-in-the-Box	10/21/93	.60	.20			1.25	250
2792	29¢ Red-Nosed Reindeer	10/21/93	.60	.20			1.25	250
2793	29¢ Snowman	10/21/93	.60	.20			1.25	250
2794	29¢ Toy Soldier	10/21/93	.60	.20			1.25	250
a	Block or strip of 4, #2791-2794		2.40	2.00	4.00	(4)	2.75	
Booklet, Perf. 11 x 10 on 2 or 3 sides								
2795	29¢ Toy Soldier (2794)	10/21/93	.85	.20			1.25	200
2796	29¢ Snowman (2793)	10/21/93	.85	.20			1.25	200
2797	29¢ Red-Nosed Reindeer (2792)	10/21/93	.85	.20			1.25	200
2798	29¢ Jack-in-the-Box (2791)	10/21/93	.85	.20			1.25	200
a	Booklet pane, 3 each #2795-2796, 2 each #2797-2798		8.50	4.00			6.50	
b	Booklet pane, 3 each #2797-2798, 2 each #2795-2796		8.50	4.00			6.50	
c	Block of 4		3.40	1.75				
Self-Adhesive, Die-Cut								
2799	29¢ Snowman	10/28/93	.65	.20			1.25	120
a	Coil with plate		—	10.00	6.00	(5)		
2800	29¢ Toy Soldier	10/28/93	.65	.20			1.25	120
2801	29¢ Jack-in-the-Box	10/28/93	.65	.20			1.25	120
2802	29¢ Red-Nosed Reindeer	10/28/93	.65	.20			1.25	120
a	Booklet pane, 3 each #2799-2802		8.00					
b	Block of 4		2.60				2.50	
2803	29¢ Snowman	10/28/93	.60	.20			1.25	18
a	Booklet pane of 18		11.00					
Tagged, Perf. 11								
2804	29¢ Northern Mariana Islands	11/04/93	.60	.20	2.50	(4)	1.25	88
Tagged, Perf. 11.2								
2805	29¢ Columbus Landing in Puerto Rico	11/19/93	.60	.20	2.75	(4)	1.25	105
2806	29¢ AIDS Awareness	12/01/93	.60	.20	2.75	(4)	2.00	100
a	Booklet version		.70	.20			2.00	250
b	Booklet pane of 5		3.50	2.00			4.00	

AMERICAN ★ COMMEMORATIVE ★ COLLECTIBLES

American Commemorative Collection

An easy and uniform way to collect and learn about issues that commemorate people, anniversaries, places and events. You'll find detailed stories on the issue and the subject and included are protective acetate mounts for your stamps.

Just mount the stamps on the specially designed sheet and place them in a three-ring binder. Just $3.25* each, depending on the value of the stamps.

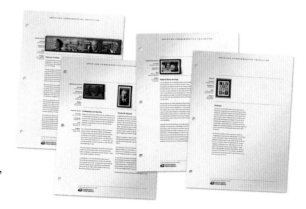

Item #29143. To order call **1 800 STAMP-24**   *Prices subject to change without notice.

Issue		Date	Un	U	PB	#	FDC	Q(M)
	Olympic Games, Winter, Tagged, Perf. 11.2							
2807	29¢ Slalom	01/06/94	.60	.20			1.25	36
2808	29¢ Luge	01/06/94	.60	.20			1.25	36
2809	29¢ Ice Dancing	01/06/94	.60	.20			1.25	36
2810	29¢ Cross-Country Skiing	01/06/94	.60	.20			1.25	36
2811	29¢ Ice Hockey	01/06/94	.60	.20			1.25	36
a	Strip of 5, #2807-2811		3.00	2.50	6.50	(10)	3.00	
	Tagged, Perf. 11.2							
2812	29¢ Edward R. Murrow	01/21/94	.60	.20	3.25	(4)	1.25	151
	Love, Tagged, Self-Adhesive, Die-Cut							
2813	29¢ Love Sunrise	01/27/94	.60	.20			1.25	358
a	Booklet of 18 (self-adhesive)		11.00					
b	Coil with plate		—	3.75	6.75	(5)		
	Love, Perf. 10.9 x 11.1 on 2 or 3 sides							
2814	29¢ Love Stamp	02/14/94	.60	.20			1.25	830
a	Booklet pane of 10		6.00	3.50			6.50	
	Tagged, Perf. 11.1							
2814C	29¢ Love Stamp	06/11/94	.70	.20	3.00	(4)	1.25	300
	Perf. 11.2							
2815	52¢ Love Birds	02/14/94	1.00	.20	5.00	(4)	1.50	273
	Black Heritage, Tagged, Perf. 11.2							
2816	29¢ Dr. Allison Davis	02/01/94	.60	.20	2.50	(4)	2.00	156
	Lunar New Year, Tagged, Perf. 11.2							
2817	29¢ Year of the Dog	02/05/94	.80	.20	3.50	(4)	2.00	105
	Tagged, Perf. 11.5 x 11.2							
2818	29¢ Buffalo Soldiers	04/22/94	.60	.20	2.50	(4)	2.75	186
	Stars of the Silent Screen, Tagged, Perf. 11.2							
2819	29¢ Rudolph Valentino	04/27/94	1.10	.30			1.50	19
2820	29¢ Clara Bow	04/27/94	1.10	.30			1.50	19
2821	29¢ Charlie Chaplin	04/27/94	1.10	.30			1.50	19
2822	29¢ Lon Chaney	04/27/94	1.10	.30			1.50	19
2823	29¢ John Gilbert	04/27/94	1.10	.30			1.50	19
2824	29¢ Zasu Pitts	04/27/94	1.10	.30			1.50	19
2825	29¢ Harold Lloyd	04/27/94	1.10	.30			1.50	19
2826	29¢ Keystone Cops	04/27/94	1.10	.30			1.50	19
2827	29¢ Theda Bara	04/27/94	1.10	.30			1.50	19
2828	29¢ Buster Keaton	04/27/94	1.10	.30			1.50	19
a	Block of 10 #2819-2828		11.00	4.00	12.00	(10)	6.50	

Issue		Date	Un	U	PB	#	FDC	Q(M)
	Garden Flowers, Booklet, Tagged, Perf. 10.9 Vertically							
2829	29¢ Lily	04/28/94	.60	.20			1.25	166
2830	29¢ Zinnia	04/28/94	.60	.20			1.25	166
2831	29¢ Gladiola	04/28/94	.60	.20			1.25	166
2832	29¢ Marigold	04/28/94	.60	.20			1.25	166
2833	29¢ Rose	04/28/94	.60	.20			1.25	166
a	Booklet pane of 5, #2829-2833		3.00	2.25			3.25	
b	As "a," imperf.		1,500.00					
c	As "a," black (engr.) omitted		225.00					
	1994 World Cup Soccer Championships, Tagged, Perf. 11.1							
2834	29¢ Soccer Player	05/26/94	.60	.20	2.50	(4)	2.00	201
2835	40¢ Soccer Player	05/26/94	.80	.20	3.20	(4)	2.00	300
2836	50¢ Soccer Player	05/26/94	1.00	.20	4.00	(4)	2.00	269
2837	Souvenir Sheet of 3, #2834-2836	05/26/94	4.00	3.00			4.00	60
	World War II, 1944: Road to Victory, Miniature, Sheet, Tagged, Perf. 10.9							
2838	Sheet of 10 and central label	06/06/94	18.00	10.00			7.00	120
a	29¢ Allies Retake New Guinea		1.80	.50			2.00	120
b	29¢ Bombing Raids		1.80	.50			2.00	120
c	29¢ Allies in Normandy, D-Day		1.80	.50			2.00	120
d	29¢ Airborne Units		1.80	.50			2.00	120
e	29¢ Submarines Shorten War		1.80	.50			2.00	120
f	29¢ Allies Free Rome, Paris		1.80	.50			2.00	120
g	29¢ Troops Clear Siapan Bunkers		1.80	.50			2.00	120
h	29¢ Red Ball Express		1.80	.50			2.00	120
i	29¢ Battle for Leyte Gulf		1.80	.50			2.00	120
j	29¢ Battle of the Bulge		1.80	.50			2.00	120

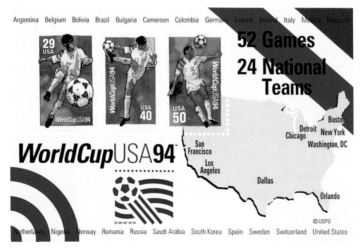

2837

2807

2808

2809

2810

2811 2811a

2812

LOVE
2813

LOVE
2814

LOVE
2814C

2815

2817

2819 2820 2821 2822 2823

2816

2818

2824 2825 2826 2827 2828 2828a

2829 2830 2831 2832 2833 2833a

2834

2835

2836

2838

a b c d e

1944: Road to Victory

f g h i j

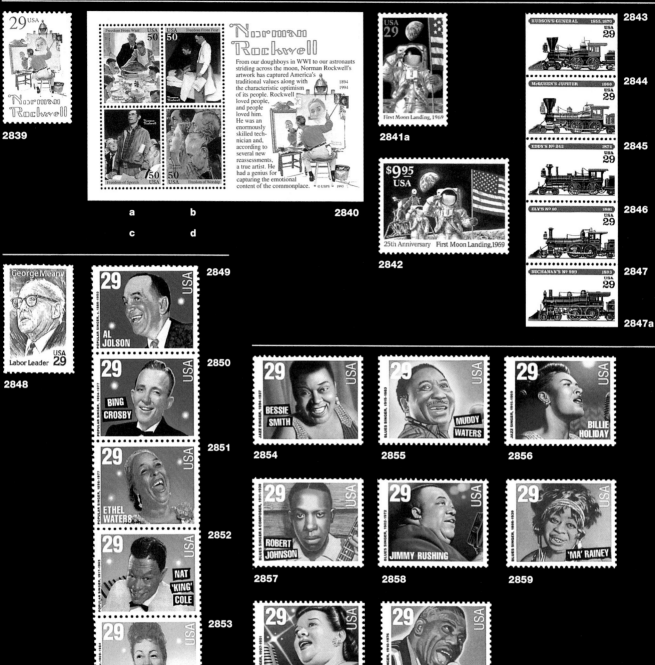

29 USA
Norman Rockwell
2839

Freedom From Want
USA 50

Freedom From Fear
USA 50

Norman Rockwell

From our doughboys in WWI to our astronauts striding across the moon, Norman Rockwell's artwork has captured America's traditional values along with the characteristic optimism of its people. Rockwell loved people, and people loved him. He was an enormously skilled technician and, according to several new reassessments, a true artist. He had a genius for capturing the emotional content of the commonplace. © USPS 1993

1894 1994

Freedom of Speech USA 50

Freedom of Worship 50

a   b
c   d
2840

USA 29
First Moon Landing, 1969
2841a

$9.95 USA
25th Anniversary   First Moon Landing, 1969
2842

HUDSON'S GENERAL   1855, 1870
USA 29
2843

McQUEEN'S JUPITER   1869
USA 29
2844

EDDY'S N° 242   1874
USA 29
2845

ELY'S N° 10   1891
USA 29
2846

BUCHANAN'S N° 999   1893
USA 29
2847

2847a

George Meany
Labor Leader   USA 29
2848

29 USA
POPULAR SINGER, c. 1886-1950
AL JOLSON
2849

29 USA
POPULAR SINGER, 1904-1977
BING CROSBY
2850

29 USA
POPULAR SINGER, 1896-1977
ETHEL WATERS
2851

29 USA
POPULAR SINGER, 1917-1965
NAT 'KING' COLE
2852

29 USA
POPULAR SINGER, c. 1909-1984
ETHEL MERMAN
2853

2853a

29 USA
JAZZ SINGER, 1894-1937
BESSIE SMITH
2854

29 USA
BLUES SINGER, 1915-1983
MUDDY WATERS
2855

29 USA
JAZZ SINGER, 1915-1959
BILLIE HOLIDAY
2856

29 USA
BLUES SINGER & COMPOSER, 1911-1938
ROBERT JOHNSON
2857

29 USA
BLUES SINGER, 1902-1972
JIMMY RUSHING
2858

29 USA
BLUES SINGER, 1886-1939
'MA' RAINEY
2859

29 USA
JAZZ SINGER, 1907-1951
MILDRED BAILEY
2860

29 USA
BLUES SINGER, 1910-1976
HOWLIN' WOLF
2861

USA 29
JAMES THURBER
2862

2863

USA 29

USA 29
2864

USA 29

2865

USA 29
2866

2866a

Black-Necked Crane
29 USA
2867

Whooping Crane
29 USA
2868   2868a

Issue		Date	Un	U	PB #	FDC	Q(M)
Norman Rockwell, Tagged, Perf. 10.9 x 11.1							
2839	29¢ Rockwell Self-Portrait	07/01/94	.60	.20	2.75 (4)	1.25	209
2840	Four Freedoms souvenir sheet	07/01/94	4.50	2.75		3.50	20
a	50¢ Freedom from Want		1.10	.65		1.50	20
b	50¢ Freedom from Fear		1.10	.65		1.50	20
c	50¢ Freedom of Speech		1.10	.65		1.50	20
d	50¢ Freedom of Worship		1.10	.65		1.50	20
Space, Tagged, Perf. 11.2 x 11.1							
2841	29¢ First Moon Landing, 1969, sheet of 12	07/20/94	11.00	—		6.50	13
a	Single stamp		.90	.60		1.50	
Space, Perf. 10.7 x 11.1							
2842	$9.95 First Moon Landing 25th Anniversary	07/20/94	20.00	16.00	82.50 (4)	20.00	101
Locomotives, Booklet, Tagged, Perf. 11 Horizontally							
2843	29¢ Hudson's General	07/28/94	.70	.20		1.75	159
2844	29¢ McQueen's Jupiter	07/28/94	.70	.20		1.75	159
2845	29¢ Eddy's No. 242	07/28/94	.70	.20		1.75	159
2846	29¢ Ely's No. 10	07/28/94	.70	.20		1.75	159
2847	29¢ Buchanan's No. 999	07/28/94	.70	.20		1.75	159
a	Booklet pane of 5, #2843-2847		3.50	2.00		4.00	
Tagged, Perf. 11.1 x 11							
2848	29¢ George Meany	08/16/94	.60	.20	2.50 (4)	1.25	151
Legends of American Music: Popular Singers, Tagged, Perf. 10.1 x 10.2							
2849	29¢ Al Jolson	09/01/94	.75	.20		1.50	35
2850	29¢ Bing Crosby	09/01/94	.75	.20		1.50	35
2851	29¢ Ethel Waters	09/01/94	.75	.20		1.50	35
2852	29¢ Nat "King" Cole	09/01/94	.75	.20		1.50	35
2853	29¢ Ethel Merman	09/01/94	.75	.20		1.50	35
a	Vert. strip of 5, #2849-2853		3.75	2.00	8.00 (6)	4.50	
b	Pane of 20, imperf.		4,600.00				

Issue		Date	Un	U	PB #	FDC	Q(M)
Legends of American Music: Jazz and Blues, Tagged, Perf. 11 x 10.8							
2854	29¢ Bessie Smith	09/17/94	.75	.20		1.25	25
2855	29¢ Muddy Waters	09/17/94	.75	.20		1.25	25
2856	29¢ Billie Holiday	09/17/94	.75	.20		1.25	25
2857	29¢ Robert Johnson	09/17/94	.75	.20		1.25	20
2858	29¢ Jimmy Rushing	09/17/94	.75	.20		1.25	20
2859	29¢ "Ma" Rainey	09/17/94	.75	.20		1.25	20
2860	29¢ Mildred Bailey	09/17/94	.75	.20		1.25	20
2861	29¢ Howlin' Wolf	09/17/94	.75	.20		1.25	20
a	Block of 9, #2854-2861 + 1 additional stamp		7.50	4.50	9.00(10)	6.00	
Literary Arts, Tagged, Perf. 11							
2862	29¢ James Thurber	09/10/94	.60	.20	2.75 (4)	1.25	151
Wonders of the Sea, Tagged, Perf. 11 x 10.9							
2863	29¢ Diver, Motorboat	10/03/94	.60	.20		1.25	56
2864	29¢ Diver, Ship	10/03/94	.60	.20		1.25	56
2865	29¢ Diver, Ship's Wheel	10/03/94	.60	.20		1.25	56
2866	29¢ Diver, Coral	10/03/94	.60	.20		1.25	56
a	Block of 4, #2963-2966		2.40	1.50	2.50 (4)	2.75	
b	As "a" imperf.		1,250.00				
Cranes, Tagged, Perf. 10.8 x 11							
2867	29¢ Black-Necked Crane	10/09/94	.70	.20		1.25	78
2868	29¢ Whooping Crane	10/09/94	.70	.20		1.25	78
a	Pair, #2867-2868		1.40	.75	3.00 (4)	2.50	
b	Black and magenta (engr.) omitted		1,650.00				
c	As "a," double impression of (engr.) black & magenta		4,750.00				

LEGENDS OF HOLLYWOOD: GARY COOPER

The 15th stamp in the Legends of Hollywood series honors Gary Cooper (1901-1961), a popular leading man who began his career during Hollywood's "Golden Age." For decades, Cooper was the all-American hero, whose believable performances and strong, silent appeal brought him a lifetime of fame. ■ Born in Helena, Montana, Frank James Cooper spent his early years on his family's ranch. Although initially pursuing a career as a political cartoonist, Cooper soon was working as an extra in Westerns. Not long after a casting agent persuaded him to adopt the name Gary—there were already two Frank Coopers in Hollywood—Cooper had his first starring role in *Arizona Bound* (1927). As talkies replaced silent films, Cooper made a seamless transition. His first all-talking movie, *The Virginian* (1929), was a box office hit. ■ Cooper won an Academy Award for his portrayal of U.S. Army Sergeant Alvin York, in *Sergeant York* (1941). In 1942, he gave another memorable performance, as baseball slugger Lou Gehrig in *The Pride of the Yankees*. He reportedly liked making Westerns, because they reminded him of his early days on the ranch. His performance as Marshal Will Kane in the classic *High Noon* (1952), considered by many to be his finest, won him his second Oscar. ■ Though he often kept to himself, Cooper was liked and respected in Hollywood, and actors and directors frequently sought him out for projects. All told, Cooper made more than a hundred movies, including such other notable films as *A Farewell to Arms* (1932), *Beau Geste* (1939), and *For Whom The Bell Tolls* (1943).

Gary Cooper licensed by 7 Bar 9 LLC., New York, New York

Issue		Date	Un	U	PB	#	FDC	Q(M)
Classic Collections: Legends of the West, Tagged, Perf. 10.1 x 10								
2869	Sheet of 20	10/18/94	15.00	10.00			15.00	
a	29¢ Home on the Range		.75	.50			2.25	20
b	29¢ Buffalo Bill Cody		.75	.50			2.25	20
c	29¢ Jim Bridger		.75	.50			2.25	20
d	29¢ Annie Oakley		.75	.50			2.25	20
e	29¢ Native American Culture		.75	.50			2.25	20
f	29¢ Chief Joseph		.75	.50			2.25	20
g	29¢ Bill Pickett		.75	.50			2.25	20
h	29¢ Bat Masterson		.75	.50			2.25	20
i	29¢ John C. Fremont		.75	.50			2.25	20
j	29¢ Wyatt Earp		.75	.50			2.25	20
k	29¢ Nellie Cashman		.75	.50			2.25	20
l	29¢ Charles Goodnight		.75	.50			2.25	20
m	29¢ Geronimo		.75	.50			2.25	20
n	29¢ Kit Carson		.75	.50			2.25	20
o	29¢ Wild Bill Hickok		.75	.50			2.25	20
p	29¢ Western Wildlife		.75	.50			2.25	20
q	29¢ Jim Beckwourth		.75	.50			2.25	20
r	29¢ Bill Tilghman		.75	.50			2.25	20
s	29¢ Sacagawea		.75	.50			2.25	20
t	29¢ Overland Mail		.75	.50			2.25	20
2870	29¢ Sheet of 20 (recalled)	10/18/94	260.00	—				0.15
Holiday Celebration: Christmas, Tagged, Perf. 11.25								
2871	29¢ Madonna and Child by Elisabetta Sira	10/20/94	.70	.20	3.00	(4)	1.25	519
2871A	Perf. 9.8 x 10.8		.60	.20			1.25	
b	As "a," booklet pane of 10		6.25	3.50				50
c	Imperf., pair		500.00					
Holiday Celebration: Holiday, Perf. 11.25								
2872	29¢ Stocking	10/20/94	.60	.20	2.50	(4)	1.25	603
a	Booklet pane of 20		12.50	4.00				
Booklet, Self-Adhesive, Die-Cut								
2873	29¢ Santa Claus	10/20/94	.70	.20	6.75	(5)	1.25	237
a	Booklet pane of 12		8.50					
2874	29¢ Cardinal in Snow	10/20/94	.60	.20			1.25	45
a	Booklet pane of 18		11.00					
Bureau of Engraving and Printing, Souvenir Sheet, Tagged, Perf.11								
2875	$2.00 Sheet of 4	11/03/94	16.00	13.50			25.00	5
a	Single stamp		4.00	2.00				
Lunar New Year, Tagged, Perf. 11.2 x 11.1								
2876	29¢ Year of the Boar	12/30/94	.70	.20	3.00	(4)	1.75	80
Untagged, Perf. 11 x 10.8								
2877	(3¢) Dove Make-Up Rate	12/13/94	.20	.20	.30	(4)	1.25	
a	Imperf., pair		135.00					
Perf. 10.8 x 10.9								
2878	(3¢) Dove Make-Up Rate	12/13/94	.20	.20	.40	(4)	1.25	
Tagged, Perf. 11.2 x 11.1								
2879	(20¢) Old Glory Postcard Rate	12/13/94	.40	.20	8.50	(4)	1.25	
Perf. 11 x 10.9								
2880	(20¢) Old Glory Postcard Rate	12/13/94	.75	.20	17.50	(4)	1.25	
Perf. 11.2 x 11.1								
2881	(32¢) "G" Old Glory	12/13/94	1.00	.20	70.00	(4)	1.25	
a	Booklet pane of 10		6.00	3.75			6.75	

Issue		Date	Un	U	PB	#	FDC	Q(M)
Perf. 11 x 10.9								
2882	(32¢) "G" Old Glory	12/13/94	.60	.20	4.00	(4)	1.25	
Booklet, Perf. 10 x 9.9 on 2 or 3 sides								
2883	(32¢) "G" Old Glory	12/13/94	.65	.20			1.25	
a	Booklet pane of 10		6.50	3.75			6.75	
Booklet, Perf. 10.9 on 2 or 3 sides								
2884	(32¢) "G" Old Glory	12/13/94	.65	.20			1.25	
a	Booklet pane of 10		6.50	3.75			6.75	
b	As "a," imperf.		1,700.00					
Booklet, Perf. 11 x 10.9 on 2 or 3 sides								
2885	(32¢) "G" Old Glory	12/13/94	.90	.20			1.25	
a	Booklet pane of 10		9.00	4.50			6.75	
Self-Adhesive, Die-Cut								
2886	(32¢) "G" Old Glory	12/13/94	.75	.20			1.25	
a	Booklet pane of 18		14.00		5.50	(5)		
b	Coil with plate		—	10.00	11.50	(5)		
2887	(32¢) "G" Old Glory	12/13/94	.75	.20			1.25	
a	Booklet pane of 18		14.00					
Coil, Perf. 9.8 Vertically								
2888	(25¢) Old Glory First-Class Presort	12/13/94	.90	.50	5.00	(5)	1.25	
2889	(32¢) Black "G"	12/13/94	1.50	.20	10.00	(5)	1.25	
a	Imperf., pair		275.00					
2890	(32¢) Blue "G"	12/13/94	.65	.20	4.75	(5)	1.25	
2891	(32¢) Red "G"	12/13/94	.85	.20	4.75	(5)	1.25	
Coil, Rouletted 9.8 Vertically								
2892	(32¢) Old Glory, red "G"	12/13/94	.75	.20	5.25	(5)	1.25	
Coil, Untagged, Perf. 9.8 Vertically								
2893	(5¢) Old Glory, green	01/12/95	.50	.20	3.50	(5)		
Coil, Tagged, Perf. 10.4								
2897	32¢ Flag Over Porch	05/19/95	.65	.20	4.25	(4)	1.25	
b	Imperf., vert. pair		65.00					
American Scenes, Coil, Untagged, Perf. 9.8 Vertically								
2902	(5¢) Butte	03/10/95	.20	.20	1.25	(5)	1.25	
a	Imperf., pair		600.00					
American Scenes, Coil, Untagged, Self-Adhesive, Serpentine Die-Cut 11.5 Vertically								
2902B	(5¢) Butte	06/15/96	.35	.20	2.10	(5)	1.25	550
American Scenes, Coil, Perf. 9.8 Vertically								
2903	(5¢) Mountain, purple and multi	03/16/96	.25	.20	1.25	(5)	1.25	150
a	Tagged (error)		4.00	3.50	65.00	(5)		
2904	(5¢) Mountain, blue and multi	03/16/96	.20	.20	1.25	(5)	1.25	150
c	Imperf., pair		425.00					
American Scenes, Coil, Self-Adhesive, Serpentine Die-Cut 11.2 Vertically								
2904A	(5¢) Mountain, purple and multi	06/15/96	.40	.20	4.00	(5)	1.25	
American Scenes, Coil, Self-Adhesive, Serpentine Die-Cut 9.8 Vertically								
2904B	(5¢) Mountain, purple and multi	01/24/97	.20	.20	1.40	(5)	1.25	148
American Transportation, Coil, Perf. 9.8 Vertically								
2905	(10¢) Automobile	03/10/95	.20	.20	2.00	(5)	1.25	
American Transportation, Coil, Self-Adhesive, Serpentine Die-Cut 11.5 Vertically								
2906	(10¢) Automobile	06/15/96	.40	.20	2.25	(5)	1.25	450
2907	(10¢) Eagle and Shield	05/21/96	.75	.20	4.00	(5)	1.25	450

2869 a b c d e
      f g h i j
      k l m n o
      p q r s t

2870g Recalled

2871

2872

2873

2874

2875

2876

2877 **2878** **2879** **2880** **2881** **2882** **2883**

2884 **2885** **2886** **2887** **2888** **2889** **2890** **2891** **2892**

2893 **2897** **2902** **2903** **2904** **2905** **2906** **2907**

2908

2909

2910

2911

2912

2913

2914

2915

2916

2919

2920

2921

2933

2934

2935

2936

2938

2940

2941

2942

2943

2948

2950

2951

2952

2953

2954

2954a

2955

2956

2961

2962

2963

2965

2964

2958

2966

2965a

Issue		Date	Un	U	PB #	FDC	Q(M)
American Culture, Coil, Perf. 9.8 Vertically							
2908	(15¢) Auto Tail Fin, bureau printing	03/17/95	.30	.30	2.50 (5)	1.25	
2909	(15¢) Auto Tail Fin, private printing	03/17/95	.30	.30	2.50 (5)	1.25	
American Culture, Coil, Self-Adhesive, Serpentine Die-Cut 11.5 Vertically							
2910	(15¢) Auto Tail Fin	06/15/96	.30	.30	2.50 (5)	1.25	
American Culture, Coil, Perf. 9.8 Vertically							
2911	(25¢) Juke Box, bureau printing	03/17/95	.50	.50	4.00 (5)	1.25	
2912	(25¢) Juke Box, private printing	03/17/95	.50	.50	3.50 (5)	1.25	
American Culture, Coil, Self-Adhesive, Serpentine Die-Cut 11.5 Vertically							
2912A	(25¢) Juke Box	06/15/96	.50	.50	3.75 (5)	1.25	550
American Culture, Coil, Self-Adhesive, Serpentine Die-Cut 9.8 Vertically							
2912B	(25¢) Juke Box	01/24/97	.75	.50	4.00 (5)	1.25	20
Coil, Tagged, Perf. 9.8 Vertically							
2913	32¢ Flag Over Porch	05/19/95	.65	.20	5.00 (5)	1.25	
a	Imperf., pair		32.50				
2914	32¢ Flag Over Porch	05/19/95	.80	.20	4.50 (3)	1.25	
Coil, Self-Adhesive, Serpentine Die-Cut 8.7 Vertically							
2915	32¢ Flag Over Porch	04/18/95	1.25	.30	10.50 (5)	1.25	
Coil, Self-Adhesive, Serpentine Die-Cut Perf. 9.8 Vertically							
2915A	32¢ Flag Over Porch	05/21/96	.65	.20	4.25 (5)	1.25	
Coil, Self-Adhesive, Serpentine Die-Cut 11.5 Vertically							
2915B	32¢ Flag Over Porch	06/15/96	1.00	.90	6.00 (5)	1.25	
Coil, Self-Adhesive, Serpentine Die-Cut 10.9 Vertically							
2915C	32¢ Flag Over Porch	06/21/96	2.00	.40	27.50 (5)	2.00	
Coil, Self-Adhesive, Serpentine Die-Cut 9.8 Vertically							
2915D	32¢ Flag Over Porch	01/24/97	2.00	.90	9.00 (5)	1.25	300
Booklet, Perf. 10.8 x 9.8 on 2 or 3 adjacent sides							
2916	32¢ Flag Over Porch	05/19/95	.65	.20		1.25	
a	Booklet pane of 10		6.50	3.25		7.50	
Booklet, Die-Cut							
2919	32¢ Flag Over Field	03/17/95	.65	.20		1.25	
a	Booklet pane of 18		12.00				
Booklet, Self-Adhesive, Serpentine Die-Cut 8.7 on 2, 3 or 4 adjacent sides							
2920	32¢ Flag Over Porch	04/18/95	.65	.20		1.25	
a	Booklet pane of 20 + label		13.00				
b	Small date		5.50	.35			
c	As "b," booklet pane of 20 + label		110.00				
f	As #2920, pane of 15 + label		10.00				
h	As #2920, booklet pane of 15		35.00				
Booklet, Self-Adhesive, Serpentine Die-Cut 11.3 on 3 sides							
2920D	32¢ Flag Over Porch	01/20/96	.80	.25			789
e	Booklet pane of 10		8.00				
Booklet, Self-Adhesive, Serpentine Die-Cut Perf. 9.8 on 2 or 3 adjacent sides							
2921	32¢ Flag Over Porch	05/21/96	.90	.20		1.25	7,344
a	Booklet pane of 10		9.00				
b	As #2921, dated red "1997"		1.20	.20			
c	As "a," dated red "1997"		12.00				
d	Booklet pane of 5 + label		7.00				
Great Americans, Tagged, Perf. 11.2							
2933	32¢ Milton S. Hershey	09/13/95	.65	.20	3.00 (4)	1.25	
2934	32¢ Cal Farley	04/26/96	.65	.20	3.00 (4)	1.25	150
2935	32¢ Henry R. Luce	04/03/98	.65	.20	3.00 (4)	1.25	
2936	32¢ Lila and DeWitt Wallace	07/16/98	.65	.20	3.00 (4)	1.25	
2938	46¢ Ruth Benedict	10/20/95	.90	.20	4.50 (4)	1.40	
2940	55¢ Alice Hamilton, MD	07/11/95	1.10	.20	5.50 (4)	1.40	
Tagged, Self-Adhesive, Serpentine Die-Cut 11.7 x 11.5							
2941	55¢ Justin S. Morrill	07/17/99	1.10	.20	4.40 (4)	1.40	

Issue		Date	Un	U	PB #	FDC	Q(M)
Tagged, Self-Adhesive, Serpentine Die-Cut 11.7 x 11.5							
2942	77¢ Mary Breckinridge	11/09/98	1.50	.40	6.00 (4)	1.75	
Tagged, Perf. 11.2							
2943	78¢ Alice Paul	08/18/95	1.60	.20	7.50 (4)	1.75	
a	Dull violet		1.60	.25	7.50 (4)		
b	Pale violet		1.75	.30	12.00 (4)		
Love, Tagged, Perf. 11.2							
2948	(32¢) Love, Cherub from Sistine Madonna, by Raphael	02/01/95	.65	.20	3.00 (4)	1.50	215
Love, Self-Adhesive, Die-Cut							
2949	(32¢) Love, Cherub from Sistine Madonna, by Raphael	02/01/95	.65	.20		1.50	1,221
a	Booklet pane of 20 + label		13.00				
b	Red (engr.) omitted		375.00				
c	As "a," red (engr.) omitted		7,500.00				
Tagged, Perf. 11.1							
2950	32¢ Florida Statehood, 150th Anniversary	03/03/95	.65	.20	2.60 (4)	1.25	95
Kids Care, Earth Day, Tagged, Perf. 11.1 x 11							
2951	32¢ Earth Clean-Up	04/20/95	.65	.20		1.25	13
2952	32¢ Solar Energy	04/20/95	.65	.20		1.25	13
2953	32¢ Tree Planting	04/20/95	.65	.20		1.25	13
2954	32¢ Beach Clean-Up	04/20/95	.65	.20		1.25	13
a	Block of 4, #2951-2954		2.60	1.75	2.60 (4)	2.75	
Tagged, Perf. 11.2							
2955	32¢ Richard Nixon	04/26/95	.65	.20	3.00 (4)	1.25	80
a	Red (engr.) omitted		1,100.00				
Black Heritage, Tagged, Perf. 11.2							
2956	32¢ Bessie Coleman	04/27/95	.85	.20	3.75 (4)	1.75	97
Love, Tagged, Perf. 11.2							
2957	32¢ Love, Cherub from Sistine Madonna, by Raphael	05/12/95	.65	.20	3.00 (4)	1.25	315
2958	55¢ Love, Cherub from Sistine Madonna, by Raphael	05/12/95	1.10	.20	5.50 (4)	1.25	300
Love, Booklet, Perf. 9.8 x 10.8							
2959	32¢ Love, Cherub from Sistine Madonna, by Raphael	05/12/95	.65	.20		1.25	
a	Booklet pane of 10		6.50	3.25		7.50	
Love, Self-Adhesive, Die-Cut							
2960	55¢ Love, Cherub from Sistine Madonna, by Raphael	05/12/95	1.10	.20		1.40	
a	Booklet pane of 20 + label		22.50				
Recreational Sports, Tagged, Perf. 11.2							
2961	32¢ Volleyball	05/20/95	.65	.20		1.50	6
2962	32¢ Softball	05/20/95	.65	.20		1.50	6
2963	32¢ Bowling	05/20/95	.65	.20		1.50	6
2964	32¢ Tennis	05/20/95	.65	.20		1.50	6
2965	32¢ Golf	05/20/95	.65	.20		1.50	6
a	Vertical strip of 5, #2961-2965		3.25	2.00	6.50(10)	3.25	
b	As "a," imperf.		2,250.00				
c	As "a," yellow omitted		2,000.00				
d	As "a," yellow, blue and magenta omitted		2,000.00				
Tagged, Perf. 11.2							
2966	32¢ Prisoners of War and Missing in Action	05/29/95	.65	.20	2.50 (4)	2.25	125
	Pane of 20		12.50	—			

Issue	Date	Un	U	PB #	FDC	Q(M)
Legends of Hollywood, Tagged, Perf. 11.1						
2967 32¢ Marilyn Monroe	06/01/95	.85	.20	5.50 (4)	3.25	400
Pane of 20		25.00				
a Imperf., pair		475.00				
Tagged, Perf. 11.2						
2968 32¢ Texas Statehood	06/16/95	.75	.20	3.00 (4)	1.75	99
Lighthouses: Great Lakes, Tagged, Perf. 11.2 Vertically						
2969 32¢ Split Rock, Lake Superior	06/17/95	1.25	.30		2.00	
2970 32¢ St. Joseph, Lake Michigan	06/17/95	1.25	.30		2.00	
2971 32¢ Spectacle Reef, Lake Huron	06/17/95	1.25	.30		2.00	
2972 32¢ Marblehead, Lake Erie	06/17/95	1.25	.30		2.00	
2973 32¢ Thirty Mile Point, Lake Ontario	06/17/95	1.25	.30		2.00	
a Booklet pane of 5, #2969-2973		6.25	3.00		5.00	120
Tagged, Perf. 11.2						
2974 32¢ United Nations, 50th Anniversary	06/26/95	.65	.20	2.60 (4)	1.50	60
Classic Collections: Civil War, Tagged, Perf. 10.1						
2975 Sheet of 20	06/29/95	35.00	17.50		16.00	300
a 32¢ *Monitor and Virginia*		1.50	.60		2.00	
b 32¢ Robert E. Lee		1.50	.60		2.00	
c 32¢ Clara Barton		1.50	.60		2.00	
d 32¢ Ulysses S. Grant		1.50	.60		2.00	
e 32¢ Battle of Shiloh		1.50	.60		2.00	
f 32¢ Jefferson Davis		1.50	.60		2.00	
g 32¢ David Farragut		1.50	.60		2.00	
h 32¢ Frederick Douglass		1.50	.60		2.00	
i 32¢ Raphael Semmes		1.50	.60		2.00	
j 32¢ Abraham Lincoln		1.50	.60		2.00	
k 32¢ Harriet Tubman		1.50	.60		2.00	
l 32¢ Stand Watie		1.50	.60		2.00	
m 32¢ Joseph E. Johnston		1.50	.60		2.00	
n 32¢ Winfield Hancock		1.50	.60		2.00	
o 32¢ Mary Chesnut		1.50	.60		2.00	
p 32¢ Battle of Chancellorsville		1.50	.60		2.00	
q 32¢ William T. Sherman		1.50	.60		2.00	
r 32¢ Phoebe Pember		1.50	.60		2.00	
s 32¢ "Stonewall" Jackson		1.50	.60		2.00	
t 32¢ Battle of Gettysburg		1.50	.60		2.00	

Issue	Date	Un	U	PB #	FDC	Q(M)
American Folk Art: Carousel Horses, Tagged, Perf. 11						
2976 32¢ Golden Horse with Roses	07/21/95	.65	.20		1.25	
2977 32¢ Black Horse with Gold Bridle	07/21/95	.65	.20		1.25	
2978 32¢ Horse with Armor	07/21/95	.65	.20		1.25	
2979 32¢ Brown Horse with Green Bridle	07/21/95	.65	.20		1.25	
a Block of 4, #2976-2979		2.60	2.00	2.60 (4)	3.25	63
Tagged, Perf. 11.1 x 11						
2980 32¢ Women's Suffrage	08/26/95	.65	.20	3.00 (4)	1.25	105
a Black (engr.) omitted		375.00				
b Imperf., pair		1,250.00				
World War II, 1945: Victory at Last, Miniature Sheet, Tagged, Perf. 11.1						
2981 Block of 10 and central label	09/02/95	15.00	7.50		7.00	100
a 32¢ Marines Raise Flag on Iwo Jima		1.50	.50		2.00	
b 32¢ Fierce Fighting Frees Manila by March 3, 1945		1.50	.50		2.00	
c 32¢ Soldiers Advancing: Okinawa, the Last Big Battle		1.50	.50		2.00	
d 32¢ Destroyed Bridge: U.S. and Soviets Link Up at Elbe River		1.50	.50		2.00	
e 32¢ Allies Liberate Holocaust Survivors		1.50	.50		2.00	
f 32¢ Germany Surrenders at Reims		1.50	.50		2.00	
g 32¢ Refugees: By 1945, World War II Has Uprooted Millions		1.50	.50		2.00	
h 32¢ Truman Announces Japan's Surrender		1.50	.50		2.00	
i 32¢ Sailor Kissing Nurse: News of Victory Hits Home		1.50	.50		2.00	
j 32¢ Hometowns Honor Their Returning Veterans		1.50	.50		2.00	

2967

2968

2969

2970

2971

2972

2973 2973a

2974

2975

a   b   c   d   e

f   g   h   i   j

k   l   m   n   o

p   q   r   s   t

2976   2977

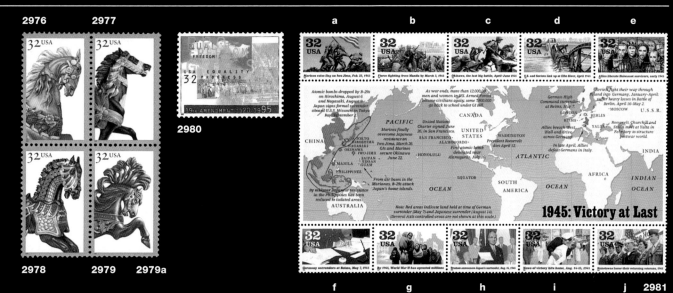

2978   2979   2979a

2980

a   b   c   d   e

f   g   h   i   j   2981

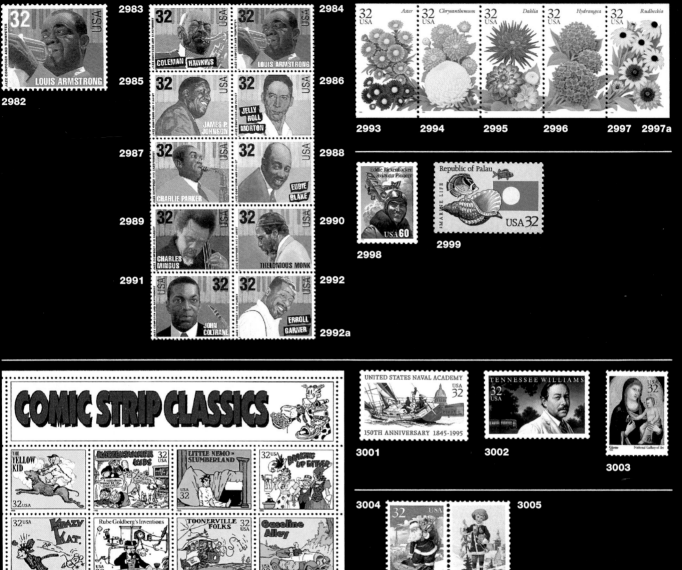

2982

2983
2984

2985
2986

2987
2988

2989
2990

2991
2992
2992a

2993 2994 2995 2996 2997 2997a

2998

2999

3001

3002

3003

3004
3005

3006
3007

3007a

3000   a   b   c   d

e   f   g   h

i   j   k   l

	Issue	Date	Un	U	PB	#	FDC	Q(M)
	Legends of American Music: Jazz Musicians, Tagged, Perf. 11.1 x 11							
2982	32¢ Louis Armstrong, white denomination	09/01/95	.80	.25	3.20	(4)	1.75	150
2983	32¢ Coleman Hawkins	09/16/95	1.50	.30			1.50	15
2984	32¢ Louis Armstrong, black denomination	09/16/95	1.50	.30			1.50	15
2985	32¢ James P. Johnson	09/16/95	1.50	.30			1.50	15
2986	32¢ Jelly Roll Morton	09/16/95	1.50	.30			1.50	15
2987	32¢ Charlie Parker	09/16/95	1.50	.30			1.50	15
2988	32¢ Eubie Blake	09/16/95	1.50	.30			1.50	15
2989	32¢ Charles Mingus	09/16/95	1.50	.30			1.50	15
2990	32¢ Thelonious Monk	09/16/95	1.50	.30			1.50	15
2991	32¢ John Coltrane	09/16/95	1.50	.30			1.50	15
2992	32¢ Erroll Garner	09/16/95	1.50	.30			1.50	15
a	Vertical block of 10, #2983-2992		15.00	7.50	15.00	(10)	6.50	
	Pane of 20		30.00	—				
	Garden Flowers, Tagged, Perf. 10.9 Vertically							
2993	32¢ Aster	09/19/95	.65	.20			1.25	
2994	32¢ Chrysanthemum	09/19/95	.65	.20			1.25	
2995	32¢ Dahlia	09/19/95	.65	.20			1.25	
2996	32¢ Hydrangea	09/19/95	.65	.20			1.25	
2997	32¢ Rudbeckia	09/19/95	.65	.20			1.25	
a	Booklet pane of 5, #2993-2997		3.25	2.25			4.00	200
	Pioneers of Aviation, Tagged, Perf. 11.25							
2998	60¢ Eddie Rickenbacker, Aviator	09/25/95	1.40	.50	9.00	(4)	1.75	300
a	Large date, 2000		2.00	.50	12.00	(4)		
	Tagged, Perf. 11.1							
2999	32¢ Republic of Palau	09/29/95	.65	.20	3.00	(4)	1.25	85
	Classic Collections: Comic Strip Classics, Tagged, Perf. 10.1							
3000	Pane of 20	10/01/95	13.00	10.00			13.00	300
a	32¢ The Yellow Kid		.65	.50			2.00	
b	32¢ Katzenjammer Kids		.65	.50			2.00	
c	32¢ Little Nemo in Slumberland		.65	.50			2.00	
d	32¢ Bringing Up Father		.65	.50			2.00	
e	32¢ Krazy Kat		.65	.50			2.00	
f	32¢ Rube Goldberg's Inventions		.65	.50			2.00	
g	32¢ Toonerville Folks		.65	.50			2.00	
h	32¢ Gasoline Alley		.65	.50			2.00	
i	32¢ Barney Google		.65	.50			2.00	

	Issue	Date	Un	U	PB	#	FDC	Q(M)
	Comic Strip Classics, Tagged, Perf. 10.1 continued							
j	32¢ Little Orphan Annie		.65	.50			2.00	
k	32¢ Popeye		.65	.50			2.00	
l	32¢ Blondie		.65	.50			2.00	
m	32¢ Dick Tracy		.65	.50			2.00	
n	32¢ Alley Oop		.65	.50			2.00	
o	32¢ Nancy		.65	.50			2.00	
p	32¢ Flash Gordon		.65	.50			2.00	
q	32¢ Li'l Abner		.65	.50			2.00	
r	32¢ Terry and the Pirates		.65	.50			2.00	
s	32¢ Prince Valiant		.65	.50			2.00	
t	32¢ Brenda Starr, Reporter		.65	.50			2.00	
	Tagged, Perf 10.9							
3001	32¢ U.S. Naval Academy, 150th Anniversary	10/10/95	.65	.20	2.60	(4)	2.00	80
	Literary Arts, Tagged, Perf 11.1							
3002	32¢ Tennessee Williams	10/13/95	.65	.20	2.80	(4)	1.25	80
	Holiday Celebration: Christmas, Tagged, Perf. 11.2							
3003	32¢ Madonna and Child, by Giotto di Bondone	10/19/95	.65	.20	3.00	(4)	1.25	300
c	Black (engr., denom.) omitted		200.00					
	Booklet, Perf. 9.8 x 10.9							
3003A	32¢ Madonna and Child	10/19/95	.65	.20			1.25	
b	Booklet pane of 10		6.50	4.00			7.25	
	Holiday Celebration: Holiday, Perf. 11.25							
3004	32¢ Santa Claus Entering Chimney	09/30/95	.70	.20			1.25	
3005	32¢ Child Holding Jumping Jack	09/30/95	.70	.20			1.25	
3006	32¢ Child Holding Tree	09/30/95	.70	.20			1.25	
3007	32¢ Santa Claus Working on Sled	09/30/95	.70	.20			1.25	
a	Block of 4, #3004-3007		2.80	1.25	3.25	(4)	3.25	75
b	Booklet pane of 10, 3 each #3004-3005, 2 each 3006-3007		7.00	4.00			7.25	
c	Booklet pane of 10, 2 each #3004-3005, 3 each 3006-3007		7.00	4.00			7.25	
d	As "a," imperf.		550.00					

"The Raven" Commemorative Edition Booklet

Commemorating one of Edgar Allan Poe's best loved poems, French artist Emmanuel Polanco graphically interprets "The Raven" in six original illustrations. This special edition Booklet also comes with a block of four stamps with mount.

Item #464473 $12.95

To order call **1 800 STAMP-24**
or visit us online at **www.usps.com**

Issue	Date	Un	U	PB #	FDC	Q(M)
Holiday Celebration: Holiday, Self-Adhesive, Serpentine Die-Cut 11.25 on 2, 3 or 4 sides continued						
3008 32¢ Santa Claus Working on Sled	09/30/95	.95	.20		1.25	350
3009 32¢ Child Holding Jumping Jack	09/30/95	.95	.20		1.25	350
3010 32¢ Santa Claus Entering Chimney	09/30/95	.95	.20		1.25	350
3011 32¢ Child Holding Tree	09/30/95	.95	.20		1.25	350
a Booklet pane of 20, 5 each #3008-3011 + label		19.00			3.25	
Serpentine Die-Cut 11.3 x 11.6 on 2, 3 or 4 sides						
3012 32¢ Midnight Angel	10/19/95	.65	.20		1.25	
a Booklet pane of 20 + label		13.00				
Self-Adhesive, Die-Cut						
3013 32¢ Children Sledding	10/19/95	.65	.20		1.25	90
a Booklet pane of 18		12.00				
Self-Adhesive Coil, Serpentine Die-Cut 11.2 Vertically						
3014 32¢ Santa Claus Working on Sled	09/30/95	2.50	.30		1.25	
3015 32¢ Child Holding Jumping Jack	09/30/95	2.50	.30		1.25	
3016 32¢ Santa Claus Entering Chimney	09/30/95	2.50	.30		1.25	
3017 32¢ Child Holding Tree	09/30/95	2.50	.30		1.25	
a Strip of 4, #3014-3017		10.00		15.00 (5)	2.50	
Serpentine Die-Cut 11.6 Vertically						
3018 32¢ Midnight Angel	10/19/95	1.10	.30	9.00 (5)	1.25	
Antique Automobiles, Tagged, Perf. 10.1 x 11.1						
3019 32¢ 1893 Duryea	11/03/95	.90	.20		1.25	
3020 32¢ 1894 Haynes	11/03/95	.90	.20		1.25	
3021 32¢ 1898 Columbia	11/03/95	.90	.20		1.25	
3022 32¢ 1899 Winton	11/03/95	.90	.20		1.25	
3023 32¢ 1901 White	11/03/95	.90	.20		1.25	
a Vertical or horizontal strip of 5, #3019-3023		4.50	2.00		3.00	30
Tagged, Perf. 11.1						
3024 32¢ Utah Statehood	01/04/96	.75	.20	4.00 (4)	1.25	120
Garden Flowers, Perf 10.9 Vertically						
3025 32¢ Crocus	01/19/96	.75	.20		1.25	
3026 32¢ Winter Aconite	01/19/96	.75	.20		1.25	
3027 32¢ Pansy	01/19/96	.75	.20		1.25	
3028 32¢ Snowdrop	01/19/96	.75	.20		1.25	
3029 32¢ Anemone	01/19/96	.75	.20		1.25	
a Booklet pane of 5, #3025-3029		3.75	2.50		3.50	160
Love, Tagged, Self-Adhesive, Serpentine Die-Cut 11.3 x 11.7						
3030 32¢ Love Cherub from Sistine Madonna, by Raphael	01/20/96	.65	.20		1.25	2,550
a Booklet pane of 20 + label		13.00				
b Booklet pane of 15 + label		10.00				
Flora and Fauna, Untagged, Self-Adhesive, Serpentine Die-Cut 10.5						
3031 1¢ American Kestrel	11/19/99	.20	.20	.25 (4)	1.50	120
Self-Adhesive, Serpentine Die-Cut 11.25						
3031A 1¢ American Kestrel	10/2000	.20	.20	.20 (4)		
Perf. 11						
3032 2¢ Red-Headed Woodpecker	02/02/96	.20	.20	.25 (4)	1.25	311
3033 3¢ Eastern Bluebird	04/03/96	.20	.20	.25 (4)	1.25	317
Tagged, Self-Adhesive, Serpentine Die-Cut 11.5 x 11.25						
3036 $1 Red Fox	08/14/98	2.00	.50	8.00 (4)	3.50	
a Serpentine Die-Cut 11.75 x 11	2002	2.75	.50	11.00 (4)		
Coil, Untagged, Perf. 9.75 Vertically						
3044 1¢ American Kestrel	01/20/96	.20	.20	.50 (5)	1.25	
a Large date		.20	.20	.70 (5)		

Issue	Date	Un	U	PB #	FDC	Q(M)
Coil, Untagged						
3045 2¢ Red-Headed Woodpecker	06/22/99	.20	.20	.60 (5)	1.25	100
Booklet, Tagged, Self-Adhesive, Serpentine Die-Cut 10.4 x 10.8 on 3 sides						
3048 20¢ Blue Jay	08/02/96	.40	.20		1.25	491
a Booklet pane of 10		4.00				
b Booklet pane of 4		22.50				
c Booklet pane of 6		37.50				
Serpentine Die-Cut 11.3 x 11.7 on 2, 3 or 4 sides						
3049 32¢ Yellow Rose	10/24/96	.65	.20		1.25	2,900
a Booklet pane of 20 and label		13.00				
b Booklet pane of 4	12/96	2.60				
c Booklet pane of 5	12/96	3.50				
d Booklet pane of 6	12/96	4.00				
Serpentine Die-Cut 11.2 on 2 or 3 sides						
3050 20¢ Ring-neck Pheasant	07/31/98	.50	.20		1.25	
a Booklet pane of 10		5.00				
Serpentine Die-Cut 10.5 x 11 on 3 sides						
3051 20¢ Ring-neck Pheasant	07/99	.75	.20			634
Serpentine Die-Cut 10.5 x 11 on 3 sides						
3051A 20¢ Ring-neck Pheasant		6.00	.50			
b Booklet pane of 5, 4 #3051, 1 #3051A turned sideways at top		9.00				
c Booklet pane of 5, 4 #3051, 1 #3051A turned sideways at bottom		9.00				
Serpentine Die-Cut 11.5 x 11.25 on 2, 3 or 4 sides						
3052 33¢ Coral Pink Rose	08/13/99	.90	.20		1.25	1,000
a Booklet pane of 4		3.60				
b Booklet pane of 5 + label		4.50				
c Booklet pane of 6		5.50				
d Booklet pane of 20		17.50				
Serpentine Die-Cut 10.75 x 10.5 on 2 or 3 sides						
3052E 33¢ Coral Pink Rose	04/07/2000	.80	.20		1.25	
f Booklet pane of 20		16.00				
g Black "33 USA" omitted		375.00				
Coil, Serpentine Die-Cut 11.5 Vertically						
3053 20¢ Blue Jay	08/02/96	.50	.20	4.00 (5)	1.25	330
Coil, Tagged, Self-Adhesive, Serpentine Die-Cut 9.75 Vertically						
3054 32¢ Yellow Rose	08/01/97	.65	.20	4.50 (5)	1.25	
a Die-cutting omitted, pair		85.00				
3055 20¢ Ring-necked Pheasant	07/31/98	.40	.20	3.00 (5)	1.25	
a Die-cutting omitted, pair		175.00				
Black Heritage, Tagged, Perf. 11.1						
3058 32¢ Ernest E. Just	02/01/96	.65	.20	2.60 (4)	1.75	92
Tagged, Perf. 11.1						
3059 32¢ Smithsonian Institution	02/07/96	.65	.20	2.60 (4)	1.25	115
Lunar New Year, Tagged, Perf. 11.1						
3060 32¢ Year of the Rat	02/08/96	.90	.20	4.25 (4)	1.75	93
a Imperf., pair		775.00				
Pioneers of Communication, Tagged, Perf. 11.1 x 11						
3061 32¢ Eadweard Muybridge	02/22/96	.65	.20		1.25	96
3062 32¢ Ottmar Mergenthaler	02/22/96	.65	.20		1.25	96
3063 32¢ Frederic E. Ives	02/22/96	.65	.20		1.25	96
3064 32¢ William Dickson	02/22/96	.65	.20		1.25	96
a Block or strip of 4, #3061-3064		2.60	2.00	2.60 (4)	2.50	24
Tagged, Perf. 11.1						
3065 32¢ Fulbright Scholarships	02/28/96	.75	.20	4.25 (4)	1.25	111
Pioneers of Aviation, Tagged, Perf. 11.1						
3066 50¢ Jacqueline Cochran	03/09/96	1.00	.40	5.00 (4)	1.75	314
a Black omitted		55.00				
Tagged, Perf. 11.1						
3067 32¢ Marathon	04/11/96	.65	.20	2.60 (4)	2.00	209

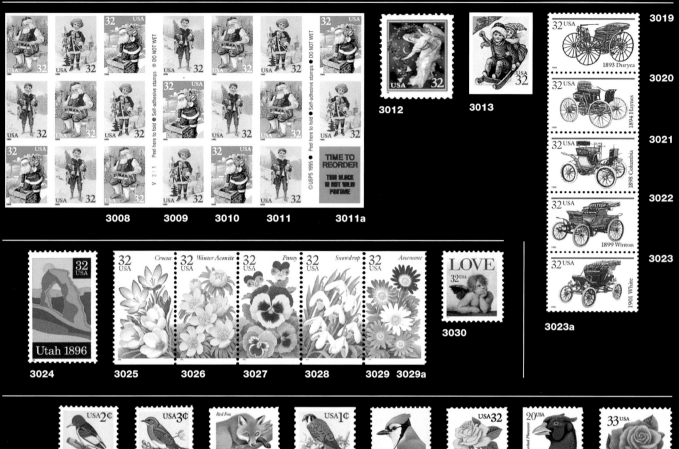

3008   3009   3010   3011   3011a

3012   3013

3019
3020
3021
3022
3023

3023a

3024

3025   3026   3027   3028   3029 3029a

LOVE
3030

USA 2¢
3032

USA 3¢
3033

Red Fox
3036

USA 1¢
3044

3048

USA 32
3049

20 USA
3050

33 USA
3052

Ernest E. Just
3058

SMITHSONIAN INSTITUTION
1846-1996
3059

HAPPY NEW YEAR!
3060

3063
3064
3061
3062

3064a

50 USA
Jacqueline Cochran
Pioneer Pilot
3066

MARATHON

3068

a b c d e

f g h i j

k l m n o

p q r s t

3069

3070

3077   3078

Eohippus   Woolly mammoth

Mastodon   Saber-tooth cat

3072   3073   3074   3075   3076   3076a

3079   3080   3080a

3083   3086

3081   3082

MIGHTY CASEY   PECOS BILL

JOHN HENRY   PAUL BUNYAN

3085   3084   3086a

3087   3088   3090

Issue		Date	Un	U	PB	#	FDC	Q(M)
Classic Collections: Atlanta Centennial Olympic Games, Tagged, Perf. 10.1								
3068	Pane of 20	05/02/96	13.00	10.00			13.00	16
a	32¢ Decathlon		.65	.50			1.25	
b	32¢ Canoeing		.65	.50			1.25	
c	32¢ Women's Running		.65	.50			1.25	
d	32¢ Women's Diving		.65	.50			1.25	
e	32¢ Cycling		.65	.50			1.25	
f	32¢ Freestyle Wrestling		.65	.50			1.25	
g	32¢ Women's Gymnastic		.65	.50			1.25	
h	32¢ Women's Sailboarding		.65	.50			1.25	
i	32¢ Shot Put		.65	.50			1.25	
j	32¢ Women's Soccer		.65	.50			1.25	
k	32¢ Beach Volleyball		.65	.50			1.25	
l	32¢ Rowing		.65	.50			1.25	
m	32¢ Sprinting		.65	.50			1.25	
n	32¢ Women's Swimming		.65	.50			1.25	
o	32¢ Women's Softball		.65	.50			1.25	
p	32¢ Hurdles		.65	.50			1.25	
q	32¢ Swimming		.65	.50			1.25	
r	32¢ Gymnastics		.65	.50			1.25	
s	32¢ Equestrian		.65	.50			1.25	
t	32¢ Basketball		.65	.50			1.25	
Artists, Tagged, Perf. 11.6 x 11.4								
3069	32¢ Georgia O'Keeffe	05/23/96	.85	.20	5.00	(4)	1.50	156
a	Imperf., pair		*135.00*					
Tagged, Perf. 11.1								
3070	32¢ Tennessee Statehood	05/31/96	.65	.20	3.00	(4)	1.25	100
Booklet, Self-Adhesive, Serpentine Die-Cut 9.9 x 10.8								
3071	32¢ Tennessee Statehood	05/31/96	.75	.30			1.25	60
a	Booklet pane of 20		15.00					
American Indian Dances, Tagged, Perf. 11.1								
3072	32¢ Fancy Dance	06/07/96	1.00	.20			1.25	
3073	32¢ Butterfly Dance	06/07/96	1.00	.20			1.25	
3074	32¢ Traditional Dance	06/07/96	1.00	.20			1.25	
3075	32¢ Raven Dance	06/07/96	1.00	.20			1.25	
3076	32¢ Hoop Dance	06/07/96	1.00	.20			1.25	
a	Strip of 5, #3072-3076		5.00	2.50	12.00	(10)	2.75	28

Issue		Date	Un	U	PB	#	FDC	Q(M)
Prehistoric Animals, Tagged, Perf. 11.1 x 11								
3077	32¢ Eohippus	06/08/96	.65	.20			1.50	
3078	32¢ Woolly Mammoth	06/08/96	.65	.20			1.50	
3079	32¢ Mastodon	06/08/96	.65	.20			1.50	
3080	32¢ Saber-tooth Cat	06/08/96	.65	.20			1.50	
a	Block or strip of 4, #3077-3080		2.60	2.00	2.60	(4)	2.75	22
	Pane of 20		13.00	—				
Tagged, Perf. 11.1								
3081	32¢ Breast Cancer Awareness	06/15/96	.65	.20	2.60	(4)	1.25	96
	Pane of 20		13.00	—				
Legends of Hollywood, Tagged, Perf. 11.1								
3082	32¢ James Dean	06/24/96	.65	.20	4.00	(4)	2.00	300
	Pane of 20		18.50	10.00				
a	Imperf., pair		*175.00*					
Folks Heroes, Tagged, Perf. 11.1 x 11								
3083	32¢ Mighty Casey	07/11/96	.65	.20			1.25	
3084	32¢ Paul Bunyan	07/11/96	.65	.20			1.25	
3085	32¢ John Henry	07/11/96	.65	.20			1.25	
3086	32¢ Pecos Bill	07/11/96	.65	.20			1.25	
a	Block or strip of 4, #3083-3086		2.60	2.00	2.60	(4)	2.75	24
	Pane of 20		13.00	—				
Centennial Olympic Games, Tagged, Perf. 11.1								
3087	32¢ Centennial Olympic Games	07/11/96	.80	.20	4.50	(4)	1.25	134
	Pane of 20		21.50	10.00				
3088	32¢ Iowa Statehood	08/01/96	.80	.20	3.75	(4)	1.25	103
Booklet, Self-Adhesive, Serpentine Die-Cut 11.6 x 11.4								
3089	32¢ Iowa Statehood	08/01/96	.70	.30			1.25	60
a	Booklet pane of 20		14.00					
Tagged, Perf. 11.2 x 11								
3090	32¢ Rural Free Delivery	08/07/96	.80	.20	3.25	(4)	1.25	134
	Pane of 20		16.50					

**CELEBRATING
LUNAR NEW YEAR:
YEAR OF THE OX**

In 2009 the U.S. Postal Service continued its Celebrating Lunar New Year series with the Year of the Ox stamp. The Year of the Ox began January 26, 2009, and ends February 13, 2010. ■ The ox is the second of twelve animals associated with the Chinese lunar calendar. According to a legend, the animals raced across a river to determine their order in the cycle. The rat won first place by riding on the back of the ox and jumping ahead at the last minute. ■ People born in the year of a particular animal are said to share characteristics with that animal.

Individuals born during the Year of the Ox are said to be hardworking, tolerant, and persistent. ■ Lunar New Year celebrations worldwide include parades, parties, and other special events. In the United States as elsewhere, dancers wearing a lion head such as the one depicted in the stamp art perform for delighted crowds. Lucky foods are served and loud noises from firecrackers and drums are used to scare off evil spirits and welcome this time of renewed hope for the future. Festive lanterns—in red, for luck—are common decorations.

	Issue	Date	Un	U	PB	#	FDC	Q(M)
	Riverboats, Tagged, Self-Adhesive, Serpentine Die-Cut 11 x 11.1							
3091	32¢ Robert E. Lee	08/22/96	.65	.20			1.25	160
3092	32¢ Sylvan Dell	08/22/96	.65	.20			1.25	160
3093	32¢ Far West	08/22/96	.65	.20			1.25	160
3094	32¢ Rebecca Everingham	08/22/96	.65	.20			1.25	160
3095	32¢ Bailey Gatzert	08/22/96	.65	.20			1.25	160
a	Vertical strip of 5, #3091-3095		3.25		6.50	(10)	3.50	
b	Strip of 5, #3091-3095 with special die-cutting		80.00	50.00	160.00	(10)	3.50	
	Legends of American Music: Big Band Leaders, Tagged, Perf. 11.1 x 11							
3096	32¢ Count Basie	09/11/96	.75	.20			1.25	92
3097	32¢ Tommy and Jimmy Dorsey	09/11/96	.75	.20			1.25	92
3098	32¢ Glenn Miller	09/11/96	.75	.20			1.25	92
3099	32¢ Benny Goodman	09/11/96	.75	.20			1.25	92
a	Block or strip of 4, #3096-3099		3.00	2.00	4.00	(4)	3.25	
	Legends of American Music: Songwriters, Tagged, Perf. 11.1 x 11							
3100	32¢ Harold Arlen	09/11/96	.75	.20			1.25	92
3101	32¢ Johnny Mercer	09/11/96	.75	.20			1.25	92
3102	32¢ Dorothy Fields	09/11/96	.75	.20			1.25	92
3103	32¢ Hoagy Carmichael	09/11/96	.75	.20			1.25	92
a	Block or strip of 4, #3100-3103		3.00	2.00	3.50	(4)	3.25	
	Literary Arts, Tagged, Perf. 11.1							
3104	23¢ F. Scott Fitzgerald	09/11/96	.55	.20	4.00	(4)	1.25	300
	Endangered Species, Tagged, Perf. 11.1 x 11							
3105	Pane of 15	10/02/96	10.50	8.00			7.50	15
a	32¢ Black-footed Ferret		.70	.50			1.25	
b	32¢ Thick-billed Parrot		.70	.50			1.25	
c	32¢ Hawaiian Monk Seal		.70	.50			1.25	
d	32¢ American Crocodile		.70	.50			1.25	
e	32¢ Ocelot		.70	.50			1.25	
f	32¢ Schaus Swallowtail Butterfly		.70	.50			1.25	
g	32¢ Wyoming Toad		.70	.50			1.25	
h	32¢ Brown Pelican		.70	.50			1.25	
i	32¢ California Condor		.70	.50			1.25	
j	32¢ Gilatrout		.70	.50			1.25	
k	32¢ San Francisco Garter Snake		.70	.50			1.25	
l	32¢ Woodland Caribou		.70	.50			1.25	
m	32¢ Florida Panther		.70	.50			1.25	
n	32¢ Piping Plover		.70	.50			1.25	
o	32¢ Florida Manatee		.70	.50			1.25	
	Tagged, Perf. 10.9 x 11.1							
3106	32¢ Computer Technology	10/08/96	.65	.20	3.00	(4)	1.75	94
	Holiday Celebration: Christmas, Tagged, Perf. 11.1 x 11.2							
3107	32¢ Madonna and Child by Paolo de Matteis	10/08/96	.65	.20	3.00	(4)	1.25	848
	Holiday Celebration: Holiday, Perf. 11.3							
3108	32¢ Family at Fireplace	10/08/96	.65	.20			1.25	226
3109	32¢ Decorating Tree	10/08/96	.65	.20			1.25	226
3110	32¢ Dreaming of Santa Claus	10/08/96	.65	.20			1.25	226
3111	32¢ Holiday Shopping	10/08/96	.65	.20			1.25	226
a	Block or strip of 4, #3108-3111		2.60	1.75	3.00	(4)	2.75	

	Issue	Date	Un	U	PB	#	FDC	Q(M)
	Holiday Celebration: Christmas, Booklet, Self-Adhesive, Serpentine Die-Cut 10 on 2, 3 or 4 sides							
3112	32¢ Madonna and Child by Paolo de Matteis	10/08/96	.75	.20			1.25	848
a	Booklet pane of 20 + label		15.00					
b	Die-cutting omitted, pair		75.00					
	Holiday Celebration: Holiday, Serpentine Die-Cut 11.8 x 11.5 on 2, 3 or 4 sides							
3113	32¢ Family at Fireplace	10/08/96	.75	.20			1.25	1,805
3114	32¢ Decorating Tree	10/08/96	.75	.20			1.25	1,805
3115	32¢ Dreaming of Santa Claus	10/08/96	.75	.20			1.25	1,805
3116	32¢ Holiday Shopping	10/08/96	.75	.20			1.25	1,805
a	Booklet pane, 5 ea #3113-3116		15.00				3.25	
b	Strip of 4, die-cutting omitted		550.00					
c	Block of 6, die-cutting omitted		775.00					
d	As "a," Die-cutting omitted		2,100.00					
	Die-Cut							
3117	32¢ Skaters	10/08/96	.65	.20			1.25	495
a	Booklet pane of 18		12.00					
	Holiday Celebrations, Tagged, Self-Adhesive, Serpentine Die-Cut 11.1							
3118	32¢ Hanukkah	10/22/96	.65	.20	2.60	(4)	1.75	104
	Cycling, Tagged, Perf. 11 x 11.1							
3119	32¢ Souvenier sheet of 2	11/01/96	2.50	2.00			4.00	
a	50¢ Orange		1.25	1.00			2.00	
b	50¢ Blue and green		1.25	1.00			2.00	
	Lunar New Year, Tagged, Perf. 11.2							
3120	32¢ Year of the Ox	01/05/97	.80	.20	3.20	(4)	1.75	106
	Black Heritage, Tagged, Self-Adhesive, Serpentine Die-Cut 11.4							
3121	32¢ Brig. Gen. Benjamin O. Davis Sr.	01/28/97	.65	.20	2.60	(4)	1.75	112
	Tagged, Self-Adhesive, Serpentine Die-Cut 11 on 2, 3 or 4 sides							
3122	32¢ Statue of Liberty, Type of 1994	02/01/97	.65	.20			1.25	2,855
a	Booklet panel of 20 + label		13.00					
b	Booklet pane of 4		2.60					
c	Booklet pane of 5 + label		3.50					
d	Booklet pane of 6		4.00					
	Self-Adhesive, Serpentine Die-Cut 11.5 x 11.8 on 2, 3 or 4 sides							
3122E	32¢ Statue of Liberty		1.25	.20				
f	Booklet pane of 20 + label		40.00					
g	Booklet pane of 6		8.00					
	Love, Tagged, Self-Adhesive, Serpentine Die-Cut 11.8 x 11.6 on 2, 3 or 4 sides							
3123	32¢ Love Swans	02/04/97	.65	.20			1.25	1,660
a	Booklet pane of 20 + label		13.00					
b	Die-cutting omitted, pair		135.00					
c	As "a," die-cutting omitted		1,350.00					
d	As "a," black omitted		575.00					
	Love, Serpentine Die-Cut 11.6 x 11.8 on 2, 3 or 4 sides							
3124	55¢ Love Swans	02/04/97	1.10	.20			1.50	814
a	Booklet pane of 20 + label		22.00					

*VISIT US ONLINE AT **THE POSTAL STORE***

*AT **WWW.USPS.COM***

*OR CALL **1 800 STAMP-24***

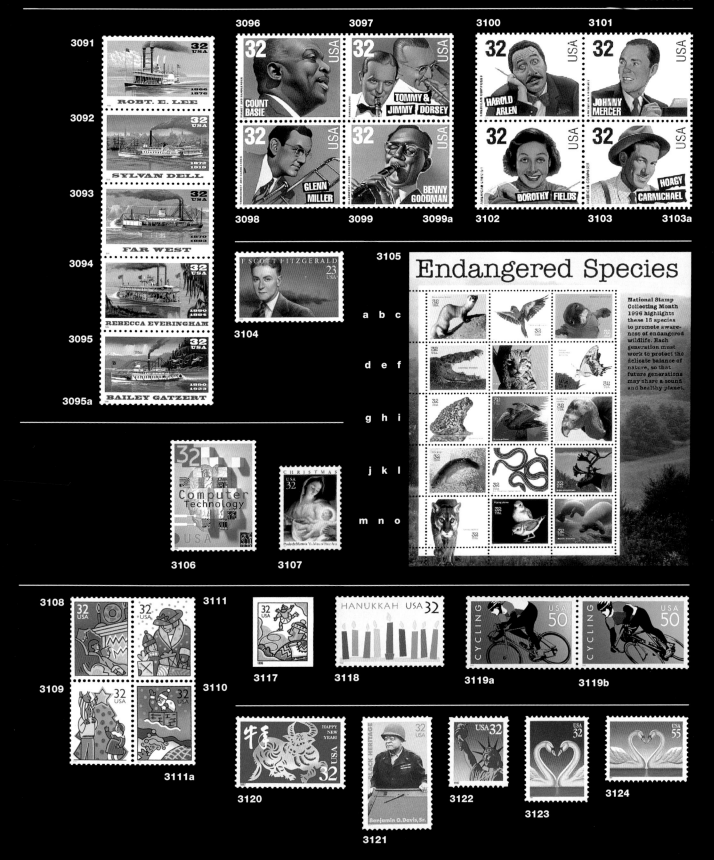

3091

ROBT. E. LEE
1866
1876

3092

SYLVAN DELL
1872
1919

3093

FAR WEST
1870
1883

3094

REBECCA EVERINGHAM
1880
1884

3095

BAILEY GATZERT
1890
1923

3095a

3096   3097

3098   3099   3099a

COUNT BASIE
TOMMY & JIMMY DORSEY
GLENN MILLER
BENNY GOODMAN

3100   3101

3102   3103   3103a

HAROLD ARLEN
JOHNNY MERCER
DOROTHY FIELDS
HOAGY CARMICHAEL

F SCOTT FITZGERALD 23 USA

3104

3105

a b c
d e f
g h i
j k l
m n o

Endangered Species

National Stamp Collecting Month 1996 highlights these 15 species to promote awareness of endangered wildlife. Each generation must work to protect the delicate balance of nature, so that future generations may share a sound and healthy planet.

Computer Technology
32
USA

3106

CHRISTMAS
USA 32
Paola de Matteis Va Adasi at Fine Arts

3107

3108   3111

3109   3110

3111a

3117

HANUKKAH USA 32

3118

CYCLING USA 50

3119a

CYCLING USA 50

3119b

HAPPY NEW YEAR!
32 USA

3120

BLACK HERITAGE 32 USA
Benjamin O. Davis, Sr.

3121

USA 32

3122

USA 32

3123

USA 55

3124

183

3125

3126

3127

3130

3131

3132

3133

3134

3135

3136

    a   **b**   **c**   **d**   **f**   **g**

3137a

	Issue	Date	Un	U	PB #	FDC	Q(M)
	Tagged, Self-Adhesive, Serpentine Die-Cut 11.6 x 11.7						
3125	32¢ Helping Children Learn	02/18/97	.65	.20	2.60 (4)	1.25	122
	Merian Botanical Prints, Tagged, Self-Adhesive, Serpentine Die-Cut 10.9 x 10.2 on 2, 3 or 4 sides						
3126	32¢ Citron, Roth, Larvae, Pupa, Beetle	03/03/97	.65	.20		1.25	2,048
3127	32¢ Flowering Pineapple, Cockroaches	03/03/97	.65	.20		1.25	2,048
a	Booklet pane, 10 each #3126-3127 + label		13.00				
b	Pair, #3126-3127		1.30				
c	Vert. pair, die-cutting omitted		475.00				
	Serpentine Die-Cut 11.2 x 10.8 on 2 or 3 sides						
3128	32¢ Citron, Roth, Larvae, Pupa, Beetle	03/03/97	1.00	.20		1.25	30
b	Booklet pane, 2 each #3128-3129		7.00				
3129	32¢ Flowering Pineapple, Cockroaches	03/03/97	1.00	.20		1.25	30
b	Booklet pane of 5, 2 each #3128-3129, 1 #3129a		9.00				
c	Pair, #3128-3129		2.00				
	Pacific 97, Tagged, Perf. 11.2						
3130	32¢ Sailing Ship	03/13/97	.65	.30		1.25	130
3131	32¢ Stagecoach	03/13/97	.65	.30		1.25	130
a	Pair #3130-3131		1.30	.75	2.60 (4)	1.75	
	American Culture, Coil, Untagged, Self-Adhesive, Imperf.						
3132	25¢ Juke Box	03/14/97	1.50	.50	8.00 (5)	1.25	24
	Coil Stamps, Tagged, Serpentine Die-Cut 9.9 Vertically						
3133	32¢ Flag Over Porch	03/14/97	1.50	.20	7.25 (5)	1.25	1
	Literary Arts, Tagged, Perf. 11.1						
3134	32¢ Thornton Wilder	04/17/97	.65	.20	2.60 (4)	1.25	98
	Tagged, Perf. 11.1						
3135	32¢ Raoul Wallenberg	04/24/97	.65	.20	2.60 (4)	2.00	96

	Issue	Date	Un	U	PB #	FDC	Q(M)
	The World of Dinosaurs, Tagged, Perf. 11 x 11.1						
3136	Sheet of 15	05/01/97	10.00	8.00		7.50	219
a	32¢ Ceratosaurus		.65	.50		1.25	
b	32¢ Camptosaurus		.65	.50		1.25	
c	32¢ Camarasaurus		.65	.50		1.25	
d	32¢ Brachiosaurus		.65	.50		1.25	
e	32¢ Goniopholis		.65	.50		1.25	
f	32¢ Stegosaurus		.65	.50		1.25	
g	32¢ Allosaurus		.65	.50		1.25	
h	32¢ Opisthias		.65	.50		1.25	
i	32¢ Edmontonia		.65	.50		1.25	
j	32¢ Einiosaurus		.65	.50		1.25	
k	32¢ Daspletosaurus		.65	.50		1.25	
l	32¢ Palaeosaniwa		.65	.50		1.25	
m	32¢ Corythosaurus		.65	.50		1.25	
n	32¢ Ornithominus		.65	.50		1.25	
o	32¢ Parasaurolophus		.65	.50		1.25	
	Looney Tunes, Tagged, Self-Adhesive, Serpentine Die-Cut 11						
3137	Bugs Bunny pane of 10	05/22/97	6.75				265
a	32¢ single		.65	.20		2.00	
b	Booklet pane of 9		6.00				
c	Booklet pane of 1		.65				
	Die-cutting on #3137b does not extend through the backing paper.						
3138	Pane of 10	05/22/97	150.00				118
a	32¢ single		3.50				
b	Booklet pane of 9		32.50				
c	Booklet pane of 1, imperf.		110.00				
	Die-cutting on #3138b extends through the backing paper.						

3137b

	Issue	Date	Un	U	PB	#	FDC	Q(M)
	Pacific 97, Tagged, Perf. 10.5 x 10.4							
3139	Benjamin Franklin, pane of 12	05/29/97	12.00	9.00			12.00	594
a	50¢ single		1.00	.50			2.00	
3140	George Washington, pane of 12	05/30/97	14.50	11.00			12.00	593
a	60¢ single		1.20	.60			2.00	
	The Marshall Plan, 50th Anniversary, Tagged, Perf. 11.1							
3141	32¢ The Marshall Plan	06/04/97	.65	.20	2.60	(4)	1.50	45
	Classic Collections: Classic American Aircraft, Tagged, Perf. 10.1							
3142	Pane of 20	07/19/97	13.00	10.00			10.00	161
a	32¢ Mustang		.65	.50			1.25	
b	32¢ Model B		.65	.50			1.25	
c	32¢ Cub		.65	.50			1.25	
d	32¢ Vega		.65	.50			1.25	
e	32¢ Alpha		.65	.50			1.25	
f	32¢ B-10		.65	.50			1.25	
g	32¢ Corsair		.65	.50			1.25	
h	32¢ Stratojet		.65	.50			1.25	
i	32¢ Gee Bee		.65	.50			1.25	
j	32¢ Staggerwing		.65	.50			1.25	

	Issue	Date	Un	U	PB	#	FDC	Q(M)
	Classic Collections: Classic American Aircraft, Tagged, Perf. 10.1 continued							
k	32¢ Flying Fortress		.65	.50			1.25	
l	32¢ Stearman		.65	.50			1.25	
m	32¢ Constellation		.65	.50			1.25	
n	32¢ Lightning		.65	.50			1.25	
o	32¢ Peashooter		.65	.50			1.25	
p	32¢ Tri-Motor		.65	.50			1.25	
q	32¢ DC-3		.65	.50			1.25	
r	32¢ 314 Clipper		.65	.50			1.25	
s	32¢ Jenny		.65	.50			1.25	
t	32¢ Wildcat		.65	.50			1.25	

JUSTICES OF THE SUPREME COURT OF THE UNITED STATES

JUSTICES OF THE SUPREME COURT OF THE UNITED STATES

The Justices of the Supreme Court of the United States stamps honor the contributions of Associate Justices Joseph Story, Louis D. Brandeis, Felix Frankfurter, and William J. Brennan, Jr. ▪ JOSEPH STORY (1779-1845), considered one of the nation's finest legal scholars, published lengthy studies about the Constitution and other legal subjects that gave shape to America's developing system of jurisprudence. His commitment to the uniform enforcement of federal regulations helped establish the preeminence of the Supreme Court. ▪ LOUIS D. BRANDEIS (1856-1941) was the associate justice most responsible for helping the Supreme Court develop the tools it needed to interpret the Constitution in light of the socioeconomic conditions of the 20th century. Devoted to social justice, Brandeis championed the right of all individuals to speak freely. ▪ FELIX FRANKFURTER (1882-1965), a spirited political activist and legal scholar, was arguably one of the most enigmatic and controversial figures to serve as an associate justice. He was the Supreme Court's strongest proponent of judicial restraint and believed that judges should disregard their own social views when making decisions. ▪ WILLIAM J. BRENNAN, JR. (1906-1997), the author of numerous landmark decisions and the inspiration behind many others, viewed the law as a force for social and political change. For more than 30 years he worked to protect and expand the rights of all citizens, especially minorities and women.

3139

3140

3141

3142 a   b   c   d

e   f   g   h

i   j   k   l

m   n   o   p

q   r   s   t

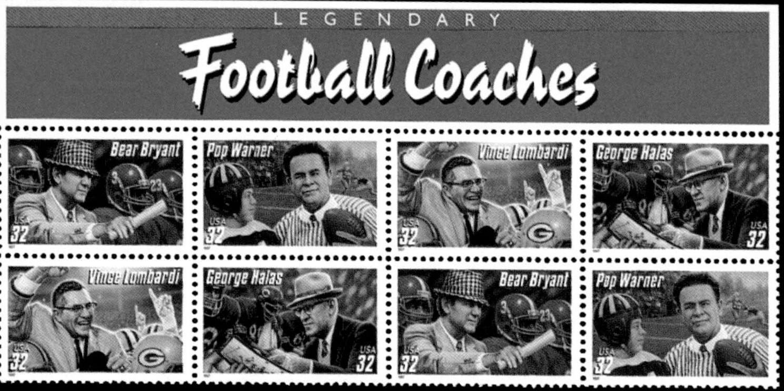

LEGENDARY
Football Coaches

3147

3148

3145

3146

3143

3144

3146a

3149

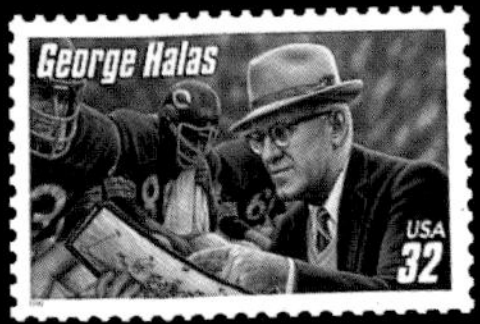

3150

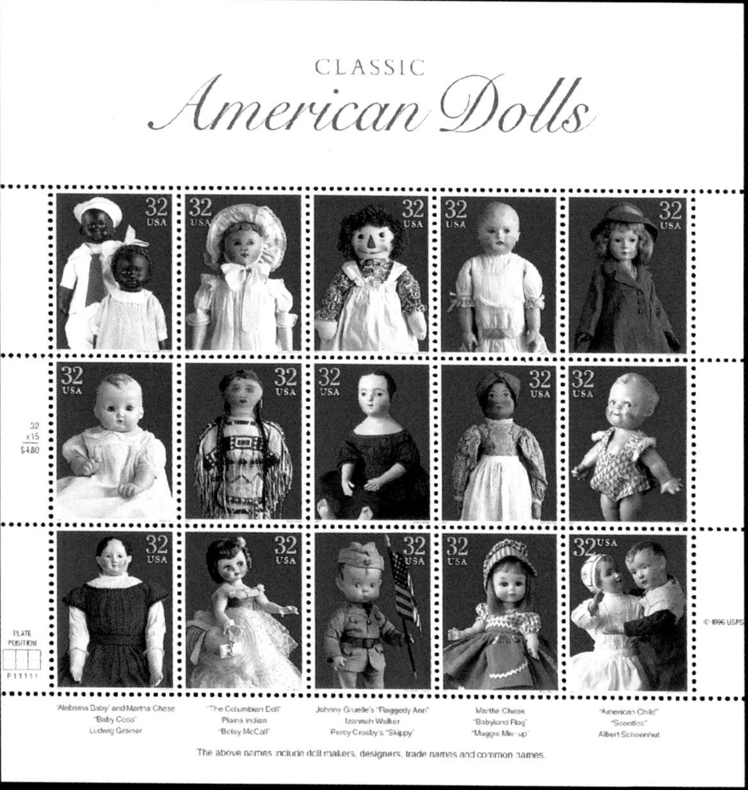

CLASSIC
American Dolls

3152

3153

3154

3155

3156

3157

3157a

32 x15
$4.80

PLATE
POSITION
F 11111

Alabama Baby and Martha Chase   "The Columbian Doll"   Johnny Gruelle's "Raggedy Ann"   Martha Chase   "American Child"
"Baby Coos"   Plains Indian   Izannah Walker   "Babyland Rag"   "Scootles"
Ludwig Greiner   "Betsy McCall"   Percy Crosby's "Skippy"   "Maggie Mix-up"   Albert Schoenhut

The above names include doll makers, designers, trade names and common names.

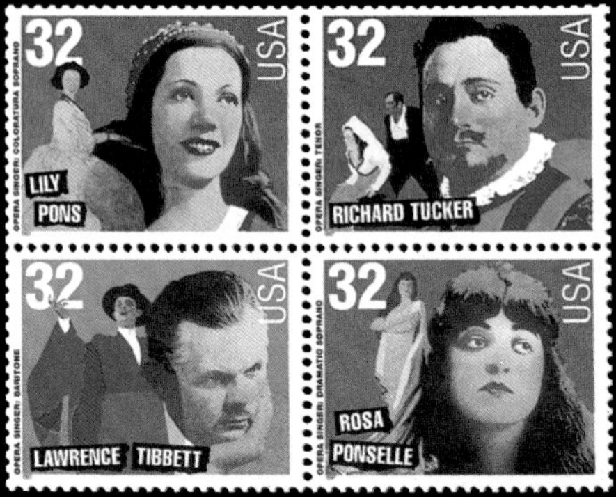

© 1996 USPS

3151

 a
 b
 c
 d
 e

 f   g   h   i   j

k   l   m   n   o

	Issue	Date	Un	U	PB	#	FDC	Q(M)
	Legendary Football Coaches, Tagged, Perf. 11.2							
3143	32¢ Bear Bryant	07/25/97	.65	.25			1.25	90
3144	32¢ Pop Warner	07/25/97	.65	.25			1.25	90
3145	32¢ Vince Lombardi	07/25/97	.65	.25			1.25	90
3146	32¢ George Halas	07/25/97	.65	.25			1.25	90
a	Block or strip of 4, #3143-3146		2.60		2.60	(4)	3.00	
	Pane of 20		13.00					
	Legendary Football Coaches (with red bar), Perf. 11							
3147	32¢ Vince Lombardi	08/05/97	.65	.45	3.00	(4)	1.75	20
3148	32¢ Bear Bryant	08/07/97	.65	.45	3.00	(4)	1.75	20
3149	32¢ Pop Warner	08/08/97	.65	.45	3.00	(4)	1.75	10
3150	32¢ George Halas	08/16/97	.65	.45	3.00	(4)	1.75	10
	Classic American Dolls, Tagged, Perf. 10.9 x 11.1							
3151	Pane of 15	07/28/97	13.50	—			8.00	105
a	32¢ "Alabama Baby," and doll by Martha Chase		.90	.60			1.25	
b	32¢ "Columbian Doll"		.90	.60			1.25	
c	32¢ Johnny Gruelle's "Raggedy Ann"		.90	.60			1.25	
d	32¢ Doll by Martha Chase		.90	.60			1.25	
e	32¢ "American Child"		.90	.60			1.25	
f	32¢ "Baby Coos"		.90	.60			1.25	
g	32¢ Plains Indian		.90	.60			1.25	

	Issue	Date	Un	U	PB	#	FDC	Q(M)
	Classic American Dolls, Tagged, Perf. 10.9 x 11.1 continued							
h	32¢ Doll by Izannah Walker		.90	.60			1.25	
i	32¢ "Babyland Rag"		.90	.60			1.25	
j	32¢ "Scootles"		.90	.60			1.25	
k	32¢ Doll by Ludwig Greiner		.90	.60			1.25	
l	32¢ "Betsy McCall"		.90	.60			1.25	
m	32¢ Percy Crosby's "Skippy"		.90	.60			1.25	
n	32¢ "Maggie Mix-up"		.90	.60			1.25	
o	32¢ Dolls by Albert Schoenhut		.90	.60			1.25	
	Legends of Hollywood, Tagged, Perf. 11.1							
3152	32¢ Humphrey Bogart	07/31/97	.85	.20	3.50	(4)	1.75	195
	Pane of 20		18.50					
	Tagged, Perf. 11.1							
3153	32¢ "The Stars and Stripes Forever"	08/21/97	.65	.20	3.00	(4)	1.25	323
	Legends of American Music: Opera Singers, Tagged, Perf. 11							
3154	32¢ Lily Pons	09/10/97	.75	.20			1.25	86
3155	32¢ Richard Tucker	09/10/97	.75	.20			1.25	86
3156	32¢ Lawrence Tibbett	09/10/97	.75	.20			1.25	86
3157	32¢ Rosa Ponselle	09/10/97	.75	.20			1.25	86
a	Block or strip of 4, #3154-3157		3.00	2.00	3.00	(4)	2.75	

THE SIMPSONS

Five stamps issued in 2009 recognize *The Simpsons* as the show enters its 20th year as a regularly scheduled half-hour series. The longest-running comedy in the history of American prime-time television, *The Simpsons* has won multiple Emmy statuettes, a Peabody Award, and numerous other accolades. *Time* magazine named it the Best TV Show in its "Best of the Century" feature. ■ A critical and popular favorite, *The Simpsons* has become a cultural institution enjoyed by fans worldwide. Intelligently written and delightfully witty, it attracts numerous guest stars, among them Elizabeth Taylor, Paul Newman, Gore Vidal, Natalie Portman, Mick Jagger, and Meryl Streep. ■ The Simpson family resides in the town of Springfield. Homer works as a safety inspector at the local nuclear power plant; his wife, Marge, tries to keep the peace in her household; their son Bart is a mischievous ten-year-old; eight-year-old Lisa is an intelligent, saxophone-playing vegetarian; and baby Maggie conveys emotions by sucking on her pacifier. ■ The animated family first appeared on *The Tracey Ullman Show* in 1987, then in a Christmas special in 1989, and had its debut as a regular series on January 14, 1990. The show became a hit in its first season. The 20th anniversary of its series launch date will be January 14, 2010. ■ Art director Derry Noyes was pleased to use original artwork by Matt Groening, the cartoonist who created the Simpson characters and named them after his own family.

	Issue	Date	Un	U	PB	#	FDC	Q(M)
	Legends of American Music: Classical Composers & Conductors, Tagged, Perf. 11							
3158	32¢ Leopold Stokowski	09/12/97	1.00	.20			1.25	3
3159	32¢ Arthur Fiedler	09/12/97	1.00	.20			1.25	3
3160	32¢ George Szell	09/12/97	1.00	.20			1.25	3
3161	32¢ Eugene Ormandy	09/12/97	1.00	.20			1.25	3
3162	32¢ Samuel Barber	09/12/97	1.00	.20			1.25	2
3163	32¢ Ferde Grofé	09/12/97	1.00	.20			1.25	2
3164	32¢ Charles Ives	09/12/97	1.00	.20			1.25	2
3165	32¢ Louis Moreau Gottschalk	09/12/97	1.00	.20			1.25	2
a	Block of 8, #3158-3165		8.00	4.00	9.00	(8)	5.25	
	Pane of 20		22.00					
	Tagged, Perf. 11.2							
3166	32¢ Padre Félix Varela	09/15/97	.65	.20	2.60	(4)	1.25	25
	Department of the Air Force, 50th Anniversary, Tagged, Perf. 11.2 x 11.1							
3167	32¢ Thunderbirds Aerial Demonstration Squadron	09/18/97	.65	.20	2.60	(4)	1.50	45
	Classic Movie Monsters, Tagged, Perf. 10.2							
3168	32¢ Lon Chaney as the Phantom of the Opera	09/30/97	.75	.20			1.50	145
3169	32¢ Bela Lugosi as Dracula	09/30/97	.75	.20			1.50	145
3170	32¢ Boris Karloff as Frankenstein's Monster	09/30/97	.75	.20			1.50	145
3171	32¢ Boris Karloff as the Mummy	09/30/97	.75	.20			1.50	145
3172	32¢ Lon Chaney, Jr. as the Wolf Man	09/30/97	.75	.20			1.50	145
a	Strip of 5, #3168-3172		3.75	2.25	7.50	(10)	3.75	
	Pane of 20		15.00	—				

Beginning with No. 3167, a hidden 3-D design can be seen on some stamps when they are viewed with a special viewer sold by the post office.

	Issue	Date	Un	U	PB	#	FDC	Q(M)
	Tagged, Self-Adhesive, Serpentine Die-Cut 11.4							
3173	32¢ First Supersonic Flight, 50th Anniversary	10/14/97	.65	.20	2.60	(4)	1.50	173
	Pane of 20		13.00					
	Tagged, Perf. 11.1							
3174	32¢ Women in Military Service	10/18/97	.65	.20	2.60	(4)	1.75	37
	Pane of 20		13.00					
	Holiday Celebrations, Tagged, Self-Adhesive, Serpentine Die-Cut 11							
3175	32¢ Kwanzaa	10/22/97	.65	.20	3.00	(4)	1.75	133
	Holiday Celebration: Christmas, Booklet, Tagged, Self-Adhesive, Serpentine Die-Cut 9.9 on 2, 3 or 4 sides							
3176	32¢ Madonna and Child by Sano di Pietro	10/09/97	.65	.20			1.25	883
a	Booklet pane of 20 + label		13.00					
	Holiday Celebration: Holiday, Booklet, Self-Adhesive, Serpentine Die-Cut 11.2 x 11.8 on 2, 3 or 4 sides							
3177	32¢ American Holly	10/30/97	.65	.20			1.25	1,621
a	Booklet pane of 20 + label		13.00					
b	Booklet pane of 4		2.60					
c	Booklet pane of 5 + label		3.25					
d	Booklet pane of 6		3.90					
	Space, Tagged, Perf. 11 x 11.1							
3178	$3 Mars Rover Sojourner	12/10/97	6.00	4.00			9.00	15
a	$3 single stamp		5.50	3.00				
b	Souvenir sheet		7.00	—				
	Lunar New Year, Tagged, Perf. 11.2							
3179	32¢ Year of the Tiger	01/05/98	.80	.20	3.75	(4)	1.75	51
	Tagged, Perf. 11.2							
3180	32¢ Winter Sports-Skiing	1/2/98	.65	.20	2.60	(4)	1.25	80
	Black Heritage, Tagged, Self-Adhesive, Serpentine Die-Cut 11.6 x 11.3							
3181	32¢ Madam C. J. Walker	1/28/98	.65	.20	2.75	(4)	1.75	45

MADONNA AND SLEEPING CHILD
BY SASSOFERRATO

Since 1978, the theme of each "traditional" Christmas stamp has been the Madonna and Child. The 2009 Christmas stamp features *Madonna and Sleeping Child,* a painting by Italian artist Giovanni Battista Salvi (1609-1685), more commonly known as Sassoferrato. The issuance of the stamp coincides with the 400th anniversary of the birth of the artist. ▧ It is customary to refer to Italian Renaissance artists by their place of birth, thus Giovanni Battista Salvi is often known simply as Sassoferrato, for a town approximately 140 miles north of Rome. Sassoferrato served as an apprentice to his father, painter Tarquinio Salvi. Few additional details are known about Sassoferrato's life, but it is believed he may have studied under the Bolognese painter Domenichino. ▧ Sassoferrato spent much of his career painting Madonna and Child portraits. Today, more than 300 examples of his artistry can be found in churches, museums, and private collections. ▧ The painting on this stamp is one of more than 20 versions of *Madonna and Sleeping Child* known to exist. Currently in the collection of Hearst Castle, the painting was purchased in 1926 by American media entrepreneur William Randolph Hearst, an avid collector and patron of the arts.

Sassoferrato, ©Hearst Castle®/California State Parks

3158 3159 3160 3161

3166 3167

3162 3163 3164 3165 3165a

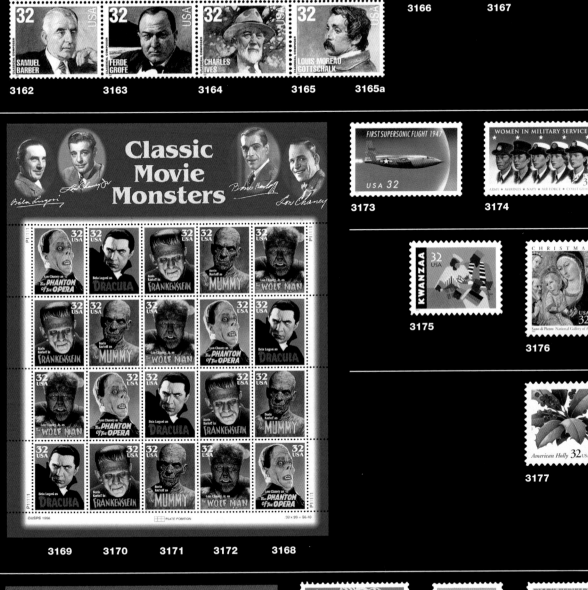

Classic Movie Monsters

3173 3174

3175

3176

3177

3169 3170 3171 3172 3168

MARS PATHFINDER
JULY 4, 1997

Mars Rover Sojourner
$3.00 USA

3178

3179

3180

3181

3182 a b c d e
        f g h
              i j
   k l   m n   o

3183 a b   c
   d   e   f
   g h i j k
      l m n   o

3184 a b c d e

3185 a b c d e

	Issue	Date	Un	U	PB #	FDC	Q(M)
	Celebrate The Century® 1900s, Tagged, Perf. 11.5						
3182	Pane of 15, 1900-1909	02/03/98	12.50	8.50		8.50	13
a	32¢ Model T Ford		.80	.65		1.50	
b	32¢ President Theodore Roosevelt		.80	.65		1.50	
c	32¢ Motion Picture, "The Great Train Robbery"		.80	.65		1.50	
d	32¢ Crayola Crayons Introduced, 1903		.80	.65		1.50	
e	32¢ St. Louis World's Fair, 1904		.80	.65		1.50	
f	32¢ Design used on Hunt's Remedy Stamp (#RS56), Pure Food & Drugs Act, 1906		.80	.65		1.50	
g	32¢ Wright Brothers First Flight, Kitty Hawk, 1903		.80	.65		1.50	
h	32¢ Boxing Match Shown in Painting "Stag at Sharkey's," by George Bellows of the Ash Can School		.80	.65		1.50	
i	32¢ Immigrants Arrive		.80	.65		1.50	
j	32¢ John Muir, Preservationist		.80	.65		1.50	
k	32¢ "Teddy" Bear Created		.80	.65		1.50	
l	32¢ W.E.B. Du Bois, Social Activist		.80	.65		1.50	
m	32¢ Gibson Girl		.80	.65		1.50	
n	32¢ First World Series, 1903		.80	.65		1.50	
o	32¢ Robie House, Chicago, Designed by Frank Lloyd Wright		.80	.65		1.50	
	Celebrate The Century® 1910s, Tagged, Perf. 11.5						
3183	Pane of 15, 1910-1919	02/03/98	12.50	8.50		8.50	13
a	32¢ Charlie Chaplin as the Little Tramp		.80	.65		1.50	
b	32¢ Federal Reserve System created, 1913		.80	.65		1.50	
c	32¢ George Washington Carver		.80	.65		1.50	
d	32¢ Avant-garde art introduced at Armory Show, 1913		.80	.65		1.50	
e	32¢ First transcontinental telephone line, 1914		.80	.65		1.50	
f	32¢ Panama Canal opens, 1914		.80	.65		1.50	
g	32¢ Jim Thorpe wins decathlon at Stockholm Olympics, 1912		.80	.65		1.50	
h	32¢ Grand Canyon National Park, 1919		.80	.65		1.50	
i	32¢ U.S. enters World War I		.80	.65		1.50	
j	32¢ Boy Scouts started in 1910, Girl Scouts formed in 1912		.80	.65		1.50	
k	32¢ President Woodrow Wilson		.80	.65		1.50	

	Issue	Date	Un	U	PB #	FDC	Q(M)
	Celebrate The Century® 1910s Tagged, Perf. 11.5 continued						
l	32¢ First Crossword Puzzle Published, 1913		.80	.65		1.50	
m	32¢ Jack Dempsey Wins Heavyweight Title, 1919		.80	.65		1.50	
n	32¢ Construction Toys		.80	.65		1.50	
o	32¢ Child Labor Reform		.80	.65		1.50	
	Celebrate The Century® 1920s, Tagged, Perf. 11.5						
3184	Pane of 15, 1920-1929	05/28/98	12.50	8.50		8.50	13
a	32¢ Babe Ruth		.80	.65		1.75	
b	32¢ The Gatsby Style		.80	.65		1.75	
c	32¢ Prohibition Enforced		.80	.65		1.75	
d	32¢ Electric Toy Trains		.80	.65		1.75	
e	32¢ Nineteenth Amendment (women voting)		.80	.65		1.75	
f	32¢ Emily Post's Etiquette		.80	.65		1.75	
g	32¢ Margaret Mead, Anthropologist		.80	.65		1.75	
h	32¢ Flappers Do the Charleston		.80	.65		1.75	
i	32¢ Radio Entertains America		.80	.65		1.75	
j	32¢ Art Deco Style (Chrysler Building)		.80	.65		1.75	
k	32¢ Jazz Flourishes		.80	.65		1.75	
l	32¢ Four Horsemen of Notre Dame		.80	.65		1.75	
m	32¢ Lindbergh Flies the Atlantic		.80	.65		1.75	
n	32¢ American Realism (*The Automat* by Edward Hopper)		.80	.65		1.75	
o	32¢ Stock Market Crash, 1929		.80	.65		1.75	
	Celebrate The Century® 1930s, Tagged, Perf. 11.5						
3185	Pane of 15, 1930-1939	09/10/98	12.50	8.50		8.50	13
a	32¢ President Franklin D. Roosevelt		.80	.65		1.75	
b	32¢ The Empire State Building		.80	.65		1.75	
c	32¢ First Issue of Life Magazine, 1936		.80	.65		1.75	
d	32¢ First Lady Eleanor Roosevelt		.80	.65		1.75	
e	32¢ FDR's New Deal		.80	.65		1.75	
f	32¢ Superman Arrives, 1938		.80	.65		1.75	
g	32¢ Household Conveniences		.80	.65		1.75	
h	32¢ "Snow White and the Seven Dwarfs," 1937		.80	.65		1.75	
i	32¢ "Gone With the Wind," 1936		.80	.65		1.75	
j	32¢ Jesse Owens		.80	.65		1.75	
k	32¢ Streamline Design		.80	.65		1.75	
l	32¢ Golden Gate Bridge		.80	.65		1.75	
m	32¢ America Survives the Depression		.80	.65		1.75	
n	32¢ Bobby Jones Wins Golf Grand Slam, 1930		.80	.65		1.75	
o	32¢ The Monopoly Game		.80	.65		1.75	

Issue	Date	Un	U	PB #	FDC	Q(M)
Celebrate The Century® 1940s, Tagged, Perf. 11.5						
3186 Pane of 15, 1940-1949	02/18/99	13.00	8.50		8.50	12.5
a 33¢ World War II		.85	.65		1.75	
b 33¢ Antibiotics Save Lives		.85	.65		1.75	
c 33¢ Jackie Robinson		.85	.65		1.75	
d 33¢ President Harry S. Truman		.85	.65		1.75	
e 33¢ Women Support War Effort		.85	.65		1.75	
f 33¢ TV Entertains America		.85	.65		1.75	
g 33¢ Jitterbug Sweeps Nation		.85	.65		1.75	
h 33¢ Jackson Pollock, Abstract Expressionism		.85	.65		1.75	
i 33¢ GI Bill, 1944		.85	.65		1.75	
j 33¢ The Big Band Sound		.85	.65		1.75	
k 33¢ International Style of Architecture		.85	.65		1.75	
l 33¢ Postwar Baby Boom		.85	.65		1.75	
m 33¢ Slinky, 1945		.85	.65		1.75	
n 33¢ "A Streetcar Named Desire", 1947		.85	.65		1.75	
o 33¢ Orson Welles' "Citizen Kane"		.85	.65		1.75	
Celebrate The Century® 1950s, Tagged, Perf. 11.5						
3187 Pane of 15, 1950-1959	05/26/99	13.00	8.50		8.50	12.5
a 33¢ Polio Vaccine Developed		.85	.65		1.75	
b 33¢ Teen Fashions		.85	.65		1.75	
c 33¢ The "Shot Heard 'Round the World"		.85	.65		1.75	
d 33¢ U.S. Launches Satellites		.85	.65		1.75	
e 33¢ Korean War		.85	.65		1.75	
f 33¢ Desegregating Public Schools		.85	.65		1.75	
g 33¢ Tail Fins and Chrome		.85	.65		1.75	
h 33¢ Dr. Seuss' "The Cat in the Hat"		.85	.65		1.75	
i 33¢ Drive-in Movies		.85	.65		1.75	
j 33¢ World Series Rivals		.85	.65		1.75	
k 33¢ Rocky Marciano, Undefeated Boxer		.85	.65		1.75	
l 33¢ "I Love Lucy"		.85	.65		1.75	
m 33¢ Rock 'n' Roll		.85	.65		1.75	
n 33¢ Stock Car Racing		.85	.65		1.75	
o 33¢ Movies Go 3-D		.85	.65		1.75	

Issue	Date	Un	U	PB #	FDC	Q(M)
Celebrate The Century® 1960s, Tagged, Perf. 11.5						
3188 Pane of 15, 1960-1969	09/17/99	13.00	8.50		8.50	8
a 33¢ "I Have a Dream"		.85	.65		1.75	
b 33¢ Woodstock		.85	.65		1.75	
c 33¢ Man Walks on the Moon		.85	.65		1.75	
d 33¢ Green Bay Packers		.85	.65		1.75	
e 33¢ Star Trek		.85	.65		1.75	
f 33¢ The Peace Corps		.85	.65		1.75	
g 33¢ The Vietnam War		.85	.65		1.75	
h 33¢ Ford Mustang		.85	.65		1.75	
i 33¢ Barbie Doll		.85	.65		1.75	
j 33¢ The Integrated Circuit		.85	.65		1.75	
k 33¢ Lasers		.85	.65		1.75	
l 33¢ Super Bowl I		.85	.65		1.75	
m 33¢ Peace Symbol		.85	.65		1.75	
n 33¢ Roger Maris, 61 in '61		.85	.65		1.75	
o 33¢ The Beatles						
Celebrate The Century® 1970s, Tagged, Perf. 11.5						
3189 Pane of 15, 1970-1979	11/18/99	13.00	8.50		8.50	6
a 33¢ Earth Day Celebrated		.85	.65		1.75	
b 33¢ TV Series "All in the Family"		.85	.65		1.75	
c 33¢ "Sesame Street"		.85	.65		1.75	
d 33¢ Disco Music		.85	.65		1.75	
e 33¢ Steelers Win Four Super Bowls		.85	.65		1.75	
f 33¢ U.S. Celebrates 200th Birthday		.85	.65		1.75	
g 33¢ Secretariat Wins the Triple Crown		.85	.65		1.75	
h 33¢ VCRs Transform Entertainment		.85	.65		1.75	
i 33¢ Pioneer 10		.85	.65		1.75	
j 33¢ Women's Rights Movement		.85	.65		1.75	
k 33¢ 1970s Fashions		.85	.65		1.75	
l 33¢ "Monday Night Football"		.85	.65		1.75	
m 33¢ America Smiles		.85	.65		1.75	
n 33¢ Jumbo Jets		.85	.65		1.75	
o 33¢ Medical Imaging		.85	.65		1.75	

ALASKA STATEHOOD

The U.S. Postal Service commemorates the 50th anniversary of Alaska statehood with this stamp featuring a photograph of a dog musher taken by Jeff Schultz near Rainy Pass in the Alaska Range. With more than 570,000 square miles of land, Alaska is the largest of the 50 states, but is the least densely populated with approximately 670,000 residents. The name of the state derives from an Aleut word meaning "great land." In 1867, the United States paid Russia $7.2 million for the land that is now Alaska. Although the plan to acquire Alaska was enthusiastically supported by William H. Seward, Secretary of State under Presidents Abraham Lincoln and Andrew Johnson, and Massachusetts Senator Charles Sumner, chair of the Senate Foreign Relations Committee, critics derided the plan, calling it "Seward's folly" and "Seward's icebox." Although there was early skepticism about the acquisition of Alaska, several well-publicized gold discoveries later in the 19th century boosted interest in the area and prompted an increase in the population. As a result, Alaska became an official U.S. territory in 1912 and the 49th state on January 3, 1959. Today, much of Alaska consists of parks, forests, and wildlife refuges managed by the federal government. The Arctic National Wildlife Refuge encompasses more than 19 million acres in northeastern Alaska, while 23 million acres of northern Alaska comprise the National Petroleum Reserve. Although around 80 percent of state revenue derives from petroleum extraction, other vital Alaskan industries include seafood, mining, timber, oil and gas, and tourism.

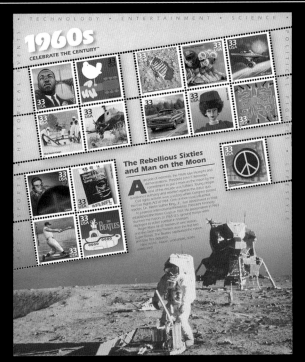

3186   a   b   c   d   e   f   g   h   i   j   k   l   m   n   o

3187 a b c d e f g h i j k l m n o

3188 a b c d e

3189 a b c

3190   a   b   c   d   e
       f   g   h   i   j
       k   l   m
       n   o

3191   a   b   c
                     d   e   f
         g   h   i   j   k
         l   m   n   o

3192

3193   3194   3195   3196   3197   3197a

3198   3199   3200   3201   3202   3202a

3203

3204a

3207A   3208A

3206

Issue		Date	Un	U	PB	#	FDC	Q(M)
Celebrate The Century® 1980s, Tagged, Perf. 11.5								
3190	Pane of 15, 1980-1989	01/12/00	13.00	8.50			8.50	6
a	33¢ Space Shuttle Program		.85	.65			1.75	
b	33¢ "Cats", Broadway show		.85	.65			1.75	
c	33¢ San Francisco 49ers		.85	.65			1.75	
d	33¢ Hostages Come Home		.85	.65			1.75	
e	33¢ Figure Skating		.85	.65			1.75	
f	33¢ Cable TV		.85	.65			1.75	
g	33¢ Vietnam Veterans Memorial		.85	.65			1.75	
h	33¢ Compact Discs		.85	.65			1.75	
i	33¢ Cabbage Patch Kids		.85	.65			1.75	
j	33¢ "The Cosby Show"		.85	.65			1.75	
k	33¢ Fall of the Berlin Wall		.85	.65			1.75	
l	33¢ Video Games		.85	.65			1.75	
m	33¢ "E.T. The Extra-Terrestrial"		.85	.65			1.75	
n	33¢ Personal Computers		.85	.65			1.75	
o	33¢ Hip-Hop Culture		.85	.65			1.75	
Celebrate The Century® 1990s, Tagged, Perf. 11.5								
3191	Pane of 15, 1990-1999	05/02/00	13.00	8.50			8.50	8
a	33¢ New Baseball Records		.85	.65			1.75	
b	33¢ Gulf War		.85	.65			1.75	
c	33¢ "Seinfeld", Television Series		.85	.65			1.75	
d	33¢ Extreme Sports		.85	.65			1.75	
e	33¢ Improving Education		.85	.65			1.75	
f	33¢ Computer Art and Graphics		.85	.65			1.75	
g	33¢ Recovering Species		.85	.65			1.75	
h	33¢ Return to Space		.85	.65			1.75	
i	33¢ Special Olympics		.85	.65			1.75	
j	33¢ Virtual Reality		.85	.65			1.75	
k	33¢ "Jurassic Park"		.85	.65			1.75	
l	33¢ "Titanic"		.85	.65			1.75	
m	33¢ Sport Utility Vehicles		.85	.65			1.75	
n	33¢ World Wide Web		.85	.65			1.75	
o	33¢ Cellular Phones		.85	.65			1.75	
Tagged, Perf. 11.2 x 11								
3192	32¢ "Remember the Maine" Spanish-American War	02/15/98	.65	.20	2.60	(4)	1.75	30

Issue		Date	Un	U	PB/PNC	#	FDC	Q(M)
Flowering Trees, Tagged, Die-Cut, Perf. 11.3								
3193	32¢ Southern Magnolia	03/19/98	.65	.20			1.50	
3194	32¢ Blue Paloverde	03/19/98	.65	.20			1.50	
3195	32¢ Yellow Poplar	03/19/98	.65	.20			1.50	
3196	32¢ Prairie Crab Apple	03/19/98	.65	.20			1.50	
3197	32¢ Pacific Dogwood	03/19/98	.65	.20			1.50	
a	Strip of 5, #3193-3197	03/19/98	3.25		6.50	(10)	3.75	250
Artists, Alexander Calder, Tagged, Perf. 10.2								
3198	32¢ Black Cascade	03/25/98	.65	.20			1.50	
3199	32¢ Untitled	03/25/98	.65	.20			1.50	
3200	32¢ Rearing Stallion	03/25/98	.65	.20			1.50	
3201	32¢ Portrait of a Young Man	03/25/98	.65	.20			1.50	
3202	32¢ Un Effet du Japonais	03/25/98	.65	.20			1.50	
a	Strip of 5, #3198-3202	03/25/98	3.25	2.25	6.50	(10)	3.75	80
Holiday Celebrations, Tagged, Self-Adhesive, Serpentine Die-Cut 11.7 x 10.9								
3203	32¢ Cinco de Mayo	04/16/98	.65	.20	2.60	(4)	1.25	85
Looney Tunes, Tagged, Self-Adhesive, Serpentine Die-Cut 11.1								
3204	Sylvester & Tweety Pane of 10	04/27/98	6.75					39
a	32¢ single		.65	.20			1.25	
b	Booklet pane of 9, #3204a		6.00					
c	Booklet pane of 1, #3204a		.65					
3205	Sylvester & Tweety Pane of 10	04/27/98	12.50					
a	32¢ single		1.00					
b	Booklet pane of 9, #3205a		*9.00*					
c	Booklet pane of 1, no die-cutting		*2.00*					
Tagged, Self-Adhesive, Serpentine Die-Cut 10.8 x 10.9								
3206	32¢ Wisconsin Statehood	05/29/98	.65	.30	3.00	(4)	1.25	32
American Scenes, Coil, Untagged, Perf. 10 Vertically								
3207	5¢ Wetlands (Nonprofit)	06/05/98	.20	.20	1.40	(5)	1.25	
Coil, Self-Adhesive, Serpentine Die-Cut 9.8 Vertically								
3207A	5¢ Wetlands (Nonprofit)	12/04/98	.20	.20	1.40	(5)	1.25	650
American Culture, Coil, Perf. 10 Vertically								
3208	25¢ Diner	06/05/98	.50	.50	3.50	(5)	1.25	400
American Culture, Coil, Self-Adhesive, Serpentine Die-Cut 9.8 Vertically								
3208A	25¢ Diner	09/30/98	.50	.50	3.50	(5)	1.25	

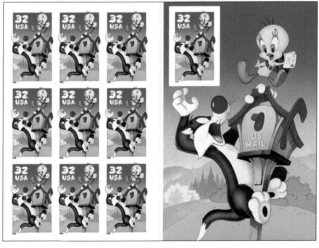

3204

	Issue	Date	Un	U	PB	#	FDC	Q(M)
	1898 Trans-Mississippi Reissue, Tagged, Perf. 12 x 12.4							
3209	Pane of 9	06/18/98	9.00	7.00			6.50	2
a	1¢ Marquette on the Mississippi		.20	.20			1.50	
b	2¢ Mississippi River Bridge		.20	.20			1.50	
c	4¢ Indian Hunting Buffalo		.20	.20			1.50	
d	5¢ Fremont on the Rocky Mountains		.20	.20			1.50	
e	8¢ Troops Guarding Train		.20	.20			1.50	
f	10¢ Hardships of Emigration		.20	.20			1.50	
g	50¢ Western Mining Prospector		1.25	.60			2.00	
h	$1 Western Cattle in Storm		2.25	1.25			2.50	
i	$2 Farm in the West		4.25	2.50			4.50	
3210	Pane of 9 #3209h, single	06/18/98	18.00	—			15.00	2
	Tagged, Perf. 11.2							
3211	32¢ Berlin Airlift	06/26/98	.65	.20	2.60	(4)	1.50	30
	Legends of American Music: Folk Musicians, Tagged, Perf. 10.1 x 10.2							
3212	32¢ Huddle "Leadbelly" Ledbetter	06/26/98	.75	.20			1.25	
3213	32¢ Woody Guthrie	06/26/98	.75	.20			1.25	
3214	32¢ Sonny Terry	06/26/98	.75	.20			1.25	
3215	32¢ Josh White	6/26/98	.75	.20			1.25	
a	Block or strip of 4, #3212-3215	06/26/98	3.00	2.00	3.00	(4)	3.25	45
	Legends of American Music: Gospel Singers, Tagged, Perf. 10.1 x 10.3							
3216	32¢ Mahalia Jackson	07/15/98	.65	.20			1.25	
3217	32¢ Roberta Martin	07/15/98	.65	.20			1.25	
3218	32¢ Clara Ward	07/15/98	.65	.20			1.25	
3219	32¢ Sister Rosetta Tharpe	07/15/98	.65	.20			1.25	
a	Block or strip of 4, #3216-3219	07/15/98	2.60	2.00	3.50	(4)	3.25	45

	Issue	Date	Un	U	PB/PNC	#	FDC	Q(M)
	Tagged, Perf. 11.2							
3220	32¢ Spanish Settlement of the Southwest	07/11/98	.65	.20	2.60	(4)	1.25	46
	Literary Arts, Tagged, Perf. 11.2							
3221	32¢ Stephen Vincent Benét	07/22/98	.65	.20	2.60	(4)	1.25	30
	Tropical Birds, Tagged, Perf. 11.2							
3222	32¢ Antillean Euphonia	07/29/98	.65	.20			1.25	
3223	32¢ Green-throated Carib	07/29/98	.65	.20			1.25	
3224	32¢ Crested Honeycreeper	07/29/98	.65	.20			1.25	
3225	32¢ Cardinal Honeyeater	07/29/98	.65	.20			1.25	
a	Block of 4, #3222-3225		2.60	2.00	2.60	(4)	3.00	70
	Legends of Hollywood, Tagged, Perf. 11.1							
3226	32¢ Alfred Hitchcock	08/03/98	.75	.20	4.50	(4)	1.50	65
	Tagged, Self-Adhesive, Serpentine Die-Cut 11.7							
3227	32¢ Organ & Tissue Donation	08/05/98	.65	.20	2.60	(4)	1.25	50
	American Transportation, Coil, Untagged, Self-Adhesive, Serpentine Die-Cut 9.8 Vertically							
3228	(10¢) Green Bicycle	08/14/98	.20	.20	2.25	(5)	1.25	
	American Transportation, Coil, Untagged, Perf. 9.9 Vertically							
3229	(10¢) Green Bicycle	08/14/98	.20	.20	2.50	(5)	1.25	
	Bright Eyes, Tagged, Self-Adhesive, Serpentine Die-Cut 9.9							
3230	32¢ Dog	08/20/98	.75	.20			1.75	
3231	32¢ Goldfish	08/20/98	.75	.20			1.75	
3232	32¢ Cat	08/20/98	.75	.20			1.75	
3233	32¢ Parakeet	08/20/98	.75	.20			1.75	
3234	32¢ Hamster	08/20/98	.75	.20			1.75	
a	Strip of 5, #3230-3234		3.75		7.50	(8)	3.25	180

HAWAI'I STATEHOOD

This 2009 stamp commemorates the 50th anniversary of Hawai'i's statehood. The "Aloha State" is made up of eight main islands and more than a hundred smaller ones, all formed by volcanic activity. The island of Hawai'i continues to grow in size with every eruption of Kilauea, the most active volcano in the world. The capital and largest city, Honolulu, is located on the island of O`ahu and is the center of transportation and business for the islands. O`ahu is home to nearly 900,000 people out of Hawai'i's 1.2 million total population. In Hawai'i there is no ethnic majority; the population includes Native Hawaiians, Caucasians, Japanese, other Pacific Islanders, Filipinos, Chinese, Vietnamese, Koreans, and many others. Hawai'i is a bilingual state. After a steep decline in the use of Hawaiian language in the early 1900s, Hawaiians started to revive their language and culture in the 1970s. Hawaiians have the utmost respect for their `ohana (extended family), land, cultural traditions, and ancestors. The geographical features of each island help create a wide range of climates. Some areas experience significant rainfall, while others are dry and desert-like. Temperatures are mild and consistent across the islands. With sandy beaches, fertile valleys, and stunning volcanic mountains, Hawai'i is a tropical paradise. With over 7 million visitors traveling to the islands annually, tourism drives Hawai'i's economy. The islands offer a serene vacation environment and a wide array of activities. In addition to tourism, the state's economy is heavily based on diversified agriculture, including pineapples, macadamia nuts, and flowers.

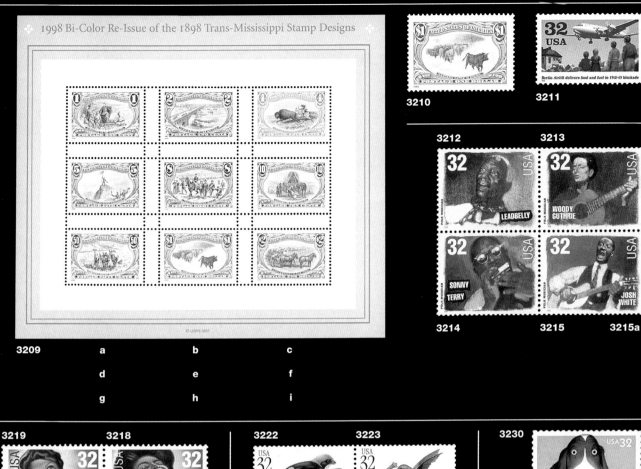

1998 Bi-Color Re-Issue of the 1898 Trans-Mississippi Stamp Designs

3209   a   b   c
       d   e   f
       g   h   i

3210

3211

3212   3213
3214   3215   3215a

3219   3218
3216   3217   3219a

3220

3221

3222   3223
3224   3225   3225a

3226

3227

3228

3230
3231
3232
3233
3234
3234a

1998

3235

KLONDIKE GOLD RUSH 1898
USA 32

3237

32 USA
B A L L E T

3236

a b c d e

f g h i j

k l m n o

p q r s t

FOUR CENTURIES OF
American Art

3238 3239 3240 3241 3242 3242a

3243

GIVING & SHARING An American Tradition
32 USA

3244

CHRISTMAS 32 USA
Florentine, n.d.   National Gallery

3245   **3246**

GREETINGS 32 USA

GREETINGS 32 USA

3247   **3248**

GREETINGS 32 USA

GREETINGS 32 USA

3258

The "H" Rate make-up stamp
USA

3259

USA 22

3260

USA H
First-Class Rate

	Issue	Date	Un	U	PB	#	FDC	Q(M)
	Tagged, Perf. 11.1							
3235	32¢ Klondike Gold Rush	08/21/98	.65	.20	2.60	(4)	1.50	28
	Classic Collections: Four Centuries of American Art, Tagged, Perf. 10.2							
3236	Pane of 20	08/27/98	17.50	10.00			9.00	4
a	32¢ "Portrait of Richard Mather," by John Foster		.85	.60			1.25	
b	32¢ "Mrs. Elizabeth Freake and Baby Mary," by The Freake Limner		.85	.60			1.25	
c	32¢ "Girl in Red Dress with Cat and Dog," by Ammi Phillips		.85	.60			1.25	
d	32¢ "Rubens Peale with a Geranium," by Rembrandt Peale		.85	.60			1.25	
e	32¢ "Long-billed Curlew, Numenius Longrostris," by John James Audubon		.85	.60			1.25	
f	32¢ "Boatmen on the Missouri," by George Caleb Bingham		.85	.60			1.25	
g	32¢ "Kindred Spirits," by Asher B. Durand		.85	.60			1.25	
h	32¢ "The Westwood Children," by Joshua Johnson		.85	.60			1.25	
i	32¢ "Music and Literature," by William Harnett		.85	.60			1.25	
j	32¢ "The Fog Warning," by Winslow Homer		.85	.60			1.25	
k	32¢ "The White Cloud, Head Chief of the Iowas," by George Catlin		.85	.60			1.25	
l	32¢ "Cliffs of Green River," by Thomas Moran		.85	.60			1.25	
m	32¢ "The Last of the Buffalo," by Alfred Bierstadt		.85	.60			1.25	
n	32¢ "Niagara," by Frederic Edwin Church		.85	.60			1.25	
o	32¢ "Breakfast in Bed," by Mary Cassatt		.85	.60			1.25	
p	32¢ "Nighthawks," by Edward Hopper		.85	.60			1.25	
q	32¢ "American Gothic," by Grant Wood		.85	.60			1.25	
r	32¢ "Two Against the White," by Charles Sheeler		.85	.60			1.25	
s	32¢ "Mahoning," by Franz Kline		.85	.60			1.25	
t	32¢ "No. 12" by Mark Rothko		.85	.60			1.25	

	Issue	Date	Un	U	PB	#	FDC	Q(M)
	Tagged, Perf. 10.9 x 11.1							
3237	32¢ Ballet	09/16/98	.65	.20	3.00	(4)	1.25	131
	Space, Tagged, Perf. 11.1							
3238	32¢ Space Discovery	10/01/98	.65	.20			1.25	
3239	32¢ Space Discovery	10/01/98	.65	.20			1.25	
3240	32¢ Space Discovery	10/01/98	.65	.20			1.25	
3241	32¢ Space Discovery	10/01/98	.65	.20			1.25	
3242	32¢ Space Discovery	10/01/98	.65	.20			1.25	
a	Strip of 5, #3238-3242		3.25	2.25	6.50	(10)	3.75	185
	Tagged, Self-Adhesive, Serpentine Die-Cut 11.1							
3243	32¢ Philanthropy, Giving and Sharing	10/07/98	.65	.20	2.60	(4)	1.25	50
	Holiday Celebration: Christmas, Booklet, Self-Adhesive, Serpentine Die-Cut 10.1 x 9.9 on 2, 3 or 4 sides							
3244	32¢ The Madonna and Child by Hans Memling	10/15/98	.65	.20			1.25	925
a	Booklet pane of 20 + label		13.00					
	Holiday Celebration: Holiday, Booklet, Self-Adhesive, Serpentine Die-Cut 11.3 x 11.7 on 2 or 3 sides							
3245	32¢ Evergreen Wreath	10/15/98	6.00	.20			1.25	
3246	32¢ Victorian Wreath	10/15/98	6.00	.20			1.25	
3247	32¢ Chili Pepper Wreath	10/15/98	6.00	.20			1.25	
3248	32¢ Tropical Wreath	10/15/98	6.00	.20			1.25	
a	Booklet pane of 4, #3245-3248		25.00				3.25	117
b	Booklet pane of 5, #3245, #3246, 3248, 2 #3247 and label		32.50					
c	Booklet pane of 6, #3247-3248, 2 each #3245-3246		40.00					
	Serpentine Die-Cut 11.4 x 11.5 on 2, 3 or 4 sides							
3249	32¢ Evergreen Wreath	10/15/98	1.75	.20			1.25	248
3250	32¢ Victorian Wreath	10/15/98	1.75	.20			1.25	248
3251	32¢ Chili Pepper Wreath	10/15/98	1.75	.20			1.25	248
3252	32¢ Tropical Wreath	10/15/98	1.75	.20			1.25	248
a	Serpentine die-cut 11.7 x 11.6 on 2, 3, or 4 sides		1.75	.20				
b	Block of 4, #3249-3252		7.00		7.50	(4)	3.00	
c	Booklet pane, 5 each #3249-3252		35.00					
	Untagged, Perf. 11.2							
3257	(1¢) Make-Up Rate Weathervane	11/09/98	.20	.20	.25	(4)	1.25	
a	Black omitted		135.00					
3258	(1¢) Make-Up Rate Weathervane	11/09/98	.20	.20	.25	(4)	1.25	

#3257 is 18mm high, has thin letters, white USA, and black 1998.
#3258 is 17mm high, has thick letters, pale blue USA, and blue 1998.

	Issue	Date	Un	U	PB	#	FDC	Q(M)
	Tagged, Self-Adhesive, Serpentine Die-Cut 10.8							
3259	22¢ Uncle Sam	11/09/98	.45	.20	2.50	(4)	1.25	
a	Die-cut 10.8 x 10.5		2.50	.25				
	Perf. 11.2							
3260	(33¢) H-Series	11/09/98	.65	.20	2.75	(4)	1.25	

Issue	Date	Un	U	PB #	FDC	Q(M)
Space, Self-Adhesive, Serpentine Die-Cut 11.5						
3261 $3.20 Space Shuttle Landing	11/09/98	6.00	1.50	24.00 (4)	5.00	245
3262 $11.75 Express Mail	11/19/98	22.50	10.00	90.00 (4)	25.00	21
Coil, Self-Adhesive, Serpentine Die-Cut 9.9 Vertically						
3263 22¢ Uncle Sam	11/09/98	.45	.20	4.00 (5)	1.25	
Perf. 9.8 Vertically						
3264 33¢ Unce Sam's Hat	11/09/98	.65	.20	6.50 (5)	1.25	
Self-Adhesive, Serpentine Die-Cut 9.9 Vertically						
3265 33¢ H-Series	11/09/98	.80	.20	7.50 (5)	1.25	
3266 33¢ Uncle Sam's Hat	11/09/98	1.75	.20	12.50 (5)	1.50	
Booklet, Self-Adhesive, Serpentine Die-Cut 9.9 on 2 or 3 sides						
3267 33¢ H-Series	11/09/98	.75	.20		1.25	
a Booklet pane of 10		7.50				
Self-Adhesive, Serpentine Die-Cut 11.25 on 3 sides						
3268 (33¢) Uncle Sam's Hat	11/09/98	.75	.20		1.25	
a Booklet pane of 10		7.50				
b Serpentine die-cut 11		.75	.20			
c As "b", booklet pane of 20 + label		15.00				
Self-Adhesive, Die-Cut 8 on 2, 3 or 4 sides						
3269 (33¢) Uncle Sam's Hat	11/09/98	.65	.20		1.25	
a Booklet pane of 18		12.00				
Coil, Untagged, Perf. 9.8 Vertically						
3270 10¢ Eagle with Shield	12/14/98	.20	.20	2.25 (5)	1.25	
a Large date		.45	.20	6.00 (5)		
Coil, Self-Adhesive, Serpentine Die-Cut 9.9 Vertically						
3271 10¢ Eagle with Shield	12/14/98	.20	.20	2.25 (5)	1.25	
a Large date		1.00	.20	5.00 (5)		
b Tagged (error)		1.25	.75	10.00 (5)		
Lunar New Year, Tagged, Perf. 11.2						
3272 33¢ Year of the Rabbit	01/05/99	.80	.20	3.25 (4)	1.75	51
Black Heritage, Tagged, Self-Adhesive, Serpentine Die-Cut 11.4						
3273 33¢ Malcolm X	01/20/99	.85	.20	3.40 (4)	2.00	100
Love, Booklet, Tagged, Self-Adhesive, Die-Cut						
3274 33¢ Love	01/28/99	.65	.20		1.25	1,500
a Booklet pane of 20		13.00				
3275 55¢ Love	01/20/99	1.10	.20	4.40 (4)	1.50	300
Tagged, Serpentine Die-Cut 11.4						
3276 33¢ Hospice Care	02/09/99	.65	.20	2.80 (4)	1.25	100
Tagged, Perf. 11.2						
3277 33¢ City Flag	02/25/99	.70	.20	47.50 (4)	1.25	200
Tagged, Self-Adhesive, Serpentine Die-Cut 11 on 2, 3 or 4 sides						
3278 33¢ City Flag	02/25/99	.65	.20	4.25 (4)	1.25	
a Booklet pane of 4		2.60				
b Booklet pane of 5 + label		3.25				
Booklet, Serpentine Die-Cut 11.5 x 11.75 on 2, 3 or 4 sides						
3278F 33¢ City Flag		1.10	.20			
g Booklet pane of 20 + label		22.50				
Self-Adhesive, Serpentine Die-Cut 9.8 on 2 or 3 sides						
3279 33¢ City Flag	02/25/99	.85	.20		1.25	
a Booklet pane of 10		8.50				
Coil, Perf. 9.9 Vertically						
3280 33¢ City Flag	02/25/99	.65	.20	4.00 (5)	1.25	
a Large date		1.25	.20	9.00 (5)		
Coil, Self-Adhesive, Serpentine Die-Cut 9.8 Vertically						
3281 33¢ City Flag (large date)	02/25/99	.65	.20	4.75 (5)	1.25	
c Small date		.65	.20	5.50 (5)		
3282 33¢ City Flag Rounded corners	02/25/99	.65	.20	4.00 (5)	1.25	

Issue	Date	Un	U	PB #	FDC	Q(M)
Booklet, Self-Adhesive, Serpentine Die-Cut 7.9 on 2, 3 or 4 sides						
3283 33¢ Flag and Chalkboard	03/13/99	.65	.20		1.25	306
a Booklet pane of 18		12.00				
Tagged, Perf. 11.2						
3286 33¢ Irish Immigration	02/26/99	.65	.20	2.60 (4)	1.50	40
Performing Arts, Tagged, Perf. 11.2						
3287 33¢ Alfred Lunt & Lynn Fontanne	03/02/99	.65	.20	2.60 (4)	1.25	43
Arctic Animals, Tagged, Perf. 11						
3288 33¢ Arctic Hare	03/12/99	.85	.20		1.25	15
3289 33¢ Arctic Fox	03/12/99	.85	.20		1.25	15
3290 33¢ Snowy Owl	03/12/99	.85	.20		1.25	15
3291 33¢ Polar Bear	03/12/99	.85	.20		1.25	15
3292 33¢ Gray Wolf	03/12/99	.85	.20		1.25	15
a Strip of 5, #3288-3292		4.25			3.25	
Nature of America: Sonoran Desert, Tagged, Self-Adhesive, Serpentine Die-Cut Perf. 11.2						
3293 Pane of 10	04/06/99	6.50			6.75	10
a 33¢ Cactus Wren, brittlebush, teddy bear cholla		.65	.50		1.25	
b 33¢ Desert tortoise		.65	.50		1.25	
c 33¢ White-winged dove		.65	.50		1.25	
d 33¢ Gambel quail		.65	.50		1.25	
e 33¢ Saguaro cactus		.65	.50		1.25	
f 33¢ Desert mule deer		.65	.50		1.25	
g 33¢ Desert cottontail, hedgehog cactus		.65	.50		1.25	
h 33¢ Gila monster		.65	.50		1.25	
i 33¢ Western diamondback rattlesnake, cactus mouse		.65	.50		1.25	
j 33¢ Gila woodpecker		.65	.50		1.25	
Fruit Berries, Tagged, Self-Adhesive, Serpentine Die-Cut 11.25 x 11.5 on 2, 3 or 4 sides, Serpentine Die-Cut 11.5 x 11.75 on 2 or 3 sides (3294a-3297a)						
3294 33¢ Blueberries	04/10/99	.75	.20		1.25	
a Dated "2000"	03/15/2000	1.00	.20		1.25	
3295 33¢ Raspberries	04/10/99	.75	.20		1.25	
a Dated "2000"	03/15/2000	1.00	.20		1.25	
3296 33¢ Strawberries	04/10/99	.75	.20		1.25	
a Dated "2000"	03/15/2000	1.00	.20		1.25	
3297 33¢ Blackberries	04/10/99	.75	.20		1.25	
a Dated "2000"	03/15/2000	1.00	.20		1.25	
b Booklet pane, 5 each #3294-3297 + label		15.00			3.25	
c Block of 4, #3294-3297		3.00				
d Booklet pane, 5 #3297e		20.00				
e Block of 4, #3294a-3297a		4.00				
Tagged, Self-Adhesive, Serpentine Die-Cut 9.5 x 10 on 2 or 3 sides						
3298 33¢ Blueberries	04/10/99	.90	.20		1.25	
3299 33¢ Raspberries	04/10/99	.90	.20		1.25	
3300 33¢ Strawberries	04/10/99	.90	.20		1.25	
3301 33¢ Blackberries	04/10/99	.90	.20		1.25	
a Booklet pane of 4 #3298-#3301		3.60			3.25	
b Booklet pane of 5 #3298, #3299, #3301 2 #3300 + label		4.50				
c Booklet pane of 6 #3300, #3301, 2 #3298, #3299		5.50				
d Block of 4, #3298-#3301		3.40				
Coil, Serpentine Die-Cut 8.5 Vertically						
3302 33¢ Blueberries	04/10/99	1.00	.20		1.25	
3303 33¢ Raspberries	04/10/99	1.00	.20		1.25	
3304 33¢ Strawberries	04/10/99	1.00	.20		1.25	
3305 33¢ Blackberries	04/10/99	1.00	.20		1.25	
a Strip of 4		4.00			3.25	

3261

3262

3272

3273

3274

3275

3276

3277

3278

3279

3283

3286

3287

3288

3289

3290

3291

3292

3292a

3293

e

c f j

a b d g h

i

3294 3296

3295 3297

3297c

3305a

3306a

3308

3309

3310 **3311**

3312 **3313** **3313a**

3314

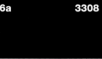

3315

3316

3317 **3318** **3319** **3320** **3320a**

3321 **3322**

3323 **3324** **3324a**

3325 **3326**

3327 **3328** **3328a**

3329 **3330**

3331

3332

3333

3334

3335

3336

3337

3337a

3338

Issue		Date	Un	U	PB #	FDC	Q(M)
Looney Tunes, Tagged, Self-Adhesive, Serpentine Die-Cut 11.1							
3306	Pane of 10	04/16/99	6.75				
a	33¢ Daffy Duck		.65	.20		1.50	43
b	Booklet pane of 9 #3306a		6.00				
c	Booklet pane of 1 #3306a		.65				
3307	Pane of 10		14.00				0.5
a	33¢ Single		1.25				
b	Booklet pane of 9 #3307a		12.00				
c	Booklet pane of 1, no die-cutting		1.75				
Literary Arts, Tagged, Perf. 11.2							
3308	33¢ Ayn Rand	04/22/99	.65	.20	2.60 (4)	2.50	43
Tagged, Self-Adhesive, Serpentine Die-Cut 11.6 x 11.3							
3309	33¢ Cinco De Mayo	04/27/99	.65	.20	2.60 (4)	1.25	113
Tropical Flowers, Tagged, Self-Adhesive, Serpentine Die-Cut 10.9 on 2 or 3 sides							
3310	33¢ Bird of Paradise	05/01/99	.65	.20		1.25	
3311	33¢ Royal Poinciana	05/01/99	.65	.20		1.25	
3312	33¢ Gloriosa Lily	05/01/99	.65	.20		1.25	
3313	33¢ Chinese Hibiscus	05/01/99	.65	.20		1.25	
a	Block of 4 #3310-3313		2.60			3.25	375
b	Booklet pane of 5 #3313a		13.00				
Tagged, Self-Adhesive, Perf. 11.5 Serpentine Die-Cut 11							
3314	33¢ John & William Bartram	05/18/99	.65	.20	2.60 (4)	1.25	145
3315	33¢ Prostate Cancer Awareness	05/28/99	.65	.20	2.60 (4)	1.25	78
Tagged, Perf. 11.25							
3316	33¢ California Gold Rush 1849	06/18/99	.65	.20	2.60 (4)	1.25	89
Aquarium Fish, Tagged, Self-Adhesive, Serpentine Die-Cut 11.5							
3317	33¢ Yellow fish, red fish, cleaner shrimp	06/24/99	.65	.20		1.25	39
a	Overall tagging		12.50	10.00			
3318	33¢ Fish, thermometer	06/24/99	.65	.20		1.25	39
a	Overall tagging		12.50	10.00			
3319	33¢ Red fish, blue & yellow fish	06/24/99	.65	.20		1.25	39
a	Overall tagging		12.50	10.00			

Issue		Date	Un	U	PB #	FDC	Q(M)
3320	33¢ Fish, heater/aerator	06/24/99	.65	.20		1.25	39
a	Overall tagging		12.50	10.00			
b	Strip of 4, #3317-3320		2.60		5.20 (8)	3.25	
c	Strip of 4, #3317a-3320a		55.00		125.00 (8)	3.25	
Extreme Sports, Tagged, Self-Adhesive, Serpentine Die-Cut 11							
3321	33¢ Skateboarding	06/25/99	.75	.20		1.25	38
3322	33¢ BMX Biking	06/25/99	.75	.20		1.25	38
3323	33¢ Snowboarding	06/25/99	.75	.20		1.25	38
3324	33¢ Inline Skating	06/15/99	.75	.20		1.25	38
a	Block of 4, #3321-3324		3.00		3.00 (4)	3.00	
American Glass, Tagged, Perf. 11							
3325	33¢ Free-Blown Glass	06/29/99	1.25	.20		1.25	29
3326	33¢ Mold-Blown Glass	06/29/99	1.25	.20		1.25	29
3327	33¢ Pressed Glass	06/29/99	1.25	.20		1.25	29
3328	33¢ Art Glass	06/29/99	1.25	.20		1.25	29
a	Strip or block of 4, #3325-3328		5.00	3.00		3.00	
Legends of Hollywood, Tagged, Perf. 11							
3329	33¢ James Cagney	07/22/99	.80	.20	4.25 (4)	1.75	76
Pioneers of Aviation, Tagged, Self-Adhesive, Serpentine Die-Cut 9.75 x 10							
3330	55¢ Gen. William "Billy" L. Mitchell	07/30/99	1.10	.30	4.40 (4)	1.50	101
Tagged, Self-Adhesive, Serpentine Die-Cut 11							
3331	33¢ Honoring Those Who Served	08/16/99	.65	.20	2.60 (4)	1.75	102
Tagged, Perf. 11							
3332	45¢ Universal Postal Union	08/25/99	.90	.45	3.60 (4)	1.25	43
All Aboard! Twentieth Century Trains, Tagged, Perf. 11							
3333	33¢ Daylight	08/26/99	.75	.20		1.50	24
3334	33¢ Congressional	08/26/99	.75	.20		1.50	24
3335	33¢ 20th Century Limited	08/26/99	.75	.20		1.50	24
3336	33¢ Hiawatha	08/26/99	.75	.20		1.50	24
3337	33¢ Super Chief	08/26/99	.75	.20		1.50	24
a	Strip of 5, #3333-3337		3.75	—	6.00 (8)	3.75	
Tagged, Perf. 11							
3338	33¢ Frederick Law Olmstead	09/13/99	.65	.20	2.60 (4)	1.25	43

PATRIOTIC BANNER

*I*n July 2007, the U.S. Postal Service issued a vibrant new Presorted Standard stamp that bulk mailers could affix to their newsletters, catalogs, and other printed matter. Dubbed "Patriotic Banner," the nondenominated stamp was issued in coils of 10,000. In 2009, the stamp will be reprinted and available in coils of 500. ■ The stamp design reflects the collaborative work of art director Ethel Kessler and stamp designer Michael Osborne, who together searched for ways to put a new spin on a familiar and popular stamp subject—the American flag. Their solution was to use elements from the flag in a design sure to stand out in a crowded mailbox. Featuring vibrant red and white stripes that bleed horizontally across vertical perforations, the design includes an eye-catching central blue field outlined in gold and sparkling with white stars. ■ Formerly known as "bulk mail," Presorted Standard mail must meet a minimum volume—200 pieces—and must be sorted by ZIP Code. While this discounted rate may be applied to business letters, postcards, magazines, and brochures, each piece in a mailing must be identical in size and weight. The rate does not apply to personal correspondence or business mail such as bills and invoices.

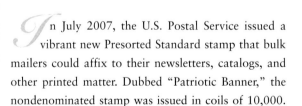

	Issue	Date	Un	U	PB	#	FDC	Q(M)
	Legends of American Music: Hollywood Composers, Tagged, Perf. 11							
3339	33¢ Max Steiner	09/16/99	1.25	.20			1.25	
3340	33¢ Dimitri Tiomkin	09/16/99	1.25	.20			1.25	
3341	33¢ Bernard Herrmann	09/16/99	1.25	.20			1.25	
3342	33¢ Franz Waxman	09/16/99	1.25	.20			1.25	
3343	33¢ Alfred Newman	09/16/99	1.25	.20			1.25	
3344	33¢ Erich Wolfgang Korngold	09/16/99	1.25	.20			1.25	
a	Block of 6, #3339-3344		7.50	4.50	7.50	(6)	3.75	85
	Legends of American Music: Broadway Songwriters, Tagged, Perf. 11							
3345	33¢ Ira & George Gershwin	09/21/99	1.25	.20			1.25	
3346	33¢ Lerner & Loewe	09/21/99	1.25	.20			1.25	
3347	33¢ Lorenz Hart	09/21/99	1.25	.20			1.25	
3348	33¢ Rodgers & Hammerstein	09/21/99	1.25	.20			1.25	
3349	33¢ Meredith Willson	09/21/99	1.25	.20			1.25	
3350	33¢ Frank Loesser	09/21/99	1.25	.20			1.25	
a	Block of 6, #3345-3350		7.50	4.50	7.50	(6)	3.75	85
	Classic Collections: Insects & Spiders, Tagged, Perf. 11							
3351	Pane of 20	10/01/99	13.00	10.00			10.00	4
a	33¢ Black Widow		.65	.50			1.25	
b	33¢ Elderberry Longhorn		.65	.50			1.25	
c	33¢ Lady Beetle		.65	.50			1.25	
d	33¢ Yellow Garden Spider		.65	.50			1.25	
e	33¢ Dogbane Beetle		.65	.50			1.25	
f	33¢ Flower Fly		.65	.50			1.25	
g	33¢ Assassin Bug		.65	.50			1.25	
h	33¢ Ebony Jewelwing		.65	.50			1.25	
i	33¢ Velvet Ant		.65	.50			1.25	
j	33¢ Monarch Caterpillar		.65	.50			1.25	
k	33¢ Monarch Butterfly		.65	.50			1.25	
l	33¢ Eastern Hercules Beetle		.65	.50			1.25	
m	33¢ Bombardier Beetle		.65	.50			1.25	
n	33¢ Dung Beetle		.65	.50			1.25	
o	33¢ Spotted Water Beetle		.65	.50			1.25	
p	33¢ True Katydid		.65	.50			1.25	
q	33¢ Spinybacked Spider		.65	.50			1.25	
r	33¢ Periodical Cicada		.65	.50			1.25	
s	33¢ Scorpionfly		.65	.50			1.25	
t	33¢ Jumping Spider		.65	.50			1.25	

	Issue	Date	Un	U	PB	#	FDC	Q(M)
	Holiday Celebrations, Tagged, Self-Adhesive, Serpentine Die-Cut 11							
3352	33¢ Hanukkah	10/08/99	.65	.20	2.60	(4)	1.50	65
	Coil, Tagged, Perf. 9.75 Vertically							
3353	22¢ Uncle Sam	10/08/99	.45	.20	3.25	(5)	1.25	150
	Tagged, Perf. 11.25							
3354	33¢ NATO 50th Anniversary	10/13/99	.65	.20	2.60	(4)	1.25	45
	Holiday Celebration: Christmas, Tagged, Self-Adhesive Booklet, Serpentine Die-Cut 11.25 on 2 or 3 sides							
3355	33¢ *Madonna and Child* by Bartolomeo Vivarini	10/20/99	1.00	.20			1.25	1,556
a	Booklet pane of 20		20.00					
	Holiday Celebration: Holiday, Self-Adhesive, Serpentine Die-Cut 11.25							
3356	33¢ Red Deer	10/20/99	1.20	.20			1.25	
3357	33¢ Blue Deer	10/20/99	1.20	.20			1.25	
3358	33¢ Purple Deer	10/20/99	1.20	.20			1.25	
3359	33¢ Green Deer	10/20/99	1.20	.20			1.25	
a	Block or strip, #3356-3359		4.80		4.80	(4)	3.00	29
	Holiday Celebration: Holiday, Booklet, Serpentine Die-Cut 11.25 on 2, 3 or 4 sides							
3360	33¢ Red Deer	10/20/99	1.50	.20			1.25	
3361	33¢ Blue Deer	10/20/99	1.50	.20			1.25	
3362	33¢ Purple Deer	10/20/99	1.50	.20			1.25	
3363	33¢ Green Deer	10/20/99	1.50	.20			1.25	
a	Booklet pane of 20		30.00				3.00	446
	Holiday Celebration: Holiday, Booklet, Serpentine Die-Cut 11.5 x 11.25 on 2 or 3 sides							
3364	33¢ Red Deer	10/20/99	2.00	.20			1.25	
3365	33¢ Blue Deer	10/20/99	2.00	.20			1.25	
3366	33¢ Purple Deer	10/20/99	2.00	.20			1.25	
3367	33¢ Green Deer	10/20/99	2.00	.20			1.25	
a	Booklet pane of 4		8.00				3.00	30
b	Block pane of 5, #3364, #3366, #3367, 2 #3365 + label		10.00					
c	Block pane of 6, #3365, #3367, 2 #3364, #3366		12.00					
	Holiday Celebrations, Tagged, Self-Adhesive, Serpentine Die-Cut 11							
3368	33¢ Kwanzaa	10/29/99	.65	.20	2.60	(4)	1.75	95

3339 **MAX STEINER** HOLLYWOOD COMPOSER — 33 USA

3340 **DIMITRI TIOMKIN** HOLLYWOOD COMPOSER — 33 USA

3341 **BERNARD HERRMANN** HOLLYWOOD COMPOSER — 33 USA

3342 **FRANZ WAXMAN** HOLLYWOOD COMPOSER — 33 USA

3343 **ALFRED NEWMAN** HOLLYWOOD COMPOSER — 33 USA

3344 **ERICH WOLFGANG KORNGOLD** HOLLYWOOD COMPOSER — 33 USA

3344a

3345 **IRA & GEORGE GERSHWIN** BROADWAY SONGWRITERS — 33 USA

3346 **LERNER & LOEWE** BROADWAY SONGWRITERS — 33 USA

3347 **LORENZ HART** BROADWAY SONGWRITER — 33 USA

3348 **RODGERS & HAMMERSTEIN** BROADWAY SONGWRITERS — 33 USA

3349 **MEREDITH WILLSON** BROADWAY SONGWRITER — 33 USA

3350 **FRANK LOESSER** BROADWAY SONGWRITER — 33 USA

3350a

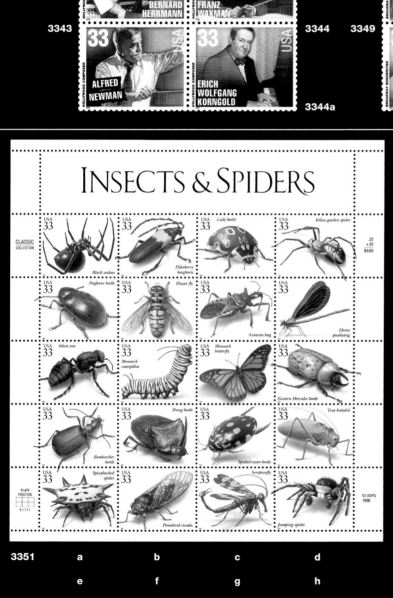

INSECTS & SPIDERS

CLASSIC COLLECTION

.33 x 20 $6.60

3351
a — Black widow
b — Elderberry longhorn
c — Lady beetle
d — Yellow garden spider
e — Dogbane beetle
f — Flower fly
g — Assassin bug
h — Ebony jewelwing
i — Velvet ant
j — Monarch caterpillar
k — Monarch butterfly
l — Eastern Hercules beetle
m — Bombardier beetle
n — Dung beetle
o — Spotted water beetle
p — True katydid
q — Spinybacked spider
r — Periodical cicada
s — Scorpionfly
t — Jumping spider

PLATE POSITION X1111
© USPS 1998

3352 HANUKKAH USA 33

3353 USA 22

3354 N 16 FIFTY YEARS 33 USA

3355 CHRISTMAS 33 USA — B. Vivarini National Gallery of Art

3356 3357

3359 3358 3359a
GREETINGS 33 USA

3368 KWANZAA 33 USA

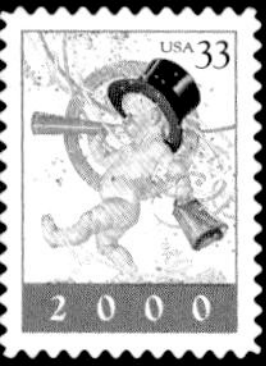
USA 33
2 0 0 0

3369

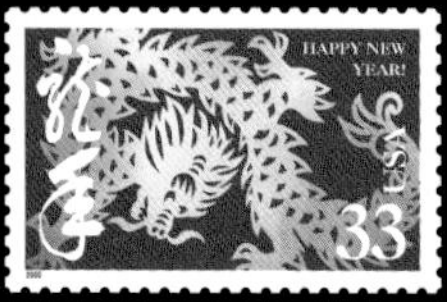
HAPPY NEW YEAR!
33

3370

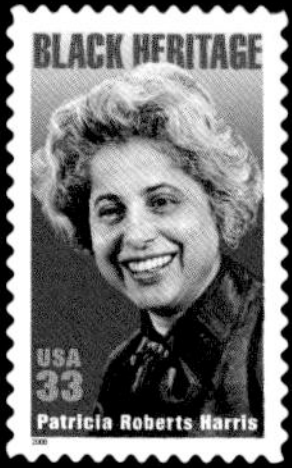
BLACK HERITAGE
USA 33
Patricia Roberts Harris

3371

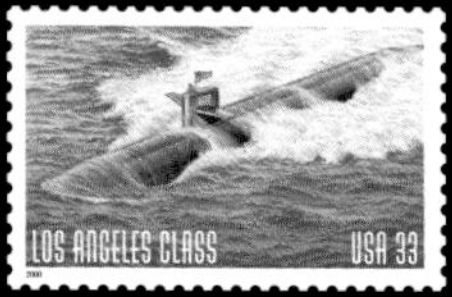
LOS ANGELES CLASS
USA 33

3372

3376 3373

3377

3374 3375

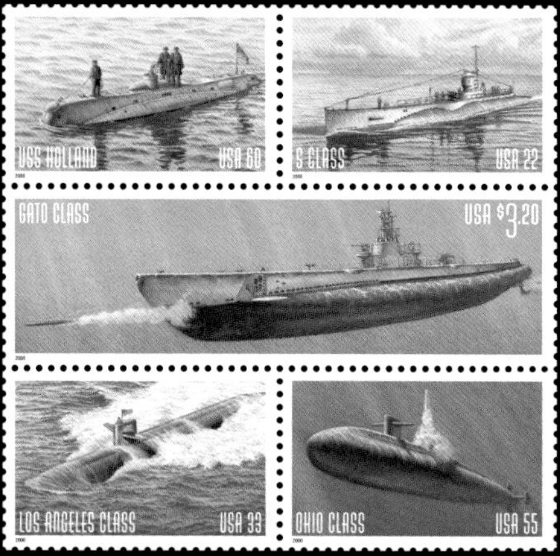
USS HOLLAND
USA 60
S CLASS
USA 22
GATO CLASS
USA $3.20
LOS ANGELES CLASS
USA 33
OHIO CLASS
USA 55

3377a

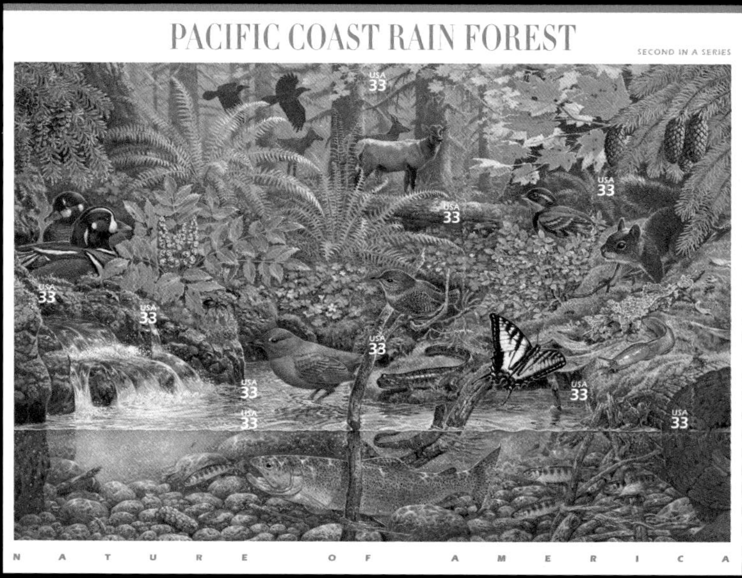
PACIFIC COAST RAIN FOREST
SECOND IN A SERIES
N A T U R E O F A M E R I C A

3378

e

a b f i

c g h j

d

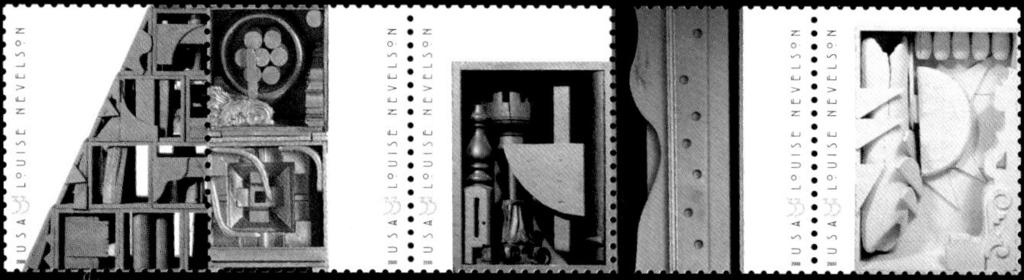
USA LOUISE NEVELSON

3379 3380 3381 3382 3383 3383a

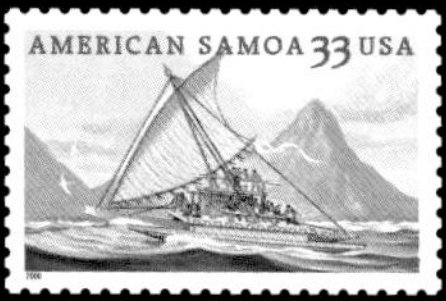
AMERICAN SAMOA 33 USA

3389

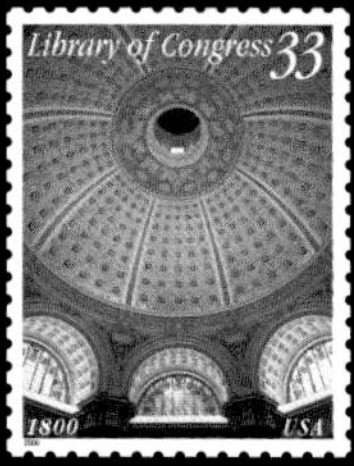
Library of Congress 33
1800
USA

3390

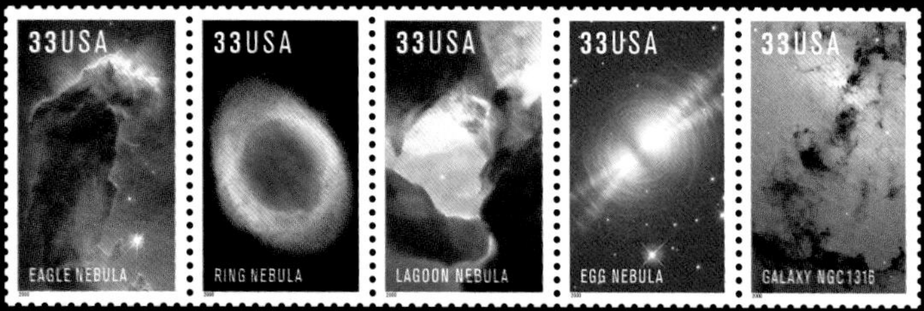
33USA
EAGLE NEBULA
33USA
RING NEBULA
33USA
LAGOON NEBULA
33USA
EGG NEBULA
33USA
GALAXY NGC1316

3384 3385 3386 3387 3388 3388a

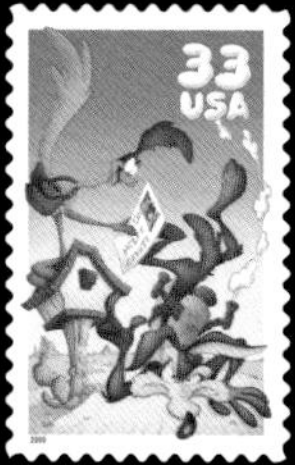
33
USA

3391a

Issue		Date	Un	U	PB	#	FDC	Q(M)
Tagged, Self-Adhesive, Serpentine Die-Cut 11.25								
3369	33¢ Year 2000	12/27/99	.65	.20	3.00	(4)	1.25	124
Lunar New Year, Tagged, Perf. 11.25								
3370	33¢ Year of the Dragon	01/06/2000	.80	.20	3.25	(4)	1.75	106
Black Heritage, Tagged, Self-Adhesive, Serpentine Die-Cut 11.5 x 11.25								
3371	33¢ Patricia Harris	01/27/2000	.65	.20	2.75	(4)	1.75	150
U.S. Navy Submarines, Tagged, Perf. 11								
3372	33¢ Los Angeles Class	03/27/2000	.75	.20	3.00	(4)	1.50	65
3373	22¢ S Class	03/27/2000	1.25	.75			1.50	3
3374	33¢ Los Angeles Class	03/27/2000	1.75	1.00			1.50	3
3375	55¢ Ohio Class	03/27/2000	2.75	1.25			1.75	3
3376	60¢ USS *Holland*	03/27/2000	3.00	1.50			1.75	3
3377	$3.20 Gato Class	03/27/2000	16.00	5.00			6.00	3
a	Booklet Pane of 5, #3373-3377		25.00	—			8.00	
Nature of America: Pacific Coast Rain Forest, Tagged, Self-Adhesive, Serpentine Die-Cut 11.25 x 11.5, 11.5 (Horiz. Stamps)								
3378	Pane of 10	03/29/2000	8.00				6.75	10
a	33¢ Harlequin Duck		.80	.50			1.25	10
b	33¢ Dwarf Oregongrape, Snail Eating Ground Beetle		.80	.50			1.25	10
c	33¢ American Dipper, horizontal		.80	.50			1.25	10
d	33¢ Cutthroat Trout, horizontal		.80	.50			1.25	10
e	33¢ Roosevelt Elk		.80	.50			1.25	10
f	33¢ Winter Wren		.80	.50			1.25	10
g	33¢ Pacific Giant Salamander, Rough-skinned Newt		.80	.50			1.25	10
h	33¢ Western Tiger Swallowtail, horizontal		.80	.50			1.25	10
i	33¢ Douglass Squirrel, Foliose Lichen		.80	.50			1.25	10
j	33¢ Foliose Lichen, Banana Slug		.80	.50			1.25	10

Issue		Date	Un	U	PB	#	FDC	Q(M)
Artists: Louise Nevelson, Tagged, Perf. 11 x 11.25								
3379	33¢ Silent Music I	04/06/2000	.65	.20	6.50	(10)	1.25	11
3380	33¢ Royal Tide I	04/06/2000	.65	.20	6.50	(10)	1.25	11
3381	33¢ Black Chord	04/06/2000	.65	.20	6.50	(10)	1.25	11
3382	33¢ Nightsphere-Light	04/06/2000	.65	.20	6.50	(10)	1.25	11
3383	33¢ Dawn's Wedding Chapel I	04/06/2000	.65	.20	6.50	(10)	1.25	11
a	Strip of 5, #3379-3383		3.25	—	6.50	(10)		
Space: Hubble Telescope, Tagged, Perf. 11								
3384	33¢ Eagle Nebula	04/10/2000	.65	.20	6.50	(10)	1.25	21
3385	33¢ Ring Nebula	04/10/2000	.65	.20	6.50	(10)	1.25	21
3386	33¢ Lagoon Nebula	04/10/2000	.65	.20	6.50	(10)	1.25	21
3387	33¢ Egg Nebula	04/10/2000	.65	.20	6.50	(10)	1.25	21
3388	33¢ Galaxy NGC 1316	04/10/2000	.65	.20	6.50	(10)	1.25	21
a	Strip of 5, #3384-3388		3.25	—	6.50	(10)	3.25	
b	As "a," imperf.		1,250.00					
Tagged, Perf. 11								
3389	33¢ American Samoa	04/17/2000	.65	.20	2.60	(4)	1.25	16
3390	33¢ Library of Congress	04/24/2000	.65	.20	2.60	(4)	1.25	55
Looney Tunes, Tagged, Self-Adhesive, Serpentine Die-Cut 11								
3391	Road Runner & Wile E. Coyote pane of 10	04/26/2000	9.00					30
a	33¢ Single		.85	.20			1.25	
3392	Road Runner & Wile E. Coyote pane of 10		40.00					
a	33¢ Single, die-cutting extends through backing paper		2.75					
c	Booklet Pane of 1, imperf.		5.00					

THANKSGIVING DAY PARADE

In 2009, the U.S. Postal Service issued four se-tenant stamps featuring iconic scenes of a Thanksgiving Day Parade. ■ Observed every year on the fourth Thursday of November, Thanksgiving is a traditional day of togetherness, when Americans of all backgrounds gather to reflect on the events of the past and give thanks for all they presently enjoy, especially family and friends. In large cities and small towns throughout the U.S., Thanksgiving Day parades have been an important part of this tradition since the early 20th century. A typical parade features marching bands, colorful floats, large balloons of favorite animals and popular characters, and, of course, crowds of delighted onlookers. ■ Thanksgiving Day stems from a rich history of American celebrations. The best known of these is the first harvest festival at Plymouth, where in autumn 1621, some 50 colonists and 90 Native Americans gathered for a three-day feast to offer thanks for a bountiful harvest. In 1863, President Abraham Lincoln issued a Proclamation of Thanksgiving, marking the beginning of national recognition of an annual U.S. Thanksgiving holiday. ■ Drawing on the long and rich visual history of Thanksgiving Day parades, artist Paul Rogers of Pasadena, California, based his design for the colorful and nostalgic images on the stamps on mid 20th-century American advertising and poster art.

	Issue	Date	Un	U	PB	#	FDC	Q(M)
	Distinguished Soldiers, Tagged, Perf. 11							
3393	33¢ Maj. Gen. John L. Hines	08/16/00	.65	.20	2.60	(4)	1.25	14
3394	33¢ Gen. Omar N. Bradley	08/16/00	.65	.20	2.60	(4)	1.25	14
3395	33¢ Sgt. Alvin C. York	08/16/00	.65	.20	2.60	(4)	1.25	14
3396	33¢ Second Lt. Audie L. Murphy	08/16/00	.65	.20	2.60	(4)	1.25	14
a	Block Strip of 4, #3393-3396		2.60	—	2.60	(4)	3.25	
	Tagged, Perf. 11							
3397	33¢ Summer Sports	05/05/00	.65	.20	2.60	(4)	1.25	91
	Tagged, Self-Adhesive, Serpentine Die-Cut 11.5							
3398	33¢ Adoption	05/10/00	.75	.20	3.00	(4)	1.25	200
	Youth Team Sports, Tagged, Perf. 11							
3399	33¢ Basketball	05/27/00	.65	.20	2.60	(4)	1.25	22
3400	33¢ Football	05/27/00	.65	.20	2.60	(4)	1.25	22
3401	33¢ Soccer	05/27/00	.65	.20	2.60	(4)	1.25	22
3402	33¢ Baseball	05/27/00	.65	.20	2.60	(4)	1.25	22
a	Block strip of 4, #3399-3402		2.60	—	2.60	(4)	3.25	
	Classic Collections: The Stars and Stripes, Tagged, Perf. 10.5 x 11							
3403	Pane of 20	06/14/00	15.00	11.00			10.00	4
a	33¢ Sons of Liberty Flag, 1775		.75	.50			1.25	
b	33¢ New England Flag, 1775		.75	.50			1.25	
c	33¢ Forster Flag, 1775		.75	.50			1.25	

	Issue	Date	Un	U	PB	#	FDC	Q(M)
	The Stars and Stripes Tagged, Perf. 10.5 x 11 continued							
d	33¢ Continental Colors, 1776		.75	.50			1.25	
e	33¢ Francis Hopkinson Flag, 1777		.75	.50			1.25	
f	33¢ Brandywine Flag, 1777		.75	.50			1.25	
g	33¢ John Paul Jones Flag, 1779		.75	.50			1.25	
h	33¢ Pierre L'Enfant Flag, 1783		.75	.50			1.25	
i	33¢ Indian Peace Flag, 1803		.75	.50			1.25	
j	33¢ Easton Flag, 1814		.75	.50			1.25	
k	33¢ Star-Spangled Banner, 1814		.75	.50			1.25	
l	33¢ Bennington Flag, c. 1820		.75	.50			1.25	
m	33¢ Great Star Flag, 1837		.75	.50			1.25	
n	33¢ 29-Star Flag, 1847		.75	.50			1.25	
o	33¢ Fort Sumter Flag, 1861		.75	.50			1.25	
p	33¢ Centennial Flag, 1876		.75	.50			1.25	
q	33¢ 38-Star Flag, 1877		.75	.50			1.25	
r	33¢ Peace Flag, 1891		.75	.50			1.25	
s	33¢ 48-Star Flag, 1912		.75	.50			1.25	
t	33¢ 50-Star Flag, 1960		.75	.50			1.25	
	Fruit Berries, Tagged, Self-Adhesive, Serpentine Die-Cut 8.5 Horizontally							
3404	33¢ Blueberries	06/16/00	2.50	.20			1.25	
3405	33¢ Strawberries	06/16/00	2.50	.20			1.25	
3406	33¢ Blackberries	06/16/00	2.50	.20			1.25	
3407	33¢ Raspberries	06/16/00	2.50	.20			1.25	
a	Strip of 4, #3404-3407		10.00		12.50	(5)	3.25	83

**OLD FAITHFUL
EXPRESS MAIL®**

The 2009 Express Mail stamp features a digital illustration by Dan Cosgrove of Old Faithful Geyser, one of the most popular attractions at Yellowstone National Park in Wyoming. Members of the 1870 Washburn Expedition, noting the large size and apparent consistency of its eruptions, named the geyser. ▓ A geyser is a type of hot spring. As underground water is heated by molten rock, it rises to the surface, where the geyser's narrow vent restricts its circulation. Pressure builds underground until the geyser erupts, throwing forth a powerful burst of hot water and steam. There are two types of geysers: Fountain geysers usually erupt from a pool of water; cone geysers, like Old Faithful, shoot a narrow and steady jet of water from a cone-shaped mound at the surface.

▓ Yellowstone National Park is home to several hundred geysers. Old Faithful is not the largest geyser in the park, but its eruptions—more frequent than other large geysers—have been carefully observed for decades. The resulting data make it possible to devise formulas to attempt to predict its eruptions. Nevertheless, from time to time, Old Faithful surprises everyone with completely unexpected behavior. ▓ Ordinarily, Old Faithful lies dormant for an average of 90 minutes between eruptions. Each eruption—which can last from more than one minute up to five minutes—throws 3,700 to 8,400 gallons of boiling water into the air at a height of 106 to 184 feet. The length of the eruption, as well as its height and volume, changes daily.

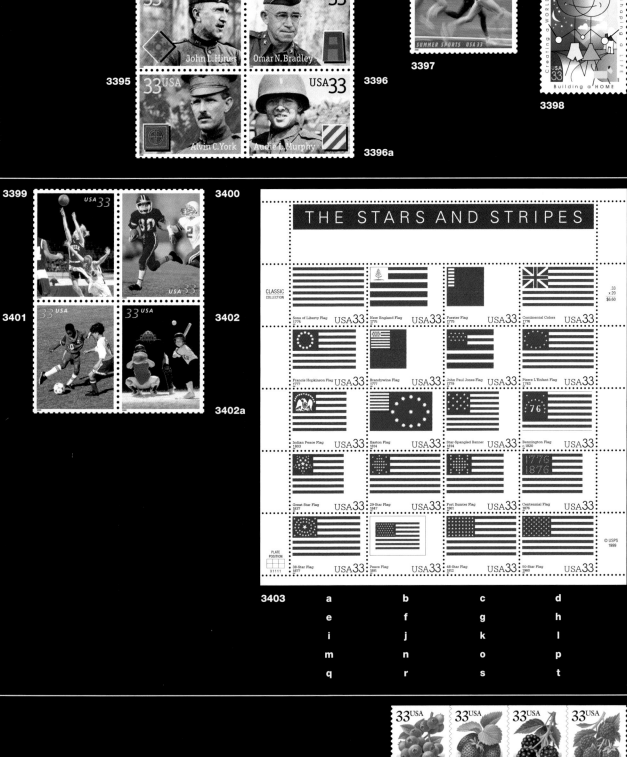

3393 33 USA John L. Hines
3394 USA 33 Omar N. Bradley
3395 33 USA Alvin C. York
3396 USA 33 Audie L. Murphy
3396a

3397 SUMMER SPORTS USA 33

3398 Adopting a CHILD / Creating a WORLD / Shaping a LIFE / Building a HOME / USA 33

3399
3400
3401
3402
3402a

THE STARS AND STRIPES

CLASSIC COLLECTION

.33 x 20 $6.60

Sons of Liberty Flag 1775 — USA 33
New England Flag 1775 — USA 33
Forster Flag 1775 — USA 33
Continental Colors 1776 — USA 33

Francis Hopkinson Flag 1777 — USA 33
Brandywine Flag 1777 — USA 33
John Paul Jones Flag 1779 — USA 33
Pierre L'Enfant Flag 1783 — USA 33

Indian Peace Flag 1803 — USA 33
Easton Flag 1814 — USA 33
Star-Spangled Banner 1814 — USA 33
Bennington Flag c.1820 — USA 33

Great Star Flag 1837 — USA 33
29-Star Flag 1847 — USA 33
Fort Sumter Flag 1861 — USA 33
Centennial Flag 1876 — USA 33

PLATE POSITION X1111
38-Star Flag 1877 — USA 33
Peace Flag 1891 — USA 33
48-Star Flag 1912 — USA 33
50-Star Flag 1960 — USA 33

© USPS 1999

3403
a b c d
e f g h
i j k l
m n o p
q r s t

33 USA
33 USA
33 USA
33 USA

3404 **3405** **3406** **3407 3407a**

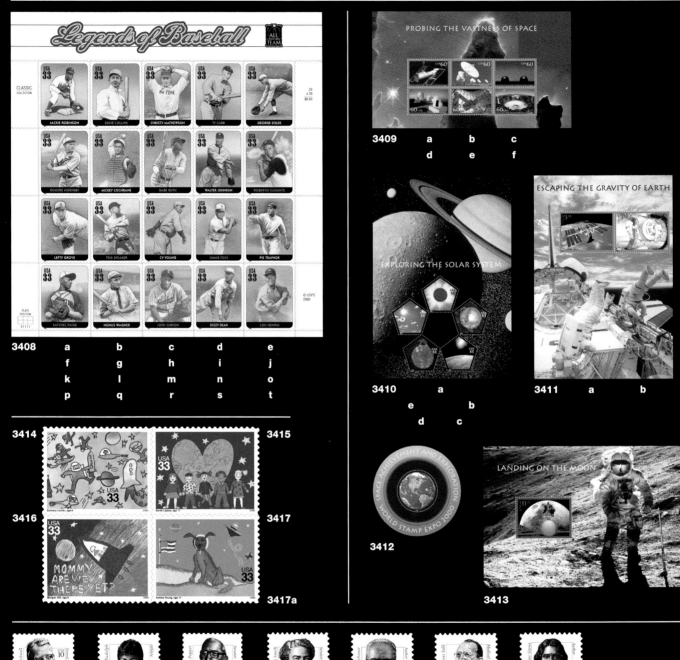

3408   a   b   c   d   e
      f   g   h   i   j
      k   l   m   n   o
      p   q   r   s   t

3409   a   b   c
      d   e   f

3410   a
      e   b
      d   c

3411   a   b

3412

3413

3414

3415

3416

3417

3417a

3420

3422

3426

3427

3427A

3428

3430

3431

3432A

3433

3435

Issue		Date	Un	U	PB	#	FDC	Q(M)
Classic Collections: Legends of Baseball, Tagged, Self-Adhesive, Serpentine Die-Cut 11.25								
3408	Pane of 20	07/06/00	13.00				10.00	11
a	33¢ Jackie Robinson		.65	.50			1.75	
b	33¢ Eddie Collins		.65	.50			1.75	
c	33¢ Christy Mathewson		.65	.50			1.75	
d	33¢ Ty Cobb		.65	.50			1.75	
e	33¢ George Sisler		.65	.50			1.75	
f	33¢ Rogers Hornsby		.65	.50			1.75	
g	33¢ Mickey Cochrane		.65	.50			1.75	
h	33¢ Babe Ruth		.65	.50			1.75	
i	33¢ Walter Johnson		.65	.50			1.75	
j	33¢ Roberto Clemente		.65	.50			1.75	
k	33¢ Lefty Grove		.65	.50			1.75	
l	33¢ Tris Speaker		.65	.50			1.75	
m	33¢ Cy Young		.65	.50			1.75	
n	33¢ Jimmie Foxx		.65	.50			1.75	
o	33¢ Pie Traynor		.65	.50			1.75	
p	33¢ Satchel Paige		.65	.50			1.75	
q	33¢ Honus Wagner		.65	.50			1.75	
r	33¢ Josh Gibson		.65	.50			1.75	
s	33¢ Dizzy Dean		.65	.50			1.75	
t	33¢ Lou Gehrig		.65	.50			1.75	
Space, Tagged, Perf. 10.5 x 11								
3409	Probing the Vastness of Space	07/10/00	12.50	7.00			6.00	2
a	60¢ Hubble Space Telescope		2.00	1.00			1.50	
b	60¢ Radio Interferometer Very Large Array, New Mexico		2.00	1.00			1.50	
c	60¢ Optical and Infrared Telescopes, Keck Observatory, Hawaii		2.00	1.00			1.50	
d	60¢ Optical Telescopes Cerro Tololo Observatory, Chile		2.00	1.00			1.50	
e	60¢ Optical Telescope, Mount Wilson Observatory, California		2.00	1.00			1.50	
f	60¢ Radio Telescope, Arecibo Observatory, Puerto Rico		2.00	1.00			1.50	
Space, Perf. 10.75								
3410	Exploring the Solar System	07/11/00	16.00	10.00			9.00	2
a	$1 Sun and Corona		3.00	1.75			2.00	
b	$1 Cross-section of Sun		3.00	1.75			2.00	
c	$1 Sun and Earth		3.00	1.75			2.00	
d	$1 Sun and Solar Flare		3.00	1.75			2.00	
e	$1 Sun and Clouds		3.00	1.75			2.00	
Space, Hologram, Untagged, Perf. 10.5, 10.75 (#3412)								
3411	Escaping the Gravity of Earth	07/09/00	21.00	10.00			9.50	2
a	$3.20 Space Shuttle and Space Station		10.00	4.00			3.75	
b	$3.20 Astronauts Working in Space		10.00	4.00			3.75	
3412	$11.75 Space Achievement and Exploration	07/07/00	37.50	17.50			17.50	2
a	$11.75 single		35.00	15.00				

Issue		Date	Un	U	PB	#	FDC	Q(M)
Space, Hologram, Untagged, Perf. 10.5 continued								
3413	$11.75 Landing on the Moon	07/08/00	37.50	17.50			17.50	2
a	$11.75 single		35.00	15.00				
d	Uncut sheet of 5 panes #3409-3412		124.50	62.00				
Stampin' The Future™, Tagged, Self-Adhesive, Serpentine Die-Cut 11.25								
3414	33¢ By Zachary Canter	07/13/00	.65	.20	5.25	(8)	1.25	
3415	33¢ By Sarah Lipsey	07/13/00	.65	.20	5.25	(8)	1.25	
3416	33¢ By Morgan Hill	07/13/00	.65	.20	5.25	(8)	1.25	
3417	33¢ By Ashley Young	07/13/00	.65	.20	5.25	(8)	1.25	
a	Horizontal Strip of 4, #3414-3417		2.60		5.25	(8)	3.25	100
Distinguished Americans, Tagged, Perf. 11								
3420	10¢ Joseph W. Stilwell	08/24/00	.20	.20	.80	(4)	1.50	100
a	Imperf, pair		500.00					
Distinguished Americans, Tagged, Self-Adhesive, Serpentine Die-Cut 11.25 x 10.75								
3422	23¢ Wilma Rudolph	07/14/04	.45	.20	1.80	(4)	1.25	
Distinguished Americans, Tagged, Perf. 11								
3426	33¢ Claude Pepper	09/07/00	.65	.20	2.60	(4)	1.25	56
Distinguished Americans, Tagged, Perf. 11								
3427	58¢ Margaret Chase Smith	06/13/07	1.25	.20	5.00	(4)	2.40	
3427A	59¢ James A. Michener	05/12/08	1.25	.20	5.00	(4)	2.40	
Distinguished Americans, Tagged, Self-Adhesive, Serpentine Die-Cut 11.25 x 11								
3428	63¢ Dr. Jonas Salk	03/08/06	1.25	.20	5.00	(4)	2.50	56
Distinguished Americans, Tagged, Self-Adhesive, Serpentine Die-Cut 11.25 x 10.75								
3430	75¢ Harriet Beecher Stowe	06/13/07	1.50	.20	6.00	(4)	2.75	56
Distinguished Americans, Tagged, Self-Adhesive, Serpentine Die-Cut 11								
3431	76¢ Hattie Caraway	02/21/01	1.50	.20	6.00	(4)	1.75	108
Distinguished Americans, Tagged, Self-Adhesive, Serpentine Die-Cut 11.5 x 11								
3432	76¢ Hattie Caraway	02/21/01	3.50	2.00	14.00	(4)		108
Distinguished Americans, Tagged, Self-Adhesive, Serpentine Die-Cut 11 x 11.75								
3432A	76¢ Edward Trudeau	05/12/08	1.50	.20	6.00	(4)	2.75	
3433	83¢ Edna Ferber	07/29/02	1.60	.30	6.50	(4)	1.75	108
Distinguished Americans, Tagged, Self-Adhesive, Serpentine Die-Cut 11.25								
3434	83¢ Edna Ferber	08/03	1.60	.30	6.50	(4)		108
3435	87¢ Dr. Albert Sabin	03/08/06	1.75	.30	7.00	(4)	3.00	56
Distinguished Americans, Booklet, Self-Adhesive, Serpentine Die-Cut 11.25 x 10.75								
3436	23¢ Wilma Rudolph	07/14/04	.45	.20			1.25	
a	Booklet pane of 4		1.80					

	Issue	Date	Un	U	PB/PNC	#	FDC	Q(M)
	Tagged, Self-Adhesive, Serpentine Die-Cut 11							
3438	33¢ California Statehood	09/08/00	.75	.20	3.00	(4)	1.25	53
	Deep Sea Creatures, Tagged, Perf. 10 x 10.25							
3439	33¢ Fanfin Anglerfish	10/02/00	.65	.20			1.25	17
3440	33¢ Sea Cucumber	10/02/00	.65	.20			1.25	17
3441	33¢ Fangtooth	10/02/00	.65	.20			1.25	17
3442	33¢ Amphipod	10/02/00	.65	.20			1.25	17
3443	33¢ Medusa	10/02/00	.65	.20			1.25	17
a	Vertical Strip 5, #3439-3443		3.25	2.00			3.75	
	Literary Arts, Tagged, Perf. 11							
3444	33¢ Thomas Wolfe	10/03/00	.65	.20	2.60	(4)	1.25	53
	Tagged, Self-Adhesive, Serpentine Die-Cut 11.25							
3445	33¢ White House	10/18/00	1.00	.20	4.00	(4)	1.25	125
	Legends of Hollywood, Tagged, Perf. 11							
3446	33¢ Edward G. Robinson	10/24/00	1.50	.20	7.00	(4)	1.75	52
	American Culture, Coil, Untagged, Serpentine Die-Cut 11.5 Vertically							
3447	(10¢) The New York Public Library	11/09/00	.20	.20	2.25	(5)	1.25	100
	Tagged, Perf. 11.25							
3448	(34¢) Flag Over Farm	12/15/00	.75	.20	3.25	(4)	1.25	25
	Self-Adhesive, Serpentine Die-Cut 11.25							
3449	(34¢) Flag Over Farm	12/15/00	1.00	.20	5.00	(4)	1.25	200
	Booklet, Self-Adhesive, Serpentine Die-Cut 8 on 2, 3 or 4 sides							
3450	(34¢) Flag Over Farm	12/15/00	.85	.20			1.25	
a	Booklet Pane of 18		16.00					300
	Booklet, Tagged, Self-Adhesive, Serpentine Die-Cut 11 on 2, 3 or 4 sides							
3451	34¢ Statue of Liberty	12/15/00	.70	.20			1.25	1.5
a	Booklet pane of 20		14.00					
	Coil, Perf. 9.75 Vertically							
3452	34¢ Statue of Liberty	12/15/00	.70	.20	5.00	(5)	1.25	200
	Coil, Self-Adhesive, Serpentine Die-Cut 10 Vertically							
3453	34¢ Statue of Liberty	12/15/00	.70	.20	6.50	(5)	1.25	
	Booklet, Tagged, Self-Adhesive, Serpentine Die-Cut 10.25 x 10.75 on 2 or 3 sides							
3454	(34¢) Purple Flower	12/15/00	1.00	.20			1.25	375
3455	(34¢) Tan Flower	12/15/00	1.00	.20			1.25	375
3456	(34¢) Green Flower	12/15/00	1.00	.20			1.25	375
3457	(34¢) Red Flower	12/15/00	1.00	.20			1.25	375
a	Block of 4		4.00				3.25	
b	Booklet pane of 4		4.00					
	Booklet, Self-Adhesive, Serpentine Die-Cut 11.5 x 11.75 on 2 or 3 sides							
3458	34¢ Purple Flower	12/15/00	3.00	.25			1.25	125
3459	34¢ Tan Flower	12/15/00	3.00	.25			1.25	125
3460	34¢ Green Flower	12/15/00	3.00	.25			1.25	125
3461	34¢ Red Flower	12/15/00	3.00	.25			1.25	125
a	Block of 4		12.00				3.25	
b	Booklet pane of 20, 2 each #3461a		36.50					

	Issue	Date	Un	U	PB/PNC	#	FDC	Q(M)
	Coil, Serpentine Die-Cut 8.5 Vertically							
3462	34¢ Green Flower	12/15/00	3.50	.20			1.25	125
3463	34¢ Red Flower	12/15/00	3.50	.20			1.25	125
3464	34¢ Tan Flower	12/15/00	3.50	.20			1.25	125
3465	34¢ Purple Flower	12/15/00	3.50	.20			1.25	125
a	Strip of 4		14.00		15.00	(5)	3.25	
	Coil, Tagged, Self-Adhesive, Serpentine Die-Cut 9.75 Vertically							
3466	34¢ Statue of Liberty	01/07/01	.70	.20	5.00	(5)	1.25	240
	Tagged, Perf. 11.25 x 11							
3467	21¢ American Buffalo	09/20/00	.50	.20	21.00	(4)	1.25	25
	Self-Adhesive, Serpentine Die-Cut 11							
3468	21¢ American Buffalo	02/22/01	.40	.20	1.60	(4)	1.25	25
	Self-Adhesive, Serpentine Die-Cut 11.25 x 11.75							
3468A	23¢ George Washington	09/20/01	.45	.20	1.80	(4)	1.25	25
	Perf. 11.25							
3469	34¢ Flag Over Farm	02/07/01	.75	.20	25.00	(4)	1.25	200
	Self-Adhesive, Serpentine Die-Cut 11.25							
3470	34¢ Flag Over Farm	03/06/01	.75	.20	3.00	(4)	1.25	204
	Self-Adhesive, Serpentine Die-Cut 10.75							
3471	55¢ Art Deco Eagle	02/22/01	1.10	.20	4.40	(4)	1.50	100
3471A	57¢ Art Deco Eagle	09/20/01	1.10	.20	4.40	(4)	1.50	100
	Self-Adhesive, Serpentine Die-Cut 11.25 x 11.5							
3472	$3.50 U. S. Capitol	01/29/01	7.00	2.00	28.00	(4)	6.25	125
	Self-Adhesive, Serpentine Die-Cut 11.25 x 11.5							
3473	$12.25 Washington Monument	01/29/01	22.50	10.00	90.00	(4)	15.00	35
	Coil, Self-Adhesive, Serpentine Die-Cut 8.5 Vertically							
3475	21¢ Buffalo	02/22/01	.50	.20	3.00	(5)	1.25	680
3475A	23¢ George Washington	09/20/01	.50	.20	3.00	(5)	1.25	680
	Perf. 9.75 Vertically							
3476	34¢ Statue of Liberty	02/07/01	.70	.20	5.00	(5)	1.25	379.8
	Self-Adhesive, Serpentine Die-Cut 9.75 Vertically							
3477	34¢ Statue of Liberty	02/07/01	.80	.20	5.00	(5)	1.25	281
	Coil, Self-Adhesive, Serpentine Die-Cut 8.5 Vertically							
3478	34¢ Green Flower	02/07/01	.70	.20			1.25	200
3479	34¢ Red Flower	02/07/01	.70	.20			1.25	200
3480	34¢ Tan Flower	02/07/01	.70	.20			1.25	200
3481	34¢ Purple Flower	02/07/01	.70	.20			1.25	200
a	Strip of 4, #3478-3481		2.80		5.50	(5)	3.25	
	Booklet, Self-Adhesive, Tagged, Serpentine Die-Cut 11.25 x 11 on 3 sides							
3482	20¢ George Washington	02/22/01	.45	.20			1.25	20.5
a	Booklet pane of 10		4.50					
b	Booklet pane of 4		1.80					

VISIT US ONLINE AT **THE POSTAL STORE**
AT **WWW.USPS.COM**
OR CALL **1 800 STAMP-24**

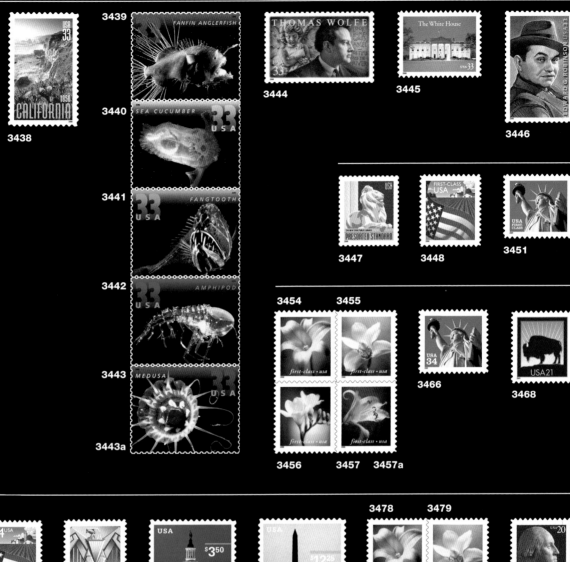

3438

3439 — FANFIN ANGLERFISH

3440 — SEA CUCUMBER

3441 — FANGTOOTH

3442 — AMPHIPOD

3443 — MEDUSA

3443a

3444

3445

3446

3447

3448

3451

3454 3455

3456 3457 3457a

3466

3468

3470

3471

3472

3473

3478 3479

3480 3481 3481a

3482

3491   3492   3492a

3497

3499

3500

3501

3503

The Nobel Prize
1901-2001

3504

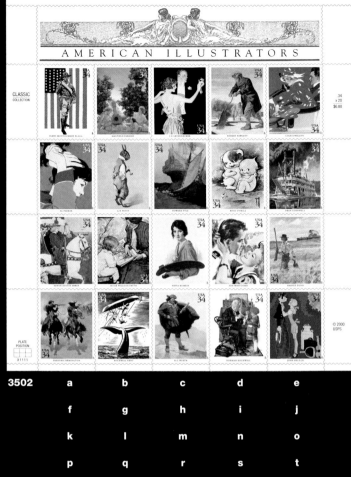

3502   a   b   c   d   e

f   g   h   i   j

k   l   m   n   o

p   q   r   s   t

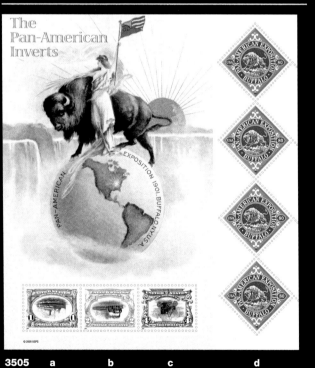

3505   a   b   c   d

3506   a   b   c   d   e   f

g   h   i   j

Issue		Date	Un	U	PB	#	FDC	Q(M)
Booklet, Serpentine Die-Cut 10.5 x 11.25 on 3 sides								
3483	20¢ George Washington	02/22/01	5.00	1.25			1.25	
a	Booklet pane of 4		12.00					
b	Booklet pane of 6		20.00					
c	Booklet pane of 10		25.00					
Serpentine Die-Cut 11.25 on 3 sides								
3484	20¢ American Buffalo	09/20/01	.50	.20			1.25	
b	Booklet pane of 4		2.00					
c	Booklet pane of 6		3.00					
d	Booklet pane of 10		5.00					
Serpentine Die-Cut 10.5 x 11.25								
3484A	20¢ American Buffalo	09/20/01	5.00	1.50			*1.25*	
Serpentine Die-Cut 11 on 2, 3 or 4 sides								
3485	34¢ Statue of Liberty	02/07/01	.70	.20			1.25	
a	Booklet pane of 10		7.00					
b	Booklet pane of 20		14.00					
c	Booklet pane of 4		3.00					
Self-Adhesive, Serpentine Die-Cut 10.25 x 10.75 on 2 or 3 sides								
3487	34¢ Purple Flower	02/07/01	.75	.20			1.25	
3488	34¢ Tan Flower	02/07/01	.75	.20			1.25	
3489	34¢ Green Flower	02/07/01	.75	.20			1.25	
3490	34¢ Red Flower	02/07/01	.75	.20			1.25	
a	Block of 4		3.00				3.25	
b	Booklet pane of 4		3.00					
c	Booklet pane of 6		4.50					
Serpentine Die-Cut 11.25 on 2, 3 or 4 sides								
3491	34¢ Apple	03/06/01	.70	.20			1.25	3
3492	34¢ Orange	03/06/01	.70	.20			1.25	3
a	Pair		1.40				2.25	
b	Booklet pane of 20		14.00					
Serpentine Die-Cut 11.5 x 10.75 on 2 or 3 sides								
3493	34¢ Apple	05/01	1.00	.20				101
3494	34¢ Orange	05/01	1.00	.20				101
a	Pair		2.00					
b	Booklet pane of 4		4.00					
c	Booklet pane of 6		6.00					
Serpentine Die-Cut 8 on 2 or 3 sides								
3495	34¢ Orange	12/17/01	.90	.20			1.25	101
a	Booklet pane of 18		16.50					
Love, Booklet, Tagged, Self-Adhesive, Serpentine Die-Cut 11.25 on 2, 3 or 4 sides								
3496	34¢ Rose and Love Letter	01/19/01	.90	.20			1.25	500
a	Booklet pane of 20		18.00					
Love, Serpentine Die-Cut 11.25 on 2, 3 or 4 sides								
3497	34¢ Rose and Love Letter	02/14/01	.90	.20			1.25	2
a	Booklet pane of 20		18.00					
Love, Self-Adhesive, Serpentine Die-Cut 11.5 x 10.75 on 2 or 3 sides								
3498	34¢ Rose and Love Letter	02/14/01	1.00	.20			1.25	80
a	Booklet pane of 4		4.00					
b	Booklet pane of 6		6.00					
Love, Serpentine Die-Cut 11.25								
3499	55¢ Rose and Love Letter	02/14/01	1.10	.20	4.50	(4)	1.50	180
Lunar New Year, Tagged, Perf. 11.25								
3500	34¢ Year of the Snake	01/20/01	.70	.20	2.80	(4)	1.75	55
Black Heritage, Tagged, Self-Adhesive, Serpentine Die-Cut 11.5 x 11.25								
3501	34¢ Roy Wilkins	01/24/01	.70	.20	2.80	(4)	1.25	200

Issue		Date	Un	U	PB	#	FDC	Q(M)
Classic Collections: American Illustrators, Tagged, Self-Adhesive, Serpentine Die-Cut 11.25								
3502	Pane of 20	02/01/01	17.50				9.50	145
a	34¢ James Montgomery Flagg		.85	.60			1.25	
b	34¢ Maxfield Parrish		.85	.60			1.25	
c	34¢ J. C. Leyendecker		.85	.60			1.25	
d	34¢ Robert Fawcett		.85	.60			1.25	
e	34¢ Coles Phillips		.85	.60			1.25	
f	34¢ Al Parker		.85	.60			1.25	
g	34¢ A. B. Frost		.85	.60			1.25	
h	34¢ Howard Pyle		.85	.60			1.25	
i	34¢ Rose O'Neill		.85	.60			1.25	
j	34¢ Dean Cornwell		.85	.60			1.25	
k	34¢ Edwin Austin Abbey		.85	.60			1.25	
l	34¢ Jessie Willcox Smith		.85	.60			1.25	
m	34¢ Neysa McMein		.85	.60			1.25	
n	34¢ Jon Whitcomb		.85	.60			1.25	
o	34¢ Harvey Dunn		.85	.60			1.25	
p	34¢ Frederic Remington		.85	.60			1.25	
q	34¢ Rockwell Kent		.85	.60			1.25	
r	34¢ N. C. Wyeth		.85	.60			1.25	
s	34¢ Norman Rockwell		.85	.60			1.25	
t	34¢ John Held, Jr.		.85	.60			1.25	
Tagged, Self-Adhesive, Serpentine Die-Cut 11.25 x 11.5								
3503	34¢ Diabetes Awareness	03/16/01	.65	.20	2.60	(4)	1.25	100
Tagged, Perf. 11								
3504	34¢ The Nobel Prize	03/22/01	.70	.20	2.80	(4)	1.50	35
The Pan-American Inverts, Untagged, Perf. 12.25 x 12 Tagged, Perf. 12 (#3505d)								
3505	34¢ Pane of 7	03/29/01	9.00	7.00			6.00	2
a	1¢ green		.60	.20			1.25	
b	2¢ carmine		.60	.20			1.25	
c	4¢ deep red brown		.60	.20			1.25	
d	80¢ red & blue		1.75	.35			1.75	
Nature of America: Great Plains Prairie, Tagged, Self-Adhesive, Serpentine Die-Cut 10								
3506	Pane of 10	04/19/01	11.00				7.00	90
a	34¢ Pronghorns, Canada geese		1.00	.50				
b	34¢ Burrowing owls, American buffalo		1.00	.50				
c	34¢ American buffalo, Black-tailed prairie dogs, wild alfalfa		1.00	.50				
d	34¢ Black-tailed prairie dog, American buffalo		1.00	.50				
e	34¢ Painted lady butterfly, American buffalo, prairie coneflowers, prairie wild roses		1.00	.50				
f	34¢ Western meadowlark, camel cricket, prairie coneflowers, prairie wild roses		1.00	.50				
g	34¢ Badger, harvester ants		1.00	.50				
h	34¢ Eastern short-horned lizard, plains pocket gopher		1.00	.50				
i	34¢ Plains spadefoot, dung beetle, prairie wild roses		1.00	.50				
j	34¢ Two-stripped grasshopper, Ord's kangaroo rat		1.00	.50				

	Issue	Date	Un	U	PB	#	FDC	Q(M)
	Peanuts Comic Strip, Tagged, Self-Adhesive, Serpentine Die-Cut 11.25 x 11.5							
3507	34¢ Snoopy	05/17/01	.75	.20	3.00	(4)	1.50	125
	Tagged, Self-Adhesive, Serpentine Die-Cut 11.25 x 11.5							
3508	34¢ Honoring Veterans	05/23/01	.70	.20	2.80	(4)	1.25	200
	Artists, Tagged, Perf. 11.25							
3509	34¢ Frida Kahlo	06/21/01	.70	.20	2.80	(4)	1.25	55
	Baseball's Legendary Playing Fields, Self-Adhesive, Serpentine Die-Cut, Perf. 11.25 x 11.5							
3510	34¢ Ebbets Field, Brooklyn	06/27/01	.90	.60			1.50	
3511	34¢ Tiger Stadium, Detroit	06/27/01	.90	.60			1.50	
3512	34¢ Crosley Field, Cincinnati	06/27/01	.90	.60			1.50	
3513	34¢ Yankee Stadium, New York City	06/27/01	.90	.60			1.50	
3514	34¢ Polo Grounds, New York City	06/27/01	.90	.60			1.50	
3515	34¢ Forbes Field, Pittsburgh	06/27/01	.90	.60			1.50	
3516	34¢ Fenway Park, Boston	06/27/01	.90	.60			1.50	
3517	34¢ Comiskey Park, Chicago	06/27/01	.90	.60			1.50	
3518	34¢ Shibe Park, Philadelphia	06/27/01	.90	.60			1.50	
3519	34¢ Wrigley Field, Chicago	06/27/01	.90	.60			1.50	
a	Block of 10, #3510-3519		9.00		9.00	(10)	6.50	125
	American Culture, Untagged, Self-Adhesive, Serpentine Die-Cut 8.5 Vertically							
3520	10¢ *Atlas* Statue	06/29/01	.20	.20	2.25	(5)	1.25	400
	Tagged, Perf. 11.25							
3521	34¢ Leonard Bernstein	07/10/01	.70	.20	2.80	(4)	1.25	55
	American Culture, Coil, Untagged, Self-Adhesive, Serpentine Die-Cut 11.5 Vertically							
3522	15¢ Woody Wagon	08/03/01	.30	.20	3.00	(5)	1.25	160
	Legends of Hollywood, Tagged, Self-Adhesive, Serpentine Die-Cut 11							
3523	34¢ Lucille Ball	08/06/01	1.00	.20	4.50	(4)	2.00	110
	American Treasures: Amish Quilts, Tagged, Self-Adhesive, Serpentine Die-Cut 11.25 x 11.5							
3524	34¢ Diamond in the Square	08/09/01	.70	.20			1.25	
3525	34¢ Lone Star	08/09/01	.70	.20			1.25	
3526	34¢ Sunshine and Shadow	08/09/01	.70	.20			1.25	
3527	34¢ Double Ninepatch	08/09/01	.70	.20			1.25	
a	Block or strip of 4 #3524-3527		2.80		2.80	(4)	3.25	96
	Carnivorous Plants, Self-Adhesive, Serpentine Die-Cut 11.5							
3528	34¢ Venus Flytrap	08/23/01	.70	.20			1.25	
3529	34¢ Yellow Trumpet	08/23/01	.70	.20			1.25	
3530	34¢ Cobra Lily	08/23/01	.70	.20			1.25	
3531	34¢ English Sundew	08/23/01	.70	.20			1.25	
a	Block or strip of 4 #3528-3531		2.80		2.80	(4)	3.25	100

	Issue	Date	Un	U	PB	#	FDC	Q(M)
	Holiday Celebrations, Tagged, Self-Adhesive, Serpentine Die-Cut 11.25							
3532	34¢ Eid	09/01/01	.70	.20	2.80	(4)	1.25	75
	Tagged, Perf. 11							
3533	34¢ Enrico Fermi	09/29/01	.70	.20	2.80	(4)	1.25	30
	Looney Tunes, Tagged, Self-Adhesive, Serpentine Die-Cut 11							
3534	Porky Pig "That's all Folks!" Pane of 10	10/01/01	7.00					
a	34¢ Single		.70	.20			1.25	275
3535	Porky Pig "That's all Folks!" Pane of 10		60.00					
a	34¢ Single, die-cutting extends through backing paper		3.00				1.25	275
c	Booklet Pane of 1, no die-cutting		30.00					
	Holiday Celebration: Christmas, Tagged, Self-Adhesive, Serpentine Die-Cut 11.5 on 2, 3 or 4 sides							
3536	34¢ Madonna and Child by Lorenzo Costa	10/10/01	.75	.20			1.25	800
a	Booklet pane of 20		15.00					
	Holiday Celebration: Holiday, Tagged, Self-Adhesive, Serpentine Die-Cut 10.75 x 11 (Black inscriptions)							
3537	34¢ Santa wearing tan hood	10/10/01	.70	.20			1.25	
3538	34¢ Santa wearing blue hat	10/10/01	.70	.20			1.25	
3539	34¢ Santa wearing red hat	10/10/01	.70	.20			1.25	
3540	34¢ Santa wearing gold hood	10/10/01	.70	.20			1.25	
b	Block of 4 #3537-3540		2.80		2.80	(4)	3.25	125
	Holiday Celebration: Holiday, Tagged, Self-Adhesive, Serpentine Die-Cut 11 on 2 or 3 sides (Red & green inscriptions)							
3541	34¢ Santa wearing tan hood	10/10/01	.70	.20			1.25	
3542	34¢ Santa wearing blue hat	10/10/01	.70	.20			1.25	
3543	34¢ Santa wearing red hat	10/10/01	.70	.20			1.25	
3544	34¢ Santa wearing gold hood	10/10/01	.70	.20			1.25	
a	Block of 4 #3541-3544		2.80		2.80	(4)	3.25	201
	Tagged, Self-Adhesive, Serpentine Die-Cut 11 x 11.25							
3545	34¢ James Madison	10/18/01	.70	.20	2.80	(4)	1.25	32
	Holiday Celebrations, Tagged, Self-Adhesive, Serpentine Die-Cut 11.25							
3546	34¢ We Give Thanks	10/19/01	.70	.20	2.80	(4)	1.25	69
	Holiday Celebrations, Tagged, Self-Adhesive, Serpentine Die-Cut 11							
3547	34¢ Hanukkah	10/21/01	.70	.20	2.80	(4)	1.25	49
3548	34¢ Kwanzaa	10/21/01	.70	.20	2.80	(4)	1.25	40
	Tagged, Self-Adhesive, Serpentine Die-Cut 11.25 on 2, 3 or 4 sides							
3549	34¢ United We Stand	10/24/01	.75	.20			1.50	70
a	Booklet pane of 20		15.00					
	Tagged, Self-Adhesive, Serpentine Die-Cut 10.5 x 10.75 on 2 or 3 sides							
3549B	34¢ United We Stand	01/02	.90	.20				70
c	Booklet pane of 4		3.60					
d	Booklet pane of 6		5.40					

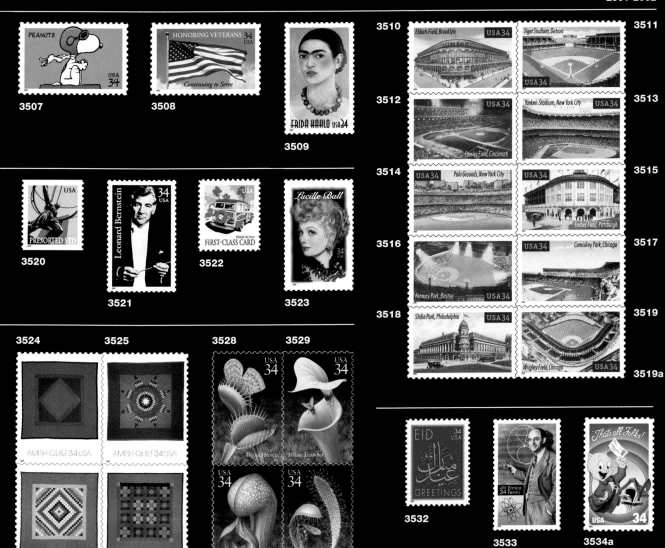

3507
3508
3509

3520
3521
3522
3523

3524   3525   3528   3529
3526   3527   3527a   3530   3531   3531a

3510
3511
3512
3513
3514
3515
3516
3517
3518
3519
3519a

3532
3533
3534a

3536

3541   3542
3543   3544   3544a

3545

3546

3547

3548

3549

3552   **3553**

SKI JUMPING USA

SNOWBOARDING USA

ICE HOCKEY USA

FIGURE SKATING USA

3554   **3555**   **3555a**

MENTORING A CHILD 34 USA

VALUES · GOALS · SKILLS

3556

BLACK HERITAGE
USA 34

Langston Hughes

3557

HAPPY BIRTHDAY 34 USA

3558

HAPPY NEW YEAR!
USA 34

3559

UNITED STATES
1802 2002 USA 34
MILITARY ACADEMY

3560

Greetings from ALABAMA · Greetings from ALASKA · 34 USA ARIZONA · Greetings from ARKANSAS 34 · Greetings from CALIFORNIA

Greetings from COLORADO · Greetings from CONNECTICUT · Greetings from DELAWARE · FLORIDA · Greetings from GEORGIA 34 USA

34 Greetings from HAWAII · GREETINGS FROM IDAHO USA · GREETINGS FROM ILLINOIS 34 · Greetings from INDIANA 34 · Greetings from IOWA USA 34

Greetings from KANSAS 34 · 34 Greetings from KENTUCKY · Greetings from LOUISIANA · Greetings from MAINE · Greetings from MARYLAND USA 34

GREETINGS FROM MASSACHUSETTS 34 USA · Greetings from MICHIGAN 34 USA · 34 USA Greetings from MINNESOTA · GREETINGS FROM MISSISSIPPI · Greetings from MISSOURI

.34 x50 $17.00   © 2001 USPS

Greetings from MONTANA USA 34 · Greetings from NEBRASKA · Greetings from NEVADA USA 34 · Greetings from NEW HAMPSHIRE USA 34 · Greetings from NEW JERSEY USA

GREETINGS FROM NEW MEXICO USA · GREETINGS FROM NEW YORK 34 · Greetings from NORTH CAROLINA · Greetings from NORTH DAKOTA 34 USA · Greetings from OHIO 34 USA

Greetings from OKLAHOMA · Greetings from OREGON 34 · Greetings from PENNSYLVANIA · Greetings from RHODE ISLAND 34 · Greetings from SOUTH CAROLINA

Greetings from SOUTH DAKOTA 34 · Greetings from TENNESSEE · Greetings from TEXAS · 34 USA Greetings from UTAH · Greetings from VERMONT USA 34

Greetings from VIRGINIA USA · GREETINGS FROM WASHINGTON USA 34 · Greetings from WEST VIRGINIA · Greetings from WISCONSIN 34 USA · Greetings from WYOMING 34 USA

X1111   PLATE POSITION   X1111

3610a	3561	3562	3563	3564	3565
	3566	3567	3568	3569	3570
	3571	3572	3573	3574	3575
	3576	3577	3578	3579	3580
	3581	3582	3583	3584	3585
	3586	3587	3588	3589	3590
	3591	3592	3593	3594	3595
	3596	3597	3598	3599	3600
	3601	3602	3603	3604	3605
	3606	3607	3608	3609	3610

Issue		Date	Un	U	PB	#	FDC	Q(M)
	Coil, Tagged, Self-Adhesive, Serpentine Die-Cut 9.75 Vertically							
3550	34¢ United We Stand, perpendicular corners	10/24/01	.95	.20	6.00	(5)		
3550A	34¢ United We Stand	10/24/01	1.10	.20	6.50	(5)	1.80 (5)	
	Tagged, Self-Adhesive, Serpentine Die-Cut 11.25							
3551	57¢ Rose and Love Letter	11/19/01	1.10	.20	5.00	(4)	1.50	100
	Olympic Games, Winter, Tagged, Self-Adhesive, Serpentine Die-Cut 11.5 x 10.75							
3552	34¢ Ski Jumping	01/08/02	.70	.20	2.60	(4)	1.25	79.64
3553	34¢ Snowboarding	01/08/02	.70	.20	2.60	(4)	1.25	79.64
3554	34¢ Ice Hockey	01/08/02	.70	.20	2.60	(4)	1.25	79.64
3555	34¢ Figure Skating	01/08/02	.70	.20	2.60	(4)	1.25	79.64
a	Block or strip of 4	01/08/02	2.80		3.00	(4)	3.25	
	Tagged, Self-Adhesive, Serpentine Die-Cut 11 x 10.75							
3556	34¢ Mentoring a Child	01/10/02	.70	.20	2.80	(4)	1.25	132.6
	Black Heritage, Tagged, Self-Adhesive, Serpentine Die-Cut 10.25 x 10.5							
3557	34¢ Langston Hughes	02/01/02	.70	.20	3.00	(4)	1.25	120
	Tagged, Self-Adhesive, Serpentine Die-Cut 11							
3558	34¢ Happy Birthday	02/08/02	.70	.20	2.80	(4)	1.25	79.6
	Lunar New Year, Tagged, Self-Adhesive, Serpentine Die-Cut 10.5 x 10.25							
3559	34¢ Year of the Horse	02/11/02	.75	.20	3.00	(4)	1.50	70
	Tagged, Self-Adhesive, Serpentine Die-Cut 10.5 x 11							
3560	34¢ U.S. Military Academy	03/16/02	.70	.20	2.80	(4)	1.75	55
	Greetings From America, Tagged, Self-Adhesive, Serpentine Die-Cut 10.75							
3561	34¢ Alabama	04/04/02	.70	.45			1.25	190
3562	34¢ Alaska	04/04/02	.70	.45			1.25	190
3563	34¢ Arizona	04/04/02	.70	.45			1.25	190
3564	34¢ Arkansas	04/04/02	.70	.45			1.25	190
3565	34¢ California	04/04/02	.70	.45			1.25	190
3566	34¢ Colorado	04/04/02	.70	.45			1.25	190
3567	34¢ Connecticut	04/04/02	.70	.45			1.25	190
3568	34¢ Delaware	04/04/02	.70	.45			1.25	190
3569	34¢ Florida	04/04/02	.70	.45			1.25	190
3570	34¢ Georgia	04/04/02	.70	.45			1.25	190
3571	34¢ Hawaii	04/04/02	.70	.45			1.25	190
3572	34¢ Idaho	04/04/02	.70	.45			1.25	190
3573	34¢ Illinois	04/04/02	.70	.45			1.25	190
3574	34¢ Indiana	04/04/02	.70	.45			1.25	190

Issue		Date	Un	U	PB	#	FDC	Q(M)
	Greetings From America continued							
3575	34¢ Iowa	04/04/02	.70	.45			1.25	190
3576	34¢ Kansas	04/04/02	.70	.45			1.25	190
3577	34¢ Kentucky	04/04/02	.70	.45			1.25	190
3578	34¢ Louisiana	04/04/02	.70	.45			1.25	190
3579	34¢ Maine	04/04/02	.70	.45			1.25	190
3580	34¢ Maryland	04/04/02	.70	.45			1.25	190
3581	34¢ Massachusetts	04/04/02	.70	.45			1.25	190
3582	34¢ Michigan	04/04/02	.70	.45			1.25	190
3583	34¢ Minnesota	04/04/02	.70	.45			1.25	190
3584	34¢ Mississippi	04/04/02	.70	.45			1.25	190
3585	34¢ Missouri	04/04/02	.70	.45			1.25	190
3586	34¢ Montana	04/04/02	.70	.45			1.25	190
3587	34¢ Nebraska	04/04/02	.70	.45			1.25	190
3588	34¢ Nevada	04/04/02	.70	.45			1.25	190
3589	34¢ New Hampshire	04/04/02	.70	.45			1.25	190
3590	34¢ New Jersey	04/04/02	.70	.45			1.25	190
3591	34¢ New Mexico	04/04/02	.70	.45			1.25	190
3592	34¢ New York	04/04/02	.70	.45			1.25	190
3593	34¢ North Carolina	04/04/02	.70	.45			1.25	190
3594	34¢ North Dakota	04/04/02	.70	.45			1.25	190
3595	34¢ Ohio	04/04/02	.70	.45			1.25	190
3596	34¢ Oklahoma	04/04/02	.70	.45			1.25	190
3597	34¢ Oregon	04/04/02	.70	.45			1.25	190
3598	34¢ Pennsylvania	04/04/02	.70	.45			1.25	190
3599	34¢ Rhode Island	04/04/02	.70	.45			1.25	190
3600	34¢ South Carolina	04/04/02	.70	.45			1.25	190
3601	34¢ South Dakota	04/04/02	.70	.45			1.25	190
3602	34¢ Tennessee	04/04/02	.70	.45			1.25	190
3603	34¢ Texas	04/04/02	.70	.45			1.25	190
3604	34¢ Utah	04/04/02	.70	.45			1.25	190
3605	34¢ Vermont	04/04/02	.70	.45			1.25	190
3606	34¢ Virginia	04/04/02	.70	.45			1.25	190
3607	34¢ Washington	04/04/02	.70	.45			1.25	190
3608	34¢ West Virginia	04/04/02	.70	.45			1.25	190
3609	34¢ Wisconsin	04/04/02	.70	.45			1.25	190
3610	34¢ Wyoming	04/04/02	.70	.45			1.25	190
a	Pane of 50, #3561-3610		35.00				32.50	

PURPLE HEART

The Purple Heart stamp, first issued by the U.S. Postal Service in 2003, honors the sacrifices of the men and women who serve in the U.S. military. The Purple Heart is awarded in the name of the President of the United States to members of the U.S. military who have been wounded or killed in action. According to the Military Order of the Purple Heart, an organization for combat-wounded veterans, the medal is "the oldest military decoration in the world in present use and the first award made available to a common soldier." ■ On August 7, 1782, during the Revolutionary War, General George Washington issued an order establishing a badge of distinction for meritorious action. The badge—a heart made of purple cloth—was known as the Badge of Military Merit. The award was distinctive because it was available to the lower ranks at a time when only officers were eligible for decoration in European armies. "The road to glory in a patriot army," Washington wrote, "is thus open to all." ■ The decoration was not continued after the Revolutionary War, but its reinstatement was announced by the U.S. War Department (now the Department of Defense) on February 22, 1932, the 200th anniversary of Washington's birth. The redesigned decoration consists of a purple heart of metal bordered by gold and suspended from a purple and white ribbon. In the center of the medal is a profile bust of George Washington beneath his family coat of arms. The words "For Military Merit" appear on the reverse.

Issue		Date	Un	U	PB	#	FDC	Q(M)
Nature of America: Longleaf Pine Forest, Tagged, Self-Adhesive, Serpentine Die-Cut 10.5 x 10.75, 10.75 x 10.5								
3611	Wildlife and Flowers, Pane of 10	04/26/02	16.00				7.00	70
a	34¢ Bachman's Sparrow		1.60	.50			1.25	
b	34¢ Northern Bobwhite, Yellow Pitcher Plants		1.60	.50			1.25	
c	34¢ Fox Squirrel, Red-bellied Woodpecker		1.60	.50			1.25	
d	34¢ Brown-headed Nuthatch		1.60	.50			1.25	
e	34¢ Broadhead Skink, Yellow Pitcher Plants, Pipeworts		1.60	.50			1.25	
f	34¢ Eastern Towhee, Yellow Pitcher Plants, Savannah Meadow Beauties, Toothache Grass		1.60	.50			1.25	
g	34¢ Gray Fox, Gopher Tortoise, horiz.		1.60	.50			1.25	
h	34¢ Blind Click Beetle, Sweetbay, Pine Woods Treefrog		1.60	.50			1.25	
i	34¢ Rosebud Orchid, Pipeworts, Southern Toad, Yellow Pitcher Plants		1.60	.50			1.25	
j	34¢ Grass-pink Orchid, Yellow-sided Skimmer, Pipeworts, Yellow Pitcher Plants, horiz.		1.60	.50			1.25	70
American Design, Coil, Untagged, Perf. 10 Vertically								
3612	5¢ American Toleware	05/31/02	.20	.20	1.25	(5)	1.25	300
Untagged, Self-Adhesive, Serpentine Die-Cut 11								
3613	3¢ Star (year at lower left)	06/07/02	.20	.20	.25	(4)	1.25	
Self-Adhesive, Serpentine Die-Cut 10								
3614	3¢ Star (year at lower right)	06/07/02	.20	.20	.25	(4)	1.25	
Coil, Perf. 10 Vertically								
3615	3¢ Star (year at lower left)	06/07/02	.20	.20	.85	(5)	1.25	
Tagged, Perf. 11.25								
3616	23¢ George Washington (green)	06/07/02	.50	.20	17.50	(4)	1.00	25
Coil, Self-Adhesive, Serpentine Die-Cut 8.5 Vertically								
3617	23¢ George Washington (gray green)	06/07/02	.45	.20	3.00	(5)	1.00	
Booklet, Self-Adhesive Serpentine Die-Cut 11.25 on 3 sides								
3618	23¢ George Washington (green)	06/07/02	.45	.20			1.00	496
a	Booklet pane of 4		1.80					
Self-Adhesive, Serpentine Die-Cut 10. 5 x 11.25 on 3 sides								
3619	23¢ George Washington (green)	06/07/02	3.00	1.75				41
a	Booklet pane of 4		6.50					
Tagged, Perf. 11.25 x 11								
3620	(37¢) U.S. Flag (First Class)	06/07/02	.85	.20	25.00	(4)	1.25	
Self-Adhesive, Serpentine Die-Cut 11.25 x 11								
3621	(37¢) U.S. Flag (First Class)	06/07/02	1.00	.20	7.50	(4)	1.25	
Coil, Self-Adhesive, Serpentine Die-Cut 10 Vertically								
3622	(37¢) U.S. Flag (First Class)	06/07/02	.75	.20	6.50	(5)	1.25	
Booklet, Self-Adhesive, Serpentine Die-Cut 11.25 on 2, 3 or 4 sides								
3623	(37¢) U.S. Flag (First Class)	06/07/02	.75	.20			1.25	
a	Booklet pane of 20		15.00					
Booklet, Self-Adhesive, Serpentine Die-Cut 10.5 x 10.75 on 2 or 3 sides								
3624	(37¢) U.S. Flag (First Class)	06/07/02	.75	.20			1.25	
a	Booklet pane of 4		3.00					
Booklet, Self-Adhesive, Serpentine Die-Cut 8 on 2, 3 or 4 sides								
3625	(37¢) U.S. Flag (First Class)	06/07/02	.75	.20			1.25	
a	Booklet pane of 18		13.50					
Antique Toys, Booklet, Self-Adhesive, Serpentine Die-Cut 11 on 2, 3 or 4 sides								
3626	(37¢) Toy Mail Wagon	06/07/02	.75	.20			1.25	120
3627	(37¢) Toy Locomotive	06/07/02	.75	.20			1.25	120
3628	(37¢) Toy Taxicab	06/07/02	.75	.20			1.25	120
3629	(37¢) Toy Fire Pumper	06/07/02	.75	.20			1.25	120
a	Block of 4		3.00				3.25	

Issue		Date	Un	U	PB	#	FDC	Q(M)
Tagged, Perf. 11.25								
3629F	37¢ U.S. Flag	11/24/03	.90	.20	25.00	(4)	1.25	120
Self-Adhesive, Serpentine Die-Cut 11.25 x 11								
3630	37¢ U.S. Flag	06/07/02	.90	.20	5.00	(4)	1.25	300
Coil, Perf. 10 Vertically								
3631	37¢ U.S. Flag	06/07/02	.95	.20	6.00	(5)	1.25	
Coil, Self-Adhesive, Serpentine Die-Cut 9.75 Vertically								
3632	37¢ U.S. Flag	06/07/02	.75	.20	4.75	(5)	1.25	
Coil, Self-Adhesive, Serpentine Die-Cut 10.25 Vertically								
3632A	37¢ U.S. Flag	08/07/03	.75	.20	5.25	(5)	1.25	
Coil, Self-Adhesive, Serpentine Die-Cut 11.75 Vertically								
3632C	37¢ U.S. Flag	06/07/02	.75	.20	5.50	(5)	1.25	
Coil, Self-Adhesive, Serpentine Die-Cut 8.5 Vertically								
3633	37¢ U.S. Flag	06/07/02	.75	.20	5.00	(5)	1.25	
3633A	37¢ U.S. Flag	04/03	2.00	.20	11.00	(5)	1.25	
3633B	37¢ U.S. Flag	06/07/05	3.00	.20	22.50	(5)	1.25	
Booklet, Serpentine Die-Cut 11 on 3 sides								
3634	37¢ U.S. Flag	06/07/02	.75	.20			1.25	
a	Booklet pane of 10		7.50					
Booklet, Self-Adhesive, Serpentine Die-Cut 11.25 on 2, 3 or 4 sides								
3635	37¢ U.S. Flag	06/07/02	.75	.20			1.25	
a	Booklet pane of 20		15.00					
Booklet, Serpentine Die-Cut 10.5 x 10.75 on 2 or 3 sides								
3636	37¢ U.S. Flag	06/07/02	.75	.20			1.25	
a	Booklet pane of 4		3.00					
Booklet, Tagged, Self-Adhesive, Serpentine Die-Cut 11.25 x 11 on 2 or 3 sides								
3636D	37¢ U.S. Flag (type of 2002)	07/04	.90	.20			1.25	
Booklet, Self-Adhesive, Serpentine Die-Cut 8 on 2, 3 or 4 sides								
3637	37¢ U.S. Flag	02/04/03	.75	.20			1.25	
a	Booklet pane of 18		13.50					
Antique Toys, Coil, Tagged, Self-Adhesive, Serpentine Die-Cut 8.5 Horizontally								
3638	37¢ Toy Locomotive	07/26/02	.85	.20			1.25	
3639	37¢ Toy Mail Wagon	07/26/02	.85	.20			1.25	
3640	37¢ Toy Fire Pumper	07/26/02	.85	.20			1.25	
3641	37¢ Toy Taxicab	07/26/02	.85	.20			1.25	
a	Strip of 4		3.40		5.00	(5)		3.25
Antique Toys, Booklet, Self-Adhesive, Serpentine Die-Cut 11 on 2, 3 or 4 sides								
3642	37¢ Toy Mail Wagon	07/26/02	.75	.20			1.25	
a	Serpentine Die-Cut 11 x 11.25 on 2 or 3 sides dated "2003"		.75	.20			1.25	
3643	37¢ Toy Locomotive	07/26/02	.75	.20			1.25	
a	Serpentine Die-Cut 11 x 11.25 on 2 or 3 sides dated "2003"		.75	.20			1.25	
3644	37¢ Toy Taxicab	07/26/02	.75	.20			1.25	
a	Serpentine Die-Cut 11 x 11.25 on 2 or 3 sides dated "2003"		.75	.20			1.25	
3645	37¢ Toy Fire Pumper	07/26/02	.75	.20			1.25	
a	Block of 4 #3642-#3645		3.00				3.25	
Tagged, Self-Adhesive, Serpentine Die-Cut 11 x 11.25								
3646	60¢ Coverlet Eagle	07/12/02	1.25	.25	5.00	(4)	1.50	100
Tagged, Self-Adhesive, Serpentine Die-Cut 11.25								
3647	$3.85 Jefferson Memorial	07/30/02	7.50	2.00	30.00	(4)	7.00	68
Tagged, Self-Adhesive, Serpentine Die-Cut 11 x 10.75								
3647A	$3.85 Jefferson Memorial (2003)	11/03	8.50	2.00	35.00	(4)	7.00	68
Tagged, Self-Adhesive, Serpentine Die-Cut 11.25								
3648	$13.65 Capitol Dome	07/30/02	27.50	10.00	110.00	(4)	25.00	23

LONGLEAF PINE FOREST

FOURTH IN A SERIES

N A T U R E   O F   A M E R I C A

3611
a
b
c
d
e
f
g
h
i
j

3612

3613

3616

3620

3626

3627

3628

3629

3629a

3630

3646

3647

3648

MASTERS OF
American Photography

3649   a   b   c   d   e

f   g   h   i   j

k   l   m   n   o

p   q   r   s   t

John James Audubon

3650

HOUDINI

3651

Andy Warhol   USA **37**

3652

3653   **3654**

Teddy Bears USA 37   Teddy Bears USA 37

Teddy Bears USA 37   Teddy Bears USA 37

3655   **3656**   **3656a**

LOVE 37 USA

3657

LOVE 60 USA

3658

OGDEN NASH

3659

USA 37

DUKE KAHANAMOKU

3660

3661   **3662**

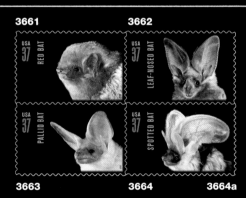

USA 37 RED BAT   USA 37 LEAF-NOSED BAT

USA 37 PALLID BAT   USA 37 SPOTTED BAT

3663   **3664**   **3664a**

3668   **3666**

37 USA Marguerite Higgins   37 USA Ida M. Tarbell

37 USA Ethel L. Payne   Nellie Bly 37

USA 37 IRVING BERLIN

3669

Spay   USA   Spay   USA

Neuter 37   Neuter 37

3670   **3671**

3667   **3665**   **3668a**

Issue		Date	Un	U	PB	#	FDC	Q(M)
Masters of American Photography, Tagged, Self-Adhesive Serpentine Die-Cut 10.5 x 10.75								
3649	Pane of 20	06/13/02	15.00				10.00	63
a	37¢ Southworth & Hawes		.75	.50			1.25	
b	37¢ Timothy H. O'Sullivan		.75	.50			1.25	
c	37¢ Carleton E. Watkins		.75	.50			1.25	
d	37¢ Gertrude Käsebier		.75	.50			1.25	
e	37¢ Lewis W. Hine		.75	.50			1.25	
f	37¢ Alvin Langdon Coburn		.75	.50			1.25	
g	37¢ Edward Steichen		.75	.50			1.25	
h	37¢ Alfred Stieglitz		.75	.50			1.25	
i	37¢ Man Ray		.75	.50			1.25	
j	37¢ Edward Weston		.75	.50			1.25	
k	37¢ James VanDerZee		.75	.50			1.25	
l	37¢ Dorothea Lange		.75	.50			1.25	
m	37¢ Walker Evans		.75	.50			1.25	
n	37¢ W. Eugene Smith		.75	.50			1.25	
o	37¢ Paul Strand		.75	.50			1.25	
p	37¢ Ansel Adams		.75	.50			1.25	
q	37¢ Imogen Cunningham		.75	.50			1.25	
r	37¢ André Kertész		.75	.50			1.25	
s	37¢ Garry Winogrand		.75	.50			1.25	
t	37¢ Minor White		.75	.50			1.25	
American Treasures, Self-Adhesive, Serpentine Die-Cut 10.75								
3650	37¢ John James Audubon	06/27/02	1.00	.20	6.00	(4)	1.25	70
Tagged, Self-Adhesive, Serpentine Die-Cut 11.25								
3651	37¢ Harry Houdini	07/03/02	.75	.20	3.00	(4)	1.50	61
Artists, Tagged, Self-Adhesive, Serpentine Die-Cut 10.5 x 10.75								
3652	37¢ Andy Warhol	08/09/02	.75	.20	3.00	(4)	1.25	61

Issue		Date	Un	U	PB	#	FDC	Q(M)
Tagged, Self-Adhesive, Serpentine Die-Cut 10.5								
3653	37¢ Bruin Teddy Bear	08/15/02	1.00	.20			1.25	
3654	37¢ "Stick" Teddy Bear	08/15/02	1.00	.20			1.25	
3655	37¢ Gund Teddy Bear	08/15/02	1.00	.20			1.25	
3656	37¢ Ideal Teddy Bear	08/15/02	1.00	.20			1.25	
a	Block or vertical strip of 4		4.00		5.00	(4)	3.25	211
Love, Tagged, Booklet, Self-Adhesive, Serpentine Die-Cut 11 on 2, 3 or 4 sides								
3657	37¢ Love	08/16/02	.75	.20			1.25	805
a	Booklet pane of 20		15.00					
Love, Self-Adhesive, Serpentine Die-Cut 11								
3658	60¢ Love	08/16/02	1.25	.25	5.00	(4)	1.50	75
Literary Arts, Tagged, Self-Adhesive, Serpentine Die-Cut 11								
3659	37¢ Ogden Nash	08/19/02	.75	.20	3.00	(4)	1.25	60
Tagged, Self-Adhesive, Serpentine Die-Cut 11.5 x 11.75								
3660	37¢ Duke Kahanamoku	08/24/02	.75	.20	3.00	(4)	1.25	63
American Bats, Tagged, Self-Adhesive, Serpentine Die-Cut 10.75								
3661	37¢ Red Bat	09/13/02	.75	.20			1.25	
3662	37¢ Leaf-nosed Bat	09/13/02	.75	.20			1.25	
3663	37¢ Pallid Bat	09/13/02	.75	.20			1.25	
3664	37¢ Spotted Bat	09/13/02	.75	.20			1.25	
a	Block or horizontal strip of 4		3.00		3.25	(4)	3.25	111
Women in Journalism, Tagged, Self-Adhesive, Serpentine Die-Cut 11 x 10.5								
3665	37¢ Nellie Bly	09/14/02	.75	.20			1.25	
3666	37¢ Ida M. Tarbell	09/14/02	.75	.20			1.25	
3667	37¢ Ethel L. Payne	09/14/02	.75	.20			1.25	
3668	37¢ Marguerite Higgins	09/14/02	.75	.20			1.25	
a	Block or horizontal strip of 4		3.00		3.25	(4)	3.25	61
3669	37¢ Irving Berlin	09/15/02	.75	.20	3.00	(4)	1.25	61
Tagged, Self-Adhesive, Serpentine Die-Cut 10.75 x 10.5								
3670	37¢ Neuter & Spay (Kitten)	09/20/02	1.00	.20			2.25	85
3671	37¢ Neuter & Spay (Puppy)	09/20/02	1.00	.20			2.25	85
a	Horizontal or vertical pair		2.00		4.00	(4)		

POLAR BEAR

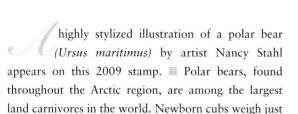

highly stylized illustration of a polar bear *(Ursus maritimus)* by artist Nancy Stahl appears on this 2009 stamp. ■ Polar bears, found throughout the Arctic region, are among the largest land carnivores in the world. Newborn cubs weigh just over one pound; full-grown males can weigh more than 1,500 pounds. ■ Polar bears have evolved to survive in the world of sea ice. Huge, flat, partially webbed paws distribute their weight like snowshoes, helping the bears travel across ice and swim between floes. The textured pads of the paws are covered with small papillae that provide good traction on the ice. Polar bears tend to overheat, so they dive into the water to cool off. Excellent swimmers, they can swim out more than 50 miles from land when necessary. ■ Most of the time, polar bears wander around in solitude or in small family groups. They may travel thousands of miles a year, searching for food. Their diet consists mainly of ringed and bearded seals. Walruses, beluga whales, and birds are also potential prey. Mating season occurs in late spring, with females giving birth to an average of two cubs in December or January. Cubs are usually about two and a half years old before they are weaned and able to venture off alone. ■ Of the estimated 25,000 polar bears in the Arctic region, approximately 3,000 to 5,000 are found in the coastal areas of Alaska. This relatively recent species, thought to have evolved from brown bears less than a million years ago, was officially designated a threatened species in 2008.

Issue	Date	Un	U	PB	#	FDC	Q(M)
Holiday Celebrations, Tagged, Self-Adhesive, Serpentine Die-Cut 11							
3672 37¢ Hanukkah (type of 1996)	10/10/02	.75	.20	3.00	(4)	1.25	35
3673 37¢ Kwanzaa (type of 1997)	10/10/02	.75	.20	3.00	(4)	1.25	48
3674 37¢ Eid (type of 2001)	10/10/02	.75	.20	3.00	(4)	1.25	35
Holiday Celebration: Christmas, Tagged, Self-Adhesive, Serpentine Die-Cut 11 x 11.25 on 2, 3 or 4 sides							
3675 37¢ Madonna and Child by Gossaert	10/10/02	.75	.20			1.25	536
a Booklet pane of 20		15.00					
Holiday Celebration: Holiday, Tagged, Self-Adhesive, Serpentine Die-Cut 11							
3676 37¢ Snowman w/red & green plaid scarf	10/28/02	.85	.20			1.25	125
3677 37¢ Snowman w/blue plaid scarf	10/28/02	.85	.20			1.25	125
3678 37¢ Snowman w/pipe	10/28/02	.85	.20			1.25	125
3679 37¢ Snowman w/top hat	10/28/02	.85	.20			1.25	125
a Block or vertical strip of 4, #3676-3679		3.40		3.40	(4)	3.25	
Coil, Self-Adhesive, Serpentine Die-Cut 8.5 Vertically							
3680 37¢ Snowman w/blue plaid scarf	10/28/02	1.75	.20			1.25	
3681 37¢ Snowman w/pipe	10/28/02	1.75	.20			1.25	
3682 37¢ Snowman w/top hat	10/28/02	1.75	.20			1.25	
3683 37¢ Snowman w/red & green plaid scarf	10/28/02	1.75	.20			1.25	
a Strip of 4, #3680-3683		7.00		9.00	(5)	3.25	
Booklet, Self-Adhesive, Serpentine Die-Cut 10.75 x 11 on 2 or 3 sides							
3684 37¢ Snowman w/red & green plaid scarf	10/28/02	1.00	.20			1.25	4
3685 37¢ Snowman w/blue plaid scarf	10/28/02	1.00	.20			1.25	4
3686 37¢ Snowman w/pipe	10/28/02	1.00	.20			1.25	4
3687 37¢ Snowman w/top hat	10/28/02	1.00	.20			1.25	4
a Block of 4, #3684-3687		4.00				3.25	
b Booklet pane of 20, 5 #3687a + label		20.00					
Colors of $3684-3687 are deeper and designs are slightly smaller than #3676-3679							
Booklet, Self-Adhesive, Serpentine Die-Cut 11 on 2 or 3 sides							
3688 37¢ Snowman w/red & green plaid scarf	10/28/02	1.00	.20			1.25	
3689 37¢ Snowman w/blue plaid scarf	10/28/02	1.00	.20			1.25	
3690 37¢ Snowman w/pipe	10/28/02	1.00	.20			1.25	
3691 37¢ Snowman w/top hat	10/28/02	1.00	.20			1.25	
a Block of 4 #3688-3691		4.00				3.25	
Legends of Hollywood, Tagged, Self-Adhesive, Serpentine Die-Cut 10.75							
3692 37¢ Cary Grant	10/15/02	.90	.20	3.60	(4)	1.50	80
American Scenes, Coil, Tagged, Self-Adhesive, Serpentine Die-Cut 8.5 Vertically							
3693 (5¢) Sea Coast	10/21/02	.20	.20	1.25	(5)	1.25	1,000
Tagged, Perf, 11							
3694 37¢ Hawaiian Missionary	10/24/02	3.50	2.50			4.00	6
a 37¢-2¢ of 1851 (Hawaii Scott 1)		.85	.50			1.25	
b 37¢-5¢ of 1851 (Hawaii Scott 2)		.85	.50			1.25	
c 37¢-13¢ of 1851 (Hawaii Scott 3)		.85	.50			1.25	
d 37¢-13¢ of 1852 (Hawaii Scott 4)		.85	.50			1.25	
Tagged, Self-Adhesive, Serpentine Die-Cut 11							
3695 37¢ Happy Birthday (type of 2002)	10/25/02	.75	.20	3.00	(4)	1.25	50

Issue	Date	Un	U	PB	#	FDC	Q(M)
Greetings From America (type of 2002)**, Tagged, Self-Adhesive, Serpentine Die-Cut 10.75**							
3696 37¢ Alabama	10/25/02	.75	.60			1.25	200
3697 37¢ Alaska	10/25/02	.75	.60			1.25	200
3698 37¢ Arizona	10/25/02	.75	.60			1.25	200
3699 37¢ Arkansas	10/25/02	.75	.60			1.25	200
3700 37¢ California	10/25/02	.75	.60			1.25	200
3701 37¢ Colorado	10/25/02	.75	.60			1.25	200
3702 37¢ Connecticut	10/25/02	.75	.60			1.25	200
3703 37¢ Delaware	10/25/02	.75	.60			1.25	200
3704 37¢ Florida	10/25/02	.75	.60			1.25	200
3705 37¢ Georgia	10/25/02	.75	.60			1.25	200
3706 37¢ Hawaii	10/25/02	.75	.60			1.25	200
3707 37¢ Idaho	10/25/02	.75	.60			1.25	200
3708 37¢ Illinois	10/25/02	.75	.60			1.25	200
3709 37¢ Indiana	10/25/02	.75	.60			1.25	200
3710 37¢ Iowa	10/25/02	.75	.60			1.25	200
3711 37¢ Kansas	10/25/02	.75	.60			1.25	200
3712 37¢ Kentucky	10/25/02	.75	.60			1.25	200
3713 37¢ Louisiana	10/25/02	.75	.60			1.25	200
3714 37¢ Maine	10/25/02	.75	.60			1.25	200
3715 37¢ Maryland	10/25/02	.75	.60			1.25	200
3716 37¢ Massachusetts	10/25/02	.75	.60			1.25	200
3717 37¢ Michigan	10/25/02	.75	.60			1.25	200
3718 37¢ Minnesota	10/25/02	.75	.60			1.25	200
3719 37¢ Mississippi	10/25/02	.75	.60			1.25	200
3720 37¢ Missouri	10/25/02	.75	.60			1.25	200
3721 37¢ Montana	10/25/02	.75	.60			1.25	200
3722 37¢ Nebraska	10/25/02	.75	.60			1.25	200
3723 37¢ Nevada	10/25/02	.75	.60			1.25	200
3724 37¢ New Hampshire	10/25/02	.75	.60			1.25	200
3725 37¢ New Jersey	10/25/02	.75	.60			1.25	200
3726 37¢ New Mexico	10/25/02	.75	.60			1.25	200
3727 37¢ New York	10/25/02	.75	.60			1.25	200
3728 37¢ North Carolina	10/25/02	.75	.60			1.25	200
3729 37¢ North Dakota	10/25/02	.75	.60			1.25	200
3730 37¢ Ohio	10/25/02	.75	.60			1.25	200
3731 37¢ Oklahoma	10/25/02	.75	.60			1.25	200
3732 37¢ Oregon	10/25/02	.75	.60			1.25	200
3733 37¢ Pennsylvania	10/25/02	.75	.60			1.25	200
3734 37¢ Rhode Island	10/25/02	.75	.60			1.25	200
3735 37¢ South Carolina	10/25/02	.75	.60			1.25	200
3736 37¢ South Dakota	10/25/02	.75	.60			1.25	200
3737 37¢ Tennessee	10/25/02	.75	.60			1.25	200
3738 37¢ Texas	10/25/02	.75	.60			1.25	200
3739 37¢ Utah	10/25/02	.75	.60			1.25	200
3740 37¢ Vermont	10/25/02	.75	.60			1.25	200
3741 37¢ Virginia	10/25/02	.75	.60			1.25	200
3742 37¢ Washington	10/25/02	.75	.60			1.25	200
3743 37¢ West Virginia	10/25/02	.75	.60			1.25	200
3744 37¢ Wisconsin	10/25/02	.75	.60			1.25	200
3745 37¢ Wyoming	10/25/02	.75	.60			1.25	200
a Pane of 50, #3696-3745		37.50				35.00	

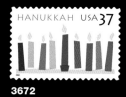

HANUKKAH USA37
2002

3672

KWANZAA
37
USA

3673

EID
37
USA
GREETINGS

3674

CHRISTMAS
37
USA
J. Gossaert Art Institute of Chicago

3675

3676 3677

37
USA
37
USA
37
USA
37
USA

3678 3679

3679a

CARY GRANT
USA
37

3692

USA
NONPROFIT ORG.

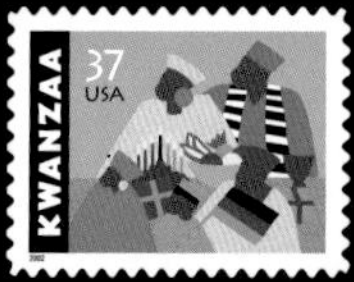

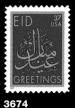

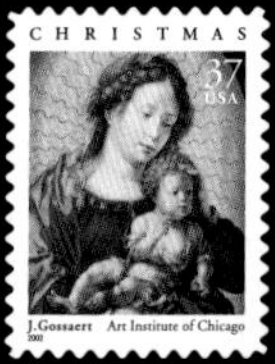

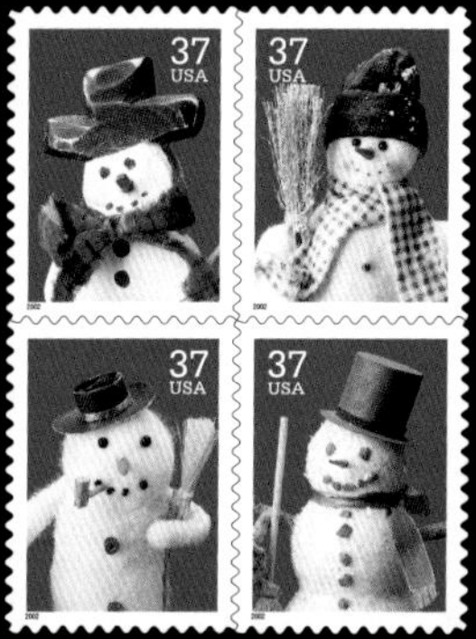

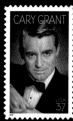

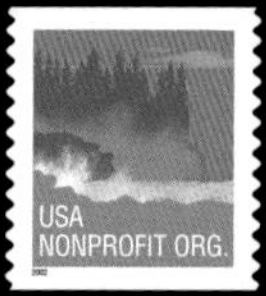

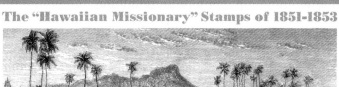

3693

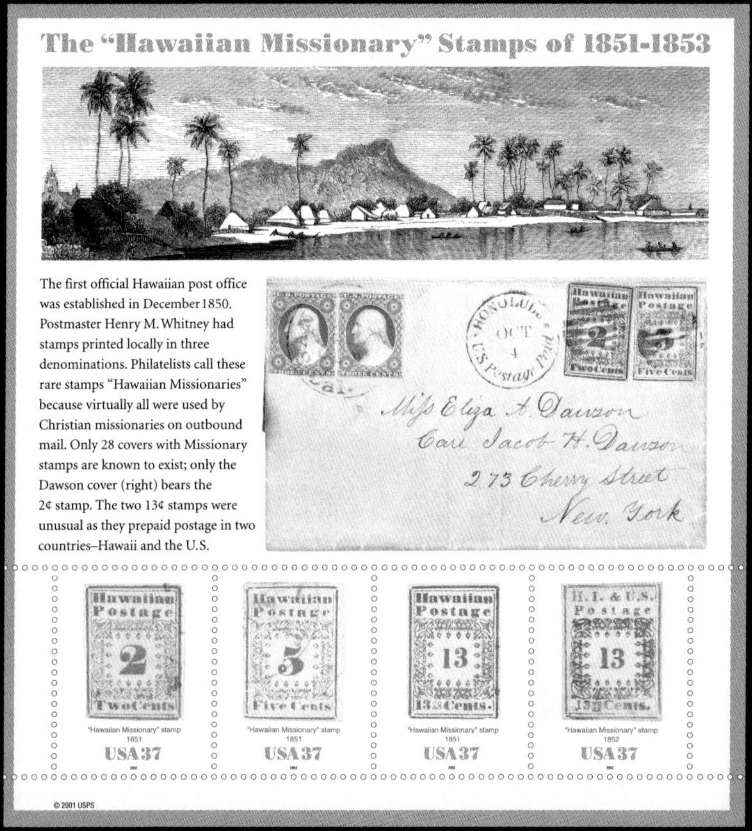

The "Hawaiian Missionary" Stamps of 1851-1853
The first official Hawaiian post office was established in December 1850. Postmaster Henry M. Whitney had stamps printed locally in three denominations. Philatelists call these rare stamps "Hawaiian Missionaries" because virtually all were used by Christian missionaries on outbound mail. Only 28 covers with Missionary stamps are known to exist; only the Dawson cover (right) bears the 2¢ stamp. The two 13¢ stamps were unusual as they prepaid postage in two countries–Hawaii and the U.S.
Miss Eliza A. Dawson
Care Jacob H. Dawson
273 Cherry Street
New. York
"Hawaiian Missionary" stamp 1851
USA37
"Hawaiian Missionary" stamp 1851
USA37
"Hawaiian Missionary" stamp 1851
USA37
"Hawaiian Missionary" stamp 1852
USA37
© 2001 USPS

3694 a b c d

HAPPY 37 USA
BIRTHDAY

3695

Greetings from
ALABAMA
USA37

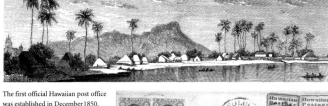

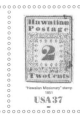

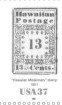

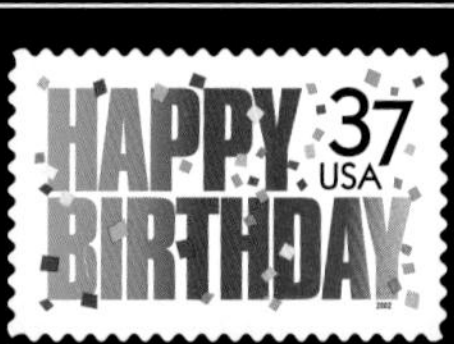

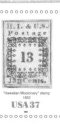

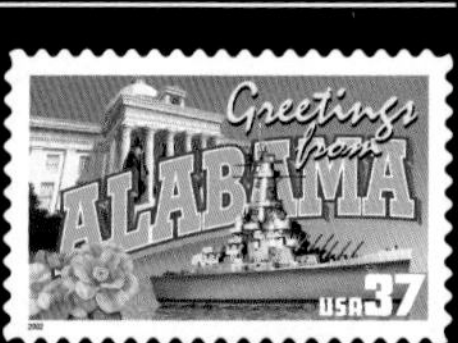

3696

3746

3747

3748

3750

3755

3756

3757

3758

3759

3766

3771

3773

3774

3772

a   f

b   g

c   h

d   i

e   j

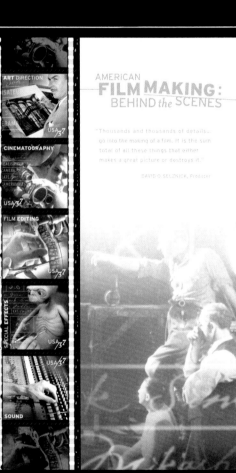

AMERICAN
FILM MAKING:
BEHIND the SCENES

"Thousands and thousands of details...
go into the making of a film. It is the sum
total of all these things that either
makes a great picture or destroys it."

DAVID O. SELZNICK, Producer

3776

3777

3778

3779

3780   **3780a**

Issue		Date	Un	U	PB	#	FDC	Q(M)
Black Heritage, Tagged, Self-Adhesive, Serpentine Die-Cut 11.5								
3746	37¢ Thurgood Marshall	01/07/03	.75	.20	3.00	(4)	1.25	150
Lunar New Year, Tagged, Self-Adhesive, Serpentine Die-Cut 11.5								
3747	37¢ Year of the Ram	01/15/03	.75	.20	3.00	(4)	1.50	70
Literary Arts, Tagged, Self-Adhesive, Serpentine Die-Cut 10.75								
3748	37¢ Zora Neale Hurston	01/24/03	.80	.20	3.25	(4)	1.25	70
American Design, Untagged, Self-Adhesive, Serpentine Die-Cut 11								
3749	1¢ Tiffany Lamp	03/16/07	.20	.20	.20	(4)	1.25	100
3750	2¢ Navajo Jewelry	08/20/04	.20	.20	.20	(4)	1.25	100
American Design, Untagged, Self-Adhesive, Serpentine Die-Cut 11.25 x 11.5								
3751	2¢ Navajo Jewelry	12/08/05	.20	.20	.20	(4)	1.25	100
American Design, Untagged, Self-Adhesive, Serpentine Die-Cut 11.25 x 11								
3752	2¢ Navajo Jewelry, with "USPS" microprinting	12/08/05	.20	.20	.20	(4)	1.25	100
American Design, Untagged, Self-Adhesive, Serpentine Die-Cut 11.25 x 10.75								
3753	2¢ Navajo Jewelry	05/12/07	.20	.20	.20	(4)	2.00	100
American Design, Untagged, Self-Adhesive, Serpentine Die-Cut 11.25 x 11								
3754	3¢ Silver Coffeepot	03/16/07	.20	.20	.25	(4)	2.00	210
3755	4¢ Chippendale Chair	03/05/04	.20	.20	.35	(4)	1.25	100
American Design, Untagged, Self-Adhesive, Serpentine Die-Cut 11.25 x 11.75								
3756	5¢ American Toleware Coffeepot	06/25/04	.20	.20	.40	(4)	1.25	
American Design, Untagged, Self-Adhesive, Serpentine Die-Cut 11.25 x 10.75								
3756A	5¢ American Toleware Coffeepot	08/08	.20	.20	.40	(4)		
American Design, Tagged, Self-Adhesive, Serpentine Die-Cut 11.25 x 11								
3757	10¢ American Clock	01/24/03	.20	.20	.80	(4)	1.25	150
American Design, Coil, Untagged, Perf. 10 Vertically								
3758	1¢ Tiffany Lamp	03/01/03	.20	.20	.50	(5)	1.25	210
American Design, Coil, Untagged, Perf. 9.75 Vertically								
3759	3¢ Silver Coffeepot	09/16/05	.20	.20	.75	(5)	2.00	210
3761	4¢ Chippendale Chair (type of 2004)	07/19/07	.20	.20	1.25	(5)	2.00	
3762	10¢ American Clock (2006)	08/04/06	.20	.20	2.00	(5)	2.00	
American Design, Coil, Tagged, Perf. 9.75 Vertically								
3763	10¢ American Clock (2008)	07/15/08	.20	.20	2.50	(4)	2.00	
American Culture, Tagged, Self-Adhesive, Serpentine Die-Cut 11.25 x 11								
3766	$1 Wisdom	02/28/03	2.00	.40	8.00	(4)	2.50	100
a	Dated "2008" (type of 2003)	2008	2.00	.40				
American Culture, Coil, Untagged, Perf. 10 Vertically								
3769	(10¢) New York Public Library Lion (type of 2000)	02/04/03	.20	.20	3.00	(5)	1.25	170

Issue		Date	Un	U	PB	#	FDC	Q(M)
American Culture, Coil, Untagged, Self-Adhesive, Serpentine Die-Cut 11, Vertically								
3770	(10¢) Atlas Statue dated "2003" (type of 2001)	11/03	.20	.20	3.00	(5)		400
American Culture, Tagged, Self-Adhesive, Serpentine Die-Cut 11								
3771	80¢ Special Olympics	02/13/03	1.60	.35	6.40	(4)	1.75	60
American Filmmaking: Behind the Scenes Tagged, Self-Adhesive, Serpentine Die-Cut 11, Horizontally								
3772	Pane of 10	02/25/03	10.00				7.25	70
a	37¢ Screenwriting (script from Gone With the Wind)		1.00	.50			1.25	
b	37¢ Directing (John Cassavetes)		1.00	.50			1.25	
c	37¢ Costume Design (Edith Head)		1.00	.50			1.25	
d	37¢ Music (Max Steiner working on score)		1.00	.50			1.25	
e	37¢ Makeup (Jack Pierce—Boris Karloff for Frankenstein)		1.00	.50			1.25	
f	37¢ Art Direction (Perry Ferguson for Citizen Kane)		1.00	.50			1.25	
g	37¢ Cinematography (Paul Hill for Nagana)		1.00	.50			1.25	
h	37¢ Film Editing (J. Watson Webb for The Razor's Edge)		1.00	.50			1.25	
i	37¢ Special Effects (Mark Siegel for E.T. Extra-Terrestriah)		1.00	.50			1.25	
j	37¢ Sound (Gary Summers)		1.00	.50			1.25	
Tagged, Self-Adhesive, Serpentine Die-Cut 11.75 x 11.5								
3773	37¢ Ohio Statehood	03/01/03	.75	.20	3.00	(4)	1.25	50
Tagged, Self-Adhesive, Serpentine Die-Cut 12 x 11.5								
3774	37¢ Pelican Island Natural Wildlife Refuge	03/14/03	.75	.20	3.00	(4)	1.25	55
Coil, Untagged, Perf. 9.75 Vertically								
3775	(5¢) Sea Coast	03/19/03	.20	.20	1.25	(5)	1.25	200
Old Glory, Booklet, Tagged, Self-Adhesive, Serpentine Die-Cut 10 x 9.75								
3776	37¢ Uncle Sam on Bicycle with Liberty Flag	04/03/03	.75	.50			1.25	
3777	37¢ 1888 Presidential Campaign	04/03/03	.75	.50			1.25	
3778	37¢ 1893 Silk Bookmark	04/03/03	.75	.50			1.25	
3779	37¢ Modern Hand Fan	04/03/03	.75	.50			1.25	
3780	37¢ Carving of Woman with Flag & Sword 19th Century	04/03/03	.75	.50			1.25	
a	Horizontal strip of 5 #3776-3780		3.75				4.00	60
b	Booklet pane, 2 #3780a		7.50					

America's Postmarks Binder

This elegant three-ring binder is the perfect way to display and preserve your Postmark collectibles. This 9¾ x 9¾ inch binder includes 20 vinyl pages with two pockets on each side sized to hold #6¾ envelopes.

Item #880660 $21.95

Item #880681 (Set of 20 Pages) $8.95

	Issue	Date	Un	U	PB/PNC	#	FDC	Q(M)
	Tagged, Self-Adhesive, Serpentine Die-Cut 11.75 x 11.5							
3781	37¢ Cesar E. Chavez	04/23/03	.75	.20	3.00	(4)	1.25	75
	Tagged, Self-Adhesive, Serpentine Die-Cut 10.75							
3782	37¢ Louisiana Purchase	04/30/03	.95	.40	4.00	(4)	1.25	54
	Booklet, Tagged, Self-Adhesive, Serpentine Die-Cut 11							
3783	37¢ First Flight	05/22/03	.75	.40			1.25	85
a	Booklet pane of 9		6.75					
b	Booklet pane of 1		.75					
	Tagged, Self-Adhesive, Serpentine Die-Cut 11.25 x 10.75							
3784	37¢ Purple Heart	05/30/03	.75	.20	3.00	(4)	1.50	120
	Tagged, Self-Adhesive, Serpentine Die-Cut 10.75 x 10.25							
3784A	37¢ Purple Heart	05/30/03	.75	.20	3.00	(4)		
	Coil, Untagged, Self-Adhesive, Serpentine Die-Cut 9.5 x 10							
3785	(5¢) Sea Coast	06/03	.20	.20	1.50	(5)		50
	Legends of Hollywood, Tagged, Self-Adhesive, Serpentine Die-Cut 10.75							
3786	37¢ Audrey Hepburn	06/11/03	.90	.20	3.75	(4)	1.75	80
	Lighthouses: Southeastern, Tagged, Self-Adhesive, Serpentine Die-Cut 10.75							
3787	37¢ Old Cape Henry, Virginia	06/13/03	1.10	.20			1.50	
3788	37¢ Cape Lookout, North Carolina	06/13/03	1.10	.20			1.50	
3789	37¢ Morris Island, South Carolina	06/13/03	1.10	.20			1.50	
3790	37¢ Tybee Island, Georgia	06/13/03	1.10	.20			1.50	
3791	37¢ Hillsboro Inlet, Florida	06/13/03	1.10	.20			1.50	
a	Strip of 5, #3787-3791		5.50				4.00	125
	American Eagle, (dated "2003"), Untagged, Coil, Serpentine Die-Cut 11.75 Vertically							
3792	(25¢) gray background & gold eagle	06/26/03	.50	.20			1.25	
3793	(25¢) gold background & red eagle	06/26/03	.50	.20			1.25	
3794	(25¢) dull blue background & gold eagle	06/26/03	.50	.20			1.25	
3795	(25¢) gold background & Prussian blue eagle	06/26/03	.50	.20			1.25	
3796	(25¢) green background & gold eagle	06/26/03	.50	.20			1.25	
3797	(25¢) gold background & gray eagle	06/26/03	.50	.20			1.25	
3798	(25¢) Prussian blue background & gold eagle	06/26/03	.50	.20			1.25	
3799	(25¢) gold background & dull blue eagle	06/26/03	.50	.20			1.25	
3800	(25¢) red background & gold eagle	06/26/03	.50	.20			1.25	
3801	(25¢) gold background & green eagle	06/26/03	.50	.20			1.25	
a	Strip of 10, #3792-3801		5.00		8.00	(11)	6.00	310

	Issue	Date	Un	U	PB/PNC	#	FDC	Q(M)
	American Eagle (dated "2005"), Coil, Serpentine Die-Cut 11.5 Vertically							
3792a	(25¢) gray background & gold eagle	08/05/05	.50	.20			1.25	
3793a	(25¢) gold background & red eagle	08/05/05	.50	.20			1.25	
3794a	(25¢) dull blue background & gold eagle	08/05/05	.50	.20			1.25	
3795a	(25¢) gold background & Prussian blue eagle	08/05/05	.50	.20			1.25	
3796a	(25¢) green background & gold eagle	08/05/05	.50	.20			1.25	
3797a	(25¢) gold background & gray eagle	08/05/05	.50	.20			1.25	
3798a	(25¢) Prussian blue background & gold eagle	08/05/05	.50	.20			1.25	
3799a	(25¢) gold background & dull blue eagle	08/05/05	.50	.20			1.25	
3800a	(25¢) red background & gold eagle	08/05/05	.50	.20			1.25	
3801a	(25¢) gold background & green eagle	08/05/05	.50	.20			1.25	
c	Strip of 10, #3792a-3801a		5.00		8.50	(11)	6.00	
	Nature of America: Arctic Tundra, Tagged, Self-Adhesive, Serpentine Die-Cut 10.75 x 10.5, 10.5 x 10.75							
3802	Pane of 10	07/02/03	7.50				7.50	60
a	37¢ Gyrfalcon		.75	.50			1.25	
b	37¢ Gray Wolf		.75	.50			1.25	
c	37¢ Common Raven		.75	.50			1.25	
d	37¢ Musk Oxen & Caribou		.75	.50			1.25	
e	37¢ Grizzly Bears, Caribou		.75	.50			1.25	
f	37¢ Caribou, Willow Ptarmigans		.75	.50			1.25	
g	37¢ Arctic Ground Squirrel		.75	.50			1.25	
h	37¢ Willow Ptarmigan, Bearberry		.75	.50			1.25	
i	37¢ Arctic Grayling		.75	.50			1.25	
j	37¢ Singing Vole, Thin-legged Wolf Spider, Lingonberry, Labrador Tea		.75	.50			1.25	
	Tagged, Self-Adhesive, Serpentine Die-Cut 11.5 x 11.75							
3803	37¢ Korean War Veterans Memorial	07/27/03	.75	.20	3.00	(4)	1.50	87
	American Treasures, Booklet, Tagged, Self-Adhesive, Serpentine Die-Cut 10.75 on 2 or 3 sides							
3804	37¢ Mary Cassatt— Young Mother	08/07/03	.75	.20			1.25	
3805	37¢ Mary Cassatt— Children Playing on the Beach	08/07/03	.75	.20			1.25	
3806	37¢ Mary Cassatt— On a Balcony	08/07/03	.75	.20			1.25	
3807	37¢ Mary Cassatt— Child in a Straw Hat	08/07/03	.75	.20			1.25	
a	Block of 4, #3804-3807		3.00				3.25	779

VISIT US ONLINE AT **THE POSTAL STORE**
AT **WWW.USPS.COM**
OR CALL **1 800 STAMP-24**

3781

3782

3783

3784

3786

3787

3788

3789

3790

3791 **3791a**

3801a

3797

3798

3799

3800

3801

3792

3793

3794

3795

3796

3802 a

b

c d f e

g

j h i

3803

3804 **3805**

3806 **3807** **3807a**

3808

3809

3810

3811

3811a

3812

3813

Scarlet Kingsnake

Blue-spotted Salamander

Reticulate Collared Lizard

Ornate Chorus Frog

Ornate Box Turtle

3820

3821

3822

3823

3824

3824a

3829

3830

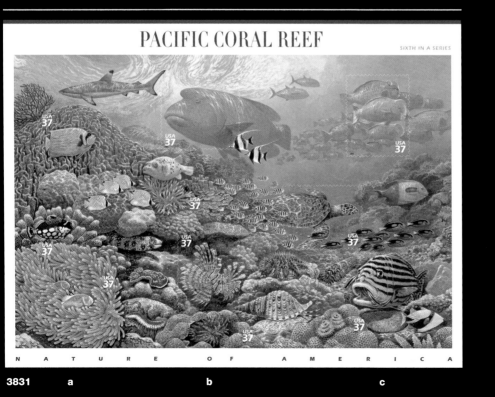

PACIFIC CORAL REEF

SIXTH IN A SERIES

N A T U R E   O F   A M E R I C A

3831   a   b   c

d   e

	Issue	Date	Un	U	PB	#	FDC	Q(M)
	Early Football Heroes, Tagged, Self-Adhesive, Serpentine Die-Cut 11.5 x 11.75							
3808	37¢ Bronko Nagurski	08/08/03	.75	.20			1.25	
3809	37¢ Ernie Nevers	08/08/03	.75	.20			1.25	
3810	37¢ Walter Camp	08/08/03	.75	.20			1.25	
3811	37¢ Red Grange	08/08/03	.75	.20			1.25	
a	Block of 4, #3808-3811		3.00		3.00	(4)	3.25	70
	Tagged, Self-Adhesive, Serpentine Die-Cut 11							
3812	37¢ Roy Acuff	09/13/03	.75	.20	3.00	(4)	1.25	52
3813	37¢ District of Columbia	09/23/03	.75	.20	3.75	(4)	1.25	72
	Reptiles and Amphibians, Tagged, Self-Adhesive, Serpentine Die-Cut 11							
3814	37¢ Scarlet Kingsnake	10/07/03	.75	.20			1.25	
3815	37¢ Blue-Spotted Salamander	10/07/03	.75	.20			1.25	
3816	37¢ Reticulate Collared Lizard	10/07/03	.75	.20			1.25	
3817	37¢ Ornate Chorus Frog	10/07/03	.75	.20			1.25	
3818	37¢ Ornate Box Turtle	10/07/03	.75	.20			1.25	
a	Vert. strip of 5, #3814-3818		3.75		7.50	(10)	4.00	100
	Tagged, Self-Adhesive, Serpentine Die-Cut 11							
3819	23¢ George Washington (type of 2002)	10//03	.70	.20	7.50	(4)	1.25	200
	Holiday Celebration: Christmas, Booklet, Tagged, Self-Adhesive, Serpentine Die-Cut 11 x 11.25 on 2 or 3 sides							
3820	37¢ Madonna and Child by Gossaert (type of 2002)	10/23/03	.75	.20			1.25	
a	Booklet pane of 20		15.00					700
	Holiday Celebration: Holiday, Music Makers, Self-Adhesive, Serpentine Die-Cut 11.75 x 11							
3821	37¢ Reindeer with Pan Pipes	10/23/03	.80	.20			1.25	
3822	37¢ Santa Claus with Drum	10/23/03	.80	.20			1.25	
3823	37¢ Santa Claus with Trumpet	10/23/03	.80	.20			1.25	
3824	37¢ Reindeer with Horn	10/23/03	.80	.20			1.25	
a	Block of 4, #3821-3824		3.20		3.20	(4)	3.25	125

	Issue	Date	Un	U	PB	#	FDC	Q(M)
	Holiday Celebration: Holiday, Music Makers, Booklet, Self-Adhesive, Serpentine Die-Cut 10.5 x 10.75 on 2 or 3 sides							
3825	37¢ Reindeer with Pan Pipes	10/23/03	.85	.20			1.25	
3826	37¢ Santa Claus with Drum	10/23/03	.85	.20			1.25	
3827	37¢ Santa Claus with Trumpet	10/23/03	.85	.20			1.25	
3828	37¢ Reindeer with Horn	10/23/03	.85	.20			1.25	
a	Block of 4, #3825-3828		3.40				3.25	200
	Coil, Tagged, Self-Adhesive, Serpentine Die-Cut 8.5 Vertically							
3829	37¢ Snowy Egret	10/24/03	.75	.20	4.50	(5)	1.25	2,000
	Die-Cut 9.5 Vertically							
3829A	37¢ Snowy Egret	03/04	.75	.20	6.00	(5)	1.25	2,000
	Booklet, Self-Adhesive, Serpentine Die-Cut 11.5 x 11 on 2, 3 or 4 sides							
3830	37¢ Snowy Egret	03/30/04	.75	.20			1.25	2,000
a	Booklet pane of 20		15.00					
	Nature of America: Pacific Coral Reef, Tagged, Self-Adhesive, Serpentine Die-Cut 10.75							
3831	Pane of 10	01/02/04	7.50				7.50	76
a	37¢ Emperor Angelfish, Blue Coral, Mound Coral		.75	.20			1.25	
b	37¢ Humphead Wrasse, Moorish Idol		.75	.20			1.25	
c	37¢ Bumphead Parrotfish		.75	.20				
d	37¢ Black-spotted Puffer, Threadfin Butterflyfish, Staghorn Coral		.75	.20			1.25	
e	37¢ Hawksbill Turtle, Palette Surgeonfish		.75	.20			1.25	
f	37¢ Pink Anemonefish, Magnificent Sea Anemone		.75	.20			1.25	
g	37¢ Snowflake Moray Eel, Spanish Dancer		.75	.20			1.25	
h	37¢ Lionfish		.75	.20			1.25	
i	37¢ Triton's Trumpet		.75	.20			1.25	
j	37¢ Oriental Sweetlips, Bluestreak Cleaner Wrasse, Mushroom Coral		.75	.20			1.25	

REDWOOD FOREST PRIORITY MAIL®

The 2009 Priority Mail stamp pays tribute to the redwood forests of the United States. Redwoods, named for the color of their bark and heartwood, are the tallest living trees in the world, and some of the oldest. The stamp features a digital illustration by Dan Cosgrove of a typical redwood forest. ■ Redwood forests consist of massive redwood trees as well as assorted tree, shrub, flower, fern, and moss species. Together they form a complex ecosystem that also includes many types of amphibians, birds, and mammals. ■ Only two types of redwood tree are native to the United States: The Coast Redwood *(Sequoia sempervirens)*, found along the coasts of extreme southwestern Oregon and northern and central California; and the Giant Sequoia *(Sequoiadendron giganteum)*, native to the western slope of the Sierra Nevada mountain range in eastern California. ■ Coast Redwoods take 400 to 500 years to reach maturity and can live for 2,000 years. With an average height of 300 feet, they boast trunks of more than 20 feet in diameter and 30 feet at the base. They survive the long, hot days of summer by absorbing moisture directly from the fog. Shorter and thicker, the Giant Sequoia lives longer than its coastal relative. The thick bark of these cone-bearing evergreens is high in tannin, which makes them resistant to insects, fungus, and fire. Nevertheless, redwood forests benefit from periodic fires, which clear the forest floor of plant debris, recycle nutrients into the soil, and allow redwood seedlings to develop.

	Issue	Date	Un	U	PB	#	FDC	Q(M)
	Lunar New Year, Tagged, Self-Adhesive, Serpentine Die-Cut 10.75							
3832	37¢ Year of the Monkey	01/13/04	.75	.20	3.00	(4)	1.50	80
	Love, Booklet, Tagged, Self-Adhesive, Serpentine Die-Cut 10.75 on 2, 3 or 4 sides							
3833	37¢ Candy Hearts	01/14/04	.75	.20			1.25	
a	Booklet pane of 20		15.00					750
	Black Heritage, Tagged, Self-Adhesive, Serpentine Die-Cut 10.75							
3834	37¢ Paul Robeson	01/20/04	.75	.20	3.00	(4)	1.25	150
	Tagged, Self-Adhesive, Serpentine Die-Cut 10.75 x 10.5							
3835	37¢ Theodor "Dr. Seuss" Geisel	03/02/04	.85	.20	3.50	(4)	1.25	172
	Garden Flowers (Wedding)**, Tagged, Booklet, Self-Adhesive, Serpentine Die-Cut 10.75 on 2, 3 or 4 sides**							
3836	37¢ White Lilacs & Pink Roses	03/04/04	.75	.20			1.25	1,500
a	Booklet pane of 20		15.00					750
	Self-Adhesive, Serpentine Die-Cut 11.5 x 11							
3837	60¢ Pink Roses	03/04/04	1.25	.25	5.00	(4)	1.50	60
	Tagged, Self-Adhesive, Serpentine Die-Cut 10.75							
3838	37¢ US Air Force Academy	04/01/04	.75	.20	3.00	(4)	1.50	60
3839	37¢ Henry Mancini	04/13/04	.75	.20	3.00	(4)	1.25	80
	American Choreographers, Tagged, Self-Adhesive, Serpentine Die-Cut 10.75							
3840	37¢ Martha Graham	05/04/04	.75	.20	3.00	(4)	1.25	
3841	37¢ Alvin Ailey	05/04/04	.75	.20	3.00	(4)	1.25	
3842	37¢ Agnes de Mille	05/04/04	.75	.20	3.00	(4)	1.25	
3843	37¢ George Balanchine	05/04/04	.75	.20	3.00	(4)	1.25	
a	Horizontal strip of 4		3.00		6.00	(8)	3.25	57
	American Eagle (types of 2003)**, Coil, Untagged, Perf. 9.75 Vertically**							
3844	(25¢) Gray Background & Gold Eagle	05/12/04	.65	.20			1.25	
3845	(25¢) Gold Background & Green Eagle	05/12/04	.65	.20			1.25	
3846	(25¢) Red Background & Gold Eagle	05/12/04	.65	.20			1.25	
3847	(25¢) Gold Background & Dull Blue Eagle	05/12/04	.65	.20			1.25	
3848	(25¢) Prussian Blue Background & Gold Eagle	05/12/04	.65	.20			1.25	
3849	(25¢) Gold Background & Gray Eagle	05/12/04	.65	.20			1.25	
3850	(25¢) Green Background & Gold Eagle	05/12/04	.65	.20			1.25	
3851	(25¢) Gold Background & Prussian Blue Eagle	05/12/04	.65	.20			1.25	

	Issue	Date	Un	U	PB	#	FDC	Q(M)
	American Eagle (types of 2003)**, Coil, Untagged, Perf. 9.75 Vertically** continued							
3852	(25¢) Dull Blue Background & Gold Eagle	05/12/04	.65	.20			1.25	
3853	(25¢) Gold Background & Red Eagle	05/12/04	.65	.20			1.25	
a	Strip of 10 #3844-3853		6.50		9.50	(11)	6.00	700
	Lewis & Clark Expedition Bicentennial, Tagged, Self-Adhesive, Serpentine Die-Cut 10.75							
3854	37¢ Lewis & Clark Bicentennial	05/14/04	.90	.20	3.75	(4)	1.25	
	Booklet, Serpentine Die-Cut 10.5 x 10.75							
3855	37¢ Meriwether Lewis	05/14/04	.90	.45			2.75	
3856	37¢ William Clark	05/14/04	.90	.45			2.75	
a	Horiz. or vert. pair #3855-3856		1.80					62
b	Booklet pane of 5 each #3855-3856		9.00					20
	Artists: Isamu Noguchi, Tagged, Self-Adhesive, Serpentine Die-Cut 10.5 x 10.75							
3857	37¢ Akari 25N	05/18/04	.75	.20			1.25	
3858	37¢ Margaret La Farge	05/18/04	.75	.20			1.25	
3859	37¢ Black Sun	05/18/04	.75	.20			1.25	
3860	37¢ Mother and Child	05/18/04	.75	.20			1.25	
3861	37¢ Figure	05/18/04	.75	.20			1.25	
a	Horizontal strip of 5 #3857-3860		3.75		4.50	(6)	4.00	57
	Tagged, Self-Adhesive, Serpentine Die-Cut 10.75							
3862	37¢ National WWII Memorial	05/29/04	.75	.20	3.00	(4)	1.50	96
	Olympic Games, Tagged, Self-Adhesive, Serpentine Die-Cut 10.75							
3863	37¢ 2004 Olympic Games Athens	06/09/04	.75	.20	3.00	(4)	1.25	71
	Coil, Untagged, Perf. 9.75 Vertically							
3864	(5¢) Sea Coast (type of 2002)	06/11/04	.20	.20	1.50	(5)	1.25	
	The Art of Disney: Friendship, Tagged, Self-Adhesive, Serpentine Die-Cut 10.5 x 10.75							
3865	37¢ Goofy, Mickey Mouse, Donald Duck	06/23/04	1.00	.20			1.25	
3866	37¢ Bambi, Thumper	06/23/04	1.00	.20			1.25	
3867	37¢ Mufasa, Simba	06/23/04	1.00	.20			1.25	
3868	37¢ Jiminy Cricket, Pinocchio	06/23/04	1.00	.20			1.25	
a	Block or vert. strip of 4		4.00		4.00	(4)	3.25	284
	Tagged, Self-Adhesive, Serpentine Die-Cut 10.5							
3869	37¢ USS Constellation	06/30/04	.75	.20	3.00	(4)	1.25	45
	Tagged, Self-Adhesive, Serpentine Die-Cut 10.5 x 10.75							
3870	37¢ R. Buckminster Fuller	07/12/04	.75	.20	3.00	(4)	1.25	60
	Literary Arts, Tagged, Self-Adhesive, Serpentine Die-Cut 10.75							
3871	37¢ James Baldwin	07/23/04	.75	.20	3.00	(4)	1.25	50

3832

3833

3834

3835

3836

3837

3838

3840 3841 3842 3843 3843a

3839

3854

3855

3856

3857

3858

3859

3860

3861 3861a

3862

3865 3866

3867

3868 3868a

3863

3869

3870

3871

3872

ART OF THE AMERICAN INDIAN

Mimbres bowl USA37	Kutenai parfleche USA37	Tlingit sculptures USA37	Ho-Chunk bag USA37	Seminole doll USA37
Mississippian effigy USA37	Acoma pot USA37	Navajo weaving USA37	Seneca carving USA37	Luiseño basket USA37

3873   a   b   c   d   e

f   g   h   i   j

3876

3877

CLOUDSCAPES

© 2003 USPS

.37 x 15 $5.55

Cirrus radiatus	Cirrostratus fibratus	Cirrocumulus undulatus	Cumulonimbus mammatus	Cumulonimbus incus
Altocumulus stratiformis	Altostratus translucidus	Altocumulus undulatus	Altocumulus castellanus	Altocumulus lenticularis
Stratocumulus undulatus	Stratus opacus	Cumulus humilis	Cumulus congestus	Cumulonimbus with tornado

X1111   PLATE POSITION   X1111

3878   a   b   c   d   e

3879

3880

3881

3882

3883   **3884**

	Issue	Date	Un	U	PB	#	FDC	Q(M)
	American Treasures, Tagged, Booklet, Self-Adhesive, Serpentine Die-Cut 10.75 on 2 or 3 sides							
3872	37¢ Martin Johnson Heade	08/12/04	.70	.20			1.25	
a	Booklet of pane of 20		15.00					794
	Art of the American Indian, Tagged, Self-Adhesive, Serpentine Die-Cut 10.75 x 11							
3873	Pane of 10	08/21/04	12.00				7.00	87
a	37¢ Mimbres Bowl		1.20	.20			1.25	
b	37¢ Kutenai Parfleche		1.20	.20			1.25	
c	37¢ Tlingit Sculptures		1.20	.20			1.25	
d	37¢ Ho-Chunk Bag		1.20	.20			1.25	
e	37¢ Seminole Doll		1.20	.20			1.25	
f	37¢ Mississippian Effigy		1.20	.20			1.25	
g	37¢ Acoma Pot		1.20	.20			1.25	
h	37¢ Navajo Weaving		1.20	.20			1.25	
i	37¢ Seneca Carving		1.20	.20			1.25	
j	37¢ Luiseño Basket		1.20	.20			1.25	
	Coil, Untagged, Self-Adhesive, Serpentine Die-Cut 10 Vertically							
3874	(5¢) Sea Coast (type of 2002)	08/04	.20	.20	1.60	(5)		
	Coil, Untagged, Self-Adhesive, Serpentine Die-Cut 11.5 Vertically							
3875	(5¢) Sea Coast (type of 2002)	08/04	.20	.20	1.50	(5)		
	Legends of Hollywood, Tagged, Self-Adhesive, Serpentine Die-Cut 10.75							
3876	37¢ John Wayne	09/09/04	.75	.20	3.00	(4)	2.00	100
	Tagged, Self-Adhesive, Serpentine Die-Cut 11							
3877	37¢ Sickle Cell Awareness	09/29/04	.75	.20	3.00	(4)	1.25	96
	Cloudscapes, Tagged, Self-Adhesive, Serpentine Die-Cut 11							
3878	Pane of 15	10/04/04	12.50				9.00	125
a	37¢ Cirrus Radiatus		.80	.20			1.25	
b	37¢ Cirrostratus Fibratus		.80	.20			1.25	
c	37¢ Cirrocumulus Undulatus		.80	.20			1.25	
d	37¢ Cumulonimbus Mammatus		.80	.20			1.25	
e	37¢ Cumulonimbus Incus		.80	.20			1.25	
f	37¢ Altocumulus Stratiformis		.80	.20			1.25	
g	37¢ Altostratus Translucidus		.80	.20			1.25	
h	37¢ Altocumulus Undulatus		.80	.20			1.25	
i	37¢ Altocumulus Castellanus		.80	.20			1.25	
j	37¢ Altocumulus Lenticularis		.80	.20			1.25	
k	37¢ Stratocumulus Undulatus		.80	.20			1.25	

	Issue	Date	Un	U	PB	#	FDC	Q(M)
	Cloudscapes Tagged, Self-Adhesive, Serpentine Die-Cut 11 continued							
l	37¢ Stratus Opacus		.80	.20			1.25	
m	37¢ Cumulus Humilis		.80	.20			1.25	
n	37¢ Cumulus Congestus		.80	.20			1.25	
o	37¢ Cumulonimbus with Tornado		.80	.20			1.25	
	Holiday Celebration: Christmas, Tagged, Self-Adhesive, Serpentine Die-Cut 10.75 x 11 on 2 or 3 sides							
3879	37¢ Madonna and Child by Lorenzo Monaco	10/14/04	.75	.20			1.25	776
a	Booklet pane of 20		15.00					
	Holiday Celebration: Tagged, Self-Adhesive, Serpentine Die-Cut 10.75							
3880	37¢ Hanukkah	10/15/04	.75	.20	3.00	(4)	1.25	43
3881	37¢ Kwanzaa	10/16/04	.75	.20	3.00	(4)	1.25	60
	Tagged, Self-Adhesive, Serpentine Die-Cut 11							
3882	37¢ Moss Hart	10/25/04	.75	.20	3.00	(4)	1.25	45
	Holiday Celebration: Holiday Ornaments, Tagged, Self-Adhesive, Serpentine Die-Cut 11.25 x 11							
3883	37¢ Purple Santa	11/16/04	.80	.20	3.00	(4)	1.25	
3884	37¢ Green Santa	11/16/04	.80	.20	3.00	(4)	1.25	
3885	37¢ Blue Santa	11/16/04	.80	.20	3.00	(4)	1.25	
3886	37¢ Red Santa	11/16/04	.80	.20	3.00	(4)	1.25	
a	Block or strip of 4 #3883-3886		3.20					
	Holiday Celebration: Holiday Ornaments, Booklet, Serpentine Die-Cut 10.25 x 10.75 on 2 or 3 sides							
3887	37¢ Purple Santa	11/16/04	.75	.20			1.25	
3888	37¢ Green Santa	11/16/04	.75	.20			1.25	
3889	37¢ Blue Santa	11/16/04	.75	.20			1.25	
3890	37¢ Red Santa	11/16/04	.75	.20			1.25	
a	Block or strip of 4 #3887-3890		3.00					
	Holiday Celebration: Holiday Ornaments, Booklet, Serpentine Die-Cut 8 on 2, 3 or 4 sides							
3891	37¢ Purple Santa	11/16/04	.90	.20			1.25	
3892	37¢ Green Santa	11/16/04	.90	.20			1.25	
3893	37¢ Blue Santa	11/16/04	.90	.20			1.25	
3894	37¢ Red Santa	11/16/04	.90	.20			1.25	
a	Block or strip of 4 #3891-3894		3.60					
b	Pane of 18, 6 each #3891,#3893, 3 each #3892, #3894		18.00					

U.S. FLAG

The U.S. flag, one of the most recognizable symbols in the world, appears on this new 2009 stamp. The American flag has regularly appeared on definitive stamps intended for mail use, and recent commemoratives have displayed the flag as well. The Stars and Stripes pane (2000), for example, highlighted the evolution of American flags over time, and the Old Glory prestige booklet (2003) featured a wide range of ephemera and folk art that incorporated American flag motifs. ■ This new stamp features a photograph by Rick Barrentine of Duluth, Georgia, that focuses on a detail of an American flag. The detail, which shows a softly folded flag, features most prominently the starry blue field, with the flag's red-and-white stripes occupying the remaining space.

Issue	Date	Un	U	PB	#	FDC	Q(M)
Lunar New Year, Tagged, Self-Adhesive, Serpentine Die-Cut 10.75							
3895 Pane of 24, 2 each	01/06/05	18.00				20.00	
a 37¢ Year of the Rat		.75	.20			1.25	
b 37¢ Year of the Ox		.75	.20			1.25	
c 37¢ Year of the Tiger		.75	.20			1.25	
d 37¢ Year of the Rabbit		.75	.20			1.25	
e 37¢ Year of the Dragon		.75	.20			1.25	
f 37¢ Year of the Snake		.75	.20			1.25	
g 37¢ Year of the Horse		.75	.20			1.25	
h 37¢ Year of the Ram		.75	.20			1.25	
i 37¢ Year of the Monkey		.75	.20			1.25	
j 37¢ Year of the Rooster		.75	.20			1.25	
k 37¢ Year of the Dog		.75	.20			1.25	
l 37¢ Year of the Boar		.75	.20			1.25	
Black Heritage, Tagged, Self-Adhesive, Serpentine Die-Cut 10.75							
3896 37¢ Marian Anderson	01/27/05	.75	.20	3.00	(4)	1.25	
Tagged, Self-Adhesive, Serpentine Die-Cut 10.75							
3897 37¢ Ronald Reagan	02/09/05	.75	.20	3.00	(4)	1.50	
Love, Tagged, Self-Adhesive, Serpentine Die-Cut 10.75 x 11 on 2, 3 or 4 sides							
3898 37¢ Love Bouquet	02/18/05	.75	.20			1.25	
a Booklet pane of 20		15.00					

Issue	Date	Un	U	PB	#	FDC	Q(M)
Northeast Deciduous Forest, Tagged, Self-Adhesive, Serpentine Die-Cut 10.75							
3899 Pane of 10	03/03/05	7.50				7.50	
a 37¢ Eastern Buckmoth		.75	.20			1.25	
b 37¢ Red-shouldered Hawk		.75	.20			1.25	
c 37¢ Eastern Red Bat		.75	.20			1.25	
d 37¢ White-tailed Deer		.75	.20			1.25	
e 37¢ Black Bear		.75	.20			1.25	
f 37¢ Long-tailed Weasel		.75	.20			1.25	
g 37¢ Wild Turkey		.75	.20			1.25	
h 37¢ Ovenbird		.75	.20			1.25	
i 37¢ Red Eft		.75	.20			1.25	
j 37¢ Eastern Chipmunk		.75	.20			1.25	
Garden Flowers, Tagged, Self-Adhesive, Serpentine Die-Cut 10.75 x 11 on 2, 3 or 4 sides							
3900 37¢ Hyacinth	03/15/05	.75	.20			1.25	
3901 37¢ Daffodil	03/15/05	.75	.20			1.25	
3902 37¢ Tulip	03/15/05	.75	.20			1.25	
3903 37¢ Iris	03/15/05	.75	.20			1.25	
a Block of 4 #3900-3903		3.00				3.25	
b Booklet pane, 5 ea. #3900-3903		15.00					
Literary Arts, Tagged, Self-Adhesive, Serpentine Die-Cut 10.75							
3904 37¢ Robert Penn Warren	04/22/05	.75	.20	3.00	(4)	1.25	
Tagged, Self-Adhesive, Serpentine Die-Cut 10.75							
3905 37¢ Edgar Y. "Yip" Harburg	04/28/05	.75	.20	3.00	(4)	1.25	

KOI STAMPED CARDS

These 2009 stamped cards feature colorful carp known as koi. Many Americans collect koi, prizing these large freshwater fish for their bold, bright colors in striking combinations and patterns. ▪ Koi collecting is thought to have begun in Asia hundreds of years ago, when farmers occasionally noticed carp *(Cyprinus carpio)* with colors other than the usual gray, brown, or black, swimming in their rice fields. In time, breeding and crossbreeding resulted in numerous varieties. Like all carp, koi are hardy fish that thrive in a range of water conditions and temperatures. This makes them ideal for shallow, year-round ornamental ponds, but it also makes them formidable competitors against other fish species if they are accidentally released into lakes and streams. ▪ In addition to hardiness, koi and other carp are traditionally associated with several highly regarded attributes and achievements. Many Asian and Asian-American families consider them to be symbols of perseverance and strength, energy and power, and prosperity and good fortune. ▪ The stamp art is based on photographs taken by the artist, Kam Mak, who left Hong Kong as a child and grew up in New York City's Chinatown. He and his family now live in Brooklyn.

HAPPY · NEW · YEAR!

3895   a   b   c

               d   e   f

               g   h   i

               j   k   l

3896

3897

3898

NORTHEAST DECIDUOUS FOREST

SEVENTH IN A SERIES

NATURE OF AMERICA

3899   a   b   c

               d   e

       f   g

   h   i   j

3900   3901

3902   3903

3904

3905

3906   **3907**

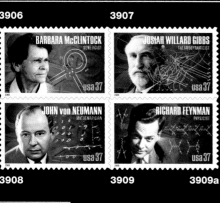

3908   **3909**   **3909a**

3911

Masterworks of Modern American Architecture

3910   a   b   c   d
         e   f   g   h
         i   j   k   l

3912   **3913**

3914   **3915**   **3915a**

3916   **3917**

3918   **3919**

3920   **3921**

3922   **3923**

3924   **3925**

3925a

3926   **3927**

3928   **3929**   **3929a**

3930

Issue		Date	Un	U	PB	#	FDC	Q(M)
American Scientists, Tagged, Self-Adhesive, Serpentine Die-Cut 10.75								
3906	37¢ Barbara McClintock	05/04/05	.75	.20			1.25	
3907	37¢ Josiah Willard Gibbs	05/04/05	.75	.20			1.25	
3908	37¢ John von Neumann	05/04/05	.75	.20			1.25	
3909	37¢ Richard Feynman	05/04/05	.75	.20	3.00	(4)	1.25	
a	Block or strip of 4		3.00				3.25	
Masterworks of Modern American Architecture, Tagged, Self-Adhesive, Serpentine Die-Cut 10.75 x 11								
3910	Pane of 12	05/19/05	9.00				9.00	
a	37¢ Guggenheim Museum, New York		.75	.20			1.25	
b	37¢ Chrysler Building, New York		.75	.20			1.25	
c	37¢ Vanna Venturi House, Philadelphia		.75	.20			1.25	
d	37¢ TWA Terminal, New York		.75	.20			1.25	
e	37¢ Walt Disney Concert Hall, Los Angeles		.75	.20			1.25	
f	37¢ 860-880 Lake Shore Drive, Chicago		.75	.20			1.25	
g	37¢ National Gallery of Art, Washington, DC		.75	.20			1.25	
h	37¢ Glass House, New Canaan, CT		.75	.20			1.25	
i	37¢ Yale Art & Architecture Building, New Haven, CT		.75	.20			1.25	
j	37¢ High Museum of Art, Atlanta		.75	.20			1.25	
k	37¢ Exeter Academy Library, Exeter, NH		.75	.20			1.25	
l	37¢ Hancock Center, Chicago		.75	.20			1.25	
Legends of Hollywood, Tagged, Self-Adhesive, Serpentine Die-Cut 11 x 10.75								
3911	37¢ Henry Fonda	05/20/05	.75	.20	3.00	(4)	1.25	
The Art of Disney: Celebration, Tagged, Self-Adhesive, Serpentine Die-Cut 10.5 x 10.75								
3912	37¢ Pluto, Mickey Mouse	06/30/05	.75	.20	3.00	(4)	1.25	
3913	37¢ Mad Hatter, Alice	06/30/05	.75	.20	3.00	(4)	1.25	
3914	37¢ Flounder, Ariel	06/30/05	.75	.20	3.00	(4)	1.25	
3915	37¢ Snow White, Dopey	06/30/05	.75	.20	3.00	(4)	1.25	
a	Block or vert. strip of 4		3.00		3.00	(4)	3.25	

Issue		Date	Un	U	PB	#	FDC	Q(M)
Advances in Aviation, Tagged, Self-Adhesive, Serpentine Die-Cut 10.75 x 10.5								
3916	37¢ Boeing 247	07/29/05	.75	.20			1.50	
3917	37¢ Consolidated PBY Catalina	07/29/05	.75	.20			1.50	
3918	37¢ Grumman F6F Hellcat	07/29/05	.75	.20			1.50	
3919	37¢ Republic P-47 Thunderbolt	07/29/05	.75	.20			1.50	
3920	37¢ Engineering and Research Corporation Ercoupe 415	07/29/05	.75	.20			1.50	
3921	37¢ Lockheed P-80 Shooting Star	07/29/05	.75	.20			1.50	
3922	37¢ Consolidated B-24 Liberator	07/29/05	.75	.20			1.50	
3923	37¢ Boeing B-29 Superfortress	07/29/05	.75	.20			1.50	
3924	37¢ Beechcraft 35 Bonanza	07/29/05	.75	.20			1.50	
3925	37¢ Northrop YB-49 Flying Wing	07/29/05	.75	.20			1.50	
a	Block of 10		7.50		7.50	(10)	7.50	
American Treasures: New Mexico Rio Grande Blankets, Tagged, Self-Adhesive, Serpentine Die-Cut 10.75 on 2 or 3 sides								
3926	37¢ Spanish design	07/30/05	.75	.20			1.25	
3927	37¢ Mexican design	07/30/05	.75	.20			1.25	
3928	37¢ Pueblo design	07/30/05	.75	.20			1.25	
3929	37¢ Navajo design	07/30/05	.75	.20			1.25	
a	Block of 4		3.00				3.25	
b	Booklet pane of 5 ea.		15.00					
Tagged, Self-Adhesive, Serpentine Die-Cut 10.75								
3930	37¢ Presidential Libraries	08/04/05	.75	.20	3.00	(4)	1.25	

SEABISCUIT STAMPED ENVELOPE

This stamped envelope features an illustration by artist John Mattos of the racehorse Seabiscuit. An unassuming champion, Seabiscuit raised the hopes and spirits of a beleaguered nation during the Great Depression with a series of unlikely victories. ■ Born in Kentucky in 1933, Seabiscuit was small, dull brown, and unattractive—belying his Thoroughbred pedigree. Although he ran in many races as a young horse, his slow times on the track did not improve with continued training. ■ Charles Howard, an entrepreneur with a passion for horses, saw the colt's potential and bought him in 1936. Flourishing under the new training regimen, by the end of the year Seabiscuit had won several races and set two records. Although he started 1937 with a loss, Seabiscuit's spectacular performance in race after race created a storm of interest across the country. ■ Seabiscuit ran perhaps his greatest race against just a single horse: the 1937 Triple Crown winner War Admiral. Held on November 1, 1938, at Pimlico in Maryland, the race drew some 40,000 spectators and was broadcast on the radio to 40 million listeners across the country, including President Franklin D. Roosevelt. Although War Admiral, the favorite, ran his fastest time at the track distance of 1 3/16 miles, Seabiscuit won the race by four lengths and set a blazing track record in the process. ■ In 1940, Seabiscuit retired to Howard's Ridgewood Ranch in Willits, California, where he died on May 17, 1947. He is buried at Ridgewood. ■ The stamp design depicts a scene from the 1938 match race between Seabiscuit and War Admiral.

Issue	Date	Un	U	PB	#	FDC	Q(M)
America on the Move: 50s Sporty Cars, Booklet, Tagged, Self-Adhesive, Serpentine Die-Cut 10.75 on 2 or 3 sides							
3931 37¢ 1953 Studebaker Starliner	08/20/05	.80	.20			2.00	
3932 37¢ 1954 Kaiser Darren	08/20/05	.80	.20			2.00	
3933 37¢ 1953 Chevrolet Corvette	08/20/05	.80	.20			2.00	
3934 37¢ 1952 Nash Healey	08/20/05	.80	.20			2.00	
3935 37¢ 1955 Ford Thunderbird	08/20/05	.80	.20			2.00	
a Vertical strip of 5 #3931-3935		4.00				5.00	
b Booklet pane of 4 ea.		16.00					
American Sports Personalities, Tagged, Self-Adhesive, Serpentine Die-Cut 10.75							
3936 37¢ Arthur Ashe	08/27/05	.75	.20	3.00	(4)	2.00	
To Form a More Perfect Union, Tagged, Self-Adhesive, Serpentine Die-Cut 10.75 x 10.5							
3937 Pane of 10	08/30/05	7.50				8.75	
a 37¢ 1948 Executive Order 9981		.75	.20			2.00	
b 37¢ 1965 Voting Rights Act		.75	.20			2.00	
c 37¢ 1960 Lunch Counter Sit-ins		.75	.20			2.00	
d 37¢ 1957 Little Rock Nine		.75	.20			2.00	
e 37¢ 1955 Montgomery Bus Boycott		.75	.20			2.00	
f 37¢ 1961 Freedom Riders		.75	.20			2.00	
g 37¢ 1964 Civil Rights Act		.75	.20			2.00	
h 37¢ 1963 March on Washington		.75	.20			2.00	
i 37¢ 1965 Selma March		.75	.20			2.00	
j 37¢ 1954 Brown v. Board of Education		.75	.20			2.00	

Issue	Date	Un	U	PB	#	FDC	Q(M)
Tagged, Self-Adhesive, Serpentine Die-Cut 10.5 x 11							
3938 37¢ Child Health	09/07/05	.75	.20	3.00	(4)	2.00	
Let's Dance/Bailemos, Tagged, Self-Adhesive, Serpentine Die-Cut 10.75							
3939 37¢ Merengue	09/17/05	.75	.20			2.00	
3940 37¢ Salsa	09/17/05	.75	.20			2.00	
3941 37¢ Cha cha cha	09/17/05	.75	.20			2.00	
3942 37¢ Mambo	09/17/05	.75	.20			2.00	
a Vert. strip of 4		3.00		6.00	(8)	4.25	
Legends of Hollywood, Tagged, Self-Adhesive, Serpentine Die-Cut 10.75							
3943 37¢ Greta Garbo	09/23/05	.75	.20	3.00	(4)	2.00	
Jim Henson and the Muppets, Tagged, Self-Adhesive, Serpentine Die-Cut 10.5, 10.5 x 10.75							
3944 Pane of 11	09/28/05	8.25				9.25	
a 37¢ Kermit the Frog		.75	.20			2.00	
b 37¢ Fozzie Bear		.75	.20			2.00	
c 37¢ Sam the Eagle and Flag		.75	.20			2.00	
d 37¢ Miss Piggy		.75	.20			2.00	
e 37¢ Statler and Waldorf		.75	.20			2.00	
f 37¢ The Swedish Chef and Fruit		.75	.20			2.00	
g 37¢ Animal		.75	.20			2.00	
h 37¢ Dr. Bunsen Honeydew and Beaker		.75	.20			2.00	
i 37¢ Rowlf the Dog		.75	.20			2.00	
j 37¢ The Great Gonzo and Camilla the Chicken		.75	.20			2.00	
k 37¢ Jim Henson		.75	.20			2.00	

ABRAHAM LINCOLN

With the issuance of these four stamps in 2009, the U.S. Postal Service recognizes the 200th anniversary of the birth of Abraham Lincoln (1809-1865), who rose from humble, frontier origins to become a prominent lawyer and politician and ultimately President of the United States. The stamp art was created by Mark Summers, who is noted for his scratchboard technique, a style distinguished by a dense network of lines etched with exquisite precision. Each stamp features a different aspect of Lincoln's life. RAIL-SPLITTER — As a youth, Lincoln split logs for rail fences on the American frontier. When he became a candidate for President in 1860, the Republican Party used the "rail-splitter" image to enhance Lincoln's appeal to the workingman. LAWYER — Lincoln practiced law in Springfield, Illinois, for nearly 25 years. He became a prominent attorney in the state and learned the concerns of citizens from all walks of life. POLITICIAN — Lincoln was little known nationally until 1858, when he ran as the Republican nominee against Democrat Stephen A. Douglas for a U.S. Senate seat from Illinois. Lincoln gained national exposure during his historic series of debates with Douglas. PRESIDENT — As President from 1861 to 1865, Lincoln faced the crisis of the Civil War. He preserved the Union, while giving added meaning to the conflict by issuing the Emancipation Proclamation and by calling for "a new birth of freedom."

3935

1955 Ford Thunderbird   USA 37

3933

1953 Chevrolet Corvette   USA 37

3931

1953 Studebaker Starliner   USA 37

3934

1952 Nash Healey   USA 37

3932

1954 Kaiser Darrin   USA 37

3935a

USA 37

3936

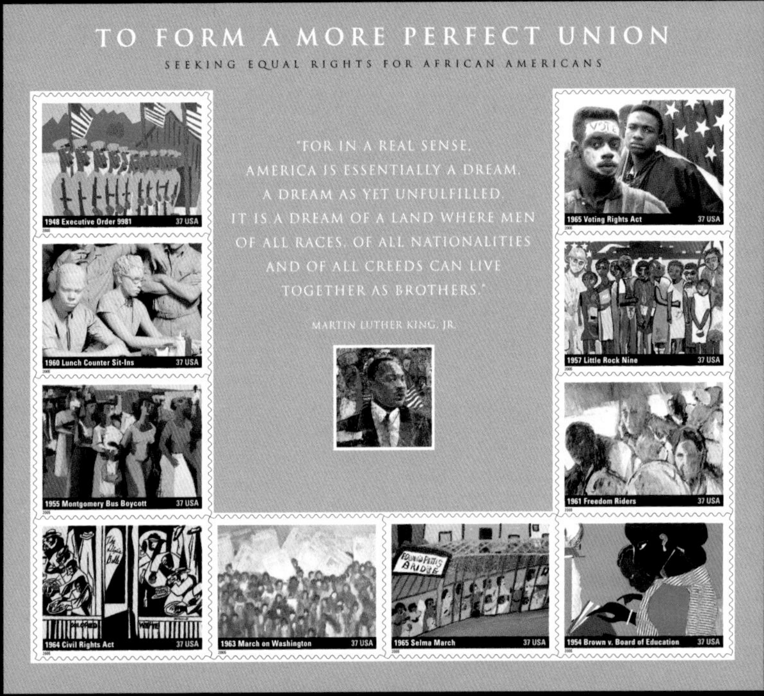

TO FORM A MORE PERFECT UNION
SEEKING EQUAL RIGHTS FOR AFRICAN AMERICANS

"FOR IN A REAL SENSE, AMERICA IS ESSENTIALLY A DREAM, A DREAM AS YET UNFULFILLED. IT IS A DREAM OF A LAND WHERE MEN OF ALL RACES, OF ALL NATIONALITIES AND OF ALL CREEDS CAN LIVE TOGETHER AS BROTHERS."

MARTIN LUTHER KING, JR.

1948 Executive Order 9981 37 USA
1965 Voting Rights Act 37 USA
1960 Lunch Counter Sit-Ins 37 USA
1957 Little Rock Nine 37 USA
1955 Montgomery Bus Boycott 37 USA
1961 Freedom Riders 37 USA
1964 Civil Rights Act 37 USA
1963 March on Washington 37 USA
1965 Selma March 37 USA
1954 Brown v. Board of Education 37 USA

3937 a b c d e f g h i j

3939

ChildHealth 37 USA

3938

3940

Merengue 37 USA

3943

GRETA GARBO USA 37

3941

SALSA 37 USA

3942

CHA CHA CHA 37 USA

3942a

MAMBO 37 USA

3944 a b k c d e f g h i j

USA 37

Jim Henson
the man behind the Muppets

"When I was young, my ambition was to be one of the people who made a difference in this world. My hope is to leave the world a little better for my having been there."

Jim Henson

3945 3946

3947 3948 3948a

3949 3950

3951 3952 3952a

3961 3962

3963 3964 3964a

3967

3976

3978

3987 3988 3989 3990

3991 3992 3993 3994 3994a

3995

3996

	Issue	Date	Un	U	PB	#	FDC	Q(M)
	Constellations, Tagged, Self-Adhesive, Serpentine Die-Cut 10.75							
3945	37¢ Leo	10/03/05	.75	.20	3.00	(4)	2.00	
3946	37¢ Orion	10/03/05	.75	.20	3.00	(4)	2.00	
3947	37¢ Lyra	10/03/05	.75	.20	3.00	(4)	2.00	
3948	37¢ Pegasus	10/03/05	.75	.20	3.00	(4)	2.00	
a	Block or vert. strip of 4		3.00		3.00	(4)	4.25	
	Holiday Celebration: Holiday, Christmas Cookies, Tagged, Self-Adhesive, Serpentine Die-Cut 10.75 x 11							
3949	37¢ Santa Claus	10/20/05	.75	.20	3.00	(4)	2.00	
3950	37¢ Snowmen	10/20/05	.75	.20	3.00	(4)	2.00	
3951	37¢ Angel	10/20/05	.75	.20	3.00	(4)	2.00	
3952	37¢ Elves	10/20/05	.75	.20	3.00	(4)	2.00	
a	Block or vert. strip of 4		3.00		3.00	(4)	4.25	
	Booklet, Self-Adhesive, Serpentine Die-Cut 10.75 x 11 on 2 or 3 sides							
3953	37¢ Santa Claus	10/20/05	.75	.20			2.00	
3954	37¢ Snowmen	10/20/05	.75	.20			2.00	
3955	37¢ Angel	10/20/05	.75	.20			2.00	
3956	37¢ Elves	10/20/05	.75	.20			2.00	
a	Block or vert. strip of 4		3.00				4.25	
	Booklet, Self-Adhesive, Serpentine Die-Cut 10.5 x 10.75 on 2 or 3 sides							
3957	37¢ Santa Claus	10/20/05	1.50	.20			2.00	
3958	37¢ Snowmen	10/20/05	1.50	.20			2.00	
3959	37¢ Angel	10/20/05	1.50	.20			2.00	
3960	37¢ Elves	10/20/05	1.50	.20			2.00	
a	Block or vert. strip of 4		6.00				4.25	
	Distinguished Marines, Tagged, Self-Adhesive, Serpentine Die-Cut 11 x 10.5							
3961	37¢ Lt. Gen. John A. Lejeune	11/10/05	1.00	.20			2.00	
3962	37¢ Lt. Gen. Lewis B. Puller	11/10/05	1.00	.20			2.00	
3963	37¢ Sgt. John Basilone	11/10/05	1.00	.20			2.00	
3964	37¢ Sgt. Major Daniel J. Daly	11/10/05	1.00	.20			2.00	
a	Block or horiz. strip of 4		4.00		4.00	(4)	4.25	
	Tagged, Perf. 11.25							
3965	(39¢) Flag and Statue of Liberty	12/08/05	.80	.20	5.00	(4)	2.00	
	Self-Adhesive, Serpentine Die-Cut 11.25 x 11							
3966	(39¢) Flag and Statue of Liberty	12/08/05	.80	.20	3.20	(4)	2.00	
	Coil, Perf. 9.75 Vertically							
3967	(39¢) Flag and Statue of Liberty	12/08/05	.80	.20	5.25	(5)	2.00	
	Self-Adhesive, Serpentine Die-Cut 8.5 Vertically							
3968	(39¢) Flag and Statue of Liberty	12/08/05	.80	.20	5.25	(5)	2.00	
	Tagged, Coil, Serpentine Die-Cut 10.25 Vertically							
3969	(39¢) Flag and Statue of Liberty, type of 2005 dated "2006"	12/08/05	.80	.20	5.25	(5)	2.00	
	Self-Adhesive, Serpentine Die-Cut 9.5 Vertically							
3970	(39¢) Flag and Statue of Liberty	12/08/05	.80	.20	7.00	(5)	2.00	
	Booklet, Serpentine Die-Cut 11.25 x 11 on 2 or 3 sides							
3971	(39¢) Flag and Statue of Liberty	12/08/05	.80	.20			2.00	
a	Booklet pane of 20		16.00					
	Booklet, Self-Adhesive, Serpentine Die-Cut 11.25 x 10.75 on 2 or 3 sides							
3972	(39¢) Flag and Statue of Liberty	12/08/05	.80	.20			2.00	
a	Booklet pane of 20		16.00					
	Booklet, Self-Adhesive, Serpentine Die-Cut 10.25 x 10.75 on 2 or 3 sides							
3973	(39¢) Flag and Statue of Liberty	12/08/05	.80	.20			2.00	
a	Booklet pane of 20		16.00					
	Booklet, Self-Adhesive, Serpentine Die-Cut 11.25 x 11 on 2 or 3 sides							
3974	(39¢) Flag and Statue of Liberty	12/08/05	.80	.20			2.00	
a	Booklet pane of 4		3.20					

	Issue	Date	Un	U	PB	#	FDC	Q(M)
	Booklet, Self-Adhesive, Serpentine Die-Cut 8 on 2, 3 or 4 sides							
3975	(39¢) Flag and Statue of Liberty	12/08/05	.80	.20			2.00	
a	Booklet pane of 18		14.50					
	Love, Booklet, Tagged, Self-Adhesive, Serpentine Die-Cut 11 on 2, 3 or 4 sides							
3976	(39¢) Love: True Blue	01/03/06	.90	.20			2.00	
a	Booklet pane of 20		18.00					
	Tagged, Self-Adhesive, Serpentine Die-Cut 11.25 x 10.75							
3978	39¢ Flag and Statue of Liberty	04/08/06	.80	.20	3.20	(4)	2.00	
a	Booklet pane of 10		8.00					
	Coil, Serpentine Die-Cut 11 Vertically							
3979	39¢ Flag and Statue of Liberty	03/08/06	.80	.20	5.25	(5)	2.00	
	Coil, Serpentine Die-Cut 11 Vertically							
3980	39¢ Flag and Statue of Liberty	01/09/06	.80	.20	5.25	(5)	2.00	
	Coil, Serpentine Die-Cut 9.5 Vertically							
3981	39¢ Flag and Statue of Liberty	04/08/06	.80	.20	6.25	(5)	2.00	
	Coil, Serpentine Die-Cut 10.25 Vertically							
3982	39¢ Flag and Statue of Liberty	04/08/06	.80	.20	5.25	(5)	2.00	
	Coil, Serpentine Die-Cut 8.25 Vertically							
3983	39¢ Flag and Statue of Liberty	04/08/06	.80	.20	5.25	(5)	2.00	
	Booklet, Serpentine Die-Cut 11.25 x 10.75 on 2 or 3 sides							
3985	39¢ Flag and Statue of Liberty	04/08/06	.80	.20			2.00	
	Favorite Children's Book Animals, Tagged, Self-Adhesive, Serpentine Die-Cut 10.75							
3987	39¢ The Very Hungry Caterpillar, from *The Very Hungry Caterpillar*	01/10/06	.80	.20			2.00	
3988	39¢ Wilbur, from *Charlotte's Web*	01/10/06	.80	.20			2.00	
3989	39¢ Fox in Socks, from *Fox in Socks*	01/10/06	.80	.20			2.00	
3990	39¢ Maisy, from *Maisy's ABC*	01/10/06	.80	.20			2.00	
3991	39¢ Wild Thing, from *Where the Wild Things Are*	01/10/06	.80	.20			2.00	
3992	39¢ Curious George, from *Curious George*	01/10/06	.80	.20			2.00	
3993	39¢ Olivia, from *Olivia*	01/10/06	.80	.20			2.00	
3994	39¢ Frederick, from *Frederick*	01/10/06	.80	.20			2.00	
a	Block of 8 #3987-3994		6.50		6.50	(8)	7.50	
	Olmpic Games, Winter, Tagged, Self-Adhesive, Serpentine Die-Cut 10.75							
3995	39¢ 2006 Winter Olympic Games	01/11/06	.80	.20	3.20	(4)	2.00	
	Black Heritage, Tagged, Self-Adhesive, Serpentine Die-Cut 10.75							
3996	39¢ Hattie McDaniel	01/25/06	.80	.20	3.20	(4)	2.00	
	Lunar New Year, Tagged, Self-Adhesive, Serpentine Die-Cut 10.75							
3997	Pane of 12 (types of 1992-2004)	01/29/06	9.75				10.50	
a	39¢ Year of the Rat		.80	.20			2.00	
b	39¢ Year of the Ox		.80	.20			2.00	
c	39¢ Year of the Tiger		.80	.20			2.00	
d	39¢ Year of the Rabbit		.80	.20			2.00	
e	39¢ Year of the Dragon		.80	.20			2.00	
f	39¢ Year of the Snake		.80	.20			2.00	
g	39¢ Year of the Horse		.80	.20			2.00	
h	39¢ Year of the Ram		.80	.20			2.00	
i	39¢ Year of the Monkey		.80	.20			2.00	
j	39¢ Year of the Rooster		.80	.20			2.00	
k	39¢ Year of the Dog		.80	.20			2.00	
l	39¢ Year of the Boar		.80	.20			2.00	

Issue	Date	Un	U	PB #	FDC	Q(M)
Booklet, Tagged, Self-Adhesive, Serpentine Die-Cut 10.75 x 11 on 2, 3 or 4 sides						
3998 39¢ Our Wedding	03/01/06	.80	.20		2.00	
a Booklet pane of 20		16.00				
Booklet, Serpentine Die-Cut 10.75 x 11						
3999 63¢ Our Wedding	03/01/06	1.25	.50		2.50	
a Booklet pane of 20, 20 each #3998-3999		37.50				
b Horiz. pair, #3998-3999, vert. gutter between		2.10	1.50			
Tagged, Perf. 11.25						
4000 24¢ Common Buckeye Butterfly	03/08/06	.50	.20	8.00 (4)	2.00	
Self-Adhesive, Serpentine Die-Cut 11						
4001 24¢ Common Buckeye Butterfly	03/08/06	.50	.20	2.00 (4)	2.00	
a Serpentine Die-cut 10.75 x 11.25 on 3 sides		.50	.20			
Coil, Serpentine Die-Cut 8.25 Horizontally						
4002 24¢ Common Buckeye Butterfly	03/08/06	.50	.20	3.75 (5)	2.00	
Crops of the Americas, Coil, Tagged, Self-Adhesive, Serpentine Die-Cut 10.25 Horizontally						
4003 39¢ Chili Peppers	03/16/06	.85	.20		2.00	
4004 39¢ Beans	03/16/06	.85	.20		2.00	
4005 39¢ Sunflower and Seeds	03/16/06	.85	.20		2.00	
4006 39¢ Squashes	03/16/06	.85	.20		2.00	
4007 39¢ Corn	03/16/06	.85	.20		2.00	
a Strip of 5 #4003-4007		4.25		5.75 (5)	5.25	
Crops of the Americas, Booklet, Serpentine Die-Cut 10.75 x 10.5 on 2 or 3 sides						
4008 39¢ Corn	03/16/06	.80	.20		2.00	
4009 39¢ Squashes	03/16/06	.80	.20		2.00	
4010 39¢ Sunflower and Seeds	03/16/06	.80	.20		2.00	
4011 39¢ Beans	03/16/06	.80	.20		2.00	
4012 39¢ Chili Peppers	03/16/06	.80	.20		2.00	
a Horiz. strip of 5 #4008-4012		4.00			5.25	
Crops of the Americas, Booklet, Serpentine Die-Cut 10.75 x 11.25 on 2 or 3 sides						
4013 39¢ Chili Peppers	03/16/06	.80	.20		2.00	
4014 39¢ Corn	03/16/06	.80	.20		2.00	
4015 39¢ Squashes	03/16/06	.80	.20		2.00	
4016 39¢ Sunflower and Seeds	03/16/06	.80	.20		2.00	
a Pane of 4, #4013-4016		3.20			5.25	
4017 39¢ Beans	03/16/06	.80	.20		2.00	
a Horiz. strip of 5 #4013-4017		4.00				
b Pane of 4, #4013-4015, 4017		3.20				
Tagged, Self-Adhesive, Serpentine Die-Cut 10.75 x 10.5						
4018 $4.05 X-Planes	03/17/06	8.00	5.00	40.00 (4)	8.00	
4019 $14.40 X-Planes	03/17/06	27.50	15.00	110.00 (4)	27.50	
Tagged, Self-Adhesive, Serpentine Die-Cut 11						
4020 39¢ Sugar Ray Robinson	04/07/06	.80	.20	3.20 (4)	2.00	
Benjamin Franklin, Tagged, Self-Adhesive, Serpentine Die-Cut 11						
4021 39¢ Statesman	04/07/06	1.10	.20		2.00	
4022 39¢ Scientist	04/07/06	1.10	.20		2.00	
4023 39¢ Printer	04/07/06	1.10	.20		2.00	
4024 39¢ Postmaster	04/07/06	1.10	.20		2.00	
a Block or Horiz. strip of 4		4.40		4.50 (4)	4.50	
Art of Disney: Romance, Tagged, Self-Adhesive, Serpentine Die-Cut 10.5 x 10.75						
4025 39¢ Mickey and Minnie Mouse	04/21/06	.80	.20		2.00	
4026 39¢ Cinderella and Prince Charming	04/21/06	.80	.20		2.00	
4027 39¢ Beauty and the Beast	04/21/06	.80	.20		2.00	
4028 39¢ Lady and Tramp	04/21/06	.80	.20		2.00	
a Block or vert. strip of 4		3.20		3.20 (4)	4.50	
Booklet, Tagged, Self-Adhesive, Serpentine Die-Cut 11 on 2, 3 or 4 sides						
4029 39¢ Love: True Blue	05/01/06	.80	.20		2.00	
b Booklet pane of 20		16.00				
Literary Arts, Tagged, Self-Adhesive, Serpentine Die-Cut 10.75						
4030 39¢ Katherine Anne Porter	05/15/06	.80	.20	3.20 (4)	2.00	
Tagged, Self-Adhesive, Serpentine Die-Cut 10.75						
4031 39¢ AMBER Alert	05/25/06	.80	.20	3.20 (4)	2.00	
Tagged, Self-Adhesive, Serpentine Die-Cut 11.25 x 11						
4032 39¢ Purple Heart (type of 2003)	05/25/06	.80	.20	3.20 (4)	2.00	

CELEBRATE!

When good times call for good wishes, the "Celebrate!" stamp, which is being reissued in 2009, adds a touch of cheer to special greeting cards, invitations, and gift-bearing packages. First issued in 2007, this colorful stamp allows a postal patron to add an extra wish to cards and letters being sent to acknowledge a host of happy occasions, from birthdays to engagements, anniversaries, graduations, and more. ■ Artist Nicholas Wilton of San Geronimo, California, designed the "Celebrate!" stamp. Twelve brightly colored blocks, much like the building blocks made for children, are arranged in four horizontal rows, with three blocks in each row. Each of the blocks in the top three rows contains a single letter of the alphabet that when read together spell out the word "Celebrate." The three blocks in the bottom row contain an exclamation point, a star, and the stamp denomination.

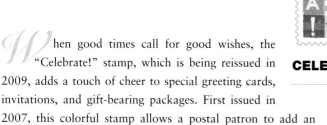

3998

3999

Common Buckeye
USA 24

4000

4003
USA 39

4004
39 USA

4005
USA 39

4006
USA 39

4007
USA 39

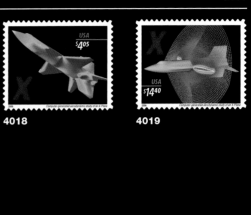

4018

4019

SUGAR RAY ROBINSON
USA 39
WORLD CHAMPION

4020

4021 BENJAMIN FRANKLIN, STATESMAN
39 USA

4022 BENJAMIN FRANKLIN, SCIENTIST
USA 39

4023 BENJAMIN FRANKLIN, PRINTER
Almanack 1733

4024 B. FREE FRANKLIN, POSTMASTER
USA 39

4024a

4025 39 USA

4026 39 USA

4027 39 USA

4028 39 USA

4028a

4029
39 USA

KATHERINE ANNE PORTER
USA 39

4030

39 USA
AMBER ALERT
saves missing children

4031

4035

4072a

4073

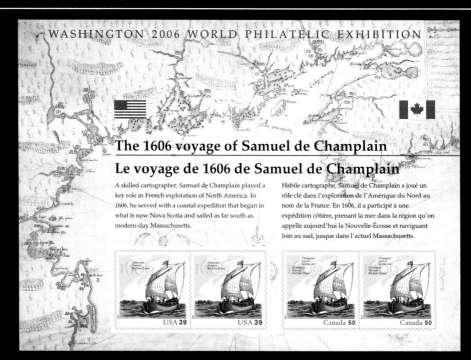

4074a

Issue	Date	Un	U	PB	#	FDC	Q(M)
Wonders of America: Land of Superlatives, Tagged, Self-Adhesive, Serpentine Die-Cut 10.75							
4033 39¢ American Alligator, Largest Alligator	05/27/06	.80	45			2.00	
4034 39¢ MoloKa'i, Highest Sea Cliffs	05/27/06	.80	45			2.00	
4035 39¢ Saguaro, Tallest Cactus	05/27/06	.80	45			2.00	
4036 39¢ Bering Glacier, Largest Glacier	05/27/06	.80	45			2.00	
4037 39¢ Great Sand Dunes, Tallest Dunes	05/27/06	.80	45			2.00	
4038 39¢ Chesapeake Bay, Largest Estuary	05/27/06	.80	45			2.00	
4039 39¢ Cliff Palace, Largest Cliff Dwelling	05/27/06	.80	45			2.00	
4040 39¢ Crater Lake, Deepest Lake	05/27/06	.80	45			2.00	
4041 39¢ American Bison, Largest Land Mammal	05/27/06	.80	45			2.00	
4042 39¢ Off the Florida Keys, Longest Reef	05/27/06	.80	45			2.00	
4043 39¢ Pacific Crest Trail, Longest Hiking Trail	05/27/06	.80	45			2.00	
4044 39¢ Gateway Arch, Tallest Man-made Monument	05/27/06	.80	45			2.00	
4045 39¢ Appalachians, Oldest Mountains	05/27/06	.80	45			2.00	
4046 39¢ American Lotus, Largest Flower	05/27/06	.80	45			2.00	
4047 39¢ Lake Superior, Largest Lake	05/27/06	.80	45			2.00	
4048 39¢ Pronghorn, Fastest Land Animal	05/27/06	.80	45			2.00	
4049 39¢ Bristlecone Pines, Oldest Trees	05/27/06	.80	45			2.00	
4050 39¢ Yosemite Falls, Tallest Waterfall	05/27/06	.80	45			2.00	
4051 39¢ Great Basin, Largest Desert	05/27/06	.80	45			2.00	
4052 39¢ Verrazano-Narrows Bridge, Longest Span	05/27/06	.80	45			2.00	
4053 39¢ Mount Washington, Windiest Place	05/27/06	.80	45			2.00	
4054 39¢ Grand Canyon, Largest Canyon	05/27/06	.80	45			2.00	
4055 39¢ American Bullfrog, Largest Frog	05/27/06	.80	45			2.00	

Issue	Date	Un	U	PB	#	FDC	Q(M)
Wonders of America: Land of Superlatives, Tagged, Self-Adhesive, Serpentine Die-Cut 10.75 continued							
4056 39¢ Oroville Dam, Tallest Dam	05/27/06	.80	45			2.00	
4057 39¢ Peregrine Falcon, Fastest Bird	05/27/06	.80	45			2.00	
4058 39¢ Mississippi River Delta, Largest Delta	05/27/06	.80	45			2.00	
4059 39¢ Steamboat, Tallest Geyser	05/27/06	.80	45			2.00	
4060 39¢ Rainbow Bridge, Largest Natural Bridge	05/27/06	.80	45			2.00	
4061 39¢ White Sturgeon, Largest Freshwater Fish	05/27/06	.80	45			2.00	
4062 39¢ Rocky Mountains, Longest Mountain Chain	05/27/06	.80	45			2.00	
4063 39¢ Coast Redwoods, Tallest Trees	05/27/06	.80	45			2.00	
4064 39¢ American Beaver, Largest Rodent	05/27/06	.80	45			2.00	
4065 39¢ Mississippi-Missouri, Longest River System	05/27/06	.80	45			2.00	
4066 39¢ Mount Wai'ale'ale, Rainiest Spot	05/27/06	.80	45			2.00	
4067 39¢ Kilauea, Most Active Volcano	05/27/06	.80	45			2.00	
4068 39¢ Mammoth Cave, Longest Cave	05/27/06	.80	45			2.00	
4069 39¢ Blue Whale, Loudest Animal	05/27/06	.80	45			2.00	
4070 39¢ Death Valley, Hottest Spot	05/27/06	.80	45			2.00	
4071 39¢ Cornish-Windsor Bridge, Longest Covered Bridge	05/27/06	.80	45			2.00	
4072 39¢ Quaking Aspen, Largest Plant	05/27/06	.80	45			2.00	
a Pane of 40 #4033-4072		32.00				32.50	
Tagged, Self-Adhesive, Serpentine Die-Cut 10.75							
4073 39¢ 1606 Voyage of Samuel de Champlain	05/28/06	.85	.20	3.50	(4)	2.00	
Souvenir Sheet, Perf. 11							
4074 39¢ 1606 Voyage of Samuel de Champlain, sheet 2 each #4074a, Canada #2156a	05/28/06	4.25	2.00			4.75	
a 39¢ 1606 Voyage of Samuel de Champlain	05/28/06	.85	.20				

An American Postal Portrait — *A Photographic Legacy*

The rich history of the U.S. Postal Service from 1860 until the present day comes to life in more than 200 dazzling photographs from behind-the-scenes stories of individual postal workers to a visual record of the growth of technology. The book also includes color reproductions of every U.S. stamp that commemorates the Post Office and its employees. Sixty-one stamp images and four stationery selections make this book a fascinating tribute to America's leading communications institution.

Item #989100 $31.50

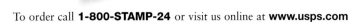

To order call **1-800-STAMP-24** or visit us online at **www.usps.com**

Issue	Date	Un	U	PB	#	FDC	Q(M)
Washington 2006 World Philatelic Exhibition, Souvenir Sheet, Tagged, Perf. 10.75 x 10.5							
4075 Pane of 3	05/29/06	16.00	6.00			16.00	
a $1 Lincoln Memorial		2.00	.50			3.25	
b $2 U.S. Capitol		4.00	1.00			5.25	
c $5 Head of Freedom Statue, Capitol Dome		10.00	2.50			10.00	
Distinguished American Diplomats, Souvenir Sheet, Tagged, Self-Adhesive, Serpentine Die-Cut 10.75							
4076 Pane of 6	05/29/06	4.80				6.00	
a 39¢ Robert D. Murphy		.80	.20			2.00	
b 39¢ Frances E. Willis		.80	.20			2.00	
c 39¢ Hiram Bingham IV		.80	.20			2.00	
d 39¢ Philip C. Habib		.80	.20			2.00	
e 39¢ Charles E. Bohlen		.80	.20			2.00	
f 39¢ Clifton R. Wharton, Sr.		.80	.20			2.00	
Legends of Hollywood, Tagged, Self-Adhesive, Serpentine Die-Cut 10.75							
4077 39¢ Judy Garland	06/10/06	.80	.20	3.20	(4)	2.00	
Tagged, Self-Adhesive, Serpentine Die-Cut 10.75							
4078 39¢ Ronald Reagan (type of 2005)	06/14/06	.80	.20	3.20	(4)	2.00	
Tagged, Self-Adhesive, Serpentine Die-Cut 11							
4079 39¢ Happy Birthday (type of 2002)	06/23/06	.80	.20	3.20	(4)	2.00	
Baseball Sluggers, Tagged, Self-Adhesive, Serpentine Die-Cut 10.75							
4080 39¢ Roy Campanella	07/15/06	.80	.20	3.20	(4)	2.00	
4081 39¢ Hank Greenberg	07/15/06	.80	.20	3.20	(4)	2.00	
4082 39¢ Mel Ott	07/15/06	.80	.20	3.20	(4)	2.00	
4083 39¢ Mickey Mantle	07/15/06	.80	.20	3.20	(4)	2.00	
a Block or vert. strip of 4 #4080-4083		3.20		3.20	(4)	4.50	

Issue	Date	Un	U	PB	#	FDC	Q(M)
DC Comics Super Heroes, Tagged, Self-Adhesive, Serpentine Die-Cut 10.5 x 10.75							
4084 Pane of 20	07/20/06	16.00				16.00	
a 39¢ Superman		.80	.20			2.00	
b 39¢ Green Lantern		.80	.20			2.00	
c 39¢ Wonder Woman		.80	.20			2.00	
d 39¢ Green Arrow		.80	.20			2.00	
e 39¢ Batman		.80	.20			2.00	
f 39¢ The Flash		.80	.20			2.00	
g 39¢ Plastic Man		.80	.20			2.00	
h 39¢ Aquaman		.80	.20			2.00	
i 39¢ Supergirl		.80	.20			2.00	
j 39¢ Hawkman		.80	.20			2.00	
k 39¢ Cover of *Superman* #11		.80	.20			2.00	
l 39¢ Cover of *Green Lantern* #15		.80	.20			2.00	
m 39¢ Cover of *Wonder Woman* #22		.80	.20			2.00	
n 39¢ Cover of *Green Arrow* #15		.80	.20			2.00	
o 39¢ Cover of *Batman* #1		.80	.20			2.00	
p 39¢ Cover of *The Flash* #111		.80	.20			2.00	
q 39¢ Cover of *Plastic Man* #4		.80	.20			2.00	
r 39¢ Cover of *Aquaman* #5		.80	.20			2.00	
s 39¢ Cover of *The Daring New Adventures of Supergirl* #1		.80	.20			2.00	
t 39¢ Cover of *The Brave and the Bold Presents* Hawkman #36		.80	.20			2.00	
American Motorcycles, Tagged, Self-Adhesive, Serpentine Die-Cut 10.75 x 10.5							
4085 39¢ 1940 Indian Four	08/07/06	.90	.20			2.00	
4086 39¢ 1918 Cleveland	08/07/06	.90	.20			2.00	
4087 39¢ Generic "Chopper" c. 1970	08/07/06	.90	.20			2.00	
4088 39¢ 1965 Harley-Davidson Electra-Glide	08/07/06	.90	.20			2.00	
a Block or horiz. strip of 4 #4085-4088		3.60		3.60	(4)	4.50	

OFFICIAL MAIL

In 2009 the U.S. Postal Service issued the latest Official Mail stamps in a design familiar to collectors. Patterned after the Great Seal of the United States, the design—by Bradbury Thompson—has been used on all Official Mail stamps since the category was resumed in 1983. ▪ The design of the Great Seal was a collaborative effort of the nation's Founding Fathers. Finalized on June 20, 1782, the design today remains the same. On the breast of the American bald eagle is a shield; an olive branch is in the eagle's right talon and a bundle of thirteen arrows is in his left. ▪ Housed in a mahogany cabinet located in the Exhibit Hall of the U.S. Department of State in Washington, D.C., the Great Seal is still in use today. It is affixed to a variety of official documents including proclamations and ratifications of treaties and appointment commissions of Ambassadors and Foreign Service officers. ▪ Official Mail stamps first appeared in the United States in the 19th century. Issued on July 1, 1873, the stamps were created in order to account for postage on mail sent by various federal departments. Although collectors may buy Official Mail stamps, they cannot use them for postage. These stamps may only be used on mail sent by U.S. government agencies and related to official business.

WASHINGTON 2006
WORLD PHILATELIC EXHIBITION

4075   a   b   c

Distinguished American Diplomats

4076   a   b   c
       d   e   f

4077

4080   4081

ROY CAMPANELLA   HANK GREENBERG

MEL OTT   MICKEY MANTLE

4082   4083   4083a

4085   4086

Indian 1940   Cleveland 1918

Chopper c.1970   Harley-Davidson 1965

4087   4088   4088a

DC Comics

SUPER HEROES

4084   a   b   c   d   e

       f   g   h   i   j

       k   l   m   n   o

       p   q

4089

4094

4093

4098

4092

4097

4091

4096

4090

4095

4098a

SOUTHERN FLORIDA WETLAND

EIGHTH IN A SERIES

NATURE OF AMERICA

4099   a   b   c   d

e   f

g   h   i   j

CHRISTMAS

4105   4106

4107   4108

4100

Issue		Date	Un	U	PB	#	FDC	Q(M)
	American Treasures: Quilts of Gee's Bend, Tagged, Self-Adhesive, Serpentine Die-Cut 10.75 on 2 or 3 sides							
4089	39¢ Housetop Variation	08/24/06	.80	.20			2.00	
4090	39¢ Pig in a Pen Medallion	08/24/06	.80	.20			2.00	
4091	39¢ Nine Patch	08/24/06	.80	.20			2.00	
4092	39¢ Housetop Four Block Half Log Cabin Variation	08/24/06	.80	.20			2.00	
4093	39¢ Roman Stripes Variation	08/24/06	.80	.20			2.00	
4094	39¢ Chinese Coins Variation	08/24/06	.80	.20			2.00	
4095	39¢ Blocks and Stripes	08/24/06	.80	.20			2.00	
4096	39¢ Medallion	08/24/06	.80	.20			2.00	
4097	39¢ Bars and String-pieced Columns	08/24/06	.80	.20			2.00	
4098	39¢ Medallion with Checkerboard Center	08/24/06	.80	.20			2.00	
a	Block of 10 #4089-4098		8.00				8.00	
	Nature of America: Southern Florida Wetland, Tagged, Self-Adhesive, Serpentine Die-Cut 10.75							
4099	Pane of 10	10/04/06	8.00				9.00	
a	39¢ Snail Kite		.80	.20			2.00	
b	39¢ Wood Storks		.80	.20			2.00	
c	39¢ Florida Panther		.80	.20			2.00	
d	39¢ Bald Eagle		.80	.20			2.00	
e	39¢ American Crocodile		.80	.20			2.00	
f	39¢ Roseate Spoonbills		.80	.20			2.00	
g	39¢ Everglades Mink		.80	.20			2.00	
h	39¢ Cape Sable Seaside Sparrow		.80	.20			2.00	
i	39¢ American Alligator		.80	.20			2.00	
j	39¢ White Ibis		.80	.20			2.00	
	Holiday Celebration: Christmas, Booklet, Tagged, Self-Adhesive, Serpentine Die-Cut 10.75 x 11 on 2 or 3 sides							
4100	39¢ *Madonna and Child with Bird*, by Ignacio Chacón	10/17/06	.80	.20			2.00	
	Holiday Celebration: Holiday Snowflakes, Serpentine Die-Cut 11.25 x 11							
4101	39¢ Snowflake A3139	10/05/06	.90	.20			2.00	
4102	39¢ Snowflake A3140	10/05/06	.90	.20			2.00	
4103	39¢ Snowflake A3141	10/05/06	.90	.20			2.00	
4104	39¢ Snowflake A3142	10/05/06	.90	.20			2.00	
a	Block or vert. strip of 4 #4101-4104		3.60				3.60	(4)

Issue		Date	Un	U	PB	#	FDC	Q(M)
	Holiday Celebration: Holiday Snowflakes, Booklet, Self-Adhesive, Serpentine Die-Cut 11.25 x 11.5 on 2 or 3 sides							
4105	39¢ Snowflake A3139	10/05/06	.80	.20			2.00	
4106	39¢ Snowflake A3140	10/05/06	.80	.20			2.00	
4107	39¢ Snowflake A3141	10/05/06	.80	.20			2.00	
4108	39¢ Snowflake A3142	10/05/06	.80	.20			2.00	
a	Block or vert. strip of 4 #4105-4108		3.20				4.50	
	Holiday Celebration: Holiday Snowflakes, Booklet, Self-Adhesive, Serpentine Die-Cut 11.25 x 11.5 on 2 or 3 sides							
4109	39¢ Snowflake A3139	10/05/06	.80	.20			2.00	
4110	39¢ Snowflake A3140	10/05/06	.80	.20			2.00	
4111	39¢ Snowflake A3141	10/05/06	.80	.20			2.00	
4112	39¢ Snowflake A3142	10/05/06	.80	.20			2.00	
a	Block of 4, #4109-4112		3.20				4.50	
	Holiday Celebration: Holiday Snowflakes, Booklet, Serpentine Die-Cut 8 on 2, 3 or 4 sides							
4113	39¢ Snowflake A3139	10/05/06	1.00	.20			2.00	
4114	39¢ Snowflake A3140	10/05/06	1.00	.20			2.00	
4115	39¢ Snowflake A3141	10/05/06	1.00	.20			2.00	
4116	39¢ Snowflake A3142	10/05/06	1.00	.20			2.00	
a	Block of 4, #4113-4116		4.00				4.50	
	Holiday Celebrations, Tagged, Self-Adhesive, Serpentine Die-Cut 11							
4117	39¢ Eid (type of 2001)	10/06/06	.80	.20	3.20	(4)	2.00	
	Holiday Celebrations, Tagged, Self-Adhesive, Serpentine Die-Cut 10.75 x 11							
4118	39¢ Hanukkah (type of 2004)	10/06/06	.80	.20	3.20	(4)	2.00	
	Holiday Celebrations, Tagged, Self-Adhesive, Serpentine Die-Cut 11 x 10.75							
4119	39¢ Kwanzaa (type of 2004)	10/06/06	.80	.20	3.20	(4)	2.00	

AMERICAN ★ COMMEMORATIVE ★ COLLECTIBLES

First Day of Issue Ceremony Programs

Receive detailed information about each First Day of Issue ceremony held for new stamp and stationery issuances.

Collect these valuable programs for only $4.95 each* when purchasing through subscription. ($6.95 if purchased individually**)   Item #29144

*If the stamp value exceeds $4.95, then the price is determined by the actual value of the stamps.

**To purchase individual Ceremony Programs see specific stamp listings.

To order call **1-800-STAMP-24** or visit us online at **www.usps.com**

	Issue	Date	Un	U	PB #	FDC	Q(M)
	Black Heritage, Tagged, Self-Adhesive, Serpentine Die-Cut 11						
4120	39¢ Ella Fitzgerald	01/10/07	.80	.20	3.20 (4)		2.00
	Tagged, Self-Adhesive, Serpentine Die-Cut 11						
4121	39¢ Oklahoma Statehood	01/11/07	.80	.20	3.20 (4)		2.00
	Love, Booklet, Tagged, Self-Adhesive, Serpentine Die-Cut 10.75 x 11 on 2, 3 or 4 sides						
4122	39¢ With Love and Kisses	01/13/07	.80	.20			2.00
a	Booklet pane of 20		16.00				
	Tagged, Self-Adhesive, Serpentine Die-Cut 10.75						
4123	84¢ International Polar Year Souvenir Sheet, pane of 2	02/21/07	3.50			4.75	
a-b	84¢ Either single		1.75	.50			3.00
4124	39¢ Henry Wadsworth Longfellow	03/15/07	.80	.20	3.20 (4)		2.00
	Forever Stamp™, Tagged, Booklet, Self-Adhesive, Serpentine Die-Cut 11.25 x 10.75 on 2 or 3 sides						
4125	(41¢) Liberty Bell, large microprinting, bell 16mm wide	04/12/07	.85	.20			2.10
a	Booklet pane of 20		17.00				
4126	(41¢) Liberty Bell, small microprinting, bell 16mm wide	04/12/07	.85	.20			2.10
a	Booklet pane of 20		17.00				
4127	(41¢) Liberty Bell, medium microprinting, bell 15mm wide	04/12/07	.85	.20			2.10
a	Booklet pane of 20		17.00				
j	(42¢) Liberty Bell, medium microprinting, bell 15mm wide dated "2008". (type of 2007)	10/25/08	.85	.20			

	Issue	Date	Un	U	PB #	FDC	Q(M)
	Forever Stamp™, Tagged, Booklet, Self-Adhesive, Serpentine Die-Cut 8 on 2, 3 or 4 sides						
4128	(41¢) Liberty Bell, large microprinting, bell 16mm wide	04/12/07	.85	.20			2.10
a	Booklet pane of 18 #4125-4128 (4)		15.50				
	Tagged, Perf 11.25						
4129	(41¢) Flag	04/12/07	.85	.40	4.50 (4)		2.10
	Tagged, Self-Adhesive, Serpentine Die-Cut 11.25 x 10.75						
4130	(41¢) Flag	04/12/07	.85	.40	3.50 (4)		2.10
	Tagged, Coil, Perf 9.75 Vertically						
4131	(41¢) Flag	04/12/07	.85	.40	6.00 (5)		2.10
	Tagged, Coil, Self-Adhesive, Perf 9.5 Vertically, with Perpendicular Corners						
4132	(41¢) Flag	04/12/07	.85	.20	6.00 (5)		2.10
	Tagged, Coil, Self-Adhesive, Serpentine Die-Cut 11 Vertically						
4133	(41¢) Flag	04/12/07	.85	.20	6.00 (5)		2.10
	Tagged, Coil, Self-Adhesive, Serpentine Die-Cut 8.5 Vertically						
4134	(41¢) Flag	04/12/07	.85	.20	6.00 (5)		2.10
	Tagged, Coil, Self-Adhesive, Serpentine Die-Cut 11 Vertically, with Rounded Corners						
4135	(41¢) Flag	04/12/07	.85	.20	6.00 (5)		2.10

EDGAR ALLAN POE

Award-winning artist Michael J. Deas created the portrait featured on this stamp commemorating the 200th birthday of Edgar Allan Poe (1809-1849). One of America's greatest poets and fiction writers and a masterful storyteller with a vivid imagination, Poe is famous for having written such gripping tales as "The Fall of the House of Usher," "The Pit and the Pendulum," "The Tell-Tale Heart," and "The Black Cat." His "Murders in the Rue Morgue" has been called the first detective story. Poe also wrote some of the most memorable poems in American literature, including "Eldorado," "Annabel Lee," "The Bells," and "The Raven," a masterpiece of rhyme and rhythm published in 1845. ■ Born "Edgar Poe" in Boston, Massachusetts, he lost both parents before age three and grew up in the care of John and Frances Allan, wealthy Richmond, Virginia, residents who shared their name with Poe but never formally adopted him. ■ Poe received his early education at private schools in England and Virginia, and briefly attended the University of Virginia. Deeply in debt, he left Virginia and spent the rest of his life living in various places along the East Coast, struggling to get by and to get his writings into print. In 1835, he returned to Richmond as editor for the *Southern Literary Messenger* and, soon after, married Virginia Clemm of Baltimore. He and his family moved to Philadelphia and then to New York, where Poe published "The Raven" in 1845. The poem made him a star of literary society, but his income was never more than barely adequate. ■ On October 3, 1849, Poe was found suffering from some unknown ailment in Baltimore, Maryland. He was taken by carriage to a hospital, where he died from "congestion of the brain" on October 7.

4120

4121

4122

International Polar Year 2007-2008

Continuing the tradition of international cooperation that began with the first IPY in 1882-1883, scientists from around the world will initiate a new era in polar research by participating in IPY 2007-2008. Working across many disciplines, they will conduct field observations, research, and analysis to build upon current knowledge and increase our understanding of the roles that both polar regions play in global processes.

USA 84
Aurora Borealis

USA 84
Aurora Australis

4123

4124

4125

Vintage Black Cinema Cultural Diary Page and Pane of 20 Stamps

Vivid reminders of a bygone era, these vintage movie posters highlight various facets of the African-American cultural experience as represented in early film. Whether spotlighting the talents of entertainment icons or documenting changing social attitudes and expectations, they are now invaluable pieces of history.

Item #463176 $12.95

For more information call **1 800 STAMP-24** or visit us online at **www.usps.com**

Duke Ellington licensed by CMG Worldwide, Indianapolis, IN.
Josephine Baker licensed by CMG Worldwide, Indianapolis, IN.
Louis Jordan name and likeness reprinted with permission.
Hallelujah art © Al Hirschfeld, licensed by The Margo Feiden Galleries Ltd., New York.

4136

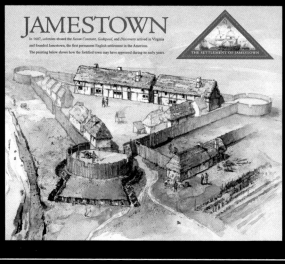

4137

4138

4143

a   b

c   d   e

f   g   h   i

j   k   l

m   n   o

	Issue	Date	Un	U	PB #	FDC Q(M)
	Tagged, Self-Adhesive, Serpentine Die-Cut 10.5 x 10.5 x 10.75					
4136	41¢ Settlement of Jamestown	05/11/07	1.00	.20		2.10
	Tagged, Perf. 11.25 x 11					
4137	26¢ Florida Panther	05/12/07	.55	.20	3.25 (4)	2.10
	Tagged, Self-Adhesive, Serpentine Die-Cut 11					
4138	17¢ Bighorn Sheep	05/14/07	.35	.20	1.40 (4)	2.10
	Tagged, Self-Adhesive, Serpentine Die-Cut 11.25 x 11					
4139	26¢ Florida Panther	05/12/07	.55	.20	2.25 (4)	2.10
	Coil, Self-Adhesive, Serpentine Die-Cut 11 Vertically					
4140	17¢ Bighorn Sheep	05/21/07	.35	.20	3.25 (5)	2.10
4141	26¢ Florida Panther	05/12/07	.55	.20	4.00 (5)	2.10
a	Die-Cutting omitted, pair		—			
	Booklet, Self-Adhesive, Serpentine Die-Cut 11.25 x 11 on 3 sides					
4142	26¢ Florida Panther	05/12/07	.55	.20		2.10
a	Booklet pane of 10		5.50			

	Issue	Date	Un	U	PB #	FDC Q(M)
	Star Wars, Tagged, Self-Adhesive, Serpentine Die-Cut 11					
4143	Pane of 15	05/27/07	13.00			12.50
a	41¢ Darth Vader		.85	.20		2.10
b	41¢ Millennium Falcon		.85	.20		2.10
c	41¢ Emperor Palpatine		.85	.20		2.10
d	41¢ Anakin Skywalker and Obi-Wan Kenobi		.85	.20		2.10
e	41¢ Luke Skywalker		.85	.20		2.10
f	41¢ Princess Leia Organa and R2-D2		.85	.20		2.10
g	41¢ C-3PO		.85	.20		2.10
h	41¢ Queen Padmé Amidala		.85	.20		2.10
i	41¢ Obi-Wan Kenobi		.85	.20		2.10
j	41¢ Boba Fett		.85	.20		2.10
k	41¢ Darth Maul		.85	.20		2.10
l	41¢ Chewbacca and Han Solo		.85	.20		2.10
m	41¢ X-wing Starfighter		.85	.20		2.10
n	41¢ Yoda		.85	.20		2.10
o	41¢ Stormtroopers		.85	.20		2.10

GULF COAST LIGHTHOUSES

The U.S. Postal Service continues its popular series of lighthouse stamps with the issuance of Gulf Coast Lighthouses. Featuring paintings by artist Howard Koslow, the five stamps depict the lighthouses of Matagorda Island, Sabine Pass, Biloxi, Sand Island, and Fort Jefferson. ■ The Gulf Coast extends about 1,000 miles from Key West, Florida, to Corpus Christi, Texas. For more than 150 years, lighthouses have guided ships and other sailing vessels through this picturesque but dangerous stretch of water. Known as "hurricane alley," the Gulf Coast weathers many powerful storms each year, including Hurricane Katrina, which devastated the region in 2005. In addition, the land along the coast is swampy and marshy in many places and given to erosion, making it doubly difficult for lighthouses to withstand heavy rains and winds. The five lighthouses featured on the stamps are some of the few that remain standing. ■ Listed on the National Register of Historic Places in 1984, Matagorda Island Lighthouse has stood proudly for more than a century near Port O'Connor,

Texas. The black conical tower is made of cast iron and features a solar-powered light. ■ Erected on soft, marshy ground in Louisiana, Sabine Pass Lighthouse features eight buttresses that stabilize the heavy brick structure and give it a distinct missile-like shape. Completed in 1856, the lighthouse was deactivated in 1952. ■ The only lighthouse still standing in Mississippi, Biloxi Lighthouse was named to the National Register of Historic Places in 1973. The white, conical tower was built in 1848, making it one of the first cast-iron lighthouses in the South. ■ First lit in 1873, Sand Island Lighthouse was an active aid to navigation for 60 years. Originally on a 400-acre island off the Alabama coast, this conical tower made of local brick now stands alone, its foundation completely surrounded by water. ■ Erected in 1876, Fort Jefferson Lighthouse (also known as Garden Key Lighthouse) helped warn sea traffic away from the dangerous shoals and reefs surrounding the Florida Keys. Today the hexagonal lighthouse is part of Dry Tortugas National Park.

	Issue	Date	Un	U	PB	#	FDC	Q(M)
	Tagged, Self-Adhesive, Serpentine Die-Cut 10.75							
4144	$4.60 Air Force One	06/13/07	9.25	5.00	37.50	(4)		9.25
4145	$16.25 Marine One	06/13/07	27.50	16.00	110.00	(4)		32.50
	Pacific Lighthouses, Tagged, Self-Adhesive, Serpentine Die-Cut 11							
4146	41¢ Diamond Head	06/21/07	.85	.20				2.10
4147	41¢ Five Finger	06/21/07	.85	.20				2.10
4148	41¢ Grays Harbor	06/21/07	.85	.20				2.10
4149	41¢ Umpqua River	06/21/07	.85	.20				2.10
4150	41¢ St. George Reef	06/21/07	.85	.20				2.10
a	Horizontal strip of five		4.25		8.50	(10)		5.50
	Hearts, Booklet, Tagged, Self-Adhesive, Serpentine Die-Cut 10.75 on 2, 3 or 4 sides							
4151	41¢ Heart With Lilac	06/27/07	.85	.20				2.10
a	Booklet of 20		17.00					
	Hearts, Booklet, Tagged, Self-Adhesive, Serpentine Die-Cut 10.75 x 11							
4152	58¢ Heart With Pink	06/27/07	1.25	.25	5.00	(4)		2.40
	Pollination, Booklet, Tagged, Self-Adhesive, Serpentine Die-Cut 11 on 2, 3 or 4 sides							
4153	41¢ Purple Nightshade, Morrison's Bumblebee, Type I	06/29/07	.85	.20				2.10
a	Type II		.85	.20				

	Issue	Date	Un	U	PB	#	FDC	Q(M)
	Pollination, Booklet, Tagged, Self-Adhesive, Serpentine Die-Cut 10.75 x 11							
4154	41¢ Hummingbird Trumpet, Calliope Hummingbird, Type I	06/29/07	.85	.20				2.10
a	Type II		.85	.20				
4155	41¢ Saguaro, Lesser Long-nosed Bat, Type I	06/29/07	.85	.20				2.10
a	Type II		.85	.20				
4156	41¢ Prairie Ironweed, Southern Dogface Butterfly, Type I	06/29/07	.85	.20				2.10
a	Type II		.85	.20				
b	Block of 4, #4153-4156		3.40					4.50
c	Block of 4, #4153a-4156a		3.40					4.50
d	Booklet pane of 20, 3 each #4153-4156, 2 each #4153a-4156a		17.00					

LITERARY ARTS: RICHARD WRIGHT

The 25th stamp in the Literary Arts series honors author Richard Wright (1908-1960). Best remembered for his controversial 1940 novel, *Native Son*, and his 1945 autobiography, *Black Boy*, Wright drew on a wide range of literary traditions, including protest writing and detective fiction, to craft unflinching portrayals of racism in American society. ▪ Born near Natchez, Mississippi, Wright gained national prominence in 1940 with the publication of *Native Son*, his controversial novel about a black man who accidentally murders a white woman. *Native Son* challenged readers to implicate society in the crimes of Bigger Thomas, a protagonist who believes that the murders he commits are acts of human freedom. Although many reviewers found Bigger Thomas highly unsympathetic, they nonetheless praised *Native Son* for its powerful and unflinching depiction of racism. Still debated in high school and college classrooms, *Native Son* is often considered the strongest race-relations protest novel of its day. ▪ Wright again gained national attention with his acclaimed autobiography, *Black Boy* (1945). While examining the omnipresent effects of racism, *Black Boy* also documents Wright's childhood clashes with his family's religion and his discovery of writing and literature as outlets for his own creativity and freedom. In an influential 1945 essay, writer Ralph Ellison compared *Black Boy* to the music of the blues and praised Wright for his ability "to evaluate his experience honestly and throw his findings unashamedly into the guilty conscience of America." ▪ The stamp artwork by Kadir Nelson features a portrait of Wright based on a circa 1945 photograph, in front of snow-swept tenements on the South Side of Chicago, a scene that recalls the setting of *Native Son*.

4144

4145

4146 **4147** **4148** **4149** **4150** **4150a**

4151

4152

4153

4155

4155

4155

4156

4156b

Ella Fitzgerald Cultural Diary Page and Maxi Card

The "first lady of song" is now the first lady of stamps. This 30th issuance in the Black Heritage series honors Ella Fitzgerald, one of the most distinctive and instantly recognizable singers of both jazz and popular tunes.

Cultural Diary Page w/ Maxi Card and Pane of 20.   Item #460776 $12.95

To order this item call **1 800 STAMP-24** *or visit us online at* **www.usps.com**

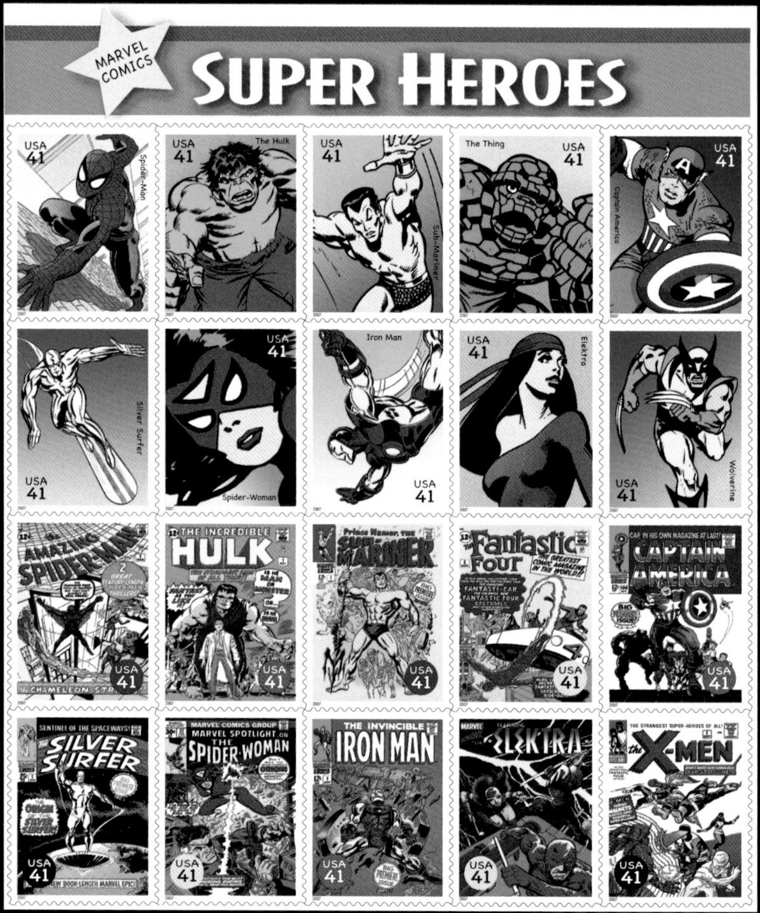

4159

a   b   c   d   e

f   g   h   i   j

k   l   m   n   o

p   q   r   s   t

4160    4161    4162    4163   4163a

4165

LOUIS COMFORT TIFFANY

Issue		Date	Un	U	PB #	FDC	Q(M)
	Coil, Untagged, Self-Adhesive, Serpentine Die-Cut 11 Vertically						
4157	(10¢) Patriotic Banner	07/04/07	.20	.20	2.50 (5)	2.00	
	Coil, Untagged, Self-Adhesive, Serpentine Die-Cut 11.75 Vertically						
4158	(10¢) Patriotic Banner	07/04/07	.20	.20	2.50 (5)	2.00	
	Marvel Comics Superheroes, Tagged, Self-Adhesive, Serpentine Die-Cut 10.5 x 10.75						
4159	Pane of 20	07/26/07	17.00			17.00	
a	41¢ Spider-Man		.85	.20		2.10	
b	41¢ The Hulk		.85	.20		2.10	
c	41¢ Sub-Mariner		.85	.20		2.10	
d	41¢ The Thing		.85	.20		2.10	
e	41¢ Captain America		.85	.20		2.10	
f	41¢ Silver Surfer		.85	.20		2.10	
g	41¢ Spider-Woman		.85	.20		2.10	
h	41¢ Iron Man		.85	.20		2.10	
i	41¢ Elektra		.85	.20		2.10	
j	41¢ Wolverine		.85	.20		2.10	
k	41¢ Cover of *The Amazing Spider-Man* #1		.85	.20		2.10	
l	41¢ Cover of *The Incredible Hulk* #1		.85	.20		2.10	
m	41¢ Cover of *The Sub-Mariner* #1		.85	.20		2.10	
n	41¢ Cover of *The Fantastic Four* #3		.85	.20		2.10	

Issue		Date	Un	U	PB #	FDC	Q(M)
	Marvel Comics Superheroes, Tagged, Self-Adhesive, Serpentine Die-Cut 10.5 x 10.75 continued						
o	41¢ Cover of *Captain America* #100		.85	.20		2.10	
p	41¢ Cover of *The Silver Surfer* #1		.85	.20		2.10	
q	41¢ Cover of *Marvel Spotlight on The Spider-Woman* #32		.85	.20		2.10	
r	41¢ Cover of *The Iron Man* #1		.85	.20		2.10	
s	41¢ Cover of *Daredevil #176 Featuring Elektra*		.85	.20		2.10	
t	41¢ Cover of *The X-Men* #1		.85	.20		2.10	
	Tagged, Self-Adhesive, Serpentine Die-Cut 10.5						
4160	41¢ 1915 Hutchinson	08/04/07	.85	.20		2.10	
4161	41¢ 1954 Chris-Craft	08/04/07	.85	.20		2.10	
4162	41¢ 1939 Hacker-Craft	08/04/07	.85	.20		2.10	
4163	41¢ 1931 Gar Wood	08/04/07	.85	.20		2.10	
a	Horizontal strip of 4, #4160-4163		3.40		6.80 (8)	4.50	
	Tagged, Self-Adhesive, Serpentine Die-Cut 11.25 x 10.75						
4164	41¢ Purple Heart, (type of 2003)	08/07/07	.85	.20	3.40 (4)	2.10	
	American Treasures, Tagged, Self-Adhesive, Serpentine Die-Cut 10.75 on 2 or 3 sides						
4165	41¢ Louis Comfort Tiffany	08/09/07	.85	.20		2.10	
a	Booklet pane of 20		17.00				

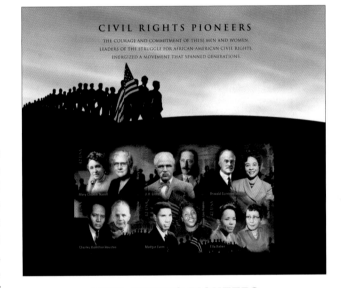

CIVIL RIGHTS PIONEERS

With these stamps, the U.S. Postal Service honors the courage, commitment, and achievements of 12 leaders of the struggle for African-American civil rights. ▪ Educator and activist MARY CHURCH TERRELL (1863-1954) published her powerful autobiography, *A Colored Woman in a White World*, in 1940. MARY WHITE OVINGTON (1865-1951) was a founder of the National Association for the Advancement of Colored People (NAACP). ▪ J. R. CLIFFORD (1848-1933), the first black attorney licensed in West Virginia, attacked racial discrimination in education. JOEL ELIAS SPINGARN (1875-1939) endowed the prestigious Spingarn Medal, awarded annually since 1915, to highlight black achievement. ▪ OSWALD GARRISON VILLARD (1872-1949) was one of the founders of the NAACP and wrote the eloquent "Call" leading to its formation. When nine black students enrolled at an all-white school in Little Rock, Arkansas, in 1957, they used the home of their mentor, DAISY GATSON BATES (1914-1999) as a hub. ▪ Lawyer and educator CHARLES HAMILTON HOUSTON (1895-1950), who believed in using laws to better the lives of underprivileged citizens, was a key figure in the movement. Blue eyes and a fair complexion enabled WALTER WHITE (1893-1955), longtime leader of the NAACP, to make daring undercover investigations of lynching. ▪ Until his assassination in 1963, MEDGAR EVERS (1925-1963) served with distinction as an official of the NAACP in Mississippi. FANNIE LOU HAMER (1917-1977) was a Mississippi sharecropper who fought to gain access to the political process for black voters. ▪ ELLA BAKER (1903-1986) was a skillful organizer who encouraged young people to assume positions of leadership in the civil rights movement. As a courageous and capable official with the NAACP, RUBY HURLEY (1909-1980) did difficult, dangerous work in the South.

Issue		Date	Un	U	PB	#	FDC	Q(M)
Coil, Tagged, Self-Adhesive, Serpentine Die-Cut 9.5 Vertically								
4166	41¢ Iris	08/10/07	.85	.20				2.10
4167	41¢ Dahlia	08/10/07	.85	.20				2.10
4168	41¢ Magnolia	08/10/07	.85	.20				2.10
4169	41¢ Red Gerbera Daisy	08/10/07	.85	.20				2.10
4170	41¢ Coneflower	08/10/07	.85	.20				2.10
4171	41¢ Tulip	08/10/07	.85	.20				2.10
4172	41¢ Water Lily	08/10/07	.85	.20				2.10
4173	41¢ Poppy	08/10/07	.85	.20				2.10
4174	41¢ Chrysanthemum	08/10/07	.85	.20				2.10
4175	41¢ Orange Gerbera Daisy	08/10/07	.85	.20				2.10
a	Strip of 10 #4166-4175		8.50		13.00	(11)		8.25
Booklet, Serpentine Die-Cut 11.25 x 11.5 on 2 or 3 sides								
4176	41¢ Chrysanthemum	08/10/07	.85	.20				2.10
4177	41¢ Orange Gerbera Daisy	08/10/07	.85	.20				2.10
4178	41¢ Iris	08/10/07	.85	.20				2.10
4179	41¢ Dahlia	08/10/07	.85	.20				2.10
4180	41¢ Magnolia	08/10/07	.85	.20				2.10
4181	41¢ Red Gerbera Daisy	08/10/07	.85	.20				2.10
4182	41¢ Water Lily	08/10/07	.85	.20				2.10
4183	41¢ Poppy	08/10/07	.85	.20				2.10
4184	41¢ Coneflower	08/10/07	.85	.20				2.10
4185	41¢ Tulip	08/10/07	.85	.20				2.10
a	Booklet pane of 20, 2 each of #4176-4185		17.00					
Coil, Untagged, Self-Adhesive, Serpentine Die-Cut 9.5 Vertically								
4186	41¢ American Flag, (type of 2007) with "USPS" microprinted on right side of flag pole	08/15/07	.85	.20	6.00	(5)		2.10

Issue		Date	Un	U	PB	#	FDC	Q(M)
Coil, Tagged, Self-Adhesive, Serpentine Die-Cut 11 Vertically								
4187	41¢ American Flag, (type of 2007) with "USPS" microprinted on left side of flag pole	08/15/07	.85	.20	6.00	(5)		2.10
Coil, Tagged, Self-Adhesive, Serpentine Die-Cut 8.5 Vertically								
4188	41¢ American Flag, with perpendicular corners	08/15/07	.85	.20	6.00	(5)		2.10
Coil, Tagged, Self-Adhesive, Serpentine Die-Cut 11 Vertically								
4189	41¢ American Flag, with rounded corners	08/15/07	.85	.20	6.00	(5)		2.10
Booklet, Tagged, Self-Adhesive, Serpentine Die-Cut 11.25 x 10.75 on 2 or 3 sides								
4190	41¢ American Flag, with "USPS" microprinted on right side of flag pole	08/15/07	.85	.20				2.10
a	Booklet pane of 10		8.50					
4191	41¢ American Flag, with "USPS" microprinted on left side of flag pole	08/15/07	.85	.20				2.10
a	Booklet pane of 20		17.00					
The Art of Disney: Magic, Tagged, Self-Adhesive, Serpentine Die-Cut 10.25 x 10.75								
4192	41¢ Mickey Mouse	08/16/07	.85	.20				2.10
4193	41¢ Peter Pan and Tinker Bell	08/16/07	.85	.20				2.10
4194	41¢ Dumbo and Timothy Mouse	08/16/07	.85	.20				2.10
4195	41¢ Aladdin and Genie	08/16/07	.85	.20				2.10
a	Block of 4 #4192-4195		3.40		3.40	(4)		4.50
Tagged, Self-Adhesive, Serpentine Die-Cut 10.75								
4196	41¢ Celebrate!	08/17/07	.85	.20	3.40	(4)		2.10
Legends of Hollywood, Tagged, Self-Adhesive, Serpentine Die-Cut 10.75								
4197	41¢ James Stewart	08/17/07	.85	.20	3.40	(4)		2.10

WEDDINGS: RINGS & CAKE

The popular Weddings series continues with two new stamps sure to add beauty and romance to modern wedding correspondence. ▮ The one-ounce stamp—perfect for returning RSVP cards and sending thank-you notes—features two gold wedding rings united by a slender ribbon of white silk atop a small white pillow. ▮ Historians tell us that the tradition of exchanging rings as part of the wedding ceremony began with the ancient Egyptians, who fashioned rings made from reeds found along the Nile River. The reeds were braided and bent into small circles; with no beginning and no end, the circle came to symbolize eternal love and devotion. During the marriage ritual, the Egyptians placed a reed band on the third finger of the left hand, as many people still do today, believing (wrongly) that a vein in that finger led directly to the heart.

▮ A wedding cake topped with white flowers appears on the two-ounce stamp, issued to accommodate the heavier weight of the invitation with its enclosures. The tiered wedding cake has its origins in the Middle Ages, when guests brought small, unsweetened bread cakes to the ceremony, piling them between the newlyweds who had to kiss each other over the stack. If the couple succeeded without toppling the cakes, it was believed that they would enjoy prosperity and good fortune. ▮ The bride and groom typically cut the wedding cake together, their first public act as a couple and symbolic of their devotion to a shared future. In a tradition that dates back to the ancient Romans, couples often feed the first pieces of cake to one another, in honor of their mutual commitment and support, before sharing it with those gathered to celebrate their union.

4175a

4170 4171 4172 4173 4174 4175 4166 4167 4168 4169

4188

4192 4193

4194 4195

4195a

4196

4197

Get Involved With Stamp Design

Find out how!

Stop by your local Post Office and pick up this free brochure *Creating U.S. Postage Stamps* which provides information on how you can propose a subject for a postage stamp or obtain information on the design process.

ALPINE TUNDRA

NINTH IN A SERIES

USA 41

USA 41

USA 41

USA 41

USA 41

USA 41

USA 41

USA 41

USA 41

USA 41

N A T U R E   O F   A M E R I C A

4198

a   b   c

d   e

f   g   h

i   j

Gerald R. Ford

41 USA

4199

JURY DUTY

SERVE WITH PRIDE
USA 41

4200

MENDEZ v. WESTMINSTER 1947

TOWARD EQUALITY IN OUR SCHOOLS

4201

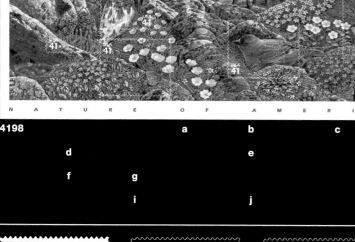

USA 41

Aurora Borealis

4203

USA 41

Aurora Australis

4204

USA 41

STAR WARS YODA

4205

CHRISTMAS

41 USA

Bernardino Luini, National Gallery of Art

4206

4207

USA 41

USA 41

USA 41

USA 41

4208

4209

4210

4210a

41

LUNAR NEW YEAR

4221

BLACK HERITAGE

Charles W. Chesnutt

41 USA

4222

	Issue	Date	Un	U	PB	#	FDC	Q(M)
	Nature of America: Alpine Tundra, Tagged, Self-Adhesive, Serpentine Die-Cut 10.75							
4198	Pane of 10	08/28/07	8.50				8.25	
a	41¢ Elk		.85	.20			2.10	
b	41¢ Golden Eagle, horiz.		.85	.20			2.10	
c	41¢ Yellow-bellied Marmot		.85	.20			2.10	
d	41¢ American Pika		.85	.20			2.10	
e	41¢ Big-horn Sheep		.85	.20			2.10	
f	41¢ Magdalena Alpine Butterfly		.85	.20			2.10	
g	41¢ White-tailed Ptarmigan		.85	.20			2.10	
h	41¢ Rocky Mountain Parnassian Butterfly		.85	.20			2.10	
i	41¢ Mellissa Arctic Butterfly, horiz.		.85	.20			2.10	
j	41¢ Brown-capped Rosy-finch, horiz.		.85	.20			2.10	
	Tagged, Self-Adhesive, Serpentine Die-Cut 11							
4199	41¢ Gerald R. Ford	08/31/07	.85	.20	3.40	(4)	2.10	
	Tagged, Self-Adhesive, Serpentine Die-Cut 10.5							
4200	41¢ Jury Duty	09/12/07	.85	.20	3.40	(4)	2.10	
	Tagged, Self-Adhesive, Serpentine Die-Cut 11							
4201	41¢ Mendez v. Westminster	09/14/07	.85	.20	3.40	(4)	2.10	
	Holiday Celebrations, Tagged, Self-Adhesive, Serpentine Die-Cut 11							
4202	41¢ Eid (type of 2001)	09/28/07	.85	.20	3.40	(4)	2.10	
	Polar Lights, Tagged, Self-Adhesive, Serpentine Die-Cut 10.75							
4203	41¢ Aurora Borealis	10/01/07	.90	.20			2.10	
4204	41¢ Aurora Australis	10/01/07	.90	.20			2.10	
a	Horiz. or vert. pair		1.80		4.00	(4)	3.00	
	Tagged, Self-Adhesive, Serpentine Die-Cut 10.5 x 10.75							
4205	41¢ Yoda	10/25/07	.85	.20	3.40	(4)	2.10	
	Holiday Celebration: Christmas, Booklet, Tagged, Self-Adhesive, Serpentine Die-Cut 10.75 x 11 on 2 or 3 sides							
4206	41¢ *Madonna of the Carnation*, by Bernardino Luini	10/25/07	.85	.20			2.10	
a	Booklet pane of 20		17.00					
	Holiday Celebration: Holiday, Tagged, Self-Adhesive, Serpentine Die-Cut 10.75							
4207	41¢ Knit Reindeer	10/25/07	.85	.20			2.10	
4208	41¢ Knit Christmas Tree	10/25/07	.85	.20			2.10	
4209	41¢ Knit Snowman	10/25/07	.85	.20			2.10	
4210	41¢ Knit Bear	10/25/07	.85	.20			2.10	
a	Block or vert. strip of 4 #4207-4210		3.40				4.50	
b	Booklet pane of 20, 5 each #4207-4210, Serpentine Die-Cut 10.75 on 2 or 3 sides		17.00					

	Issue	Date	Un	U	PB	#	FDC	Q(M)
	Holiday Celebration: Holiday, Booklet, Tagged, Self-Adhesive, Serpentine Die-Cut 11.25 x 11 on 2 or 3 sides							
4211	41¢ Knit Reindeer	10/25/07	.85	.20			2.10	
4212	41¢ Knit Christmas Tree	10/25/07	.85	.20			2.10	
4213	41¢ Knit Snowman	10/25/07	.85	.20			2.10	
4214	41¢ Knit Bear	10/25/07	.85	.20			2.10	
a	Block of 4 #4211-4214		3.40				4.50	
b	Booklet pane of 4 #4211-4214, Serpentine Die-Cut 11.25 x 11 on 2 or 3 sides		3.40					
	Holiday Celebration: Holiday, Booklet, Tagged, Self-Adhesive, Serpentine Die-Cut 8 on 2 or 3 sides							
4215	41¢ Knit Reindeer	10/25/07	.85	.20			2.10	
4216	41¢ Knit Christmas Tree	10/25/07	.85	.20			2.10	
4217	41¢ Knit Snowman	10/25/07	.85	.20			2.10	
4218	41¢ Knit Bear	10/25/07	.85	.20			2.10	
a	Block of 4 #4215-4218		3.40				4.50	
b	Booklet pane of 18, 4 each #4215, #4218, 5 each #4216, #4217, Serpentine Die-Cut 8 on 2, 3 or 4 sides		15.50					
	Holiday Celebrations, Tagged, Self-Adhesive, Serpentine Die-Cut 10.75 x 11							
4219	41¢ Hanukkah (type of 2004)	10/26/07	.85	.20	3.40	(4)	2.10	
	Holiday Celebrations, Tagged, Self-Adhesive, Serpentine Die-Cut 11 x 10.75							
4220	41¢ Kwanzaa (type of 2004)	10/26/07	.85	.20	3.40	(4)	2.10	
	Lunar New Year, Tagged, Self-Adhesive, Serpentine Die-Cut 10.75							
4221	41¢ Year of the Rat	01/09/08	.85	.20			2.10	
	Black Heritage, Tagged, Self-Adhesive, Serpentine Die-Cut 11							
4222	41¢ Charles W. Chesnutt	01/31/08	.85	.20	3.40	(4)	2.10	

Issue	Date	Un	U	PB	#	FDC	Q(M)
Literary Arts, Tagged, Self-Adhesive, Serpentine Die-Cut 11							
4223 41¢ Marjorie Kinnan Rawlings	02/21/08	.85	.20	3.40	(4)	2.10	
American Scientists, Tagged, Self-Adhesive, Serpentine Die-Cut 11							
4224 41¢ Gerty Cori	03/06/08	.85	.20	3.40	(4)	2.10	
4225 41¢ Linus Pauling	03/06/08	.85	.20	3.40	(4)	2.10	
4226 41¢ Edwin Hubble	03/06/08	.85	.20	3.40	(4)	2.10	
4227 41¢ John Bardeen	03/06/08	.85	.20	3.40	(4)	2.10	
a Horizontal strip of four		3.40		6.80	(8)		
Coil, Tagged, Perf. 10 Vertically							
4228 42¢ Flag at Dusk	04/18/08	.85	.40			2.10	
4229 42¢ Flag at Night	04/18/08	.85	.40			2.10	
4230 42¢ Flag at Dawn	04/18/08	.85	.40			2.10	
4231 42¢ Flag at Midday	04/18/08	.85	.40			2.10	
a Horizontal strip of four		3.40	1.60	6.00	(5)		
Coil, Self-Adhesive, Perpendicular Corners, Serpentine Die-Cut 9.5 Vertically							
4232 42¢ Flag at Dusk	04/18/08	.85	.20			2.10	
4233 42¢ Flag at Night	04/18/08	.85	.20			2.10	
4234 42¢ Flag at Dawn	04/18/08	.85	.20			2.10	
4235 42¢ Flag at Midday	04/18/08	.85	.20			2.10	
a Horizontal strip of four		3.40		6.00	(5)		
Coil, Self-Adhesive, Serpentine Die-Cut 11 Vertically							
4236 42¢ Flag at Dusk	04/18/08	.85	.20			2.10	
4237 42¢ Flag at Night	04/18/08	.85	.20			2.10	
4238 42¢ Flag at Dawn	04/18/08	.85	.20			2.10	
4239 42¢ Flag at Midday	04/18/08	.85	.20			2.10	
a Horizontal strip of four		3.40		6.00	(5)		
Coil, Self-Adhesive, Serpentine Die-Cut 8.5 Vertically							
4240 42¢ Flag at Dusk	04/18/08	.85	.20			2.10	
4241 42¢ Flag at Night	04/18/08	.85	.20			2.10	
4242 42¢ Flag at Dawn	04/18/08	.85	.20			2.10	
4243 42¢ Flag at Midday	04/18/08	.85	.20			2.10	
a Horizontal strip of four		3.40		6.00	(5)		
Coil, Self-Adhesive, Rounded Corners, Serpentine Die-Cut 11 Vertically							
4244 42¢ Flag at Dusk	04/18/08	.85	.30			2.10	
4245 42¢ Flag at Night	04/18/08	.85	.30			2.10	
4246 42¢ Flag at Dawn	04/18/08	.85	.30			2.10	
4247 42¢ Flag at Midday	04/18/08	.85	.30			2.10	
a Horizontal strip of four		3.40		6.00	(5)		

Issue	Date	Un	U	PB	#	FDC	Q(M)
American Journalists, Tagged, Self-Adhesive, Serpentine Die-Cut 10.75 x 10.5							
4248 42¢ Martha Gellhorn	04/22/08	.85	.20			2.10	
4249 42¢ John Hersey	04/22/08	.85	.20			2.10	
4250 42¢ George Polk	04/22/08	.85	.20			2.10	
4251 42¢ Ruben Salazar	04/22/08	.85	.20			2.10	
4252 42¢ Eric Sevareid	04/22/08	.85	.20			2.10	
a Vertical strip of five		4.25		8.50	(10)		
Tropical Fruit, Tagged, Self-Adhesive, Serpentine Die-Cut 11.25 x 10.75							
4253 27¢ Pomegranate	04/25/08	.55	.20			2.10	
4254 27¢ Star Fruit	04/25/08	.55	.20			2.10	
4255 27¢ Kiwi	04/25/08	.55	.20			2.10	
4256 27¢ Papaya	04/25/08	.55	.20			2.10	
4257 27¢ Guava	04/25/08	.55	.20			2.10	
a Horizontal strip of five		2.75		5.50	(10)		
Tropical Fruit, Coil, Serpentine Die-Cut 8.5 Vertically							
4258 27¢ Papaya	04/25/08	.55	.20			2.10	
4259 27¢ Guava	04/25/08	.55	.20			2.10	
4260 27¢ Pomegranate	04/25/08	.55	.20			2.10	
4261 27¢ Star Fruit	04/25/08	.55	.20			2.10	
4262 27¢ Kiwi	04/25/08	.55	.20			2.10	
a Horizontal strip of five		2.75		4.00	(5)		
Tagged, Perf. 11.25							
4263 42¢ Purple Heart (type of 2003)	04/30/08	.85	.25	3.40	(4)	2.10	
Tagged, Self-Adhesive, Serpentine Die-Cut 11.25 x 10.75							
4264 42¢ Purple Heart (type of 2003)	04/30/08	.85	.20	3.40	(4)	2.10	
Tagged, Self-Adhesive, Serpentine Die-Cut 10.75							
4265 42¢ Frank Sinatra	05/13/08	.85	.20	3.40	(4)	2.10	
Statehood, Tagged, Self-Adhesive, Serpentine Die-Cut 10.75							
4266 42¢ Minnesota	05/13/08	.85	.20	3.40	(4)	2.10	
Tagged, Self-Adhesive, Serpentine Die-Cut 11.25 x 11							
4267 42¢ Dragonfly	05/19/08	1.25	.20	5.00	(4)	2.10	
Tagged, Self-Adhesive, Serpentine Die-Cut 10.75 x 10.5							
4268 $4.80 Mount Rushmore	06/06/08	9.75	5.00	40.00	(4)	2.10	
4269 $16.50 Hoover Dam	06/20/08	30.00	17.00	120.00	(4)	2.10	
Love, Booklet, Tagged, Self-Adhesive, Serpentine Die-Cut 10.75 on 2, 3 or 4 sides							
4270 42¢ All Heart	06/10/08	.85	.20			2.10	
Booklet, Tagged, Self-Adhesive, Serpentine Die-Cut 10.75 on 2, 3 or 4 sides							
4271 42¢ Heart With Green	06/10/08	.85	.20			2.10	
Tagged, Self-Adhesive, Serpentine Die-Cut 10.75							
4272 59¢ Heart With Buff	06/10/08	1.25	.25	5.00	(4)	2.10	

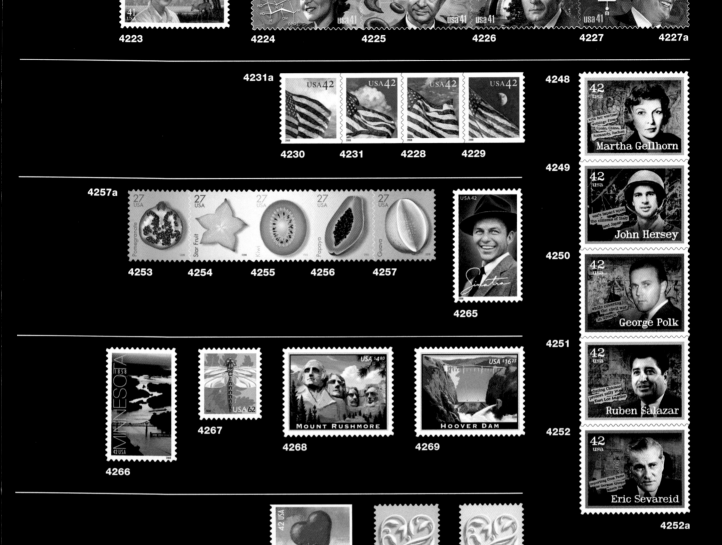

MARJORIE KINNAN RAWLINGS
4223

GERTY CORI BIOCHEMIST
4224

LINUS PAULING CHEMIST
4225

EDWIN HUBBLE ASTRONOMER
4226

JOHN BARDEEN PHYSICIST
4227

4227a

4231a
4230 4231 4228 4229

4257a
Pomegranate 4253
Star Fruit 4254
Kiwi 4255
Papaya 4256
Guava 4257

4265

4248 Martha Gellhorn
4249 John Hersey
4250 George Polk
4251 Ruben Salazar
4252 Eric Sevareid

4252a

4266 MINNESOTA 1858

4267

MOUNT RUSHMORE 4268

HOOVER DAM 4269

4270

4271 USA 42

4272 USA 59

VISIT US ONLINE AT *THE POSTAL STORE*
AT *WWW.USPS.COM*
OR CALL *1 800 STAMP-24*

4277a

4273   **4274**   **4275**   **4276**   **4277**

4282a

4278   **4279**   **4280**   **4281**   **4282**

4287a

4283   **4284**   **4285**   **4286**   **4287**

4292a

4288   **4289**   **4290**   **4291**   **4292**

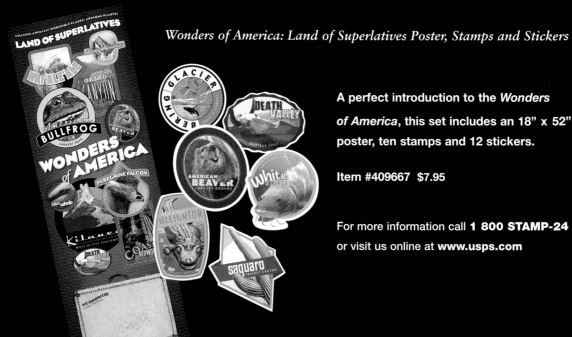

Wonders of America: Land of Superlatives Poster, Stamps and Stickers

A perfect introduction to the *Wonders of America*, this set includes an 18" x 52" poster, ten stamps and 12 stickers.

Item #409667 $7.95

For more information call **1 800 STAMP-24** or visit us online at **www.usps.com**

Issue		Date	Un	U	PB	#	FDC	Q(M)
Flags of Our Nation: Set 1, Coil, Tagged, Self-Adhesive, Serpentine Die-Cut 11 Vertically								
4273	42¢ American Flag and Clouds	06/14/08	.85	.25			2.10	
4274	42¢ Alabama Flag and Shrimp	06/14/08	.85	.25			2.10	
4275	42¢ Alaska Flag and Humpback Whale	06/14/08	.85	.25			2.10	
4276	42¢ American Samoa Flag and Island Peaks and Trees	06/14/08	.85	.25			2.10	
4277	42¢ Arizona Flag and Saguaro Cacti	06/14/08	.85	.25			2.10	
a	Horizontal strip of five		4.25				8.50	
4278	42¢ Arkansas Flag and Wood Duck	06/14/08	.85	.25			2.10	
4279	42¢ California Flag and Coast	06/14/08	.85	.25			2.10	
4280	42¢ Colorado Flag and Mountain	06/14/08	.85	.25			2.10	
4281	42¢ Connecticut Flag, Sailboats and Buoy	06/14/08	.85	.25			2.10	
4282	42¢ Delaware Flag and Beach	06/14/08	.85	.25			2.10	
a	Horizontal strip of five		4.25				8.50	
b	P # set of 10 (#4277a + #4282a)		8.50		12.50 (11)			

Issue		Date	Un	U	PB	#	FDC	Q(M)
Flags of Our Nation: Set 2, Coil, Tagged, Self-Adhesive, Serpentine Die-Cut 11 Vertically								
4283	42¢ District of Columbia Flag and Cherry Tree	09/02/08	.85	.25			2.10	
4284	42¢ Florida Flag and Anhinga	09/02/08	.85	.25			2.10	
4285	42¢ Georgia Flag, Fence and Lamppost	09/02/08	.85	.25			2.10	
4286	42¢ Guam Flag, Fish and Tropicbird	09/02/08	.85	.25			2.10	
4287	42¢ Hawaii Flag and Ohia Lehua Flowers	09/02/08	.85	.25			2.10	
a	Horizontal strip of five		4.25				8.50	
4288	42¢ Idaho Flag and Rainbow Trout	09/02/08	.85	.25			2.10	
4289	42¢ Illinois Flag and Windmill	09/02/08	.85	.25			2.10	
4290	42¢ Indiana Flag and Tractor	09/02/08	.85	.25			2.10	
4291	42¢ Iowa Flag, Farm Field and Cornstalks	09/02/08	.85	.25			2.10	
4292	42¢ Kansas Flag and Farm Buildings	09/02/08	.85	.25			2.10	
a	Horizontal strip of five		4.25				8.50	
b	P # set of 10 (#4287a + #4292a)		8.50		12.50 (11)			

#4293-4332 unassigned

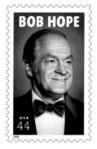

BOB HOPE

*I*n 2009, the U.S. Postal Service honors entertainer Bob Hope (1903-2003), a man who devoted his life to making people laugh. Well-known for his many television appearances, Hope also found success on the live stage, in radio shows, and in motion pictures. He became one of the most honored and beloved performers of the 20th century. ▪ In his twenties, Hope sang, danced, and told jokes on the vaudeville circuit, reaching the pinnacle of vaudeville success in 1931 and 1932 when he played the Palace Theatre in New York City. In his thirties, Hope appeared in major Broadway productions such as *Roberta*, the 1936 *Ziegfeld Follies*, and *Red, Hot, and Blue*. He also began headlining his own radio program and impressed audiences and producers in his first major film role, as Buzz Fielding in *Big Broadcast of 1938*. Hope went on to star in more than 50 feature films, including *Road to Singapore* and six more *Road* series movies with Bing Crosby. ▪ For almost five decades, Hope hosted numerous comedy-variety TV specials and made hundreds of guest appearances on other shows. He served as master of ceremonies for more Academy Awards presentations than anyone else, including the first live telecast on March 19, 1953, and the first colorcast in 1966. ▪ Although Hope never officially served in the U.S. Armed Forces, he dedicated a significant part of his life to entertaining America's men and women in uniform, starting in 1941 and continuing through Operation Desert Storm five decades later. In 1997, Hope became the first person recognized by the U.S. Congress as an "honorary veteran of the United States Armed Forces." He received thousands of honors during his lifetime, among them the Congressional Gold Medal, the Presidential Medal of Freedom, and five awards from the Academy of Motion Picture Arts and Sciences.

Bob Hope® Hope Enterprises, Inc.

Issue		Date	Un	U	PB	#	FDC	Q(M)
Charles + Ray Eames, Tagged, Self-Adhesive, Serpentine Die-Cut 10.75 x 10.5								
4333	Pane of 16 + label	06/17/08	14.00					13.50
a	42¢ Christmas Card Depicting Charles and Ray Eames		.85	.20				2.10
b	42¢ "Crosspatch" Fabric Design		.85	.20				2.10
c	42¢ Stacking Chairs		.85	.20				2.10
d	42¢ Case Study House #8, Pacific Palisades, CA		.85	.20				2.10
e	42¢ Wire-base Table		.85	.20				2.10
f	42¢ Lounge Chair and Ottoman		.85	.20				2.10
g	42¢ Hang-it-all		.85	.20				2.10
h	42¢ La Chaise		.85	.20				2.10
i	42¢ Scene From Film, "Tops"		.85	.20				2.10
j	42¢ Wire Mesh Chair		.85	.20				2.10
k	42¢ Cover of May 1993 Edition of *California Arts & Architecture* Magazine		.85	.20				2.10
l	42¢ House of Cards		.85	.20				2.10
m	42¢ Molded Plywood Sculpture		.85	.20				2.10
n	42¢ Eames Storage Unit		.85	.20				2.10
o	42¢ Aluminum Group Chair		.85	.20				2.10
p	42¢ Molded Plywood Chair		.85	.20				2.10
Olympic Games: Summer, Tagged, Self-Adhesive, Serpentine Die-Cut 10.75								
4334	42¢ Olympic Games	06/19/08	.85	.20	3.40	(4)		2.10

Issue		Date	Un	U	PB	#	FDC	Q(M)
Tagged, Self-Adhesive, Serpentine Die-Cut 10.75								
4335	42¢ Celebrate! (type of 2007)	07/10/08	.85	.20	3.40	(4)		2.10
Vintage Black Cinema, Tagged, Self-Adhesive, Serpentine Die-Cut 10.75								
4336	42¢ Poster for "Black and Tan"	07/16/08	.85	.20				2.10
4337	42¢ Poster for "The Sport of the Gods"	07/16/08	.85	.20				2.10
4338	42¢ Poster for "Prinsesse Tam-Tam"	07/16/08	.85	.20				2.10
4339	42¢ Poster for "Caldonia"	07/16/08	.85	.20				2.10
4340	42¢ Poster for "Hallelujah"	07/16/08	.85	.20				2.10
a	Horizontal strip of five		4.25		5.50	(10)		8.50
Tagged, Self-Adhesive, Serpentine Die-Cut 11								
4341	42¢ "Take Me Out To The Ball Game"	07/16/08	.85	.20	3.40	(4)		2.10
The Art of Disney: Imagination, Tagged, Self-Adhesive, Serpentine Die-Cut 10.5 x 10.75								
4342	42¢ Pongo and Pup	08/07/08	.85	.20				2.10
4343	42¢ Steamboat Willie	08/07/08	.85	.20				2.10
4344	42¢ Princess Aurora, Flora, Fauna and Merryweather	08/07/08	.85	.20				2.10
4345	42¢ Mowgil and Baloo	08/07/08	.85	.20				2.10
a	Block of four		3.40		3.40	(4)		4.75
American Treasures, Tagged, Self-Adhesive, Serpentine Die-Cut 11 on 2 or 3 sides								
4346	42¢ Albert Bierstadt, Valley of the Yosemite	08/14/08	.85	.20				2.10

A *Flags of Our Nation* Collector's Folder & Set 1 Stamps

Specifically designed to preserve and display the entire *Flags of Our Nation* series,
the Collector's Folder comes with a coil of 50 stamps featuring the flags of Alabama,
Alaska, American Samoa, Arizona, Arkansas, California, Colorado,
Connecticut, Delaware, plus Stars and Stripes (5 repeats of each),
and mounts for all 60 stamps in the series.

Item #786575 $29.95

Sets 2 & 3 are also now available.
Watch for additional sets coming
in 2010, 2011 and 2012.

To order this item call **1 800 STAMP-24**
or visit us online at **www.usps.com**

4333

a   b   c   d

e   f

g   h

i   j   k   l

m   n   o   p

ARCHITECTURE • FURNITURE • FILM • GRAPHIC DESIGN • INDUSTRIAL DESIGN • SCULPTURE • TOYS • EXHIBITS

4334

4336   4337   4338   4339   4340   4340a

4342   4343

4346

4341   4344   4345

4345a

4347

4349

4350

GREAT LAKES DUNES

TENTH IN A SERIES

N A T U R E   O F   A M E R I C A

4352   a   b   c

         d   e   f

     g   h   i   j

4353

4354

4355

4356

4357

4357a

4258

4259

4260  **4261**

4262  **4263**

4263a

Issue	Date	Un	U	PB	#	FDC	Q(M)
Booklet, Tagged, Self-Adhesive, Serpentine Die-Cut 11.25 x 10.75 on 2 or 3 sides							
4347 42¢ Sunflower	08/15/08	.85	.20				2.10
Coil, Untagged, Perf. 9.75 Vertically							
4348 (5¢) Sea Coast "2008" (type of 2002)	09/05/08	.20	.20	1.25	(5)		2.10
Tagged, Self-Adhesive, Serpentine Die-Cut 11 x 10.75							
4349 42¢ Latin Jazz	08/08/08	.85	.20	3.40	(4)		2.10
Legends of Hollywood, Tagged, Self-Adhesive, Serpentine Die-Cut 10.75							
4350 42¢ Bette Davis	08/18/08	.85	.20	3.40	(4)		2.10
Holiday Celebrations, Tagged, Self-Adhesive, Serpentine Die-Cut 11							
4351 42¢ Eid (type of 2001)	08/23/08	.85	.20	3.40	(4)		2.10
Nature of America: Great Lakes Dunes, Tagged, Self-Adhesive, Serpentine Die-Cut 10.75							
4352 Pane of 10	10/02/08						8.50
a 42¢ Vesper Sparrow		.85	.20				2.10
b 42¢ Red Fox		.85	.20				2.10
c 42¢ Piping Plover		.85	.20				2.10
d 42¢ Eastern Hognose Snake		.85	.20				2.10
e 42¢ Common Mergansers		.85	.20				2.10
f 42¢ Spotted Sandpiper		.85	.20				2.10
g 42¢ Tiger Beetle		.85	.20				2.10
h 42¢ White-footed Mouse		.85	.20				2.10
i 42¢ Piping Plover Nestlings		.85	.20				2.10
j 42¢ Red Admiral Butterfly		.85	.20				2.10
America on the Move: 50s Fins and Chrome, Tagged, Self-Adhesive, Serpentine Die-Cut 10.75							
4353 42¢ 1959 Cadillac Eldorado	10/03/08	.85	.20				2.10
4354 42¢ 1957 Studebaker Golden Hawk	10/03/08	.85	.20				2.10
4355 42¢ 1957 Pontiac Safari	10/03/08	.85	.20				2.10
4356 42¢ 1957 Lincoln Premiere	10/03/08	.85	.20				2.10
4357 42¢ 1957 Chrysler 300C	10/03/08	.85	.20				2.10
a Vertical strip of five		4.25		8.50	(10)		5.50

Issue	Date	Un	U	PB	#	FDC	Q(M)
Tagged, Self-Adhesive, Serpentine Die-Cut 10.75							
4358 42¢ Alzheimer's Awareness	10/17/08	.85	.20	3.40	(4)		2.10
Holiday Celebration: Christmas, Booklet, Tagged, Self-Adhesive, Serpentine Die-Cut 10.75 x 11 on 2 or 3 sides							
4359 42¢ Virgin and Child with the Young John the Baptist, by Sandro Botticelli	10/23/08	.85	.20				2.10
Holiday Celebration: Holiday, Booklet, Tagged, Self-Adhesive, Serpentine Die-Cut 10.75 x 11 on 2 or 3 sides							
4360 42¢ Drummer Nutcracker	10/23/08	.85	.20				2.10
4361 42¢ Santa Claus Nutcracker	10/23/08	.85	.20				2.10
4362 42¢ King Nutcracker	10/23/08	.85	.20				2.10
4363 42¢ Soldier Nutcracker	10/23/08	.85	.20				2.10
a Block of four		3.40					4.75
Holiday Celebration: Holiday, Booklet, Tagged, Self-Adhesive, Serpentine Die-Cut 11.25 x 11 on 2 or 3 sides							
4364 42¢ Drummer Nutcracker	10/23/08	.85	.20				2.10
4365 42¢ Santa Claus Nutcracker	10/23/08	.85	.20				2.10
4366 42¢ King Nutcracker	10/23/08	.85	.20				2.10
4367 42¢ Soldier Nutcracker	10/23/08	.85	.20				2.10
a Block of four		3.40					4.75
Holiday Celebration: Holiday, Booklet, Tagged, Self-Adhesive, Serpentine Die-Cut 8 on 2, 3 or 4 sides							
4368 42¢ Drummer Nutcracker	10/23/08	.85	.20				2.10
4369 42¢ Santa Claus Nutcracker	10/23/08	.85	.20				2.10
4370 42¢ King Nutcracker	10/23/08	.85	.20				2.10
4371 42¢ Soldier Nutcracker	10/23/08	.85	.20				2.10
a Block of four		3.40					4.75
Holiday Celebrations: Tagged, Self-Adhesive, Serpentine Die-Cut 10.75 x 11							
4372 42¢ Hanukkah (type of 2004)	10/24/08	.85	.20	3.40	(4)		2.10
Holiday Celebrations: Tagged, Self-Adhesive, Serpentine Die-Cut 11 x 10.75							
4373 42¢ Kwanzaa (type of 2004)	10/24/08	.85	.20	3.40	(4)		2.10

WINTER HOLIDAYS

In 2009, the U.S. Postal Service celebrates the winter holiday season with stamps featuring a reindeer, snowman, gingerbread man, and toy soldier. ■ These popular figures are seen throughout the holidays, decorating homes, schools, and stores from Thanksgiving to New Year's. They also appear in gift-wrap designs and are the subjects of several favorite songs and stories. As stamp art, they will add a festive touch to letters and cards sent to friends and family. ■ Reindeer have long been associated with Santa's Christmas Eve journey and his sleigh full of toys, while toy soldiers have been holiday heroes for generations. After a big winter snowstorm, snowmen sporting hats, scarves, and carrot noses stand guard on neighborhood lawns. Indoors, the enticing aroma of gingerbread cookies baking in the oven fills the air while parents, children, and holiday guests await a first taste of these traditional holiday sweets. ■ This is the first stamp project for artist Joseph Cudd of Brushworks Studio, in Greensboro, North Carolina.

	Issue	Date	Un	U	PB	#	FDC	Q(M)
	Semi-Postal, Tagged, Self-Adhesive, Serpentine Die-Cut 11							
B1	(32¢ + 8¢) Breast Cancer Research	07/29/1998	.80	.20	3.25	(4)	2.00	618

The proceeds went for cancer research. Sales were suspended Jan. 1, 2004 but were resumed Feb. 2, 2004 when congress extended the sales period through Dec. 31, 2011.

Date	Sales Price	Postage Value	Proceeds
07/29/1998	.40	.32	.08
01/10/1999	.40	.33	.07
01/07/2001	.40	.34	.06
03/23/2002	.45	.34	.11
06/30/2002	.45	.37	.08
01/08/2006	.45	.39	.06
05/14/2007	.55	.41	.14
05/12/2008	.55	.42	.13
05/11/2009	.55	.44	.11

	Issue	Date	Un	U	PB	#	FDC	Q(M)
	Semi-Postal, Tagged, Self-Adhesive, Serpentine Die-Cut 11.25							
B2	(34¢ + 11¢) Heroes of 2001	06/07/02	.80	.35	3.25	(4)	2.00	255

The 11¢ proceeds went for assistance to families of emergency relief personnel killed or permanently disabled in the line of duty in connection with the terrorists attacks of Sept. 11, 2001. The face value became 37¢ and the surtax 8¢ June 30, 2002.

	Issue	Date	Un	U	PB	#	FDC	Q(M)
	Semi-Postal, Tagged, Self-Adhesive, Serpentine Die-Cut 11							
B3	(37¢ + 8¢) Stop Family Violence	10/08/03	.85	.45	3.50	(4)	1.60	125

EARLY TV MEMORIES

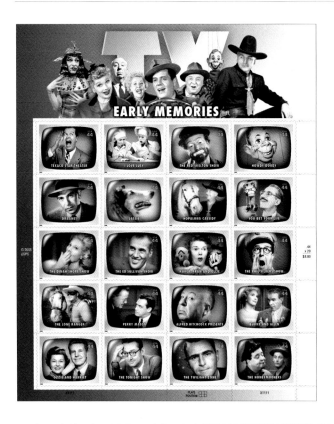

With these stamps, the U.S. Postal Service commemorates 20 great shows from TV's golden age. For more than half a century, Americans have turned to television for entertainment and information. To those watching in its early days, TV offered the additional excitement of the new. Whether laughing at the first situation comedies, tingling at crime dramas, or identifying with ordinary people who had their day in the spotlight on game shows, audiences were charmed by the novelty of the young medium. Today, memories from television's "childhood"—often especially vivid—are a pure pleasure. Art director Carl Herrman worked with twenty2product, a San Francisco-based studio, to give the archival photos used in the stamp art a suitably "retro" look. ■ Featured on the stamps are the following memorable shows: *Texaco Star Theater; I Love Lucy; The Red Skelton Show; Howdy Doody; Dragnet; Lassie; Hopalong Cassidy; You Bet Your Life; The Dinah Shore Show; The Ed Sullivan Show; Kukla, Fran and Ollie; The Phil Silvers Show; The Lone Ranger; Perry Mason; Alfred Hitchcock Presents; The George Burns and Gracie Allen Show; The Adventures of Ozzie and Harriet; The Tonight Show; The Twilight Zone;* and *The Honeymooners.*

B1   **B2**   **B3**

Flags of Our Nation — An Exciting New Multi-Stamp Series!

In 2008, the U.S. Postal Service introduced a new multi-stamp series featuring the Stars and Stripes,
the fifty state flags, five territorial flags, and the District of Columbia flag. A total of sixty stamps will be issued
in sets of ten, with the last issuance in 2012. Start your collection today with these exciting sets!

Flags of Our Nation (Set 1)

Flags of Our Nation Set 1: Coil of 50 (only)   Item #786540 $21.00

Confederate States of America

1861-1863

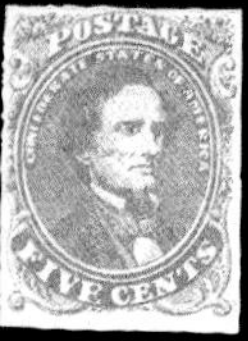

1

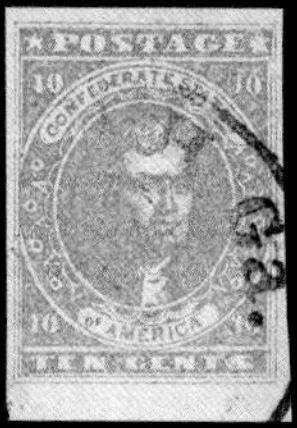

2

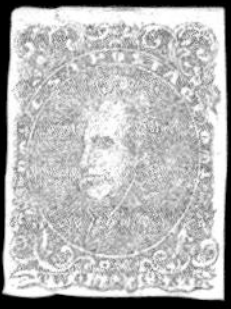

3

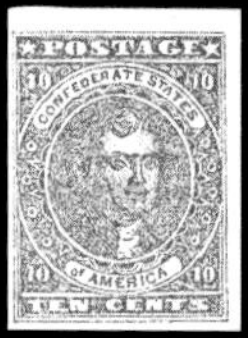

5

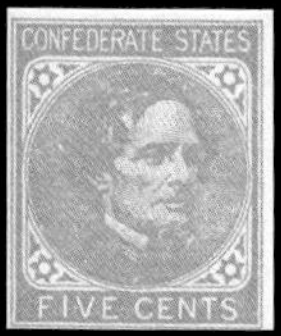

6

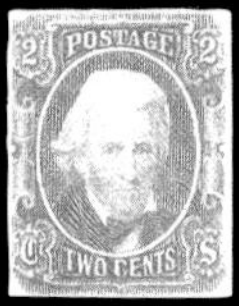

8

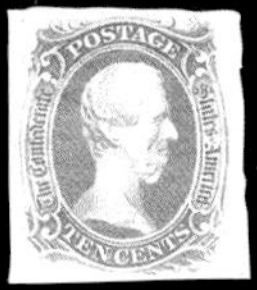

9

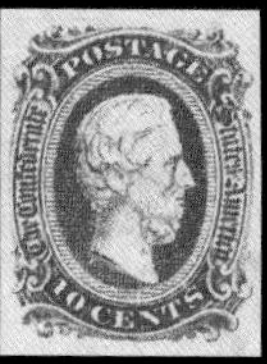

11

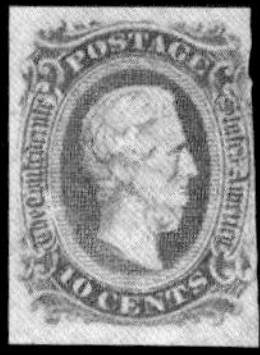

12

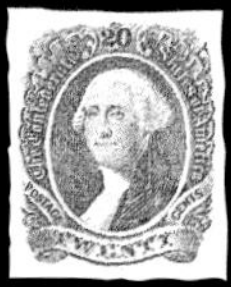

13

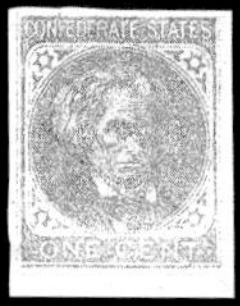

14

Newspaper/Periodical

1865-1897

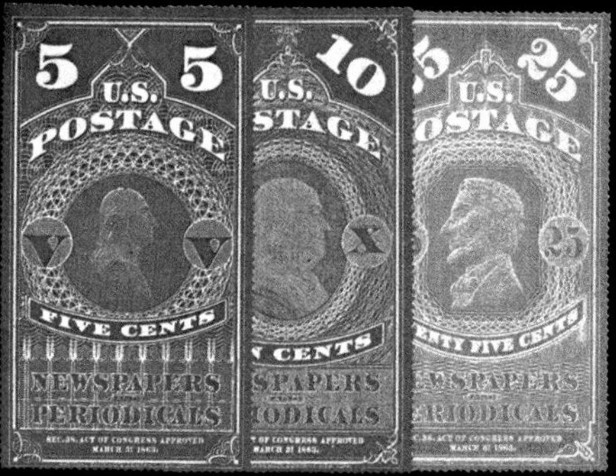

PR1 PR2 PR3

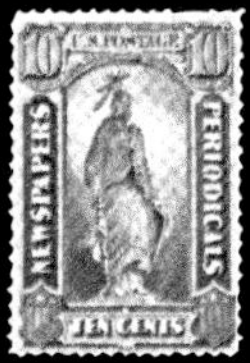

PR15

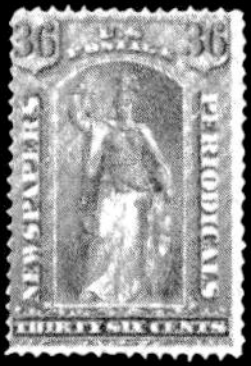

PR18

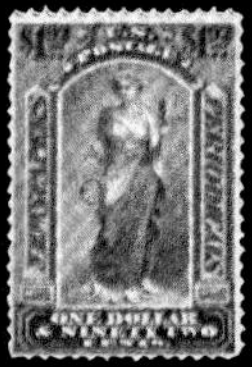

PR24

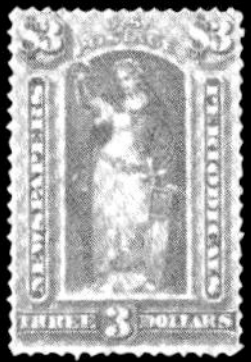

PR25

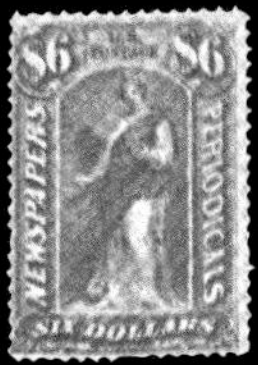

PR26

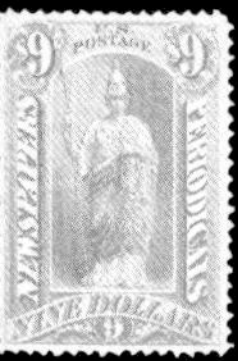

PR27

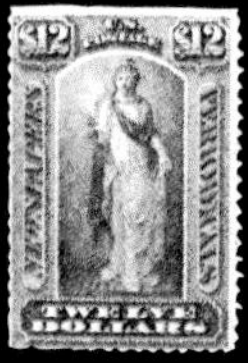

PR28

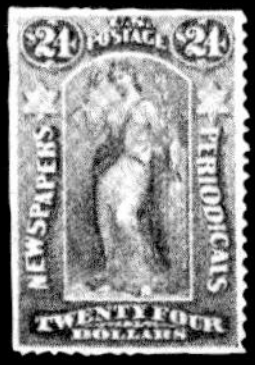

PR29

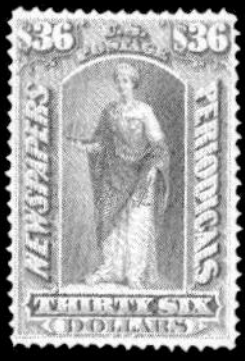

PR30

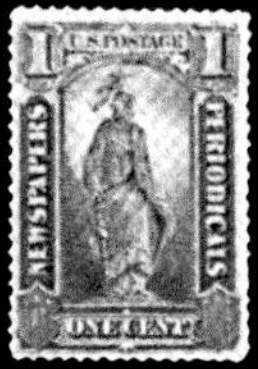

PR78

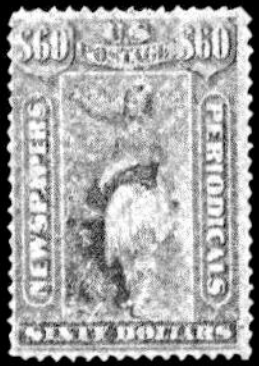

PR79

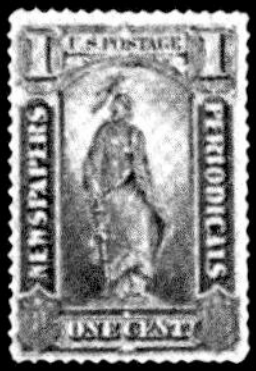

PR90

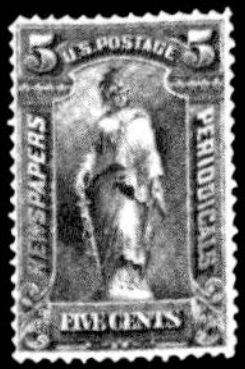

PR116

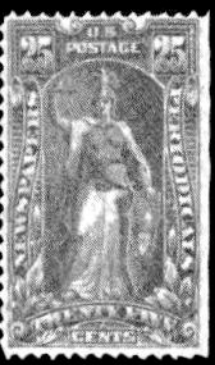

PR118

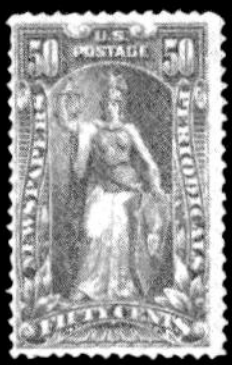

PR119

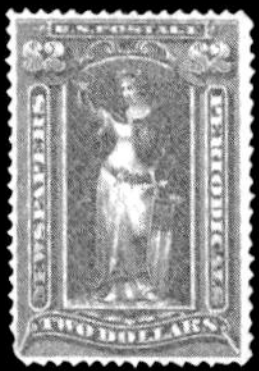

PR120

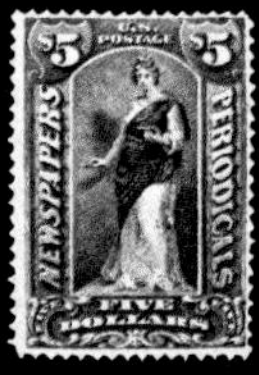

PR121

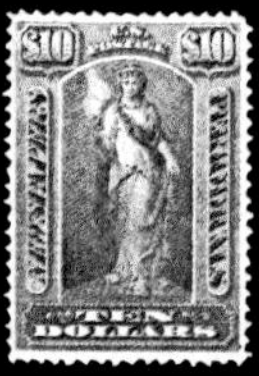

PR122

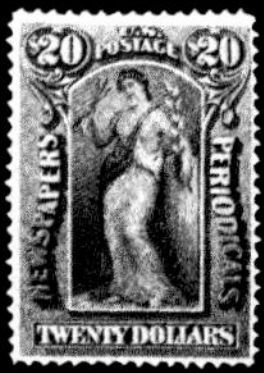

PR123

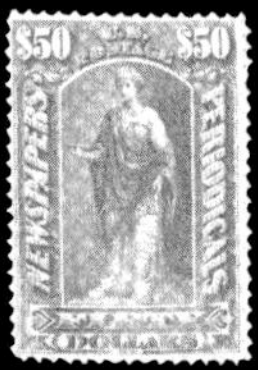

PR124

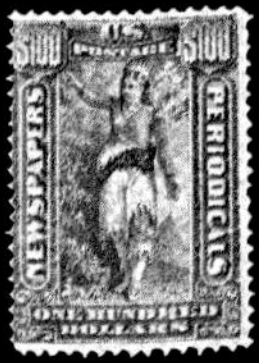

PR125

Confederate States of America

Issue	Date	Un	U
Imperf., Lithographed, Soft Porous Paper			
1 5¢ Jefferson Davis	1861	275.00	175.00
2 10¢ Thomas Jefferson	1861	300.00	200.00
3 2¢ Andrew Jackson	1862	900.00	750.00
4 5¢ Jefferson Davis (6)	1862	225.00	125.00
5 10¢ Thomas Jefferson	1862	1,500.00	500.00
Imperf., Typographed, Hard Medium Paper			
6 5¢ Jefferson Davis, (London print)	1862	15.00	27.50

Issue	Date	Un	U
Imperf., Typographed, Thin to Thick Paper			
7 5¢ Jefferson Davis (6) (Local print)	1862	18.00	20.00
Imperf., Engraved, Soft Porous Paper			
8 2¢ Andrew Jackson	1863	70.00	*350.00*
9 10¢ Jefferson Davis	1863	900.00	550.00
10 10¢ Jefferson Davis (9), (with rect. frame showing parts of lines outside at least 3 sides of frame)	1863	5,000.00	1,800.00

Issue	Date	Un	U
Imperf., Engraved, Thick or Thin Paper			
11 10¢ Jefferson Davis, die A	1863	15.00	20.00
12 10¢ Jefferson Davis die B (11), with extra line outside corner ornament	1863	18.00	20.00
13 20¢ George Washington	1863	40.00	*400.00*
Imperf., Typographed			
14 1¢ John C. Calhoun This stamp was never put into use	1862	110.00	

Newspaper/Periodical

Issue	Date	Un	U
Typographed, Perf. 12:			
Colored Border, Thin Hard Paper			
PR1 5¢ Washington	1865	750.00	*2,000.00*
PR2 10¢ Franklin	1865	300.00	*1,800.00*
PR3 25¢ Lincoln	1865	375.00	*2,400.00*
White Border, Yellowish Paper			
PR4 5¢ Washington	1865	250.00	*2,400.00*
White Border, Hard White Paper			
PR5 5¢ Washington	1875	200.00	
Colored Border, Hard White Paper			
PR6 10¢ Franklin	1875	225.00	
PR7 25¢ Lincoln	1875	250.00	
White Border, Soft Porous Paper			
PR8 5¢ Washington	1881	800.00	
Engraved, Perf. 12, Thin Hard Paper			
PR9 2¢ Statue of Freedom	1875	280.00	30.00
PR10 3¢ Statue of Freedom	1875	280.00	32.50
PR11 4¢ Statue of Freedom	1875	280.00	30.00
PR12 6¢ Statue of Freedom	1875	280.00	32.50
PR13 8¢ Statue of Freedom	1875	325.00	47.50
PR14 9¢ Statue of Freedom	1875	475.00	95.00
PR15 10¢ Statue of Freedom	1875	350.00	37.50
PR16 12¢ "Justice"	1875	800.00	100.00
PR17 24¢ "Justice"	1875	875.00	125.00
PR18 36¢ "Justice"	1875	875.00	150.00
PR19 48¢ "Justice"	1875	1,250.00	200.00
PR20 60¢ "Justice"	1875	1,250.00	115.00
PR21 72¢ "Justice"	1875	1,250.00	250.00
PR22 84¢ "Justice"	1875	1,850.00	375.00
PR23 96¢ "Justice"	1875	1,350.00	250.00
PR24 $1.92 Ceres	1875	1,650.00	250.00
PR25 $3 "Victory"	1875	1,800.00	450.00
PR26 $6 Clio	1875	3,600.00	550.00
PR27 $9 Minerva	1875	4,000.00	600.00
PR28 $12 Vesta	1875	4,500.00	750.00
PR29 $24 "Peace"	1875	4,750.00	800.00
PR30 $36 "Commerce"	1875	5,000.00	950.00
PR31 $48 Hebe	1875	6,250.00	1,150.00
PR32 $60 Indian Maiden	1875	6,500.00	1,250.00
Special Printing, Perf. 12, Hard White Paper			
PR33 2¢ Statue of Freedom	1875	600.00	
PR34 3¢ Statue of Freedom	1875	600.00	
PR35 4¢ Statue of Freedom	1875	650.00	
PR36 6¢ Statue of Freedom	1875	850.00	
PR37 8¢ Statue of Freedom	1875	950.00	
PR38 9¢ Statue of Freedom	1875	1,050.00	
PR39 10¢ Statue of Freedom	1875	1,300.00	

Issue	Date	Un	U
PR40 12¢ "Justice"	1875	1,500.00	
PR41 24¢ "Justice"	1875	2,100.00	
PR42 36¢ "Justice"	1875	2,800.00	
PR43 48¢ "Justice"	1875	4,000.00	
PR44 60¢ "Justice"	1875	4,000.00	
PR45 72¢ "Justice"	1875	4,500.00	
PR46 84¢ "Justice"	1875	5,000.00	
PR47 96¢ "Justice"	1875	*8,500.00*	
PR48 $1.92 Ceres	1875	*22,500.00*	
PR49 $3 "Victory"	1875	*45,000.00*	
PR50 $6 Clio	1875	*80,000.00*	
PR51 $9 Minerva	1875	*160,000.00*	
PR52 $12 Vesta	1875	*125,000.00*	
PR53 $24 "Peace"	1875	—	
PR54 $36 "Commerce"	1875	*250,000.00*	
PR55 $48 Hebe	1875	—	
PR56 $60 Indian Maiden	1875	—	
Soft Porous Paper, Perf. 12			
PR57 2¢ Statue of Freedom	1879	50.00	8.50
PR58 3¢ Statue of Freedom	1879	60.00	10.50
PR59 4¢ Statue of Freedom	1879	60.00	10.50
PR60 6¢ Statue of Freedom	1879	105.00	21.00
PR61 8¢ Statue of Freedom	1879	115.00	21.00
PR62 10¢ Statue of Freedom	1879	115.00	21.00
PR63 12¢ "Justice"	1879	475.00	85.00
PR64 24¢ "Justice"	1879	475.00	85.00
PR65 36¢ "Justice"	1879	1,000.00	240.00
PR66 48¢ "Justice"	1879	1,000.00	180.00
PR67 60¢ "Justice"	1879	1,000.00	160.00
PR68 72¢ "Justice"	1879	1,250.00	300.00
PR69 84¢ "Justice"	1879	1,250.00	225.00
PR70 96¢ "Justice"	1879	1,200.00	160.00
PR71 $1.92 Ceres	1879	550.00	135.00
PR72 $3 "Victory"	1879	625.00	150.00
PR73 $6 Clio	1879	1,050.00	230.00
PR74 $9 Minerva	1879	800.00	160.00
PR75 $12 Vesta	1879	850.00	210.00
PR76 $24 "Peace"	1879	800.00	260.00
PR77 $36 "Commerce"	1879	850.00	280.00
PR78 $48 Hebe	1879	900.00	390.00
PR79 $60 Indian Maiden	1879	850.00	360.00
Special Printing of 1879			
PR80 2¢ Statue of Freedom	1883	1,350.00	
Perf. 12			
PR81 1¢ Statue of Freedom	1885	85.00	8.50
PR82 12¢ "Justice"	1885	180.00	20.00

Issue	Date	Un	U
PR83 24¢ "Justice"	1885	180.00	22.50
PR84 36¢ "Justice"	1885	280.00	37.50
PR85 48¢ "Justice"	1885	400.00	55.00
PR86 60¢ "Justice"	1885	525.00	80.00
PR87 72¢ "Justice"	1885	525.00	85.00
PR88 84¢ "Justice"	1885	800.00	200.00
PR89 96¢ "Justice"	1885	700.00	160.00
Soft Wove Paper, Perf. 12			
PR90 1¢ Stat. of Freedom	1894	425.00	*750.00*
PR91 2¢ Stat. of Freedom	1894	475.00	
PR92 4¢ Stat. of Freedom	1894	500.00	—
PR93 6¢ Stat. of Freedom	1894	3,750.00	
PR94 10¢ Stat. of Freedom	1894	1,150.00	
PR95 12¢ "Justice"	1894	2,600.00	*1,500.00*
PR96 24¢ "Justice"	1894	3,750.00	*1,750.00*
PR97 36¢ "Justice"	1894	50,000.00	
PR98 60¢ "Justice"	1894	55,000.00	*7,500.00*
PR99 96¢ "Justice"	1894	52,500.00	
PR100 $3 "Victory"	1894	60,000.00	
PR101 $6 Clio	1894	60,000.00	—
PR102 1¢ Stat. of Freedom	1895	230.00	*100.00*
PR103 2¢ Stat. of Freedom	1895	230.00	*100.00*
PR104 5¢ Stat. of Freedom	1895	300.00	*150.00*
PR105 10¢ Stat. of Freedom	1895	550.00	*350.00*
PR106 25¢ "Justice"	1895	750.00	*500.00*
PR107 50¢ "Justice"	1895	1,500.00	*800.00*
PR108 $2 "Victory"	1895	1,500.00	*600.00*
PR109 $5 Clio	1895	2,100.00	*1,100.00*
PR110 $10 Vesta	1895	2,500.00	*1,300.00*
PR111 $20 "Peace"	1895	3,250.00	*2,000.00*
PR112 $50 "Commerce"	1895	2,900.00	*750.00*
PR113 $100 Indian Maiden	1895	3,500.00	*2,500.00*
Wmkd. 191, Perf. 12			
PR114 1¢ Stat. of Freedom	1895	8.00	*25.00*
PR115 2¢ Stat. of Freedom	1896	8.00	*25.00*
PR116 5¢ Stat. of Freedom	1896	13.00	*40.00*
PR117 10¢ Stat. of Freedom	1895	13.00	*25.00*
PR118 25¢ "Justice"	1895	20.00	*65.00*
PR119 50¢ "Justice"	1895	25.00	*75.00*
PR120 $2 "Victory"	1897	30.00	*110.00*
PR121 $5 Clio	1896	40.00	*160.00*
PR122 $10 Vesta	1896	42.50	*160.00*
PR123 $20 "Peace"	1896	45.00	*180.00*
PR124 $50 "Commerce"	1897	75.00	*225.00*
PR125 $100 Indian Maiden	1896	65.00	*240.00*

Issue	Date	Un	U	PB #	FDC	Q(M)
Unwmk., Engr., Perf. 11						
For prepayment of postage on all mailable matter sent by airmail. All unwatermarked.						
C1 6¢ Curtiss Jenny	12/10/18	65.00	30.00	775.00 (6)	*25,000.00*	3
Double transfer		90.00	45.00			
C2 16¢ Curtiss Jenny	07/11/18	70.00	35.00	1,000.00 (6)	*32,500.00*	4
C3 24¢ Curtiss Jenny	05/13/18	70.00	35.00	400.00 (4)	*27,500.00*	2
a Center Inverted		500,000.00		3,500,000.00 (4)		0.0001
Unwmk., Perf. 11						
C4 8¢ Airplane Radiator and Wooden Propeller	08/15/23	21.00	14.00	250.00 (6)	400.00	6
C5 16¢ Air Service Emblem	08/17/23	70.00	30.00	1,550.00 (6)	600.00	5
C6 24¢ De Havilland Biplane	08/21/23	75.00	30.00	2,050.00 (6)	750.00	5
C7 10¢ Map of U.S. and Two Mail Planes	02/13/26	2.50	.35	35.00 (6)	70.00	42
Double transfer		5.75	1.10			
C8 15¢ olive brown (C7)	09/18/26	2.75	2.50	35.00 (6)	85.00	16
C9 20¢ yellow green (C7)	01/25/27	7.00	2.00	75.00 (6)	100.00	18
C10 10¢ Lindbergh's "Spirit of St. Louis"	06/18/27	7.00	2.50	90.00 (6)	25.00	20
a Booklet pane of 3	05/26/28	80.00	*65.00*		875.00	
C11 5¢ Beacon on Rocky Mountains	07/25/28	5.00	.75	200.00 (8)	50.00	107
Recut frame line at left		7.50	1.50			
a Vertical pair, imperf. between		*7,000.00*				
C12 5¢ Winged Globe	02/10/30	9.50	.50	140.00 (6)	12.00	98
a Horizontal pair, imperf. between		*4,500.00*				
Graf Zeppelin, Unwmk., Perf. 11						
C13 65¢ *Graf Zeppelin* over Atlantic Ocean	04/19/30	240.00	160.00	2,300.00 (6)	1,200.00	0.09
C14 $1.30 *Graf Zeppelin* Between Continents	04/19/30	500.00	375.00	5,750.00 (6)	1,100.00	0.07
C15 $2.60 *Graf Zeppelin* Passing Globe	04/19/30	700.00	575.00	8,500.00 (6)	1,200.00	0.06
Unwmk., Perf. 10.5 x 11						
C16 5¢ violet (C12)	08/19/31	5.00	.60	75.00 (4)	175.00	57
C17 8¢ olive bister (C12)	09/26/32	2.25	.40	27.50 (4)	15.00	77
Century of Progress, Unwmk., Perf. 11						
C18 50¢ Zeppelin, Federal Building at Chicago Exposition and Hangar at Friedrichshafen	10/02/33	55.00	55.00	500.00 (6)	200.00	0.3
Beginning with #C19, unused values are for never-hinged stamps.						
Unwmk., Perf. 10.5 x 11						
C19 6¢ dull orange (C12)	06/30/34	3.50	.25	20.00 (4)	*190.00*	302
Trans-Pacific, Unwmk., Perf. 11						
C20 25¢ "China Clipper" over the Pacific	11/22/35	1.40	1.00	22.50 (6)	40.00	10
C21 20¢ "China Clipper" over the Pacific	02/15/37	11.00	1.75	90.00 (6)	45.00	13
C22 50¢ carmine (C21)	02/15/37	11.00	5.00	90.00 (6)	50.00	9
C23 6¢ Eagle Holding Shield, Olive Branch and Arrows	05/14/38	.50	.20	8.00 (4)	15.00	350
a Vertical pair, imperf. horizontally		*325.00*		*1,250.00* (4)		
b Horizontal pair, imperf. vertically		*12,500.00*		*37,500.00* (4)		
c Ultramarine and carmine		*150.00*	*1,500.00*	*1,500.00* (4)		

Issue	Date	Un	U	PB/LP #	FDC	Q(M)
Transatlantic, Unwmk., Perf. 11						
C24 30¢ Winged Globe	05/16/39	12.00	1.50	130.00 (6)	47.50	20
Unwmk., Perf. 11 x 10.5						
C25 6¢ Twin-Motor Transport Plane	06/25/41	.20	.20	.60 (4)	3.75	4,747
a Booklet pane of 3	03/18/43	5.00	1.50		25.00	
Singles of #C25a are imperf. at sides or imperf. at sides and bottom.						
b Horizontal pair, imperf. between		*2,250.00*				
C26 8¢ olive green (C25)	03/21/44	.20	.20	1.10 (4)	3.75	1,745
C27 10¢ violet (C25)	08/15/41	1.25	.20	5.50 (4)	8.00	67
C28 15¢ brn. carmine (C25)	08/19/41	2.25	.35	9.50 (4)	10.00	78
C29 20¢ bright green (C25)	08/27/41	2.25	.30	9.50 (4)	12.50	42
C30 30¢ blue (C25)	09/25/41	2.25	.35	9.50 (4)	20.00	60
C31 50¢ orange (C25)	10/29/41	11.00	3.25	50.00 (4)	40.00	11
C32 5¢ DC-4 Skymaster	09/25/46	.20	.20	.45 (4)	2.00	865
Unwmk., Perf. 10.5 x 11						
C33 5¢ DC-4 Skymaster	03/26/47	.20	.20	.60 (4)	2.00	972
Unwmk., Perf. 11 x 10.5						
C34 10¢ Pan American Union Bldg., Washington, D.C. and Martin 2-0-2	08/30/47	.25	.20	1.10 (4)	2.00	208
a Dry printing		.40	.20	1.75 (4)		
C35 15¢ Statue of Liberty, N.Y. Skyline and Lockheed Constellation	08/20/47	.35	.20	1.50 (4)	1.75	756
a Horizontal pair, imperf. between		*2,750.00*				
b Dry printing		.55	.20	2.50 (4)		
C36 25¢ San Francisco-Oakland Bay Bridge and Boeing Stratocruiser	07/30/47	.90	.20	4.00 (4)	2.25	133
a Dry printing		1.20	.20	5.25 (4)		
Unwmk., Perf. 10 Horizontally						
C37 5¢ carmine (C33)	01/15/48	1.00	.80	10.00 (2)	1.75	33
Unwmk., Perf. 11 x 10.5						
C38 5¢ New York City	07/31/48	.20	.20	3.50 (4)	1.75	38
Unwmk., Perf. 10.5 x 11						
C39 6¢ carmine (C33)	01/18/49	.20	.20	.50 (4)	1.50	5,070
a Booklet pane of 6	11/18/49	10.00	5.00		10.00	
b Dry printing		.50	.20	2.25 (4)		
c As "a," dry printing		25.00	—			
Unwmk., Perf. 11 x 10.5						
C40 6¢ Alexandria, Virginia	05/11/49	.20	.20	.50 (4)	1.50	75
Coil, Unwmk., Perf. 10 Horizontally						
C41 6¢ carmine (C33)	08/25/49	3.00	.20	14.00 (2)	1.25	260
Universal Postal Union, Unwmk., Perf. 11 x 10.5						
C42 10¢ Post Office Dept. Bldg.	11/18/49	.20	.20	1.40 (4)	1.75	21
C43 15¢ Globe and Doves Carrying Messages	10/07/49	.30	.25	1.25 (4)	2.75	37
C44 25¢ Boeing Stratocruiser and Globe	11/30/49	.60	.40	4.00 (4)	3.75	16
C45 6¢ Wright Brothers	12/17/49	.20	.20	.70 (4)	2.75	80
C46 80¢ Diamond Head, Honolulu, Hawaii	03/26/52	5.00	1.25	22.50 (4)	20.00	19
C47 6¢ Powered Flight	05/29/53	.20	.20	.55 (4)	1.50	78
C48 4¢ Eagle in Flight	09/03/54	.20	.20	1.10 (4)	1.00	50

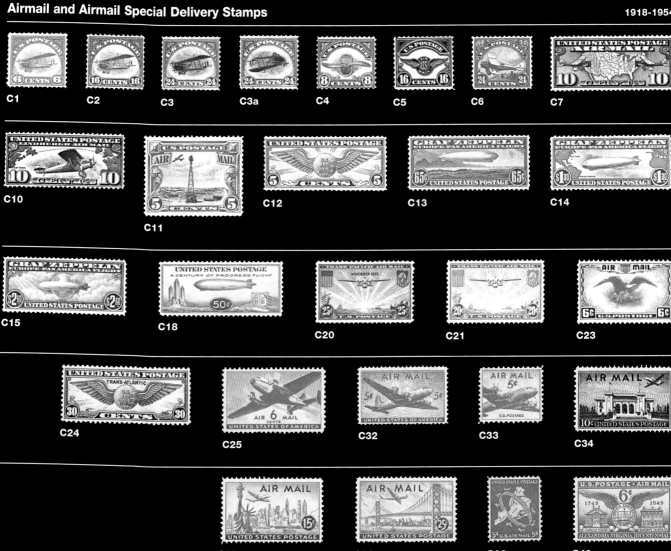

C1   C2   C3   C3a   C4   C5   C6   C7

C10   C11   C12   C13   C14

C15   C18   C20   C21   C23

C24   C25   C32   C33   C34

C35   C36   C38   C40

C42   C43   C44   C45

C46   C47   C48

C49

C51

C53

C54

C55

C56

C57

C58

C59

C61

C62

C63

C64

C66

C67

C68

C69

C70

C71

C72

C74

C75

FIRST MAN ON THE MOON

C76

C77

C78

C79

C80

C81

C84

C85

C86

C87

C88

C89

C90

	Issue	Date	Un	U	PB/LP	#	FDC	Q(M)
	Unwmk., Perf. 11 x 10.5							
C49	6¢ Air Force	08/01/57	.20	.20	.70	(4)	2.75	63
C50	5¢ rose red (C48)	07/31/58	.20	.20	1.00	(4)	1.00	72
	Unwmk., Perf. 10.5 x 11							
C51	7¢ Jet Airliner	07/31/58	.20	.20	.60	(4)	1.00	1,327
a	Booklet pane of 6		9.00	7.00			9.00	221
	Coil, Perf. 10 Horizontally							
C52	7¢ blue (C51)	07/31/58	2.00	.20	14.00	(2)	1.00	157
	Unwmk., Perf. 11 x 10.5							
C53	7¢ Alaska Statehood	01/03/59	.20	.20	.75	(4)	1.50	90
	Unwmk., Perf. 11							
C54	7¢ Balloon Jupiter	08/17/59	.30	.20	1.40	(4)	1.75	79
	Unwmk., Perf. 11 x 10.5							
C55	7¢ Hawaii Statehood	08/21/59	.20	.20	.75	(4)	1.00	85
	Unwmk., Perf. 11							
C56	10¢ Pan American Games	08/27/59	.25	.25	1.25	(4)	1.00	39
C57	10¢ Liberty Bell	06/10/60	1.00	.70	6.00	(4)	1.50	40
C58	15¢ Statue of Liberty	11/20/59	.35	.20	1.50	(4)	1.50	98
C59	25¢ Abraham Lincoln	04/22/60	.50	.20	2.00	(4)	1.50	
a	Tagged	12/29/66	.60	.30	2.50	(4)	50.00	
	Unwmk., Perf. 10.5 x 11							
C60	7¢ carmine (C61)	08/12/60	.20	.20	.60	(4)	1.00	1,289
	Pair with full horizontal gutter between		125.00					
a	Booklet pane of 6	08/19/60	10.00	8.00			8.00	
b	Vertical pair, imperf. between		5,500.00					
	Coil, Unwmk., Perf. 10 Horizontally							
C61	7¢ Jet Airliner	10//22/60	4.00	.25	35.00	(2)	1.00	87
	Unwmk., Perf. 11							
C62	13¢ Liberty Bell	06/28/61	.40	.20	1.65	(4)	1.00	
a	Tagged	02/15/67	.75	.50	6.00	(4)	50.00	
C63	15¢ Statue of Liberty	01/13/61	.30	.20	1.25	(4)	1.00	
a	Tagged	01/11/67	.35	.20	1.50	(4)	50.00	
b	As "a," horiz. pair, imperf. vertically		15,000.00					
	#C63 has a gutter between the two parts of the design; C58 does not.							
	Unwmk., Perf. 10.5 x 11							
C64	8¢ Jetliner over Capitol	12/05/62	.20	.20	.65	(4)	1.00	
a	Tagged	08/01/63	.20	.20	.65	(4)	2.00	
b	Booklet pane of 5 + label		7.00	3.00			3.50	
c	As "b," tagged	1964	2.00	.75				
	Coil, Perf. 10 Horizontally							
C65	8¢ carmine (C64)	12/05/62	.40	.20	3.75	(2)	1.00	
a	Tagged	01/14/65	.35	.20	1.75	(2)		
	Unwmk., Perf. 11							
C66	15¢ Montgomery Blair	05/03/63	.60	.55	2.50	(4)	1.50	42
	Unwmk., Perf. 11 x 10.5							
C67	6¢ Bald Eagle	07/12/63	.20	.20	1.40	(4)	1.00	
a	Tagged	02/15/67	4.00	3.00	62.50	(4)	50.00	
	Unwmk., Perf. 11							
C68	8¢ Amelia Earhart	07/24/63	.20	.20	1.00	(4)	4.00	64
	Tagged, Perf. 11							
C69	8¢ Robert H. Goddard	10/05/64	.40	.20	1.75	(4)	3.00	62
	Unwmk., Perf. 11							
C70	8¢ Alaska Purchase	03/30/67	.25	.20	1.10	(4)	1.50	56
	Perf. 11							
C71	20¢ "Columbia Jays," by Audubon, (See also #1241)	04/26/67	.80	.20	3.50	(4)	2.00	50
a	Tagging omitted		10.00					

	Issue	Date	Un	U	PB/LP	#	FDC	Q(M)
	Unwmk., Perf. 11 x 10.5							
C72	10¢ 50-Star Runway	01/05/68	.20	.20	.90	(4)	1.00	
b	Booklet pane of 8		2.00	.75			3.75	
c	Booklet pane of 5 + label	01/06/68	3.75	.75			125.00	
	Coil, Perf. 10 Vertically							
C73	10¢ carmine (C72)	01/05/68	.30	.20	1.75	(2)	1.00	
a	Imperf., pair		600.00		900.00	(2)		
	Perf. 11							
C74	10¢ U.S. Air Mail Service	05/15/68	.25	.20	1.40	(4)	1.50	60
b	Tagging omitted		8.00					
C75	20¢ USA and Jet	11/22/68	.35	.20	1.75	(4)	1.25	
a	Tagging omitted		10.00					
C76	10¢ Moon Landing	09/09/69	.25	.20	1.10	(4)	5.00	152
a	Rose red omitted		525.00	—				
	Perf. 10.5 x 11							
C77	9¢ Delta Wing Plane	05/15/71	.20	.20	.90	(4)	1.00	
	Perf. 11 x 10.5							
C78	11¢ Silhouette of Jet	05/07/71	.20	.20	.90	(4)	1.00	
a	Booklet pane of 4 + 2 labels		1.25	.75			2.25	
b	Untagged (Bureau precanceled)		.85	.85				
c	Tagging omitted (not Bureau precanceled)		7.50					
C79	13¢ Winged Airmail Envelope	11/16/73	.25	.20	1.10	(4)	1.00	
a	Booklet pane of 5 + label	12/27/73	1.50	.75			2.25	
b	Untagged (Bureau precanceled)		.85	.85				
	Perf. 11							
C80	17¢ Statue of Liberty	07/13/71	.35	.20	1.60	(4)	1.50	
a	Tagging omitted		10.00	—				
C81	21¢ USA and Jet	05/21/71	.40	.20	2.00	(4)	1.00	
a	Tagging omitted		10.00					
	Coil, Perf. 10 Vertically							
C82	11¢ carmine (C78)	05/07/71	.25	.20	.85	(2)	1.00	
a	Imperf., pair		250.00		425.00	(2)		
C83	13¢ carmine (C79)	12/27/73	.30	.20	1.10	(2)	1.00	
a	Imperf., pair		75.00		150.00	(2)		
	National Parks Centennial, Perf. 11							
C84	11¢ Kii Statue and Temple at City of Refuge Historical National Park, Honaunau, Hawaii	05/03/72	.20	.20	.90	(4)	1.00	78
a	Blue and green omitted		750.00					
	Olympic Games, Perf. 11 x 10.5							
C85	11¢ Skiers and Olympic Rings	08/17/72	.20	.20	2.40	(10)	1.00	96
	Progress in Electronics, Perf. 11							
C86	11¢ DeForest Audions	07/10/73	.30	.20	1.25	(4)	1.00	59
a	Vermilion and green omitted		900.00					
b	Tagging omitted		25.00					
	Perf. 11							
C87	18¢ Statue of Liberty	01/11/74	.35	.30	1.50	(4)	1.25	
a	Tagging omitted		20.00					
C88	26¢ Mount Rushmore National Memorial	01/02/74	.60	.20	2.30	(4)	1.50	
a	Tagging omitted		17.50					
C89	25¢ Plane and Globes	01/02/76	.50	.20	2.25	(4)	1.00	
C90	31¢ Plane, Globes and Flag	01/02/76	.60	.20	2.60	(4)	1.25	
a	Tagging omitted		10.00					

	Issue	Date	Un	U	PB	#	FDC	Q(M)
	Pioneers of Aviation, Perf. 11							
C91	31¢ Wright Brothers, Flyer A	09/23/78	.65	.30			3.00	157
C92	31¢ Wright Brothers, Flyer A and Shed	09/23/78	.65	.30			3.00	157
a	Vert. pair, #C91-92		1.30	1.20	3.00	(4)	4.00	
b	As "a," ultramarine and black omitted		700.00					
c	As "a," black omitted		2,500.00					
d	As "a," black, yellow, magenta, blue and brown omitted		2,250.00					
	Pioneers of Aviation, Tagged, Perf. 11							
C93	21¢ Octave Chanute and Biplane Hang-Glider	03/29/79	.70	.35			3.00	29
C94	21¢ Biplane Hang-Glider and Chanute	03/29/79	.70	.35			3.00	29
a	Attached pair, #C93-C94		1.40	1.20	3.00	(4)	4.00	
b	As "a," ultramarine and black omitted		3,750.00					
C95	25¢ Wiley Post and "Winnie Mae"	11/20/79	1.10	.45			3.00	32
C96	25¢ NR-105-W, Post in Pressurized Suit and Portrait	11/20/79	1.10	.45			3.00	32
a	Vert. pair, #C95-C96		2.25	1.50	4.75	(4)	4.00	
	Olympic Games, Tagged, Perf. 11							
C97	31¢ High Jumper	11/01/79	.70	.30	9.50	(12)	1.50	47
	Tagged, Perf. 11							
C98	40¢ Philip Mazzei	10/13/80	.80	.20	10.00	(12)	1.50	81
b	Imperf., pair		3,500.00					
d	Tagging omitted		11.00					
	Tagged, Perf. 10.5 x 11.25							
C98A	40¢ Philip Mazzei	1982	8.00	1.50	125.00	(12)		
	Pioneers of Aviation, Tagged, Perf. 11							
C99	28¢ Blanche Stuart Scott and Biplane	12/30/80	.60	.20	8.50	(12)	1.50	20
a	Imperf., pair		2,500.00					
C100	35¢ Glen Curtiss and "Pusher" Biplane	12/30/80	.65	.20	9.00	(12)	1.50	23
	Olympic Games, Tagged, Perf. 11							
C101	28¢ Gymnast	06/17/83	1.00	.30			1.75	43
C102	28¢ Hurdler	06/17/83	1.00	.30			1.75	43
C103	28¢ Basketball Player	06/17/83	1.00	.30			1.75	43
C104	28¢ Soccer Player	06/17/83	1.00	.30			1.75	43
a	Block of 4, #C101-C104		4.25	2.50	5.50	(4)	3.75	
b	As "a," imperf., vert.		7,500.00					
	Olympic Games, Perf. 11.2 Bullseye							
C105	40¢ Shotputter	04/08/83	.90	.40			1.75	67
a	Perf. 11 line		1.00	.45				
C106	40¢ Gymnast	04/08/83	.90	.40			1.75	67
a	Perf. 11 line		1.00	.45				

	Issue	Date	Un	U	PB	#	FDC	Q(M)
	Olympic Games, Perf. 11.2 Bullseye continued							
C107	40¢ Swimmer	04/08/83	.90	.40			1.75	67
a	Perf. 11 line		1.00	.45				
C108	40¢ Weightlifter	04/08/83	.90	.40			1.75	67
a	Perf. 11 line		1.00	.45			5.00	
b	Block of 4, #C105-C108		4.25	3.00	5.00	(4)		
c	Block of 4, #C105a-C108a		5.00	4.00	7.50	(4)		
d	Block of 4, imperf.		1,000.00					
	Olympic Games, Tagged, Perf. 11							
C109	35¢ Fencer	11/04/83	.90	.55			1.75	
C110	35¢ Bicyclist	11/04/83	.90	.55			1.75	
C111	35¢ Volleyball Players	11/04/83	.90	.55			1.75	
C112	35¢ Pole Vaulter	11/04/83	.90	.55			1.75	
a	Block of 4, #C109-C112		4.00	3.25	6.50	(4)	4.50	175
	Pioneers of Aviation, Tagged, Perf. 11							
C113	33¢ Alfred Verville and Airplane Diagram	02/13/85	.65	.20	3.25	(4)	1.50	168
a	Imperf., pair		850.00					
C114	39¢ Lawrence and Elmer Sperry	02/13/85	.80	.25	3.75	(4)	1.50	168
a	Imperf., pair		1,750.00					
C115	44¢ Transpacific Airmail	02/15/85	.85	.25	4.00	(4)	1.75	209
a	Imperf., pair		750.00					
	Tagged, Perf. 11							
C116	44¢ Junipero Serra	08/22/85	1.00	.35	7.50	(4)	2.00	164
a	Imperf., pair		1,500.00					
C117	44¢ New Sweden	03/29/88	1.00	.25	6.50	(4)	1.50	137
	Pioneers of Aviation, Tagged, Perf. 11							
C118	45¢ Samuel P. Langley	05/14/88	.90	.20	4.00	(4)	1.50	406
a	Overall tagging		3.00	.50	30.00	(4)		
C119	36¢ Igor Sikorsky	06/23/88	.70	.25	3.25	(4)	2.50	179
	Tagged, Perf. 11.5 x 11							
C120	45¢ French Revolution	07/14/89	.95	.20	4.75	(4)	1.50	38
	America/PUAS, Perf. 11							
C121	45¢ Southeast Carved Wood Figure, Emblem of the Postal Union of the Americas and Spain	10/12/89	.90	.20	5.25	(4)	1.50	39
	20th UPU Congress, Tagged, Perf. 11							
C122	45¢ Hypersonic Airliner	11/27/89	1.00	.50			1.75	27
C123	45¢ Air-Cushion Vehicle	11/27/89	1.00	.50			1.75	27
C124	45¢ Surface Rover	11/27/89	1.00	.50			1.75	27
C125	45¢ Shuttle	11/27/89	1.00	.50			1.75	27
a	Block of 4, #C122-C125		4.00	3.00	5.50	(4)	6.50	
b	As "a," light blue (engr.) omitted		750.00					

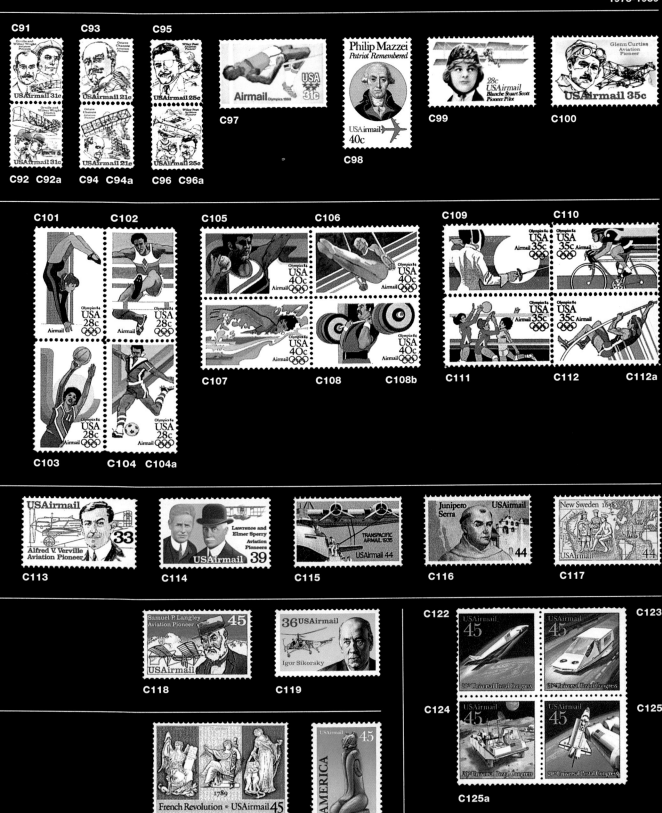

C91   **C93**   **C95**

C97

C98

C99

C100

C92 **C92a**   **C94** **C94a**   **C96** **C96a**

C101   **C102**   **C105**   **C106**   **C109**   **C110**

C103   **C104** **C104a**   **C107**   **C108** **C108b**   **C111**   **C112** **C112a**

C113   **C114**   **C115**   **C116**   **C117**

C118   **C119**   **C122**   **C123**

C124   **C125**

C120   **C121**   **C125a**

20th Universal Postal Congress

A glimpse at several potential mail delivery methods of the future is the theme of these four stamps issued by the U.S. in commemoration of the convening of the 20th Universal Postal Congress in Washington, D.C. from November 13 through December 14, 1989. The United States, as host nation to the Congress for the first time in ninety-two years, welcomed more than 1,000 delegates from most of the member nations of the Universal Postal Union to the major international event.

©USPS 1989

C126

C127

C128

C129

C130

C131

C133

C134

C135

C136

C137

C138

C139

C140

C141

C142

C143

C144

C145

CE1

CE2

VISIT US ONLINE AT **THE POSTAL STORE**
AT *WWW.USPS.COM*
OR CALL **1 800 STAMP-24**

	Issue	Date	Un	U	PB	#	FDC	Q(M)
	20th UPU Congress Souvenir Sheet, Tagged, Imperf.							
C126	Designs of #C122-C125	11/24/1989	5.00	4.00			6.50	2
a-d	Single stamp from sheet		1.25	.50				
	America/PUAS, Tagged, Perf. 11 (See also #2512)							
C127	45¢ Tropical Coast	10/12/1990	.90	.20	7.00	(4)	1.50	48
	Pioneers of Aviation, Tagged, Perf. 11							
C128	50¢ Harriet Quimby and Early Plane	04/27/1991	1.00	.25	5.25	(4)	1.50	250
a	Vertical pair, imperf. horizontally		1,750.00					
b	Perf. 11.2	04/27/1991	1.10	.25	5.75	(4)		
C129	40¢ William T. Piper and Piper Cub Airplane	05/17/1991	.80	.20	3.75	(4)	1.50	182
	Tagged, Perf. 11							
C130	50¢ Antarctic Treaty	06/21/1991	1.00	.35	5.00	(4)	1.50	113
	America/PUAS, Tagged, Perf. 11							
C131	50¢ Eskimo and Bering Land Bridge	10/12/1991	1.00	.35	5.25	(4)	1.50	15
	Tagged, Perf. 11.2							
C132	40¢ William T. Piper, (type of 1991)	1993	2.75	.65	52.50	(4)		100
	Scenic American Landscapes, Tagged, Self-Adhesive, Perf. 11							
C133	48¢ Niagara Falls	05/12/1999	.95	.20	4.00	(4)	1.75	101
	Scenic American Landscapes, Tagged, Self-Adhesive, Serpentine Die-Cut 11							
C134	40¢ Rio Grande	07/30/1999	.80	.60	3.20	(4)	1.75	101
	Scenic American Landscapes, Tagged, Self-Adhesive, Serpentine Die-Cut 11.25 x 11.5							
C135	60¢ Grand Canyon	01/20/2000	1.25	.25	5.00	(4)	2.00	101
C136	70¢ Nine-Mile Prairie	03/06/2001	1.40	.30	5.60	(4)	2.00	85
	Scenic American Landscapes, Tagged, Self-Adhesive, Serpentine Die-Cut 11							
C137	80¢ Mount McKinley	04/17/2001	1.60	.35	6.40	(4)	2.00	85
	Scenic American Landscapes, Tagged, Self-Adhesive, Serpentine Die-Cut 11.25 x 11.5							
C138	60¢ Acadia National Park	05/30/2001	1.25	.25	5.00	(4)	1.75	100
a	Overall tagging	03/2003	1.25	.25	5.00	(4)		
b	As "a," with "2005"	01/2005	1.25	.25	5.00	(4)		

	Issue	Date	Un	U	PB	#	FDC	Q(M)
	Scenic American Landscapes, Tagged, Self-Adhesive, Serpentine Die-Cut 10.75							
C139	63¢ Bryce Canyon National Park	02/24/2006	1.25	.25	5.00	(4)	2.50	100
C140	75¢ Great Smoky Mountains National Park	02/24/2006	1.50	.35	6.00	(4)	2.75	100
	Scenic American Landscapes, Tagged, Self-Adhesive, Serpentine Die-Cut 11							
C141	84¢ Yosemite National Park	02/24/2006	1.75	.35	7.00	(4)	3.00	100
	Scenic American Landscapes, Tagged, Self-Adhesive, Serpentine Die-Cut 10.75							
C142	69¢ Okefenokee Swamp, Georgia/Florida	06/01/2007	1.40	.30	5.60	(4)	2.60	100
	Scenic American Landscapes, Tagged, Self-Adhesive, Serpentine Die-Cut 11							
C143	90¢ Hagåtña Bay, Guam	06/01/2007	1.80	.40	7.20	(4)	3.00	100
	Scenic American Landscapes, Tagged, Self-Adhesive, Serpentine Die-Cut 10.75							
C144	72¢ 13-Mile Woods, New Hampshire	05/16/2008	1.50	.30	6.00	(4)	3.00	100
	Scenic American Landscapes, Tagged, Self-Adhesive, Serpentine Die-Cut 11							
C145	94¢ Trunk Bay, St. John, Virgin Islands	06/01/2007	1.90	.45	7.60	(4)	3.00	100
	Airmail Special Delivery							
	Unwmk. Perf. 11							
CE1	16¢ Great Seal of the United States	08/30/1934	.60	.70	15.00	(6)	25.00	
	For imperforate variety see #771							
CE2	16¢ red and blue	02/10/1936	.45	.25	8.50	(4)	17.50	
a	Horizontal pair, imperf. vertically		3,750.00					

MIAMI UNIVERSITY STAMPED CARD

The Historic Preservation series continues with this stamped card commemorating the bicentennial of Ohio's Miami University. Artist Tom Engeman of Bethany Beach, Delaware, created the illustration of MacCracken Hall— a residence hall on the main campus in Oxford—featured on the card. The hall is named for distinguished 19th-century educator Henry Mitchell MacCracken, a Miami University alumnus who became chancellor of New York University. ■ In 1809, the Ohio state legislature passed an act incorporating Miami University in the Miami valley region of southwestern Ohio. By 1824, the university trustees had hired a small faculty and erected a couple of buildings. Approximately twenty students attended opening classes that fall. ■ Today, Miami University boasts an overall enrollment of twenty thousand students and maintains regional campuses in Hamilton and Middletown, Ohio, as well as the Miami University European Center in Luxembourg. Recognized as one of the top public universities in the country, Miami defines itself as a "place of involved scholarship and teaching where all students are grounded in the liberal arts, encouraged to become citizen leaders, and infused with an excitement for learning and critical thinking." The university's impressive roster of alumni includes Benjamin Harrison, class of 1852, our nation's 23rd President.

	Issue	Date	Un	U	PB	#	FDC
	Special Delivery						
	1885, Unwmkd., Perf. 12						
E1	10¢ Messenger Running	10/01/1885	550.00	70.00	17,500.00	(8)	20,000.00
E2	10¢ blue Messenger Running (E3)	09/06/1888	500.00	35.00	16,000.00	(8)	
E3	10¢ Messenger Running	01/24/1893	260.00	40.00	11,000.00	(8)	
E4	10¢ Messenger Running (Line under "Ten Cents")	10/10/1894	850.00	55.00	17,500.00	(6)	
	Wmkd. (191), Perf. 12						
E5	10¢ bl. Messenger Running (E4)	08/16/1895	210.00	10.00	4,750.00	(6)	
	Double transfer		—	32.50			
	Line of color through "POSTAL DELIVERY"		300.00	35.00			
a	Dots in curved frame above messenger		300.00	20.00			
	Special Delivery, Wmkd. (191), Perf. 12						
E6	10¢ ultramarine Messenger on Bicycle	12/09/1902	230.00	10.00			
	Damaged transfer under "N" of "CENTS"		250.00	15.00			
a	Blue		250.00	10.00	3,500.00	(6)	
E7	10¢ Mercury Helmet and Olive Branch	12/12/1908	70.00	45.00	1,000.00	(6)	
	Wmkd. (190), Perf. 12						
E8	10¢ ultramarine Messenger on Bicycle (E6)	01/1911	110.00	10.00			
	Top frame line missing		150.00	22.50			
b	Violet blue		125.00	12.00	1,950.00	(6)	
	Perf. 10						
E9	10¢ ultramarine Messenger on Bicycle (E6)	09/1914	190.00	12.00	3,000.00	(6)	
a	Blue		240.00	15.00	5,000.00	(6)	
	Unwmkd., Perf. 10						
E10	10¢ ultramarine Messenger on Bicycle (E6)	10/19/1916	320.00	45.00	5,500.00	(6)	
a	Blue		350.00	50.00	5,750.00	(6)	
	Unwmkd., Perf. 11						
E11	10¢ ultramarine Messenger on Bicycle (E6)	05/02/1917	20.00	.75	725.00	(6)	
b	Gray violet		30.00	3.00	850.00	(6)	
c	Blue		65.00	4.00	625.00	(6)	
E12	10¢ Postman and Motorcycle	07/12/1922	42.50	1.25	475.00	(6)	500.00
a	Deep ultramarine		50.00	2.00	525.00	(6)	
E13	15¢ Postman and Motorcycle	04/11/1925	27.50	1.75	350.00	(6)	350.00
E14	20¢ Post Office Truck	04/25/1925	2.00	1.00	40.00	(6)	125.00
	Unwmkd., Perf. 11 x 10.5						
E15	10¢ gray violet Postman and Motorcycle (E12)	11/29/1927	.65	.25			110.00
c	Horizontal pair, imperf. between		325.00				
E16	15¢ orange Postman and Motorcycle (E13)	08/13/1931	.70	.25	2.75	(4)	125.00
	Beginning with #E17, unused values are for never-hinged stamps.						
E17	13¢ Postman and Motorcycle	10/30/1944	.60	.20	2.75	(4)	15.00
E18	17¢ Postman and Motorcycle	10/30/1944	3.50	2.50	24.00	(4)	12.00
E19	20¢ blk. Post Office Truck (E14)	11/30/1951	1.25	.20	5.50	(4)	5.00
E20	20¢ Delivery of Letter	10/13/1954	.40	.20	2.00	(4)	3.00
E21	30¢ Delivery of Letter	09/03/1957	.50	.20	2.25	(4)	2.25

	Issue	Date	Un	U	PB	#	FDC
	Unwmkd., Perf. 11						
E22	45¢ Arrows	11/21/1969	1.25	.25	5.50	(4)	4.00
E23	60¢ Arrows	05/10/1971	1.25	.20	5.50	(4)	3.50
	Registration Stamp						
	Issued for the prepayment of registry; not usable for postage. Sale discontinued May 28, 1913.						
	Wmkd. (190), Perf. 12						
F1	10¢ Bald Eagle	12/01/1911	70.00	10.00	1,600.00	(6)	17,500.00
	Certified Mail Stamp						
	For use on First-Class mail for which no indemnity value was claimed, but for which proof of mailing and proof of delivery were available at less cost than registered mail.						
	Unwmkd., Perf. 10.5 x 11						
FA1	15¢ Letter Carrier	06/06/1955	.45	.30	4.25	(4)	7.50
	Quantities Issued in millions, 54						
	Postage Due Stamps						
	For affixing by a postal clerk to any mail to denote amount to be collected from addressee because of insufficient prepayment of postage.						
	Printed by American Bank Note Co., Design of #J2, Unwmkd., Perf. 12						
J1	1¢ brown	1879	95.00	14.00	1,650.00	(10)	
J2	2¢ brown	1879	425.00	18.00			
J3	3¢ brown	1879	105.00	6.00	1,800.00	(10)	
J4	5¢ brown	1879	825.00	70.00			
J5	10¢ brown	09/19/1879	1,000.00	70.00			
a	Imperf., pair		3,000.00				
J6	30¢ brown	09/19/1879	400.00	65.00	5,000.00	(10)	
J7	50¢ brown	09/19/1879	650.00	90.00	12,500.00	(10)	
	Special Printing, Soft Porous Paper, Unwmkd., Perf. 12						
J8	1¢ deep brown	1879	22,500.00				
J9	2¢ deep brown	1879	20,000.00				
J10	3¢ deep brown	1879	25,000.00				
J11	5¢ deep brown	1879	15,000.00				
J12	10¢ deep brown	1879	9,000.00				
J13	30¢ deep brown	1879	10,000.00				
J14	50¢ deep brown	1879	9,000.00				
	Design of #J19, Unwmkd., Perf. 12						
J15	1¢ red brown	1884	75.00	7.00	1,450.00	(10)	
J16	2¢ red brown	1884	90.00	6.00	1,650.00	(10)	
J17	3¢ red brown	1884	1,150.00	300.00			
J18	5¢ red brown	1884	625.00	45.00			
J19	10¢ Figure of Value	1884	625.00	35.00	14,000.00	(10)	
J20	30¢ red brown	1884	225.00	60.00	3,500.00	(10)	
J21	50¢ red brown	1884	1,900.00	225.00			
	Design of #J25, Unwmkd., Perf. 12						
J22	1¢ bright claret	1891	35.00	2.00	625.00	(10)	
J23	2¢ bright claret	1891	37.50	2.00	700.00	(10)	
J24	3¢ bright claret	1891	75.00	16.00	1,100.00	(10)	
J25	5¢ Figure of Value	1891	110.00	16.00	1,500.00	(10)	
J26	10¢ bright claret	1891	180.00	30.00	2,500.00	(10)	
J27	30¢ bright claret	1891	650.00	225.00	8,750.00	(10)	
J28	50¢ bright claret	1891	700.00	210.00	10,500.00	(10)	
	Design of #J33, Unwmkd., Perf. 12						
J29	1¢ vermilion	1894	2,750.00	725.00			
J30	2¢ vermilion	1894	850.00	350.00	7,000.00	(6)	
J31	1¢ deep claret	08/14/1894	80.00	12.00	675.00	(6)	
J32	2¢ deep claret	07/20/1894	70.00	10.00	625.00	(6)	
J33	3¢ Figure of Value	04/27/1895	220.00	50.00	2,750.00	(6)	
J34	5¢ deep claret	04/27/1895	350.00	55.00	3,000.00	(6)	
J35	10¢ deep claret	09/24/1894	400.00	40.00	3,250.00	(6)	
J36	30¢ deep claret	04/27/1895	600.00	225.00	4,750.00	(6)	
a	Carmine		750.00	275.00	5,750.00	(6)	
b	Pale rose		500.00	200.00	4,250.00	(6)	

E1

E3

E4

E6

E7

E12

E13

E14

E18

E20

E21

E22

E23

F1

FA1

J2

J19

J25

J33

1930-1959

J69

J78

J88

J98

J101

Nature of America: Kelp Forest Souvenir Sheet

Discover the beauty and complexity of major plant and animal
communities in the U.S. on this pane of 10 stamps issued in this year's
Nature of America series.   Souvenir Sheet   Item #464040 $4.40

To order item call **1 800 STAMP-24** *or visit us online at* **www.usps.com**

	Issue	Date	Un	U	PB # Q(M)
	Design of #J33, Unwmkd., Perf. 12 continued				
J37	50¢ deep claret	04/27/1895	2,000.00	800.00	
a	Pale rose		1,800.00	725.00	*13,000.00* (6)
	Design of #J33, Wmkd. (191), Horizontally or Vertically, Perf. 12				
J38	1¢ deep claret	08/29/1895	15.00	1.00	275.00 (6)
J39	2¢ deep claret	09/14/1895	15.00	1.00	275.00 (6)
J40	3¢ deep claret	10/30/1895	110.00	4.00	1,000.00 (6)
J41	5¢ deep claret	10/15/1895	120.00	4.00	1,050.00 (6)
J42	10¢ deep claret	09/14/1895	120.00	6.00	1,050.00 (6)
J43	30¢ deep claret	08/21/1897	700.00	70.00	*6,500.00* (6)
J44	50¢ deep claret	03/17/1896	450.00	50.00	*4,750.00* (6)
	Design of #J33, Wmkd. (190), Perf. 12				
J45	1¢ deep claret	08/30/1910	45.00	5.00	
a	Rose carmine		40.00	5.00	525.00 (6)
J46	2¢ deep claret	11/25/1910	45.00	2.00	
a	Rose carmine		40.00	2.00	500.00 (6)
J47	3¢ deep claret	08/31/1910	675.00	50.00	6,000.00 (6)
J48	5¢ deep claret	08/31/1910	130.00	12.00	
a	Rose carmine		130.00	12.00	1,150.00 (6)
J49	10¢ deep claret	08/31/1910	140.00	20.00	1,500.00 (6)
J50	50¢ deep claret	09/23/1912	1,150.00	175.00	*10,000.00* (6)
	Design of #J33, Perf. 10				
J52	1¢ carmine lake	1914	90.00	15.00	750.00 (6)
a	Dull rose		95.00	15.00	775.00 (6)
J53	2¢ carmine lake	1914	70.00	1.00	650.00 (6)
a	Dull rose		75.00	2.00	
b	Vermillion		75.00	2.00	675.00 (6)
J54	3¢ carmine lake	1914	1,150.00	75.00	*9,500.00* (6)
a	Dull rose		1,100.00	75.00	*9,000.00* (6)
J55	5¢ carmine lake	1914	55.00	5.00	475.00 (6)
a	Dull rose		50.00	4.00	450.00 (6)
J56	10¢ carmine lake	1914	85.00	4.00	825.00 (6)
a	Dull rose		90.00	5.00	950.00 (6)
J57	30¢ carmine lake	1914	250.00	55.00	2,900.00 (6)
J58	50¢ carmine lake	1914	*17,500.00*	1,500.00	*125,000.00* (6)
	Design of #J33, Unwmkd., Perf. 10				
J59	1¢ rose	1916	4,500.00	700.00	*31,500.00* (6)
	Experimental Bureau precancel, New Orleans			*350.00*	
J60	2¢ rose	1916	300.00	75.00	2,500.00 (6)
	Design of #J33, Unwmkd., Perf. 11				
J61	1¢ carmine rose	1917	3.00	.25	
b	Deep claret		3.00	.25	45.00 (6)
J62	2¢ carmine rose	1917	3.00	.25	
b	Deep claret		3.00	.25	55.00 (6)
J63	3¢ carmine rose	1917	15.00	.80	
b	Deep claret		15.00	.80	150.00 (6)
J64	5¢ carmine	1917	12.50	.80	
b	Deep claret		12.50	.80	125.00 (6)
J65	10¢ carmine rose	1917	25.00	1.00	
b	Deep claret		25.00	1.00	220.00 (6)
J66	30¢ carmine rose	1917	90.00	2.00	
a	Deep claret		90.00	2.00	750.00 (6)
J67	50¢ carmine rose	1917	150.00	1.00	
b	Deep claret		150.00	1.00	1,150.00 (6)
J68	½¢ dull red	04/13/25	1.00	.25	12.50 (6)
	Design of #J69, Unwmkd., Perf. 11				
J69	½¢ Figure of Value	1930	4.50	1.90	50.00 (6)
J70	1¢ carmine	1930	3.00	.35	55.00 (6)
J71	2¢ carmine	1930	4.00	.35	50.00 (6)
J72	3¢ carmine	1930	21.00	2.75	300.00 (6)
J73	5¢ carmine	1930	19.00	5.00	300.00 (6)

	Issue	Date	Un	U	PB # Q(M)
	Design of #J69, Unwmkd., Perf. 11 continued				
J74	10¢ carmine	1930	45.00	2.00	475.00 (6)
J75	30¢ carmine	1930	150.00	4.00	1,150.00 (6)
J76	50¢ carmine	1930	200.00	2.00	1,750.00 (6)
	Design of #J78				
J77	$1 carmine	1930	35.00	.35	250.00 (6)
a	$1 scarlet		30.00	.35	275.00 (6)
J78	$5 "FIVE" on $	1930	40.00	.35	300.00 (6)
a	$5 scarlet		35.00	.35	260.00 (6)
b	As "a," wet printing		40.00	.35	300.00 (6)
	Design of #J69, Unwmkd., Perf. 11 x 10.5				
J79	½¢ dull carmine	1931	.90	.20	
a	½¢ scarlet		.90	.20	20.00 (4)
J80	1¢ dull carmine	1931	.20	.20	
a	Scarlet		.20	.20	1.50 (4)
J81	2¢ dull carmine	1931	.20	.20	
a	Scarlet		.20	.20	1.50 (4)
J82	3¢ dull carmine	1931	.25	.20	
a	Scarlet		.25	.20	2.25 (4)
b	Scarlet, wet printing		.30	.20	2.50 (4)
J83	5¢ dull carmine	1931	.40	.20	
a	Scarlet		.40	.20	3.00 (4)
b	As "a," wet printing		.50	.20	3.50 (4)
J84	10¢ dull carmine	1931	1.10	.20	
a	Scarlet		1.10	.20	6.50 (4)
b	Scarlet, wet printing		1.25	.20	7.00 (4)
J85	30¢ dull carmine	1931	7.50	.25	
a	Scarlet		7.50	.25	35.00 (4)
J86	50¢ dull carmine	1931	9.00	.25	
a	Scarlet		9.00	.25	52.50 (4)
	Design of #J78, Perf. 10.5 x 11				
J87	$1 scarlet	1956	30.00	.25	190.00 (4)
	Beginning with #J88, unused values are for never-hinged stamps.				
	Designs of #J88, #J98 and #J101, Unwmkd., Perf. 11 x 10.5				
J88	½¢ Figure of Value	06/19/59	1.50	1.10	130.00 (4)
J89	1¢ carmine rose	06/19/59	.20	.20	.35 (4)
a	"1 CENT" omitted		225.00		
b	Pair, one without "1 CENT"		*475.00*		
J90	2¢ carmine rose	06/19/59	.20	.20	.45 (4)
J91	3¢ carmine rose	06/19/59	.20	.20	.50 (4)
a	Pair, one without "3 CENTS"		*675.00*		
J92	4¢ carmine rose	06/19/59	.20	.20	.60 (4)
J93	5¢ carmine rose	06/19/59	.20	.20	.65 (4)
a	Pair, one without "5 CENTS"		*1,500.00*		
J94	6¢ carmine rose	06/19/59	.20	.20	.70 (4)
a	Pair, one without "6 CENTS"		*850.00*		
J95	7¢ carmine rose	06/19/59	.20	.20	.80 (4)
J96	8¢ carmine rose	06/19/59	.20	.20	.90 (4)
a	Pair, one without "8 CENTS"		*850.00*		
J97	10¢ carmine rose	06/19/59	.20	.20	1.00 (4)
J98	30¢ Figure of Value	06/19/59	.75	.20	3.50 (4)
J99	50¢ carmine rose	06/19/59	1.10	.20	5.00 (4)
	Design of #J101				
J100	$1 carmine rose	06/19/59	2.00	.20	8.50 (4)
J101	$5 Outline Figure of Value	06/19/59	9.00	.20	40.00 (4)
	Design of #J98, Perf. 11 x 10.5				
J102	11¢ carmine rose	01/02/78	.25	.20	2.00 (4)
J103	13¢ carmine rose	01/02/78	.25	.20	2.00 (4)
J104	17¢ carmine rose	06/10/85	.40	.35	22.50 (4)

Official and Penalty Mail Stamps

Official Stamps
Thin, Hard Paper, Unwmkd., Perf. 12

The franking privilege having been abolished as of July 1, 1873, these stamps were provided for each of the departments of government for the prepayment on official matter. These stamps were supplanted on May 1, 1879, by penalty envelopes and on July 5, 1884, were declared obsolete.

Issues of 1873

Department of Agriculture: Yellow

	Issue	Un	U
O1	1¢ Franklin	280.00	*180.00*
	Ribbed paper	340.00	200.00
O2	2¢ Jackson	240.00	85.00
O3	3¢ Washington	220.00	16.00
O4	6¢ Lincoln	260.00	60.00
O5	10¢ Jefferson	525.00	200.00
O6	12¢ Clay	450.00	260.00
O7	15¢ Webster	425.00	230.00
O8	24¢ Scott	425.00	220.00
O9	30¢ Hamilton	550.00	270.00

Executive Dept.: Carmine

	Issue	Un	U
O10	1¢ Franklin	850.00	475.00
O11	2¢ Jackson	550.00	240.00
O12	3¢ Washington	700.00	210.00
O13	6¢ Lincoln	900.00	550.00
O14	10¢ Jefferson	1,200.00	650.00

Dept. of the Interior: Vermilion

	Issue	Un	U
O15	1¢ Franklin	75.00	10.00
	Ribbed paper	85.00	20.00
O16	2¢ Jackson	70.00	12.00
O17	3¢ Washington	80.00	6.00
O18	6¢ Lincoln	70.00	10.00
O19	10¢ Jefferson	70.00	20.00
O20	12¢ Clay	90.00	12.00
O21	15¢ Webster	200.00	25.00
	Double transfer of left side	275.00	37.50
O22	24¢ Scott	180.00	20.00
O23	30¢ Hamilton	290.00	20.00
O24	90¢ Perry	325.00	50.00

Dept. of Justice: Purple

	Issue	Un	U
O25	1¢ Franklin	250.00	100.00
O26	2¢ Jackson	310.00	110.00
O27	3¢ Washington	320.00	35.00
O28	6¢ Lincoln	310.00	45.00
O29	10¢ Jefferson	310.00	100.00
O30	12¢ Clay	260.00	75.00
O31	15¢ Webster	475.00	200.00
O32	24¢ Scott	1,250.00	425.00
O33	30¢ Hamilton	1,300.00	350.00
	Double transfer at top	1,450.00	375.00
O34	90¢ Perry	1,900.00	900.00

Navy Dept.: Ultramarine

	Issue	Un	U
O35	1¢ Franklin	160.00	50.00
a	1¢ dull blue	160.00	50.00
O36	2¢ Jackson	160.00	25.00
a	Dull blue	160.00	25.00
O37	3¢ Washington	170.00	15.00
a	Dull blue	170.00	15.00
O38	6¢ Lincoln	150.00	25.00
	Vertical line through "N" of "NAVY"	175.00	35.00
a	Dull blue	150.00	25.00
O39	7¢ Stanton	650.00	230.00
a	Dull blue	650.00	230.00
O40	10¢ Jefferson	210.00	45.00
	Plate scratch	*325.00*	—
a	Dull blue	210.00	45.00
O41	12¢ Clay	220.00	45.00
	Double transfer of left side	400.00	250.00
O42	15¢ Webster	375.00	75.00
O43	24¢ Scott	400.00	85.00
a	Dull blue	375.00	80.00
O44	30¢ Hamilton	325.00	50.00
O45	90¢ Perry	1,050.00	375.00
a	Double impression		*20,000.00*

Post Office Dept.: Black

	Issue	Un	U
O47	1¢ Figure of Value	25.00	12.00
O48	2¢ Figure of Value	30.00	10.00
a	Double impression	600.00	400.00
O49	3¢ Figure of Value	10.00	2.00
a	Printed on both sides	*7,500.00*	
O50	6¢ Figure of Value	30.00	8.00
	Vertical ribbed paper	—	12.50
a	Diagonal half used as 3¢ on cover	*4,750.00*	
O51	10¢ Figure of Value	140.00	55.00
O52	12¢ Figure of Value	120.00	12.00
O53	15¢ Figure of Value	140.00	20.00
O54	24¢ Figure of Value	200.00	25.00
O55	30¢ Figure of Value	200.00	25.00
O56	90¢ Figure of Value	220.00	25.00

Dept. of State: Green, Perf. 12

	Issue	Un	U
O57	1¢ Franklin	260.00	75.00
O58	2¢ Jackson	310.00	100.00
O59	3¢ Washington	220.00	25.00
O60	6¢ Lincoln	220.00	30.00
O61	7¢ Stanton	290.00	65.00
	Ribbed paper	310.00	70.00
O62	10¢ Jefferson	230.00	55.00
	Short transfer	275.00	67.50
O63	12¢ Clay	310.00	125.00
O64	15¢ Webster	320.00	90.00
O65	24¢ Scott	525.00	230.00
O66	30¢ Hamilton	500.00	180.00
O67	90¢ Perry	1,050.00	325.00
O68	$2 Seward	1,500.00	1,500.00
O69	$5 Seward	7,500.00	*12,000.00*
O70	$10 Seward	5,000.00	*7,000.00*
O71	$20 Seward	5,250.00	5,000.00

Treasury Dept.: Brown

	Issue	Un	U
O72	1¢ Franklin	120.00	10.00
	Double transfer	135.00	12.50
O73	2¢ Jackson	125.00	8.00
	Double transfer	—	12.50
O74	3¢ Washington	110.00	2.00
a	Double impression	*5,000.00*	
O75	6¢ Lincoln	120.00	4.00
	Dirty plate	120.00	6.00
O76	7¢ Stanton	250.00	35.00
O77	10¢ Jefferson	240.00	12.00
O78	12¢ Clay	300.00	10.00
O79	15¢ Webster	300.00	12.00
O80	24¢ Scott	675.00	100.00
O81	30¢ Hamilton	400.00	12.00
	Short transfer top right	450.00	25.00
O82	90¢ Perry	400.00	15.00

War Dept.: Rose

	Issue	Un	U
O83	1¢ Franklin	240.00	15.00
O84	2¢ Jackson	240.00	15.00
	Ribbed paper	250.00	17.50
O85	3¢ Washington	240.00	5.00
O86	6¢ Lincoln	625.00	10.00
O87	7¢ Stanton	160.00	90.00
O88	10¢ Jefferson	140.00	25.00
O89	12¢ Clay	275.00	12.00
	Ribbed paper	300.00	20.00
O90	15¢ Webster	85.00	15.00
	Ribbed paper	92.50	20.00
O91	24¢ Scott	85.00	12.00
O92	30¢ Hamilton	130.00	12.00
O93	90¢ Perry	225.00	50.00

O3 O7 O11 O14

O16 O18 O25 O34

O37 O44 O47 O52 O57

O74 O76 O87 O91

Sugar Ray Robinson
Cultural Diary Page and Pane of 20 Stamps

Start your own cultural diary by
collecting all of the pages created for the
Expressions of African-Americans binder.

Item #460276 $12.95

To order this item call **1 800 STAMP-24**
or visit us online at **www.usps.com**

O121

O124

O125

O126

Official Mail USA
USA 1c
Penalty for private use $300
O127

Official Mail USA
USA 14
Penalty for private use $300
O129A

Official Mail USA
Domestic Letter Rate D
Penalty for private use $300
O139

Official Mail USA
Domestic Mail E
Penalty for private use $300
O140

Official Mail USA
1
Penalty for private use $300
O143

Official Mail USA
10
Penalty for private use $300
O146A

Official Mail USA
$1
Penalty for private use $300
O151

Official Mail USA
For U.S. addresses only G
Penalty for private use $300
O152

Official Mail USA
32
Penalty for private use $300
O153

Official Mail USA
1¢
Penalty for private use $300
O154

Official Mail USA
20
Penalty for private use $300
O155

Official Mail USA
23
Penalty for private use $300
O156

Official Mail USA
33
Penalty for private use $300
O157

Official Mail USA
34
Penalty for private use $300
O158

Official Mail USA
37
Penalty for private use $300
O159

Official Mail USA
39
Penalty for private use $300
O160

Official Mail USA
$1
Penalty for private use $300
O161

Official Mail USA
41
Penalty for private use $300
O162

Marvel Comics Super Heroes Stamp Collecting & Creativity Set

This unique kit contains biographies of favorite Marvel characters, storyline of early-edition Marvel comics, and templates to design your own Super Heroes and create a comic book. Also includes a pane of 20 *Marvel Comics Super Heroes* stamps.

Item #461474 $18.50

To order call 1 800 STAMP-24
or visit us online at www.usps.com

Issue		Date	Un	U
Soft Porous Paper				
Dept. of Agriculture: Yellow				
O94	1¢ Franklin, issued without gum	1879	6,000.00	
O95	3¢ Washington		550.00	110.00
Dept. of the Interior: Vermilion				
O96	1¢ Franklin	1879	300.00	*275.00*
O97	2¢ Jackson	1879	10.00	3.00
O98	3¢ Washington	1879	10.00	3.00
O99	6¢ Lincoln	1879	10.00	12.50
O100	10¢ Jefferson	1879	110.00	75.00
O101	12¢ Clay	1879	230.00	115.00
O102	15¢ Webster	1879	400.00	260.00
	Double transfer		450.00	—
O103	24¢ Scott	1879	4,500.00	—
O104-05	Not assigned			
Dept. of Justice: Bluish Purple				
O106	3¢ Washington	1879	175.00	100.00
O107	6¢ Lincoln		475.00	275.00
Post Office Dept.: Black				
O108	3¢ Figure of Value	1879	30.00	10.00
Treasury Dept.: Brown				
O109	3¢ Washington	1879	80.00	10.00
O110	6¢ Lincoln	1879	200.00	50.00
O111	10¢ Jefferson	1879	260.00	80.00
O112	30¢ Hamilton	1879	2,400.00	425.00
O113	90¢ Perry	1879	4,500.00	525.00
War Dept.: Rose Red				
O114	1¢ Franklin	1879	6.00	4.00
O115	2¢ Jackson	1879	12.00	4.00
O116	3¢ Washington	1879	12.00	2.00
	Double transfer		17.50	6.00
a	Imperf. pair		*5,000.00*	
b	Double impression		*6,500.00*	
O117	6¢ Lincoln	1879	11.00	3.00
O118	10¢ Jefferson	1879	65.00	50.00
O119	12¢ Clay	1879	60.00	14.00
O120	30¢ Hamilton	1879	225.00	100.00

Issue		Date	Un	U
Official Postal Savings Mail				

These stamps were used to prepay postage on official correspondence of the Postal Savings Division of the Post Office Department. Discontinued Sept. 23, 1914.

Issue		Date	Un	U
Engr., Wmkd. (191)				
O121	2¢ Postal Savings	12/22/1910	17.50	2.00
	Double transfer		22.50	4.00
O122	50¢ dark green	02/01/1911	160.00	60.00
O123	$1 ultramarine	02/01/1911	200.00	15.00
Wmkd. (190)				
O124	1¢ dark violet	03/27/1911	10.00	2.00
O125	2¢ Postal Savings (O121)		55.00	7.00
O126	10¢ carmine	02/01/1911	20.00	2.00
Penalty Mail Stamps				

Stamps for use by government departments were reinstituted in 1983. Now known as Penalty Mail stamps, they help provide a better accounting of actual mail costs for official departments and agencies, etc.

Beginning with #O127, unused values are for never-hinged stamps.

Issue		Date	Un	U
Engr., Unwmkd., Perf. 11				
O127	1¢ red, blue & blk	01/12/1983	.20	.20
O128	4¢ red, blue & blk	01/12/1983	.20	.25
O129	13¢ red, blue & blk	01/12/1983	.45	15.00
O129A	14¢ red, blue & blk	05/15/1985	.45	.50
O130	17¢ red, blue & blk	01/12/1983	.60	.40
O131, O134, O137, O142 Not assigned				
O132	$1 red, blue & blk	01/12/1983	2.25	1.00
O133	$5 red, blue & blk	01/12/1983	9.00	5.00
Coil, Perf. 10 Vertically				
O135	20¢ red, blue & blk	01/12/1983	1.75	2.00
a	Imperf. pair		*2,000.00*	
O136	22¢ red, blue & blk	05/15/1985	1.00	*2.00*
Perf. 11				
O138	"D" postcard rate (14¢)	02/04/1985	5.25	*10.00*

Issue		Date	Un	U
Coil, Perf. 10 Vertically				
O138A	15¢ red, blue & blk	06/11/1988	.45	.50
O138B	20¢ red, blue & blk	05/19/1988	.45	.30
O139	"D" (22¢) red, blue & blk	02/04/1985	5.25	*10.00*
O140	"E" (25¢) red, blue & blk	03/22/1988	.75	*2.00*
O141	25¢ red, blue & blk	06/11/1988	.65	.50
Litho., Perf. 11				
O143	1¢ red, blue & blk	07/05/1989	.20	.20
Coil, Litho., Perf. 10 Vertically				
O144	"F" (29¢) red, blue & blk	01/22/1991	.80	.50
O145	29¢ red, blue & blk	05/24/1991	.65	.30
Litho., Perf. 11				
O146	4¢ red, blue & blk	04/06/1991	.20	*.30*
O146A	10¢ red, blue & blk	10/19/1993	.25	*.30*
O147	19¢ red, blue & blk	05/24/1991	.40	*.50*
O148	23¢ red, blue & blk	05/241991	.45	.30
O151	$1 red, blue & blk	09/1993	4.75	.75
Coil, Perf. 9.8 Vertically				
O152	(32¢) red, blue & blk	12/13/1994	.65	.50
O153	32¢ red, blue & blk	05/09/1995	1.25	.50
Coil, Perf. 11.2				
O154	1¢ red, blue & blk	05/09/1995	.20	*.50*
O155	20¢ red, blue & blk	05/09/1995	.45	*.50*
O156	23¢ red, blue & blk	05/09/1995	.55	.50
Coil, Litho., Perf. 9.75 Vertically				
O157	33¢ red, blue & blk	10/08/1999	.65	—
Coil, Tagged, Litho., Perf. 9.75 Vertically				
O158	34¢ red, blue & blk	02/27/2001	.65	.50
Coil, Tagged, Photo., Perf. 10 Vertically				
O159	37¢ red, blue & blk	08/02/2002	.70	.50
O160	39¢ red, blue & blk	03/08/2006	.80	.40
Tagged, Perf. 11.25				
O161	$1 red, blue & blk	09/29/2006	2.00	.75
Tagged, Perf. 9.75				
O162	41¢ red, blue & blk	06/25/2007	.85	.40

Variable Rate Coil Stamps

These are coil postage stamps printed without denominations. The denomination is imprinted by the dispensing equipment called a Postage and Mailing Center (PMC). Denominations can be set between 1¢ and $99.99. In 1993, the minimum denomination was adjusted to 19¢ (the postcard rate at the time).

Date of Issue:
August 20, 1992
Printing: Intaglio

Date of Issue:
February 19, 1994
Printing: Gravure

Date of Issue:
January 26, 1996
Printing: Gravure

Parcel Post Stamps

Engr., Wmkd. (190), **Perf. 12**

Issued for the prepayment of postage on parcel post packages only.
Beginning July 1, 1913 these stamps were valid for all postal purposes.

Issue		Date	Un	U	PB #	FDC	Q(M)
Q1	1¢ Post Office Clerk	07/01/13	5.75	1.75	110.00 (6)		*1,500.00*
	Double transfer		9.50	4.00			
Q2	2¢ City Carrier	07/01/13	6.75	1.40	145.00 (6)		*1,750.00*
a	Lake		*1,750.00*				
b	Carmine lake		*350.00*				
Q3	3¢ Railway Postal Clerk	04/05/13	13.50	6.50	235.00 (6)		*3,500.00*
	Retouched at lower right corner		26.00	14.50			
	Double transfer		26.00	14.50			
Q4	4¢ Rural Carrier	07/01/13	37.50	3.50	1,000.00 (6)		*3,500.00*
	Double transfer		—	—			
Q5	5¢ Mail Train	07/01/13	32.50	2.50	975.00 (6)		*3,500.00*
	Double transfer		45.00	6.25			
Q6	10¢ Steamship and Mail Tender	07/01/13	52.50	3.50	1,000.00 (6)		*12,500.00*
Q7	15¢ Automobile Service	07/01/13	67.50	15.00	2,300.00 (6)		—
Q8	20¢ Aeroplane Carrying Mail	1913	150.00	30.00	6,500.00 (6)		
Q9	25¢ Manufacturing	1913	67.50	8.50	2,400.00 (6)		
Q10	50¢ Dairying	03/15/13	300.00	50.00	*22,500.00* (6)		
Q11	75¢ Harvesting		110.00	40.00	3,000.00 (6)		
Q12	$1 Fruit Growing	01/03/13	375.00	45.00	*18,000.00* (6)		

Special Handling Stamps

Issued for use on parcel post packages to secure the same expeditious handling
accorded first class mail matter.

Unwmkd., Perf. 11

Issue		Date	Un	U	PB #	FDC	Q(M)
QE1	10¢ Special Handling, yellow grn. wet printing	*06/25/28*	2.50	1.00	25.00 (6)	45.00	
a	Dry printing	*1955*	3.75	—	40.00 (6)		
QE2	15¢ Special Handling, yellow grn. wet printing	*06/25/28*	3.00	.90	30.00 (6)	45.00	
a	Dry printing	*1955*	5.00	—	50.00 (6)		
QE3	20¢ Special Handling, yellow grn. wet printing	*06/25/28*	4.50	1.50	37.50 (6)	45.00	
a	Dry printing	*1955*	7.50	—	57.50 (6)		
QE4	25¢ Special Handling, deep green	*04/11/25*	25.00	3.75	350.00 (6)	225.00	
	"A" and second "T" of "STATES" joined at top		70.00	30.00			
	"T" and "A" of "POSTAGE" joined at top		110.00	100.00		225.00	
a	25¢ yellow green	*1928*	20.00	15.00	250.00 (6)		

Parcel Post Postage Due Stamps

Issued for affixing by a postal clerk to any parcel post package to denote the
amount to be collected from the addressee because of insufficient prepayment of
postage. Beginning July 1, 1913 these stamps were valid for use as regular
postage due stamps.

Engr., Wmkd. (190), **Perf. 12**

Issue		Date	Un	U	PB #	FDC	Q(M)
JQ1	1¢ Figure of Value	11/27/13	10.50	4.50	550.00 (6)		
JQ2	2¢ dark green	12/09/13	85.00	17.50	*3,750.00* (6)		
JQ3	5¢ dark green	11/27/13	14.00	5.50	600.00 (6)		
JQ4	10¢ dark green	12/12/13	175.00	45.00	*9,750.00* (6)		
JQ5	25¢ Figure of Value	12/16/13	100.00	5.00	*5,000.00* (6)		

FLAGS OF OUR NATION (SET 3)

*I*n 2009, the U.S. Postal Service continued its Flags of Our Nation series by issuing 10 more stamp designs. This new multi-stamp series, which was introduced in 2008, consists of sixty stamp designs featuring the Stars and Stripes, the fifty state flags, five territorial flags, and the District of Columbia flag. Two sets of ten stamps were issued in 2008; beginning in 2009, one set of 10 stamps will be issued each year with the final ten stamps scheduled for issuance in 2012. ▤ Each stamp design includes artwork that provides a "snapshot view" of the state or other area represented by a particular flag. "Snapshot" art for the Stars and Stripes stamps was inspired by the opening lines of "America the Beautiful," written by Katharine Lee Bates (1859-1929). ▤ The third set of ten features a stamp for each of the following: Kentucky, Louisiana, Maine, Maryland, Massachusetts, Michigan, Minnesota, Mississippi, Missouri, and the Stars and Stripes.

Abraham Lincoln Digital Color Postmarks

Celebrate the 200th anniversary of Abraham Lincoln's birth with these four unique digital color postmarks featuring Lincoln as rail-splitter, lawyer, politician and President.

Item #464768 (Set of four) $6.00

To order this item and other related philatelic products call **1 800 STAMP-24** *or visit us on-line at* **www.usps.com**

RW1

RW3

RW10

RW13

RW15

RW16

RW23

RW26

RW33

RW36

RW38

RW39

RW46

Migratory Bird Hunting and Conservation Stamps (commonly known as "Duck Stamps") are sold as hunting permits. While they are sold at many Post Offices, they are not usable for postage.

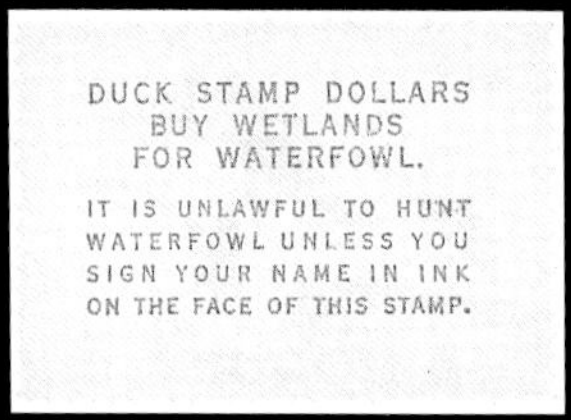

DUCK STAMP DOLLARS
BUY WETLANDS
FOR WATERFOWL.

IT IS UNLAWFUL TO HUNT
WATERFOWL UNLESS YOU
SIGN YOUR NAME IN INK
ON THE FACE OF THIS STAMP.

RW26-34

BUY DUCK STAMPS
SAVE WETLANDS

SEND IN *ALL* BIRD BANDS

SIGN YOUR DUCK STAMP

IT IS UNLAWFUL TO HUNT WATERFOWL UNLESS YOU
SIGN YOUR NAME IN INK ON THE FACE OF THIS STAMP

RW37-53

TAKE PRIDE IN AMERICA
BUY DUCK STAMPS
SAVE WETLANDS

SEND IN ALL BIRD BANDS

SIGN YOUR DUCK STAMPS

IT IS UNLAWFUL TO HUNT WATERFOWL OR USE THIS STAMP
AS A NATIONAL WILDLIFE ENTRANCE PASS UNLESS YOU
SIGN YOUR NAME IN INK ON THE FACE OF THIS STAMP

RW57

TAKE PRIDE IN AMERICA
BUY DUCK STAMPS
SAVE WETLANDS

SEND IN ALL BIRD BANDS

IT IS UNLAWFUL TO HUNT WATERFOWL OR USE THIS STAMP
AS A NATIONAL WILDLIFE REFUGE ENTRANCE PASS UNLESS
YOU SIGN YOUR NAME IN INK ON THE FACE OF THIS STAMP.

RW58-present

Migratory Bird Hunting and Conservation Stamps

	Issue	Date	Un	U	PB	#	Q(M)
	Department of Agriculture, Unwmkd., Perf 11						
RW1	$1 Mallards Alighting	1934	800.00	140.00	16,500.00	(6)	0.6
RW2	$1 Canvasbacks	1935	750.00	160.00	11,500.00	(6)	0.4
RW3	$1 Canada Geese	1936	350.00	75.00	4,000.00	(6)	0.6
RW4	$1 Scaup Ducks	1937	375.00	60.00	3,250.00	(6)	0.8
RW5	$1 Pintail Drake and Hen Alighting	1938	475.00	60.00	4,500.00	(6)	1
	Department of the Interior, Unwmkd., Perf 11						
RW6	$1 Green-winged Teal	1939	275.00	45.00	2,900.00	(6)	1
RW7	$1 Black Mallards	1940	250.00	45.00	2,900.00	(6)	1
RW8	$1 Ruddy Ducks	1941	250.00	45.00	2,900.00	(6)	1
RW9	$1 Baldpates	1942	250.00	45.00	2,900.00	(6)	1
RW10	$1 Wood Ducks	1943	125.00	35.00	700.00	(6)	1
RW11	$1 White-fronted Geese	1944	135.00	45.00	750.00	(6)	1
RW12	$1 Shoveller Ducks	1945	110.00	25.00	475.00	(6)	2
RW13	$1 Redhead Ducks	1946	55.00	16.00	325.00	(6)	2
RW14	$1 Snow Geese	1947	57.50	17.50	350.00	(6)	2
RW15	$1 Buffleheads in Flight	1948	60.00	16.00	425.00	(6)	2
RW16	$2 Goldeneye Ducks	1949	70.00	15.00	450.00	(6)	2
RW17	$2 Trumpeter Swans	1950	95.00	12.00	575.00	(6)	2
RW18	$2 Gadwall Ducks	1951	95.00	12.00	575.00	(6)	2
RW19	$2 Harlequin Ducks	1952	95.00	12.00	575.00	(6)	2
RW20	$2 Blue-winged Teal	1953	95.00	12.00	600.00	(6)	2
RW21	$2 Ring-necked Ducks	1954	85.00	10.50	600.00	(6)	2
RW22	$2 Blue Geese	1955	85.00	10.50	600.00	(6)	2
a	Black inscription inverted		5,500.00	4,500.00			
RW23	$2 American Merganser	1956	85.00	10.50	625.00	(6)	2

	Issue	Date	Un	U	PB	#	Q(M)
	Department of the Interior continued, **Unwmkd., Perf 11**						
RW24	$2 American Eider	1957	85.00	10.50	600.00	(6)	2
a	Black inscription inverted		5,000.00				
RW25	$2 Canada Geese	1958	85.00	10.50	600.00	(6)	2
RW26	$3 Labrador Retriever Carrying Mallard Drake	1959	125.00	11.00	550.00	(4)	2
a	Black inscription inverted		35,000.00				
RW27	$3 Redhead Ducks	1960	95.00	10.50	475.00	(4)	2
RW28	$3 Mallard Hen and Ducklings	1961	110.00	10.50	525.00	(4)	1
RW29	$3 Pintail Drakes	1962	125.00	10.50	600.00	(4)	1
RW30	$3 Pair of Brant Landing	1963	120.00	12.50	500.00	(4)	1
RW31	$3 Hawaiian Nene Geese	1964	110.00	12.50	2,300.00	(6)	2
RW32	$3 Three Canvasback Drakes	1965	110.00	12.50	550.00	(4)	2
RW33	$3 Whistling Swans	1966	110.00	12.50	550.00	(4)	2
RW34	$3 Old Squaw Ducks	1967	125.00	12.50	600.00	(4)	2
RW35	$3 Hooded Mergansers	1968	70.00	10.50	325.00	(4)	2
RW36	$3 White-winged Scoters	1969	65.00	8.00	300.00	(4)	2
RW37	$3 Ross's Geese	1970	70.00	8.00	300.00	(4)	2
RW38	$3 Three Cinnamon Teal	1971	45.00	7.75	200.00	(4)	2
RW39	$5 Emperor Geese	1972	25.00	7.00	110.00	(4)	2
RW40	$5 Steller's Eiders	1973	20.00	7.00	95.00	(4)	2
RW41	$5 Wood Ducks	1974	18.00	6.00	80.00	(4)	2
RW42	$5 Canvasbacks Decoy, 3 Flying Canvasbacks	1975	17.50	6.00	65.00	(4)	2
RW43	$5 Canada Geese	1976	17.50	6.00	65.00	(4)	2
RW44	$5 Pair of Ross's Geese	1977	17.50	6.00	65.00	(4)	2
RW45	$5 Hooded Merganser Drake	1978	15.00	6.00	57.50	(4)	2
RW46	$7.50 Green-winged Teal	1979	17.50	7.00	75.00	(4)	2

The First Federal Duck Stamp

Jay Norwood "Ding" Darling (1876 - 1962), the designer of the first Federal Duck Stamp, was a Pulitzer Prize-winning cartoonist. He was one of the leading advocates of the Migratory Bird Hunting Stamp Act.

Ding Darling's etching, *Mallards Dropping In*, became the design for the first Federal Duck Stamp issued in 1934.

"Ding" Darling purchased the first sheet of the 1934 Federal Duck Stamp on August 22, 1934, from C.B. Eilenberger, the third assistant postmaster general. Behind Darling is William M. Mooney, postmaster of Washington, D.C.

History of the Federal Duck Stamp Contest

The first Federal Duck Stamp, designed by Jay "Ding" Darling in 1934 at President Franklin D. Roosevelt's request, depicts two mallards about to land on a marsh pond. In subsequent years, other noted wildlife artists were asked to submit designs. The first contest in 1949 was open to any U.S. artist who wished to enter. The number of entries rose to 2,099 in 1981. This is the only art competition of its kind sponsored by the U.S. Government. A panel of noted art, waterfowl, and philatelic authorities is appointed by the Secretary of the Interior to judge each competition. Winners receive no compensation for their work, other than a pane of stamps carrying their design. The U.S. Fish and Wildlife Service mails contest regulations to interested artists each spring.

	Issue	Date	Un	U	PB	#	Q(M)
	Department of the Interior, Unwmkd., Perf 11 continued						
RW47	$7.50 Mallards	1980	17.50	7.00	75.00	(4)	2
RW48	$7.50 Ruddy Ducks	1981	17.50	7.00	75.00	(4)	2
RW49	$7.50 Canvasbacks	1982	17.50	7.00	75.00	(4)	2
a	Orange & violet omitted		7,500.00				
RW50	$7.50 Pintails	1983	17.50	7.00	75.00	(4)	2
RW51	$7.50 Widgeons	1984	17.50	7.00	75.00	(4)	2
RW52	$7.50 Cinnamon Teal	1985	17.50	8.00	75.00	(4)	
a	Light blue omitted		22,500.00				
RW53	$7.50 Fulvous Whistling Duck	1986	17.50	7.00	75.00	(4)	2
a	Black omitted		3,750.00				
	Perf. 11.5 x 11						
RW54	$10 Redheads	1987	17.50	9.50	75.00	(4)	2
RW55	$10 Snow Goose	1988	17.50	10.00	75.00	(4)	1
RW56	$12.50 Lesser Scaup	1989	20.00	10.00	85.00	(4)	1
RW57	$12.50 Black Bellied Whistling Duck	1990	20.00	10.00	85.00	(4)	1
a	Back inscription omitted		375.00				
RW58	$15 King Eiders	1991	30.00	11.00	140.00	(4)	1
a	Black omitted		20,000.00				
RW59	$15 Spectacled Eider	1992	30.00	11.00	140.00	(4)	1
RW60	$15 Canvasbacks	1993	27.50	11.00	130.00	(4)	1
a	Black omitted		3,000.00				
	Perf. 11.25 x 11						
RW61	$15 Red-breasted Merganser	1994	30.00	11.00	140.00	(4)	1
RW62	$15 Mallards	1995	30.00	11.00	140.00	(4)	1
RW63	$15 Surf Scoters	1996	30.00	11.00	140.00	(4)	1
RW64	$15 Canada Goose	1997	30.00	11.00	125.00	(4)	1

	Issue	Date	Un	U	PB	#	Q(M)
	Department of the Interior continued						
	Perf. 11.25						
RW65	$15 Barrow's Goldeneye	1998	45.00	20.00	190.00	(4)	1
	Self-Adhesive, Die-Cut Perf. 10						
RW65A	$15 Barrow's Goldeneye	1998	25.00	15.00			1
	Perf. 11.25						
RW66	$15 Greater Scaup	1999	40.00	15.00	170.00	(4)	
	Perf. 10, Self-Adhesive, Die-Cut						
RW66A	$15 Greater Scaup	1999	25.00	12.00			1
	Perf. 11.25						
RW67	$15 Mottled Duck	2000	30.00	14.00	130.00	(4)	1
	Perf. 10, Self-Adhesive, Die-Cut						
RW67A	$15 Mottled Duck	2000	22.50	14.00			1
	Perf. 11.25						
RW68	$15 Northern Pintail	2001	27.50	15.00	110.00	(4)	1
	Self-Adhesive, Die-Cut Perf. 10						
RW68A	$15 Northern Pintail	2001	25.00	10.00			1
	Perf. 11.25						
RW69	$15 Black Scoters	2002	27.50	15.00	110.00	(4)	1
	Self-Adhesive, Serpentine Die-Cut 11 x 10.75						
RW69A	$15 Black Scoters	2002	25.00	10.00			1
	Perf. 11						
RW70	$15 Snow Geese	2003	27.50	15.00	120.00	(4)	1
b	Imperf., pair		7,500.00				
c	Black inscription omitted		4,500.00				
	Self-Adhesive, Serpentine Die-Cut 11 x 10.75						
RW70A	$15 Snow Geese	2003	25.00	10.00			1
	Perf. 11						
RW71	$15 Redheads	2004	27.50	11.00	100.00	(4)	1
	Self-Adhesive, Serpentine Die-Cut 11 x 10.75						
RW71A	$15 Redheads	2004	25.00	10.00			1
	Perf. 11						
RW72	$15 Hooded Mergansers	2005	22.50	11.00	100.00	(4)	1
	Self-Adhesive, Serpentine Die-Cut 11 x 10.75						
RW72A	$15 Hooded Mergansers	2005	22.50	11.00			1
	Self-Adhesive, Perf. 11						
RW73	$15 Ross's Goose	2006	22.50	11.00	100.00	(4)	1
b	Souvenir sheet		160.00	—			
c	As "b" no artist's signature		4,500.00				
	Self-Adhesive, Serpentine Die-Cut 11 x 10.75						
RW73A	$15 Ross's Goose	2006	22.50	11.00			1
	Perf. 11						
RW74	$15 Ring-necked Ducks	2007	22.50	11.00	100.00	(4)	1
b	Souvenir sheet		150.00				
	Self-Adhesive, Serpentine Die-Cut 11 x 10.75						
RW74A	$15 Ring-necked Ducks	2007	22.50	11.00			1
	Perf. 13.25						
RW75	$15 Northern Pintails	2008	22.50	11.00			
b	Souvenir sheet		85.00				
	Self-Adhesive, Serpentine Die-Cut 10.75						
RW75A	$15 Northern Pintails	2008	22.50	15.00			1

The Most Successful Conservation Program

Few conservation programs rival the success of the Federal Duck Stamp Program. The Federal Duck Stamp is the longest running series of stamps issued by the United States government. Stamp collectors, hunters, conservationists and lovers of wildlife art all prize the stamps for their beauty and their role in saving wetlands.

The success of the Federal Duck Stamp has been a result of its unique efficiency, made possible by the cooperation between the U.S. Postal Service and the Department of Interior. The stamp is produced by the Department of Interior and distributed and sold primarily by the U.S. Postal Service.

RW49

RW54

RW57

RW58

RW59

RW60

RW61

RW62

RW63

RW65

RW66

RW67

RW68

RW69

RW70

RW71

RW72

RW73

RW74

RW75

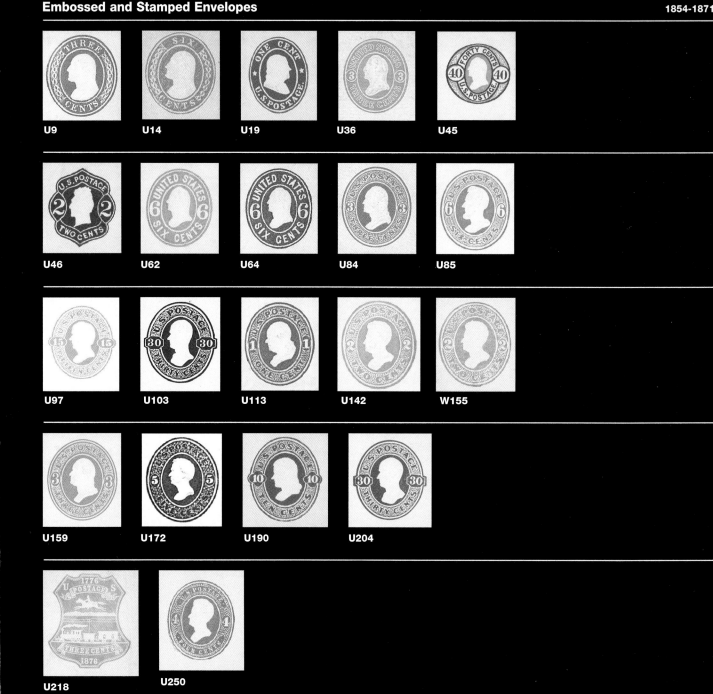

U9

U14

U19

U36

U45

U46

U62

U64

U84

U85

U97

U103

U113

U142

W155

U159

U172

U190

U204

U218

U250

Embossed and Stamped Envelopes

Represented below is only a partial listing of stamped envelopes. At least one example is listed for most die types; most die types exist on several colors of envelope paper. Values are for cut squares; prices for entire envelopes are higher. Color in italic is the color of the envelope paper; when no color is specified, envelope paper is white. "W" with catalog number indicates wrapper instead of envelope.

1853-1861

	Issue	Un	U
U1	3¢ red Washington (top label 13mm wide)	400.00	35.00
U2	3¢ red Washington (top label 13mm wide), *buff*	100.00	25.00
U3	3¢ red Washington (top label 15½mm wide)	900.00	40.00
U4	3¢ red Washington, (top label 15½mm wide), *buff*	350.00	40.00
U5	3¢ red Washington, (label has octagonal ends)	5,500.00	550.00
U6	3¢ red Washington, (label has octagonal ends), *buff*	4,750.00	75.00
U7	3¢ red Washington, (label 20mm wide)	5,500.00	150.00
U8	3¢ red Washington, (label 20mm wide), *buff*	*8,750.00*	175.00
U9	3¢ red (label 14½mm)	40.00	4.00
U10	3¢ red (label 14½mm), *buff*	22.50	4.00
U11	6¢ red Washington	175.00	90.00
U12	6¢ red Washington, *buff*	175.00	90.00
U13	6¢ green Washington	300.00	125.00
U14	6¢ green Washington, *buff*	225.00	100.00
U15	10¢ green Washington (label 15½mm wide)	550.00	100.00
U16	10¢ green Washington, (label 15½mm wide), buff	190.00	75.00
U17	10¢ green Washington, (label 20mm)	475.00	140.00
U18	10¢ green Washington, (label 20mm), buff	250.00	90.00
U19	1¢ blue Franklin (period after "POSTAGE"), *buff*	40.00	15.00
U21A	1¢ blue Franklin, *orange*, entire	*2,750.00*	
U23	1¢ blue Franklin (bust touches inner frame line), *orange*	600.00	350.00
U24	1¢ blue Franklin (no period after "POSTAGE"), *amber*	200.00	100.00
U26	3¢ red Washington	35.00	20.00
U27	3¢ red Washington, *buff*	26.00	13.00
U28	3¢ + 1¢ (U12 and U9)	300.00	225.00
U29	3¢ + 1¢ (U12 and U9), *buff*	300.00	250.00
U30	6¢ red Washington	1,750.00	1,250.00
U31	6¢ red Washington, *buff*	2,500.00	1,250.00
U32	10¢ green Washington	1,000.00	400.00
U33	10¢ green Washington, *buff*	1,100.00	350.00

1861-1870

	Issue	Un	U
U34	3¢ pink Washington (outline lettering)	32.50	6.00
U35	3¢ pink Washington (outline lettering), *buff*	32.50	6.00
U36	3¢ pink Washington, blue (letter sheet)	75.00	60.00
U38	6¢ pink Washington	125.00	80.00
U39	6¢ pink Washington, *buff*	70.00	62.50
U40	10¢ yellow green Washington	47.50	30.00
U41	10¢ yellow green Washington, *buff*	47.50	30.00
U42	12¢ red & brown Washington, *buff*	225.00	175.00
U43	20¢ red & blue Washington, *buff*	250.00	200.00
U44	24¢ Washington, *buff*	240.00	200.00
U45	40¢ black & red Washington, *buff*	375.00	350.00
U46	2¢ black Jackson ("U.S. POSTAGE" downstroke, tail of "2" unite near point)	55.00	21.00
U49	2¢ black Jackson ("POSTAGE" downstroke and tail of "2" touch but do not merge), *orange*	2,750.00	
U50	2¢ black Jackson ("U.S. POST." 24-25mm wide), *buff*	19.00	9.50
U52	2¢ black Jackson ("U.S. POST." 24-25mm wide), *orange*	19.00	9.50
U54	2¢ black Jackson ("U.S. POST." 25½-26½mm), *buff*	19.00	9.50
U56	2¢ black Jackson ("U.S. POST." 25½-26½mm), *orange*	22.00	8.50
U58	3¢ pink Washington	12.00	1.60
U59	3¢ pink Washington, *buff*	12.00	1.25
U60	3¢ brown Washington	75.00	40.00
U61	3¢ brown Washington, *buff*	60.00	30.00
U62	6¢ pink Washington	110.00	29.00
U63	6¢ pink Washington, *buff*	55.00	27.50
U64	6¢ purple Washington	70.00	26.00
U65	6¢ purple Washington, *buff*	60.00	20.00
U66	9¢ lemon Washington, *buff*	450.00	250.00
U67	9¢ orange Washington, *buff*	160.00	90.00
U68	12¢ brown Washington, *buff*	275.00	275.00
U69	12¢ red brown Washington, *buff*	150.00	55.00
U70	18¢ red Washington, *buff*	95.00	95.00
U71	24¢ blue Washington, *buff*	100.00	95.00
U72	30¢ green Washington, *buff*	125.00	80.00
U73	40¢ rose Washington, *buff*	125.00	*250.00*
U74	1¢ blue Franklin (bust points to end of "N" of "ONE")	45.00	30.00
U75	1¢ blue Franklin (bust points to end of "N" of "ONE"), *amber*	37.50	27.50
U76	1¢ blue Franklin (bust points to end of "N" of "ONE"), *orange*	20.00	15.00

1870-1871

	Issue	Un	U
U78	2¢ brown Jackson (bust narrow at back; small, thick numerals)	40.00	16.00
U79	2¢ brown Jackson (bust narrow at back; small, thick numerals), *amber*	22.50	10.00
U80	2¢ brown Jackson (bust narrow at back; small, thick numerals), *orange*	12.00	6.50
U82	3¢ green Washington ("ponytail" projects below bust)	8.50	1.00
U83	3¢ green Washington ("ponytail" projects below bust), *amber*	7.25	2.00
U84	3¢ green Washington ("ponytail" projects below bust), *cream*	11.00	4.50
U85	6¢ dark red Lincoln (neck very long at back)	32.50	16.00
U86	6¢ dark red Lincoln (neck very long at back), *amber*	40.00	20.00
U87	6¢ dark red Lincoln (neck very long at back), *cream*	40.00	20.00
U88	7¢ vermillion Stanton (figures "7" normal), *amber*	55.00	*190.00*
U89	10¢ olive black Jefferson	800.00	900.00
U90	10¢ olive black Jefferson, *amber*	950.00	900.00
U91	10¢ brown Jefferson	92.50	72.50
U92	10¢ brown Jefferson, *amber*	110.00	52.50
U93	12¢ plum Clay (ear partly covered, chin prominent)	125.00	82.50
U94	12¢ plum Clay (ear partly covered, chin prominent), *amber*	140.00	110.00
U95	12¢ plum Clay (ear partly covered, chin prominent), *cream*	225.00	225.00
U96	15¢ red orange Webster (has side whiskers)	85.00	85.00
U97	15¢ red orange Webster (has side whiskers), *amber*	150.00	*300.00*
U98	15¢ red orange Webster (has side whiskers), *cream*	350.00	350.00
U99	24¢ purple Scott (locks of hair project, top of head)	150.00	150.00
U100	24¢ purple Scott (locks of hair project, top of head), *amber*	200.00	*325.00*
U101	24¢ purple Scott (locks of hair project, top of head), *cream*	275.00	*500.00*
U102	30¢ black Hamilton (back of bust very narrow)	80.00	*110.00*
U103	30¢ black Hamilton (back of bust very narrow), *amber*	250.00	*500.00*
U104	30¢ black Hamilton (back of bust very narrow), *cream*	250.00	*500.00*
U105	90¢ carmine Perry (front of bust very narrow, pointed)	175.00	*350.00*
U106	90¢ carmine Perry (front of bust very narrow, pointed), *amber*	325.00	*450.00*
U107	90¢ carmine Perry (front of bust very narrow, pointed), *cream*	200.00	*2,500.00*

Issue		Un	U
1874-1886			
U108	1¢ dark blue Franklin (circle in "O" of "Postage")	210.00	70.00
U109	1¢ dark blue Franklin (circle in "O" of "Postage"), *amber*	190.00	75.00
U110	1¢ dark blue Franklin (circle in "O" of "Postage"), *cream*	1,000.00	
U111	1¢ dark blue Franklin (circle in "O" of "Postage"), *orange*	25.00	17.50
U113	1¢ light blue Franklin (lower part of bust points to end of "E" in "ONE")	1.50	1.00
U114	1¢ light blue (lower part of bust points to end of "E" in "Postage"), *amber*	4.00	4.00
1874-1886			
U115	1¢ blue Franklin (lower part of bust points to end of "E" in "ONE"), *cream*	5.25	4.50
U116	1¢ blue Franklin (lower part of bust points to end of "E" in "ONE"), *orange*	.80	.40
U117	1¢ light blue Franklin (lower part of bust points to end of "E" in "ONE"), *blue*	8.50	5.25
U118	1¢ light blue Franklin (lower part of bust points to end of "E" in "ONE"), *fawn*	8.50	5.25
U119	1¢ light blue Franklin (lower part of bust points to end of "E" in "ONE"), *manila*	9.00	3.25
U121	1¢ light blue Franklin (lower part of bust points to end of "E" in "ONE"), *amber manila*	19.00	10.00
U122	2¢ brown Jackson (bust narrow at back; numerals thin)	150.00	50.00
U123	2¢ brown Jackson (bust narrow at back; numerals thin), *amber*	72.50	40.00
U124	2¢ brown Jackson (bust narrow at back; numerals thin), *cream*	1,000.00	
U125	2¢ brown Jackson (bust narrow at back; numerals thin), *orange*	25,000.00	
U128	2¢ brown Jackson (numerals in long ovals)	60.00	35.00
U129	2¢ brown Jackson (numerals in long ovals), *amber*	85.00	45.00
U130	2¢ brown Jackson (numerals in long ovals), *cream*	50,000.00	
U132	2¢ brown Jackson, (left numeral touches oval)	82.50	29.00
U133	2¢ brown Jackson, (left numeral touches oval), *amber*	525.00	70.00

Issue		Un	U
1875-1881			
U134	2¢ brown Jackson (numerals in long ovals and "O" of "TWO" has center netted instead of plain)	1,500.00	160.00
U135	2¢ brown Jackson (numerals in long ovals and "O" of "TWO" has center netted instead of plain), *amber*	375.00	125.00
U136	2¢ brown Jackson (numerals in long ovals and "O" of "TWO" has center netted instead of plain), *orange*	57.50	29.00
U139	2¢ brown Jackson (bust broad; numerals short, thick)	62.50	37.50
U140	2¢ brown Jackson (bust broad; numerals short, thick), *amber*	97.50	62.50
U142	2¢ vermillion Jackson (bust broad; numerals short, thick)	10.00	5.00
U143	2¢ vermillion Jackson (bust broad; numerals short, thick), *amber*	10.00	4.50
U144	2¢ vermillion Jackson (bust broad; numerals short, thick), *cream*	21.00	7.50
U146	2¢ vermillion Jackson (bust broad; numerals short, thick), *blue*	140.00	40.00
U147	2¢ vermillion Jackson (bust broad; numerals short, thick), *fawn*	11.00	5.00
U149	2¢ vermillion Jackson (similar to U139-147 but circles around ovals much heavier)	62.50	32.50
U150	2¢ vermillion Jackson (similar to U139-147 but circles around ovals much heavier), *amber*	42.50	17.50
U151	2¢ vermillion Jackson (similar to U139-147 but circles around ovals much heavier), *blue*	14.00	10.00
U152	2¢ vermillion Jackson (similar to U139-147 but circles around ovals much heavier), *fawn*	15.00	4.75
U153	2¢ vermillion Jackson (similar to U139-147 but middle stroke of "N" is thin)	77.50	27.50
U154	2¢ vermillion Jackson (similar to U139-147 but middle stroke of "N" as thin as verticals), *amber*	350.00	90.00
W155	2¢ vermillion Jackson (similar to U139-147 but middle stroke of "N" as thin as verticals), *manilla*	24.00	11.00
U156	2¢ vermillion Jackson (bottom of bust cut almost semi-circularly)	1,750.00	175.00
U157	2¢ vermillion Jackson (bottom of bust cut almost semi-circularly), *amber*	57,500.00	35,000.00

Issue		Un	U
1875-1881			
U159	3¢ green Washington (thin letters, long numerals)	40.00	11.50
U160	3¢ green Washington (thin letters, long numerals), *amber*	37.50	10.50
U161	3¢ green Washington (thin letters, long numerals), *cream*	42.50	15.00
U163	3¢ green Washington (thick letters, "ponytail" does not project below bust)	1.50	.30
U164	3¢ green Washington (thick letters, "ponytail" does not project below bust), *amber*	1.60	.70
U165	3¢ green Washington (thick letters, "ponytail" does not project below bust), *cream*	9.50	6.50
U166	3¢ green Washington (thick letters, "ponytail" does not project below bust), *blue*	8.50	6.25
U167	3¢ green Washington (thick letters, "ponytail" does not project below bust), *fawn*	5.25	3.50
U168	3¢ green Washington (top of head egg-shaped; "ponytail" knot projects as point)	1,500.00	80.00
U169	3¢ green Washington (top of head egg-shaped; "ponytail" knot projects as point), *amber*	625.00	110.00
U170	3¢ green Washington (top of head egg-shaped; "ponytail" knot projects as point), *blue*	12,500.00	3,250.00
U171	3¢ green Washington (top of head egg-shaped; "ponytail" knot projects as point), *fawn*	45,000.00	3,250.00
U172	5¢ blue Taylor, (numerals have thick, curved tops)	15.00	11.00
U173	5¢ blue Taylor, die 1, (numerals have thick, curved tops), *amber*	15.00	12.50
U174	5¢ blue Taylor, die 1, (numerals have thick, curved tops), *cream*	125.00	47.50
U175	5¢ blue Taylor, die 1, (numerals have thick, curved tops), *blue*	40.00	19.00
U176	5¢ blue Taylor, die 1, (numerals have thick, curved tops), *blue*	160.00	70.00
U177	5¢ blue Taylor, die 2, (numerals have long, thin tops)	14.00	10.00
U178	5¢ blue Taylor, die 2, (numerals have long, thin tops), *amber*	12.00	10.00
U179	5¢ blue Taylor, die 2, (numerals have long, thin tops), *blue*	32.50	13.50
U180	5¢ blue Taylor, die 2, (numerals have long, thin tops), *fawn*	140.00	47.50

Issue	Un	U
1899-1903		
U360 2¢ carmine Washington, bust points to first notch of inner oval), *amber*	24.00	12.50
U361 2¢ carmine Washington, bust points to first notch of inner oval), *blue*	65.00	35.00
U362 2¢ carmine Washington, bust points to middle of second notch of inner oval, "ponytail"	.35	.20
U363 2¢ carmine Washington, bust points to middle of second notch of inner oval, "ponytail"), *amber*	1.40	.20
U364 2¢ carmine Washington, bust points to middle of second notch of inner oval, "ponytail"), *oriental buff*	1.20	.20
U365 2¢ carmine Washington, bust points to middle of second notch of inner oval, "ponytail"), *blue*	1.50	.55
U367 2¢ carmine Washington, (same as U362 but hair flowing; no ribbon "ponytail")	6.00	2.75
U368 2¢ carmine Washington, (same as U362 but hair flowing; no ribbon "ponytail"), *amber*	9.00	6.75
U369 2¢ carmine Washington, (same as U362 but hair flowing; no ribbon "ponytail"), *oriental buff*	25.00	12.50
U370 2¢ carmine Washington, (same as U362 but hair flowing; no ribbon "ponytail"), *blue*	12.50	10.00
U371 4¢ brown Lincoln (bust pointed, undraped)	20.00	13.00
U372 4¢ brown Lincoln (bust pointed, undraped), *amber*	20.00	13.00
U373 4¢ brown Lincoln, (broad bust and draped)	13,500.00	1,250.00
U374 4¢ brown (head larger; inner oval has no notches)	15.00	8.00
U375 4¢ brown (head larger; inner oval has no notches), *amber*	65.00	25.00
U377 5¢ blue Grant (like U331, U335 but smaller)	13.00	10.00
U378 5¢ blue Grant (like U331, U335 but smaller), *amber*	17.00	10.50
U379 1¢ green Franklin, horizontal oval	.80	.20
U380 1¢ green Franklin, horizontal oval, *amber*	16.00	2.00
U381 1¢ green Franklin, horizontal oval, *oriental buff*	19.00	2.50
U382 1¢ green Franklin, horizontal oval, *blue*	24.00	2.50
U383 1¢ green Franklin, horizontal oval, *manila*	4.50	.90

Issue	Un	U
1903-1916		
U385 2¢ carmine Washington (1 short, 2 long vertical lines at right of "CENTS")	.50	.20
U386 2¢ carmine Washington (1 short, 2 long vertical lines at right of "CENTS"), *amber*	2.50	.20
U387 2¢ carmine Washington (1 short, 2 long vertical lines at right of "CENTS"), *oriental buff*	2.25	.30
U388 2¢ carmine Washington (1 short, 2 long vertical lines at right of "CENTS"), *blue*	2.00	.50
U390 4¢ chocolate Grant	22.50	12.50
U391 4¢ chocolate Grant, *amber*	24.00	12.50
U393 5¢ blue Lincoln	24.00	12.50
U394 5¢ blue Lincoln, *amber*	24.00	12.50
U395 2¢ carmine Washington, recut die (lines at end of "TWO CENTS" all short), *blue*	.75	.20
U396 2¢ carmine Washington, recut die (lines at end of "TWO CENTS" all short), *amber*	9.00	1.00
U397 2¢ carmine Washington, recut die (lines at end of "TWO CENTS" all short), *oriental buff*	6.00	1.10
U398 2¢ carmine Washington, recut die (lines at end of "TWO CENTS" all short), *blue*	4.50	.90
U400 1¢ green Franklin, oval, die 1 (wide "D" in "UNITED")	.35	.20
U401 1¢ green Franklin, oval, die 1 (wide "D" in "UNITED"), *amber*	2.10	.40
U402 1¢ green Franklin, oval, die 1 (wide "D" in "UNITED"), *oriental buff*	10.50	1.00
U403 1¢ green Franklin, oval, die 1 (wide "D" in "UNITED"), *blue*	10.50	1.50
U404 1¢ green Franklin, oval, die 1 (wide "D" in "UNITED"), *manila*	3.50	1.90
U406 2¢ brown red Washington, die 1 (oval "O" in "TWO" and "C" in "CENTS")	1.00	.20
U407 2¢ brown red Washington, die 1 (oval "O" in "TWO" and "C" in "CENTS"), *amber*	6.50	2.00
U408 2¢ brown red Washington, die 1 (oval "O" in "TWO" and "C" in "CENTS"), *oriental buff*	8.75	1.50
U409 2¢ brown red Washington, die 1 (oval "O" in "TWO" and "C" in "CENTS"), *blue*	5.75	2.00

Issue	Un	U
1916-1932		
U411 2¢ carmine Washington, die 1 (oval "O" in "TWO" and "C" in "CENTS"), *blue*	.35	.20
U412 2¢ carmine Washington, die 1 (oval "O" in "TWO" and "C" in "CENTS"), *amber*	.30	.20
U413 2¢ carmine Washington, die 1 (oval "O" in "TWO" and "C" in "CENTS"), *oriental buff*	.55	.20
U414 2¢ carmine Washington, die 1 (oval "O" in "TWO" and "C" in "CENTS"), *blue*	.60	.20
U416 4¢ black Washington, die 2 ("F" is 1¾mm from left "4")	6.00	3.00
U417 4¢ black Washington, die 2 ("F" is 1¾mm from left "4"), *amber*	7.50	2.50
U418 5¢ blue Washington, die 2 (short "F" in FIVE)	7.00	2.25
U419 5¢ blue Washington, die 2 (short "F" in FIVE), *amber*	16.50	11.00
U420 1¢ green Franklin, round, die 1 ("UNITED" nearer inner circle than outer circle)	.25	.20
U421 1¢ green Franklin, round, die 1 ("UNITED" nearer inner circle than outer circle), *amber*	.55	.30
U422 1¢ green Franklin, round, die 1 ("UNITED" nearer inner circle than outer circle), *oriental buff*	2.40	.90
U423 1¢ green Franklin, round, die 1 ("UNITED" nearer inner circle than outer circle), *blue*	.50	.35
U424 1¢ green Franklin, round, die 1 ("UNITED" nearer inner circle than outer circle), *manila*	7.00	4.00
U426 1¢ green Franklin, round, die 1 ("UNITED" nearer inner circle than outer circle), glazed, *brown*	45.00	15.00
U428 1¢ green Franklin, round, die 1 ("UNITED" nearer inner circle than outer circle), unglazed, *brown*	16.50	7.50

Issue	Un	U
1915-1921		
U429 2¢ carmine Washington, die 1 (letters broad, numerals vertical, "E" closer than "N" to inner circle)	.25	.20
U430 2¢ carmine Washington, die 1 (letters broad, numerals vertical, "E" closer than "N" to inner circle), *amber*	.30	.20
U431 2¢ carmine Washington, die 1 (letters broad, numerals vertical, "E" closer than "N" to inner circle), *oriental buff*	2.25	.65
U432 2¢ carmine Washington, die 1 (letters broad, numerals vertical, "E" closer than "N" to inner circle), *blue*	.30	.20
U436 3¢ purple Washington, die 1 (as 2¢)	.30	.20
U437 3¢ purple Washington, die 1 (as 2¢), *amber*	.35	.20
U438 3¢ dark violet Washington, die 1 (as 2¢), *oriental buff*	27.50	1.65
U439 3¢ purplet Washington, die 1 (as 2¢), *blue*	.35	.20
U440 4¢ black Franklin, die 1, ("UNITED" closer to inner circle)	1.75	.60
U441 4¢ black Franklin, die 1, ("UNITED" closer to inner circle), *amber*	3.00	.85
U442 4¢ black Franklin, die 1, ("UNITED" closer to inner circle), *blue*	3.50	.85
U443 5¢ blue Washington, die 1, (letters are broad)	3.50	2.75
U444 5¢ blue Washington, die 1, (letters are broad), *amber*	4.00	1.60
U445 5¢ blue Washington, die 1, (letters are broad), *blue*	4.25	3.25
U446 2¢ on 3¢ dark violet Washington, die 1, black surcharge	16.00	10.00
U447 2¢ on 3¢ dark violet Washington, die 1, rose surcharge	10.00	6.50
U448 2¢ on 3¢ dark violet Washington, die 1, black surcharge	2.75	2.00
U449 2¢ on 3¢ dark violet Washington, die 1, black surcharge, *amber*	7.50	6.00
U450 2¢ on 3¢ dark violet Washington, die 1, black surcharge, *oriental buff*	20.00	15.00
U451 2¢ on 3¢ dark violet Washington, die 1, black surcharge, *blue*	16.00	10.50
U452 2¢ on 1¢ green Franklin, die 1, ("UNITED" nearer inner circle than outer circle)	3,750.00	

Issue	Un	U
1921		
U453 2¢ on 2¢ carmine Washington, die 3, (round "O" and "C", coarse lettering)	5,000.00	
U454 2¢ on 2¢ carmine Washington, die 6, ("T" and "S" far apart at bottom)	150.00	
U455 2¢ on 2¢ carmine Washington, die 1, (letters broad, numerals vertical, "E" closer than "N" to inner circle), *amber*	1,750.00	
U456 2¢ on 2¢ carmine Washington, die 2, ("U" far from left circle), *oriental buff*	300.00	
U457 2¢ on 2¢ carmine Washington, die 6, ("T" and "S" far apart at bottom), *blue*	250.00	
U458 2¢ on 3¢ dark violet Washington, die 1, black surcharge, (bars 2mm apart)	.55	.35
U459 2¢ on 3¢ dark violet Washington, die 6, ("T" and "S" far apart at bottom), *amber*	3.25	1.00
U460 2¢ on 3¢ dark violet Washington, die 6, ("T" and "S" far apart at bottom), *oriental buff*	4.00	2.00
U461 2¢ on 3¢ dark violet Washington, die 1, (letters broad, numerals vertical, "E" closer than "N" to inner circle), *blue*	6.50	1.00
U462 2¢ on 4¢ chocolate Grant	350.00	260.00
U463 2¢ on 4¢ chocolate Grant, *amber*	550.00	350.00
U464 2¢ on 5¢ blue Washington, die 1, (letters are broad)	1,200.00	
U465 2¢ on 1¢ green Franklin, die 1, (letters are broad)	1,400.00	
U466 2¢ on 2¢ carmne Franklin, die 1, (letters are broad)	*15,000.00*	
U467 2¢ on 3¢ green Washington, die 2 (thick letters, "ponytail" does not project below bust), *blue*	425.00	
U468 2¢ on 3¢ dark violet Washington, die 1, black surcharge, (bars 1½mm apart)	.70	.45
U469 2¢ on 3¢ dark violet Washington, die 1, (letters broad, numerals vertical, "E" closer than "N" to inner circle), *amber*	3.75	2.25
U470 2¢ on 3¢ dark violet Washington, die 1, (letters broad, numerals vertical, "E" closer than "N" to inner circle), *oriental buff*	6.00	2.50
U471 2¢ on 3¢ dark violet Washington, die 1, (letters broad, numerals vertical, "E" closer than "N" to inner circle), *blue*	7.50	1.75

Issue	Un	U
1921-1925		
U472 2¢ on 4¢ chocolate Grant	15.00	8.00
U473 2¢ on 4¢ chocolate Grant, *amber*	16.50	10.00
U474 2¢ on 1¢ on 3¢ dark violet Washington, die 1, double surcharge, (letters broad, numerals vertical, "E" closer than "N" to inner circle)	300.00	
U475 2¢ on 1¢ on 3¢ dark violet Washington, die 1, double surcharge, (letters broad, numerals vertical, "E" closer than "N" to inner circle), *amber*	150.00	
U476 2¢ on 3¢ dark violet Washington, die 1, double surcharge, (letters broad, numerals vertical, "E" closer than "N" to inner circle), *amber*	300.00	
U477 2¢ on 3¢ dark violet Washington, die 1, double surcharge, (letters broad, numerals vertical, "E" closer than "N" to inner circle)	140.00	
U478 2¢ on 3¢ dark violet Washington, die 1, double surcharge, (letters broad, numerals vertical, "E" closer than "N" to inner circle), *amber*	350.00	
U479 2¢ on 3¢ dark violet Washington, (bk) die 1, double surcharge, (letters broad, numerals vertical, "E" closer than "N" to inner circle), *amber*	300.00	
U480 2¢ on 3¢ dark violet Washington, (bk) die 7, double surcharge, (letters broad, numerals vertical, "E" closer than "N" to inner circle), *amber*	*6,000.00*	
U481 1½¢ brown Washington, die 1 (letters broad, numerals vertical, "E" closer than "N" to inner circle)	.25	.20
U482 1½¢ brown Washington, die 1 (letters broad, numerals vertical, "E" closer than "N" to inner circle), *amber*	.95	.40
U483 1½¢ brown Washington, die 1 (letters broad, numerals vertical, "E" closer than "N" to inner circle), *blue*	1.60	.95
U484 1½¢ brown Washington, die 1 (letters broad, numerals vertical, "E" closer than "N" to inner circle), *manila*	6.50	3.00
W485 1½¢ brown Washington, *manila*	.85	.20
U486 1½¢ on 2¢ green Washington, ("G" has bar, ear indicated by 1 heavy line)	800.00	
U487 1½¢ on 2¢ green Washington, ("G" has bar, ear indicated by 1 heavy line), *amber*	1,000.00	

Issue		Un	U
1925			
U488	1½¢ on 1¢ green Franklin, (no wavy lines)	400.00	
U489	1½¢ on 1¢ green Franklin, (no wavy lines), *amber*	125.00	60.00
U490	1½¢ on 1¢ green Franklin, die 1, (wide "D" in "UNITED")	6.75	3.50
U491	1½¢ on 1¢ green Franklin, die 4, (sharp angle at back of bust), *amber*	8.00	2.25
U492	1½¢ on 1¢ green Franklin, die 2, (narrow "D" in "UNITED"), *oriental buff*	500.00	150.00
U493	1½¢ on 1¢ green Franklin, die 4, (sharp angle at back of bust), *blue*	125.00	65.00
U494	1½¢ on 1¢ green Franklin, die 1, (wide "D" in "UNITED"), *manila*	275.00	100.00
U495	1½¢ on 1¢ green Franklin, die 1, ("UNITED" nearer inner circle than outer circle)	.80	.25
U496	1½¢ on 1¢ green Franklin, die 1, ("UNITED" nearer inner circle than outer circle), *amber*	21.00	12.50
U497	1½¢ on 1¢ green Franklin, die 1, ("UNITED" nearer inner circle than outer circle), *oriental buff*	3.75	1.90
U498	1½¢ on 1¢ green Franklin, die 1, ("UNITED" nearer outer circle than inner circle), *blue*	1.60	.75
U499	1½¢ on 1¢, green Franklin, ("UNITED" nearer inner circle than outer circle), unglazed, *manila*	13.00	6.00
U500	1½¢ on 1¢, green Franklin, ("UNITED" nearer inner circle than outer circle), unglazed, *brown*	85.00	30.00
U501	1½¢ on 1¢, green Franklin, round, die 1 ("UNITED" nearer inner circle than outer circle), glazed, *brown*	85.00	30.00
U502	1½¢ on 2¢, carmine Washington, die 1 (letters broad, numerals vertical, "E" closer than "N" to inner circle)	300.00	—
U503	1½¢ on 2¢, carmine Washington, die 5 ("T" and "S" of CENTS close at bottom), *oriental buff*	300.00	—

Issue		Un	U
1920-1925			
U504	1½¢ on 2¢, carmine Washington, die 1 (letters broad, numerals vertical, "E" closer than "N" to inner circle), *blue*	300.00	—
U505	1½¢ on 1½¢, brown Washington, die 1 (letters broad, numerals vertical, "E" closer than "N" to inner circle), *blue*	500.00	
U506	1½¢ on 1½¢, brown Washington, die 8 (large head, clean letters, all "T"s long top strokes), *blue*	300.00	
U507	1½¢ on 1½¢, brown Washington, die 8 (large head, clean letters, all "T"s long top strokes), *blue*	2,250.00	
U508	1½¢ on 1¢ green Franklin, no wavy lines, *amber*	70.00	
U509	1½¢ on 1¢ green Franklin, horizontal oval, *amber*	16.00	10.00
U510	1½¢ on 1¢ green Franklin, oval, die 1, (wide "D" in "UNITED")	2.90	1.25
U511	1½¢ on 1¢ green Franklin, oval, die 1, (wide "D" in "UNITED"), *amber*	250.00	100.00
U512	1½¢ on 1¢ green Franklin, oval, die 1, (wide "D" in "UNITED"), *oriental buff*	9.00	4.00
U513	1½¢ on 1¢ green Franklin, oval, die 1, (wide "D" in "UNITED"), *blue*	6.50	4.00
U514	1½¢ on 1¢ green Franklin, oval, die 1, (wide "D" in "UNITED")	34.00	9.00
U515	1½¢ on 1¢ green Franklin, die 1, (wide "D" in "UNITED"), *manila*	.40	.20
U516	1½¢ on 1¢ green Franklin, die 4, ("UNITED" nearer to outer circle), *amber*	50.00	25.00
U517	1½¢ on 1¢ green Franklin, die 4, ("UNITED" nearer to inner circle), *oriental buff*	6.25	1.25
U518	1½¢ on 1¢ green Franklin, die 4, ("UNITED" nearer to outer circle), *blue*	5.50	1.25
U519	1½¢ on 1¢ green Franklin, die 4, ("UNITED" nearer to inner circle), *manila*	32.50	10.00
U520	1½¢ on 1¢ green Washington, die 1, (letters broad, numerals vertical, "E" closer than "N" to inner circle)	350.00	—
U521	1½¢ on 1¢ green Franklin, die 3, (knob of hair at back of neck)	4.75	3.50
U522	2¢ carmine Liberty Bell, die 1	1.10	.50
U523	1¢ olive green Mount Vernon	1.00	.80
U524	1½¢ chocolate Mount Vernon	2.00	1.50
U525	2¢ carmine Mount Vernon	.40	.20
U526	3¢ violet Mount Vernon	2.00	.35

Issue		Un	U
1926-1971			
U527	4¢ black Mount Vernon	16.50	*20.00*
U528	5¢ dark blue Mount Vernon	4.00	3.50
U529	6¢ orange Washington, die 7, both numerals slope to right	5.50	4.00
U530	6¢ orange Washington, die 7, both numerals slope to right, *amber*	11.00	10.00
U531	6¢ orange Washington, die 7, both numerals slope to right, *blue*	11.00	10.00
U532	1¢ green Franklin, die 1, (thick "I" in thick circle)	4.75	1.75
U533	2¢ carmine Washington, die 3, (thin "2" in thin circle, short "N" in UNITED, thin crossbar in "A" of STATES)	.75	.25
U534	3¢ dark violet Washington, die 4, (thin "3" in thin circle, short "N" in UNITED, thin crossbar in "A" of STATES)	.40	.20
U535	1½¢ brown Washington	4.75	3.50
U536	4¢ red violet Franklin, die 1 (thick "I" in thick circle)	.80	.20
U537	2¢ + 2¢ carmine Washington, die 1, (letters broad, numerals vertical, "E" closer than "N" to inner circle)	3.00	1.50
U538	2¢ + 2¢ carmine Washington, die 1, (thick "2" in thick circle)	.75	*1.25*
U539	3¢ + 1¢ purple, Washington, die 1, (thick "3" in thick circle)	14.00	11.00
U540	3¢ + 1¢ dark violet Washington, die 3, (thin "3" in thin circle)	.50	*1.00*
U541	1¼¢ turquoise Franklin	.75	.50
U542	2½¢ dull blue Washington	.85	.50
U543	4¢ brown Pony Express Rider	.60	.30
U544	5¢ dark blue Lincoln	.85	.20
U545	4¢ + 1¢ red violet Franklin	1.40	*1.25*
U546	5¢ maroon New York World's Fair	.60	.40
U547	1¼¢ brown Liberty Bell		.20
U548	1 4/10¢ brown Liberty Bell		.20
U548A	1 6/10¢ orange Liberty Bell		.20
U549	4¢ bright blue Old Ironsides	.75	.20
U550	5¢ bright purple Eagle	.75	.20
U551	6¢ light green Statue of Liberty, tagged	.70	.20
U552	4¢ + 2¢ bright blue Old Ironsides	3.25	2.00
U553	5¢ + 1¢ bright purple Eagle	3.00	2.75
U554	6¢ blue Herman Melville	.50	.20
U555	6¢ light blue Youth Conference	.75	.20
U556	1 7/10¢ deep lilac Liberty Bell		.20

Issue	Date	Un	U
U557 8¢ ultramarine Eagle	05/06/71	.40	.20
U561 6¢ + (2¢) light green Statue of Liberty	05/16/71	1.00	1.25
U562 6¢ + (2¢) light blue Youth Conference	05/16/71	2.00	2.50
U563 8¢ rose red Bowling	08/21/71	.70	.20
U564 8¢ Aging Conference	11/15/71	.50	.20
U565 8¢ ultramarine and rose red Transpo '72	05/02/72	.50	.20
U566 8¢ + 2¢ bright ultramarine Eagle	12/01/73	.40	1.25
U567 10¢ emerald Liberty Bell	12/05/73	.40	.20
U568 1⁸⁄₁₀¢ blue green Volunteer Yourself	08/23/74		.20
U569 10¢ Tennis Centenary	08/31/74	.65	.20
U571 10¢ Compass Rose	10/13/75	.30	.20
U572 13¢ Quilt Pattern	02/02/76	.35	.20
U573 13¢ Sheaf of Wheat	03/15/76	.35	.20
U574 13¢ Mortar and Pestle	06/30/76	.35	.20
U575 13¢ Tools	08/06/76	.35	.20
U576 13¢ Liberty Tree	11/08/75	.30	.20
U577 2¢ red Nonprofit Star and Pinwheel	09/10/76		.20
U578 2.1¢ yellow green Nonprofit	06/03/77		.20
U579 2.7¢ green Nonprofit	07/05/78		.20
U580 15¢ orange Eagle, A	05/22/78	.40	.20
U581 15¢ red Uncle Sam	06/03/78	.40	.20
U582 13¢ emerald bi-centennial	10/15/76	.35	.20
U583 13¢ Golf	04/07/77	.65	.20
U584 13¢ Energy Conservation	10/20/77	.40	.20
U585 13¢ Energy Development	10/20/77	.40	.20
U586 15¢ on 16¢ blue USA	07/28/78	.35	.20
U587 15¢ Auto Racing	10/02/78	.35	.20
U588 15¢ on 13¢ Liberty Tree	11/28/78	.35	.20
U589 3.1¢ ultramarine Nonprofit	05/18/79		.50
U590 3.5¢ purple Violins	06/23/80		.50
U591 5.9¢ brown nonprofit	02/17/82		.50
U592 (18¢) violet Eagle, B	03/15/81	.45	.25
U593 18¢ dark blue Star	04/02/81	.45	.25
U594 (20¢) brown Eagle, C	10/11/81	.45	.25
U595 15¢ Veterinary Medicine	07/24/79	.50	.20
U596 15¢ Summer Olympic Games	12/10/79	.60	.20
U597 15¢ blue and rose claret Highwheeler Bicycle	05/16/80	.40	.20
U598 15¢ America's Cup	09/15/80	.40	.20

Issue	Date	Un	U
U599 15¢ brown, green and yellow Honeybee	10/10/80	.35	.20
U600 18¢ red and blue Blind Veterans	08/13/81	.45	.20
U601 20¢ Capitol Dome	11/13/81	.45	.20
U602 20¢ dark blue, black and magenta Great Seal of US	06/15/82	.45	.20
U603 20¢ purple and black Purple Heart	08/06/82	.65	.20
U604 5.2¢ orange Nonprofit	03/21/83		.20
U605 20¢ red, blue and black Paralyzed Veterans	08/03/83	.45	.20
U606 20¢ Small Business	05/07/84	.50	.20
U607 22¢ deep green Eagle, D	02/01/85	.55	.30
U608 22¢ violet brown Bison	02/25/85	.55	.20
U609 6¢ nonprofit USS Constitution	05/03/85		.20
U610 8.5¢ nonprofit Mayflower	12/04/86		.20
U611 25¢ dark red and deep blue Stars	03/26/88	.60	.20
U612 8.4¢ nonprofit US Frigate Constellation	04/12/88		.20
U613 25¢ Snowflake	09/08/88	1.00	20.00
U614 25¢ dark red and deep blue Stars (Philatelic Mail)	03/10/89	.50	.25
U615 25¢ dark red and blue Stars (lined paper)	07/10/89	.50	.25
U616 25¢ dark red and bright blue, Love	09/22/89	.50	.75
U617 25¢ ultramarine Space hologram	12/03/89	.90	.60
U618 25¢ Football hologram	09/09/90	.90	.60
U619 29¢ ultramarine and rose Star	01/24/91	.60	.30
U620 11.1¢ Birds	05/03/91		.50
U621 29¢ light blue, maroon and bright rose, Love	05/09/91	.60	.60
U622 29¢ Magazine Industry	10/07/91	.60	.50
U623 29¢ ultramarine and rose Star	07/20/91	.60	.30
U624 29¢ Country Geese	11/08/91	.60	.60
U625 29¢ Space Shuttle, (type of 1989), die-cut	01/21/92	.90	.50
U626 29¢ Western Americana, die-cut	04/10/92	.60	.90
U627 29¢ Protect the Environment	04/22/92	.60	.30

Issue	Date	Un	U
U628 19.8¢ Bulk Rate star precanceled	05/19/92		.40
U629 29¢ Disabled Americans	07/22/92	.60	.30
U630 29¢ Kitten, die-cut	10/02/93	.90	1.00
U631 29¢ brown and black Football	09/17/94	.60	.90
U632 32¢ greenish blue and blue Liberty Bell, embossed	01/03/95	.65	.30
U633 (32¢) Old Glory, #6¾	1995	.75	.90
U634 (32¢) Old Glory, #10	1995	.75	.90
U635 (5¢) green and red brown Nonprofit	03/10/95		.50
U636 (10¢) Graphic Eagle	03/10/95		.20
U637 32¢ red, light blue, Spiral Heart	05/12/95	.65	.30
U638 32¢ greenish blue and blue Liberty Bell	05/16/95	.65	.30
U639 32¢ Space Shuttle, (type of 1989), die-cut	09/22/95	.65	.35
U640 32¢ Save Our Environment	04/20/96	.60	.30
U641 32¢ multicolored 1996 Paralympic Games	05/02/96	.60	.30
U642 33¢ yellow, blue and red Flag	01/11/99	.65	.30
U643 33¢ red and blue Flag	01/11/99	.65	.30
U644 33¢ Victorian, Love	01/28/99	.65	.30
U645 33¢ Lincoln	06/05/99	.65	.30
U646 34¢ blue gray and gray Federal Eagle, tagged	01/07/01	.65	.30
U647 34¢ Lovebirds, tagged	01/14/01	.65	.30
U648 34¢ Community Colleges, tagged	02/20/01	.65	.30
U649 37¢ red, blue and gray Ribbon Star	06/07/02	.75	.35
U650 (10¢) Presorted Graphic Eagle	08/08/02		.20
U651 37¢ Nuturing, Love	01/25/03	.75	.35
U652 $3.85 Jefferson Memorial	01/25/03	7.75	6.25
U653-U657 (See Premium Stamped Stationery and Cards)			
U658 $4.05 X-Planes	01/05/06	8.25	6.50
U659 36¢ Benjamin Franklin	01/09/06	.80	.40
U660 $4.60 Air Force One	05/06/07	9.25	7.00
U661 $16.25 Marine One	05/06/07	33.00	17.00
U662 41¢ Horses	05/12/07	.85	.40
U663 42¢ Elk	05/02/08	.85	.40
U664 $4.80 Mount Rushmore	05/12/08	9.75	7.00
U665 (See Premium Stamped Stationery and Cards)			

U634

U635

U636

U637

U639

U640

U641

U642

U643

U644

U645

U646

U647

U648

U649

U650

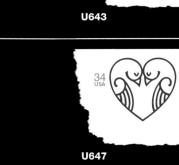

U651

U658

U659

U660

U661

U662

U663

U664

UC1

UC3

UC7

UC8

UC14

UC21

UC25

UC26

UC30

UC39

UC46

UC48

UC52

UC53

UC56

UC57

UC59

VISIT US ONLINE AT **THE POSTAL STORE**
AT **WWW.USPS.COM**
OR CALL **1 800 STAMP-24**

Issue	Date	Un	U
UC1 5¢ blue Airplane, die 1 (vertical rudder is not semi-circular)	01/12/29	3.50	2.00
1933 wmk., entire		750.00	750.00
1937 wmk., entire		—	2,500.00
Bi-colored border omitted, entire		1,300.00	
UC2 5¢ blue, die 2 (vertical rudder is semi-circular)	01/12/29	11.50	5.00
1929 wmk., entire		—	1,500.00
1933 wmk., entire		650.00	—
UC3 6¢ orange Airplane, die 2a ("6" is 6½mm wide)	07/01/34	1.50	.40
UC4 6¢ orange Airplane, die 2b ("6" is 6mm wide)	1942	3.00	2.00
UC5 6¢ orange, Airplane, die 2c ("6" is 5½mm wide)	1944	.75	.30
UC6 6¢ orange, Airplane, die 3 (vertical rudder leans forward)	1942	1.00	.35
a 6¢ orange, Airplane, blue, entire		3,500.00	2,400.00
UC7 8¢ olive green Airplane	09/26/32	12.00	3.50
UC8 6¢ on 2¢ carmine Washington, (letters broad, numerals vertical, "E" closer than "N" to inner circle)	1945	1.25	.65
UC9 6¢ on 2¢ Mount Vernon	1945	65.00	35.00
UC10 5¢ on 6¢ orange Airplane	1946	2.75	1.50
a Double surcharge	1946	75.00	
UC11 5¢ on 6¢ orange Airplane, die 2b ("6" is 6mm wide)	1946	9.00	5.50
UC12 5¢ on 6¢ orange Airplane	1946	.75	.50
a Double surcharge	1946	75.00	300.00
UC13 5¢ on 6¢ orange Airplane, die 3 (vertical rudder leans forward)	1946	.80	.60
a Double surcharge		75.00	
UC14 5¢ carmine DC-4, die 1 (end of wing on right is smooth curve)	09/25/46	.85	.25
UC15 5¢ carmine DC-4, die 2 (end of wing on right is a straight line)	1946	.85	.25
UC16 10¢ red, DC-4 2-line back inscription, entire, *pale blue*	04/29/47	8.50	10.00
a "Air Letter" on face, 4-line inscription on back		17.50	14.00
Die-cutting reversed		275.00	
UC17 5¢ carmine Postage Centenary	05/21/47	.50	.30
UC18 6¢ carmine DC-4, type I (6's lean right)	09/22/50	.40	.25
a Type II (6's upright)		.75	.25

Issue	Date	Un	U
UC19 6¢ on 5¢ carmine DC-4, die 1, (end of wing on right is smooth curve)	1951	.85	1.00
UC20 6¢ on 5¢ carmine DC-4, die 2, (end of wing on right is a straight line)	1951	.85	1.00
a 6¢ on 6¢ carmine, (error) entire		1,500.00	
b Double surcharge		975.00	—
UC21 6¢ on 5¢ carmine DC-4 die 1, (end of wing on right is smooth curve)	1952	27.50	17.50
UC22 6¢ on 5¢ carmine DC-4 die 2, (end of wing on right is a straight line)	08/29/52	4.25	2.50
a Double surcharge		200.00	
UC23 6¢ on 5¢ carmine Postage Centenary	1952	900.00	
UC25 6¢ red Eagle	05/02/56	.75	.50
UC26 7¢ blue DC-4, type of 1946	07/31/58	.65	.50
UC27 6¢ + 1¢ orange Airplane die 2a ("6" is 6½mm wide)	1958	325.00	250.00
UC28 6¢ + 1¢ orange DC-4, die 2b ("6" is 6mm wide)	1958	80.00	80.00
UC29 6¢ + 1¢ orange Airplane, die 2c ("6" is 5½mm wide)	1958	40.00	50.00
UC30 6¢ + 1¢ carmine DC-4, type I	1958	1.00	.50
UC31 6¢ + 1¢ red Eagle	1958	1.00	.50
UC32 10¢ blue and red Jet Airliner, *blue,* type II (back inscription in 2 lines)	05/1959	6.00	5.00
a Type I, entire		10.00	5.00
UC33 7¢ blue Jet Airliner, embossed	11/21/58	.60	.25
UC34 7¢ carmine Jet Airliner	08/18/60	.60	.25
UC35 11¢ red and blue Jet Airliner and Globe, *blue,* entire	06/16/61	2.75	3.50
a Red omitted		1,150.00	
Die-cutting reversed		35.00	
UC36 8¢ red Jet Airliner, embossed	11/17/62	.55	.20
UC37 8¢ red Jet Airliner in Triangle	01/07/65	.45	.20
a Tagged		3.75	.30
UC38 11¢ red and dark blue, John Kennedy, *blue,* entire	05/29/65	3.25	4.00
UC39 13¢ red and dark blue, John Kennedy, *blue,* entire	05/29/67	3.25	4.00
a Red omitted		750.00	

Issue	Date	Un	U
UC40 10¢ red Jet Airliner in Triangle, embossed	01/08/68	.50	.20
UC41 8¢ + 2¢ red Jet Airliner in Triangle	02/05/68	.65	.20
UC42 13¢ Human Rights, tagged, entire	12/03/68	8.00	5.00
Die-cutting reversed		75.00	
UC43 11¢ red and blue Jet Plane in Circle, embossed	05/06/71	.50	.90
UC44 15¢ gray, red, white and blue Birds in Flight	05/28/71	1.50	3.00
UC45 10¢ + (1¢) red Jet Airliner in Triangle, embossed	06/28/71	1.50	.20
UC46 15¢ red, white and blue Birds in Flight, tagged	02/10/73	1.00	.40
UC47 13¢ rose red Bird in Flight	12/01/73	.30	.20
UC48 18¢ red and blue USA, entire	01/04/74	1.00	2.00
UC49 18¢ red and blue USA, *blue,* entire, tagged	04/04/74	1.00	.40
UC50 22¢ red and blue USA, *blue,* entire, tagged	01/16/76	.95	1.50
UC51 22¢ blue USA, *blue,* entire, tagged	11/03/78	.90	.25
Die-cutting reversed		25.00	
UC52 22¢ Summer Olympic Games, *bluish,* entie tagged	12/05/79	1.50	.25
UC53 30¢ blue, red, and brown USA, Tour the United States, *blue,* entire, tagged	12/29/80	.85	1.50
a Red "30" omitted		70.00	
UC54 30¢ yellow, magenta, blue and black USA, Tour the United States, *blue,* entire, tagged	09/21/81	.65	1.00
Die-cutting reversed		20.00	
UC55 30¢ Made in USA, *blue,* entire, tagged	09/16/82	.80	2.75
UC56 30¢ World Communications Year, *blue,* entire, tagged	01/07/83	.90	3.00
Die-cutting reversed		25.00	
UC57 30¢ Olympic Games, *blue,* entire, tagged	10/14/83	.85	3.00
UC58 36¢ Landsat, *blue,* entire, tagged	02/14/85	.85	3.00
UC59 36¢ Tourism Week, blue, entire, tagged	05/21/85	.85	3.00

Issue		Date	Un	U
UC60	36¢ Mark Twain/ Halley's Comet, entire, tagged	12/04/85	1.00	4.00
UC61	39¢ Envelope entire, tagged	05/09/88	.95	2.25
UC62	39¢ Montgomery Blair/Lincoln, entire, tagged	11/20/89	.95	2.25
UC63	45¢ Eagle, blue, entire, tagged	05/17/91	.95	1.50
a	White paper		.95	1.50
UC64	50¢ Thaddeus Lowe, Balloonist, blue, entire, tagged	09/23/1995	1.25	2.25
UC65	60¢ Voyageurs Nat'l Park, Minnesota blue, entire, tagged	05/15/1999	1.25	2.25

Official Envelopes
Post Office Department
Numeral 9mm high

Issue		Date	Un	U
UO1	2¢ black, lemon	1873	24.00	10.00
UO2	3¢ black, lemon		16.00	6.50

Numeral 9½mm high

UO4	6¢ black, lemon	1873	26.00	16.00

Numeral 9¼mm high

UO5	2¢ black, lemon	1874	10.50	4.25
UO6	2¢ black		140.00	35.00
UO7	3¢ black, lemon		3.25	.85
UO8	3¢ black		1,500.00	1,200.00
UO9	3¢ black, amber		150.00	40.00
UO10	3¢ black, blue		45,000.00	
UO11	3¢ blue, blue	1875	45,000.00	

Numeral 10½mm high

UO12	6¢ black, lemon	1875	16.00	6.50
UO13	6¢ black		1,750.00	1,750.00

Postal Service

UO14	black	1877	7.00	4.50
UO15	black, amber		225.00	40.00
UO16	blue, amber		210.00	40.00
UO17	blue, blue		9.00	6.75

War Department

UO18	1¢ dark red Franklin	1873	700.00	300.00
UO19	2¢ dark red Jackson		1,000.00	400.00
UO20	3¢ dark red Washington		72.50	42.50
UO21	3¢ dark red Washington, amber		40,000.00	
UO22	3¢ dark red Washington, cream		800.00	300.00
UO23	6¢ dark red Lincoln		325.00	100.00
UO24	6¢ dark red Lincoln, cream		9,250.00	425.00
UO25	10¢ dark red Jefferson		17,500.00	2,250.00

Issue		Date	Un	U
UO26	12¢ dark red Clay	1873	175.00	50.00
UO27	15¢ dark red Webster		160.00	55.00
UO28	24¢ dark red Scott		175.00	50.00
UO29	30¢ dark red Hamilton		550.00	150.00
UO30	1¢ dark red Franklin		100.00	
UO34	3¢ vermilion Washington		100.00	40.00
UO35	3¢ vermilion Washington, amber		125.00	
UO36	3¢ vermilion Washington, cream		17.00	12.50
UO37	6¢ vermilion Lincoln		100.00	
UO39	10¢ vermilion Jefferson		200.00	
UO40	12¢ vermilion Clay		175.00	
UO41	15¢ vermilion Webster		250.00	
UO42	24¢ vermilion Scott		400.00	
UO43	30¢ vermilion Hamilton		475.00	
UO44	1¢ red Franklin	1875	190.00	85.00
UO47	2¢ red Jackson		140.00	—
UO48	2¢ red Jackson, amber		37.50	17.50
UO49	2¢ red Jackson, orange		70.00	17.50
UO51	3¢ red Washington		17.50	10.00
UO52	3¢ red Washington, amber		22.50	10.00
UO53	3¢ red Washington, cream		6.00	3.75
UO54	3¢ red Washington, blue		4.00	2.75
UO55	3¢ red Washington, fawn		6.50	2.75
UO56	6¢ red Lincoln		65.00	30.00
UO57	6¢ red Lincoln, amber		95.00	40.00
UO58	6¢ red Lincoln, cream		225.00	85.00
UO59	10¢ red Jefferson		250.00	80.00
UO60	10¢ red Jefferson, amber		800.00	
UO61	12¢ red		65.00	40.00
UO62	12¢ red, amber		775.00	
UO63	12¢ red, cream		700.00	
UO64	15¢ red		250.00	140.00
UO65	15¢ red, amber		925.00	
UO66	15¢ red, cream		775.00	
UO67	30¢ red		190.00	140.00
UO68	30¢ red, amber		925.00	
UO69	30¢ red, cream		950.00	

Postal Savings Envelopes

UO70	1¢ green	1911	77.50	25.00
UO71	1¢ green, oriental buff		200.00	75.00
UO72	2¢ carmine		13.50	4.00

Official Mail

UO73	20¢ blue Great Seal, embossed	01/12/1983	1.25	30.00
UO74	22¢ blue Great Seal, embossed	02/26/1985	.90	30.00
UO75	22¢ blue Great Seal	03/02/1987	1.25	35.00
UO76	(25¢) black and blue "E" Great Seal	03/22/1988	1.25	35.00

Issue		Date	Un	U
Official Mail continued				
UO77	25¢ black and blue Great Seal, embossed	04/11/1988	.80	25.00
UO78	25¢ black and blue Great Seal	1988	.90	35.00
UO79	45¢ black and blue Great Seal (stars illegible)	03/17/1990	1.25	—
UO80	65¢ black and blue Great Seal (stars illegible)	03/17/1990	1.75	—
UO81	45¢ black and blue Great Seal, (stars clear)	08/10/1990	1.25	100.00
UO82	65¢ black and blue Great Seal, (stars clear)	08/10/1990	1.60	150.00
UO83	(29¢) "F" black and blue Great Seal, watermarked	01/22/1991	1.25	35.00
UO84	29¢ black and blue Great Seal, watermarked	04/06/1991	.75	20.00
UO85	29¢ black and blue Great Seal, watermarked	04/17/1991	.70	20.00
UO86	52¢ blue and red Consular Service	07/10/1992	5.00	125.00
UO87	75¢ blue and red Consular Service	07/10/1992	10.00	125.00
UO88	32¢ blue and red Great Seal, embossed	05/09/1995	.80	20.00
UO89	33¢ blue and red Great Seal	02/22/1999	.70	20.00
UO90	34¢ blue and red Great Seal, type of 1995, tagged	02/27/2001	.85	20.00
UO91	37¢ blue and red Great Seal, type of 1995, tagged	08/02/2002	.90	—
UO92	39¢ blue and red Great Seal, type of 1995, tagged	01/09/2006	.95	—
UO93	41¢ blue and red Great Seal, type of 1995, tagged	05/12/07	1.00	.50
UO94	21¢ blue and red Great Seal, type of 1995, tagged	06/20/08	1.00	.50

UC63

UC64

UC65

UO1

UO16

UO20

UO73

UO84

UO88

UO89

UO90

UO91

UO92

UO93

UO94

UX5

UX6

UX11

UX14

UX16

UX18

UX25

UX27

UX28

UX37

UX43

UX44

UX45

UX46

UX48

UX49

UX50

UX56

Postal, Official, Stamped and Paid Reply Cards

Issue		Date	Un	U

Represented below is a listing of postal cards. Values are for entire cards. Color in italic is color of card. Cards preprinted with written address or message usually sell for much less.

Issue		Date	Un	U
UX1	1¢ brown Liberty, wmkd. (90 x 60mm)	05/1873	375.00	25.00
UX3	1¢ brown Liberty, wmkd. (53 x 36mm), *buff*	07/06/1873	80.00	2.50
UX4	1¢ black Liberty, wmkd., USPOD in monogram, *buff*	09/28/1875	3,500.00	350.00
UX5	1¢ black Liberty, *buff*	09/30/1875	82.50	.45
UX6	2¢ blue Liberty, *buff*	12/01/1879	35.00	25.00
a	2¢ dark blue, *buff*		35.00	25.00
UX7	1¢ black Liberty, inscribed "Nothing But The Address", *buff*	10/17/1881	70.00	.40
a	23 teeth below "One Cent"		1,350.00	65.00
b	Printed on both sides		*1,000.00*	*750.00*
UX8	1¢ brown Jefferson, large "one-cent" wreath, *buff*	08/24/1885	55.00	1.25
c	1¢ dark chocolate, *buff*		300.00	40.00
UX9	1¢ black Jefferson, *buff*	12/01/1886	25.00	.55
a	1¢ black, *dark buff*		75.00	5.00
UX10	1¢ black Grant, *buff*	12/16/1891	45.00	1.50
UX11	1¢ blue Grant, *grayish white*	12/16/1891	22.50	3.00
UX12	1¢ black Jefferson, small wreath, *buff*	01/02/1894	45.00	.65
UX13	2¢ blue Liberty, *cream*	01/25/1897	225.00	85.00
UX14	1¢ black Jefferson, large wreath, *buff*	12/01/1897	40.00	.45
UX15	1¢ black John Adams, *buff*	03/31/1898	47.50	15.00
UX16	2¢ black Liberty, *buff*	1898	15.00	17.00
UX17	1¢ black McKinley, *buff*	1902	9,000.00	
UX18	1¢ black McKinley, (in oval), *buff*	1902	17.50	.35
UX19	1¢ black McKinley, (triangles in top corners), *buff*	1907	45.00	.50
UX20	1¢ black McKinley, (correspondence space at left), *buff*	01/02/1908	57.50	4.25
UX21	1¢ blue McKinley, (shaded background), *bluish*	1910	105.00	13.00
a	1¢ bronze blue, *bluish*		400.00	100.00

Issue		Date	Un	U
UX22	1¢ blue McKinley, (white background), *bluish*	04/13/1910	20.00	.35
UX23	1¢ red Lincoln, *cream*	01/21/1911	10.00	5.50
UX24	1¢ red McKinley, *cream*	08/10/1911	11.00	.35
UX25	2¢ red Grant, *cream*	10/27/1911	1.50	*20.00*
UX26	1¢ green Lincoln, *cream*	07/29/1913	13.00	7.50
UX27	1¢ green Jefferson, die I (end of ponytail small) *buff*	06/04/1914	.25	.25
a	1¢ green, *cream*		5.00	.65
UX27C	1¢ green Jefferson, die I	1916	*4,000.00*	250.00
UX27D	1¢ dark green Jefferson, die II (end of ponytail large and rounded)	12/22/1916	*24,000.00*	160.00
UX28	1¢ green Lincoln, *cream*	03/14/1917	.60	.30
a	1¢ green, *dark buff*		1.50	.60
UX29	2¢ red Jefferson, die I (coarse impression), *buff*	10/22/1917	42.50	2.10
a	2¢ lake, *cream*		50.00	4.00
c	2¢ vermilion, *buff*		925.00	75.00
UX30	2¢ red Jefferson, die II (fine lines), *cream*	01/23/1918	30.00	1.60
	Surcharged in one line by canceling machine			
UX31	1¢ on 2¢ red Jefferson, die II (fine lines), *cream*	01/23/1918	*3,750.00*	*4,250.00*
	Surcharged in two lines by canceling machine.			
UX32	1¢ on 2¢ red Jefferson, die I (coarse impression), *buff*	1920	52.50	12.50
a	1¢ on 2¢ vermilion, *buff*		150.00	60.00
b	Double surcharge		150.00	100.00
UX33	1¢ on 2¢ red Jefferson, die I (coarse impression), *cream*	1920	13.00	2.00
a	Inverted surcharge		150.00	*200.00*
b	Double surcharge		150.00	*175.00*
	Surcharged in two lines by press printing			
UX34	1¢ on 2¢ red Jefferson, die I (coarse impression), *buff*	1920	800.00	52.50
UX35	1¢ on 2¢ red Jefferson, *cream*	1920	225.00	37.50
UX36	1¢ on 2¢ red Grant, *cream*	1920		57,500.00
UX37	3¢ red McKinley, *buff*	02/01/1926	4.50	15.00
a	3¢ red, *yellow*		6.00	15.00
UX38	2¢ carmine rose Franklin, *buff*	11/16/1951	.35	.25
a	Double impression		500.00	
	Surcharged by canceling machine in light green			

Issue		Date	Un	U
UX39	2¢ on 1¢ green Jefferson, *buff*	01/01/1952	.50	.35
a	Surcharge vertical		8.00	*10.00*
b	Double surcharge		20.00	*25.00*
UX40	2¢ on 1¢ green Lincoln, *cream*	03/22/1952	.65	.45
a	Surcharge vertical		7.00	5.50
	Surcharged typographically in dark green			
UX41	2¢ on 1¢ green Jefferson, *buff*	1952	4.50	2.00
a	Inverted surcharge lower left		60.00	125.00
UX42	2¢ on 1¢ green Lincoln, *cream*	1952	5.00	2.50
b	Surcharged on back		300.00	
UX43	2¢ carmine Lincoln, *buff*	07/31/1952	.30	1.00
UX44	2¢ deep carmine and dark violet blue FIPEX, *buff*	05/04/1956	.25	1.00
a	Dark violet blue omitted		525.00	600.00
UX45	4¢ deep red and ultramarine Statue of Liberty, *buff*	11/16/1956	1.50	*90.00*
UX46	3¢ purple Statue of Liberty, *buff*	08/01/1958	.50	.20
a	"N GOD WE TRUST"		12.00	*25.00*
UX47	2¢ + 1¢ carmine rose Franklin, *buff*	1958	235.00	700.00
UX48	4¢ red violet Lincoln	11/19/1962	.50	.20
UX49	7¢ blue and red World Vacationland	08/30/1963	4.00	*65.00*
UX50	4¢ red and blue U.S. Customs	02/22/1964	.50	*1.00*
a	Blue omitted		650.00	
UX51	4¢ dull blue and red Social Security	09/26/1964	.40	*1.00*
b	Blue omitted		*650.00*	*650.00*
UX52	4¢ blue & red Coast Guard	08/04/1965	.30	*1.00*
UX53	4¢ bright blue and black Bureau of the Census	10/21/1965	.30	*1.00*
UX54	8¢ blue and red World Vacationland	12/04/1967	4.00	*65.00*
UX55	5¢ emerald Lincoln	01/04/1968	.30	*.60*
UX56	5¢ rose and red green Women Marines	07/26/1968	.35	*1.00*
UX57	5¢ blue, yellow, red and black Weather Services	09/01/1970	.30	*1.00*
a	Yellow, black omitted		*1,000.00*	*900.00*
b	Blue omitted		*1,000.00*	*5,000.00*
c	Black omitted		*1,000.00*	*850.00*

Issue	Date	Un	U
UX58 6¢ brown Paul Revere	05/15/1971	.30	1.00
a Double impression		300.00	
UX59 10¢ blue and red World Vacationland	06/10/1971	4.50	65.00
UX60 6¢ blue and multicolored America's Hospitals	09/16/71	.30	1.00
a Blue, yellow omitted		1,000.00	
UX61 6¢ black USF Constellation	06/29/72	.85	10.00
a Address side blank		300.00	
UX62 6¢ black Gloucester, MA, buff	06/29/72	.40	10.00
UX63 6¢ black Monument Valley, buff	06/29/72	.40	6.00
UX64 6¢ blue John Hanson	09/01/72	.50	1.00
UX65 6¢ magenta Liberty	09/14/73	.25	1.00
UX66 8¢ orange Samuel Adams	12/16/73	.50	1.00
UX67 12¢ multicolored Visit USA/ Ship's Figurehead	01/04/74	.35	50.00
UX68 7¢ emerald Charles Thomson	09/14/75	.30	10.00
UX69 9¢ yellow brown John Witherspoon	11/10/75	.30	1.00
UX70 9¢ blue Caesar Rodney	07/01/76	.30	1.00
Historic Preservation (UX71, UX73)			
UX71 9¢ multicolored Federal Court House	07/20/77	.25	1.00
UX72 9¢ green Nathan Hale	10/14/77	.25	1.00
UX73 10¢ Cincinnati Music Hall	05/12/78	.30	1.00
UX74 (10¢) brown orange John Hancock	05/19/78	.30	1.00
UX75 10¢ John Hancock	06/20/78	.30	1.00
UX76 14¢ Coast Guard Eagle	08/04/78	.40	35.00
UX77 10¢ Molly Pitcher	09/08/78	.30	1.60
UX78 10¢ George Rogers Clark	02/23/79	.30	1.50
UX79 10¢ Casimir Pulaski	11/11/79	.30	1.50
UX80 10¢ Olympic Summer Games	09/17/80	.60	1.50
Historic Preservation (UX81, UX83)			
UX81 10¢ Iolani Palace	10/01/79	.30	1.50
UX82 14¢ Olympic Winter Games	01/15/80	.60	25.00
UX83 10¢ Salt Lake Temple	04/05/80	.25	1.50
UX84 10¢ Landing of Rochambeau	07/11/80	.25	1.50
UX85 10¢ Battle of Kings Mountain	10/07/80	.25	1.50

Issue	Date	Un	U
UX86 19¢ Drake's Golden Hinde	11/21/80	.70	35.00
UX87 10¢ Battle of Cowpens	01/07/81	.25	17.50
UX88 (12¢) violet Eagle	03/15/81	.30	.65
UX89 12¢ light blue Isaiah Thomas	05/05/81	.30	.75
UX90 12¢ Nathanael Greene	09/08/81	.30	22.50
UX91 12¢ Lewis and Clark	09/23/81	.30	30.00
UX92 13¢ buff Robert Morris	01/11/81	.30	.60
UX93 13¢ buff Robert Morris	11/10/81	.30	.60
UX94 13¢ "Swamp Fox" Francis Marion	04/03/82	.30	1.00
UX95 13¢ LaSalle Claims Louisiana	04/07/82	.30	1.00
Historic Preservation (UX96, UX97)			
UX96 13¢ Academy of Music	06/18/82	.30	1.00
UX97 13¢ Old Post Office, St. Louis, Missouri	10/14/82	.30	1.00
UX98 13¢ Landing of Ogelthorpe	02/12/83	.30	1.00
UX99 13¢ Old Post Office, Washington, DC	04/19/83	.30	1.00
UX100 13¢ Olympic Yachting	08/05/83	.30	1.00
UX101 13¢ Ark and Dove, Maryland	03/25/84	.30	1.00
UX102 13¢ Olympic Torch	04/30/84	.30	1.25
UX103 13¢ Frederic Baraga	06/29/84	.30	1.00
UX104 13¢ Dominguez Adobe	09/16/84	.30	1.00
UX105 (14¢) pale green Charles Carroll	02/01/85	.45	.65
UX106 14¢ green Charles Carroll	03/06/85	.45	.55
UX107 25¢ Clipper Flying Cloud	02/27/85	.70	22.50
UX108 14¢ bright apple green George Wythe	06/20/85	.30	.75
UX109 14¢ Settlement of Connecticut	04/18/86	.30	1.50
UX110 14¢ Stamp Collecting	05/23/86	.30	1.25
UX111 14¢ Francis Vigo	05/24/86	.30	1.25
UX112 14¢ Settling of Rhode Island	06/26/86	.30	1.50
UX113 14¢ Wisconsin Territory	07/03/86	.30	1.00
UX114 14¢ National Guard	12/12/86	.30	1.25
UX115 14¢ Self-Scouring Plow	05/22/87	.30	1.25
UX116 14¢ Constitutional Convention	05/25/87	.30	.75

Issue	Date	Un	U
UX117 14¢ Stars and Stripes	06/14/87	.30	.60
UX118 14¢ Take Pride in America	09/22/87	.30	1.25
Historic Preservation (UX119, UX121)			
UX119 14¢ Timberline Lodge	09/28/87	.30	1.25
UX120 15¢ Bison and Prairie	03/28/88	.30	.60
UX121 15¢ Blair House	05/04/88	.30	1.00
UX122 28¢ Yorkshire	06/29/88	.60	20.00
UX123 15¢ Iowa Territory	07/02/88	.30	1.00
UX124 15¢ Settling of Ohio, Northwest Territory	07/15/88	.30	1.00
Historic Preservation (UX125, UX128)			
UX125 15¢ Hearst Castle	09/20/88	.30	1.00
UX126 15¢ The Federalist Papers	10/27/88	.30	1.00
UX127 15¢ Hawk and Desert	01/13/89	.30	1.00
UX128 15¢ Healy Hall, Georgetown University	01/23/89	.30	1.00
UX129 15¢ America the Beautiful, Great Blue Heron	03/17/89	.30	1.00
UX130 15¢ Settling of Oklahoma	04/22/89	.30	1.00
UX131 21¢ America the Beautiful, Canadian Geese	05/05/89	.40	20.00
UX132 15¢ America the Beautiful, Seagull and Seashore	06/17/89	.30	1.00
UX133 15¢ America the Beautiful, Deer and Waterfall	08/26/89	.30	1.00
Historic Preservation (UX134)			
UX134 15¢ Hull House, Chicago	09/16/89	.30	1.00
UX135 15¢ America the Beautiful Independence Hall, PA	09/25/89	.30	1.00
UX136 15¢ America the Beautiful, Inner Harbor, Baltimore	10/07/89	.30	1.00
UX137 15¢ America the Beautiful, Beautiful 59th St. Bridge, NY	11/08/89	.30	1.00
UX138 15¢ America the Beautiful, Capitol, Washington DC	11/26/89	.30	1.00
#UX139-UX142 issued in sheets of 4 plus 2 inscribed labels, rouletted 9½ on 2 or 3 sides			
UX139 15¢ (UX135)	12/01/89	3.25	4.00
UX140 15¢ (UX136)	12/01/89	3.25	4.00
UX141 15¢ (UX137)	12/01/89	3.25	4.00
UX142 15¢ (UX138)	12/01/89	3.25	4.00
a Sheet of 4, #UX139-UX142		14.00	
UX143 15¢ The White House	11/30/89	1.50	2.50
UX144 15¢ Jefferson Memorial	12/02/89	1.50	2.00

UX70

UX79

UX81

UX83

UX94

UX109

UX112

UX113

UX115

UX116

UX118

UX119

UX131

UX143

UX144

UX143 (picture side)

UX144 (picture side)

UX174   UX175   UX176   UX177

UX198   UX199   UX219A   UX220

UX241   UX262   UX263   UX280

UX282   UX283   UX290   UX292

UX298   UX299   UX301   UX302

VISIT US ONLINE AT *THE POSTAL STORE*
AT *WWW.USPS.COM*
OR CALL *1 800 STAMP-24*

Issue	Date	Un	U
UX145 15¢ Rittenhouse Paper Mill, Germantown, PA	03/13/90	.30	1.00
UX146 15¢ World Literacy Year	03/22/90	.30	.90
UX147 15¢ George Caleb Bingham	05/04/90	1.50	2.50
Historic Preservation (UX148, UX150-UX152)			
UX148 15¢ Isaac Royall House	06/16/90	.30	1.00
UX149 Unassigned			
UX150 15¢ Stanford University	09/30/90	.30	1.00
UX151 15¢ Constitution Hall	10/11/90	1.50	2.00
UX152 15¢ Chicago Orchestra Hall	10/19/90	.30	1.00
UX153 19¢ Flag	01/24/91	.40	.75
Historic Preservation (UX154, UX155, UX157)			
UX154 19¢ Carnegie Hall	04/01/91	.40	1.00
UX155 19¢ Old Red, UT-Galveston	06/14/91	.40	1.00
UX156 19¢ Bill of Rights	09/25/91	.40	.90
UX157 19¢ Notre Dame	10/15/91	.40	1.00
UX158 30¢ Niagara Falls	08/21/90	.75	13.00
Historic Preservation (UX159-UX162)			
UX159 19¢ The Old Mill	10/29/91	.40	1.00
UX160 19¢ Wadsworth Atheneum	01/16/92	.40	1.00
UX161 19¢ Cobb Hall	01/23/92	.40	1.00
UX162 19¢ Waller Hall	02/01/92	.40	1.00
UX163 19¢ America's Cup	05/06/92	1.75	3.00
UX164 19¢ Columbia River Gorge	05/09/92	.40	1.00

Issue	Date	Un	U
Historic Preservation (UX165-UX172)			
UX165 19¢ Ellis Island	05/11/92	.40	1.00
UX166 19¢ National Cathedral	01/06/93	.40	1.00
UX167 19¢ Wren Building	02/08/93	.40	1.00
UX168 19¢ Holocaust Memorial	03/23/93	1.75	3.00
UX169 19¢ Fort Recovery	06/13/93	.40	.90
UX170 19¢ Playmakers Theatre	09/14/93	.40	1.00
UX171 19¢ O'Kane Hall	09/17/93	.40	.90
UX172 19¢ Beecher Hall	10/09/93	.40	.90
UX173 19¢ Massachusetts Hall	10/14/93	.40	.90
UX174 19¢ Lincoln's Home	02/12/94	.40	.90
Historic Preservation (UX175-UX177)			
UX175 19¢ Wittenberg University	03/11/94	.40	.90
UX176 19¢ Canyon de Chelly	08/11/94	.40	1.00
UX177 19¢ St. Louis Union Station	09/03/94	.40	1.00
UX178-UX197 (See Premium Stamped Cards)			
Scenic America (UX198, UX199)			
UX198 20¢ Red Barn	01/03/95	.40	.60
UX199 20¢ Old Glory	1995	3.25	2.50
UX200-UX219 (See Premium Stamped Cards)			
UX219A 50¢ Soaring Eagle	08/24/95	1.25	9.00
UX220 20¢ American Clipper Ships	09/03/95	.40	.75
UX221-UX240 (See Premium Stamped Cards)			
Scenic America			
UX241 20¢ Winter Scene		.40	.40
UX242-UX261 (See Premium Stamped Cards)			

Issue	Date	Un	U
Historic Preservation (UX262, UX263)			
UX262 20¢ St. John's College	06/01/96	.50	.75
UX263 20¢ Princeton University	09/20/96	.50	.75
UX264-UX279 (See Premium Stamped Cards)			
Historic Preservation (UX280, UX284)			
UX280 20¢ City College of New York	05/07/97	.50	.75
UX281 20¢ Bugs Bunny	05/22/97	1.25	2.00
UX282 20¢ Pacific 97 Golden Gate Bridge in Daylight	06/02/97	.40	.80
UX283 50¢ Pacific 97 Golden Gate Bridge at Sunset	06/03/97	1.10	5.00
UX284 20¢ Fort McHenry	09/07/97	.40	.75
UX285-UX289 (See Premium Stamped Cards)			
Historic Preservation (UX290, UX292)			
UX290 20¢ University of Mississippi	04/20/98	.50	.75
UX291 (See Premium Stamped Cards)			
UX292 20¢ Girard College	05/01/98	.50	.75
UX293-UX297 (See Premium Stamped Cards)			
Historic Preservation (UX298, UX299, UX301, UX302)			
UX298 20¢ Northeastern University	10/03/98	.50	.75
UX299 20¢ Brandeis University	10/17/98	.50	.75
UX300 (See Premium Stamped Cards)			
Historic Preservation (UX301-UX303, UX305)			
UX301 20¢ University of Wisconsin-Madison	02/05/99	.50	.50
UX302 20¢ Washington and Lee University	02/11/99	.50	.50

The Art of Disney: Magic Print Set & Stamped Cards

Discover the magic of the dreams within your heart! This beautiful print set contains four 8" x 10" prints ready for framing along with its matching stamp.

Print Set (four different designs)
Item #569788 $14.95

Booklet of 20 stamped cards*
(four different designs)
Item #569766 $12.95

Additional postage required for mailing.

Disney Materials © Disney

To order call 1 800 STAMP-24
or visit us on-line at www.usps.com

Issue	Date	Un	U
Historic Preservation (UX303, UX305)			
UX303 20¢ Redwood Library & Athenæum	03/11/99	.50	.50
UX304 (See Premium Stamped Cards)			
UX305 20¢ Mount Vernon	05/14/99	.50	*.50*
Scenic America			
UX306 20¢ Block Island Lighthouse	07/24/99	.40	*.50*
UX307-UX311 (See Premium Stamped Cards)			
Historic Preservation (UX312, UX313, UX316)			
UX312 20¢ Univ. of Utah	02/28/2000	.40	*.50*
UX313 20¢ Ryman Auditorium	03/18/2000	.40	*.50*
UX314-UX315 (See Premium Stamped Cards)			
UX316 20¢ Middlebury College	05/19/2000	.40	*.50*
UX317-UX360 (See Premium Stamped Cards)			

Issue	Date	Un	U
Historic Preservation (UX361-UX364)			
UX361 20¢ Yale University	03/30/2001	.40	.60
UX362 20¢ Univ. of South Carolina	04/26/2001	.40	*.75*
UX363 20¢ Northwestern University	04/28/2001	.40	*.75*
UX364 20¢ University of Portland	05/01/2001	.40	*.65*
UX365-UX374 (See Premium Stamped Cards)			
Scenic America (UX375, UX381)			
UX375 21¢ White Barn	09/20/2001	.45	.45
UX376-UX380 (See Premium Stamped Cards)			
UX381 23¢ Carlsbad Caverns National Park	06/07/2002	.50	.50
UX382-UX399 (See Premium Stamped Cards)			
Historic Preservation			
UX400 23¢ Ohio University	10/10/2003	.50	.50
UX401-UX404 (See Premium Stamped Cards)			

Issue	Date	Un	U
Historic Preservation (UX405, UX406, UX449, UX533)			
UX405 23¢ Columbia Univ.	03/25/2004	.50	.50
UX406 23¢ Harriton House	06/10/2004	.50	.50
UX407-UX448 (See Premium Stamped Cards)			
UX449 24¢ Pikes Peak	01/09/2006	.55	.55
UX450-UX487 (See Premium Stamped Cards)			
UX488 26¢ Pineapple	05/12/2007	.60	.60
UX489-UX532 (See Premium Stamped Cards)			
UX533 27¢ Mount St. Mary's University	04/26/2008	.60	.60
UX534 27¢ Corinthian Capital	05/12/2008	.60	.60
UX535-UX548 (See Premium Stamped Cards)			

NATURE OF AMERICA: KELP FOREST

*T*he 2009 Nature of America stamp pane—eleventh in an educational series that focuses on the beauty and complexity of major plant and animal communities in the United States—features a kelp forest in the Monterey Bay National Marine Sanctuary off the central California coast. This federally protected area encompassing 5,322 square miles of ocean protects one of the most diverse marine ecosystems in the world. A kelp forest is a remarkable undersea ecosystem dominated by very large marine algae more commonly known as seaweeds or kelp. Kelp forests thrive in shallow, cool coastal areas where upwelling—a process that brings nutrient-rich waters from the deep sea to the coast—occurs. These highly productive coastal waters sustain hundreds of species of marine algae and animals that make their home in the kelp forest. Along California's central coast, intense upwelling and moderate conditions combine to support an incredible diversity of marine life. Small creatures such as snails and crabs climb on rocks or up blades of giant kelp where sea slugs cling, as colorful species of rockfish swim past. Several kinds of perch, a striped treefish, a bright yellow señorita, and a school of anchovies are watched by a harbor seal and blue shark cruising by. At the surface, pelicans, gulls, and cormorants swoop and dive and feed on fish while a California sea lion and a southern sea otter find food and shelter among the kelp.

UX303   UX305   UX306

UX312   UX313   UX316   UX361   UX362

UX363   UX364   UX375   UX381   UX400

UX405   UX406   UX449   UX488

UX533   UX534

VISIT US ONLINE AT *THE POSTAL STORE*
AT *WWW.USPS.COM*
OR CALL *1 800 STAMP-24*

U655   U657   U665

UX178   UX200   UX221

UX242

Civil Rights Pioneers
Cultural Diary Page and Souvenir Sheet

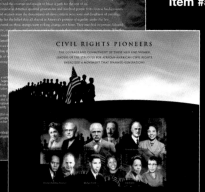

The U.S. Postal Service honors
12 leaders in the struggle for African-
American civil rights with this Cultural
Diary Page. Two pages and souvenir
sheet of six stamps.

Item #573976 $8.95

To order this item
call **1 800 STAMP-24**
or visit us on-line at
www.usps.com

Premium Stamped Stationery

Issue		Date	Un	U
Art of Disney: Friendship (U653-U657)				
U653	37¢ Goofy, Mickey Mouse, Donald Duck	06/23/2004	2.50	2.10
U654	37¢ Bambi, Thumper	06/23/2004	2.50	2.10
U655	37¢ Mufasa, Simba	06/23/2004	2.50	2.10
U656	37¢ Jiminy Cricket, Pinocchio	06/23/2004	2.50	2.10
Garden Bouquet				
U657	37¢ White Lilacs & Pink Roses	03/03/2005	2.50	2.50
U665	42¢ Sunflower	08/15/2008	3.00	3.00

Premium Stamped Cards

Issue		Date	Un	U
Legends of the West (UX178-UX197)				
UX178	19¢ Home on the Range		1.10	*3.00*
UX179	19¢ Buffalo Bill		1.10	*3.00*
UX180	19¢ Jim Bridger		1.10	*3.00*
UX181	19¢ Annie Oakley		1.10	*3.00*
UX182	19¢ Native American Culture		1.10	*3.00*
UX183	19¢ Chief Joseph		1.10	*3.00*
UX184	19¢ Bill Pickett (revised)		1.10	*3.00*
UX185	19¢ Bat Masterson		1.10	*3.00*
UX186	19¢ John Fremont		1.10	*3.00*
UX187	19¢ Wyatt Earp		1.10	*3.00*
UX188	19¢ Nellie Cashman		1.10	*3.00*
UX189	19¢ Charles Goodnight		1.10	*3.00*
UX190	19¢ Geronimo		1.10	*3.00*
UX191	19¢ Kit Carson		1.10	*3.00*
UX192	19¢ Wild Bill Hickok		1.10	*3.00*
UX193	19¢ Western Wildlife		1.10	*3.00*
UX194	19¢ Jim Beckwourth		1.10	*3.00*
UX195	19¢ Bill Tilghman		1.10	*3.00*
UX196	19¢ Sacagawea		1.10	*3.00*
UX197	19¢ Overland Mail		1.10	*3.00*
a	Pack of 20	10/18/94	22.00	
Civil War (UX200-UX219)				
UX200	20¢ Monitor and Virginia		1.75	*3.00*
UX201	20¢ Robert E. Lee		1.75	*3.00*
UX202	20¢ Clara Barton		1.75	*3.00*
UX203	20¢ Ulysses S. Grant		1.75	*3.00*
UX204	20¢ Battle of Shiloh		1.75	*3.00*
UX205	20¢ Jefferson Davis		1.75	*3.00*
UX206	20¢ David Farragut		1.75	*3.00*
UX207	20¢ Frederick Douglas		1.75	*3.00*
UX208	20¢ Raphael Semmes		1.75	*3.00*
UX209	20¢ Abraham Lincoln		1.75	*3.00*
UX210	20¢ Harriet Tubman		1.75	*3.00*
UX211	20¢ Stand Watie		1.75	*3.00*
UX212	20¢ Joseph E. Johnson		1.75	*3.00*
UX213	20¢ Winfield Hancock		1.75	*3.00*
UX214	20¢ Mary Chesnut		1.75	*3.00*
UX215	20¢ Battle of Chancellorsville		1.75	*3.00*
UX216	20¢ William T. Sherman		1.75	*3.00*
UX217	20¢ Phoebe Pember		1.75	*3.00*
UX218	20¢ Stonewall Jackson		1.75	*3.00*
UX219	20¢ Battle of Gettysburg		1.75	*3.00*
a	Pack of 20	06/29/95	35.00	

Issue		Date	Un	U
Comic Strip Characters (UX221-UX240)				
UX221	20¢ The Yellow Kid		2.50	*3.00*
UX222	20¢ Katzenjammer Kids		2.50	*3.00*
UX223	20¢ Little Nemo in Slumberland		2.50	*3.00*
UX224	20¢ Bringing Up Father		2.50	*3.00*
UX225	20¢ Krazy Kat		2.50	*3.00*
UX226	20¢ Rube Goldberg's Inventions		2.50	*3.00*
UX227	20¢ Toonerville Folks		2.50	*3.00*
UX228	20¢ Gasoline Alley		2.50	*3.00*
UX229	20¢ Barney Google		2.50	*3.00*
UX230	20¢ Little Orphan Annie		2.50	*3.00*
UX231	20¢ Popeye		2.50	*3.00*
UX232	20¢ Blondie		2.50	*3.00*
UX233	20¢ Dick Tracey		2.50	*3.00*
UX234	20¢ Alley Oop		2.50	*3.00*
UX235	20¢ Nancy		2.50	*3.00*
UX236	20¢ Flash Gordan		2.50	*3.00*
UX237	20¢ Li'l Abner		2.50	*3.00*
UX238	20¢ Terry and the Pirates		2.50	*3.00*
UX239	20¢ Prince Valiant		2.50	*3.00*
UX240	20¢ Brenda Starr Reporter		2.50	*3.00*
a	Pack of 20	10/01/95	50.00	
Olympic Games (UX242-UX261)				
UX242	20¢ Men's Cycling		2.75	*3.00*
UX243	20¢ Women's Diving		2.75	*3.00*
UX244	20¢ Women's Running		2.75	*3.00*
UX245	20¢ Women's Canoeing		2.75	*3.00*
UX246	20¢ Decathlon		2.75	*3.00*
UX247	20¢ Women's Soccer		2.75	*3.00*
UX248	20¢ Men's Shot Put		2.75	*3.00*
UX249	20¢ Women's Sailboarding		2.75	*3.00*
UX250	20¢ Women's Gymnastics		2.75	*3.00*
UX251	20¢ Freestyle Wrestling		2.75	*3.00*
UX252	20¢ Women's Softball		2.75	*3.00*
UX253	20¢ Women's Swimming		2.75	*3.00*
UX254	20¢ Men's Sprints		2.75	*3.00*
UX255	20¢ Men's Rowing		2.75	*3.00*
UX256	20¢ Beach Volleyball		2.75	*3.00*
UX257	20¢ Men's Basketball		2.75	*3.00*
UX258	20¢ Equestrian		2.75	*3.00*
UX259	20¢ Men's Gymnastics		2.75	*3.00*
UX260	20¢ Men's Swimming		2.75	*3.00*
UX261	20¢ Men's Hurdles		2.75	*3.00*
a	Pack of 20	05/02/96	55.00	

VISIT US ONLINE AT *THE POSTAL STORE*

AT *WWW.USPS.COM*

OR CALL *1 800 STAMP-24*

Issue	Date	Un	U
Endangered Species (UX264-UX278)			
UX264 20¢ Florida Panther		3.50	1.75
UX265 20¢ Black-footed Ferret		3.50	1.75
UX266 20¢ American Crocodile		3.50	1.75
UX267 20¢ Piping Plover		3.50	1.75
UX268 20¢ Gila Trout		3.50	1.75
UX269 20¢ Florida Manatee		3.50	1.75
UX270 20¢ Schaus Swallowtail Butterfly		3.50	1.75
UX271 20¢ Woodland Caribou		3.50	1.75
UX272 20¢ Thick-billed Parrot		3.50	1.75
UX273 20¢ San Francisco Garter Snake		3.50	1.75
UX274 20¢ Ocelot		3.50	1.75
UX275 20¢ Wyoming Toad		3.50	1.75
UX276 20¢ California Condor		3.50	1.75
UX277 20¢ Hawaiian Monk Seal		3.50	1.75
UX278 20¢ Brown Pelican		3.50	1.75
a Pack of 20	10/02/1996	55.00	
UX279 20¢ Love Swans	02/04/1997	.80	1.10
Classic Movie Monsters (UX285-UX289)			
UX285 20¢ Lon Chaney as Phantom of the Opera		1.50	1.40
UX286 20¢ Bela Lugosi as Dracula		1.50	1.40
UX287 20¢ Boris Karloff as Frankenstein's Monster		1.50	1.40
UX288 20¢ Boris Karloff as The Mummy		1.50	1.40
UX289 20¢ Lon Chaney, Jr. as The Wolfman		1.50	1.40
a Booklet of 20	09/30/1997	30.00	
UX291 20¢ Sylvester & Tweety	04/27/1998	1.40	*2.00*
Tropical Birds (UX293-UX296)			
UX293 20¢ Antillean Euphonia		1.00	1.75
UX294 20¢ Green-throated Carib		1.00	1.75
UX295 20¢ Crested Honeycreeper		1.00	1.75
UX296 20¢ Cardinal Honeyeater		1.00	1.75
a Booklet of 20	07/28/1998	20.00	
UX297 20¢ American Ballet	09/16/1998	1.25	*1.40*
UX300 20¢ Love	01/28/1999	1.25	1.50
UX304 Daffy Duck	04/16/1999	1.40	1.40

Issue	Date	Un	U
All Aboard! Twentieth Century Trains (UX307-UX311)			
UX307 Super Chief		1.50	1.50
UX308 Hiawatha		1.50	1.50
UX309 Daylight		1.50	1.50
UX310 Congressional		1.50	1.50
UX311 20th Century Limited		1.50	1.50
a Booklet of 20	08/26/1999	25.00	
UX314 20¢ Road Runner & Wilie E. Coyote	04/26/2000	1.40	1.40
UX315 Adoption	05/10/2000	1.40	1.50
Stars and Stripes (UX317-UX336)			
UX317 20¢ Sons of Liberty Flag, 1775		2.00	2.00
UX318 20¢ New England Flag, 1775		2.00	2.00
UX319 20¢ Forster Flag, 1775		2.00	2.00
UX320 20¢ Continental Colors, 1776		2.00	2.00
UX321 20¢ Francis Hopkinson Flag, 1777		2.00	2.00
UX322 20¢ Brandywine Flag, 1777		2.00	2.00
UX323 20¢ John Paul Jones Flag, 1779		2.00	2.00
UX324 20¢ Pierre L'Enfant Flag, 1783		2.00	2.00
UX325 20¢ Indian Peace Flag, 1803		2.00	2.00
UX326 20¢ Easton Flag, 1814		2.00	2.00
UX327 20¢ Star Spangled Banner, 1814		2.00	2.00
UX328 20¢ Bennington Flag, c. 1820		2.00	2.00
UX329 20¢ Great Star Flag, 1837		2.00	2.00
UX330 20¢ 29-Star Flag, 1847		2.00	2.00
UX331 20¢ Fort Sumter Flag, 1861		2.00	2.00
UX332 20¢ Sentennial Flag, 1876		2.00	2.00
UX333 20¢ 38-Star Flag, 1877		2.00	2.00
UX334 20¢ Peace Flag, 1891		2.00	2.00
UX335 20¢ 48-Star Flag, 1912		2.00	2.00
UX336 20¢ 50-Star Flag, 1960		2.00	2.00
a Five sheets of four	06/14/2000	40.00	40.00

Issue	Date	Un	U
Legends of Baseball (UX337-UX356)			
UX337 20¢ Jackie Robinson		1.50	1.50
UX338 20¢ Eddie Collins		1.50	1.50
UX339 20¢ Christy Matthewson		1.50	1.50
UX340 20¢ Ty Cobb		1.50	1.50
UX341 20¢ George Sisler		1.50	1.50
UX342 20¢ Rogers Hornsby		1.50	1.50
UX343 20¢ Mickey Cochrane		1.50	1.50
UX344 20¢ Babe Ruth		1.50	1.50
UX345 20¢ Walter Johnson		1.50	1.50
UX346 20¢ Roberto Clemente		1.50	1.50
UX347 20¢ Lefty Grove		1.50	1.50
UX348 20¢ Tris Speaker		1.50	1.50
UX349 20¢ Cy Young		1.50	1.50
UX350 20¢ Jimmie Foxx		1.50	1.50
UX351 20¢ Pie Traynor		1.50	1.50
UX352 20¢ Satchel Paige		1.50	1.50
UX353 20¢ Honus Wagner		1.50	1.50
UX354 20¢ Josh Gibson		1.50	1.50
UX355 20¢ Dizzy Dean		1.50	1.50
UX356 20¢ Lou Gehrig		1.50	1.50
a Booklet of 20	07/06/2000	30.00	
Holiday Celebrations: Holiday, Deer (UX357-UX360)			
UX357 20¢ gold & blue		1.25	1.25
UX358 20¢ gold & red		1.25	1.25
UX359 20¢ gold & purple		1.25	1.25
UX360 20¢ gold & green		1.25	1.25
a Sheet of four	10/12/2000	5.00	
Legendary Playing Fields (UX365-UX374)			
UX365 21¢ Ebbets Field		2.00	2.00
UX366 21¢ Tiger Stadium		2.00	2.00
UX367 21¢ Crosley Field		2.00	2.00
UX368 21¢ Yankee Stadium		2.00	2.00
UX369 21¢ Polo Grounds		2.00	2.00
UX370 21¢ Forbes Field		2.00	2.00
UX371 21¢ Fenway Park		2.00	2.00
UX372 21¢ Comiskey Park		2.00	2.00
UX373 21¢ Shibe Park		2.00	2.00
UX374 21¢ Wrigley Field		2.00	2.00
a Booklet of 10	06/27/2001	22.50	
UX376 21¢ That's All Folks!	10/01/2001	1.50	1.50
Holiday Celebrations: Holiday, Santas (UX377-UX380)			
UX377 21¢ Santa with tan hood		1.25	1.25
UX378 21¢ Santa with blue hat		1.25	1.25
UX379 21¢ Santa with red hat		1.25	1.25
UX380 21¢ Santa with gold hood		1.25	1.25
a Sheet of four	10/10/2001	5.00	

VISIT US ONLINE AT **THE POSTAL STORE**

AT **WWW.USPS.COM**

OR CALL **1 800 STAMP-24**

UX264

UX279

UX289

UX293

UX307

UX317

UX337

UX357

UX365

UX377

50s Fins and Chrome Premium Stamped Cards

Rev up your collection with these cultural icons from the 50s. Add the dazzle of five high-powered luxury cars with their prominent tail fins and shiny chrome detailing!

Item #463666 $13.95

To order this item and other related philatelic products call **1 800 STAMP-24** *or visit us online at* **www.usps.com**

UX382   UX386   UX390   UX396

UX401   UX407   UX411

UX421   UX436   UX440   UX445

UX450   UX454   UX458

VISIT US ONLINE AT **THE POSTAL STORE**
AT **WWW.USPS.COM**
OR CALL **1 800 STAMP-24**

Issue		Date	Un	U
Teddy Bears (UX382-UX385)				
UX382	23¢ Ideal Bear		1.25	1.25
UX383	23¢ Gund Bear		1.25	1.25
UX384	23¢ Bruin Bear		1.25	1.25
UX385	23¢ "Stick" Bear		1.25	1.25
a	Pack of five	08/15/2002	5.50	
Holiday Celebrations: Holiday, Snowmen				
UX386	23¢ Snowman w/red & green scarf		1.25	1.25
UX387	23¢ Snowman w/blue plaid scarf		1.25	1.25
UX388	Snowman w/pipe		1.25	1.25
UX389	Snowman w/top hat		1.25	1.25
a	Pack of five	10/28/2002	5.00	
Old Glory (UX390-UX394)				
UX390	23¢ Uncle Sam on Bicycle with Liberty Flag		1.25	1.25
UX391	23¢ 1888 Presidential Campaign		1.25	1.25
UX392	23¢ 1893 Silk Bookmark		1.25	1.25
UX393	23¢ 1888 Modern Hand Fan		1.25	1.25
UX394	23¢ 1888 Carving of Woman with Flag & Sword 19th Century		1.25	1.25
a	Booklet of 20	04/03/2003	25.00	
Southeastern Lighthouses (UX395-UX399)				
UX395	23¢ Old Cape Henry, Virginia		1.10	1.10
UX396	23¢ Cape Lookout, North Carolina		1.10	1.10
UX397	23¢ Morris Island, South Carolina		1.10	1.10
UX398	23¢ Tybee Island, Georgia		1.10	1.10
UX399	23¢ Hillsboro Inlet, Florida		1.10	1.10
a	Booklet of 20	06/13/2003	22.50	
Holiday Celebrations: Holiday, Music Makers (UX401-UX404)				
UX401	23¢ Reindeer with Pan Pipes		1.10	1.10
UX402	23¢ Santa Claus with Drum		1.10	1.10
UX403	23¢ Santa Claus with Trumpet		1.10	1.10
UX404	23¢ Reindeer with Horn		1.10	1.10
a	Sheet of four	10/23/2003	4.50	
Art of Disney: Friendship (UX407-UX410)				
UX407	23¢ Bambi, Thumper		1.25	1.25
UX408	23¢ Mufasa, Simba		1.25	1.25
UX409	23¢ Goofy, Mickey Mouse, Donald Duck		1.25	1.25
UX410	23¢ Jiminy Cricket, Pinocchio		1.25	1.25
a	Booklet of 20	06/23/2004	25.00	

Issue		Date	Un	U
Art of the American Indian (UX411-UX420)				
UX411	23¢ Mimbres Bowl		1.25	1.25
UX412	23¢ Kutenai Parfleche		1.25	1.25
UX413	23¢ Tlinget Scultures		1.25	1.25
UX414	23¢ Ho-Chunk Bag		1.25	1.25
UX415	23¢ Seminole Doll		1.25	1.25
UX416	23¢ Mississippian Effigy		1.25	1.25
UX417	23¢ Acoma Pot		1.25	1.25
UX418	23¢ Navajo Weaving		1.25	1.25
UX419	23¢ Seneca Carving		1.25	1.25
UX420	23¢ Luiseño Basket		1.25	1.25
a	Booklet of 20	08/21/2004	25.00	
Cloudscapes (UX421-UX435)				
UX421	23¢ Cirrus Radiatus		1.25	1.25
UX422	23¢ Cirrostratus Fibratus		1.25	1.25
UX423	23¢ Cirrocumulus Undulatus		1.25	1.25
UX424	23¢ Cumulonimbus Mammatus		1.25	1.25
UX425	23¢ Cumulonimbus Incus		1.25	1.25
UX426	23¢ Altocumulus Stratiformis		1.25	1.25
UX427	23¢ Altostratus Translucidus		1.25	1.25
UX428	23¢ Altocumulus Undulatus		1.25	1.25
UX429	23¢ Altocumulus Castellanus		1.25	1.25
UX430	23¢ Altocumulus Lenticularis		1.25	1.25
UX431	23¢ Stratocumulus Undulatus		1.25	1.25
UX432	23¢ Stratus Opacus		1.25	1.25
UX433	23¢ Cumulus Humilis		1.25	1.25
UX434	23¢ Cumulus Congestus		1.25	1.25
UX435	23¢ Cumulonimbus with Tornado		1.25	1.25
a	Booklet of 20	10/04/2004	25.00	
Art of Disney: Celebration (UX436-UX439)				
UX436	23¢ Pluto, Mickey Mouse		1.10	1.10
UX437	23¢ Mad Hatter		1.10	1.10
UX438	23¢ Flounder, Ariel		1.10	1.10
UX439	23¢ Snow White, Dopey		1.10	1.10
a	Booklet of 20	06/30/2005	22.50	
America on the Move: 50s Sporty Cars				
UX440	23¢ Ford Thunderbird		1.00	1.00
UX441	23¢ Nash Healey		1.00	1.00
UX442	23¢ Chevrolet Corvette		1.00	1.00
UX443	23¢ Studebaker Starliner		1.00	1.00
UX444	23¢ Kaiser Darrin		1.00	1.00
a	Booklet of 20	08/20/2005	20.00	

Issue		Date	Un	U
Let's Dance (UX445-UX448)				
UX445	23¢ Cha cha cha		1.00	1.00
UX446	23¢ Mambo		1.00	1.00
UX447	23¢ Salsa		1.00	1.00
UX448	23¢ Merengue		1.00	1.00
a	Booklet of 20	09/17/2005	20.00	
Art of Disney: Romance (UX450-UX453)				
UX450	24¢ Mickey and Minnie Mouse		1.00	1.00
UX451	24¢ Cinderella and Prince Charming		1.00	1.00
UX452	24¢ Lady and Tramp		1.00	1.00
UX453	24¢ Beauty and the Beast		1.00	1.00
a	Booklet of 20	04/21/2006	20.00	
Baseball Sluggers (Type of 2006) (UX454-UX457)				
UX454	24¢ Mickey Mantle		1.25	1.25
UX455	24¢ Roy Campanella		1.25	1.25
UX456	24¢ Hank Greenberg		1.25	1.25
UX457	24¢ Mel Ott		1.25	1.25
a	Booklet of 20	07/15/2006	25.00	
DC Comics Superheroes (Type of 2006) (UX458-UX477)				
UX458	24¢ Superman Cover		1.50	1.50
UX459	24¢ Superman		1.50	1.50
UX460	24¢ Batman Cover		1.50	1.50
UX461	24¢ Batman		1.50	1.50
UX462	24¢ Wonder Woman Cover		1.50	1.50
UX463	24¢ Wonder Woman		1.50	1.50
UX464	24¢ Green Lantern Cover		1.50	1.50
UX465	24¢ Green Lantern		1.50	1.50
UX466	24¢ Green Arrow Cover		1.50	1.50
UX467	24¢ Green Arrow		1.50	1.50
UX468	24¢ The Flash Cover		1.50	1.50
UX469	24¢ The Flash		1.50	1.50
UX470	24¢ Plastic Man Cover		1.50	1.50
UX471	24¢ Plastic Man		1.50	1.50
UX472	24¢ Aquaman Cover		1.50	1.50
UX473	24¢ Aquaman		1.50	1.50
UX474	24¢ Supergirl Cover		1.50	1.50
UX475	24¢ Supergirl		1.50	1.50
UX476	24¢ Hawkman Cover		1.50	1.50
UX477	24¢ Hawkman		1.50	1.50
a	Booklet of 20	07/20/2006	30.00	

VISIT US ONLINE AT THE POSTAL STORE AT WWW.USPS.COM OR CALL 1 800 STAMP-24

Issue		Date	Un	U
Nature of America:				
Southern Florida Wetland (UX478-UX487)				
UX478	39¢ Snail Kite		3.50	3.50
UX479	39¢ Cape Sable Seaside Sparrow		3.50	3.50
UX480	39¢ Wood Storks		3.50	3.50
UX481	39¢ Florida Panther		3.50	3.50
UX482	39¢ Bald Eagle		3.50	3.50
UX483	39¢ White Ibis		3.50	3.50
UX484	39¢ American Crocodile		3.50	3.50
UX485	39¢ Everglades Mink		3.50	3.50
UX486	39¢ Roseate Spoonbills		3.50	3.50
UX487	39¢ American Alligator		3.50	3.50
a	Booklet of 10	10/04/06	35.00	
Star Wars (UX489-UX4503)				
UX489	26¢ Darth Vader		1.75	1.75
UX490	26¢ Luke Skywalker		1.75	1.75
UX491	26¢ C-3PO		1.75	1.75
UX492	26¢ Queen Padmé Amidala		1.75	1.75
UX493	26¢ Millennium Falcon		1.75	1.75
UX494	26¢ Emperor Palpatine		1.75	1.75
UX495	26¢ Anakin Skywalker and Obi-Wan Kenobi		1.75	1.75
UX496	26¢ Obi-Wan Kenobi		1.75	1.75
UX497	26¢ Boba Fett		1.75	1.75
UX498	26¢ Darth Maul		1.75	1.75
UX499	26¢ Yoda		1.75	1.75
UX500	26¢ Princess Leia Organa and R2-D2		1.75	1.75
UX501	26¢ Chewbacca and Han Solo		1.75	1.75
UX502	26¢ X-wing Starfighter		1.75	1.75
UX503	26¢ Stormtroopers		1.75	1.75
a	Booklet of 15	04/27/07	26.00	
Pacific Lighthouses (UX504-UX508)				
UX504	26¢ Grays Harbor		1.25	1.25
UX505	26¢ Five Finger		1.25	1.25
UX506	26¢ Umpqua River		1.25	1.25
UX507	26¢ Diamond Head		1.25	1.25
UX508	26¢ St. George Reef			
a	Booklet of 20	06/21/07	26.00	

Issue		Date	Un	U
Marvel Comics Superheroes				
(Type of 2006), (UX509-UX508)				
UX509	26¢ Spider-Man		1.25	1.25
UX510	26¢ The Hulk		1.25	1.25
UX511	26¢ Sub-Mariner		1.25	1.25
UX512	26¢ The Thing		1.25	1.25
UX513	26¢ Captain America		1.25	1.25
UX514	26¢ Silver Surfer		1.25	1.25
UX515	26¢ Spider-Woman		1.25	1.25
UX516	26¢ Iron Man		1.25	1.25
UX517	26¢ Elektra		1.25	1.25
UX518	26¢ Wolverine		1.25	1.25
UX519	26¢ *The Amazing Spider-Man* Cover		1.25	1.25
UX520	26¢ *The Incredible Hulk* Cover		1.25	1.25
UX521	26¢ *The Sub-Mariner* Cover		1.25	1.25
UX522	26¢ *The Fantastic Four* Cover		1.25	1.25
UX523	26¢ *Captain America* Cover		1.25	1.25
UX524	26¢ *The Silver Surfer* Cover		1.25	1.25
UX525	26¢ *The Spider-Woman* Cover		1.25	1.25
UX526	26¢ *The Invincible Iron Man* Cover		1.25	1.25
UX527	26¢ *Daredevil #176 Featuring Elektra* Cover		1.25	1.25
UX528	26¢ *The X-Men* Cover		1.25	1.25
a	Booklet of 20	07/26/07	26.00	
Art of Disney: Magic (UX529-UX532)				
UX529	26¢ Mickey Mouse		1.25	1.25
UX530	26¢ Peter Pan and Tinker Bell		1.25	1.25
UX531	26¢ Dumbo and Timothy Mouse		1.25	1.25
UX532	26¢ Aladdin and Genie		1.25	1.25
a	Booklet of 20	08/16/07	26.00	
Art of Disney: Imagination (UX535-UX538)				
UX535	27¢ Steamboat Willie		1.40	1.40
UX536	27¢ Pongo and Pup		1.40	1.40
UX537	27¢ Princess Aurora, Flora, Fauna, Merryweather		1.40	1.40
UX538	27¢ Mowgil and Baloo		1.40	1.40
a	Booklet of 20	08/07/08	28.00	

Issue		Date	Un	U
Nature of America: Great Lakes Dunes				
(UX539-UX548)				
UX539	42¢ Vesper Sparrow		1.90	1.90
UX540	42¢ Piping Plover		1.90	1.90
a	Sheet of 2	10/03/08	4.00	
UX541	42¢ Eastern Hognose Snake		1.90	1.90
UX542	42¢ Common Mergansers		1.90	1.90
a	Sheet of 2	10/03/08	4.00	
UX543	42¢ Piping Plover Nestlings		1.90	1.90
UX544	42¢ Red Fox		1.90	1.90
a	Sheet of 2	10/03/08	4.00	
UX545	42¢ Tiger Beetle		1.90	1.90
UX546	42¢ White-footed Mouse		1.90	1.90
a	Sheet of 2	10/03/08	4.00	
UX547	42¢ Spotted Sandpiper		1.90	1.90
UX548	42¢ Red Admiral Butterfly		1.90	1.90
a	Sheet of 2	10/03/08	4.00	
America on the Move: 50s Fins and Chrome (UX549-UX553)				
UX549	27¢ 1957 Lincoln Premier		1.40	1.40
UX550	27¢ 1957 Chrysler 300C		1.40	1.40
UX551	27¢ 1957 Cadillac Eldorado		1.40	1.40
UX552	27¢ 1957 Studebaker Golden Hawk		1.40	1.40
UX553	27¢ 1957 Pontiac Safari		1.40	1.40
a	Booklet of 20	10/03/08	28.00	

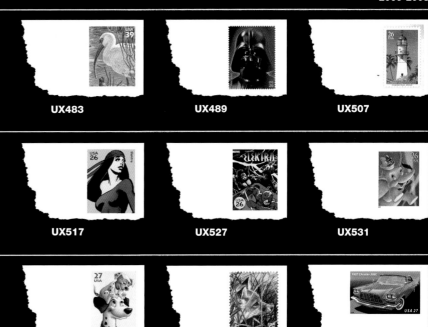

UX483 UX489 UX507

UX517 UX527 UX531

UX536 UX544 UX550

Celebrate with Your Personal Pictorial Postmarks

Make your own mark on history! Create a pictorial postmark that you've designed especially to commemorate your event.

For information on how you can create your own idea for a pictorial postmark stop by your local Post Office and inquire about this free brochure.

Celebrating with Pictorial Postmarks, Pub. 186.

1926-2008

UXC1

UXC2

UXC4

UXC5

UXC6

UXC7

UXC8

UXC9

UXC10

UXC11

UXC12

UXC13

UXC19

UXC20

UXC23

UXC25

UXC27

UXC28

UY12

UY41

UY43

UY44

UY45

UY46

Issue		Date	Un	U
	Airmail Postal Cards			
UXC1	4¢ red orange Eagle in Flight	01/10/1949	.50	*.75*
UXC2	5¢ red Eagle in Flight (type of 1954), buff	07/31/1958	1.75	.75
UXC3	5¢ UXC2 redrawn, bi-colored border	06/18/1960	6.50	2.00
UXC4	6¢ red Bald Eagle	02/15/1963	1.10	*2.50*
UXC5	11¢ Visit The USA	05/27/1966	.65	*25.00*
UXC6	6¢ Virgin Islands	03/31/1967	.75	*10.00*
a	Red, yellow omitted		*1,700.00*	
UXC7	6¢ Boy Scout World Jamboree	08/04/1967	.75	*15.00*
a	Blue omitted		*11,000.00*	
UXC8	13¢ Visit The USA	09/08/1967	1.50	*25.00*
UXC9	8¢ Stylized Eagle, precanceled w/3 red lines	03/01/1968	.75	*2.50*
UXC10	9¢ Stylized Eagle, precanceled w/3 red lines	05/15/1971	.50	*1.25*
UXC11	15¢ Visit The USA	06/10/1971	1.75	*45.00*
UXC12	9¢ black Grand Canyon, *buff*	06/29/1972	.75	*75.00*
UXC13	15¢ black Niagara Falls, *buff*	06/29/1972	.75	*75.00*
UXC14	11¢ Stylized Eagle	01/04/1974	1.10	*25.00*
UXC15	18¢ Eagle Weather Vane		1.10	*25.00*
UXC16	21¢ Angel Weather Vane	12/17/1975	.85	*22.50*
UXC17	21¢ Curtiss Jenny	09/16/1978	1.00	*22.50*
UXC18	21¢ Olympic Gymnast	12/01/1979	1.25	*20.00*
UXC19	28¢ First Transpacific Flight	01/02/1981	1.00	*22.50*
UXC20	28¢ Gliders	03/05/1982	1.00	*22.50*
UXC21	28¢ Olympic Speed Skater	12/29/1983	1.00	*22.50*
UXC22	33¢ China Clipper	02/15/1985	1.00	*22.50*
	Scenic American Landscapes (UXC27-UXC28)			
UXC23	33¢ AMERIPEX '86	02/01/1986	1.00	*22.50*
UXC24	36¢ DC-3	05/14/1988	.85	*22.50*
UXC25	40¢ Yankee Clipper	06/28/1991	.90	*22.50*
UXC27	55¢ Mt. Rainier	05/15/1999	1.25	20.00
UXC28	70¢ Badlands	02/22/2001	1.40	10.00
	Paid Reply Postal Cards			
	Prices are: Un=unsevered, U=severed card			
UY1	1¢ + 1¢ black Grant	10/25/1892	40.00	9.00
UY2	2¢ + 2¢ blue Liberty		22.50	20.00
UY3	1¢ + 1¢ black Grant	09/1898	67.50	12.50
UY4	1¢ + 1¢ black Sherman	03/31/1904	57.50	6.50
UY5	1¢ + 1¢ blue Washington	09/14/1910	175.00	25.00
UY6	1¢ + 1¢ green George and Martha Washington, double frame line	10/27/1911	175.00	25.00
UY7	1¢ + 1¢ Green George and Martha Washington, single frame line	09/18/1915	1.25	.50
UY8	2¢ + 2¢ red George and Martha Washington, *buff*	08/02/1918	90.00	40.00
UY9	1¢ on 2¢ + 1¢ on 2¢ red George and Martha Washington, *buff, (canceling machine type)*	04/1920	22.50	11.00
UY10	1¢ on 2¢ + 1¢ on 2¢ red George and Martha Washington, *buff, (press printed type)*	04/1920	375.00	200.00
UY11	2¢ + 2¢ red Liberty	03/18/1924	2.50	*50.00*
UY12	3¢ + 3¢ red McKinley	02/01/1926	12.00	*27.50*
UY13	2¢ + 2¢ carmine Washington, *buff*	12/29/1951	1.25	*2.00*
UY14	2¢ on 1¢ + 2¢ on 1¢ green George and Martha Washington, *buff, (canceling machine type)*	01/01/1952	1.25	*2.00*
UY15	2¢ on 1¢ + 2¢ on 1¢ green George and Martha Washington, *buff, (press printed type)*	1952	115.00	45.00
UY16	4¢ + 4¢ carmine and dark violet blue Statue of Liberty	11/16/1956	1.25	*75.00*
UY17	3¢ + 3¢ purple Statue of Liberty, *buff*	07/31/1958	3.00	*2.00*
UY18	4¢ + 4¢ red violet Lincoln	11/19/1962	3.00	*2.50*
UY19	7¢ + 7¢ blue and red World Vacationland	08/30/1963	2.50	*60.00*
UY20	8¢ + 8¢ blue and red World Vacationland	12/04/1967	2.50	*60.00*
UY21	5¢ + 5¢ emerald Lincoln	01/04/1968	1.25	*2.00*
UY22	6¢ + 6¢ brown Paul Revere	05/15/1971	.85	*2.00*
UY23	6¢ + 6¢ blue John Hanson	09/01/1972	1.00	*2.00*
UY24	8¢ + 8¢ orange Samuel Adams	09/01/1972	.75	*2.00*
UY25	7¢ + 7¢ emerald Charles Thomson	09/14/1975	.75	*8.00*
UY26	9¢ + 9¢ yellow brown John Witherspoon	11/10/1975	.75	*2.00*
UY27	9¢ + 9¢ blue Caesar Rodney	07/01/1976	1.00	*2.00*
UY28	9¢ + 9¢ green Nathan Hale	10/14/1977	1.00	*2.00*
UY29	(10¢ + 10¢) brown orange John Hancock	05/19/1978	7.50	*9.00*
UY30	10¢ + 10¢ brown orange John Hancock	06/20/1978	1.00	.25
UY31	(12¢ + 12¢) violet Eagle	03/15/1981	1.00	*2.00*
UY32	12¢ + 12¢ light blue Isaiah Thomas	05/05/1981	5.00	*2.00*
UY33	(13¢ + 13¢) buff Robert Morris	10/11/1981	1.50	*2.00*
UY34	13¢ + 13¢ buff Robert Morris	11/10/1981	.85	.20
UY35	(14¢ + 14¢) pale green Charles Carroll	02/01/1985	2.50	*2.00*
UY36	14¢ + 14¢ pale green Charles Carroll	03/06/1985	1.00	*2.00*
UY37	14¢ + 14¢ bright green George Wythe	06/20/1985	.75	*2.00*
UY38	14¢ + 14¢ black, blue & red Stars and Stripes	09/01/1987	.75	*2.00*
UY39	15¢ + 15¢ Bison and Prairie	07/11/1988	.75	*1.50*
UY40	19¢ + 19¢ Flag	03/27/1991	.80	*1.50*
	Scenic America (UY41, UY43, UY44, UY45)			
UY41	20¢ + 20¢ Red Barn	02/01/1995	.80	*1.50*
UY42	20¢ + 20¢ Block Island Lighthouse	11/10/1999	.85	*1.50*
UY43	21¢ + 21¢ White Barn	09/20/2001	.90	*1.50*
UY44	23¢ + 23¢ Carlsbad Caverns	06/07/2002	1.00	*1.25*
UY45	24¢ + 24¢ Pikes Peak	01/09/2006	1.10	*1.25*
UY46	26¢ + 26¢ Pineapple	05/12/2007	1.25	*1.40*
UY47	27¢ + 27¢ Corinthian Capital	05/12/2008	1.25	*1.40*
	Official Mail Postal Cards			
UZ1	1¢ black Numeral	07/1913	700.00	475.00
UZ2	13¢ blue Great Seal	01/12/1983	.75	*100.00*
UZ3	14¢ blue Great Seal	02/26/1985	.80	*80.00*
UZ4	15¢ blue Great Seal	06/10/1988	.80	*90.00*
UZ5	19¢ blue Great Seal	05/24/1991	.80	*90.00*
UZ6	20¢ Official Mail	05/09/1995	.90	*90.00*

American Commemorative Cancellations

The Postal Service offers American Commemorative Cancellations (formerly known as Souvenir Pages) for new stamps. The series began with a page for the Yellowstone Park Centennial stamp issued March 1, 1972. The pages feature one or more stamps tied by the first day cancel, along with technical data and information on the subject of the issue. More than just collectors' items, American Commemorative Cancellations make wonderful show and conversation pieces. These pages are issued in limited editions. Number in parentheses ( ) indicates the number of stamps on page if there are more than one.

The identifying numbers used below are based on the Postal Service's numbering system for American Commemorative Cancellations; therefore, they do not follow the Scott numbering system.

1972

72-00	Family Planning	675.00
72-01	Yellowstone Park	110.00
72-02	2¢ Cape Hatteras	80.00
72-03	14¢ Fiorello LaGuardia	100.00
72-04	11¢ City of Refuge Park	95.00
72-05	6¢ Wolf Trap Farm Park	32.50
72-06	Colonial Craftsmen (4)	13.00
72-07	15¢ Mount McKinley	20.00
72-08	6¢-15¢ Olympic Games (4)	10.00
72-09	PTA	6.00
72-10	Wildlife Conservation (4)	7.00
72-11	Mail Order	4.50
72-12	Osteopathic Medicine	5.50
72-13	Tom Sawyer	8.00
72-14	7¢ Benjamin Franklin	5.00
72-15	Christmas (2)	6.00
72-16	Pharmacy	7.00
72-17	Stamp Collecting	5.00

1973

73-01	$1 Eugene O'Neill	15.00
73-02	Love	7.00
73-03	Pamphleteer Printing	5.00
73-04	George Gershwin	6.00
73-05	Broadside	5.00
73-06	Copernicus	5.75
73-07	Postal Employees	5.75
73-08	Harry S. Truman	5.00
73-09	Post Rider	5.00
73-10	21¢ Amadeo Gianninni	4.50
73-11	Boston Tea Party (4)	6.00
73-12	6¢-15¢ Electronics (4)	9.00
73-13	Robinson Jeffers	5.25
73-14	Lyndon B. Johnson	4.75
73-15	Henry O. Tanner	6.00
73-16	Willa Cather	7.00
73-17	Colonial Drummer	3.25
73-18	Angus Cattle	3.75
73-19	Christmas (2)	6.25
73-20	13¢ Winged Envelope airmail	4.00
73-21	10¢ Crossed Flags	3.50
73-22	10¢ Jefferson Memorial	3.50
73-23	13¢ Winged Envelope airmail coil (2)	4.00

1974

74-01	26¢ Mount Rushmore airmail	5.25
74-02	10¢ ZIP Code	5.00
74-03	18¢ Statue of Liberty airmail	7.50
74-04	18¢ Elizabeth Blackwell	3.50
74-05	10¢ VFW	3.25
74-06	Robert Frost	5.25
74-07	Expo '74	6.00
74-08	Horse Racing	6.00
74-09	Skylab	5.75
74-10	UPU (8)	6.00
74-11	Mineral Heritage (4)	6.00
74-12	Fort Harrod	3.25
74-13	Continental Congress (4)	5.25
74-14	10¢ Chautauqua	3.25
74-15	10¢ Kansas Wheat	3.00
74-16	Energy Conservation	3.25
74-17	6.3¢ Liberty Bell coil (2)	4.00
74-18	Sleepy Hollow	5.25
74-19	Retarded Children	3.25
74-20	Christmas (3)	5.25

1975

75-01	Benjamin West	3.75
75-02	Pioneer/Jupiter	6.00
75-03	Collective Bargaining	3.25
75-04	Salem Poor	4.00
75-05	8¢ Sybil Ludington	3.25
75-06	Haym Salomon	3.75
75-07	15¢ Peter Francisco	3.75
75-08	Mariner 10	6.00
75-09	Lexington & Concord	3.75
75-10	Paul Dunbar	5.00
75-11	D.W. Griffith	5.25
75-12	Bunker Hill	3.75
75-13	Military Uniforms (4)	6.00
75-14	Apollo Soyuz (2)	7.50
75-15	International Women's Year	3.25
75-16	10¢ Postal Service Bicentennial (4)	4.00
75-17	World Peace Through Law	3.25

75-18	Banking & Commerce (2)	3.75
75-19	Christmas (2)	4.25
75-20	3¢ Francis Parkman	4.00
75-21	11¢ Printing Press	3.50
75-22	24¢ Old North Church	3.50
75-23	13¢ Flag over Independence Hall (2)	3.25
75-24	9¢ Freedom to Assemble #1591 (2) Capitol Dome	3.25
75-25	13¢ Liberty Bell coil (2)	3.25
75-26	13¢ Eagle & Shield #1596	5.00

1976

76-01	13¢ Spirit of '76 (3)	5.00
76-02	25¢ and 31¢ Plane and Globes airmails (2)	3.50
76-03	Interphil '76	3.75
76-04	State Flags, DE to VA (10)	9.00
76-05	State Flags, NY to MS (10)	9.00
76-06	State Flags, IL to WI (10)	9.00
76-07	State Flags, CA to SD (10)	9.00
76-08	State Flags, MT to HI (10)	9.00
76-09	9¢ Freedom to Assemble coil #1616 (2) Capitol Dome	3.25
76-10	13¢ Telephone Centennial	3.50
76-11	13¢ Commercial Aviation	3.50
76-12	13¢ Chemistry	3.50
76-13	7.9¢ Drum coil (2)	3.25
76-14	13¢ Bicentennial souvenir sheet	10.00
76-15	18¢ Bicentennial souvenir sheet	10.00
76-16	24¢ Bicentennial souvenir sheet	10.00
76-17	31¢ Bicentennial souvenir sheet	10.00
76-18	13¢ Benjamin Franklin	3.00
76-19	13¢ Declaration of Independence (4)	4.75
76-20	13¢ Olympics (4)	4.75
76-21	13¢ Clara Maass	6.50
76-22	13¢ Adolph S. Ochs	3.50
76-23	13¢ Christmas (3)	3.75
76-24	7.7¢ Saxhorns coil (2)	3.25

1977

77-01	13¢ Washington at Princeton	3.25
77-02	Flag over Capitol booklet pane (9¢ and 13¢) Perf. 10 (8)	17.50
77-03	13¢ Sound Recording	4.00
77-04	Pueblo Pottery (4)	7.00
77-05	Lindbergh Flight	4.00
77-06	Colorado Centennial	3.00
77-07	Butterflies (4)	5.00
77-08	Lafayette	3.00
77-09	Skilled Hands (4)	4.00
77-10	Peace Bridge	3.50
77-11	Battle of Oriskany	3.50
77-12	Alta, CA, First Civil Settlement	3.50
77-13	Articles of Confederation	4.50

77-14	Talking Pictures	4.50
77-15	Surrender at Saratoga	3.25
77-16	13¢ Energy (2)	3.50
77-17	Christmas Valley Forge, and Christmas Mailbox (2) Omaha cancel	3.25
77-18	Same, Valley Forge cancel	3.25
77-19	10¢ Petition for Redress #1617 coil (2)	3.25
77-20	10¢ Petition for Redress #1592 sheet (2)	3.25
77-21	1¢-4¢ Americana (5)	4.00

1978

78-01	13¢ Carl Sandburg	4.00
78-02	Indian Head Penny	3.25
78-03	Captain Cook Anchorage cancel (2) #1732	4.50
78-04	Captain Cook, Honolulu cancel (2)	4.50
78-05	Harriet Tubman	4.00
78-06	American Quilts (4)	5.00
78-07	16¢ Statue of Liberty sheet and coil (2)	3.50
78-08	29¢ Sandy Hook Lighthouse #1605	5.00
78-09	13¢ American Dance (4)	6.00
78-10	French Alliance	3.50
78-11	Early Cancer Detection	4.50
78-12	"A" (15¢) sheet and coil (2)	5.50
78-13	Jimmie Rodgers	4.50
78-14	CAPEX '78 (8)	7.75
78-15	15¢ Oliver Wendell Holmes coil #1288	10.00
78-16	15¢ Photography	5.00
78-17	Fort McHenry Flag #1597 15¢ sheet and coil (2)	3.25
78-18	15¢ George M. Cohan	4.50
78-19	15¢ Rose booklet single	4.25
78-20	8.4¢ Piano coil (2) #1615C	4.25
78-21	15¢ Viking Missions	6.25
78-22	28¢ Ft. Nisqually	4.00
78-23	15¢ American Owls (4)	5.50
78-24	31¢ Wright Brothers airmails (2) C91-C92	4.00
78-25	American Trees (4)	4.00
78-26	15¢ Christmas, Madonna	3.50
78-27	15¢ Christmas, Hobby Horse	3.50
78-28	$2 Kerosene Lamp #1611	6.00

1979

79-01	15¢ Robert F. Kennedy	4.25
79-02	15¢ Martin Luther King, Jr.	5.00
79-03	15¢ International Year of the Child	3.25
79-04	15¢ John Steinbeck	6.50
79-05	15¢ Albert Einstein	6.50
79-06	21¢ Octave Chanute airmails (2)	4.00
79-07	15¢ Pennsylvania Toleware (4)	5.50
79-08	American Architecture (4)	4.00
79-09	15¢ Endangered Flora (4)	4.00
79-10	Seeing Eye Dogs	3.25
79-11	$1 Candle & Holder	4.75
79-12	15¢ Special Olympics	3.25
79-13	$5 Lantern #1612	11.00
79-14	30¢ Schoolhouse	4.75
79-15	10¢ Summer Olympics	3.50
79-16	50¢ "Betty" Lamp	4.25
79-17	15¢ John Paul Jones	3.25
79-18	15¢ Summer Olympics (4)	5.00
79-19	15¢ Christmas, Madonna	3.25
79-20	Christmas, Santa Claus	3.25
79-21	3.1¢ Guitar coil (2)	6.50
79-22	31¢ Summer Olympics airmail	4.50
79-23	Will Rogers	4.00
79-24	Vietnam Veterans	5.50
79-25	25¢ Wiley Post airmails (2)	4.50

1980

80-01	15¢ W.C. Fields	5.00
80-02	15¢ Winter Olympics (4)	5.25
80-03	15¢ Windmills booklet pane (10) #1742a	9.50
80-04	Benjamin Banneker	4.25
80-05	Letter Writing (6)	4.00
80-06	1¢ Ability to Write #1811 (2)	3.50
80-07	15¢ Frances Perkins	3.25
80-08	Dolley Madison	4.50
80-09	Emily Bissell	4.50
80-10	3.5¢ Violins #1813 coil (2)	3.25
80-11	Helen Keller/ Anne Sullivan	3.25
80-12	Veterans Administration	3.25
80-13	General Bernardo de Galvez	3.25
80-14	Coral Reefs (4)	5.50
80-15	Organized Labor	4.00
80-16	Edith Wharton	4.00
80-17	Education	3.50
80-18	Indian Masks (4)	5.00
80-19	American Architecture (4)	4.00
80-20	40¢ Philip Mazzei airmail	3.75
80-21	15¢ Christmas, Madonna	3.25
80-22	Christmas, Antique Toys	4.00
80-23	19¢ Sequoyah	3.25
80-24	28¢ Blanche Scott airmail	3.75
80-25	35¢ Glenn Curtiss airmail	3.75

1981

81-01	15¢ Everett Dirksen	3.25
81-02	15¢ Whitney M. Young	5.50
81-03	"B" (18¢ sheet and coil (3) #1818, #1820	3.25
81-04	"B" (18¢) booklet pane (8) #1818	3.25
81-05	12¢ Torch Sheet and coil (3) #1594, #1816	3.50
81-06	18¢ Flowers #1879a (4)	4.00
81-07	18¢ Flag and Anthem sheet and coil (3) #1890-1891	3.25
81-08	Flag and Anthem booklet pane (8 - 6¢ and 18¢)	3.25
81-09	18¢ American Red Cross	3.25
81-10	18¢ George Mason	3.25
81-11	Savings & Loans	3.25
81-12	Wildlife booklet #1889a pane (10)	6.50
81-13	18¢ Surrey coil (2) #1907	4.75
81-14	18¢ Space Achievement (8)	8.00
81-15	17¢ Rachel Carson #1857	3.25
81-16	35¢ Charles Drew, MD	3.25
81-17	18¢ Professional Management	3.25
81-18	17¢ Electric Auto coil (2)	3.25
81-19	Wildlife Habitat (4) #1924a	4.00
81-20	18¢ Disabled	3.25
81-21	Edna St. Vincent Millay	3.25
81-22	18¢ Alcoholism	3.25
81-23	American Architecture (4)	4.50
81-24	Babe Zaharias	17.50
81-25	Bobby Jones	20.00
81-26	Frederic Remington	5.00
81-27	(20¢) "C" sheet and coil (3)	4.00
81-28	"C" booklet #1948a pane (10)	3.75
81-29	18¢ and 20¢ Hoban (2)	3.25
81-30	Yorktown/ Virginia Capes (2)	4.00
81-31	20¢ Christmas, Madonna	3.25
81-32	Christmas, Bear on Sleigh	4.75
81-33	20¢ John Hanson	3.25
81-34	20¢ Fire Pumper coil (2)	5.25
81-35	20¢ Desert Plants (4)	4.50
81-36	9.3¢ Mail Wagon coil (3)	4.25
81-37	20¢ Flag over Supreme Court sheet and coil (3) #1894-1895	3.25
81-38	Flag over Supreme Court booklet pane (6) #1896a	3.25

1982

82-01	20¢ Bighorn Sheep booklet pane (10)	4.00
82-02	20¢ Ralph Bunche	5.25
82-03	13¢ Crazy Horse (2)	4.00
82-04	37¢ Robert Millikan	3.25
82-05	20¢ Franklin D. Roosevelt	3.25
82-06	20¢ Love	3.25
82-07	5.9¢ Bicycle coil (4)	6.50
82-08	20¢ George Washington	4.00
82-09	10.9¢ Hansom Cab coil (2)	4.50
82-10	20¢ Birds & Flowers, AL-GE (10)	12.00
82-11	20¢ Birds & Flowers, HI-MD (10)	12.00
82-12	20¢ Birds & Flowers, MA-NJ (10)	12.00
82-13	20¢ Birds & Flowers, NM-SC (10)	12.00
82-14	20¢ Birds & Flowers, SD-WY (10)	12.00
82-15	20¢ USA/Netherlands	3.25
82-16	20¢ Library of Congress	3.25
82-17	20¢ Consumer Education coil (2)	4.25
82-18	Knoxville World's Fair (4)	3.25
82-19	Horatio Alger	3.25
82-20	2¢ Locomotive coil (2)	4.50
82-21	Aging Together	3.25
82-22	The Barrymores	4.25
82-23	Mary Walker	3.25
82-24	Peace Garden	3.25
82-25	America's Libraries	3.25
82-26	Jackie Robinson	14.00
82-27	4¢ Stagecoach coil (3)	4.25
82-28	20¢ Touro Synagogue	3.25
82-29	Wolf Trap Farm Park	3.25
82-30	American Architecture (4)	4.50
82-31	Francis of Assisi	3.25
82-32	Ponce de Leon	3.25
82-33	13¢ Kitten & Puppy (2)	4.25
82-34	20¢ Christmas, Madonna	4.00
82-35	Christmas, Seasons Greetings (4)	4.50
82-36	2¢ Igor Stravinsky (2)	3.75

1983

83-01	1¢, 4¢, 13¢ Penalty Mail (5)	4.00
83-02	17¢ Penalty Mail (4)	4.00
83-03	20¢ Penalty Mail coil (2)	4.00
83-04	$1 Penalty Mail	5.50
83-05	$5 Penalty Mail	10.00
83-06	Science & Industry	3.25
83-07	5.2¢ Antique Sleigh coil (4)	4.75
83-08	Sweden/USA Treaty	3.25
83-09	3¢ Handcar coil (3)	4.00
83-10	20¢ Balloons (4)	3.25
83-11	20¢ Civilian Conservation Corps	3.25
83-12	40¢ Olympics airmails (4)	4.00
83-13	20¢ Joseph Priestley	3.25
83-14	Volunteerism	3.25
83-15	Concord/German Immigration	3.25
83-16	Physical Fitness	3.25
83-17	Brooklyn Bridge	3.25
83-18	TVA	3.25
83-19	4¢ Carl Schurz (5)	4.25
83-20	Medal of Honor	6.50
83-21	Scott Joplin	3.25
83-22	20¢ Thomas H. Gallaudet	3.25
83-23	28¢ Olympics (4)	4.00
83-24	5¢ Pearl S. Buck (4)	4.00
83-25	20¢ Babe Ruth	12.00
83-26	Nathaniel Hawthorne	3.25
83-27	3¢ Henry Clay (7)	3.50
83-28	13¢ Olympics (4)	4.00
83-29	$9.35 Eagle booklet single	80.00
83-30	$9.35 Eagle booklet pane (3)	195.00
83-31	1¢ Omnibus coil (3)	3.25
83-32	20¢ Treaty of Paris	3.25
83-33	Civil Service	3.25
83-34	Metropolitan Opera	3.75
83-35	Inventors (4)	3.75
83-36	1¢ Dorothea Dix (3)	3.50
83-37	20¢ Streetcars (4)	4.75
83-38	5¢ Motorcycle coil (4)	5.75
83-39	Christmas, Madonna	3.25
83-40	Christmas, Santa Claus	3.25
83-41	35¢ Olympics airmails (4)	4.00
83-42	Martin Luther	5.25
83-43	20¢ Flag over Supreme Court booklet #1896b (10)	4.50

1984

84-01	20¢ Alaska Statehood	3.25
84-02	20¢ Winter Olympics (4)	4.00
84-03	20¢ FDIC	3.25
84-04	20¢ Harry S. Truman	3.25
84-05	20¢ Love	3.25
84-06	Carter G. Woodson	4.00
84-07	11¢ RR Caboose coil (2)	4.25
84-08	Soil & Water Conservation	3.25
84-09	20¢ Credit Union Act	3.25
84-10	40¢ Lillian M. Gilbreth	3.25
84-11	20¢ Orchids (4)	5.25
84-12	Hawaii Statehood	3.75
84-13	7.4¢ Baby Buggy coil (3)	4.00
84-14	20¢ National Archives	3.25
84-15	20¢ Summer Olympics (4)	4.00
84-16	New Orleans World's Expo	3.25
84-17	Health Research	3.25
84-18	Douglas Fairbanks	5.25
84-19	Jim Thorpe	10.00
84-20	10¢ Richard Russell (2)	3.25
84-21	20¢ John McCormack	5.25
84-22	St. Lawrence Seaway	3.25
84-23	20¢ Migratory Bird Hunting and Pre-Conservation Stamp Act #2092	5.25
84-24	20¢ Roanoke Voyages	3.25
84-25	20¢ Herman Melville	3.50
84-26	20¢ Horace Moses	3.25
84-27	Smokey Bear	10.00
84-28	Roberto Clemente	13.00
84-29	30¢ Frank C. Laubach	3.25
84-30	20¢ Dogs (4)	5.25
84-31	20¢ Crime Prevention	3.75
84-32	20¢ Family Unity	3.25
84-33	Eleanor Roosevelt	4.75
84-34	Nation of Readers	3.25
84-35	Christmas, Madonna	3.25
84-36	Christmas, Santa Claus	3.25
84-37	Hispanic Americans	3.25
84-38	Vietnam Veterans Memorial	5.25

1985

85-01	20¢ Jerome Kern	3.25
85-02	7¢ Abraham Baldwin (3)	3.25
85-03	"D" (22¢) sheet and coil	3.25
85-04	"D" (22¢) booklet pane (10)	4.25
85-05	"D" (22¢) Penalty Mail sheet and coil	3.25
85-06	11¢ Alden Partridge (2)	3.25
85-07	33¢ Alfred Verville airmail	3.25
85-08	39¢ Lawrence & Elmer Sperry airmail	3.75
85-09	44¢ Transpacific airmail	3.25
85-10	50¢ Chester Nimitz	4.00
85-11	22¢ Mary McLeod Bethune	5.25
85-12	39¢ Grenville Clark	3.25
85-13	14¢ Sinclair Lewis (2)	5.50
85-14	22¢ Duck Decoys (4)	6.00
85-15	14¢ Iceboat coil (2)	4.00
85-16	22¢ Winter Special Olympics	3.25
85-17	22¢ Flag over Capitol sheet and coil (3) #2114-2115	3.25
85-18	22¢ Flag over Capitol booklet pane (5)	3.25
85-19	12¢ Stanley Steamer coil (2)	4.00
85-20	22¢ Seashells #2121a booklet pane (10)	5.50
85-21	22¢ Love	3.50
85-22	10.1¢ Oil Wagon coil (3)	3.25
85-23	12.5¢ Pushcart coil (2)	3.75
85-24	22¢ John J. Audubon	4.25
85-25	$10.75 Eagle booklet single	47.50
85-26	$10.75 Eagle booklet pane (3)	100.00
85-27	6¢ Tricycle coil (4)	3.75
85-28	22¢ Rural Electrification Administration #2144	3.25
85-29	14¢ and 22¢ Penalty Mail sheet and coil (4)	3.25
85-30	22¢ AMERIPEX '86	3.25
85-31	9¢ Sylvanus Thayer (3)	3.25
85-32	3.4¢ School Bus coil (7)	4.00
85-33	11¢ Stutz Bearcat coil (2)	3.75
85-34	22¢ Abigail Adams	3.25
85-35	4.9¢ Buckboard coil (5)	3.75
85-36	8.3¢ Ambulance coil (3)	3.25
85-37	22¢ Frederic Bartholdi	3.75
85-38	8¢ Henry Knox (3)	3.25
85-39	22¢ Korean War Veterans	4.00
85-40	Social Security Act	3.25
85-41	44¢ Father Junipero Serra airmail	3.25
85-42	World War I Veterans	5.25
85-43	6¢ Walter Lippmann (4)	4.25
85-44	22¢ Horses (4)	5.75
85-45	Public Education	3.25
85-46	International Youth Year (4)	5.75
85-47	Help End Hunger	3.25
85-48	21.1¢ Letters coil (2)	3.75
85-49	22¢ Christmas, Madonna	3.25
85-50	Christmas, Poinsettias	3.25
85-51	18¢ Washington/ Washington Monument coil (2) #2149	3.25

1986

86-01	22¢ Arkansas Statehood	3.25
86-02	25¢ Jack London	3.25
86-03	22¢ Stamp Collecting booklet pane (4)	4.50
86-04	22¢ Love	4.00
86-05	Sojourner Truth	5.50
86-06	5¢ Hugo L. Black (5)	4.00
86-07	Republic of Texas (2)	3.25
86-08	$2 William Jennings Bryan	5.00
86-09	22¢ Fish booklet pane (5)	6.00
86-10	22¢ Public Hospitals	2.75
86-11	22¢ Duke Ellington	6.00
86-12	Presidents, Washington-Harrison (9)	5.75
86-13	Presidents, Tyler-Grant (9)	5.75
86-14	Presidents, Hayes-Wilson (9)	5.75
86-15	Presidents, Harding-Johnson (9)	5.75
86-16	22¢ Polar Explorers (4)	5.25
86-17	17¢ Belva Ann Lockwood (2)	4.00
86-18	1¢ Margaret Mitchell (3)	5.50
86-19	22¢ Statue of Liberty	3.75
86-20	4¢ Father Flanagan (3)	3.25
86-21	17¢ Dog Sled coil (2)	3.25
86-22	56¢ John Harvard	3.50
86-23	Navajo Blankets (4)	5.25
86-24	3¢ Paul Dudley White, MD (8)	3.25
86-25	$1 Bernard Revel	3.75
86-26	22¢ T.S. Eliot	5.25
86-27	Wood-Carved Figurines (4)	5.50
86-28	22¢ Christmas, Madonna	3.25
86-29	Christmas, Village Scene	3.25
86-30	5.5¢ Star Route Truck coil (4)	4.00
86-31	25¢ Bread Wagon coil	4.00

1987

87-01	8.5¢ Tow Truck coil (5)	3.25
87-02	22¢ Michigan Statehood	3.75
87-03	Pan American Games	3.25
87-04	Love	3.25
87-05	7.1¢ Tractor coil (5)	3.25
87-06	14¢ Julia Ward Howe (2)	3.25
87-07	22¢ Jean Baptiste Pointe Du Sable	6.50
87-08	22¢ Enrico Caruso	3.75
87-09	2¢ Mary Lyon (3)	3.25
87-10	Reengraved 2¢ Locomotive coil (6)	4.50
87-11	22¢ Girl Scouts	6.00
87-12	10¢ Canal Boat coil (5)	3.75
87-13	22¢ Special Occasions booklet pane (10)	4.50
87-14	United Way	3.25
87-15	22¢ Flag with Fireworks	3.25
87-16	22¢ Flag over Capitol coil, prephosphored paper (2) #2214-#2215	3.25
87-17	Wildlife, Swallow-Squirrel (10)	6.50
87-18	Wildlife, Armadillo-Rabbit (10)	6.50
87-19	Wildlife, Tanager-Ladybug (10)	6.50
87-20	Wildlife, Beaver-Prairie Dog (10)	6.50
87-21	Wildlife, Turtle-Fox (10)	6.50
87-22	22¢ Delaware Statehood	3.75
87-23	U.S./Morocco Friendship	3.25
87-24	22¢ William Faulkner	6.25
87-25	22¢ Lacemaking (4)	6.75
87-26	10¢ Red Cloud (3)	5.50
87-27	$5 Bret Harte	10.00
87-28	Pennsylvania Statehood	3.25
87-29	Drafting of the Constitution booklet pane (5) #2359a	4.00
87-30	New Jersey Statehood	3.75
87-31	Signing of Constitution	3.25
87-32	22¢ Certified Public Accountants	6.00
87-33	5¢ Milk Wagon and 17.5¢ Racing Car coils (4)	3.25
87-34	22¢ Locomotives #2366a booklet pane (5)	9.00
87-35	Christmas, Madonna	3.25
87-36	Christmas, Ornaments	3.25
87-37	22¢ Flag with Fireworks booklet-pair #2276	3.25

1988

88-01	22¢ Georgia Statehood	3.75
88-02	Connecticut Statehood	3.75
88-03	22¢ Winter Olympics	3.25
88-04	Australia Bicentennial	4.00
88-05	James Weldon Johnson	3.75
88-06	Cats (4)	6.50
88-07	Massachusetts Statehood	3.75
88-08	Maryland Statehood	3.75
88-09	3¢ Conestoga Wagon coil (8)	3.25
88-10	Knute Rockne	10.00
88-11	"E" (25¢) Earth sheet and coil (3) #2277, #2279	4.00
88-12	"E" (25¢) Earth booklet pane (10) #2282a	4.00
88-13	"E" (25¢) Penalty Mail coil (2) #O140	3.25
88-14	44¢ New Sweden airmail	3.25
88-15	25¢ Pheasant booklet pane (10)	5.25
88-16	25¢ Jack London booklet pane (6)	3.25
88-17	Jack London booklet pane (10)	5.75
88-18	Flag with Clouds #2278	3.25
88-19	45¢ Samuel Langley airmail	3.25
88-19A	20¢ Penalty Mail coil (2)	3.25
88-20	Flag over Yosemite coil (2)	3.25
88-21	South Carolina Statehood	3.25
88-22	25¢ Owl & Grosbeak booklet pane (10)	4.00
88-23	15¢ Buffalo Bill Cody (2)	3.25
88-24	15¢ and 25¢ Penalty Mail coils (4)	3.25
88-25	25¢ Francis Ouimet	12.00
88-26	45¢ Harvey Cushing, MD	3.25
88-27	New Hampshire Statehood	3.25
88-28	36¢ Igor Sikorsky airmail	3.25
88-29	22¢ Virginia Statehood	3.75
88-30	10.1¢ Oil Wagon coil, precancel (3)	3.25
88-31	25¢ Love #2378	3.25
88-32	25¢ Flag with Clouds booklet pane (6) #2285c	3.75
88-33	16.7¢ Popcorn Wagon coil (2)	3.75
88-34	15¢ Tugboat coil (2)	3.75
88-35	13.2¢ Coal Car coil (2)	5.25
88-36	New York Statehood	3.25
88-37	45¢ Love #2379	3.25
88-38	8.4¢ Wheelchair coil (3)	3.50
88-39	21¢ Railroad Mail Car coil (2)	4.75
88-40	25¢ Summer Olympics	3.25
88-41	Classic Cars booklet pane (5)	6.00
88-42	7.6¢ Carreta coil (4)	3.50
88-43	25¢ Honeybee coil (2)	4.75
88-44	25¢ Antarctic Explorers (4)	3.75
88-45	5.3¢ Elevator coil (5)	3.50
88-46	20.5¢ Fire Engine coil (2)	4.75
88-47	25¢ Carousel Animals (4)	5.25
88-48	$8.75 Eagle	22.00
88-49	25¢ Christmas, Madonna	3.25
88-50	Christmas, Snow Scene	3.25
88-51	21¢ Chester Carlson	3.25
88-52	Special Occasions booklet pane (6), Love You, Thinking of You #2396a	20.00
88-53	Special Occasions booklet pane (6), Happy Birthday, Best Wishes #2398a	20.00
88-54	24.1¢ Tandem Bicycle coil (2)	3.50
88-55	20¢ Cable Car coil (2)	3.75
88-56	13¢ Patrol Wagon coil (2)	5.25
88-57	23¢ Mary Cassatt	3.25
88-58	65¢ H.H. "Hap" Arnold	4.50

1989

89-01	25¢ Montana Statehood	3.25
89-02	25¢ A. Philip Randolph	4.25
89-03	25¢ Flag over Yosemite coil, prephosphored paper (2)	3.25
89-04	North Dakota Statehood	3.25
89-05	25¢ Washington Statehood	3.25
89-06	25¢ Steamboats booklet pane (5) #2409a	6.50
89-07	25¢ World Stamp Expo '89	3.25
89-08	Arturo Toscanini	5.25
89-09	U.S. House of Representatives	3.25
89-10	U.S. Senate	3.25
89-11	Executive Branch	3.25
89-12	South Dakota Statehood	3.25
89-13	7.1¢ Tractor coil, precancel (4)	3.25
89-14	$1 Johns Hopkins	3.75
89-15	25¢ Lou Gehrig	12.00
89-16	1¢ Penalty Mail #O143	3.25
89-17	45¢ French Revolution airmail	5.25
89-18	Ernest Hemingway	6.00
89-19	$2.40 Moon Landing	20.00
89-20	North Carolina Statehood	3.75
89-21	25¢ Letter Carriers	3.25
89-22	28¢ Sitting Bull	4.75
89-23	25¢ Drafting of the Bill of Rights	3.25
89-24	Prehistoric Animals (4)	8.00
89-25	25¢ and 45¢ PUAS/ America (2)	3.25
89-26	Christmas, Madonna	3.25
89-27	Christmas, Antique Sleigh	3.25
89-28	25¢ Eagle and Shield, self-adhesive	3.25
89-29	90¢ World Stamp Expo '89 souvenir sheet	12.00
89-30	25¢ Classic Mail Transportation (4)	5.00
89-31	Future Mail Transportation 45¢ souvenir sheet	6.00
89-32	45¢ Future Mail Transportation airmails (4)	6.00
89-33	Classic Mail Transportation souvenir sheet	6.50

1990

90-01	25¢ Idaho Statehood	3.25
90-02	25¢ Love sheet and booklet pane (10)	5.25
90-03	25¢ Ida B. Wells	5.25
90-04	25¢ U.S. Supreme Court	3.25
90-05	15¢ Beach Umbrella booklet pane (10)	5.25
90-06	5¢ Luis Muñoz Marín (5)	3.25
90-07	25¢ Wyoming Statehood	4.00
90-08	Classic Films (4)	9.00
90-09	Marianne Moore	4.00
90-10	$1 Seaplane coil (2)	6.50
90-11	25¢ Lighthouses booklet pane (5)	9.00
90-12	25¢ Plastic Flag	3.75
90-13	Rhode Island Statehood	3.25
90-14	$2 Bobcat	5.25
90-15	25¢ Olympians (5)	5.75
90-16	Indian Headdresses booklet pane (10)	6.75
90-17	5¢ Circus Wagon coil (5)	3.75
90-18	40¢ Claire Lee Chennault	4.25
90-19	25¢ Federated States of Micronesia/Marshall Islands (2)	3.25
90-20	Creatures of the Sea (4)	7.00
90-21	25¢ and 45¢ PUAS/ America (2) #2426	3.25
90-22	25¢ Dwight D. Eisenhower	3.75
90-23	25¢ Christmas, Madonna, sheet and booklet pane (10)	6.00
90-24	Christmas, Yule Tree, sheet and booklet pane (10)	6.00

1991

91-01	"F" (29¢) Flower sheet and coil (3)	3.25
91-02	"F" (29¢) Flower booklet panes (20)	10.00
91-03	(4¢) Makeup	3.25
91-04	"F" (29¢) Flag ATM booklet single	3.75
91-05	"F" (29¢) Penalty Mail coil (2)	3.25
91-06	4¢ Steam Carriage coil (7)	3.50
91-07	50¢ Switzerland	3.25
91-08	20¢ Vermont Statehood	3.50
91-09	19¢ Fawn (2)	3.50
91-10	29¢ Flag over Mount Rushmore coil (2) #2523	3.75
91-11	35¢ Dennis Chavez	4.00
91-12	29¢ Flower sheet and booklet pane (10)	6.25
91-13	4¢ Penalty Mail (8)	3.50
91-14	29¢ Wood Duck booklet panes (10)	12.00
91-15	23¢ Lunch Wagon coil (2)	3.75
91-16	29¢ Flag with Olympic Rings booklet pane (10)	6.50

91-17	50¢ Harriet Quimby	3.75
91-18	29¢ Savings Bond	3.25
91-19	Love sheet and booklet pane, 52¢ Love (12)	12.00
91-20	19¢ Balloon booklet pane (10)	5.25
91-21	40¢ William Piper airmail	3.25
91-22	William Saroyan	6.00
91-23	Penalty Mail coil and 19¢ and 23¢ sheet (4)	3.50
91-24	5¢ Canoe and 10¢ Tractor Trailer coils (4)	3.50
91-25	29¢ Flags on Parade	3.50
91-26	29¢ Fishing Flies booklet pane (5)	19.00
91-27	52¢ Hubert H. Humphrey	3.50
91-28	29¢ Cole Porter	3.75
91-29	50¢ Antarctic Treaty airmail	3.75
91-30	1¢ Kestrel, 3¢ Bluebird and 30¢ Cardinal (3)	3.50
91-31	39¢ Liberty Torch	3.50
91-32	29¢ Desert Shield/Desert Storm sheet and booklet pane (11)	10.00
91-33	29¢ Flag over Mount Rushmore coil, #2523	3.75
91-34	29¢ Summer Olympics (5)	7.00
91-35	29¢ Flower coil, slit perforations (3)	3.25
91-36	Numismatics	5.20
91-37	29¢ Basketball	8.00
91-38	through 91-47 are unassigned	
91-48	19¢ Fishing Boat coil (3)	5.25
91-49	29¢ Comedians booklet pane (10)	8.75
91-50	29¢ World War II miniature sheet (10)	11.00
91-51	District of Columbia	3.25
91-52	29¢ Jan Matzeliger	6.00
91-53	$1 USPS/Olympic Logo	4.00
91-54	29¢ Space Exploration booklet pane (10)	11.00
91-55	50¢ PUASP/America airmail #C131	3.25
91-56	29¢ Christmas, Madonna sheet and booklet pane (10)	11.00
91-57	Christmas, Santa Claus sheet and booklet pane (11)	18.00
91-58	5¢ Canoe coil, gravure printing (red, 6)	3.75
91-59	29¢ Eagle and Shield, self-adhesive (3)	4.50
91-60	23¢ Flag presort #2606	4.00
91-61	$9.95 Express Mail #2541	12.00
91-62	$2.90 Priority Mail #2540	32.00
91-63	$14.00 Express Mail International #2542	42.50

1992

92-01	Winter Olympic Games (5)	5.25
92-02	29¢ World Columbian Stamp Expo '92	4.50
92-03	W.E.B. DuBois	6.00
92-04	Love	3.25
92-05	75¢ Wendell Willkie	4.50
92-06	(29¢) Flower coil, round perforations (2)	3.25
92-07	29¢ Earl Warren	3.75
92-08	Olympic Baseball	14.00
92-09	Flag over White House, coil (2) #2609	3.50
92-10	First Voyage of Christopher Columbus (4)	4.50
92-11	New York Stock Exchange	3.50
92-12	Christopher Columbus	12.00
92-13	Columbus - Seeking Royal Support (3) #2626	9.00
92-14	Columbus - First Sighting of Land (3) #2624	10.00
92-15	Columbus - Claiming New World (3) #2625	11.00
92-16	Columbus - Reporting Discoveries (3) #2628	10.00
92-17	Columbus - Royal Favor Restored (3) #2627	11.00
92-18	29¢ Space Adventures (4)	7.50
92-19	29¢ Alaska Highway	3.75
92-20	29¢ Kentucky Statehood	3.50
92-21	29¢ Summer Olympic Games (5)	5.25
92-22	Hummingbirds booklet pane (5)	8.00
92-22A	23¢ Presort USA (3)	4.00
92-23	29¢ Wildflowers (10)	8.00
92-24	Wildflowers (10)	8.00
92-25	Wildflowers (10)	8.00
92-26	Wildflowers (10)	8.00
92-27	Wildflowers (10)	8.00
92-28	World War II miniature sheet (10)	9.00
92-29	29¢ Variable Rate	3.50
92-30	Dorothy Parker	3.75
92-31	Theodore von Karman	6.00
92-32	Pledge of Allegiance (10)	5.00
92-33	Minerals (4)	5.75
92-34	Eagle and Shield (3)	4.50
92-35	Juan Rodriguez Cabrillo	3.75
92-36	Wild Animals booklet pane (5)	7.25
92-37	23¢ Presort (3)	4.00
92-38	Christmas Contemporary, sheet and booklet pane (8)	6.00
92-39	Christmas Traditional, sheet and booklet pane (11)	10.00
92-40	45¢ Pumpkinseed Sunfish	3.75
92-41	5¢ Circus Wagon	3.75
92-42	Year of the Rooster	11.00

1993

93-01	29¢ Elvis	14.00
93-02	Space Fantasy (5)	10.00
93-03	Percy Lavon Julian	5.25
93-04	Oregon Trail	3.25
93-05	World University Games	3.25
93-06	Grace Kelly	9.00
93-07	Oklahoma!	3.25
93-08	Circus	6.00
93-09	29¢ Thomas Jefferson	3.25
93-10	Cherokee Strip	5.00
93-11	Dean Acheson	3.25
93-12	Sporting Horses	7.00
93-13	USA Coil	3.25
93-14	Garden Flowers, booklet pane (5)	5.25
93-15	Eagle and Shield, coil, #2595	4.50
93-16	World War II miniature sheet (10)	9.00
93-17	Futuristic Space Shuttle #2745a	10.00
93-18	Hank Williams, sheet	15.00
93-19	Rock & Roll/Rhythm & Blues, sheet single, booklet pane (8)	24.00
93-20	29¢ Joe Louis	12.00
93-21	29¢ Red Squirrel	3.75
93-22	Broadway Musicals, booklet pane (4)	6.75
93-23	National Postal Museum, strip (4)	4.50
93-24	29¢ Red Rose #2490	3.25
93-25	American Sign Language, pair	3.25
93-26	Country & Western Music, sheet and booklet pane (4)	15.00
93-27	African Violets, booklet pane (10)	5.00
93-28	10¢ Official Mail	3.50
93-29	Contemporary Christmas, booklet pane (10), sheet and self-adhesive stamps	18.00
93-30	Traditional Christmas, sheet, booklet pane (4)	6.75
93-31	Classic Books, strip (4)	4.25
93-32	Mariana Islands	3.25
93-33	29¢ Pine Cone #2491	3.75
93-34	29¢ Columbus' Landing in Puerto Rico	4.00
93-35	AIDS Awareness	6.50

1994

94-01	29¢ Winter Olympics	6.75
94-02	Edward R. Murrow	4.25
94-03	Love, self-adhesive	4.25
94-04	Dr. Allison Davis	6.50
94-05	29¢ Eagle, self-adhesive	3.50
94-06	Year of the Dog	4.75
94-07	Love, booklet pane (10), single sheet	9.00
94-08	29¢ Postage and Mailing Center	4.00
94-09	Buffalo Soldiers	7.00
94-10	Silent Screen Stars	8.00
94-11	Garden Flowers, booklet pane (5)	8.00
94-12	$1 Victory at Saratoga #2590	5.00
94-13	10¢ Tractor Trailer gravure printing	5.00
94-14	World Cup Soccer	8.00
94-15	World Cup Soccer souvenir sheet	8.00
94-16	World War II miniature sheet (10)	7.25
94-17	Love, sheet stamp	4.00
94-18	Statue of Liberty #2599	3.50
94-19	Fishing Boat, reissue	4.00
94-20	Norman Rockwell	14.00
94-21	$9.95 and 29¢ Moon Landing	25.00
94-22	Locomotives (5)	8.75
94-23	George Meany	4.00
94-24	$5.00 Washington/ Jackson #2592	13.00
94-25	Popular Singers (5)	8.00
94-26	James Thurber	5.25
94-27	Jazz Singers/ Blues Singers (10)	11.00
94-28	Wonders of the Sea (4)	6.50
94-29	Chinese/Joint Issue (2)	4.00
94-30	Holiday Traditional (10)	9.75
94-31	Holiday Contemporary (4)	6.75
94-32	Holiday, self-adhesive	8.00
94-33	20¢ Virginia Apgar	4.75
94-34	$2 BEP Centennial #2875	18.00
94-35	Year of the Boar	6.75
94-G1	G1 (4) Rate Change	5.25
94-G2	G2 (6) Rate Change	5.25
94-G3	G3 (5) Rate Change	5.25
94-G4	G4 (2) Rate Change	10.00
94-36	29¢ Legends of West	21.50

1995

95-01	29¢ Love (2)	4.00
95-02	Florida Statehood	3.25
95-03	(5¢) Butte (6)	6.50
95-04	(10¢) Automobile (4)	5.25
95-05	Flag Over Field, self-adhesive #2919	6.00
95-06	Juke Box (2+2) (25¢)	4.25
95-07	Tail Fin (2+2) (15¢)	5.25
95-08	(5¢) Circus Wagon	5.25
95-09	32¢ Kids Care (4)	4.00
95-10	32¢ Richard Nixon	4.00
95-11	32¢ Bessie Coleman	5.25
95-12	Official Mail #O153-#O156	3.50
95-13	1¢ Kestrel with cent sign #2477	3.50
95-14	Love 1 oz. and 2 oz.	4.00
95-15	32¢ Flag Over Porch	6.50
95-16	Recreational Sports (5)	10.00
95-17	POW / MIA	4.50
95-18	Marilyn Monroe	14.00
95-19	32¢ Pink Rose #2492	5.25
95-20	32¢ Ferry Boat (3) #2466	4.00
95-21	20¢ Cog Railway Car (3) #2463	4.00
95-22	20¢ Blue Jay #2483	3.50
95-23	Texas Statehood	5.00
95-24	Great Lake Lighthouses (5)	10.00
95-25	$3 Challenger Shuttle #2544	14.00
95-26	32¢ United Nations	3.25
95-27	Civil War (front and back)	16.00
95-28	32¢ Peach & Pear	5.25
95-29	55¢ Alice Hamilton	3.25
95-30	Carousel Horses	7.00
95-31	$10.75 Endeavor Shuttle	25.00
95-32	78¢ Alice Paul	3.25
95-33	32¢ Women's Suffrage	3.25
95-34	Louis Armstrong	5.00
95-35	World War II	8.00
95-36	Milton Hershey	3.25
95-37	Jazz Musicians	9.00
95-38	Fall Garden Flowers (5)	8.00
95-39	Eddie Rickenbacker (airmail)	5.00
95-40	Republic of Palau	4.00
95-41	Holiday Contemporary/ Santa (4)	6.00
95-42	American Comic Strips	16.00
95-43	Naval Academy	5.00
95-44	Tennessee Williams	5.00
95-45	Holiday Children Sledding	6.00
95-46	Holiday Traditional sheet and booklet pane (10)	7.25
95-47	Holiday Midnight Angel	5.25
95-48	46¢ Ruth Benedict	4.00
95-49	32¢ James K. Polk #2587	7.00
95-50	Antique Automobiles, strip (5) #3023a	7.50

1996

96-01	32¢ Utah Statehood	4.00
96-02	Garden Flowers	7.25
96-03	32¢ Flag Over Porch/ Love/Kestrel	16.00
96-04	32¢ Postage and Mailing Center (3)	5.50
96-05	Ernest E. Just #3058	6.00
96-06	2¢ Woodpecker #3032	4.00
96-07	Smithsonian Institution	4.00
96-08	32¢ Year of the Rat	7.25
96-09	Pioneers of Communication	5.50
96-10	Fulbright Scholarships	4.00
96-11	50¢ Jacqueline Cochran	4.00
96-12	(5¢) Mountain #2903-#2904	6.50
96-13	3¢ Bluebird #3033	4.00
96-14	Marathon	4.00
96-15	32¢ Flag over Porch/ Eagle & Shield	6.50
96-16	32¢ Cal Farley	4.00
96-17	32¢ Classic Olympic Collection	17.50
96-18	Georgia O'Keefe Art	5.25
96-19	Tennessee	4.00
96-20	American Indian Dances	5.25
96-21	Prehistoric Animals	5.25
96-22	Breast Cancer Awareness	5.75
96-23	Flag Over Porch/Juke Box/ Butte/Tail Fin Automobile/Mountain	5.50
96-24	James Dean	7.25
96-25	Folk Heroes	6.25
96-26	Centennial Olympic Games #3087	5.75
96-27	Iowa	5.75
96-28	20¢ Blue Jay #3048	5.75
96-29	Rural Free Delivery	4.50
96-30	Riverboats #3095a	7.50
96-31	Big Band Leaders	7.25
96-32	Songwriters	7.25
96-33	F. Scott Fitzgerald	4.50
96-34	Endangered Species	18.00
96-35	Computer Technology	4.50
96-36	Holiday, Family Scenes	7.25
96-37	Skaters	7.25
96-38	Hanukkah	5.75
96-39	Madonna and Child	7.25
96-40	32¢ Yellow Rose #3049	6.00
96-41	Cycling	7.25

1997

97-01	32¢ Year of the Ox	8.75
97-02	Flag Over Porch/	
	Juke Box/ Mountain	5.50
97-03	Benjamin O. Davis Sr.	7.25
97-04	Statue of Liberty	6.50
97-05	Love Swans	6.50
97-06	Helping Children Learn	5.75
97-07	Merian Botanical Plants	6.50
97-08	Pacific 97 -	
	Stagecoach and Ship	7.25
97-09	Linerless Flag	
	Over Porch/ Juke Box	6.50
97-10	Thornton Wilder	5.75
97-11	Raoul Wallenberg	5.75
97-12	Dinosaurs	18.00
97-13	Pacific '97 - Franklin	16.00
97-14	Pacific '97 - Washington	16.00
97-15	Bugs Bunny	18.00
97-16	The Marshall Plan	6.50
97-17	Humphrey Bogart	7.25
97-18	Classic Aircraft	18.00
97-19	Classic American Dolls	15.00
97-20	Football Coaches	16.00
97-20A	George Halas	11.00
97-20B	Vince Lombardi	11.00
97-20C	Pop Warner	11.00
97-20D	Bear Bryant	11.00
97-21	Yellow Rose #3054	7.25
97-22	"Stars and Stripes Forever"	7.25
97-23	Padre Félix Varela	7.20
97-24	Composers and	
	Conducters	12.00
97-25	Opera Singers	11.00
97-26	Air Force	11.00
97-27	Movie Monsters	14.00
97-28	Supersonic Flight	11.00
97-29	Women in Military	7.25
97-30	Kwanzaa	8.00
97-31	Holiday Traditional,	
	Madonna and Child	9.00
97-32	Holly	9.00
97-33	Mars Pathfinder	18.00

1998

98-01	32¢ Year of the Tiger	8.00
98-02	Winter Sports #3180	8.00
98-03	Madam C. J. Walker	8.00
98-03A	Celebrate The Century®	
	1900s	17.50
98-03B	Celebrate The Century®	
	1910s	17.50
98-04	"Remember the Maine"	8.00
98-05	Flowering Trees	9.75
98-06	Alexander Calder	9.75
98-07	Henry R. Luce	7.25
98-08	Cinco De Mayo	7.25
98-09	Sylvester & Tweety	9.75
98-09A	Celebrate The Century®	
	1920s	17.50
98-10	Wisconsin Statehood	8.00
98-11	Trans-Mississippi	
	Reissue of 1898	20.00
98-12	$1 Trans-Mississippi	
	(single stamp)	15.00
98-13	Folk Musicians	10.00
98-14	Berlin Airlift	7.25
98-15	(5¢) Diner/	
	(25¢) Wetlands coil	7.25
98-16	Spanish Settlement	
	of the Southwest	7.25
98-17	Gospel Singers	9.00
98-18	The Wallaces	5.75
98-19	Stephen Vincent Benét	7.25
98-20	Tropical Birds #3225a	11.00
98-21	Breast Cancer Research	
	(semi-postal) #B1	8.00
98-22	20¢ Ring-Neck Pheasant	7.25
98-23	Alfred Hitchcock	8.00
98-24	Organ Donations	7.25
98-24A	$1 Red Fox	9.00
98-24B	Bicycle coil (10¢) #3229	7.25
98-25	Bright Eyes	10.00
98-26	Klondike Gold Rush	8.00
98-26A	Celebrate The Century®	
	1930s	17.50
98-27	32¢ American Art	16.00
98-28	Ballet	8.00
98-28A	(25¢) Diner coil #3208a	7.25
98-29	Space Discovery	9.75
98-30	Philanthropy #3243	7.25
98-31	Holiday Traditional	7.25
98-32	Holiday Contemporary	9.75
98-33	Hat Rate Change	
	"H" Series/ Makeup Rate	8.00
98-34	Uncle Sam - Rate Change	7.25
98-35	Hat Rate Change	
	"H" Series	8.50
98-36	Hat Rate Change	
	"H" Series	9.00
98-37	Mary Breckinridge	6.50
98-38	Space Shuttle Landing	17.50
98-39	Shuttle Piggyback	27.50
98-40	Wetlands non-denominated	
	nonprofit coil and Eagle	
	& Shield non-denominated	
	presort coil	8.00

1999

99-01	33¢ Year of the Hare	9.75
99-02	Malcolm X	13.00
99-03	33¢ Victorian - Love	8.00
99-04	55¢ Victorian - Love	8.00
99-05	Hospice Care	7.25
99-06	Celebrate The Century®	
	1940s	17.50
99-07	City Flag	8.00
99-08	Irish Immigration	7.25
99-09	Alfred Lunt and	
	Lynn Fontanne	7.25
99-10	Arctic Animals	9.75
99-10A	Flag Over Chalkboard	
	#3283	7.25
99-11	Nature of America	
	Sonoran Desert	16.00
99-11A	33¢ Fruit Berries	9.00
99-12	Daffy Duck	9.75
99-13	Ayn Rand	8.00
99-14	Cinco de Mayo	7.25
99-15	Tropical Flowers	9.00
99-16	Niagara Falls	8.50
99-17	John and William Bartram	7.25
99-18	Celebrate The Century®	17.50
	1950s	
99-19	Prostate Cancer	7.25
99-20	California Gold Rush	7.25
99-20A	2¢ Woodpecker #3032	4.00
99-21	Aquarium Fish	9.00
99-22	Extreme Sports	8.75
99-23	American Glass	9.00
99-24	Justin Morrill	7.25
99-25	James Cagney	9.00
99-26	55¢ Billy Mitchell	8.75
99-27	40¢ Rio Grande #C134	7.25
99-28	Pink Coral Rose	7.25
99-29	Honoring Those	
	Who Served	7.25
99-29A	UPU	7.25
99-30	All Aboard!	10.00
99-31	Frederick Law Olmsted	7.25
99-32	Hollywood Composers	15.00
99-33	Celebrate The Century®	
	1960s	17.50
99-34	Broadway Songwriters	14.50
99-35	Insects and Spiders	18.00
99-36	Hanukkah	7.25
99-37	Official Mail #O157	7.25
99-38	Uncle Sam	7.25
99-39	NATO #3354	7.25
99-40	Holiday Traditional,	
	Madonna & Child	7.25
99-41	Holiday Contemporary,	
	Deer	8.75
99-42	Kwanzaa	7.25
99-43	Celebrate The Century®	
	1970s	17.50
99-44	1¢ Kestrel #3031	7.25
99-45 through 99-49 are unassigned		
99-50	Year 2000	7.25

2000

00-01	33¢ Year of the Dragon	9.75
00-02	Celebrate The Century®	
	1980s	17.50
00-03	60¢ Grand Canyon	7.25
00-04	Patricia Roberts Harris	8.00
00-05	Fruit Berries	8.00
00-06	U.S. Navy Submarine –	
	Los Angeles Class	16.00
00-07	Pacific Coast	
	Rain Forest	18.50
00-08	Louise Nevelson	9.25
00-09	Coral Pink Rose	7.25
00-10	Edwin Powell Hubble	9.25
00-11	American Somoa	7.25
00-12	Library of Congress	7.25
00-13	Wile E. Coyote/	
	Road Runner	10.00
00-14	Celebrate The Century®	
	1990s	17.50
00-15	Summer Sports	7.25
00-16	Adoption	11.00
00-17	Youth Team Sports	8.00
00-18	Distinguished Soldiers	9.75
00-19	The Stars and Stripes	16.00
00-20	Legends of Baseball	20.00
00-21	Stampin' The Future™	8.00
00-22	10¢ Joseph Stilwell	7.25
00-23	33¢ Claude Pepper	7.25
00-24	California Statehood	7.25
00-25	Edward G. Robinson	8.00
00-26	Deep Sea Creatures	9.25
00-27	Thomas Wolfe	8.00
00-28	White House	7.25
00-29	(10¢) New York Public Library	
	Lion Presort #3447	7.25

2001

No.	Description	Value
01-01	(34¢) Farm Flag (1 oz.)	7.25
01-02	Statue of Liberty #3466	6.50
01-03	34¢ Flowers	7.25
01-04	34¢ Statute of Liberty	6.50
01-05	Love Letters #3496	6.50
01-06	Year of the Snake	8.75
01-07	Roy Wilkins	10.00
01-08	Washington Monument	27.50
01-09	U.S. Capitol	13.50
01-10	American Illustrators (front & back)	26.00
01-11	Farm Flag #3470	7.25
01-12	Statute of Liberty	7.50
01-13	Flowers	7.50
01-14	Love Letters #3497, #3499	9.00
01-15	76¢ Hattie Caraway	7.25
01-16	21¢ Buffalo	6.50
01-17	George Washington	7.25
01-18	Art Deco Eagle (2 oz.)	7.25
01-19	Official Mail #O158	6.50
01-20	34¢ Apple and Orange	7.25
01-21	Nine-Mile Prairie	7.25
01-22	Farm Flag #3495	8.00
01-23	Diabetes Awareness	8.00
01-24	The Nobel Prize	8.00
01-25	The Pan- American Inverts (front and back)	18.00
01-26	Mt. McKinley (Int'l PC)	9.00
01-27	34¢ Great Plains Prairie (front and back)	17.50
01-28	Peanuts	12.00
01-29	Honoring Veterans	9.00
01-30	Acadia National Park	8.00
01-31	Frida Kahlo	12.00
01-32	Baseball's Legendary Playing Fields (front and back)	27.50
01-33	(10¢) Atlas Statue	6.50
01-34	Leonard Bernstein	8.00
01-35	(15¢) Woody Wagon	6.50
01-36	Lucille Ball	10.00
01-37	The Amish Quilts	8.75
01-38	Carnivorous Plants	8.75
01-39	Holiday Celebration–Eid	6.50
01-40	Dr. Enrico Fermi	8.00
01-41	Bison #3467, #3484	6.50
01-42	20¢ George Washington	6.50
01-43	Art Deco Eagle	7.50
01-44	"That's All Folks!"	10.00
01-45	Holiday Traditional: Lorenza Costa– Virgin and Child	6.50
01-46	Holiday Celebration: Santas	8.00
01-47	Holiday Celebration: Thanksgiving	6.50
01-48	James Madison	6.50
01-49	Kwanzaa	6.50
01-50	Hanukkah	6.50
01-51	Farm Flag (1 oz.)	8.00
01-52	Love Letters #3551	7.50
01-53	United We Stand	13.50

2002

No.	Description	Value
02-01	34¢ Winter Sports	9.75
02-02	Mentoring a Child	6.50
02-03	Langston Hughes	9.75
02-04	Happy Birthday	6.50
02-05	Year of the Horse	8.00
02-06	U.S. Military Academy	8.00
02-07	Greetings From America	37.50
02-08	Longleaf Pine Forest	17.50
02-09	5¢ American Toleware	6.50
02-10	37¢ U.S. Flag	8.75
02-11	Antique Toys	8.00
02-12	3¢ Star #3613-#3615	6.50
02-13	U.S. Flag	6.50
02-14	George Washington	7.50
02-15	Heroes 2001	16.00
02-16	Masters of American Photography	25.00
02-17	John James Audubon	7.25
02-18	Harry Houdini	7.25
02-19	60¢ Eagle Coverlet	6.50
02-20	Antique Toys	8.75
02-21	83¢ Edna Ferber	7.25
02-22	$3.85 Jefferson Memorial	12.00
02-23	$13.65 Capitol at Dusk	27.50
02-24	Official Mail #O159	7.00
02-25	Andy Warhol	7.25
02-26	Teddy Bears	8.00
02-27	Love #3657-#3658	8.00
02-28	37¢ Ogden Nash	7.25
02-29	Duke Kahanamoku	7.50
02-30	American Bats	8.00
02-31	Women in Journalism	9.75
02-32	Irving Berlin	7.25
02-33	Neuter or Spay	7.75
02-34	Christmas: Gossaert	7.25
02-35	Eid	7.00
02-36	Kwanzaa	7.00
02-37	Hanukkah	7.00
02-38	Cary Grant	9.25
02-39	Sea Coast Nonprofit (5¢)	7.25
02-40	Hawaiian Missionaries	13.00
02-41	Happy Birthday	7.25
02-42	Greetings From America	37.50
02-43	Holiday Celebrations: Snowmen	8.00

2003

No.	Description	Value
03-01	37¢ Thurgood Marshall	7.50
03-02	Year of the Ram	7.50
03-03	Zora Neale Hurston	7.50
03-04	American Clock	7.00
03-05	U.S. Flag	6.50
03-06	(10¢) The New York Public Library Lion	7.50
03-07	80¢ Special Oylmpics	8.50
03-08	American Filmmaking: Behind the Scenes	13.50
03-09	$1 Wisdom	9.00
03-10	1¢ Tiffany Lamp	7.00
03-11	Ohio Statehood	7.50
03-12	Pelican Island National Wildlife Refuge	7.50
03-13	(5¢) Sea Coast	7.50
03-14	Old Glory	8.00
03-15	Cesar E. Chavez	7.50
03-16	Louisiana Purchase	7.50
03-17	First Flight	7.50
03-18	Purple Heart	7.50
03-19	Audrey Hepburn	8.50
03-20	Southeastern Lighthouses	9.00
03-21	American Eagle (2)	6.50
03-21A	American Eagle (10)	10.00
03-22	Arctic Tundra	12.50
03-23	Korean War Veterans Memorial	7.00
03-24	Purple Heart	7.50
03-25	37¢ Mary Cassatt	8.00
03-26	Early Football Heroes	10.00
03-27	37¢ Antique Toys	8.75
03-28	Roy Acuff	7.00
03-29	District of Columbia	6.50
03-30	Reptiles and Amphibians	9.00
03-31	Stop Family Violence	7.25
03-32	Holiday Music Makers	7.50
03-33	Christmas: Gossaert	6.50
03-34	Snowy Egret	6.50
03-35	U.S. Flag #3631	6.50

2004

No.	Description	Value
04-01	37¢ Pacific Coral Reef	17.50
04-02	Lunar New Year: Monkey	7.25
04-03	Love: Candy Hearts	6.50
04-04	Paul Robeson	6.00
04-05	Snowy Egret	6.50
04-06	Theodor "Dr. Seuss" Geisel	8.00
04-07	Garden Bouquet	6.00
04-08	Garden Botanical	6.00
04-09	4¢ Chippendale Chair	7.00
04-10	U.S. Air Force Academy	6.50
04-11	Sea Coast #3785	6.00
04-12	Henry Mancini	6.50
04-13	American Choreographers	8.00
04-14	American Eagle	10.00
04-15	Lewis & Clark Prestige Booklet	12.00
04-16	Lewis & Clark Pane	12.00
04-17	Isamu Noguchi	7.50
04-18	National WWII Memorial	6.00
04-19	2004 Olympic Games	6.00
04-20	Sea Coast (5¢) Coil	6.00
04-21	Art of Disney: Friendship	9.00
04-22	American Toleware #3756	6.50
04-23	USS Constellation	6.00
04-24	R. Buckminster Fuller	6.00
04-25	23¢ Wilma Rudolph	7.25
04-26	James Baldwin	6.00
04-27	Martin Johnson Heade	6.00
04-28	Navajo Jewelry	7.00
04-29	Art of American Indian	11.00
04-30	John Wayne	9.00
04-30a	(10¢) Atlas Statue #3770	7.00
04-31	Sickle Cell Awareness	6.00
04-32	Cloudscapes	11.00
04-33	Madonna & Child	6.50
04-34	Hanukkah	6.00
04-35	Kwanzaa	6.00
04-36	Moss Hart	6.00
04-37	Holiday Ornaments	10.00

2005

No.	Description	Value
05-01	37¢ Lunar New Year	20.00
05-02	Marian Anderson	6.00
05-03	Ronald Reagan	11.00
05-04	Love Bouquet	6.00
05-05	Northeast Deciduous Forest	13.50
05-06	Spring Flowers	7.50
05-07	Robert Penn Warren	6.00
05-08	Yip Harburg	6.00
05-09	American Scientists	7.50
05-10	Modern American Architecture	12.00
05-11	Henry Fonda	6.00
05-12	Art of Disney: Celebration	9.00
05-13	Advances in Aviation	15.00
05-14	New Mexico Rio Grande Blankets	7.50
05-15	Presidential Libraries	10.00
05-16	American Eagle	10.00
05-17	Sporty Cars	8.75
05-18	Arthur Ashe	6.50
05-19	Perfect Union	10.00
05-20	Child Health	6.00
05-21	3¢ Silver Coffee Pot	7.00
05-22	Let's Dance/Bailemos	8.00
05-23	Greta Garbo	7.75
05-24	Jim Henson & Muppets	11.00
05-25	Constellations	7.50
05-26	Holiday Cookies	10.00
05-27	Distinguished Marines	8.00
05-28	(39¢) Lady Liberty Non-Denominated	10.00
05-29	Navajo Jewelry	7.00

	2006			2007			2008	
06-01	(39¢) Love: True Blue	6.00	07-01	Ella Fitzgerald 39¢	6.00	08-01	Celebrating Lunar New	
06-02	39¢ Lady Liberty and		07-02	Oklahoma Statehood	6.00		Year: Year of the Rat	6.00
	U.S. Flag 39¢ (10k)	7.50	07-03	With Love and Kisses	6.00	08-02	Charles W. Chesnutt	6.00
06-03	Favorite Children's		07-04	International Polar Year		08-03	Marjorie Kinnan Rawlings	6.00
	Book Animals	10.00		(Auroras) 84¢	7.50	08-04	American Scientists	7.50
06-04	2006 Olympic Winter		07-05	Henry W. Longfellow	6.00	08-05	Tiffany Lamp	6.00
	Games	6.00	07-06	Tiffany Lamp 1¢	6.00	08-06	Flags 24/7	7.50
06-05	Black Heritage:		07-07	3¢ Silver Coffeepot	6.00	08-07	Flags 24/7	7.50
	Hattie McDaniel	6.00	07-08	"Forever" Stamp	7.50	08-08	American Journalists	7.50
06-06	Lunar New Year	10.00	07-09	American Flag (non-denom.)		08-09	Tropical Fruit	10.00
06-07	Lady Liberty and			(41¢) #4129-4135	10.00	08-10	Purple Heart	6.00
	U.S. Flag 39¢ (3k)	7.50	07-10	Settlement of Jamestown	6.00	08-11	Forever	6.00
06-08	Great Smoky Mountains	6.00	07-11	Navajo Jewelry 2¢	6.00	08-12	James A. Michener	7.50
06-09	Yosemite National Park	6.00	07-12	Florida Panther 26¢	7.50	08-13	Edward Trudeau	7.50
06-10	Bryce Canyon		07-13	Bighorn Sheep (pane) 17¢	6.00	08-14	Frank Sinatra	6.00
	National Park	6.00	07-14	Bighorn Sheep (coil) 17¢	6.00	08-15	13 Mile Woods,	
06-11	Our Wedding (39¢ & 63¢)	7.50	07-15	Star Wars (2-sided)	10.00		New Hampshire	6.00
06-12	39¢ Official Mail	6.00	07-16	Hagåtña Bay, Guam	6.00	08-16	St. John, U.S.	
06-13	Lady Liberty and		07-17	Okefenokee Swamp,			Virgin Islands	7.50
	U.S. Flag (3k & 10k)	10.00		Georgia	6.00	08-17	Minnesota Statehood	6.00
06-14	Dr. Jonas Salk	7.50	07-18	Margaret Chase Smith	7.50	08-18	Dragonfly	7.50
06-15	Dr. Albert Sabin	7.50	07-19	Harriet Beecher Stowe	7.50	08-19	Mount Rushmore	12.00
06-16	Common Buckeye	7.50	07-20	Air Force One	12.00	08-20	Tiffany Lamp	6.00
06-17	Crops of America	12.00	07-21	Marine One	27.50	08-21	Love: All Heart	6.00
06-18	X-Planes: $4.05	10.00	07-22	Pacific Lighthouses	7.50	08-22	Hearts (1 oz. & 2 oz.)	7.50
06-19	X-Planes: $14.40	22.50	07-23	Official Mail (coil) 41¢	6.00	08-23	Flags of Our Nation #1	10.00
06-20	Sugar Ray Robinson	6.00	07-24	Hearts 41¢ and 58¢	7.50	08-24	Charles + Ray Eames	15.00
06-21	Benjamin Franklin	7.50	07-25	Pollination (bklt.)	10.00	08-25	Olympic Games	6.00
06-22	Lady Liberty and		07-26	Patriotic Banner	6.00	08-26	Hoover Dam	25.00
	U.S. Flag (bk)	7.50	07-27	Chippendale Chair 4¢	6.00	08-27	Celebrate!	6.00
06-23	Art of Disney: Romance	7.50	07-28	Marvel Comics		08-28	American Clock	6.00
06-24	Love: True Blue	6.00		Super Heroes	15.00	08-29	Vintage Black Cinema	7.50
06-25	Katherine Anne Porter	6.00	07-29	Vintage Mahogany		08-30	"Take Me Out to	
06-26	AMBER Alert	6.00		Speedboats	7.50		the Ball Game"	6.00
06-27	Purple Heart	6.00	07-30	41¢ Purple Heart #4164	6.00	08-31	The Art of Disney:	
06-28	Wonders of America:		07-31	Louis Comfort Tiffany	6.00		Imagination	7.50
	Land of Superlatives	40.00	07-32	Beautiful Blooms		08-32	Albert Bierstadt	6.00
06-29	1606 Voyage of Samuel			#4166-4185	15.00	08-33	Sunflower	6.00
	de Champlain (sov. sht)	7.50	07-33	American Flag 41¢		08-34	Forever	6.00
06-30	1606 Voyage of			#4186-4191	10.00	08-35	Flags of Our Nation #2	10.00
	Samuel de Champlain	7.50	07-34	Art of Disney: Magic	7.50	08-36	Sea Coast	6.00
06-31	Washington 2006		07-35	James Stewart	6.00	08-37	Latin Jazz	6.00
	World Philatelic Exhibition	16.00	07-36	Celebrate!	6.00	08-38	Bette Davis	6.00
06-32	Distinguished American		07-37	Nature of America:		08-39	EID	6.00
	Diplomats	7.50		Alpine Tundra	10.00	08-40	Nature of America:	
06-33	Judy Garland	6.00	07-38	Gerald R. Ford	6.00		Great Lakes Dunes	10.00
06-34	Ronald Reagan	6.00	07-39	Jury Duty	6.00	08-41	50s Fins and Chrome	7.50
06-35	Happy Birthday	6.00	07-40	Mendez v. Westminster	6.00	08-42	Alzheimer's Awareness	6.00
06-36	Baseball Sluggers	7.50	07-41	Eid 41¢	6.00	08-43	Holiday Nutcrackers	6.00
06-37	DC Comics Super Heroes	15.00	07-42	Polar Lights	6.00	08-44	Christmas: Botticelli	
06-38	American Clock	7.00	07-43	Holiday Knits	7.50		Virgin and Child	6.00
06-39	American Motorcycles	7.50	07-44	Luini: Madonna of the		08-45	Hanukkah	6.00
06-40	American Treasures:			Carnation	6.00	08-46	Kwanzaa	6.00
	Quilts of Gee's Bend	10.00	07-45	Yoda	6.00			
06-41	$1.00 Official Mail	7.50	07-46	Hanukkah	6.00			
06-42	Nature of America:		07-47	Kwanzaa	6.00			
	Southern Florida Wetlands	10.00						
06-43	Holiday Snowflakes	10.00						
06-44	Eid	6.00						
06-45	Hanukkah	6.00						
06-46	Kwanzaa	6.00						
06-47	Chacón: Madonna and							
	Child with Bird	6.00						
06-48	Lady Liberty and Flag							
	(bklt. of 20)	6.00						

American Commemorative Panels

The Postal Service offers American Commemorative Panels for each new commemorative stamp and special Holiday and Love stamp issued. The series began in 1972 with the Wildlife Commemorative Panel.

The panels feature mint stamps complemented by intaglio elements and the stories behind the commemorated subjects.

The identifying numbers used below are based on the Postal Service's numbering system for American Commemorative Panels; therefore, they do not follow the Scott numbering system.

1972

1	Wildlife	7.00
2	Mail Order	7.00
3	Osteopathic Medicine	14.00
4	Tom Sawyer	13.00
5	Pharmacy	9.50
6	Christmas, Angels	9.50
7	Santa Claus	9.50
8	Stamp Collecting	7.00

1973

9	Love	9.00
10	Pamphleteers	7.00
11	George Gershwin	9.00
12	Posting a Broadside	6.50
13	Copernicus	6.50
14	Postal Employees	6.50
15	Harry S. Truman	11.00
16	Postrider	9.00
17	Boston Tea Party	25.00
18	Electronics	11.00
19	Robinson Jeffers	6.50
20	Lyndon B. Johnson	9.00
21	Henry O. Tanner	6.50
22	Willa Cather	6.50
23	Drummer	12.00
24	Angus Cattle	9.00
25	Christmas, Madonna	13.50
26	Christmas Tree, Needlepoint	11.50

1974

27	VFW	6.50
28	Robert Frost	7.50
29	Expo '74	9.50
30	Horse Racing	12.00
31	Skylab	14.00
32	Universal Postal Union	9.00
33	Mineral Heritage	12.00
34	First Kentucky Settlement	7.00
35	Continental Congress	9.00
36	Chautauqua	9.00
37	Kansas Wheat	9.00
38	Energy Conservation	7.00
39	Sleepy Hollow	9.00
40	Retarded Children	6.50
41	Christmas, Currier & Ives	9.50
42	Christmas, Angel Altarpiece	9.50

1975

43	Benjamin West	9.00
44	Pioneer	15.00
45	Collective Bargaining	7.50
46	Contributors to the Cause	9.00
47	Mariner 10	17.50
48	Lexington & Concord	7.00
49	Paul Laurence Dunbar	9.00
50	D.W. Griffith	12.00
51	Bunker Hill	9.00
52	Military Uniforms	8.75
53	Apollo Soyuz	16.00
54	World Peace Through Law	7.00
55	Women's Year	7.00
56	Postal Service Bicentennial	7.00
57	Banking and Commerce	9.00
58	Early Christmas, Card	9.00
59	Christmas, Madonna	9.00

1976

60	Spirit of '76	12.50
61	*Interphil* 76	11.00
62	State Flags	25.00
63	Telephone	9.00
64	Commercial Aviation	11.00
65	Chemistry	9.00
66	Benjamin Franklin	10.00
67	Declaration of Independence	9.00
68	12th Winter Olympics	11.50
69	Clara Maass	16.00
70	Adolph S. Ochs	11.00
71	Christmas, Winter Pastime	11.00
72	Christmas, Nativity	13.00

1977

73	Washington at Princeton	14.00
74	Sound Recording	40.00
75	Pueblo Art	90.00
76	Solo Transatlantic Lindbergh Flight	95.00
77	Colorado	16.50
78	Butterflies	19.00
79	Lafayette	16.00
80	Skilled Hands	16.00
81	Peace Bridge	16.00
82	Battle of Oriskany	16.00
83	Alta, CA, Civil Settlement	16.00
84	Articles of Confederation	24.00
85	Talking Pictures	19.00
86	Surrender at Saratoga	20.00
87	Energy	16.00
88	Christmas, Valley Forge	18.50
89	Christmas, Mailbox	35.00

1978

90	Carl Sandburg	9.50
91	Captain Cook	15.50
92	Harriet Tubman	12.00
93	Quilts	19.00
94	Dance	14.00
95	French Alliance	11.50
96	Early Cancer Detection	12.00
97	Jimmie Rodgers	14.50
98	Photography	14.50
99	George M. Cohan	19.00
100	Viking Missions	42.50
101	Owls	42.50
102	Trees	34.00
103	Christmas, Madonna	16.00
104	Christmas, Hobby Horse	16.50

1979

105	Robert F. Kennedy	14.50
106	Martin Luther King, Jr.	11.00
107	International Year of the Child	9.00
108	John Steinbeck	8.50
109	Albert Einstein	11.50
110	Pennsylvania Toleware	14.00
111	Architecture	11.00
112	Endangered Flora	11.50
113	Seeing Eye Dogs	9.50
114	Special Olympics	9.00
115	John Paul Jones	11.00
116	15¢ Olympics	11.00
117	Christmas, Madonna	12.00
118	Christmas, Santa Claus	12.00
119	Will Rogers	13.00
120	Vietnam Veterans	11.50
121	10¢, 31¢ Olympics	12.00

1980

122	W.C. Fields	16.00
123	Winter Olympics	9.00
124	Benjamin Banneker	9.00
125	Frances Perkins	7.00
126	Emily Bissell	12.00
127	Helen Keller/ Anne Sullivan	7.00
128	Veterans Administration	7.00
129	General Bernardo de Galvez	7.00
130	Coral Reefs	10.00
131	Organized Labor	7.00
132	Edith Wharton	7.00
133	Education	7.00
134	Indian Masks	17.00
135	Architecture	9.00
136	Christmas, Window	11.50
137	Christmas, Toys	12.00

1981

138	Everett Dirksen	8.00
139	Whitney Moore Young	12.00
140	Flowers	12.00
141	Red Cross	9.00
142	Savings & Loans	9.00
143	Space Achievements	16.50
144	Professional Management	7.00
145	Wildlife Habitats	11.50
146	Int'l. Year of the Disabled	7.00
147	Edna St. Vincent Millay	7.00
148	Architecture	9.00
149	Babe Zaharias/ Bobby Jones	42.50
150	James Hoban	7.00
151	Frederic Remington	12.00
152	Battle of Yorktown/ Virginia Capes	7.00
153	Christmas, Madonna	10.00
154	Christmas, Bear and Sleigh	11.00
155	John Hanson	7.00
156	U.S. Desert Plants	11.50

1982

157	Roosevelt	11.50
158	Love	14.00
159	George Washington	15.00
160	State Birds & Flowers	42.50
161	U.S./Netherlands	16.50
162	Library of Congress	14.00
163	Knoxville World's Fair	12.00
164	Horatio Alger	13.00
165	Aging Together	13.00
166	The Barrymores	16.00
167	Dr. Mary Walker	12.00
168	Peace Garden	13.00
169	America's Libraries	12.00
170	Jackie Robinson	40.00
171	Touro Synagogue	12.00
172	Architecture	15.00
173	Wolf Trap Farm Park	14.00
174	Francis of Assisi	14.00
175	Ponce de Leon	14.00
176	Christmas, Madonna	19.00
177	Christmas, Season's Greetings	19.00
178	Kitten & Puppy	22.50

1983

179	Science and Industry	7.00
180	Sweden/USA Treaty	7.00
181	Balloons	9.00
182	Civilian Conservation Corps	7.00
183	40¢ Olympics	9.50
184	Joseph Priestley	7.00
185	Voluntarism	19.00
186	Concord/German Immigration	7.00
187	Physical Fitness	7.00
188	Brooklyn Bridge	9.50
189	TVA	7.00
190	Medal of Honor	11.50
191	Scott Joplin	9.50
192	28¢ Olympics	9.00
193	Babe Ruth	32.50
194	Nathaniel Hawthorne	7.00
195	13¢ Olympics	9.00
196	Treaty of Paris	8.00
197	Civil Service	8.00
198	Metropolitan Opera	12.00
199	Inventors	10.00
200	Streetcars	12.00
201	Christmas, Madonna	11.50
202	Christmas, Santa Claus	11.50
203	35¢ Olympics	11.50
204	Martin Luther	10.00

1984

205	Alaska	7.00
206	Winter Olympics	9.00
207	FDIC	7.00
208	Love	7.00
209	Carter G. Woodson	9.00
210	Soil and Water Conservation	7.00
211	Credit Union Act	6.50
212	Orchids	9.00
213	Hawaii	9.00
214	National Archives	6.50
215	20¢ Olympics	9.00
216	Louisiana World Exposition	7.00
217	Health Research	6.50
218	Douglas Fairbanks	9.00
219	Jim Thorpe	9.00
220	John McCormack	9.00
221	St. Lawrence Seaway	9.00
222	Preserving Waterfowl	13.50
223	Roanoke Voyages	6.50
224	Herman Melville	9.00
225	Horace Moses	6.50
226	Smokey Bear	32.50
227	Roberto Clemente	42.50
228	Dogs	12.00
229	Crime Prevention	7.00
230	Family Unity	6.50
231	Christmas, Madonna	9.00
232	Christmas, Santa Claus	9.00
233	Eleanor Roosevelt	16.00
234	Nation of Readers	6.50
235	Hispanic Americans	6.50
236	Vietnam Veterans Memorial	14.50

1985

237	Jerome Kern	9.00
238	Mary McLeod Bethune	9.00
239	Duck Decoys	22.50
240	Winter Special Olympics	6.50
241	Love	7.00
242	Rural Electrification Administration	6.50
243	AMERIPEX '86	7.50
244	Abigail Adams	6.50
245	Frederic Auguste Bartholdi	12.00
246	Korean War Veterans	12.50
247	Social Security Act	6.50
248	World War I Veterans	8.00
249	Horses	17.00
250	Public Education	7.00
251	Youth	16.00
252	Help End Hunger	6.50
253	Christmas, Madonna	10.00
254	Christmas, Poinsettias	10.00

1986

255	Arkansas	7.00
256	Stamp Collecting Booklet	9.00
257	Love	11.50
258	Sojourner Truth	11.50
259	Republic of Texas	9.00
260	Fish Booklet	11.50
261	Public Hospitals	7.00
262	Duke Ellington	11.00
263	U.S. Presidents' Sheet #1	10.00
264	U.S. Presidents' Sheet #2	10.00
265	U.S. Presidents' Sheet #3	10.00
266	U.S. Presidents' Sheet #4	10.00
267	Arctic Explorers	11.50
268	Statue of Liberty	11.50
269	Navajo Art	15.00
270	T.S. Eliot	9.00
271	Wood-Carved Figurines	11.50
272	Christmas, Madonna	8.00
273	Christmas, Village Scene	8.00

1987

274	Michigan	9.00
275	Pan American Games	6.50
276	Love	9.00
277	Jean Baptiste Pointe Du Sable	9.00
278	Enrico Caruso	11.50
279	Girl Scouts	14.50
280	Special Occasions Booklet	8.00
281	United Way	7.00
282	#1 American Wildlife	10.00
283	#2 American Wildlife	10.00
284	#3 American Wildlife	10.00
285	#4 American Wildlife	10.00
286	#5 American Wildlife	10.00
287	Delaware	12.00
288	Morocco/U.S. Diplomatic Relations	7.00

289	William Faulkner	7.00
290	Lacemaking	12.00
291	Pennsylvania	9.00
292	Constitution Booklet	9.00
293	New Jersey	9.00
294	Signing of the Constitution	9.00
295	Certified Public Accountants	52.50
296	Locomotives Booklet	12.00
297	Christmas, Madonna	8.00
298	Christmas, Ornaments	7.00

1988

299	Georgia	9.00
300	Connecticut	9.00
301	Winter Olympics	9.00
302	Australia Bicentennial	11.50
303	James Weldon Johnson	9.00
304	Cats	12.00
305	Massachusetts	9.00
306	Maryland	9.00
307	Knute Rockne	18.50
308	New Sweden	9.00
309	South Carolina	9.00
310	Francis Ouimet	27.50
311	New Hampshire	9.00
312	Virginia	9.00
313	Love #2378, #2379	9.00
314	New York	9.00
315	Summer Olympics #2380	9.00
316	Classic Cars Booklet	12.00
317	Antarctic Explorers	9.00
318	Carousel Animals	12.00
319	Christmas, Madonna, Sleigh	9.00
320	Special Occasions Booklet	9.00

1989

321	Montana	9.00
322	A. Philip Randolph	11.00
323	North Dakota	9.00
324	Washington	9.00
325	Steamboats Booklet	11.50
326	World Stamp Expo '89	7.00
327	Arturo Toscanini	11.50
328	U.S. House of Representatives	11.50
329	U.S. Senate	11.50
330	Executive Branch	11.50
331	South Dakota	9.00
332	Lou Gehrig	40.00
333	French Revolution	9.00
334	Ernest Hemingway	16.00
335	North Carolina	9.00
336	Letter Carriers	9.00
337	Drafting of the Bill of Rights	9.00
338	Prehistoric Animals	21.00
339	Southwest Carved Figure, America/PUAS	9.25
340	Christmas: Madonna and Child, Sleigh with Presents	11.00
341	Classic Mail Transportation	9.00
342	Future Mail Transportation	11.00

1990

343	Idaho	9.00
344	Love #2440	9.00
345	Ida B. Wells	15.00
346	U.S. Supreme Court	11.50
347	Wyoming	9.00
348	Classic Films	22.00
349	Marianne Moore	6.50
350	Lighthouses Booklet	22.00
351	Rhode Island	9.00
352	Olympians #2500a	15.00
353	Indian Headdresses Booklet	14.00
354	Micronesia/ Marshall Islands	9.00
355	Grand Canyon Tropical Coastline America/PUAS	11.00
356	Eisenhower	11.50
357	Creatures of the Sea	19.00
358	Christmas, Traditional and Contemporary	11.00

1991

359	Switzerland	12.00
360	Vermont	9.00
361	Savings Bonds	8.00
362	29¢ and 52¢ Love	11.00
363	Saroyan	21.00
364	Fishing Flies Booklet	19.00
365	Cole Porter	9.00
366	Antarctic Treaty	9.00
367	Desert Shield/ Desert Storm	40.00
368	Summer Olympics #2557a	11.00
369	Numismatics	9.00
370	Basketball	21.00
371	World War II Miniature Sheet	17.00
372	Comedians Booklet	17.00
373	District of Columbia	9.00
374	Jan Matzeliger	11.00
375	Space Exploration Booklet	16.50
376	America/PUAS #C131	9.00
377	Christmas, Traditional and Contemporary	14.00

1992

378	Winter Olympics	10.00
379	World Columbian Stamp Expo '92	11.00
380	W.E.B. Du Bois	17.00
381	Love #2618	10.00
382	Olympic Baseball	42.50
383	Columbus' First Voyage	70.00
384	Space Accomplishments	17.00
385	New York Stock Exchange	22.50
386	Alaska Highway	9.00
387	Kentucky Statehood	9.00
388	Summer Olympics #2641a	11.00
389	Hummingbirds Booklet	17.00
390	World War II Miniature Sheet	17.00
391	Dorothy Parker	9.00
392	Theodore von Karman	15.00
393	Minerals	17.00
394	Juan Rodriguez Cabrillo	11.00
395	Wild Animals Booklet	15.00
396	Christmas, Traditional and Contemporary	15.00
397	Columbus Souvenir Sheets	70.00
398	Columbus Souvenir Sheets	70.00
399	Columbus Souvenir Sheets	70.00
400	Wildflowers #1	40.00
401	Wildflowers #2	40.00
402	Wildflowers #3	40.00
403	Wildflowers #4	40.00
404	Wildflowers #5	40.00
405	Chinese New Year	30.00

1993

406	Elvis	32.50
407	Space Fantasy	19.00
408	Percy Julian	15.00
409	Oregon Trail	11.00
410	World Univ.Games	11.00
411	Grace Kelly	28.00
412	Oklahoma!	11.00
413	Circus	14.50
414	Cherokee Strip	11.00
415	Dean Acheson	15.00
416	Sport Horses	16.00
417	Garden Flowers	11.00
418	World War II	16.00
419	Hank Williams	29.00
420	Rock & Roll/R&B	32.50
421	Joe Louis	39.00
422	Broadway Musicals	16.00
423	National Postal Museum	14.00
424	American Sign Language	13.00
425	Country Western	28.50
426	Christmas, Traditional	16.50
427	Youth Classics	16.50
428	Mariana Islands	13.00
429	Columbus Landing In Puerto Rico	14.00
430	AIDS Awareness	14.00

1994

431	Winter Olympics	12.50
432	Edward R. Murrow	14.00
433	Dr. Allison Davis	17.50
434	Year of the Dog	20.00
435	Love #2814	16.00
436	Buffalo Soldiers	17.50
437	Silent ScreenStars	20.00
438	Garden Flowers	16.00
439	World Cup Soccer	17.50
440	World War II	17.50
441	Norman Rockwell	29.50
442	Moon Landing	27.50
443	Locomotives	17.50
444	George Meany	11.00
445	Popular Singers	17.50
446	James Thurber	11.00
447	Jazz/Blues	22.50
448	Wonders of the Sea	17.50
449	Birds (Cranes)	17.50
450	Christmas, Madonna	11.00
451	Christmas, Stocking	11.00
452	Year of the Boar	17.50

1995

453	Florida	13.00
454	Bessie Coleman	18.00
455	Kids Care!	13.00
456	Richard Nixon	22.50
457	Love #2957-2958	18.00
458	Recreational Sports	18.00
459	POW & MIA	16.00
460	Marilyn Monroe	37.50
461	Texas	16.00
462	Great Lakes Lighthouses	18.00
463	United Nations	13.00
464	Carousel Horses	20.00
465	Jazz Musicians	22.50
466	Women's Suffrage	13.00
467	Louis Armstrong	22.50
468	World War II	20.00
469	Fall Garden Flowers	13.00
470	Republic of Palau	13.00
471	Christmas, Contemporary	18.00
472	Naval Academy	18.00
473	Tennessee Williams	16.00
474	Christmas, Traditional	18.00
475	James K. Polk	13.00
476	Antique Automobiles	22.50

1996

477	Utah	13.00
478	Garden Flowers	13.00
479	Ernest E. Just	18.00
480	Smithsonian Institution	13.00
481	Year of the Rat	22.50
482	Pioneers of Communication	18.00
483	Fulbright Scholarships	13.00
484	Summer Olympics	50.00
485	Marathon	18.00
486	Georgia O'Keefe	13.00
487	Tennessee	13.00
488	James Dean	22.50
489	Prehistoric Animals	22.50

490	Breast Cancer Awareness	13.00
491	American Indian Dances	22.50
492	Folk Heroes	22.50
493	Centennial Olympic Games	16.00
494	Iowa Statehood	13.00
495	Rural Free Delivery	13.00
496	Riverboats	22.50
497	Big Band Leaders	21.00
498	Songwriters	21.00
499	Endangered Species	37.50
500	Family Scenes (4 designs)	18.00
501	Hanukkah	16.00
502	Madonna and Child	18.00
503	Cycling	45.00
503A	F. Scott Fitzgerald	22.50
503B	Computer Technology	22.50

1997

504	Year of the Ox	24.00
505	Benjamin O. Davis	21.00
506	Love #3123-3124	16.00
507	Helping Children Learn	13.00
508	Pacific '97 Triangle Stamps	20.00
509	Thornton Wilder	18.00
510	Raoul Wallenberg	16.00
511	Dinosaurs	30.00
512	Bugs Bunny	24.00
513	Pacific '97 Franklin	55.00
514	Pacific '97 Washington	55.00
515	The Marshall Plan	16.00
516	Classic American Aircraft	36.00
517	Football Coaches	30.00
518	American Dolls	55.00
519	Humphrey Bogart	20.00
520	Stars and Stripes	16.00
521	Opera Singers	19.00
522	Composers and Conductors	20.00
523	Padre Varela	16.00
524	Dept. of the Air Force	20.00
525	Movie Monsters	22.50
526	Supersonic Flight	22.50
527	Women in the Military	18.00
528	Holiday Kwanzaa	16.00
529	Holiday, Traditional	21.00
530	Holiday, Contemporary	21.00

1998

531	Year of the Tiger	17.50
532	Winter Sports-Skiing	15.50
533	Madam C.J. Walker	18.00
533A	Celebrate The Century® 1900s	27.00
533B	Celebrate The Century® 1910s	27.00
534	Remember The Maine	16.00
535	Flowering Trees	18.00
536	Alexander Calder	18.00
537	Cinco de Mayo	16.00
538	Sylvester & Tweety	22.50
538A	Celebrate The Century® 1920s	27.00

539	Wisconsin	17.50
540	Trans-Mississippi	27.50
541	Folk Singers	20.00
542	Berlin Airlift	15.00
543	Spanish Settlement of the Southwest	16.00
544	Gospel Singers	20.00
545	Stephen Vincent Benét	15.00
546	Tropical Birds	17.00
546A	Breast Cancer Research	25.00
547	Alfred Hitchcock	19.00
548	Organ Donations	17.00
549	Bright Eyes	17.00
550	Klondike Gold Rush	15.00
551	American Art	30.00
551A	Celebrate The Century® 1930s	30.00
552	American Ballet	16.00
553	Space Discovery	20.00
554	Philanthropy #3243	15.00
555	Holiday, Traditional	20.00
556	Holiday, Contemporary	16.00

1999

557	Year of the Hare #3272	17.50
558	Malcolm X	16.00
559	33¢ Love #3274a	22.50
560	55¢ Love #3275	17.00
561	Hospice Care	16.00
562	Celebrate The Century® 1940s	35.00
563	Irish Immigration	21.00
564	Alfred Lunt and Lynn Fontanne	16.00
565	Arctic Animals	18.00
566	Nature of America Sonoran Desert	25.00
567	Daffy Duck	25.00
568	Ayn Rand	32.50
569	Cinco de Mayo	17.00
570	John and William Bartram	18.00
571	Celebrate The Century® 1950s	29.00
572	Prostate Cancer	18.00
573	California Gold Rush	18.00
574	Aquarium Fish	18.00
575	Xtreme Sports	18.00
576	American Glass	18.00
577	James Cagney	18.00
578	Honoring Those Who Served	16.00
579	All Aboard! #3337a	22.50
580	Frederick Law Olmsted	18.00
581	Hollywood Composers	20.00
582	Celebrate The Century® 1960s	32.50
583	Broadway Songwriters	20.00
584	Insects and Spiders	30.00
585	Hanukkah	18.00
586	Nato	18.00
587	Holiday Celebrations: Bartolomeo Vivarini	18.00
588	Holiday Celebrations: Deer	18.00
589	Kwanzaa	18.00
590	Celebrate The Century® 1970s	30.00
591	Year 2000	22.50

2000

592	Year of the Dragon #3370	16.00
593	Celebrate The Century® 1980s	29.00
594	Patricia Roberts Harris	22.50
595	U.S. Navy Submarines – *Los Angeles* Class #3372	25.00
596	Pacific Coast Rain Forest	29.00
597	Louise Nevelson	20.00
598	Edwin Powell Hubble	23.00
599	American Samoa	18.00
600	Library of Congress	18.00
601	Wile E. Coyote/ Road Runner	20.00
602	Celebrate The Century® 1990s	29.00
603	Summer Sports #3397	18.00
604	Adoption	22.00
605	Youth Team Sports	22.00
606	Distinguished Soldiers	22.00
607	The Stars and Stripes	34.50
608	Legends of Baseball	40.00
609	Stampin' The Future™	20.00
610	Edward G. Robinson	10.00
611	California Statehood	18.00
612	Deep Sea Creatures	21.00
613	Thomas Wolfe	17.50
614	The White House	21.50

2001

615	Love #3497	19.00
615A	Love #3499	21.00
616	Year of the Snake	25.00
617	Roy Wilkins	29.00
618	American Illustrators	37.50
619	34¢ Love Letters (1 oz)	19.00
620	55¢ Love Letters (2 oz)	21.00
621	Nine-Mile Prairie	19.00
622	Diabetes Awareness	19.00
623	The Nobel Prize	22.50
624	Mt. McKinley	20.00
625	The Pan-American Inverts	40.00
626	Great Plains Prairie	37.50
627	Peanuts	27.50
628	Honoring Veterans	20.00
629	Frida Kahlo	26.00
630	Baseball's Legendary Playing Fields	45.00
631	Leonard Bernstein	22.50
632	Lucille Ball	22.50
633	The Amish Quilts	22.50
634	Carnivorous Plants	20.00

635	Holiday Celebrations: Eid	16.00
636	Enrico Fermi	20.00
637	That's All Folks!	22.50
638	Holiday Celebrations: Lorenzo Costa's Virgin and Child	16.50
639	Holiday Celebrations: Santas	19.00
640	James Madison	20.00
641	Holiday Celebrations: Thanksgiving	20.00
642	Kwanzaa	21.00
643	Hanukkah	19.00
644	57¢ Love #3551	19.00

2002

645	Winter Olympics #3555a	19.00
646	Mentoring a Child	19.00
647	Langston Hughes	19.00
648	Happy Birthday	19.00
649	Year of the Horse	25.00
650	U.S. Military Academy	21.00
651	Greetings From America	45.00
652	Longleaf Pine Forest	40.00
653	Heroes of 2001	25.00
654	Masters of American Photography	45.00
655	John James Audubon	21.00
656	Harry Houdini	21.00
657	Andy Warhol	21.00
658	Teddy Bears	16.50
659	37¢ Love #3657	19.00
660	60¢ Love #3658	19.00
661	Ogden Nash	20.00
662	Duke Kahanamoku	27.50
663	American Bats	27.50
664	Women in Journalism	24.00
665	Irving Berlin	19.00
666	Neuter or Spay	22.50
667	Christmas: Gossaert	19.00
668	Hanukkah	20.00
669	Eid	16.00
670	Kwanzaa	20.00
671	Cary Grant	22.50
672	Hawaiian Missionaries	40.00
673	Happy Birthday	17.50
674	Greetings From America	52.50
675	Holiday Celebrations: Snowmen	16.50

2003

676	Thurgood Marshall	19.00
677	Year of the Ram	21.00
678	Zora Neale Hurston	24.00
679	Special Oylmpics #3771	21.00
680	American Filmmaking: Behind the Scenes	42.50
681	Ohio Statehood	21.00
682	Pelican Island National Wildlife Refuge	21.00
683	Old Glory	24.00
684	Cesar E. Chavez	21.00
685	Louisiana Purchase	21.00
686	First Flight	21.00
687	Audrey Hepburn	25.00
688	Southeastern Lighthouses	21.00
689	Arctic Tundra	40.00
690	Korean War Veterans Memorial	21.00
691	Mary Cassatt	21.00
692	Early Football Heroes	27.50
693	Roy Acuff	21.00
694	District of Columbia	21.00
695	Reptiles and Amphibians	27.50
696	Stop Family Violence	21.00
697	Holiday Celebrations: Music Makers	21.00
698	Holiday Celebrations: Gossaert	21.00

2004

699	Pacific Coral Reef	40.00
700	Lunar New Year: Year of the Monkey	21.00
701	Love #3833	21.00
702	Paul Robeson	22.50
703	Ted "Dr. Seuss" Geisel	27.50
704	Garden Bouquet: Weddings	19.00
705	Garden Botanical: Weddings	19.00
706	US Air Force Academy	21.00
707	Henry Mancini	21.00
708	American Choreographers	22.50
709	Lewis & Clark Prestige Booklet	25.00
710	Lewis & Clark Pane	25.00

711	Isamu Noguchi	19.00
712	National World War II Memorial	22.50
713	2004 Olympic Games	20.00
714	Art of Disney: Friendship	24.00
715	USS *Constellation*	22.50
716	R. Buckminster Fuller	19.00
717	James Baldwin	18.00
718	Martin Johnson Heade	18.00
719	Art of the American Indian	42.50
720	John Wayne	26.00
721	Sickle Cell Disease	19.00
722	Cloudscapes	40.00
723	Holiday Celebrations: Madonna & Child	19.00
724	Hanukkah	16.50
725	Kwanzaa	16.50
726	Moss Hart	19.00
727	Holiday Celebrations: Holiday Ornaments	19.00

2005

728	Lunar New Year #3895	35.00
729	Marian Anderson	25.00
730	Ronald Reagan	27.50
731	Love #3898	21.00
732	Northeast Deciduous Forest	37.50
733	Spring Flowers	19.00
734	Robert Penn Warren	16.00
735	Yip Harburg	16.00
736	American Scientists	16.00
737	Modern American Architecture	42.50
738	Henry Fonda	17.50
739	Art of Disney: Celebration	30.00
740	American Advances in Aviation	42.50
741	New Mexico Rio Grande Blankets	16.00
742	Presidential Libraries	16.00
743	American on the Move: 50s Sporty Cars	30.00
744	Arthur Ashe	20.00
745	To Form a More Perfect Union	32.50
746	Child Health	16.00
747	Let's Dance/Bailemos	16.00
748	Greta Garbo	25.00
749	Jim Henson & Muppets	42.50
750	Constellations	29.00
751	Holiday Celebrations: Holiday Cookies	15.00
752	Distinguished Marines	29.00

VISIT US ONLINE AT **THE POSTAL STORE**

AT *WWW.USPS.COM*

OR CALL **1 800 STAMP-24**

2006		
753	Love #3976	14.00
754	Favorite Children's Book Animals	32.50
755	Olympic Games #3995	15.00
756	Hattie McDaniel	17.50
757	Lunar New Year	30.00
758	Our Wedding #3998	14.00
759	Our Wedding #3999	14.00
760	Sugar Ray Robinson	14.00
761	Benjamin Franklin	14.00
762	Art of Disney: Romance	14.00
763	Love: True Blue	14.00
764	Katherine Anne Porter	14.00
765	AMBER Alert	14.00
766	Wonders of America: Land of Superlatives	37.50
767	1606 Voyage of Samuel de Champlain	14.00
768	Washington 2006 World Philatelic Exhibition	17.50
769	Distinguished American Diplomats	14.00
769A	Judy Garland	14.00
770	Ronald Reagan	15.00
771	Happy Birthday	14.00
772	Baseball Sluggers	14.00
773	DC Comics Superheroes	32.50
774	American Motorcycles	15.00
775	American Treasures: Quilts of Gee's Bend	16.00
776	Nature of America: Southern Florida Wetland	35.00
777	Holiday Snowflakes	12.00
778	Eid	12.00
779	Hanukkah	12.00
780	Kwanzaa	12.00
781	Chacón: Madonna and Child with Bird	12.00

2007		
782	Ella Fitzgerald	12.00
783	Oklahoma Statehood	12.00
784	With Love and Kisses	12.00
785	International Polar Year	12.00
786	Henry Wadsworth Longfellow	12.00
787	Settlement of Jamestown	30.00
788	Star Wars	30.00
789	Pacific Lighthouses	12.00
790	Wedding Hearts 41¢	12.00
791	Wedding Hearts 58¢	12.00
792	Pollination	16.50
793	Marvel Comics Super Heroes	30.00
794	Vintage Mahogany Speedboats	12.00
795	Louis Comfort Tiffany	12.00
795A	Art of Disney: Magic	12.00
796	James Stewart	12.00
796A	Celebrate!	12.00
797	Alpine Tundra	30.00
798	Gerald Ford	12.00
799	Jury Duty	12.00
800	Mendez v. Westminster School District	12.00
801	Eid	12.00
802	Polar Lights	12.00
803	Holiday Knits	12.00
804	Luini: Madonna of the Carnation	12.00
805	Yoda	12.00
806	Hanukkah	12.00
807	Kwanzaa	12.00

2008		
808	Celebrating Lunar New Year: Year of the Rat	12.00
809	Charles W. Chesnutt	12.00
810	Marjorie Kinnan Rawlings	12.00
811	American Scientists	12.00
812	American Journalists	12.00
813	Frank Sinatra	12.00
814	Minnesota Statehood	12.00
815	Love: All Heart	12.00
816	Hearts (1 oz. & 2 oz.)	12.00
817	Charles + Ray Eames	30.00
818	Olympic Games	12.00
819	Vintage Black Cinema	12.00
820	"Take Me Out to the Ball Game"	12.00
821	The Art of Disney: Imagination	12.00
822	Albert Bierstadt	12.00
823	Latin Jazz	12.00
824	Bette Davis	12.00
825	Nature of America: Great Lakes Dunes	30.00
826	50s Fins and Chrome	12.00
827	Alzheimer's Awareness	12.00
828	Holiday Nutcrackers	12.00
829	Christmas: Botticelli Virgin and Child	12.00

The Art of Disney: Imagination Premium Stamped Cards & Prints*

With help from a few beloved Disney characters, it's easy to add an imaginative touch to your correspondence and collection with this booklet of stamped cards or 8"x 10" prints.

Booklet of 20 cards (four different designs)   Item #571466 $13.95

Print Set (four different designs w/matching stamp)   Item #571488 $14.95

*Additional postage required

Disney Materials © Disney

To order call **1 800 STAMP-24** or visit us online **www.usps.com**

Organizations, Publications and Resources

Please enclose a stamped, self-addressed envelope when writing to these organizations.

American Air Mail Society
Rudy Roy
PO Box 5367
Virginia Beach, VA 23471-0367
(p) 757/499-5234
AAMSinformation@aol.com
http://www.americanairmailsociety.org

Specializes in all phases of aerophilately. Membership services include Advance Bulletin Service, Auction Service, free want ads, Sales Department, monthly journal, discounts on Society publications, translation service.

American First Day Cover Society
PO Box 16277
Tucson, AZ 85732-6277
(p) 520/321-0880
afdcs@aol.com
http://www.afdcs.org
Contact Doug Kelsey, Executive Director

A full-service, not-for-profit, noncommercial society devoted exclusively to First Day Covers and First Day Cover collecting. Publishes 80-page magazine, First Day, eight times a year. Offers information on 300 current cachet producers, expertizing, foreign covers, translation service, color slide programs and archives covering First Day Covers.

Claude C. Ries Chapter #48
American First Day Cover Society
Kathy Clements
Membership Secretary Treasurer
3976 Olmsted Avenue
Los Angeles, CA 90008-2626
(323)292-5460 home
(213)703-7809 mobile
curfmeistr@aol.com
www.rieschapterafdcs.com

Visit us online or contact us by phone or e-mail for more information.

American Ceremony Program Society
John E. Peterson
ACPS Secretary/Treasurer
6987 Coleshill Drive
San Diego, CA 92119-1953
jkpete@cox.net
www.webacps.org

The American Ceremony Program Society is a place to learn about First Day and Supplemental (Second Day or later) stamp Ceremonies and Ceremony Programs. The Society publishes a journal, The Ceremonial.

American Philatelic Society
Peter Mastrangelo
Department PG
100 Match Factory Place
Bellefonte, PA 16823-1367
(p) 814/933-3803
(f) 814/933-6128
apsinfo@stamps.org
http://www.stamps.org

America's national stamp society. Membership benefits include various publications, services, and more. Sponsors national stamp exhibitions annually in partnership with the ASDA and USPS. 40,000+ members worldwide.

American Society for Philatelic Pages and Panels
Gerald Blankenship
PO Box 475
Crosby, TX 77532-0475
(p) 281/324-2709
membership@asppp.org
www.asppp.org

The only society with a focus on commemorative cancellations (formerly souvenir pages) and commemorative panels. Free ads, member auction, quarterly publication sent to all members with reports on new issues, varieties, errors, oddities and discoveries. Active web site.

American Stamp Dealers Association
3 School St., Suite 205
Glen Cove, NY 11542-2548
(p) 516/759-7000
(f) 516/759-7014
asda@asdaonline.com
http://www.asdaonline.com

Association of dealers engaged in every facet of philately, with 6 regional chapters nationwide. Sponsors national and local shows. Will send you a complete listing of dealers in your area or collecting specialty. A #10 SASE must accompany your request.

American Topical Association
Vera Felts
Executive Director
PO Box 8
Carterville, IL 62918-0008
(p) 618/985-5100
(f) 618/985-5131
americantopical@msn.com
www.americantopicalassn.org

A service organization concentrating on the specialty of topical stamp collecting. Offers handbooks and checklists on specific topics; exhibition awards; Topical Time, a bimonthly publication highlighting topical interest areas. ATA has ~30 affiliated study units and ~20 local chapters.

Ebony Society of Philatelic Events and Reflections
Manuel Gilyard, President
PO Box 1757
Lincolnton Station
New York, NY 10037-1757
(p) 212-928-5165
(f) 212-928-1477
gilyardmani@aol.com
http://www.esperstamps.org

Mailer's Postmark Permit Club
Charles F. Myers
Central Office
PO Box 3
Portland, TN 37148-0003
(p) 615/325-9478
cfmyers@mindspring.com
www.mppclub.org

Publishes bimonthly newsletter, Permit Patter, which covers all aspects of mailer's postmark permits. Also available, an 8-page step by step brochure "How to obtain a Mailer's Postmark Permit… a basic guide."

Plate Number Coil Collectors Club
Ronald E. Maifeld
President
PO Box 54622
Cincinnati, OH 45254-0622
Rmaifeld@fuse.net
www.pnc3.org

The Plate Number Coil Collectors Club (PNC[3]) is an organization that studies the plate numbers and plate varieties of United States coil stamps issued since 1981. The PNC[3] publishes a monthly newsletter, Coil Line. The website includes a membership application and discusses plate number coils and PNC[3] at length.

Postal History Society
Kalman V. Illyefalvi
869 Bridgewater Drive
New Oxford, PA 17350-8206
(p) 717/624-5941
kalphyl@juno.com

Devoted to the study of various aspects of the development of the mails and local, national and international postal systems; postal treaties; and the means and methods of transporting mail.

Precancel Stamp Society
Promotional Secretary
Jerry Hejduk
PO Box 490450
Leesburg, FL 34749-0450
psspromosec@comcast.com
www.precancels.com

Devoted to the collecting and study of precanceled stamps done by the Bureau of Printing & Engraving and by local post offices across the U.S.

Scott Stamp Monthly
PO Box 828
Sidney, OH 45365-0828
(p) 937/498-0846
(f) 937/498-0886
dhouseman@scottonline.com
www.scottstampmonthly.com

Scott Stamp Monthly is the premier magazine for collectors at every level, from advanced specialists to beginners. Established by John Walter Scott in 1868 as the American Journal of Philately, the magazine has been published continuously for 140 years. A sample copy of the monthly magazine is available upon request.

The Souvenir Card Collectors Society, Inc.
Dana M. Marr
PO Box 4155
Tulsa, OK 74159-0155
(p) 918/664-6724
DMARR5569@aol.com

Provides member auctions, a quarterly journal and access to limited-edition souvenir cards.

Spring-Ford Philatelic Society
First United Church of Christ
145 Chestnut St.
Spring City, PA 19475-1804
(p) 610/970-5408
DickRoslie@aol.com

Meeting the last Thursday of the month at 7:00 p.m.

Stamp Camp USA
(teaching children using world-wide stamps)
117 Court Street, Suite A
Elkland, PA 16920-1447
814-258-5601
Fax 814-258-5601
sstampcampusa@stny.rr.com
www.stampcampusa.org

United Postal Stationery Society
Stuart Leven
Membership Office
1445 Foxworthy Ave. #187
San Jose, CA 954118-1119
poststat@gmail.com
www.upss.org

Postal stationary is made up of the post office-issued postal cards, envelopes, letter sheets and other postal products having the stamp already printed. The UPSS is the largest society devoted to the collecting and study of postal stationery of the world with members throughout the U.S. and many foreign countries.

U.S. Postal Card Catalog

Contemporary Account of 1st U.S. Postal Card

Transitive Relationship to Family Tree of Proofs

19th, 20th Century Envelopes Catalog

U.S. Commemorative Stamped Envelopes, 1867-1965

U.S. Envelope Essays and Proofs

Plating of U.S. International Cards

Stamped Envelopes & Wrappers

Universal Ship Cancellation Society
Steve Shay
747 Shard Court
Fremont, CA 94539-7419
e-mail: Shaymur@flash.net
http://www.uscs.org

Specializes in naval ship postmarks and cachets.

**U.S. Postal Service
Stamp Services**
1735 N. Lynn St, 5th Floor, Room 5018
Arlington, VA 22209-6432

U.S. Stamp Society
Executive Secretary
PO Box 6634
Katy, TX 77491-6634
http://www.usstamps.org

*An association of collectors to promote
the study of all postage and revenue
stamps and stamped paper of the United
States and U.S.-administered areas produced by the Bureau of Engraving and
Printing and other contract printers.*

Durland Plate Number Catalog

Expertisers

**American Philatelic Expertizing
Service (APEX)**
Mercer Bristow
Director of Expertizing
100 Match Factory Place
Bellefonte, PA 16823-1367
(p) 814/933-3803
(f) 814/933-6128
Mercer@stamps.org

Krystal Harter
Expertizing Coordinator
Krharter@stamps.org
(p) 814/933-3803
(f) 814/933-6128
http://www.stamps.org

*A service of the American Philatelic
Society since 1903, APEX utilizes the
outstanding reference collections at APS
headquarters in conjunction with the
nation's best philatelic scholars to pass
judgement on the identification, authenticity and condition of stamps from
around the world.*

Philatelic Foundation
Attention: Chairman
George J. Kramer
70 W 40th Street 15th Floor
New York, NY 10018-2615
(p) 212/221-6555
(f) 212/221-6208
www.philatelicfoundation.org

*A nonprofit organization known for its
excellent expertization service. The
Foundation's broad resources, including
extensive reference collections, 5,000-
volume library and Expert Committee,
provide collectors with comprehensive
consumer protection. Book series include
expertizing case histories in Opinions,
Foundation seminar subjects in "text-
books" and specialized U.S. subjects in
monographs.*

Professional Stamp Experts
PO Box 6170
Newport Beach, CA 92658-6170
(p) 877/782-6788
http://www.psestamp.com
pse@collectors.com

*Organization specializing in identifica-
tion, expertization and grading of U.S.
Postage Stamps, Covers, Revenues etc....
PSE issues a Certificate of Authenticity
accepted by all auction firms, dealers and
collectors. PSE publishes a Guide to the
Grading of U.S. Stamps and The Stamp
Market Quarterly Price Guide. Either is
free upon request.*

Periodicals

*The following publications will send you
a free copy of their magazine or newspaper upon request.*

Global Stamp News
PO Box 97
Sidney, OH 45365-0097
(p) 937/492-3183
globalstampnews@embaygmail.com

*America's largest-circulation monthly
stamp magazine featuring U.S. and
foreign issues.*

Linn's Stamp News
PO Box 29
Sidney, OH 45365-0029
(p) 937/498-0801
(f) 937/498-0876
(f) 888/340-8388 (toll free)
linns@linns.com
www.linns.com

*Linn's Stamp News, the world's largest
weekly stamp newspaper, contains breaking news stories of major importance to
stamp collectors, features on a variety of
stamp-collecting topics, the monthly U.S.
Stamp Market Index, Stamp Market Tips
and much more. A sample copy of the
weekly news-paper is available upon
request.*

Linn's U.S. Stamp Yearbook
(p) 937/498-0802
(f) 800/572-6885 (US only)
(f) 937/498-0807 (outside US)
linns@linns.com
www.linns.com

Stamp Collecting Made Easy

Mekeel's & Stamps Magazine-fa
John Dunn
42 Sentry Way
Merrimack, NH 03054-4407
subs@StampNewsNow.com
www.StampNewsNow.com

*Weekly magazine for collectors of U.S.
& worldwide stamps & covers.*

U.S. Stamp News-fb
42 Sentry Way
Merrimack, NH 03054-4407
subs@StampNewsNow.com
www.StampNewsNow.com

*Monthly magazine for all collectors of
U.S. stamps, covers and postal history.*

Stamp Fulfillment Services
U.S. Postal Service
8300 NE Underground Dr
Pillar 210
Kansas City, MO 64144-0001
(p) 1-800-STAMP-24

**Scott Specialized Catalogue of
United States Stamps and Covers**
PO Box 828
Sidney, OH 45365-0828
(p) 937/498-0831
(p) 800/572-6885
(f) 937/498-0807
cuserv@amosadvantage.com
www.amosadvantage.com

**Scott Standard Postage Stamp
Catalogue**

**Scott Classic Specialized Catalogue:
Stamps and Covers of the World
including U.S., 1840-1940 (British
Commonwealth to 1952)**

Scott Stamp Monthly

Museums, Libraries and Displays

*Please contact the institutions before visit-
ing to confirm hours and any entry fees.*

American Philatelic Research Library
100 Match Factory Place
Bellefonte, PA 16823-1367
(p) 814/933-3803
(f) 814/933-6128
aprl@stamps.org
www.stamplibrary.org

*The largest philatelic library in the US,
the APRL receives more than 400 period-
icals, and houses extensive collections of
philatelic literature.*

The Collectors Club
Irene Bromberg
Executive Secretary
22 E. 35th Street
New York, NY 10016-3806
(p) 212/683-0559
(f) 212/481-1269
collectorsclub@verizon.net
www.collectorsclub.org

*Bimonthly journal, publication of various
reference works, one of the most extensive reference libraries in the world, read-
ing and study rooms. Regular meetings
on the first and third Wednesdays of each
month at 6:30 p.m., except July and
August.*

Corporate Library
United States Postal Service
475 L'Enfant Plaza SW
Washington, DC 20260-1540
(p) 202/268-2904
(f) 202/268-4423
carolina.menendez@usps.gov

*Offers a wide collection of past and pres-
ent postal publications, including the
Postal Bulletin, Annual Report, news and
philatelic releases, the Postal Guide and
Postal Laws and Regulations.*

National Postal Museum
Office of the Director
Smithsonian National Postal Museum
2 Massachusetts Ave, NE
Washington, D.C. 20013-0570
(p) 202/633-5555
allegrettie@si.edu

*Located in the Old City Post Office
building at 2 Massachusetts Avenue, NE
National Postal Museum houses more
than 6 million items for exhibition and
study purposes. Collections research may
be conducted separately or jointly with
library materials. Call the museum and
its library (202/633-5544) separately to
schedule an appointment.*

The Postal History Foundation
Betsy Towle
PO Box 40725
Tucson, AZ 85717-0725
(p) 520/623-6652
(f) 520/623-6652
phf3@mindspring.com
www.postalhistoryfoundation.org
Hours: M-F 8 a.m.-3 p.m.

*The Postal History Foundation is located
in Tucson, Arizona. Established in 1960,
the Foundation has a world class collection of postal history information and
artifacts and is a pioneer in its provision
of youth philatelic education programs.
It offers museum tours, research library,
USPS contract post office, philatelic
sales, archives and stamp collections.*

**Spellman Museum of Stamps and
Postal History**
235 Wellesley Street
Weston, MA 02493-1538
(p) 781/768-8367
(f) 781/768-7332
info@spellman.org
http://www.spellman.org

*America's first fully accredited museum
devoted to the display, collection and
preservation of stamps and postal
history. Exhibitions feature rarities, U.S.,
and worldwide collections. Philatelic
library and family activity center open
with admission. School and scout programs by appointment. Museum store
and post office carries gifts, collecting
supplies, and stamps.*

Western Philatelic Library
PO Box 2219
Sunnyvale, CA 94087-2219
(p) 408/733-0336
stulev@ix.netcom.com
http://www.pbbooks.com/wpl.htm
http://www.fwpl.org

Friends of the Western Philatelic Library

Wineburgh Philatelic Research Library
Special Collections Department
Paul Oelkrug
McDermott Library
The University of Texas at Dallas
PO Box 830643
Mailstation: MC33
Richardson, TX 75083-0643
(p) 972/883-2553
http://www.utdallas.edu/library/special/wprl.html
Hours: M-Th 9 a.m.–6 p.m.;
Fri 9 a.m.-5 p.m.

Literature

ArtCraft First Day Cover Price List
Washington Press
2 Vreeland Road
Florham Park, NJ 07932-1501
(p) 877/966-0001 (toll free)
(f) 973/966-0888
info@washpress.com
http://www.washpress.com

Includes Presidential Inaugural covers.

Legends of the West
Washington Press

How some collectors struck it rich!

The Inverted Jenny

A Dream Come True

Operation HUSH – HUSH

How the Project Mercury Stamp was Planned and Issued

The Hammarskjold Invert

Tells the story of the Dag Hammarskjold error/invert

The U.S. Transportation Coils

How some collectors struck it rich!

The White Ace Album Format Guide

A Listing of Stamps Required for The 2003 United States White Ace Album Supplements

ANY ABOVE FREE for #10 SASE

Brookman's 1st Edition Black Heritage First Day Cachet Cover Catalog
Arlene Dunn
Brookman/Barrett & Worthen
167 So. River Rd Unit 3
Bedford, NH 03110-5566
(p) 603/472-5575
(f) 603/472-8795

Illustrated 176-page perfect bound book.

Brookman's 2nd Edition Price Guide for Disney Stamps

Illustrated 256-page perfect bound book.

2009 Brookman Price Guide of U.S., and Canada Stamps and Postal Collectibles

Illustrated 408-page perfect and spiral bound catalog.

Postmark Advisory
Paul Brenner
General Image, Inc.
10 East Sumner Avenue
Roselle Park, NJ 07204
Postmark1@earthlink.net
There is also a web site announcing these postmarks. The address is:
http://www.pictorialpostmarks.com
This site is updated twice a month. (How-to-do-it is excellent for beginners)

A weekly newsletter is available which provides descriptive information on U.S. pictorial postmarks that you can send away for. A free sample newsletter is available if you send a SASE and ask for a copy. If you are interested in postmarks, you might like to visit the web site.

Black Heritage Postmarks
This is a web site describing U.S. postmarks relating to Black heritage, pictorial and first day.
http://www.blackheritagepostmarks.com

Fleetwood's Standard First Day Cover Catalog
Fleetwood
Unicover Corporation
1 Unicover Center
Cheyenne, WY 82008-0001
(p) 307/771-3000
(p) 800/443-4225 (toll free)
(f) 307/771-3134
http://www.unicover.com

Precancel Stamp Society Catalogs
Dick Laetsch
3 Shady Creek Lane
Scarborough, ME 04074
(p) 207/883-2505
precancel@aol.com
www.precanceledstamps.com

Precancel approvals available.

Stamp Collecting Made Easy
Amos Hobby Publishing Co.
PO Box 828
Sidney, OH 045365-0097
(p) 937/498-0807
(p) 800/572-6885
(f) 937/498-0807

An illustrated, easy-to-read, 96-page booklet for beginning collectors.

The United States Postal Service: An American History, *Pub. 100*
Historian
United States Postal Service
475 L'Enfant Plaza SW
Washington, DC 20260-0012
(p) 202/268-2507
mausman@usps.gov
www.usps.com

Tells the history of the U.S. Postal Service from 1775 to the present. Includes bibliography, First-Class rate history. One free copy.

Sources of Historical Information on Post Offices, Postal Employees, Mail Routes and Mail Contractors
Pub. 119

Lists all known federal sources of information on topics covered in the title. Includes a bibliography of books on state postal histories. One free copy.

The Art of Stamp Collecting
Pub. 225

Celebrating with Pictorial Postmarks
Pub. 186

Creating U.S. Postage Stamps

Lists all known federal sources of information on topics covered in the title. Includes a bibliography of books on state postal histories. One free copy.
www.usps.com/postmasterfinder

Provides complete lists of Postmasters for more than 14,000 Post Offices and partial lists for all current Post Offices. Can be researched by Postmaster name, Post Office, state and establishment and discontinuance dates. Post Offices are researched upon request.

International

AUSTRALIA
Max Stern
234 Flinders Street
Box 997 H
GPO Melbourne 3001

CANADA
Canada Post
2701 Riverside Dr.
Suite N0420
Ottawa ON K1A 0B1

CHINA
China National Philatelic Corporation
14, Taipinghu Dongli, Xicheng District
Beijing, 100031

DENMARK
Nordfrim
DK 5450 Otterup

GERMANY
Georg Roll Stamps LTD
Hafenstrasse 8
D-26931 Elsfleth

Hermann Sieger GMBH
Venusberg 32-34
D73545 Lorch Wurttemberg

HONG KONG
Hongkong Post
1706-7, ING Tower
308-320 Des Voeux Road Central
Sheung Wan

ITALY
Alberto Bolaffi
Via Cavour 17
10123 Torino

JAPAN
Japan Philatelic Agency
PO Box 96 Toshima
Tokyo 170-8668

NETHERLANDS
TPG Post
Prinses Beatrixlann 23
P O Box 30250
2500 GC The Hague

SPAIN
Philagroup, S. L.
Manuel Tovar, 1, 4 izda
28034 Madrid

THAILAND
International House of Stamps
98/2 Soi Tonson
Langsuan Rd
Lumpinee, Pathumwan
Bangkok 10330

UNITED KINGDOM
Harry Allen
PO Box 5
Watford Herts WD2 5SW

We always welcome orders from international customers at
http://www.usps.com/shop

Philatelic Centers
In addition to the more than 20,000 postal facilities authorized to sell philatelic products, the Postal Service also maintains Philatelic Centers located in major population centers. These Philatelic Centers have been established to serve stamp collectors and make it convenient for them to acquire an extensive range of current postage stamps, postal stationery and philatelic products issued by the Postal Service.

For questions, location and hours of operation about a Philatelic Center near you, please call **800-275-8777** or visit us online at **www.usps.com**.

U.S. Postal Service Stamp Series

Stamps are listed with Scott Numbers

First Pictorial 1869

113	2¢ Post Horse and Rider
114	3¢ Locomotive
116	10¢ Shield and Eagle
117	12¢ S.S. *Adriatic*
118	15¢ Landing of Columbus
120	24¢ Declaration of Independence
121	30¢ Shield, Eagle, and Flags

Columbian Exposition 1893

230	1¢ Columbus in Sight of Land
231	2¢ Landing of Columbus
232	3¢ *Santa Maria,* Flagship
233	4¢ Fleet of Columbus
234	5¢ Columbus Soliciting Aid from Queen Isabella
235	6¢ Columbus Welcomed at Barcelona
236	8¢ Columbus Restored to Favor
237	10¢ Columbus Presenting Natives
238	15¢ Columbus Announcing His Discovery
239	30¢ Columbus at La Rábida
240	50¢ Recall of Columbus
241	$1 Queen Isabella Pledging Her Jewels
242	$2 Columbus in Chains
243	$3 Columbus Describing His Third Voyage
244	$4 Queen Isabella and Columbus
245	$5 Portrait of Columbus

America 1922-1925

551	1/2¢ Nathan Hale
552	1¢ Franklin
553	1-1/2¢ Warren G. Harding
554	2¢ Washington
555	3¢ Lincoln
556	4¢ Martha Washington
557	5¢ Theodore Roosevelt
558	6¢ Garfield
559	7¢ McKinley
560	8¢ Grant
561	9¢ Jefferson
562	10¢ Monroe
563	11¢ Rutherford B. Hayes
564	12¢ Grover Cleveland
565	14¢ American Indian
566	15¢ Statue of Liberty
567	20¢ Golden Gate
568	25¢ Niagara Falls
569	30¢ Buffalo
570	50¢ Arlington Amphitheater
571	$1 Lincoln Memorial
572	$2 U.S. Capitol
573	$5 Head of *Freedom*, Capitol Dome

American Revolution Sesquicentennial 1925-1933

617	1¢ Washington at Cambridge
618	2¢ "The Birth of Liberty"
619	5¢ "The Minute Man"
627	2¢ Independence Sesquicentennial Exposition
629	2¢ Alexander Hamilton's Battery
630	2¢ Battle of White Plains
644	2¢ Burgoyne at Saratoga
645	2¢ Valley Forge
646	2¢ Battle of Monmouth/ Molly Pitcher
651	2¢ George Rogers Clark
657	2¢ Sullivan Expedition
680	2¢ Battle of Fallen Timbers
688	2¢ Battle of Braddock's Field
689	2¢ General von Steuben
690	2¢ General Pulaski
703	2¢ Yorktown
727	3¢ Peace of 1783
734	5¢ General Tadeusz Kosciuszko
752	3¢ violet Peace of 1783 (#727)

National Parks 1934-1935

740	1¢ El Capitan, Yosemite (CA)
741	2¢ Grand Canyon (AZ)
742	3¢ Mt. Rainier and Mirror Lake (WA)
743	4¢ Cliff Palace, Mesa Verde (CO)
744	5¢ Old Faithful, Yellowstone (WY)
745	6¢ Crater Lake (OR)
746	7¢ Great Head, Acadia Park (ME)
747	8¢ Great White Throne, Zion Park (UT)
748	9¢ Glacier National Park (MT)
749	10¢ Great Smoky Mountains (NC)
750	3¢ Souvenir Sheet, American Philatelic Society (#742)
751	1¢ Souvenir Sheet, Trans-Mississippi Philatelic Exposition (#740)
756	1¢ green Yosemite (#740)
757	2¢ red Grand Canyon (#741)
758	3¢ deep violet Mt. Rainier (#742)
759	4¢ brown Mesa Verde (#743)
760	5¢ blue Yellowstone (#744)
761	6¢ dark blue Crater Lake (#745)
762	7¢ black Acadia (#746)
763	8¢ sage green Zion (#747)
764	9¢ red orange Glacier (#748)
765	10¢ gray black Great Smoky Mountains (#749)

Army Navy 1936-1937

785 1¢ George Washington, Nathanael Greene and Mount Vernon
786 2¢ Andrew Jackson, Winfield Scott and The Hermitage
787 3¢ Generals Sherman, Grant and Sheridan
788 4¢ Generals Robert E. Lee and "Stonewall" Jackson and Stratford Hall
789 5¢ U.S. Military Academy at West Point
790 1¢ John Paul Jones, John Barry, *Bon Homme Richard* and *Lexington*
791 2¢ Stephen Decatur, Thomas MacDonough and *Saratoga*
792 3¢ David G. Farragut and David D. Porter, *Hartford* and *Powhatan*
793 4¢ Admirals William T. Sampson, George Dewey and Winfield S. Schley
794 5¢ Seal of U.S. Naval Academy and Naval Cadets

Territorial 1937

799 3¢ Hawaii
800 3¢ Alaska
801 3¢ Puerto Rico
802 3¢ Virgin Islands

Presidential 1938-1939

803 1/2¢ Benjamin Franklin
804 1¢ George Washington
805 1-1/2¢ Martha Washington
806 2¢ John Adams
807 3¢ Thomas Jefferson
808 4¢ James Madison
809 4-1/2¢ The White House
810 5¢ James Monroe
811 6¢ John Quincy Adams
812 7¢ Andrew Jackson
813 8¢ Martin Van Buren
814 9¢ William H. Harrison
815 10¢ John Tyler
816 11¢ James K. Polk
817 12¢ Zachary Taylor
818 13¢ Millard Fillmore
819 14¢ Franklin Pierce
820 15¢ James Buchanan
821 16¢ Abraham Lincoln
822 17¢ Andrew Johnson
823 18¢ Ulysses S. Grant
824 19¢ Rutherford B. Hayes
825 20¢ James A. Garfield
826 21¢ Chester A. Arthur
827 22¢ Grover Cleveland
828 24¢ Benjamin Harrison
829 25¢ William McKinley
830 30¢ Theodore Roosevelt
831 50¢ William Howard Taft
832 $1 Woodrow Wilson
833 $2 Warren G. Harding
834 $5 Calvin Coolidge

Famous Americans 1940

859 1¢ Washington Irving
860 2¢ James Fenimore Cooper
861 3¢ Ralph Waldo Emerson
862 5¢ Louisa May Alcott
863 10¢ Samuel L. Clemens (Mark Twain)
864 1¢ Henry W. Longfellow
865 2¢ John Greenleaf Whittier
866 3¢ James Russell Lowell
867 5¢ Walt Whitman
868 10¢ James Whitcomb Riley
869 1¢ Horace Mann
870 2¢ Mark Hopkins
871 3¢ Charles W. Eliot
872 5¢ Frances E. Willard
873 10¢ Booker T. Washington
874 1¢ John James Audubon
875 2¢ Dr. Crawford W. Long
876 3¢ Luther Burbank
877 5¢ Dr. Walter Reed
878 10¢ Jane Addams
879 1¢ Stephen Collins Foster
880 2¢ John Philip Sousa
881 3¢ Victor Herbert
882 5¢ Edward A. MacDowell
883 10¢ Ethelbert Nevin
884 1¢ Gilbert Charles Stuart
885 2¢ James A. McNeill Whistler
886 3¢ Augustus Saint-Gaudens
887 5¢ Daniel Chester French
888 10¢ Frederic Remington
889 1¢ Eli Whitney
890 2¢ Samuel F.B. Morse
891 3¢ Cyrus Hall McCormick
892 5¢ Elias Howe
893 10¢ Alexander Graham Bell

Win the War 1940-1946

899 1¢ Statue of Liberty
900 2¢ 90mm Antiaircraft Gun
901 3¢ Torch of Enlightenment
905 3¢ Win the War
906 5¢ Chinese Resistance
907 2¢ Allied Nations
908 1¢ Four Freedoms
925 3¢ Philippine
928 5¢ United Nations Conference
929 3¢ Iwo Jima (Marines)
930 1¢ Roosevelt and Hyde Park Residence
931 2¢ Roosevelt and "The Little White House" at Warm Springs, GA
932 3¢ Roosevelt and White House

933 5¢ Roosevelt, Map of Western Hemisphere and Four Freedoms
934 3¢ Army
935 3¢ Navy
936 3¢ Coast Guard
939 3¢ Merchant Marine
940 3¢ Veterans of World War II

Overrun Countries 1943-1944

909 5¢ Poland
910 5¢ Czechoslovakia
911 5¢ Norway
912 5¢ Luxembourg
913 5¢ Netherlands
914 5¢ Belgium
915 5¢ France
916 5¢ Greece
917 5¢ Yugoslavia
918 5¢ Albania
919 5¢ Austria
920 5¢ Denmark
921 5¢ Korea

National Capital Sesquicentennial 1950

989 3¢ Statue of *Freedom* on Capitol Dome
990 3¢ Executive Mansion
991 3¢ Supreme Court
992 3¢ U.S. Capitol

Liberty 1954-1961

1030 1/2¢ Benjamin Franklin
1031 1¢ George Washington
1031A 1-1/4¢ Palace of the Governors
1032 1-1/2¢ Mount Vernon
1033 2¢ Thomas Jefferson
1034 2-1/2¢ Bunker Hill Monument and Massachusetts Flag
1035 3¢ Statue of Liberty
1036 4¢ Abraham Lincoln
1037 4-1/2¢ The Hermitage
1038 5¢ James Monroe
1039 6¢ Theodore Roosevelt
1040 7¢ Woodrow Wilson
1041 8¢ Statue of Liberty
1042 8¢ Statue of Liberty, redrawn
1042A 8¢ General John J. Pershing
1043 9¢ The Alamo
1044 10¢ Independence Hall
1044A 11¢ Statue of Liberty
1045 12¢ Benjamin Harrison
1046 15¢ John Jay
1047 20¢ Monticello
1048 25¢ Paul Revere
1049 30¢ Robert E. Lee
1050 40¢ John Marshall
1051 50¢ Susan B. Anthony
1052 $1 Patrick Henry
1053 $5 Alexander Hamilton

Wildlife Conservation 1956-1978

1077 3¢ Wild Turkey
1078 3¢ Pronghorn Antelope
1079 3¢ King Salmon
1098 3¢ Wildlife Conservation
1427 8¢ Trout
1428 8¢ Alligator
1429 8¢ Polar Bear and Cubs
1430 8¢ California Condor
1464 8¢ Fur Seals
1465 8¢ Cardinal
1466 8¢ Brown Pelican
1467 8¢ Bighorn Sheep
1760 15¢ Great Gray Owl
1761 15¢ Saw-Whet Owl
1762 15¢ Barred Owl
1763 15¢ Great Horned Owl
1764 15¢ Giant Sequoia
1765 15¢ White Pine
1766 15¢ White Oak
1767 15¢ Gray Birch

Champion of Liberty 1957-1961

1096 8¢ Ramon Magsaysay
1110 4¢ Simon Bolivar
1111 8¢ Simon Bolivar
1117 4¢ Lajos Kossuth
1118 8¢ Lajos Kossuth
1125 4¢ José de San Martin
1126 8¢ José de San Martin
1136 4¢ Ernst Reuter
1137 8¢ Ernst Reuter
1147 4¢ Thomas Masaryk
1148 8¢ Thomas Masaryk
1159 4¢ Ignacy Jan Paderewski
1160 8¢ Ignacy Jan Paderewski
1165 4¢ Gustaf Mannerheim
1166 8¢ Gustaf Mannerheim
1168 4¢ Giuseppe Garibaldi
1169 8¢ Giuseppe Garibaldi
1174 4¢ Mahatma Gandhi
1175 8¢ Mahatma Gandhi

American Credo 1960-1961

1139 4¢ Quotation from Washington's Farewell Address
1140 4¢ Benjamin Franklin Quotation
1141 4¢ Thomas Jefferson Quotation
1142 4¢ Francis Scott Key Quotation
1143 4¢ Abraham Lincoln Quotation
1144 4¢ Patrick Henry Quotation

Civil War Centennial 1961-1965

1178 4¢ Fort Sumter
1179 4¢ Shiloh
1180 5¢ Gettysburg
1181 5¢ The Wilderness
1182 5¢ Appomattox

Prominent Americans 1968-1974

1278 1¢ Thomas Jefferson
1279 1-1/4¢ Albert Gallatin
1280 2¢ Frank Lloyd Wright
1281 3¢ Francis Parkman
1282 4¢ Abraham Lincoln
1283 5¢ George Washington
1283B 5¢ George Washington redrawn
1284 6¢ Franklin D. Roosevelt
1285 8¢ Albert Einstein
1286 10¢ Andrew Jackson
1286A 12¢ Henry Ford
1287 13¢ John F. Kennedy
1288 15¢ Oliver Wendell Holmes
1289 20¢ George C. Marshall
1290 25¢ Frederick Douglass
1291 30¢ John Dewey
1292 40¢ Thomas Paine
1293 50¢ Lucy Stone
1294 $1 Eugene O'Neill
1295 $5 John Bassett Moore
1297 3¢ violet Parkman (#1281)
1298 6¢ Franklin D. Roosevelt (1284)
1299 1¢ green Jefferson
1303 4¢ black Lincoln (#1282)
1304 5¢ blue Washington (#1283)
1304C 5¢ Washington redrawn (#1283B)
1305 6¢ gray brown Roosevelt
1305C $1 dull purple Eugene O'Neill
1305E 15¢ magenta Oliver Wendell
      Holmes, Type I (#1288)
1393 6¢ Dwight D. Eisenhower
1393D 7¢ Benjamin Franklin
1394 8¢ Dwight D. Eisenhower
1397 14¢ Fiorello H. LaGuardia
1398 16¢ Ernie Pyle
1399 18¢ Dr. Elizabeth Blackwell
1400 21¢ Amadeo P. Giannini

American Folklore 1966-1974

1317 5¢ Johnny Appleseed
1330 5¢ Davy Crockett
1357 6¢ Daniel Boone
1370 6¢ Grandma Moses
1470 8¢ Tom Sawyer
1548 10¢ The Legend of Sleepy Hollow

Space 1962-2000

1193 4¢ Project Mercury
1331 5¢ Space-Walking Astronaut
1332 5¢ Gemini Capsule
1371 6¢ Apollo 8
1434 8¢ Earth, Sun and Landing Craft
      on Moon
1435 8¢ Lunar Rover and Astronauts
1529 10¢ Skylab
1556 10¢ Pioneer 10 Passing Jupiter
1557 10¢ Mariner 10, Venus and Mercury
1569 10¢ Apollo and Soyuz after
      Link-up and Earth
1570 10¢ Spacecraft before Link-up,
      Earth and Project Emblem
1759 15¢ Viking Missions to Mars
1912 18¢ Exploring the Moon—
      Moon Walk
1913 18¢ Benefiting Mankind,
      Columbia Space Shuttle
1914 18¢ Benefiting Mankind,
      Space Shuttle Deploying Satellite
1915 18¢ Understanding the Sun—
      Skylab
1916 18¢ Probing the Planets—
      Pioneer 11
1917 18¢ Benefiting Mankind, Space
      Shuttle Lifting Off
1918 18¢ Benefiting Mankind, Space
      Shuttle Preparing to Lane
1919 18¢ Comprehending the
      Universe—Telescope
2419 $2.40 Moon Landing
2543 $2.90 Space Vehicle
2544 $3.00 Space Shuttle *Challenger*
2544A $10.75 Space Shuttle *Endeavour*
2568 29¢ Mercury, Mariner 10
2569 29¢ Venus, Mariner 2
2570 29¢ Earth, Landsat
2571 29¢ Moon, Lunar Orbiter
2572 29¢ Mars, Viking Orbiter
2573 29¢ Jupiter, Pioneer 11
2574 29¢ Saturn, Voyager 2
2575 29¢ Uranus, Voyager 2
2576 29¢ Neptune, Voyager 2
2577 29¢ Pluto
2631 29¢ Cosmonaut, U.S. Space Shuttle
2632 29¢ Astronaut, Russian Space
      Station
2633 29¢ Sputnik, Vostok, Apollo
      Command and Lunar Modules
2634 29¢ Soyuz, Mercury and Gemini
      Spacecraft
2741 29¢ Space Fantasy
2742 29¢ Space Fantasy
2743 29¢ Space Fantasy
2744 29¢ Space Fantasy
2745 29¢ Space Fantasy
2841A 29¢ First Moon Landing 1969
2842 $9.95 First Moon Landing,
      25th Anniversary
3178 $3.00 Mars Rover Sojourner
3238 32¢ Space Discovery
3239 32¢ Space Discovery
3240 32¢ Space Discovery
3241 32¢ Space Discovery
3242 32¢ Space Discovery
3261 $3.20 Space Shuttle Landing
3262 $11.75 Piggyback Space Shuttle
3384 33¢ Eagle Nebula
3385 33¢ Ring Nebula
3386 33¢ Lagoon Nebula
3387 33¢ Egg Nebula
3388 33¢ Galaxy NGC1316
3409 Probing the Vastness of Space
3409A 60¢ Hubble Space Telescope
409B 60¢ Radio Interferometer, NM
3409C 60¢ Telescopes, Keck
      Observatory, HI
3409D 60¢ Telescopes, Cerro Tololo
      Observatory, Chile
3409E 60¢ Telescope, Mount Wilson
      Observatory, CA
3409F 60¢ Telescope, Arecibo
      Observatory, Puerto Rico
3410 Exploring the Solar System
3410A $1 Sun and Corona
3410B $1 Cross-section of Sun
3410C $1 Sun and Earth
3410D $1 Sun and solar flare
3410E $1 Sun and clouds
3411 Escaping the Gravity of Earth
3411A $3.20 Space Shuttle and
      Space Station
3411B $3.20 Astronauts working in space
3412 $11.75 Space Achievement
      and Exploration
3413 $11.75 Landing on the Moon

American Bicentennial 1971-1983

1432 8¢ Bicentennial Commission
      Emblem
1456 8¢ Glass Blower
1457 8¢ Silversmith
1458 8¢ Wigmaker
1459 8¢ Hatter
1476 8¢ Printer and Patriots
      Examining Pamphlet
1477 8¢ Posting a Broadside
1478 8¢ Postrider
1479 8¢ Drummer
1480 8¢ British Merchantman
1481 8¢ British Three-Master
1482 8¢ Boats and Ship's Hull
1483 8¢ Boat and Dock
1543 10¢ Carpenters' Hall
1544 10¢ "We Ask but for Peace,
      Liberty and Safety"
1545 10¢ "Deriving Their Just
      Powers from the Consent
      of the Governed"
1546 10¢ Independence Hall
1559 8¢ Sybil Ludington
1560 8¢ Salem Poor
1561 10¢ Haym Salomon
1562 18¢ Peter Francisco
1563 10¢ Lexington-Concord 1775
1564 10¢ Bunker Hill 1775
1565 10¢ Continental Army
1566 10¢ Continental Navy
1567 10¢ Continental Marines
1568 10¢ American Militia
1629 13¢ Drummer Boy
1630 13¢ Old Drummer
1631 13¢ Fifer
1633 13¢ Delaware State Flag
1634 13¢ Pennsylvania State Flag
1635 13¢ New Jersey
1636 13¢ Georgia
1637 13¢ Connecticut
1638 13¢ Massachusetts
1639 13¢ Maryland
1640 13¢ South Carolina
1641 13¢ New Hampshire
1642 13¢ Virginia
1643 13¢ New York
1644 13¢ North Carolina

American Bicentennial continued

1645 13¢ Rhode Island
1646 13¢ Vermont
1647 13¢ Kentucky
1648 13¢ Tennessee
1649 13¢ Ohio
1650 13¢ Louisiana
1651 13¢ Indiana
1652 13¢ Mississippi
1653 13¢ Illinois
1654 13¢ Alabama
1655 13¢ Maine
1656 13¢ Missouri
1657 13¢ Arkansas
1658 13¢ Michigan
1659 13¢ Florida
1660 13¢ Texas
1661 13¢ Iowa
1662 13¢ Wisconsin
1663 13¢ California
1664 13¢ Minnesota
1665 13¢ Oregon
1666 13¢ Kansas
1667 13¢ West Virginia
1668 13¢ Nevada
1669 13¢ Nebraska
1670 13¢ Colorado
1671 13¢ North Dakota
1672 13¢ South Dakota
1673 13¢ Montana
1674 13¢ Washington
1675 13¢ Idaho
1676 13¢ Wyoming
1677 13¢ Utah
1678 13¢ Oklahoma
1679 13¢ New Mexico
1680 13¢ Arizona
1681 13¢ Alaska
1682 13¢ Hawaii
1686 13¢ *Surrender of Lord Cornwallis at Yorktown*
1687 18¢ *Declaration of Independence, 4 July 1776 at Philadelphia*
1688 23¢ *Washington Crossing the Delaware*
1689 31¢ *Washington Reviewing His Ragged Army at Valley Forge*
1690 13¢ Bust of Benjamin Franklin, Map of North America, 1776
Declaration of Independence #1691-1694
1691 13¢ Delegates

1692 13¢ Delegates and John Adams
1693 13¢ Roger Sherman, Robert R. Livingston, Thomas Jefferson and Benjamin Franklin
1694 13¢ John Hancock, Charles Thomson, George Read, John Dickinson and Edward Rutledge
1704 13¢ *Washington at Princeton*
1716 13¢ Marquis de Lafayette
1717 13¢ Seamstress
1718 13¢ Blacksmith
1719 13¢ Wheelwright
1720 13¢ Leatherworker
1722 13¢ *Herkimer at Oriskany*
1726 13¢ Members of Continental Congress in Conference
1728 13¢ *Surrender at Saratoga*
1753 13¢ *King Louis XVI and Benjamin Franklin*
1789 15¢ *John Paul Jones*
1826 15¢ General Bernardo de Gálvez, Battle of Mobile 1780
1937 18¢ Battle of Yorktown 1781
1938 18¢ Battle of the Virginia Capes 1781
1941 20¢ John Hanson
1952 20¢ George Washington
2052 20¢ Treaty of Paris

National Parks Centennial 1972

1448 2¢ Ship at Sea
1449 2¢ Cape Hatteras
1450 2¢ Laughing Gulls on Driftwood
1451 2¢ Laughing Gulls and Dune
1452 6¢ Wolf Trap Farm, Virginia
1453 8¢ Old Faithful, Yellowstone
1454 15¢ Mount McKinley, Alaska
C84 11¢ City of Refuge, Hawaii

Black Heritage 1978-Present

1744 13¢ Harriet Tubman
1771 15¢ Dr. Martin Luther King, Jr.
1804 15¢ Benjamin Banneker
1875 15¢ Whitney Moore Young
2016 20¢ Jackie Robinson
2044 20¢ Scott Joplin
2073 20¢ Carter G. Woodson
2137 22¢ Mary McLeod Bethune
2203 22¢ Sojourner Truth
2249 22¢ Jean Baptiste Point Du Sable
2371 22¢ James Weldon Johnson
2402 25¢ A. Philip Randolph
2442 25¢ Ida B. Wells
2567 29¢ Jan E. Matzeliger
2617 29¢ W.E.B. DuBois

2746 29¢ Percy Lavon Julian
2816 29¢ Dr. Allison Davis
2956 32¢ Bessie Coleman
3058 32¢ Ernest E. Just
3121 32¢ Brig. Gen. Benjamin O. Davis, Sr.
3181 32¢ Madam C.J. Walker
3273 33¢ Malcolm X
3371 33¢ Patricia Roberts Harris
3501 34¢ Roy Wilkins
3557 34¢ Langston Hughes
3746 37¢ Thurgood Marshall
3834 37¢ Paul Robeson
3896 37¢ Marian Anderson
3996 39¢ Hattie McDaniel
4120 39¢ Ella Fitzgerald
4222 41¢ Charles W. Chesnutt
—   42¢ Anna Julia Cooper (2009)

American Arts 1973-1975

1484 8¢ George Gershwin, Composer
1485 8¢ Robinson Jeffers, Poet
1486 8¢ Henry Ossawa Tanner, Artist
1487 8¢ Willa Cather, Novelist
1553 10¢ Benjamin West, Artist
1554 10¢ Paul Laurence Dunbar, Poet
1555 10¢ D. W. Griffith, Moviemaker

Rural America 1973

1504 8¢ Angus and Longhorn
1505 10¢ Chautauqua Tent & Buggies
1506 10¢ Wheat Fields & Train

Americana 1977-1981

1581 1¢ Inkwell and Quill
1582 2¢ Speaker's Stand
1584 3¢ Early Ballot Box
1585 4¢ Books, Bookmark, Eyeglasses
1590 9¢ Capitol Dome
1591 9¢ Capitol Dome
1592 10¢ Contemplation of Justice
1593 11¢ Printing Press
1594 12¢ Torch, Statue of Liberty
1595 13¢ Liberty Bell
1596 13¢ Eagle and Shield
1597 15¢ Fort McHenry Flag
1598 15¢ Fort McHenry Flag
1599 16¢ Head, Statue of Liberty
1603 24¢ Old North Church
1604 28¢ Fort Nisqually
1605 29¢ Sandy Hook Lighthouse
1606 30¢ Morris Township School # 2

1608 50¢ Iron "Betty" Lamp
1610 $1 Rush Lamp and Candle
1611 $2 Kerosene Table Lamp
1612 $5 Railroad Conductor's Lantern
1613 3.1¢ String Guitar
1614 7.7¢ Saxhorns
1615 7.9¢ Drum
1615C 8.4¢ Steinway Grand Piano
1616 9¢ slate green Capitol Dome
1617 10¢ purple Contemplation of Justice
1618 13¢ brown Liberty Bell
1618C 15¢ Fort McHenry Flag
1619 16¢ blue Head of Liberty
1622 13¢ Flag over Independence Hall
1622C 13¢ Star Flag over Independence Hall
1623 13¢ Flag over Capitol
1811 1¢ dark blue Inkwell and Quill
1813 3.5¢ Weaver Violins
1816 12¢ red brown, beige Torch from Statue of Liberty

American Folk Art 1977-1995

1706 13¢ Zia Pot
1707 13¢ San Ildefonso Pot
1708 13¢ Hopi Pot
1709 13¢ Acoma Pot
1745 13¢ Basket Design, Quilts
1746 13¢ Basket Design, Quilts
1747 13¢ Basket Design, Quilts
1748 13¢ Basket Design, Quilts
1775 15¢ Straight-Spout Coffeepot
1776 15¢ Tea Caddy
1777 15¢ Sugar Bowl
1778 15¢ Curved-Spout Coffeepot
1834 15¢ Heiltsuk, Bella Tribe
1835 15¢ Chilkat Tlingit Tribe
1836 15¢ Tlingit Tribe
1837 15¢ Bella Coola Tribe
2138 22¢ Broadbill Decoy
2139 22¢ Mallard Decoy
2140 22¢ Canvasback Decoy
2141 22¢ Redhead Decoy
2235 22¢ Navajo Art
2236 22¢ Navajo Art
2237 22¢ Navajo Art
2238 22¢ Navajo Art
2240 22¢ Highlander Figure
2241 22¢ Ship Figurehead
2242 22¢ Nautical Figure
2243 22¢ Cigar Store Figure
2351 22¢ Squash Blossoms, Lacemaking
2352 22¢ Floral Piece, Lacemaking

American Folk Art continued

2353 22¢ Floral Piece, Lacemaking
2354 22¢ Dogwood Blossoms,
      Lacemaking

Carousel Animals

2390 25¢ Deer
2391 25¢ Horse
2392 25¢ Camel
2393 25¢ Goat

Carousel Horses

2976 32¢ Golden Horse with Roses
2977 32¢ Black Horse with Gold Bridle
2978 32¢ Horse with Armor
2979 32¢ Brown Horse with Green Bridle

Performing Arts 1978-1991

1755 13¢ Jimmie Rodgers
1756 15¢ George M. Cohan
1801 15¢ Will Rogers
1803 15¢ W. C. Fields
2012 20¢ John, Ethel, &
      Lionel Barrymore
2088 20¢ Douglas Fairbanks
2090 20¢ John McCormack
2110 22¢ Jerome Kern
2211 22¢ Duke Ellington
2250 22¢ Enrico Caruso
2411 25¢ Arturo Toscanini
2550 29¢ Cole Porter

Literary Arts 1979-Present

1773 15¢ John Steinbeck
1832 15¢ Edith Wharton
2047 20¢ Nathaniel Hawthorne
2094 20¢ Herman Melville
2239 22¢ T. S. Eliot
2350 22¢ William Faulkner
2418 25¢ Ernest Hemingway
2449 25¢ Marianne Moore
2538 29¢ William Saroyan
2698 29¢ Dorothy Parker
2862 29¢ James Thurber
3002 32¢ Tennessee Williams
3104 23¢ F. Scott Fitzgerald
3134 32¢ Thornton Wilder
3221 32¢ Stephen Vincent Benét
3308 33¢ Ayn Rand
3444 33¢ Thomas Wolfe
3659 37¢ Ogden Nash
3748 37¢ Zora Neale Hurston
3871 37¢ James Baldwin
3904 37¢ Robert Penn Warren
4030 39¢ Katherine Anne Porter
4124 39¢ Henry Wadsworth Longfellow
4223 41¢ Marjorie Kinnan Rawlings
—   61¢ Richard Wright (2009)

Architecture 1979-1982

1779 15¢ Virginia Rotunda
1780 15¢ Baltimore Cathedral
1781 15¢ Boston State House
1782 15¢ Philadelphia Exchange
1838 15¢ Smithsonian Institution
1839 15¢ Trinity Church
1840 15¢ Pennsylvania Academy
      of Fine Arts
1841 15¢ Lyndhurst
1928 18¢ NYU Library, New York
1929 18¢ Biltmore House
1930 18¢ Palace of the Arts
1931 18¢ National Farmer's Bank
2019 20¢ Fallingwater
2020 20¢ Illinois Institute of Technology
2021 20¢ Gropius House
2022 20¢ Dulles Airport

Lighthouses 1990-2009

2470 25¢ Admiralty Head, WA
2471 25¢ Cape Hatteras, NC
2472 25¢ West Quoddy Head, ME
2473 25¢ American Shoals, FL
2474 25¢ Sandy Hook, NJ

Great Lakes Lighthouses

2969 32¢ Split Rock, Lake Superior
2970 32¢ St. Joseph, Lake Michigan
2971 32¢ Spectacle Reef, Lake Huron
2972 32¢ Marblehead, Lake Erie
2973 32¢ Thirty Mile Point, Lake Ontario

Southeastern Lighthouses

3787 37¢ Old Cape Henry, VA
3788 37¢ Cape Lookout, NC
3789 37¢ Morris Island, SC
3790 37¢ Tybee Island, GA
3791 37¢ Hillsboro Inlet, FL

Pacific Coast Lighthouses

4146 41¢ Diamond Head, Hawaii
4147 41¢ Five Finger, Alaska
4148 41¢ Grays Harbor, Washington
4149 41¢ Umpqua River, Oregon
4150 41¢ St. George Reef, California

Gulf Coast Lighthouses (2009)

—   44¢ Matagorda Island, Texas
—   44¢ Sabine Pass, Louisiana
—   44¢ Biloxi, Mississippi
—   44¢ Sand Island, Alabama
—   44¢ Fort Jefferson, Florida

Love 1973-Present

1475 8¢ Love
1951 20¢ Love
2072 20¢ Love
2143 22¢ Love
2202 22¢ Love
2248 22¢ Love
2378 25¢ Love
2379 45¢ Love
2440 25¢ Love
2535 29¢ Love
2537 52¢ Love
2618 29¢ Love
2813 29¢ Love Sunrise
2814 29¢ Love

*Cherub from Sistine Madonna
by Raphael #2948-3030*

2948 32¢ Love, Cherub from Sistine
2949 32¢ Love, Cherub from Sistine
2957 32¢ Love, Cherub from Sistine
2958 55¢ Love, Cherub from Sistine
2959 32¢ Love, Cherub from Sistine
      (Booklet)
2960 55¢ Love, Cherub from Sistine
      (Booklet)
3030 32¢ Love, Cherub from Sistine
3123 32¢ Love Swans
3124 55¢ Love Swans
3274 33¢ Love
3275 55¢ Love
3496 34¢ Rose and Love Letter
3497 34¢ Rose and Love Letter
3498 34¢ Rose and Love Letter
3499 55¢ Rose and Love Letter
3657 37¢ Love
3658 60¢ Love
3833 37¢ Love: Candy Hearts
3898 37¢ Love Bouquet
3976 39¢ True Blue
4122 39¢ With Love and Kisses
4270 42¢ Love: All Heart
—   44¢ King and Queen of Hearts
      (2009)

Love Stamped Envelopes 1989-2003

U616 25¢ Love
U621 29¢ Love
U637 32¢ Spiral Heart
U644 33¢ Victorian Love
U647 34¢ Lovebirds
U651 37¢ Nurturing Love

Nature of America 1999-Present

3293 33¢ Sonoran Desert
3378 33¢ Pacific Coast Rain Forest
3506 34¢ Great Plains Prairie
3611 34¢ Longleaf Pine Forest
3802 37¢ Arctic Tundra
3831 37¢ Pacific Coral Reef
3899 37¢ Northeast Deciduous Fores
4099 39¢ Southern Florida Wetland
4198 41¢ Alpine Tundra
4352 42¢ Great Lakes Dunes
—   44¢ Kelp Forest (2009)

Legends of Hollywood 1995-Present

2967 32¢ Marilyn Monroe
3082 32¢ James Dean
3152 32¢ Humphrey Bogart
3226 32¢ Alfred Hitchcock
3329 33¢ James Cagney
3446 33¢ Edward G. Robinson
3523 34¢ Lucille Ball
3692 37¢ Cary Grant
3786 37¢ Audrey Hepburn
3876 37¢ John Wayne
3911 37¢ Henry Fonda
4077 39¢ Judy Garland
4197 41¢ James Stewart
4350 42¢ Bette Davis
—   44¢ Gary Cooper (2009)

Lunar New Year 1992-2007

2720 29¢ Year of the Rooster
2817 29¢ Year of the Dog
2876 29¢ Year of the Boar
3060 32¢ Year of the Rat
3120 32¢ Year of the Ox
3179 32¢ Year of the Tiger
3272 33¢ Year of the Rabbit
3370 33¢ Year of the Dragon
3500 34¢ Year of the Snake
3559 34¢ Year of the Horse
3747 37¢ Year of the Ram
3832 37¢ Year of the Monkey
3895 37¢ Lunar New Year
      Souvenir Sheet
3997 39¢ Lunar New Year
      Souvenir Sheet

Transportation 1981-1995

1897 1¢ Omnibus 1880s
1897A 2¢ Locomotive 1870s
1898 3¢ Handcar 1880s
1898A 4¢ Stagecoach 1890s
1899 5¢ Motorcycle 1913
1900 5.2¢ Sleigh 1880s
1901 5.9¢ Bicycle 1870s
1902 7.4¢ Baby Buggy 1880s
1903 9.3¢ Mail Wagon 1880s
1904 10.9¢ Hansom Cab 1890s
1905 11¢ RR Caboose 1890s
1906 17¢ Electric Auto 1917
1907 18¢ Surrey 1890s
1908 20¢ Fire Pumper 1860s
2123 3.4¢ School Bus 1920s
2124 4.9¢ Buckboard 1880s
2125 5.5¢ Star Route Truck 1910s
2126 6¢ Tricycle 1880s
2127 7.1¢ Tractor 1920s
2128 8.3¢ Ambulance 1860s
2129 8.5¢ Tow Truck 1920s
2130 10.1¢ Oil Wagon 1890s
2131 11¢ Stutz Bearcat 1933
2132 12¢ Stanley Steamer 1909
2133 12.5¢ Pushcart 1880s
2134 14¢ Iceboat 1880s
2135 17¢ Dog Sled 1920s
2136 25¢ Bread Wagon 1880s
2252 3¢ Conestoga Wagon 1800s
2253 5¢ Milk Wagon 1900s
2254 5.3¢ Elevator 1900s
2255 7.6¢ Carreta 1770s
2256 8.4¢ Wheel Chair 1920s
2257 10¢ Canal Boat 1880s
2258 13¢ Patrol Wagon 1880s
2259 13.2¢ Coal Car 1870s
2260 15¢ Tugboat 1900s
2261 16.7¢ Popcorn Wagon 1902
2262 17.5¢ Racing Car 1911
2263 20¢ Cable Car 1880s
2264 20.5¢ Fire Engine 1900s
2265 21¢ Railroad Mail Car 1920s
2266 24.1¢ Tandem Bicycle 1890s
2451 4¢ Steam Carriage 1866
2452 5¢ Circus Wagon 1900s
2452D 5¢ Circus Wagon gravure printing
2453 5¢ Canoe 1800s intaglio printing
2454 5¢ Canoe 1800s gravure printing
2457 10¢ Tractor Trailer 1930s
2463 20¢ Cog Railway 1870s
2464 23¢ Lunch Wagon 1890s
2466 32¢ Ferryboat 1900s
2468 $1 Seaplane 1914

Great Americans 1980-1995

1844 1¢ Dorothea Dix
1845 2¢ Igor Stravinsky
1846 3¢ Henry Clay
1847 4¢ Carl Schurz
1848 5¢ Pearl Buck
1849 6¢ Walter Lippmann
1850 7¢ Abraham Baldwin
1851 8¢ Henry Knox
1852 9¢ Sylvanus Thayer
1853 10¢ Richard Russell
1854 11¢ Alden Partridge
1855 13¢ Crazy Horse
1856 14¢ Sinclair Lewis
1857 17¢ Rachel Carson
1858 18¢ George Mason
1859 19¢ Sequoyah
1860 20¢ Ralph Bunche
1861 20¢ Thomas H. Gallaudet
1862 20¢ Harry S. Truman
1863 22¢ John J. Audubon
1864 30¢ Frank C. Laubach
1865 35¢ Charles R. Drew M.D.
1866 37¢ Robert Millikan
1867 39¢ Grenville Clark
1868 40¢ Lillian M. Gilbreth
1869 50¢ Chester W. Nimitz
2182 25¢ Jack London
2172 5¢ Hugo L. Black
2195 $2 William Jennings Bryan
2178 17¢ Belva Ann Lockwood
2168 1¢ Margaret Mitchell
2171 4¢ Father Flanagan
2180 56¢ John Harvard
2170 3¢ Paul Dudley White MD
2193 $1 Bernard Revel
2176 14¢ Julia Ward Howe
2169 2¢ Mary Lyon
2175 10¢ Red Cloud
2196 $5 Bret Harte
2177 15¢ Buffalo Bill Cody
2188 45¢ Harvey Cushing MD
2180 21¢ Chester Carlson
2181 23¢ Mary Cassatt
2191 65¢ H.H. 'Hap' Arnold
2194 $1 Johns Hopkins
2183 28¢ Sitting Bull
2173 5¢ Luis Muñoz Marin
2187 40¢ Claire Chennault
2186 35¢ Dennis Chavez

2189 52¢ Hubert H. Humphrey
2192 75¢ Wendell Willkie
2184 29¢ Earl Warren
2185 29¢ Thomas Jefferson
2179 20¢ Virginia Apgar
2940 55¢ Alice Hamilton, MD
2934 32¢ Cal Farley
2933 32¢ Milton S. Hershey
2943 78¢ Alice Paul
2938 46¢ Ruth Benedict
2936 32¢ Lila and DeWitt Wallace
2935 32¢ Henry R. Luce, Editor
2942 77¢ Mary Breckinridge
2941 55¢ Justin S. Morrill

American Culture 1995-2003

2908-2910 (15¢) Auto Tail Fin
2911 (25¢) Juke Box
2912 (25¢) Juke Box
3132 (25¢) Juke Box
3208 25¢ Diner
3208A 25¢ Diner
3447 (10¢) New York Public Library Lion
3520 10¢ Atlas Statue
3522 15¢ Woody Wagon
3766 $1 Wisdom

American Design 2002-Present

3612 5¢ American Toleware (reissued as #3756 and #3756A)
3757 10¢ American Clock (reissued as #3762 and #3763)
3758 1¢ Tiffany Lamp (reissued as #3749, #3758A and #3749A)
3750 2¢ Navajo Jewelry (reissued as #3751, #3752 and #3753)
3755 4¢ Chippendale Chair (reissued as #3761)
3759 3¢ Silver Coffeepot (reissued as #3754)

American Treasures 2001-Present

3524 34¢ Amish Quilts, Diamond in the Square
3525 34¢ Amish Quilts, Lone Star
3526 34¢ Amish Quilts, Sunshine and Shadow
3527 34¢ Amish Quilts, Double Ninepatch
3650 37¢ John James Audubon
Mary Cassatt #3804-3807
3804 37¢ Young Mother
3805 37¢ Children Playing on the Beach
3806 37¢ On a Balcony
3807 37¢ Child in a Straw Hat
3872 37¢ Martin Johnson Heade "Magnolias"
3926-3929 37¢ New Mexico Rio Grande Blankets (4 designs)
4089-4098 39¢ Quilts of Gee's Bend (10 designs)
4165 41¢ Louis Comfort Tiffany
4346 42¢ Albert Bierstadt

American Sports Personalities 1981-Present

1932 18¢ Babe Zaharias
1933 18¢ Bobby Jones
2046 20¢ Babe Ruth
2089 20¢ Jim Thorpe
2097 20¢ Roberto Clemente
2376 22¢ Knute Rockne
2377 25¢ Francis Ouimet
2417 25¢ Lou Gehrig
2766 29¢ Joe Louis
3936 37¢ Arthur Ashe
4020 39¢ Sugar Ray Robinson

Distinguished Americans 2000-Present

3420 10¢ Joseph W. Stilwell
3422 23¢ Wilma Rudolph
3426 33¢ Claude Pepper
3428 63¢ Jonas Salk
3431 76¢ Hattie Caraway
3432 76¢ Hattie Caraway
3433 83¢ Edna Ferber
3434 83¢ Edna Ferber
3435 87¢ Albert Sabin
3436 23¢ Wilma Rudolph
3427 58¢ Margaret Chase Smith
3428 75¢ Harriet Beecher Stowe
3427A 59¢ James A. Michener
3432A 76¢ Edward Trudeau
— 78¢ Mary Lasker (2009)

Celebrate The Century® 1998-2000

3182 32¢ 1900-1909 Pane of 15
3183 32¢ 1910-1919 Pane of 15
3184 32¢ 1920-1929 Pane of 15
3185 32¢ 1930-1939 Pane of 15
3186 33¢ 1940-1949 Pane of 15
3187 33¢ 1950-1959 Pane of 15
3188 33¢ 1960-1969 Pane of 15
3189 33¢ 1970-1979 Pane of 15
3190 33¢ 1980-1989 Pane of 15
3191 33¢ 1990-1999 Pane of 15

World War II 1991-1995

2559 29¢ WWII, 1941: A World at War
2697 29¢ WWII, 1942: Into the Battle
2765 29¢ WWII, 1943: Turning the Tide
2838 29¢ WWII, 1944: Road to Victory
2981 32¢ WWII, 1945: Victory at Last

Ratification of the Constitution 1987-1990

2336 22¢ Delaware
2337 22¢ Pennsylvania
2338 22¢ New Jersey
2339 22¢ Georgia
2340 22¢ Connecticut
2341 22¢ Massachusetts
2342 22¢ Maryland
2343 22¢ South Carolina
2344 22¢ New Hampshire
2345 22¢ Virginia
2346 22¢ New York
2347 22¢ North Carolina
2348 22¢ Rhode Island

Pioneers of Aviation 1978-1999

C91 31¢ Wright Brothers
C92 31¢ Wright Brothers
C93 21¢ Octave Chanute
C94 21¢ Octave Chanute
C95 25¢ Wiley Post
C96 25¢ Wiley Post
C99 28¢ Blanche Stuart Scott
C100 35¢ Glenn Curtiss
C113 33¢ Alfred Verville
C114 39¢ Lawrence and Elmer Sperry
C115 44¢ Transpacific Airmail
C118 45¢ Samuel Langley
C119 36¢ Igor Sikorsky
C128 50¢ Harriet Quimby
C129 40¢ William T. Piper
2998 60¢ Eddie Rickenbacker
3066 50¢ Jacqueline Cochran
3330 55¢ Billy Mitchell

Garden Flowers 1993-1996

2760 29¢ Hyacinth
2761 29¢ Daffodil
2762 29¢ Tulip
2763 29¢ Iris
2764 29¢ Lilac
2829 29¢ Lilly
2830 29¢ Zinnia
2831 29¢ Gladiola
2832 29¢ Marigold
2833 29¢ Rose
2993 32¢ Aster

2994 32¢ Chrysanthemum
2995 32¢ Dahlia
2996 32¢ Hydrangea
2997 32¢ Rudbeckia
3025 32¢ Crocus
3026 32¢ Winter Aconite
3027 32¢ Pansy
3028 32¢ Snowdrop
3029 32¢ Anemone

Looney Tunes 1997-2001

3137 32¢ Bugs Bunny
3204 32¢ Sylvester & Tweety
3306 33¢ Daffy Duck
3391 33¢ Road Runner & Wile E. Coyote
3534 34¢ Porky Pig "That's All Folks!"

American Scenes 1995-2009

2902 (5¢) Butte
2903 (5¢) Mountain
2904 (5¢) Mountain
3207 (5¢) Wetlands
3693 (5¢) Sea Coast (reissued as #3864 and #4348)
— 44¢ Seabiscuit Envelope (2009)

American Transportation 1995-1998

2905 (10¢) Automobile
2906 (10¢) Automobile
3228 (10¢) Green Bicycle
3229 (10¢) Green Bicycle

Classic Collections 1994-2001

2869 29¢ Legends of the West
2975 32¢ Civil War
3000 32¢ Comic Strip Classics
3068 32¢ Atlanta Centennial Olympic Games
3142 32¢ Classic American Aircraft
3236 32¢ Four Centuries of American Art
3351 33¢ Insects & Spiders
3403 33¢ The Stars and Stripes
3408 33¢ Legends of Baseball
3502 34¢ American Illustrators

America/PUAS 1989-1992

2426 25¢ Southwest Carved Figure
C121 45¢ Southeast Carved Wood Figure
C127 45¢ Tropical Coast
2512 25¢ Grand Canyon
C131 50¢ Eskimo and Bering Land Bridge

Artists 1996-Present

3069 32¢ Georgia O'Keeffe
3202a 32¢ Alexander Calder
3383a 33¢ Louise Nevelson
3509 34¢ Frida Kahlo
3652 37¢ Andy Warhol
3861a 37¢ Isamu Noguchi

Scenic American Landscapes, International Rate 1999-Present

C133 48¢ Niagara Falls
C134 40¢ Rio Grande
C135 60¢ Grand Canyon
C136 70¢ Nine-Mile Prairie
C137 80¢ Mount McKinley
C138 60¢ Acadia National Park
C139 63¢ Bryce Canyon
C140 75¢ Great Smoky Mountains
C141 84¢ Yosemite National Park
UXC27 55¢ Mt. Rainier Stamped Card
UXC28 70¢ Badlands
C142 69¢ Okefenokee Swamp, Georgia/Florida
C143 90¢ Hagåtña Bay, Guam
C144 72¢ 13 Mile Woods, New Hampshire
C145 94¢ St. John, U.S. Virgin Islands
— 79¢ Zion National Park, Utah (2009)
— 98¢ Grand Teton National Park, Wyoming (2009)

Scenic America Stamped Cards 1994-Present

UX198 20¢ Red Barn
UY41 20¢ + 20¢ Red Barn
UX241 20¢ Winter Scene
UX306 20¢ Block Island Lighthouse
UX375 21¢ White Barn
UX381 23¢ Carlsbad Caverns
UX449 24¢ Pikes Peak
UY43 21¢ + 21¢ White Barn
UY44 23¢ + 23¢ Carlsbad Caverns
UY45 24¢ Pikes Peak

Historic Preservation Stamped Cards 1977-Present

UX71 9¢ Federal Court House
UX73 10¢ Cincinnati Music Hall
UX81 10¢ Iolani Palace
UX83 10¢ Salt Lake Temple
UX96 13¢ Academy of Music
UX97 13¢ Old Post Office, St. Louis, MO
UX119 14¢ Timberline Lodge
UX121 15¢ Blair House
UX125 15¢ Hearst Castle
UX128 15¢ Healy Hall
UX134 15¢ Hull House, Chicago
UX135 15¢ Independence Hall, Philadelphia
UX148 15¢ Isaac Royall House
UX150 15¢ Stanford University
UX151 15¢ Constitution Hall
UX152 15¢ Chicago Orchestral Hall
UX154 19¢ Carnegie Hall
UX155 19¢ Old Red, UT-Galveston
UX157 19¢ Notre Dame
UX159 19¢ The Old Mill

UX160 19¢ Wadsworth Atheneum
UX161 19¢ Cobb Hall
UX162 19¢ Waller Hall
UX165 19¢ Ellis Island
UX166 19¢ National Cathedral
UX167 19¢ Wren Building
UX168 19¢ Holocaust Memorial
UX169 19¢ Fort Recovery
UX170 19¢ Playmakers Theater
UX171 19¢ Massachusetts Hall
UX172 19¢ Lincoln's Home
UX175 19¢ Wittenberg University
UX177 19¢ St. Louis Union Station
UX262 20¢ St. John's College
UX263 20¢ Princeton University
UX280 20¢ City College of New York
UX284 20¢ Fort McHenry
UX290 20¢ University of Mississippi
UX292 20¢ Girard College
UX298 20¢ Northeastern University
UX299 20¢ Brandeis University
UX301 20¢ University of Wisconsin— Madison
UX302 20¢ Washington and Lee University
UX303 20¢ Redwood Library and Athenaeum
UX305 20¢ Mount Vernon
UX312 20¢ University of Utah
UX313 20¢ Ryman Auditorium
UX316 20¢ Middlebury College
UX361 20¢ Yale University
UX362 20¢ University of South Carolina
UX363 20¢ Northwestern University
UX364 20¢ University of Portland
UX400 23¢ Ohio University
UX405 23¢ Columbia University
UX406 23¢ Harriton House
UX533 27¢ Mount St. Mary's University
UX554 27¢ Miami University

Legends of American Music 1993-1999

2721 29¢ Elvis Presley
2722 29¢ Oklahoma!
2723 29¢ Hank Williams
Rock & Roll/Rhythm & Blues
2724 29¢ Elvis Presley
2725 29¢ Bill Haley
2726 29¢ Clyde McPhatter
2727 29¢ Ritchie Valens
2728 29¢ Otis Redding
2729 29¢ Buddy Holly
2730 29¢ Dinah Washington
Broadway Musicals
2767 29¢ Show Boat
2768 29¢ Porgy & Bess
2769 29¢ Oklahoma
2770 29¢ My Fair Lady

Legends of American Music continued
Country & Western
2771 29¢ Hank Williams
2772 29¢ Patsy Cline
2773 29¢ The Carter Family
2774 29¢ Bob Wills
Popular Singers
2849 29¢ Al Jolson
2850 29¢ Bing Crosby
2851 29¢ Ethel Waters
2852 29¢ Nat "King" Cole
2853 29¢ Ethel Merman
Jazz & Blues Singers
2854 29¢ Bessie Smith
2855 29¢ Muddy Waters
2856 29¢ Billie Holiday
2857 29¢ Robert Johnson
2858 29¢ Jimmy Rushing
2859 29¢ "Ma" Rainey
2860 29¢ Mildred Bailey
2861 29¢ Howlin' Wolf
Jazz Musicians
2982 32¢ Louis Armstrong
2983 32¢ Coleman Hawkins
2984 32¢ Louis Armstrong
2985 32¢ James P. Johnson
2986 32¢ Jelly Roll Morton
2987 32¢ Charlie Parker
2988 32¢ Eubie Blake
2989 32¢ Charles Mingus
2990 32¢ Thelonious Monk
2991 32¢ John Coltrane
2992 32¢ Erroll Garner
Big Band Leaders
3096 32¢ Count Basie
3097 32¢ Tommy and Jimmy Dorsey
3098 32¢ Glenn Miller
3099 32¢ Benny Goodman
Songwriters
3100 32¢ Harold Arlen
3101 32¢ Johnny Mercer
3102 32¢ Dorothy Fields
3103 32¢ Hoagy Carmichael
Opera Singers
3154 32¢ Lily Pons
3155 32¢ Richard Tucker
3156 32¢ Lawrence Tibbett
3157 32¢ Rosa Ponselle
Classical Composers & Conductors
3158 32¢ Leopold Stokowski
3159 32¢ Arthur Fiedler
3160 32¢ George Szell
3161 32¢ Eugene Ormandy
3162 32¢ Samuel Barber
3163 32¢ Ferde Grofé
3164 32¢ Charles Ives
3165 32¢ Louis Moreau Gottschalk

Folk Musicians
3212 32¢ Huddle "Leadbelly" Ledbetter
3213 32¢ Woody Guthrie
3214 32¢ Sonny Terry
3215 32¢ Josh White
Gospel Singers
3216 32¢ Mahalia Jackson
3217 32¢ Roberta Martin
3218 32¢ Clara Ward
3219 32¢ Sister Rosetta Tharpe
Hollywood Composers
3339 33¢ Max Steiner
3340 33¢ Dimitri Tiomkin
3341 33¢ Bernard Herrmann
3342 33¢ Franz Waxman
3343 33¢ Alfred Newman
3344 33¢ Erich Wolfgang Korngold
Broadway Songwriters
3345 33¢ Ira & George Gershwin
3346 33¢ Lerner & Loewe
3347 33¢ Lorenz Hart
3348 33¢ Rodgers & Hammerstein
3349 33¢ Meredith Willson
3350 33¢ Frank Loesser

The Art of Disney 2004-2008
3865-3868 37¢ Friendship
3912-3915 37¢ Celebration
4025-4028 39¢ Romance
4192-4195 41¢ Magic
4342-4345 42¢ Imagination

Official Mail 1983-Present
O121 2¢ Postal Savings
O122 50¢ dark green
O123 $1 ultramarine
O124 1¢ dark violet
O125 2¢ Postal Savings (0121)
O126 10¢ carmine
O127 1¢ January 12, 1983
O128 4¢ January 12, 1983
O129 13¢ January 12, 1983
O129A 14¢ May 15, 1985
O130 17¢ January 12, 1983
O132 $1 January 12, 1983
O133 $5 January 12, 1983
O135 20¢ January 12, 1983
O136 22¢ May 15, 1985
O138 "D" Postcard rate (14¢) February 4,1985
O138A 15¢ June 11, 1988
O138B 20¢ May 19, 1988
O139 "D" (22¢) February 4, 1985
O140 "E" (25¢) March 22, 1988
O141 25¢ June 11, 1988
O143 1¢ July 5, 1989

O144 "F" (29¢) January 22, 1991
O145 29¢ May 24, 1991
O146 4¢ April 6, 1991
O146A 10¢ October 19, 1993
O147 19¢ May 24, 1991
O148 23¢ May 24, 1991
O151 $1 September 1993
O152 (32¢) December 13, 1994
O153 32¢ May 9, 1995
O154 1¢ May 9, 1995
O155 20¢ May 9, 1995
O156 23¢ May 9, 1995
O157 33¢ October 8, 1999
O158 34¢ February 27, 2001
O159 37¢ August 2, 2002
O160 39¢ March 8, 2006
O161 $1 September 29, 2006
O162 41¢ June 25, 2007
O163 1¢ February 24, 2009

Official Mail Envelopes
UO73 20¢ blue Great Seal
UO74 22¢ blue Great Seal, embossed
UO75 22¢ blue Great Seal
UO76 (25¢) "E" Great Seal
UO77 25¢ black, blue Great Seal, embossed
UO78 25¢ black, blue Great Seal
UO79 45¢ black, blue Great Seal (stars illegible)
UO80 65¢ black, blue Great Seal (stars illegible)
UO81 45¢ black, blue Great Seal (stars clear)
UO82 65¢ black, blue Great Seal (stars clear)
UO83 (29¢) "F" Great Seal
UO84 29¢ black, blue, Great Seal
UO88 32¢ Great Seal
UO89 33¢ Great Seal
UO90 34¢ Great Seal
UO91 37¢ Great Seal
UO92 39¢ Great Seal
UO93 41¢ Great Seal
UO94 42¢ Great Seal
Official Mail Postal Cards
UZ6 20¢ Great Seal

Statehood 1936-Present
782 3¢ Arkansas
858 3¢ 50th Anniversary of Statehood— Montana, North Dakota, South Dakota, Washington
896 3¢ Idaho
897 3¢ Wyoming
903 3¢ Vermont
904 3¢ Kentucky
927 3¢ Florida
938 3¢ Texas

941 3¢ Tennessee
942 3¢ Iowa
957 3¢ Wisconsin
997 3¢ California
1001 3¢ Colorado
1018 3¢ Ohio
1106 3¢ Minnesota
1124 4¢ Oregon
1191 4¢ New Mexico
1192 4¢ Arizona
1197 4¢ Louisiana
1232 5¢ West Virginia
1248 5¢ Nevada
1308 5¢ Indiana
1328 5¢ Nebraska
1339 6¢ Illinois
1375 6¢ Alabama
1391 6¢ Maine
1426 8¢ Missouri
1711 13¢ Colorado
2066 20¢ Alaska
2167 22¢ Arkansas
2246 22¢ Michigan
2336 22¢ Delaware
2337 22¢ Pennsylvania
2338 22¢ New Jersey
2339 22¢ Georgia
2340 22¢ Connecticut
2341 22¢ Massachusetts
2342 22¢ Maryland
2343 22¢ South Carolina
2344 22¢ New Hampshire
2345 22¢ Virginia
2346 22¢ New York
2347 22¢ North Carolina
2348 22¢ Rhode Island
2401 25¢ Montana
2403 25¢ North Dakota
2404 25¢ Washington
2416 25¢ South Dakota
2439 25¢ Idaho
2444 25¢ Wyoming
2533 29¢ Vermont
2561 29¢ District of Columbia Bicentennial
2636 29¢ Kentucky
2950 32¢ Florida
2968 32¢ Texas
3024 32¢ Utah
3070 32¢ Tennessee
3088 32¢ Iowa
3206 32¢ Wisconsin
3438 33¢ California
3773 37¢ Ohio
4121 39¢ Oklahoma
4266 42¢ Minnesota
4374 42¢ Alaska
4376 42¢ Oregon
— 44¢ Hawaii (2009)

Stamp Series

Olympic Games 1932–Present

716	2¢	Ski Jumper
718	3¢	Runner at Starting Mark
719	5¢	Myron's Discobolus
1146	4¢	Olympic Rings and Snowflake (1960)
1460	6¢	Bicycling and Olympic Rings
1461	8¢	Bobsledding and Olympic Rings
1462	15¢	Running and Olympic Rings
C85	11¢	Skiers and Olympic Rings
1695	13¢	Diver and Olympic Rings
1696	13¢	Skier and Olympic Rings
1697	13¢	Runner and Olympic Rings
1698	13¢	Skater and Olympic Rings
1790	10¢	Javelin Thrower
1791	15¢	Runner
1792	15¢	Swimmer
1793	15¢	Rowers
1794	15¢	Equestrian Contestant
C97	31¢	High Jumper
1795	15¢	Speed Skater
1796	15¢	Downhill Skier
1797	15¢	Ski Jumper
1798	15¢	Ice Hockey
2048	13¢	Discus Thrower
2049	13¢	High Jumper
2050	13¢	Archer
2051	13¢	Boxers
C101	28¢	Gymnast
C102	28¢	Hurdler
C103	28¢	Basketball Player
C104	28¢	Soccer Player
C105	40¢	Shotputter
C106	40¢	Gymnast
C107	40¢	Swimmer
C108	40¢	Weightlifter
C109	35¢	Fencer
C110	35¢	Bicyclist
C111	35¢	Volleyball Players
C112	35¢	Pole Vaulter
2067	20¢	Ice Dancing (1984)
2068	20¢	Downhill Skiing
2069	20¢	Cross-Country Skiing
2070	20¢	Ice Hockey
2082	20¢	Diving
2083	20¢	Long Jump
2084	20¢	Wrestling
2085	20¢	Kayak
2369	22¢	Skier and Olympic Rings
2380	25¢	Gymnast on Ring
2528	29¢	U.S. Flag, Olympic Rings
2539	$1	USPS Logo/ Olympic Rings
2553	29¢	Pole Vaulter
2554	29¢	Discus Thrower
2555	29¢	Women Sprinters
2556	29¢	Javelin Thrower
2557	29¢	Women Hurdlers
2611	29¢	Hockey (1992)
2612	29¢	Figure Skating
2613	29¢	Speed Skating
2614	29¢	Skiing
2615	29¢	Bobsledding
2637	29¢	Soccer
2638	29¢	Gymnastics
2639	29¢	Volleyball
2640	29¢	Boxing
2641	29¢	Swimming
2807	29¢	Slalom (1994)
2808	29¢	Luge
2809	29¢	Ice Dancing
2810	29¢	Cross-Country Skiing
2811	29¢	Ice Hockey
3863	37¢	2004 Olympic Games Athens
UC52	22¢	Summer Olympic Games
UC57	30¢	Olympic Games
3995	39¢	Olympic Winter Games Torino
4334	42¢	Olympic Games

Holiday Celebration: Christmas 1966–Present

1321	5¢	Madonna and Child by Hans Memling
1336	5¢	Madonna and Child by Hans Memling
1363	6¢	Angel Gabriel from The Annunciation by Jan Van Eyck
1414	6¢	Nativity by Lorenzo Lotto
1444	8¢	Adoration of the Shepherds by Giorgione
1471	8¢	Angels from Mary, Queen of Heaven by the Master of the St. Lucy Legend
1507	8¢	Small Cowper Madonna by Raphael
1550	10¢	Angel from Pérussis Altarpiece
1579	(10¢)	Madonna and Child by Domenico Ghirlandaio
1701	13¢	Nativity by John Singleton Copley
1729	13¢	Washington at Valley Forge by J.C. Leyendecker
1768	15¢	Madonna and Child with Cherubim by Andrea della Robbia
1799	15¢	Virgin and Child with Cherubim by Gerard David
1842	15¢	Madonna and Child from Epiphany Window, Washington Cathedral
1939	20¢	Madonna and Child by Botticelli
2026	20¢	Madonna and Child by Tiepolo
2063	20¢	Niccolini-Cowper Madonna by Raphael
2107	20¢	Madonna and Child by Fra Filippo Lippi
2165	22¢	Genoa Madonna by Luca Della Robbia
2244	22¢	Madonna and Child by Perugino
2367	22¢	Madonna and Child by Moroni
2399	25¢	Madonna and Child by Botticelli
2427	25¢	Madonna and Child by Caracci
2514	25¢	Madonna and Child by Antonello
2578	29¢	Madonna and Child by Antoniazzo Romano
2710	29¢	Madonna and Child by Giovanni Bellini
2789	29¢	Madonna and Child by Giovanni Battista Cima
2871	29¢	Madonna and Child by Elisabetta Sira
3003	32¢	Madonna and Child by Giotto de Bondone
3107	32¢	Madonna and Child by Paolo de Matteis
3176	32¢	Madonna and Child by Sano di Pietro
3244	32¢	The Madonna and Child by Hans Memling
3355	33¢	Madonna and Child by Bartolomeo Vivarini
3536	34¢	Madonna and Child by Lorenzo Costa
3675	37¢	Madonna and Child by Gossaert
3820	37¢	Madonna and Child by Gossaert
3879	37¢	Madonna and Child by Lorenzo Monaco
4100	39¢	Madonna and Child with Bird by I. Chacón
4206	41¢	Madonna of the Carnation, by B. Luini
4359	42¢	Virgin and Child with the Young John the Baptist, by Sandro Botticelli
—	44¢	Madonna and Sleeping Child by Sassoferrato (2009)

Holiday Celebration: Holiday 1962–Present

1205	4¢	Wreath and Candles
1240	5¢	National Christmas Tree and White House
1254	5¢	Holly
1255	5¢	Mistletoe
1256	5¢	Poinsettia
1257	5¢	Sprig of Conifer
1276	5¢	Angel with Trumpet (1840 Weather Vane)
1384	6¢	Winter Sunday in Norway, ME
1415	6¢	Tin and Cast-Iron Locomotive
1416	6¢	Toy Horse on Wheels
1417	6¢	Mechanical Tricycle
1418	6¢	Doll Carriage
1445	8¢	Partridge in a Pear Tree
1472	8¢	Santa Claus
1508	8¢	Christmas Tree in needlepoint
1551	10¢	*The Road—Winter* by Currier and Ives
1552	10¢	Dove Weather Vane atop Mount Vernon
1580	(10¢)	Early Christmas Card by Louis Prang, 1878
1702	13¢	*Winter Pastime* by Nathaniel Currier
1730	13¢	Rural Mailbox
1769	15¢	Child on Hobby Horse
1800	15¢	Santa Claus, Christmas Tree Ornament
1843	15¢	Wreath and Toys
1940	20¢	Felt Bear on Sleigh
2025	13¢	Puppy and Kitten
2027	20¢	Children Sledding
2028	20¢	Children Building a Snowman
2029	20¢	Children Skating
2030	20¢	Children Trimming a Tree
2064	20¢	Santa Claus
2108	20¢	Santa Claus
2166	22¢	Poinsettia Plants

Holiday Celebration: Holiday continued

2245	22¢	Village Scene
2368	22¢	Christmas Ornaments
2400	25¢	One-Horse Open Sleigh and Village Scene
2428	25¢	Sleigh Full of Presents
2515	25¢	Christmas Tree
2579	29¢	Santa Claus in Chimney
2582	29¢	Santa Claus Checking List
2583	29¢	Santa Claus with Present Under Tree
2584	29¢	Santa Claus at Fireplace
2585	29¢	Santa Claus and Sleigh
2711	29¢	Horse and Rider
2712	29¢	Toy Train
2713	29¢	Toy Steamer
2714	29¢	Toy Ship
2715	29¢	Horse and Rider
2716	29¢	Toy Train
2717	29¢	Toy Steamer
2718	29¢	Toy Ship
2719	29¢	Toy Train (self-adhesive)
2791	29¢	Jack-in-the-Box
2792	29¢	Red-Nosed Reindeer
2793	29¢	Snowman
2794	29¢	Toy Soldier
2795	29¢	Toy Soldier (2794)
2796	29¢	Snowman (2793)
2797	29¢	Red-Nosed Reindeer (2792)
2798	29¢	Jack-in-the-Box (2791)
2799	29¢	Snowman
2800	29¢	Toy Soldier
2801	29¢	Jack-in-the-Box
2802	29¢	Red-Nosed Reindeer
2803	29¢	Snowman
2872	29¢	Stocking
2873	29¢	Santa Claus
2874	29¢	Cardinal in Snow
3004	32¢	Santa Claus Entering Chimney
3005	32¢	Child Holding Jumping Jack
3006	32¢	Child Holding Tree
3007	32¢	Santa Claus Working on Sled
3008	32¢	Santa Claus Working on Sled

3009	32¢	Child Holding Jumping Jack
3010	32¢	Santa Claus Entering Chimney
3011	32¢	Child Holding Tree
3012	32¢	Midnight Angel
3013	32¢	Children Sledding
3108	32¢	Family at Fireplace
3109	32¢	Decorating Tree
3110	32¢	Dreaming of Santa Claus
3111	32¢	Holiday Shopping
3113	32¢	Family at Fireplace
3114	32¢	Decorating Tree
3115	32¢	Dreaming of Santa Claus
3116	32¢	Holiday Shopping
3117	32¢	Skaters
3177	32¢	American Holly
3245	32¢	Evergreen Wreath
3246	32¢	Victorian Wreath
3247	32¢	Chili Pepper Wreath
3248	32¢	Tropical Wreath
3249	32¢	Evergreen Wreath
3250	32¢	Victorian Wreath
3251	32¢	Chili Pepper Wreath
3252	32¢	Tropical Wreath
3356	33¢	Red Deer
3357	33¢	Blue Deer
3358	33¢	Purple Deer
3359	33¢	Green Deer
3360	33¢	Red Deer
3361	33¢	Blue Deer
3362	33¢	Purple Deer
3363	33¢	Green Deer
3364	33¢	Red Deer
3365	33¢	Blue Deer
3366	33¢	Purple Deer
3367	33¢	Green Deer
3537	34¢	Santa wearing Tan Hood
3538	34¢	Santa wearing Blue Hat
3539	34¢	Santa wearing Red Hat
3540	34¢	Santa wearing Gold Hood
3676	37¢	Snowman w/red & green plaid scarf
3677	37¢	Snowman w/blue plaid scarf
3678	37¢	Snowman w/pipe

3679	37¢	Snowman w/top hat
3680	37¢	Snowman w/blue plaid scarf
3681	37¢	Snowman w/pipe
3682	37¢	Snowman w/top hat
3683	37¢	Snowman w/red & green plaid scarf
3684	37¢	Snowman w/red & green plaid scarf
3685	37¢	Snowman w/blue plaid scarf
3686	37¢	Snowman w/pipe
3687	37¢	Snowman w/top hat
3688	37¢	Snowman w/red & green plaid scarf
3689	37¢	Snowman w/blue plaid scarf
3690	37¢	Snowman w/pipe
3691	37¢	Snowman w/top hat
3821	37¢	Reindeer with Pan Pipes
3822	37¢	Santa Claus with Drum
3823	37¢	Santa Claus with Trumpet
3824	37¢	Reindeer with Horn
3825	37¢	Reindeer with Pan Pipes
3826	37¢	Santa Claus with Drum
3827	37¢	Santa Claus with Trumpet
3828	37¢	Reindeer with Horn
3883	37¢	Santa Ornament, purple
3884	37¢	Santa Ornament, green
3885	37¢	Santa Ornament, blue
3886	37¢	Santa Ornament, red
3949-3952	37¢	Holiday Cookies
4101-4104	39¢	Snowflakes
4207-4210	41¢	Holiday Knits
4360-4363	42¢	Nutcrackers
—	44¢	Winter Holidays (2009)

Hoilday Celebrations 1996-Present

3118	32¢	Hanukkah (reissued as #3352 33¢, #3547 34¢ and #3672 37¢)
3175	32¢	Kwanzaa (reissued as #3368 33¢, #3548 34¢ and #3673 37¢)
3203	32¢	Cinco de Mayo (reissued as #3309 33¢)

3532	34¢	Eid (reissued as #3674 37¢, #4117 39¢, #4202 41¢ and #4351 42¢)
3546	34¢	We Give Thanks
3880	37¢	Hanukkah (reissued as #4118 39¢, #4219 41¢ and #4372 42¢)
3881	37¢	Kwanzaa (reissued as #4119 39¢, #4220 41¢ and #4373 42¢)
—	44¢	Kwanzaa (2009)
—	44¢	Hanukkah (2009)

Weddings 2004-Present

3836	37¢	Garden Bouquet
3837	60¢	Garden Botanical
3998	39¢	Our Wedding
3999	63¢	Our Wedding
4151	41¢	Hearts
4152	58¢	Hearts
4271	42¢	Hearts
4272	59¢	Hearts
—	44¢	Wedding Rings (2009)
—	61¢	Wedding Cake (2009)

America On The Move 2005-Present

50s Sporty Cars

3931	37¢	1953 Studebaker Starliner
3932	37¢	1954 Kaiser Darrin
3933	37¢	1953 Chevrolet Corvette
3934	37¢	1952 Nash Healey
3935	37¢	1955 Ford Thunderbird

50s Fins and Chrome (2008)

4353	42¢	1959 Cadillac Eldorado
4354	42¢	1957 Studebaker Golden Hawk
4355	42¢	1957 Pontiac Safari
4356	42¢	1957 Lincoln Premiere
4357	42¢	1957 Chrysler 300C

Celebrating Lunar New Year 2008-Present

4221	41¢	Year of the Rat
4375	42¢	Year of the Ox

Flags of Our Nation 2008-Present

4273-4282	42¢	Set 1
4283-4292	42¢	Set 2
—	44¢	Set 3 (2009)

American Commemorative Collections Three-Ring Binder

Glossary

Accessories
The tools used by stamp collectors, such as tongs, hinges, etc.

Aerogrammes
Air letters designed to be letters and envelopes all in one. They are specially stamped and ready for folding.

Aerophilately
Stamp collecting that focuses on airmail stamps or postage.

Album
A book designed to hold stamps and covers.

Approvals
Stamps sent by a dealer to a collector for examination. Approvals must either be bought or returned to the dealer within a specified time.

Block
A group of unseparated stamps, at least two stamps high and two stamps wide.

Bogus
A completely fictitious, worthless "stamp," created only for sale to collectors. Bogus stamps include labels for nonexistent values added to regularly issued sets, issues for nations without postal systems, etc.

Booklet Pane
A small sheet of stamps specially cut to be sold in booklets.

Bourse
A marketplace, such as a stamp exhibition, where stamps are bought, sold, or exchanged.

Cachet (ka-shay´)
A stamp related design on an envelope.

Cancellation
A mark placed on a stamp by a postal authority to show that the stamp has been used.

Centering
The position of the design on a postage stamp. On perfectly centered stamps the design is exactly in the middle.

Cinderella
Any stamp-like label without an official postal value.

Classic
An early stamp issue.

Coils
Stamps issued in rolls (one stamp wide) for use in dispensers or vending machines.

Coil Stamps
Stamps that are produced in a long vertical or horizontal strip

Commemoratives
Stamps that honor anniversaries, important people, special events, or aspects of national culture.

Compound Perforations
Different gauge perforations on different sides (normally adjacent) of a single stamp.

Condition
Condition is the most important characteristic in determining the value of a stamp. It refers to the state of a stamp regarding such details as centering, color and gum.

Cover
An envelope that has been sent through the mail.

Cracked Plate
A term used to describe stamps which show evidence that the plate from which they were printed was cracked.

Definitives
Regular issues of postage stamps, usually sold over long periods of time. They tend to be fairly small and printed in large quantities often more than once.

Denomination
The postage value appearing on a stamp.

Die Cut
Scoring of self-adhesive stamps that allows a stamp to be separated from the liner.

Directory Markings
Postal markings that indicate a failed delivery attempt, stating reasons such as "No Such Number" or "Address Unknown."

Double Transfer
The condition on a printing plate that shows evidence of a duplication of all or part of the design.

Duplicates
Extra copies of stamps that can be sold or traded. Duplicates should be examined carefully for color and perforation variations.

Entire
An intact piece of postal stationery, in contrast to a cut-out of the printed design.

Error
A stamp with something incorrect in its design or manufacture.

Face Value
The monetary value, or denomination, of a stamp.

Fake
A genuine stamp that has been altered in some way to make it more attractive to collectors. It may be repaired, reperfed, or regummed to resemble a more valuable variety.

First Day Cover (FDC)
An envelope or card bearing a stamp cancelled to show its issuance date and place.

First Day Ceremony Program
A program given to those who attend first day of issue stamp ceremonies. It contains the actual stamp affixed and postmarked, a list of participants and information on the stamp subject.

Foreign Entry
When original transfers are erased incompletely from a plate, they can appear with new transfers of a different design which are subsequently entered on the plate.

Franks
Written, hand-stamped, or imprinted markings on the face of a cover indicating that it is carried free of postage. Franking is usually limited to official government correspondence.

Freak
An abnormal variety of a stamp occurring because of paper fold, over-inking, perforation shift, etc., as opposed to a continually appearing variety or an error.

Grill
A pattern of small, square pyramids in parallel rows impressed or embossed on the stamp to break paper fibers, allowing cancellation ink to soak in and preventing washing and reuse.

Gum
The coating of glue on the back of a stamp.

Hinges
Small strips of gummed material used by some collectors to affix stamps to album pages.

Hologram
An image that appears to be three-dimensional when viewed from an angle. Holograms have appeared on some modern stamps and stationery.

Imperforate
Indicates stamps without perforations.

Laid Paper
When held to the light, the paper shows alternate light and dark crossed lines.

Line Pairs (LP)
Most coil stamp rolls prior to 1981 feature a line of ink (known as a "joint line") printed between two stamps at various intervals, caused by the joining of two or more curved plates around the printing cylinder.

Liner
The backing paper for self-adhesive stamps.

Loupe
A magnifying glass used to examine details of stamps more closely.

On Paper
Stamps "on paper" are those that still have portions of the original envelope or wrapper attached.

Overprint
Additional printing on a stamp that was not part of the original design.

Packet
A presorted group of different stamps, a common and economical way to begin a stamp collection.

Pane
A full "sheet" of stamps as sold by a Post Office.

Par Avion
French for mail transported "by air."

Pictorials
Stamps with a picture of some sort, other than portraits or static designs such as coats of arms.

Perforations
Lines of small holes or cuts between stamps that make them easy to separate.

Perforation Gauge
A tool used to measure perforations along the edges of stamps or the distance between peaks or ridges.

Philately
The collection and study of postage stamps and other postal materials.

Plate Block (PB) (or Plate Number Block)
A block of stamps with the margin attached that bears the plate number used in printing that sheet.

Plate Number Coils (PNC)
For most coil stamp rolls beginning with #1891, a small plate number appears at varying intervals in the roll in the design of the stamp.

Postal Stationery
Envelopes, aerogrammes, stamped postal cards, and letter sheets with printed or embossed stamp designs.

Postal Cards
See "stamped postal cards."

Postcards
Commercially-produced mailable cards without imprinted postage.

Postmark
A mark put on envelopes or other mailing pieces showing the date and location of mailing.

Precancels
Stamps cancelled by a proper authority prior to their use on mail.

Presort Stamp
A discounted stamp used by business mailers who presort their mail.

Prestige Booklet
A booklet commemorating a special topic and containing stamps, narrative, and images.

Reissue
An official reprinting of a stamp that was no longer being printed.

Reprint
A stamp printed from the original plate after the issue is no longer valid for postage. Official reprints are sometimes made for presentation purposes, official collections, etc., and are often distinguished in some way from the "real" ones.

Revenue Stamps
Stamps issued as proof of payment of certain taxes but not valid for postage.

Rouletting
The piercing of the paper between stamps to facilitate their separation, often giving the appearance of a series of dashes.

Scrambled Indicia®
A patented process that conceals encoded text or graphics within the visible design. These hidden images can only be viewed through a special lens, the Stamp Decoder™, available from the U.S. Postal Service.

Se-tenant
An attached pair, strip or block of stamps that differ in design, value or surcharge.

Self-Adhesive Stamp
A stamp with pressure sensitive adhesive.

Selvage
The paper around panes of stamps, sometimes called the margin.

Semipostal Stamp
A First-Class Mail stamp priced to include an additional charge earmarked for a specific purpose, e.g., breast cancer research.

Series
A number of individual stamps or sets of stamps having a common purpose or theme, issued over an extended period of time (generally a year or more), including all variations of design and/or denomination.

Set
A group of stamps with a common design or theme issued at one time for a common purpose or over a limited period of time (generally less than a year).

Souvenir Sheet
A small sheet of stamps with a commemorative inscription.

Special Issues
Stamps with a commemorative appearance that supplement definitives and meet specific needs. These include Christmas, Love, Holiday Celebrations, airmail, Express Mail, and Priority Mail stamps.

Speculative
A stamp or issue released primarily for sale to collectors, rather than to meet any legitimate postal need.

Stamp Decoder™
A device with a special lens that reveals hidden images on stamps. It is available from the U.S. Postal Service.

Stamped Postal Card
The current term for a mailable card with postage imprinted on it.

Stamped Envelope
A mailable envelope with postage embossed or imprinted on it.

Star Route
A mail route serviced by an outside contractor rather than a postal employee.

Strip
Three or more unseparated stamps in a row.

Surcharge
An overprint that changes the denomination of a stamp.

Sweatbox
A closed box with a grill over which stuck-together unused stamps are placed. A wet, sponge-like material under the grill creates humidity so the stamps can be separated without removing the gum.

Tagging
The marking of stamps with a phosphor or similar coating (which may be in lines, bars, letters, overall design area or entire stamp surface), done by many countries for use with automatic mail-handling equipment. When a stamp is issued both with and without this marking, catalogs will often note varieties as "tagged" or "untagged."

Tied On
Describes a stamp whose postmark touches the envelope.

Tongs
A tweezer-like tool with rounded or flattened tips used to handle stamps.

Topicals
A group of stamps with the same theme—space travel, for example.

Unhinged
A stamp without hinge marks.

Unused
The condition of a stamp that has no cancellation or other sign of use.

Used
The condition of a stamp that has been canceled.

Variety
A stamp that varies in some way from its standard or original form. Varieties can include missing colors or perforations, constant plate flaws, changes in ink or paper, differences in printing method or in format.

Watermark
A design sometimes pressed into stamp paper during its manufacture.

Water-Activated Gum
Water-soluble adhesives such as sugar-based starches on the back of an unused stamp.

Wove Paper
A uniform paper which, when held to the light, shows no light or dark figures.

Index

The numbers listed next to the stamp description are the Scott numbers and the numbers in parentheses are numbers of the pages on which the stamps are listed.

Liberty Flag, 3776 (229), UX390 (329)
Liberty Ship, 2559h (153)
Liberty Torch, 2531A (150)
Liberty Tree, U576 (310), U588 (310)
Libraries:
America's, 2015 (118)
The New York Public, 3447 (214)
Presidential, 3930 (241)
Library & Athenæum, Redwood, UX303
(322)
Library of Congress, 2004 (118), 3390
(209)
Lichen, Foliose, 3378i-j (209)
Life Magazine, First Issue 1936, 3185c
(193)
Lighthouses, 2470-2474 (146), UX306
(322)
Block Island, UY42 (333)
Cape Hatteras, 1449 (85)
Great Lakes, 2969-2973 (174)
Pacific, 4146-4150 (258),
UX504-UX508 (330)
Sandy Hook, 1605 (93)
Southeastern, 3787-3791 (230),
UX395-UX399 (329)
Lightning, 3142n (186)
Lightning Whelk, 2121 (125)
Li'l Abner, 3000q (177), UX237 (325)
Lilac, 1981 (117), 2764 (162)
lilacs, White, & Pink Roses, 3836 (234),
U657 (325)
Lily, 1879 (109), 2829 (166)
Cobra, 3530 (218)
Gloriosa, 3312 (205)
Indian Pond, 2680 (158)
Sego, 1996 (117), 2667 (158)
Turk's Cap, 2681 (158)
Water, 4172 (262), 4182 (262)
Limner, The Freake, "Mrs. Elizabeth
Freake and Baby Mary,"
3236b (201)
Lincoln, Abraham, 77 (18), 85F (18), 91
(18), 98 (21), 108 (21), 122 (21),
132 (21), 137 (22), 148 (22), 159
(22), 170 (22), 186 (25), 195 (25),
208 (25), 222 (25), 254 (26), 269
(29), 280 (29), 304 (30), 315
(30), 317 (30), 367 (33), 368-369
(33), 555 (41), 584 (42), 600 (42),
635 (45), 661 (46), 672 (46), 821
(53), 1036 (62), 1058 (65), 1113-
1116 (66), 1143 (69), 1282 (74),
1303 (74), 2217g (130), 2433
(145), 2975j (174), C59 (281),
PR3 (277), PR7 (277), U85-U87
(301), U181-U184 (303),
U371-U375 (307), U393-U394
(307), U544 (309), U645 (310),
UO23-UO24 (314), UO37 (314),
UO56-UO58 (314), UX23 (317),
UX26 (317), UX28 (317), UX40
(317), UX42-UX43 (317), UX48
(317), UX55 (317), UX174 (321),
UX209 (325), UY18 (333),
UY21 (333)
Lincoln, Gen. Benjamin, 1686b (97)
Lincoln Memorial, 571 (42), 4075a (250)
Lincoln Premiere, 1957, 4356 (273),
UX549 (330)
Lincoln-Douglas Debates, 1115 (66)

Lindbergh, Charles, 2781 (165)
flies the Atlantic, 3184m (193)
"Spirit of St. Louis," C10 (278)
Lingonberry, 3802j (230)
Lion, Mountain, 2292 (137)
Lionfish, 3831h (233)
Liotard, Jean Etienne, "The Lovely
Reader," 1533 (89)
Lippi, Fra Filippo, Madonna and Child,
2107 (125)
Lippmann, Walter, 1849 (109)
Lipsey, Sarah, 3415 (213)
Literary Arts 1773 (102), 1832 (106), 2047
(121), 2094 (125), 2239 (133),
2350 (138), 2418 (145), 2449
(146), 2538 (150), 2698 (158),
2862 (169), 3002 (177), 3104
(182), 3134 (185), 3221 (198),
3308 (205), 3444 (214), 3659
(225), 3748 (229), 3871 (234),
3904 (238), 4030 (246), 4124
(254), 4223 (266)
Little House on the Prairie, 2786 (165)
Little Nemo in Slumberland, 3000c (177),
UX223 (325)
Little Orphan Annie, 3000j (177), UX230
(325)
Little Rock nine, 1957, 3937d (242)
Little Women, 2788 (165)
Livingston, Robert R., 323 (30), 1687a
(97), 1693 (98)
Lizard, Eastern Short-horned, 3506h
(217)
Lizard, Reticulate Collared, 3816 (233)
Lloyd, Harold, 2825 (166)
Loading Mail on Truck, 1496 (86)
Lobster, American, 2304 (137)
Lockheed Constellation, C35 (278)
Lockheed P-80 Shooting Star, 3921
(241)
Lockwood, Belva Ann, 2178 (129)
Locomobile, 1928, 2381 (141)
Locomotives, 114 (21), 125 (21), 295
(30), 922 (57), 1006 (62), 2226
(133), 2362-2366 (141), 2843-
2847 (169)
1870s, 1897A (110)
Old and New, 1573 (90)
Tin and Cast-iron, 1415 (82)
Toy, 3627 (222), 3638 (222), 3643
(222)
see also Trains
Loesser, Frank, 3350 (206)
Lombardi, Vince, 3145 (189), 3147 (189)
London, Jack, 2182 (129), 2197 (129)
Lone Star, 3525 (218)
Long, Dr. Crawford W., 875 (54)
Long Jump, 2083 (122)
"Long-billed Curlew, Numenius
Longirostris" (Audubon), 3236e
(201)
Long-tailed weasel, 3899f (238)
longest:
cave, Mammoth Cave, 4068 (249)
covered bridge, Cornish-Windsor
Bridge, 4071 (249)
hiking trail, Pacific Crest Trail, 4043
(249)
mountain chain, Rocky Mountains,
4062 (249)

reef, Off the Florida Keys, 4042 (249)
river system, Mississippi-Missouri,
4065 (249)
span, Verrazano-Narrows Bridge,
4052 (249)
Longfellow, Henry Wadsworth 864 (54),
4124 (254)
Longhorn, Elderberry, 3351b (206)
Longhorn Cattle, Angus and, 1504 (86)
Longleaf Pine Forest, 3611a-j (222)
Loon, Common, 1975 (114)
Looney Tunes, 3137-3138 (185), 3204-
3205 (197), 3306a (205), 3307
(205), 3391-3392 (209), 3534-
3535 (218)
Los Angeles Class Submarine, 3372
(209), 3374 (209)
Lotto, Lorenzo, Nativity, 1414 (82)
Lotus, American, largest flower, 4046
(249)
loudest animal, Blue Whale, 4069 (249)
Louis, Joe, 2766 (162)
Louis XVI, King, and Benjamin Franklin
(Sauvage), 1753 (102)
Louisiana, 3578 (221), 3713 (226)
Brown Pelican and Magnolia, 1970
(114)
LaSalle Claims, UX95 (318)
State Flag, 1650 (94)
Statehood, 1197 (70)
World Exposition, 2086 (122)
Louisiana Purchase, 1020 (62), 3782
(230)
Exposition, 323-327 (30)
Map of, 327 (30)
Lounge Chair and Ottoman, 4333f (270)
Love, 1475 (85), 1951 (113), 1951A (113),
2072 (122), 2143 (126), 2202
(129), 2248 (134), 2378-2379
(141), 2440-2441 (146), 2535-
2537 (150), 2618 (154), 2813
(166), 2814 (166), 2814C (166),
3274 (202), 3275 (202), 3657
(225), 3658 (225), U616 (310),
U621 (310), U637 (310), U644
(310), U647 (310), U651 (310),
UX300 (326)
All Heart, 4270 (266)
Bouquet, 3898 (238)
Candy Hearts, 3833 (234)
Cherub from Sistine Madonna
(Raphael), 2948-2949 (173),
2957-2960 (173), 3030 (178)
Nurturing, U651 (310)
Rose and Love Letters, 3496-3499
(217), 3551 (221)
Sunrise, 2813 (166)
Swans, 3123-3124 (182), UX279
(326)
True Blue, 3976 (245), 4029 (246)
Victorian, U644 (310)
With Love and Kisses, 4122 (254)
Love Birds, 2815 (166), U647 (310)
Love You, 2398 (142)
Love You, Dad!, 2270 (134)
Love You, Mother!, 2273 (134)
"Lovely Reader, The" (Liotard), 1533 (89)
Low, Juliette Gordon, 974 (61)
Lowe, Thaddeus, Balloonist, UC64 (314)
Lowell, James Russell, 866 (54)

Luce, Henry, 2935 (173)
Ludington, Sybil, Riding Horse, 1559
(90)
Luge, 2808 (166)
Lugosi, Bela, as Dracula, 3169 (190),
UX286 (326)
Luini, Bernardino, *Madonna of the
Carnation,* 4206 (265)
Luiseño Basket, 3873j (237), UX420
(329)
Luke Skywalker, 4143e (257), UX490
(330)
Luna Moth, 2293 (137)
Lunar New Year, 2720 (161), 2817 (166),
2876 (170), 3060 (178), 3120
(182), 3179 (190), 3272 (202),
3370 (209), 3500 (217), 3559
(221), 3747 (229), 3832 (234),
4221 (265)
Souvenir Sheet, 3895a-l (238),
3997a-l (245)
Lunar Orbiter, 1435 (82), 2571 (153)
Lunar Rover, and Astronauts, 1435 (82)
Lunch counter sit-ins, 1960, 3937c (242)
Lunch Wagon, 1890s, 2464 (146)
Lunt, Alfred and Lynn Fontanne, 3287
(202)
Lupine, Harlequin, 2664 (157)
Lupines, 1367 (78)
Luther, Martin, 2065 (122)
Luxembourg, 912 (57)
Lyndhurst (Davis), 1841 (106)
Lyon, Mary, 2169 (129)
Lyra the Lyre, 3947 (245)

Maass, Clara, 1699 (98)
MacArthur, Gen. Douglas, 1424 (82)
MacDonough, Thomas, 791 (53)
MacDowell, Edward A., 882 (54)
Mackinac Bridge, 1109 (66)
Mad Hatter, UX437 (329)
Alice, 3913 (241)
Made in USA, UC55 (313)
Madison, Dolley, 1822 (106)
Madison, Helene, 2500 (149)
Madison, James, 262 (29), 277 (29), 312
(30), 479 (37), 808 (53), 843
(54), 2216d (130), 3545 (218)
Madonna, Small Copwer (Raphael),
1507 (86)
Madonna and Child, 1321 (77), 1336
(78), 1579 (90), 1768 (102), 1842
(106), 1939 (113), 2026 (118),
2107 (125), 2244 (133), 2367
(141), 2399 (142), 2427 (145),
2514 (149), 2578 (153), 2710
(161), 2789-2790 (165), 2871
(170), 3003 (177), 3107 (182),
3112 (182), 3176 (190), 3244
(201), 3355 (206), 3536 (218),
3675 (226), 3820 (233), 3879
(237)
Madonna and Child with Bird (Chacón),
4100 (253)
Madonna of the Carnation (Luini), 4206
(265)
Magazine Industry, U22 (310)
Magdalena Alpine Butterfly, 4198f (265)
"Maggie Mix-up," 3151n (189)

Acknowledgments

This stamp collecting catalog was produced by Government Relations and Public Policy, Stamp Services, United States Postal Service.

UNITED STATES POSTAL SERVICE

John E. Potter
Postmaster General and
Chief Executive Officer

Marie Therese Dominguez
Vice President, Government
Relations and Public Policy

David E. Failor
Executive Director,
Stamp Services

Terrence W. McCaffrey
Manager,
Stamp Development

Cindy Tackett
Manager,
Stamp Products and Exhibitions

Sonja D. Edison
Project Manager and Editor

Jean D. Schlademan
Project Assistant

HARPERCOLLINS PUBLISHERS

Stephanie Meyers
Associate Editor,
Collins Reference

Bruce Nichols
Publisher,
Collins Reference

Lucy Albanese
Design Director,
General Books Group

Tom McNellis
Senior Production Editor,
General Books Group

Susan Kosko
Director of Production,
General Books Group

DESIGN SERVICES

Design and Project Manager
Roberta Wojtkowski Design
10992 Thrush Ridge Road
Reston, VA 20191

Cover Design
Journey Group, Inc.
418 Fourth Street, NE
Charlottesville, VA 22902

RESEARCH AND WRITING

PhotoAssist, Inc.
Regina Swygert-Smith
7735 Old Georgetown Road
Bethesda, MD 20814

SCANNING AND DIGITAL PREPRESS SERVICES

Journey Group, Inc.
418 Fourth Street NE
Charlottesville, VA 22902

PRINTING AND BINDING

C.J. Krehbiel Company
3962 Virginia Ave
Cincinnati, OH 45227

The Art of Disney Postmark Collectibles

Proprietary Notices 1999-2008

1999

Daffy Duck ™/©1999 Warner Bros.; James Cagney ™/© Estate of Frances Cagney licensed by Global Icons, Los Angeles, CA.; and Malcolm X ™/©1999 under license authorized by CMG Worldwide, Indianapolis, IN.

2000

Edward G. Robinson ™ & © Francesca Robinson Sanchez licensed by Global Icons, Los Angeles, CA. Licensed by George Sidney, Represented by Thomas A. White, Beverly Hills, CA.; Legends of Baseball: Major League Baseball trademarks and copyrights are used with permission of Major League Baseball; and Wile E. Coyote and Road Runner ™/©2000 Warner Bros.

2001

American Illustrators: Maxfield Parrish illustration authorized by The Maxfield Parrish Family Trust. Rockwell Kent illustration ©Plattsburgh State Art Museum, Rockwell Kent Gallery, Plattsburgh, NY. Norman Rockwell illustration ©1929 The Curtis Publishing Company. John Held, Jr., illustration courtesy of Judy Held; Image of Lucille Ball is used with permission of Desilu, too, LLC; Baseball's Legendary Playing Fields: Major League Baseball trademarks and copyrights are used with permission of Major League Baseball; The name, likeness and signature of Leonard Bernstein© are registered trademarks of Amberson Inc.; PEANUTS © United Feature Syndicate, Inc.; and Porky Pig "That's All Folks!" ™/®2001 Warner Bros. LOONEY TUNES, characters, names and all related indicia are trademarks of and ©Warner Bros.

2002

Andy Warhol ©2001 The Andy Warhol Foundation/ARS, NY; Antique Toys courtesy of Strong Museum; and Olympic Winter Games 36 U.S.C. Sec. 220506. Official Licensed Product of the United States Olympic Committee.

2003

Audrey Hepburn™ Licensed by Sean Ferrer and Luca Dotti. This license represented by The Roger Richman Agency, Inc., Beverly Hills, CA; Cesar E. Chavez name and likeness™ Cesar E. Chavez Foundation; and The Wright Bros.™ Licensed by The Wright Family Fund. Represented by The Roger Richman Agency, Inc., Beverly Hills, CA.

2004

BALANCHINE is a trademark of The George Balanchine Trust. The appellation *Agnes de Mille* belongs to de mille Productions. Martha Graham is a registered trademark. Alvin Ailey is a trademark of Alvin Ailey Dance Foundation, Inc.; THE PINK PANTHER and associated marks and characters ™ & ©2004 METRO-GOLD-WYN-MAYER STUDIOS INC. All rights reserved; Isamu Noguchi: Reproduced with permission of The Isamu Noguchi Foundation Inc., New York; Olympic Games, 36 U.S.C. Sec. 220506. Official Licensed Product of the United States Olympic Committee; The Art of Disney: Friendship Disney Materials ©Disney; Buckminster Fuller™, Dymaxion™ and World Game® are trademarks of the Estate of Buckminster Fuller. Spaceship Earth® is a registered trademark of the Buckminster Fuller Institute. This license represented by The Roger Richman Agency, Inc.; *The Man Who Shot Liberty Valance* ©Paramount Pictures. All Rights Reserved. Name, image and likeness of John Wayne licensed by Wayne Enterprises, Newport Beach, CA. All Rights Reserved; and Dr. Seuss properties ™ & ©2003 Dr. Seuss Enterprises, L.P. All Rights Reserved.

2005

50s Sporty Cars: General Motors Corvette Trademarks used under license to the USPS. Kaiser Darrin and Nash Healey are trademarks of DaimlerChrysler Corporation. Ford and Thunderbird ™Ford Motor Company; American Advances in Aviation: 247 and B-29 used with the permission of Boeing; Arthur Ashe™ c/o CMG Worldwide, Indianapolis, IN.; Greta Garbo™2005 Harriett Brown & Company, Inc. Licensed by Global Icons. All Rights Reserved. *As You Desire Me* ©1932 Turner Entertainment Co. A Warner Bros. Entertainment Company. All Rights Reserved; Muppet Characters ©Muppets Holding Company, LLC., a subsidiary of The Walt Disney Company. The JIM HENSON image, trademark and signature are used with permission from Henson Family Properties LLC.; The name and image of the Guggenheim Museum are registered trademarks. Used by permission; The Art of Disney: Celebration Disney Materials ©Disney; and To Form A More Perfect Union: The name, likeness, and copyrighted words of Dr. Martin Luther King, Jr., are used by permission of Intellectual Properties Management, Atlanta, Georgia, as exclusive licensor of the King estate; Brown v. Board of Education, *The Lamp* (1984) ©Romare Bearden Foundation.

2006

®2005 Harley-Davidson. All rights reserved; Indian® Indian Motorcycle International, LLC.; Baseball Sluggers: Major League Baseball trademarks and copyrights are used with permission of Major League Baseball Properties, Inc.; Roy Campanella licensed by CMG Worldwide, Indianapolis, IN; Mel Ott licensed by CMG Worldwide, Indianapolis, IN; Name and likeness of Hank Greenberg used with permission; Mickey Mantle™ & ©2006, Mantle I.P. Holdings, Ltd. All rights reserved. Licensed exclusively through Encore Sports & Entertainment, LLC.; DC Comics Super Heroes All characters and related elements ™ & © DC Comics. SUPER HEROES is a jointly owned trademark; The Very Hungry Caterpillar™ Eric Carle; Maisy™©2006 Lucy Cousins. Published by Candlewick Press, Cambridge, MA; Curious George™ & © HMCo.; Olivia ©2005 by Ian Falconer; Where the Wild Things Are™ & © Maurice Sendak; Wilbur from *Charlotte's Web* Illustration © renewed 1980 Estate of Garth Williams. Used with permission; Frederick ©1967, 1995 Leo Lionni. Used by Permission; Dr. Seuss Properties ™ & ©2006 Dr. Seuss Enterprises, L.P. Used with permission; Judy Garland™ & ©2006 Estate of Judy Garland. Licensed by Global Icons, LLC. All Rights Reserved; Olympic Winter Games, 36 U.S.C. Sec. 220506. Official Licensed Product of the United States Olympic Committee; Sugar Ray Robinson licensed by CMG Worldwide, Indianapolis, IN.; and The Art of Disney: Romance Disney Materials ©Disney

2007

Ella Fitzgerald® licensed by CMG Worldwide, Indianapolis, IN; Marvel Comics Super Heroes: Name(s) of character(s) and the distinctive likeness(es) thereof are Trademarks of Marvel Characters, Inc. and are used with permission. ©2006 Marvel Characters, Inc. All Rights Reserved. Super Heroes is a co-owned registered trademark; Star Wars & Yoda ©2006 Lucasfilm Ltd. & TM. All rights reserved. Used under authorization; The Art of Disney: Magic Disney Materials ©Disney; and With Love and Kisses: HERSHEY'S, KISSES, the plume and the product configuration are registered trademarks used with permission from The Hershey Company.

2008

50s Fins and Chrome: General Motors Cadillac Eldorado and Pontiac Safari Trademarks used under license to the USPS. Chrysler 300C and Hemi® are trademarks of Chrysler LLC and are used under license. ©Chrysler LLC 2007. LINCOLN is a registered trademark of Ford Motor Company. ©Eames Office, LLC 2007. Disney Materials ©Disney. 36 U.S.C. Sec. 220506. Official Licensed Product of the United States Olympic Committee. Edwin Hubble image is based on a photograph from the collection of The Huntington Library in San Marino, California. Duke Ellington licensed by CMG Worldwide, Indianapolis, IN. Josephine Baker licensed by CMG Worldwide, Indianapolis, IN. Louis Jordan name and likeness reprinted with permission. *Hallelujah* art ©Al Hirschfeld, licensed by the Margo Feiden Galleries Ltd., New York. Albert Bierstadt: Photograph ©2007 Museum of Fine Arts, Boston. Bette Davis licensed by CMG Worldwide, Indianapolis, IN. *All About Eve* TM & ©1950, 2007 Twentieth Century Fox Film Corporation. All rights reserved. Frank Sinatra™ Sheffield Enterprises, Los Angeles, CA. Ruben Salazar, from the Los Angeles Times Photographic Archive (Collection 1429), Department of Special Collections, Charles E. Young Research Library, UCLA.

Postmasters General of the United States

Appointed by the Continental Congress

Year	Name
1775	Benjamin Franklin, PA
1776	Richard Bache, PA
1782	Ebenezer Hazard, NY

Appointed by the President with the advice and consent of the Senate

Year	Name
1789	Samuel Osgood, MA
1791	Timothy Pickering, PA
1795	Joseph Habersham, GA
1801	Gideon Granger, CT
1814	Return J. Meigs, Jr., OH
1823	John McLean, OH
1829	William T. Barry, KY
1835	Amos Kendall, KY
1840	John M. Niles, CT
1841	Francis Granger, NY
1841	Charles A. Wickliffe, KY
1845	Cave Johnson, TN
1849	Jacob Collamer, VT
1850	Nathan K. Hall, NY
1852	Samuel D. Hubbard, CT
1853	James Campbell, PA
1857	Aaron V. Brown, TN
1859	Joseph Holt, KY
1861	Horatio King, ME
1861	Montgomery Blair, DC
1864	William Dennison, OH
1866	Alexander W. Randall, WI
1869	John A.J. Creswell, MD
1874	James W. Marshall, NJ
1874	Marshall Jewell, CT
1876	James N. Tyner, IN
1877	David McK. Key, TN
1880	Horace Maynard, TN
1881	Thomas L. James, NY
1882	Timothy O. Howe, WI
1883	Walter Q. Gresham, IN
1884	Frank Hatton, IA
1885	William F. Vilas, WI
1888	Don M. Dickinson, MI
1889	John Wanamaker, PA
1893	Wilson S. Bissell, NY
1895	William L. Wilson, WV
1897	James A. Gary, MD
1898	Charles Emory Smith, PA
1902	Henry C. Payne, WI
1904	Robert J. Wynne, PA
1905	George B. Cortelyou, NY
1907	George von L. Meyer, MA
1909	Frank H. Hitchcock, MA
1913	Albert S. Burleson, TX
1921	Will H. Hays, IN
1922	Hubert Work, CO
1923	Harry S. New, IN
1929	Walter F. Brown, OH
1933	James A. Farley, NY
1940	Frank C. Walker, PA
1945	Robert E. Hannegan, MO
1947	Jesse M. Donaldson, IL
1953	Arthur E. Summerfield, MI
1961	J. Edward Day, CA
1963	John A. Gronouski, WI
1965	Lawrence F. O'Brien, MA
1968	W. Marvin Watson, TX
1969	Winton M. Blount, AL

Selected by the Presidentially appointed U.S. Postal Service Board of Governors

Year	Name
1971	Elmer T. Klassen, MA
1975	Benjamin Franklin Bailar, MD
1978	William F. Bolger, CT
1985	Paul N. Carlin, WY
1986	Albert V. Casey, MA
1986	Preston R. Tisch, NY
1988	Anthony M. Frank, CA
1992	Marvin Runyon, TN
1998	William J. Henderson, NC
2001	John E. Potter, NY